OXFORD EC LAW LIBRARY

General Editor: Francis G. Jacobs
Professor of Law, King's College London
former Advocate General, European Court of Justice

THE GENERAL PRINCIPLES OF EU LAW

Second Edition

OXFORD EC LAW LIBRARY

The aim of this series is to publish important and original studies of the various branches of EC Law. Each work provides a clear, concise, and original critical exposition of the law in its social, economic, and political context, at a level which will interest the advanced student, the practitioner, the academic, and government and Community officials.

Other Titles in the Library

The European Union and its Court of Justice
Anthony Arnull

EU Anti-Discrimination Law
Evelyn Ellis

EC Company Law
Vanessa Edwards

Workers, Establishment, and Services in the European Union
Robin C.A. White

European Community Law of State Aid
Andrew Evans

EC Competition Law
fourth edition
Daniel G. Goyder

EC Agricultural Law
second edition
John A. Usher

Intellectual Property Rights in EU Law Volume 1
Free Movement and Competition Law
David T. Keeling

Directives in EC Law
second edition
Sacha Prechal

The European Internal Market and International Trade
A Legal Analysis
Piet Eeckhout

Trade and Environment Law in the European Community
Andreas R. Ziegler

EC Employment Law
third edition
Catherine Barnard

EC Customs Law
Timothy Lyons

The Law of Money and Financial Services in the EC
second edition
John A. Usher

EC Securities Regulation
Niamh Moloney

External Relations of the European Union
Legal and Constitutional Foundations
Piet Eeckhout

The General Principles
of EU Law

Second Edition

TAKIS TRIDIMAS

OXFORD
UNIVERSITY PRESS

OXFORD
UNIVERSITY PRESS

Great Clarendon Street, Oxford OX2 6DP

Oxford University Press is a department of the University of Oxford.
It furthers the University's objective of excellence in research, scholarship,
and education by publishing worldwide in

Oxford New York

Auckland Cape Town Dar es Salaam Hong Kong Karachi
Kuala Lumpur Madrid Melbourne Mexico City Nairobi
New Delhi Shanghai Taipei Toronto

With offices in

Argentina Austria Brazil Chile Czech Republic France Greece
Guatemala Hungary Italy Japan Poland Portugal Singapore
South Korea Switzerland Thailand Turkey Ukraine Vietnam

Oxford is a registered trade mark of Oxford University Press
in the UK and in certain other countries

Published in the United States
by Oxford University Press Inc., New York

British Library Cataloguing in Publication Data

Data available

Library of Congress Cataloging in Publication Data

Tridimas, Takis.
The general principles of EU law / Takis Tridimas.—2nd ed.
p. cm.—(Oxford EC law library)
ISBN-13: 978–0–19–925806–2 (alk. paper) 1. Constitutional law—European
Union countries. 2. Justice, Administration of—European Union countries.
3. European Union. I. Title. II. Series.
KJE947.T75 2006
341.242'2—dc22   2006005363

Typeset by Newgen Imaging Systems (P) Ltd., Chennai, India
Printed in Great Britain
on acid-free paper by
Biddles Ltd., King's Lynn, Norfolk

ISBN 0–19–925806–6   978–0–19–925806–2

1 3 5 7 9 10 8 6 4 2

To Kristin, Emily, and Beatrice

Καὶ μὴν τοῦτό γε αὐτό, ἡ εὐβουλία, δῆλον ὅτι ἐπιστήμη τίς ἐστιν· οὐ γάρ που ἀμαθίᾳ γε ἀλλ' ἐπιστήμῃ εὖ βουλεύονται.

Plato, *The Republic*, Book δ, para 428a

General Editor's Foreword

It is a great pleasure to welcome the new edition of this book, which has been very well received since the publication of the first edition. This wholly revised edition will certainly be studied with the greatest interest by all concerned with the operation of EC and EU law. The subject of the book is a crucial one; indeed the importance of general principles of law in the European Union's legal system can scarcely be overstated.

Although Athene sprang fully armed from the head of Zeus, a new legal order—such as the European Community legal system—cannot emerge fully fledged from a treaty. The Treaties establishing the European Communities and the European Union, and the amending treaties, elaborate and complex as they now are, have never been sufficient to resolve many fundamental issues. To take an early example: was a Community measure invalid if it infringed fundamental rights, in the absence of any general requirement in the Treaty for protection of such rights? Lacking the matrix of a fully developed legal system, Community law provided no express answer to such questions. Nor could the gaps be filled by a large and growing corpus of Community legislation—the regulations, directives, decisions, and other measures adopted by the Community institutions. On the contrary, that legislation, which usually addresses the particular rather than the general, constantly raises new issues.

Faced very frequently with that situation, the European Court of Justice, which is given a general mandate to rule on all questions of interpretation of the Community Treaties and on the interpretation and validity of Community legislation, finds it necessary and appropriate to draw on general principles outside the formal sources of Community law.

In that task the Court of Justice—and indeed the Court of First Instance—gain inspiration, naturally enough, from the legal systems of the Member States. Examples which by now may seem obvious, but which are nonetheless still of great practical everyday significance, are the principles of equality before the law, legal certainty, and the protection of fundamental rights. Such principles were not spelt out in the Treaties, in any event not as fundamental principles of general application. It seems clear however that all Treaty provisions should be construed so as to give effect to such principles and that all Community legislation must have effect subject to them and, in the case of conflict, be declared invalid. Thus the general principles rank alongside the Treaties as primary sources of Community law, prevailing over conflicting legislation. They have provided a particularly fertile and constantly evolving field for the judicial development of the law.

The principle of proportionality deserves special mention, as a key principle which operates across the whole field of Community law. Moreover, as this new edition shows, the category of general principles is not closed: new principles constantly emerge, and old principles evolve.

An understanding of these fundamental principles—often now called 'general principles of Community law' rather than 'general principles of law'—is therefore vital to any study of the Community legal system itself. Moreover the impact of these principles is pervasive: they are relevant in all branches and at all levels of Community law, and they condition not only the actions of the Community institutions, but also those of the Member States wherever they implement Community law. In that respect the principle of proportionality plays a particularly important role.

The publication of this thorough examination of some of the most fundamental principles will therefore be of great value to scholar and practitioner alike. The principles are relevant in illustrating the development of a legal system and the interaction of Community law with national law. They provide what is perhaps the best example of judicial techniques in the construction of the Community legal order, but they are also of great practical importance in the everyday application of the law. In that respect, as the author recognizes, the role of general principles cannot be assessed in the abstract, but only by reference to results reached in concrete cases: to be of any use, the study of such principles has to be a study of outcomes.

On all counts, therefore, this new edition will be warmly welcomed by students, scholars, practitioners and officials.

December 2005   Francis G. Jacobs

Author's Preface to the Second Edition

The purpose of this book is to examine the general principles of law recognized by the European Court of Justice and the Court of First Instance as sources of European Union law. In this edition, I have endeavoured to update and improve the text without fundamentally changing the character of the first edition. I have sought to identify trends and focus on the most important issues rather than to attempt an exhaustive analysis of the case law. Among the most important developments in recent years have been the enhanced presence of the ECJ in the protection of fundamental rights, the tendency towards the formalization of Community law, i.e. the rise in statutory and constitutional or quasi-constitutional rights, and the increase in the number of cases dealing with the application of general principles to national measures. Although I have not been exhaustive, the sheer volume of the case law has inevitably made this edition much longer. The book follows the structure of the first edition but two chapters have been added. There is a new chapter examining the interaction between proportionality, subsidiarity and competence. Also, the liability of the Community institutions is treated in a separate chapter and no longer as part of the chapter on liability in damages, which focuses on state liability. Given the affinity of the process rights involved, the right to good administration is dealt with together with the rights of defence. Owing to space and time considerations, I have decided not to deal with the principle of transparency and the right of access to documents. The focus remains firmly on the case law of the Community courts. National case law is only taken into account sparingly. The law is stated as of 30 June 2005 but, wherever possible, subsequent developments have been taken into account.

In preparing the second edition, I have benefited from the support of many colleagues and friends, too numerous to mention here. My particular thanks go to Francis Jacobs who first initiated my interest in this area and has been a steadfast supporter of this project. Walter van Gerven has been a constant source of inspiration. I am grateful to Dean McConnaughay and the Faculty at the Dickinson School of Law of the Pennsylvania State University for hosting me and giving me the opportunity to spend long hours on this project whilst in Carlisle. My special thanks to the staff of the Press, especially John Louth and Gwen Booth for their enormous support, and to José Antonio Gutierrez-Fons for his research assistance. Last but not least to my wife, Kristin, for her encouragement and unfailing patience. Needless to say, any mistakes, errors or inaccuracies remain entirely my own responsibility.

T.T.

London
October 2005

Contents—Summary

Contents—Outline

**Chapter 3: The Principle of Proportionality: Review of
             Community Measures**   136

Chapter 4: The Principle of Proportionality: Relationship with Competence and Subsidiarity 175

Chapter 5: The Principle of Proportionality: Review of National Measures 193

Table of Cases

European Community (chronological order)

Court of First Instance

European Court of Human Rights (alphabetical order)

United States (alphabetical order)

Table of Legislation

Decisions

Statutory Instruments

1

The General Principles of
Law in the European Union
Legal Order

1.1. Introduction

What is a general principle of law and how can it be distinguished from a specific
rule? As a starting point, it may be said that a principle is a general proposition of
law of some importance from which concrete rules derive.[1] According to this
definition, the constituent elements of a principle are two: it must be general and it
must carry added weight. 'General' means that it operates at a level of abstraction
that distinguishes it from a specific rule. The term 'general' may have other
meanings. It may refer to principles which transcend specific areas of law and
underlie the legal system as a whole. It may also refer to the degree of recognition
or acceptance. In that sense, an unwritten legal postulate cannot enjoy the status
of a general principle unless it can somehow objectively be verified that it enjoys
a minimum degree of recognition by a relevant constituency, e.g. the courts, or
political actors, or the citizenry, or the constituent members of a supra-national
legal order. The second element of the definition is that the principle must be of
some importance. It must express a core value of an area of law or the legal system
as a whole. There are clearly degrees of importance. Thus, in a narrower sense, the
term general principles may be reserved for fundamental propositions of law which
underlie a legal system and from which concrete rules or outcomes may be derived.
Most of the principles which form the subject-matter of this book can be classified
as general principles in the above sense.

General principles may be expressly stated, e.g. in a constitutional text, or
deduced by a process of interpretation on the basis of legislative texts, the objectives
of legislation, or the underlying values of the legal system. Where reference is made
to the general principles of law as a source of law in national or supra-national legal
systems, such reference usually connotes principles which are derived by the courts
from specific rules or from the legal system as a whole and exist beyond written
law. In that sense, the process of discovery of a general principle is *par excellence* a

---

[1] *The Shorter Oxford Dictionary* (ed 1993) defines the term 'principle' as meaning 'a fundamental . . . proposition on which others depend; a general statement or tenet forming the basis of
a system of belief . . . a primary assumption forming the basis of a chain of reasoning'. See also in
the same sense, *Oxford Dictionary of English*, Second Ed., 1989, entry 5a.

creative exercise and may involve an inductive process, where a court derives a principle from specific rules or precedent, or a deductive one, where it derives it from the objectives of law and its underlying values, or a combination of the two processes.

Principles provide justification for concrete rules. In his Hague lectures on international law, Sir Gerald Fitzmaurice observed that a principle of law, as opposed to a rule, underlies a rule and explains the reasons for its existence. A rule answers the question 'what' whereas a principle answers the question 'why'.[2] The importance of general principles as reasons for specific rules is aptly demonstrated in Dworkin's analysis of rights.[3] Dworkin remarks that both principles and rules point to particular decisions about legal obligations but differ in the character of the direction that they give.[4] Rules, because of their specificity and concrete character, stipulate answers. Principles do not set out legal consequences that follow automatically from them. A principle states a reason which gives arguments in one direction but does not necessitate a particular result.[5] For example, the principle that the burdens imposed on the individual must not exceed what is necessary to achieve their objective (proportionality) does not mean that a penalty imposed on an individual in specific circumstances is necessarily illegal. It does however tell us something about the values which the courts believe underlie the legal system. In short, principles incorporate a minimum substantive content and guide the judicial enquiry on that basis. They provide strong arguments for a certain solution, they may even raise a presumption, but rarely do they dictate results in themselves. It follows that a principle must be judged on the basis of two parameters: the intrinsic value of the right that it embodies, and how well it structures the judicial enquiry.

Academic commentators tend to distinguish various types of general principles in a legal system and make classifications on the basis of diverse criteria. In EU law, the term 'general principles' is manifold.[6] Depending on the criterion used, one may identify many such principles and draw various distinctions among them.[7] Schermers and Waelbroeck[8] identify the following: (a) compelling or constitutional

---

[2] Sir Gerald Fitzmaurice, 'The General Principles of International Law' (1957) 92 Collected Courses of the Hague Academy of International Law, p. 7.

[3] R. Dworkin, *Taking Rights Seriously*, 1994, pp. 24 *et seq*. And see also C. R. Sunstein, *Legal Reasoning and Political Conflict* (OUP, 1996) at 30 and chapter 2 *passim*.

[4] Dworkin, *ibid.*, p. 24.   [5] *ibid.*, p. 26.

[6] For general works on the subject see X. Groussot, *Creation, Development and Impact of the General Principles of Community Law: Towards a jus commune europeum?* (Lund University Press, 2005); U. Bernitz and J. Nergelius (Eds), *General Principles of European Community Law* (Kluwer, 2000); J. A. Usher, *General Principles of EC Law* (Longmans, 1998); R.E. Papadopoulou, *Principes Généraux du Droit et Droit Communautaire* (Bruylant, 1996); J. Schwarze, *European Administrative Law* (Sweet & Maxwell, 1992); A. Arnull, *The General Principles of EEC Law and the Individual* (Leicester University Press, 1990).

[7] For a detailed discussion of the classification of general principles in EU law, see Groussot, *op. cit.*, pp. 12 *et seq*.

[8] H.G. Schermers and D. Waelbroeck, *Judicial Protection in the European Union* (Sixth Ed) (Kluwer, 2001) pp. 28–30.

legal principles; (b) regulatory principles common to the laws of the Member States; and (c) general principles native to the Community legal order. The first category encompasses principles which stem from the common European constitutional heritage and are perceived by the authors to form part of natural law, such as the protection of fundamental rights. The second and third category are defined in somewhat vague terms.[9] On the basis of their origins, Boulouis[10] distinguishes between (a) *principes généraux communs aux droits des Etats membres*; (b) *principes inhérents à tout système juridique organisé*, and (c) *principes détuits de la nature des Communautés*.[11] A similar classification is followed by another author who draws a distinction among the following:[12]

(a) *Principes axiomatiques*, that is to say, principles which are inherent in the very notion of a legal order and represent 'les exigences suprêmes du droit et de la conscience collective'.[13] They are similar to the compelling legal principles referred to above;

(b) *Principes structurels*, that is to say, principles which derive from the distinct characteristics of a specific legal system. In Community law this category includes, for example, the principles of primacy and direct effect; and

(c) *Principes communs*. This category is distinct to supra-national legal systems and comprises principles common to the constituent parts of the legal system. The reference to 'the general principles common to the laws of the Member States' in Article 288(2) EC and to 'the general principles of law recognised by civilised nations' in Article 38(1)(c) of the Statute of the International Court of Justice belong to this category.

The above classifications may be helpful in certain contexts, but overall, their value seems limited. In fact, the term general principle has a relative character and, often, classifications raise more questions than they answer. It may not be easy to agree, for example, on what comes under the category of so-called *principes axiomatiques*. Also, classifications by themselves tell us little about implications and outcomes in concrete cases especially where principles conflict with each other. The importance of general principles cannot be assessed in the abstract but only by reference to

[9] For example, the third category does not seem to include, as one might expect, the principles of free movement which have their basis in the Treaty and, for that reason, are perceived by the authors to be separate sources of law: see, *op. cit.*, pp. 29–30.

[10] B. J. Boulois, *Droit Institutionnel des Communautés Européennes*, Paris, 4th Ed., (Montcherstein, 1993) p. 208 *et seq.*

[11] The first category includes principles developed in the case law of the ECJ on the basis of a comparative analysis of the laws of the Member States and includes, for example, principles of due process. The second includes fundamental principles deriving from the rule of law, such as legal certainty. The distinction between those categories however is not so clear-cut. See further Groussot, *op. cit.*, 12 n. 31.

[12] See Papadopoulou, *op. cit.*, p. 8 where further references are given. See further P. Pescatore, '*Les objectifs de la CEE comme principes d'interprétation dans la jurisprudence de la Cour de justice*', in *Miscellanea Ganshof van der Meersch*, (Brussels, Bruylant, 1972) II, p. 325.

[13] G. Issac, *Droit Communautaire Général*, 3rd Ed., (Masson, 1992) p. 145.

results reached in concrete cases. It is suggested that the following types of general principles may be distinguished:

(a) *Principles which derive from the rule of law.* In this category belong, for example, the protection of fundamental rights, equality, proportionality, legal certainty, the protection of legitimate expectations, and the rights of defence. The distinct features of these principles are the following: first, they have been derived by the ECJ from the fundamental premise that the Community legal order is based on the rule of law. This is a concept akin to the German notion of *Rechtsstaat* and it means that the exercise of public power is subject to substantive and procedural limitations.[14] They are therefore quintessentially principles of public law. They refer primarily to the relationship between the individual and the public authorities (both Community and national) but find diverse applications and, because of their all-embracing character, they may also be relied upon by Member States and even Community institutions.[15] Second, given that the EC Treaty did not provide expressly for such principles, they have been derived by the Court of Justice primarily from the laws of the Member States and used by it to supplement and refine the Treaties. They therefore developed, in the first instance, out of necessity to fill the gaps left by written law. As we shall see, the intervention of the ECJ has been creative both in terms of methodology and in terms of outcomes. Third, principles which belong to this category can be said to pre-exist written law in that provisions of the Treaty which expressly provide for them are understood to be their specific expressions.

(b) *Systemic principles which underlie the constitutional structure of the Community and define the Community legal edifice.* These refer to the relationship between the Community and Member States, and include primacy, attribution of competences,[16] subsidiarity,[17] and the duty of cooperation provided for in Article 10 EC. They may also refer to the legal position of the individual, such as the principle of direct effect, or to relations between the institutions of the Community, such as the principle of institutional balance.[18] It is indicative of the extraordinary influence which the Court of Justice has had on the development of Community law that the main principles which define the constitutional structure of the Community are not provided for expressly in the Treaty but were 'discovered' by the Court by an inductive process. This applies in particular to the principles of primacy and direct effect, which in the Court's own language form the 'essential characteristics of the Community legal order'.[19]

---

[14] See M. Herdegen, 'The Origins and Development of the General Principles of Community Law' in Bernitz and Nergelius (Eds), *op. cit.*, 3–23, at 3.

[15] This applies, for example, in certain contexts to the rights of defence.

[16] Article 5(1) EC.   [17] Article 5(3) EC.

[18] The principle was referred to by the Court in Case C-70/88 *Parliament v Council (Chernobyl)* [1990] ECR I-2041.

[19] Opinion 1/91 on *Draft Agreement relating to the creation of the European Economic Area* [1991] ECR I-6079, para 21.

The two categories mentioned above are so closely intertwined in the context of the Union polity that their separation would be liable to convey a misleading impression. It is through their parallel development that the ECJ set in motion a process towards the 'constitutionalization' of the Treaties.[20] A prime example is provided here by the so-called principle of effectiveness and State liability in damages for breach of Community law. These principles were developed by the ECJ as an essential attribute of the new EU polity and were perceived in judicial reasoning as the meeting point between the principle of primacy and the fundamental right to judicial protection.

In addition to the above categories, one may distinguish other types of general principle. There are principles of substantive Community law, such as those underlying the fundamental freedoms or specific Community policies, e.g. competition or environmental law. These make up the main body of Community and Union law and are based on written law. The function of the ECJ here is different. It is not based on a process of extrapolation of principles from sources internal or external to the Treaty but on Treaty and statutory interpretation.

This book concentrates primarily on the first category mentioned above, i.e. principles emanating from the rule of law. It also covers selectively the second category, i.e. principles which underlie the constitutional structure of the European Union, although it does not aspire to cover them exhaustively.

1.2. The general principles of law derived from the laws of Member States: An overview

This section seeks to examine in more detail the development and salient features of the rule of law-based principles. Among the sources of Community law, they occupy a distinct position. They are unwritten principles extrapolated by the Court from the laws of the Member States by a process similar to that of the development of the common law by the English courts.[21] They derive from the legal systems of the

---

[20] The term 'constitutionalisation' is used here to signify the process by which the EC Treaties have asserted their normative independence *vis-à-vis* the Member States, who created them in the first place, and evolved into the founding charter of a supranational system of government. Under this process, Community law and national law are no longer viewed as separate legal orders but as tiers of the same order operating under an overarching system of principles and values. Judge Timmermans identifies the following key developments in this process: (a) the characterisation of the Community as an autonomous legal system which is integrated to the national legal systems but retains its own distinct features (see Case 26/62 *Van Gend en Loos* [1963] ECR 1); (b) the establishment of primacy and direct effect; (c) the extrapolation from national laws of general principles of law and fundamental rights which govern both Community and Member State action; and (d) the elaboration of principles and rules governing remedies for the protection of Community rights in the national legal systems. See C. Timmermans, 'The Constitutionalisation of the European Union', 21 (2002) YEL 1.

[21] See S. de Smith, H. Woolf and J. Jowell, *Judicial Review of Administrative Action*, Fifth Ed., (Sweet & Maxwell, 1995) p. 833.

Member States but their content as sources of Community law is determined by the distinct features of the Community polity. Thus, the Court may recognize a general principle as part of Community law although it is not recognized in the laws of all Member States. Also, the scope of a principle as applied by the Court may differ from that which it has in the law of a Member State. In short, the general principles of law are children of national law but, as brought up by the Court, they become *enfants terribles*: they are extended, narrowed, restated, transformed by a creative and eclectic judicial process. Their importance as a source of Community law lies primarily in two elements: in terms of positive law, they pose significant limitations on the policy-making powers of the Community institutions and the Member States; as judicially developed rules, they show eminently the creative function of the Court and, more generally, its contribution to the development of the Community from a supra-national organization to 'a constitutional order of States'.[22]

The Court has recognized, among others, the following as general principles of Community law:

- the right to judicial protection;
- the principle of equal treatment or non-discrimination;
- the principle of proportionality;
- the principle of legal certainty;
- the principle of the protection of legitimate expectations;
- the protection of fundamental rights;
- the rights of defence.

These principles have constitutional status. They are binding on the Community institutions and a measure, whether legislative or administrative, which infringes one of them is illegal and may be annulled by the Court. They are also binding on Member States.[23] A common characteristic of the principles referred to above is that they have been derived by the Court from the laws of the Member States, sometimes with little assistance from the text of the Treaty. Respect for human rights was recognized by the Court as a general principle of Community law in the early 1970s[24] although there is no express reference in the Treaty to the protection of such rights. Various Treaty provisions prohibit discrimination on certain grounds but, according to the established case law, those provisions are merely specific illustrations of a general principle of non-discrimination which underlies the Community legal order.[25] Similarly, although a number of Treaty provisions included in the original Treaty establishing the European Economic Community could be said to incorporate the principle of proportionality, the case law developed

---

[22] The term is used by A. Dashwood, 'The Limits of European Community Power', (1996) 21 ELR 113 at 114.   [23] See below, 1.6.

[24] Case 11/70 *Internationale Handelsgesellschaft v Einfuhr-und Vorratsstelle Getreide* [1970] ECR 1125.

[25] See e.g. Joined Cases 117/76 and 16/77 *Ruckdeschel v Hauptzollamt Hamburg-St. Annen* [1977] ECR 1753, para 7.

proportionality to a general principle of law transcending specific provisions. The same is true for the principles of legal certainty and protection of legitimate expectations. Many principles first developed in the case law were incorporated in the Treaties in subsequent amendments.

The principles referred to above are principles of public law. They have been developed by the Court in order to protect the individual and, more generally, to ensure that Community institutions and national authorities act within the remit of the rule of law. It is pertinent to point out at this juncture the dual function of equality and proportionality. Those principles operate both in the sphere of public law and in the sphere of substantive law. As principles of public law, they have been derived by the Court from the rule of law, with a view to protecting the individual *vis-à-vis* Community and national authorities. As principles of substantive law, they underlie the provisions of the Treaty on free movement, their function being to facilitate integration and promote the establishment of the internal market. As we shall see in subsequent chapters, the dual function of equality and proportionality underlies diverse trends in the case law.[26]

1.3. Origins and development of general principles

Recourse to general principles of law was first made by the Court in early cases decided under the Coal and Steel Community Treaty. The origins of non-discrimination and proportionality are to be found in the case law of the 1950s, where the Court invoked them to control the restrictive effects on economic freedom of market regulation measures introduced by the High Authority.[27] In that early case law the Court confronted in an embryonic form some of the problems which it was later to face more acutely in the context of the common agricultural policy. Another area where the general principles were applied at an early stage was staff cases.[28] In the early years, disputes between the Communities and their employees accounted for a comparatively high percentage of the case law and provided fruitful ground for the development of Community administrative law.[29] As the Community evolved, the application of general principles expanded

---

[26] See below, 2.3, 3.1. and 4.1.

[27] See e.g. on proportionality, Case 8/55 *Fédération Charbonnière Belgique v High Authority* [1954–56] ECR 292, and on equality, Case 14/59 *Pont-à-Mousson v High Authority* [1959] ECR 215.

[28] See e.g. for the rights of defence, Case 32/62 *Alvis v Council* [1963] ECR 49.

[29] As the Community legal order developed and litigation in other areas increased, the importance of staff cases decreased correspondingly. In 1989, jurisdiction to hear staff cases at first instance was transferred to the Court of First Instance (CFI). Since 1994, the judgments of the CFI on staff cases have not been published in the official court reports but separately in the Reports of European Community Staff Cases, the full text of the judgment being available only in the language of the case. In November 2004, the Council decided to establish a judicial panel (the European Union Civil Service Tribunal) attached to the CFI with responsibility to hear staff cases

in other areas. The decade of the 1970s saw a proliferation of cases in a number of areas, including agricultural law. The basic features of equality, proportionality, and protection of legitimate expectations were laid down in the case law of that period. The recognition of fundamental rights as binding on the Community institutions also dates from that time.[30]

Subsequently, the case law of the 1980s established that the general principles bind not only the Community institutions but also the Member States where they implement Community law.[31] The application of general principles to national measures further expanded in the 1990s.[32] The extension of general principles to action taken by national authorities has had important repercussions as regards the powers of national courts and, more widely, the public laws of the Member States. It enabled national courts, often following a reference to the Court of Justice, to review the compatibility of a wide range of national measures with standards higher than those ordinarily applicable under national administrative law, thus opening the way for reverse discrimination against claims based purely on national law. This is particularly the case with the United Kingdom where the Diceyan tradition and the doctrine of parliamentary supremacy imposed strict limitations on the power of the courts to review the discretion of public authorities. The late 1980s saw a separate but related development in the sphere of constitutional law, namely the gradual transformation of primacy from a general principle of constitutional law to a specific obligation on national courts to provide full and effective protection of Community rights, if necessary, by establishing new remedies.[33] This shift of emphasis from rights to remedies and the gradual inroads of Community law into the national systems of remedies triggered a trend towards convergence of national public laws.[34]

The most important developments in recent years have been the increased resonance of fundamental rights, the expansion of the application of general principles to national measures and the further colonization of the law of remedies through a broad interpretation of the principle of effectiveness and the right to judicial protection. The most remarkable development is undoubtedly the first. Never in the history of the European Communities has the Court attributed so much importance to the protection of fundamental rights. As we shall see, human rights have expanded both as regards their scope of application and as regards the intensity of review exercised by the ECJ.[35]

---

at first instance. See Council Decision 2004/752, OJ 2004, L 333/7. This is a welcome and long overdue move.

[30] *Internationale Handelsgesellschaft, op. cit.*, n. 24; Case 4/73 *Nold* [1974] ECR 491; Case 44/79 *Hauer v Land Rheinland-Pfalz* [1979] ECR 3727.

[31] See Joined Cases 201 and 202/85 *Klensch v Secrétaire d'État à l'Agriculture et à la Viticulture* [1986] ECR 3477.   [32] See Case C-260/89 *ERT* [1991] ECR I-2925.

[33] See e.g. the obligation of national courts to grant interim measures: Case C- 213/89 *Factortame and Others* [1990] ECR I-2433; and the development of Member State liability in damages for breach of Community law first introduced in Joined Cases C-6 and C-9/90 *Francovich* [1991] ECR I-5357. Those developments are discussed in Chapters 9 and 11.

[34] See further J. Schwarze (ed.), *European Influences in Administrative Law*, Sweet & Maxwell, 1998.   [35] See below Chapter 7.

Since its establishment in 1989,[36] the Court of First Instance also applies the general principles of law within the limits of its jurisdiction.[37] Far from being merely a fact-finding tribunal, the CFI has made its own mark in the case law.[38] In some areas, it has applied a higher standard of scrutiny than hitherto applied by the Court of Justice, adopting a more critical stance towards the discretion of the Community institutions and requiring more exacting standards in their decision-making.[39] Overall, however, in the sphere of general principles, the case law seems balanced. In some cases the Court of Justice has reversed decisions of the CFI taking a more restrictive view of the rights of the individual[40] but in others it has reversed decisions of the lower court giving a broader definition

---

[36] See Council Decision 88/591/ECSC, EEC, Euratom of 24 October 1988 establishing a Court of First Instance of the European Communities, OJ 1988 L 319, p. 1, as amended.

[37] Currently, the CFI has jurisdiction to hear in first instance the following actions:

- actions for judicial review and for failure to act brought by individuals (natural persons and companies) under Articles 230 and 232 EC;
- actions based on the non-contractual liability of the Community brought by individuals under Article 235 EC;
- actions in contract brought by individuals against the Community pursuant to an arbitration clause under Article 238 EC;
- staff cases, i.e. disputes between the Community and its staff (Article 236 EC).

In addition, since July 2004, jurisdiction to hear some actions brought by Member States has been transferred to the CFI. In particular, the CFI hears actions for judicial review and for failure to act brought by Member States against:

- acts of the Commission, excluding decisions on further cooperation provided for in Article 11(a)EC;
- decisions of the Council on state aid under Article 88(2) EC;
- acts of the Council adopted pursuant to a Council regulation concerning measures to protect trade under Article 133 EC;
- acts of the Council by which it exercises implementing powers in accordance with the third indent of Article 202 EC.

See Article 51 of the Statute of the ECJ as amended by Council Decision 2004/407 (OJ L 132/5) which came into force on 1 June 2004, and subsequent amendments. This extension of the jurisdiction of the CFI is to be welcomed.

[38] For an initial assessment, see N. Brown, 'The First Five Years of the Court of First Instance and Appeals to the Court of Justice: Assessment and Statistics', (1995) 32 CMLRev 743.

[39] See e.g. Joined Cases T-163 and T-165/94 *Koyo Seiko v Council* [1995] ECR II-1381 where the CFI annulled an anti-dumping regulation of the Council. Upheld on appeal: Case C-245/95 P [1998] ECR I-401. See also Joined Cases T-79/89 etc. *BASF AG and Others v Commission* [1992] ECR II-315, reversed on appeal: Case C-137/92 *Commission v BASF and Others* [1994] ECR I-2555; Case T-54/99 *max.mobil Telekommunikation Service GmbH v Commission* [2002] ECR II-313; reversed on appeal: Case C-141/02 P *Commission v T-Mobile Austria GmbH*, judgment of 22 February 2005; Case T-177/01 *Jégo-Quéré v Commission* [2002] ECR II-02365, reversed on appeal: Case C-263/02 P *Commission v Jégo Quéré*, judgment of 1 April 2004.

[40] See e.g. on the requirement to give reasons, Case T-289/94 *Innamorati v Parliament* [1995] ECR SC II-393; reversed on appeal: Case C-254/95 P *Parliament v Innamorati* [1996] ECR I-3423. For a prime recent example, see Case T-227/95 *AssiDomän Kraft Products and Others v Commission (Woodpulp III)* [1997] ECR II-1185; reversed on appeal: Case C-310/97 P *Commission v AssiDomän Kraft Products aB and Others* [1999] ECR I-5363. Subsequently, however the CFI interpreted the ECJ's judgment restrictively, see Case T-7/99 *Medici Grimm v Council* [2000] ECR II-2671. The cases are discussed at pp. 31 and 262 below.

to general principles.[41] The CFI has contributed not only by applying established principles of law but also by interpreting new principles recognized by the Community legal order such as the citizen's right of access to information held by Community authorities.[42] An area where the CFI has played a distinct rôle is in determining the requirements of the rights of defence mainly in the context of competition law. The influence of the CFI in applying the general principles of law is aptly demonstrated in *Altmann and Casson v Commission*.[43] There, the CFI effectively reversed the earlier judgment of the Court of Justice in *Ainsworth*[44] and annulled on grounds of incompatibility with the general principle of equal treatment a provision of Community law which the Court of Justice had found to be lawful at the time of its adoption.[45] *Altmann* demonstrates the considerable impact of the CFI in the application of general principles and more widely its contribution to the development of Community jurisprudence. More recently, the CFI has favoured a more liberal interpretation of the *locus standi* of individuals under Article 230(4) than the ECJ[46] and a rift has appeared between the two courts as regards the conditions of Community liability in damages under Article 288(2) following the judgment of the ECJ in *Bergaderm*.[47] In some cases, the two courts differ in their understanding as to the scope and content of general principles but not in the outcomes which they reach.[48]

Two conclusions may perhaps be drawn from this brief historical survey. First, although the general principles of law were initially invoked to cover gaps in the Treaty and the written law of the Community, their importance has not lessened as the Community legal order develops. The proliferation of Community measures and, in some areas of law, the resulting polynomy have made recourse to general principles equally necessary. Second, the application of general principles has

[41] See e.g. in relation to the rights of defence, Case C-294/95 P *Ojha v Commission* [1996] ECR I-5863 reversing the decision of the CFI in T-36/93; Case C-404/92 P, *X v Commission* [1994] ECR I-4737 where the Court of Justice defined more broadly than the CFI the right to medical confidentiality; and more recently, Case C-389/98 P *Gevaert v Commission* [2001] ECR I-65 and Case C-459/98 P *Martinez del Peral Cagigal v Commission* [2001] ECR I-135, where the ECJ annulled Commission decisions on staff cases as being contrary to the principle of equal treatment; Case C-174/98 P *Netherlands v van der Wal* [2000] ECR I-1, where the ECJ interpreted more extensively the right of access to documents.

[42] Treatment of this right is beyond the scope of this book.

[43] Joined Cases T-177 and T-377/94 *Altmann and Casson v Commission* [1996] ECR II-2041.

[44] Joined Cases 271/83 and 15, 36, 113, 158 and 203/84 and 13/85 *Ainsworth v Commission and Council* [1987] ECR 167.

[45] The judgments of the Court of Justice do not constitute binding precedent for the CFI except to the extent provided in Article 54 of the Statute of the Court of Justice or where the principle of *res judicata* applies. See also Case T-162/94 *NMB* [1996] ECR II-427.

[46] See *Jégo-Quéré, op. cit.*, n. 39.

[47] See Case C-352/98 P *Laboratoires Pharmaceutiques Bergaderm and Goupil v Commission* [2000] ECR I-5291 and below Chapter 10.

[48] See e.g. Case C-315/99 P *Ismeri Europa v Court of Auditors* [2001] ECR I-5281, where the ECJ expressly held, reversing the CFI, that the right to a hearing can be invoked against the Court of Auditors by individuals or entities which are expressly criticized in its reports. The ECJ however dismissed the appeal on the ground that the illegality committed was not capable of influencing the content of the report.

gradually expanded both with regard to the areas where they apply and with regard to the requirements that they impose. One area of law, for example, where equality, proportionality, and protection of legitimate expectations have increasingly been applied since the 1980s is the external relations law of the Community.[49] Also, recent years saw moves towards the recognition of a new generation of human rights, both in the political sphere (such as the obligation of transparency and the cognate right of access to information held by public authorities) and the social sphere (such as the rights of trans-sexuals under the notion of sex discrimination).[50] Such developments are instructive of the general principles as instruments of judicial methodology. They are flexible, lend themselves to an evolutive interpretation of the law, and make for a judiciary more responsive to social change.

1.4. From general principles to constitutional texts: The gradual formalization of EU Law

One of the most striking features in recent years has been the trend towards the formalization of Community law. This refers to the tendency to provide for the express recognition and entrenchment of rights in Treaty texts. There has been an increase in the adoption of legislative instruments, principally of a 'constitutional' nature, outlining the limits of lawful government and asserting rights. As Professor Sunstein has noted in a different context, we are 'in the midst of a period of enormous enthusiasm for rule-bound justice'.[51] The origins of this process can be traced in the Treaty of Maastricht. The TEU enshrined for the first time respect for fundamental rights at Treaty level and provided expressly for fundamental constitutional doctrines, namely the attribution of powers, subsidiarity, and proportionality.[52] The Treaty of Amsterdam reiterated this tendency. Along with declaring commitment to the principles of liberty, democracy, respect for human rights, and the rule of law,[53] it introduced a system for the enforcement of those principles in the event that a Member State failed to respect them.[54] Further, it accorded constitutional status to the right of access to documents,[55] a right not traditionally recognised in the constitutions of the Member States, and expanded the principle of non-discrimination.[56]

[49] See e.g. Case C-24/90 *Werner Faust* [1991] ECR I-4905.
[50] See Case C-13/91 *P v S and Cornwall County Council* [1996] ECR I-2143.
[51] C. Sunstein, *Legal Reasoning, op. cit.*, n. 3 ix.
[52] See Article 6(2) (formerly Article F(2)) TEU and Article 5 EC.
[53] See Article 6(1) TEU as amended by the Treaty of Amsterdam.
[54] See Article 7 TEU which has now been amended, and further extended, by the Treaty of Nice. [55] Article 255 EC.
[56] Article 13 EC. This all-embracing provision provides the legal basis for adopting measures 'to combat discrimination based on sex, racial or ethnic origin, religion or belief, disability, age or sexual orientation'.

This trend was reiterated by the adoption of the EU Charter of Fundamental Rights in 2000[57] which sought to enshrine 'the very essence of European acquis regarding fundamental rights'.[58] It was further followed by the adoption of secondary Community legislation.[59] The EU Constitution, of which the Charter now forms part, represents the culmination of the process of formalization.[60]

Although the above developments have been based to some extent on diverse political motives and serve a variety of objectives, taken together they illustrate that we live in the era of legislative general principles. To a great extent, statutory recognition of individual and Member State rights illustrates the quest for Union legitimacy in the post-Maastricht era. But its bases may lie deeper. It represents a new political awareness on the part of the politicians and the citizens, a cry for participation in an era of globalization, where sovereignty eludes the nation state and exposes it to new centres of power, leaving it unaided by the veil of national law. In an era of subtle but far-reaching political change, enshrinement of values in constitutional texts seeks to achieve protection, legitimacy, legal certainty and historical continuity. At the heart of this new European constitutionalism lies an aspiration that a new social and political order can be attained and that the transfer of powers to supra-national organizations is acceptable provided that it is accompanied by shared commitment to abstract principles imbued by liberal ideals. Whether such aspirations are justified remains to be seen. The recent referenda on the EU Constitution in France and the Netherlands suggest that the people are not in tune with the politicians and the project of European integration may be going too fast.[61]

How do these developments relate to the general principles of law and the Court of Justice? Two points may be made here. The first refers to the interaction between

[57] The Charter received the unanimous agreement of the Heads of State in the Biarritz European Council held on 13 and 14 October 2000. It has been solemnly proclaimed by, and binds, the Community institutions. Given, however, the strong objections raised by some Member States, it was decided in the Nice summit that the Charter will not have binding effect on the Member States. For a discussion, see p. 356 below.

[58] See Commission Communication on the Legal Nature of the draft Charter dated 18 October 2000, para 1.

[59] See e.g. the equality directives: Directive 2000/78 establishing a general framework for equal treatment in employment and occupation, OJ 2000, L 303/16; Directive 2000/43 implementing the principle of equal treatment between persons irrespective of racial or ethnic origin, OJ 2000, L 180/22; Directive 2002/73 on the implementation of the principle of equal treatment for men and women as regards access to employment, vocational training and promotion, and working conditions, OJ 2002, L 269/15. Note also that a number of directives amending previous directives incorporate principles of the existing case law: see e.g. Article 27(2) of Directive 2004/38 on the right of the citizens of the Union and their family members to move and reside freely within the territory of the Member States amending Regulation No 1612/68 and repealing Directives 64/221, 68/360, 72/194. 73/148, 75/34, 75/35, 90/364, 90/365 and 93/96, OJ 2004, L 158/77; Directive 2002/73/EC of the European Parliament and of the Council of 23 September 2002 amending Council Directive 76/207/EEC on the implementation of the principle of equal treatment for men and women as regards access to employment, vocational training and promotion, and working conditions, OJ 2002, L 269/15, Article 5(2).

[60] For the EU Constitution, see 1.5 below.   [61] See n. 72 below.

the Court and the Member States, which as sovereign political actors, are competent to amend the founding treaties. The second relates to the workload of the Court.

Many of the principles which have been entrenched by successive Treaty amendments were first recognized by the Court of Justice. This is true, for example, in relation to fundamental rights and the principle of proportionality. At a more concrete level, it is also true with regard to the iconoclastic judgment in *Chernobyl*.[62] In that case, led by the Opinion of Advocate General van Gerven, the Court held that the Parliament had *locus standi* to challenge the validity of Community acts although, at that time, Article 173 EEC, the predecessor to Article 230 EC, did not mention the Parliament as a potential plaintiff.[63] The *Chernobyl* judgment itself was based on the fundamental right to judicial protection and the principle of institutional balance. The judgment subsequently found express recognition in the Treaty of European Union which amended Article 173 EC in accordance with the pronouncements of the Court. Thus, in relation to the general principles, the Court has followed a pro-active approach. The case law has showed the way, with subsequent Treaty amendments endorsing in many cases judicial developments.[64] The fact that the case law has prompted law reform in that way is telling of the Court's contribution to the political process and the evolution of the Union. This is not to say that the Member States have always *willingly* endorsed judicial developments nor that the Court is always a step ahead of the legislature. In some cases, the ECJ has anticipated legislative amendments by interpreting existing provisions in the light of forthcoming changes[65] or has heeded interpretations formally endorsed by the Member States[66] or has refused to take a step forward, seeking instead guidance from the politicians.[67] Yet in other areas, Member States have sought to limit the remit of the Court as a *quid pro quo* for allowing Community competence.[68] The relationship between the ECJ and the other organs of government is a dialectical one and the formalization of Community law has been the result of their interaction.

---

[62] *Op. cit.*, n. 18.

[63] See also the earlier Opinion of Darmon AG in Case 302/87 *Parliament v Council (Comitology Case)* [1988] ECR 5615.

[64] For another such example, see Case 294/83 *Partie Ecologiste 'Les Verts' v European Parliament* [1986] ECR 1339. The ruling of the Court in that case was inserted in Article 173(1) (now 230(1)) EC by the TEU.

[65] See e.g. Case C-361/91 *Parliament v Council (Fourth Lomé Convention Case)* [1994] ECR I-625.

[66] See e.g. the post-*Barber* case law which interpreted the *Barber* judgment in accordance with the *Barber* Protocol. See Case C-109/91 *Ten Oever* [1993] ECR I-4879, C-110/91 *Moroni* [1993] ECR I-6591, Case C-152/91 *Neath* [1993] ECR I-6935, and Case C-262/88 *Barber* [1990] ECR I-1889.

[67] See e.g. Opinion 2/94 on the Accession of the EC to the ECHR [1996] ECR I-1759; Case C-249/96 *Grant v South West Trains Ltd* [1998] ECR I-621; Joined Cases C-122/99 P and C-125/99 P *D and Sweden v Council* [2001] ECR I-4319.

[68] Note in this context the limitations imposed on the Court's jurisdiction by the Treaty of Amsterdam as regards Title IV of the EC Treaty (visas, asylum and immigration, Article 68 EC) and Third Pillar matters (Article 35 TEU).

The second point is the following. The recognition of new rights has profound repercussions for the Court of Justice. It enhances its constitutional jurisdiction. More importantly, it adds to its workload which, in turn, has both quantitative and qualitative consequences. In quantitative terms, it affects the length of the proceedings.[69] Its qualitative effects are more subtle. Inevitably, an increase in legislation, countenanced by greater awareness of Community law among citizens and successive enlargements, leads to more litigation. In terms of judicial time, new rights compete with existing ones. To give an example, the right of access to documents has already generated considerable case law. The case law itself has a tendency to generate more litigation as a judicial pronouncement which solves one problem may itself give rise to others. Shortly stated, the point is this: excessive workload forces a court to rely on precedent more than it might otherwise do and poses the risk that such reliance may be mechanical. A busy Court favours self-restraint over activism but this is a self-restraint which is the result of neither conviction nor studied deference to the legislature. It is rather one which is liable to hinder conceptual innovation and disadvantage liberal causes.[70] One could counter-argue that excessive case law produces the opposite effect. The uncontrollable proliferation of judgments may have a liberating effect, in that, faced with too much precedent, the judges may be tempted to ignore it. In such a case, precedent ceases to fulfil its function. The losers are clear, namely coherence and certainty, but the winners are not. Either way, judicial protection may suffer. It is not suggested here that new rights should not be recognized. Nor is there any intention to criticize the Court. In fact, the Court of Justice and the Court of First Instance have coped admirably with the overwhelming increase in their case load and have made a major effort to push forward proposals for reform. The discussion is intended to illustrate precisely the need for reform in the Community judicial architecture so as to enable the Court to perform its function as the Supreme Court of the Union. This reform is currently taking place through the broadening of the jurisdiction of the CFI and the establishment of judicial panels.[71]

1.5. The Constitution and its values

The process of formalization of Community law reached its apex with the adoption of the Treaty establishing a Constitution for Europe.[72] Following its

---

[69] See the detailed study of C. Turner and R. Munoz, 'Revisiting the Judicial Architecture of the European Union', (1999–2000) 19 YEL 1.

[70] See R.A. Posner, *The Federal Courts: Challenge and Reform* (Harvard University Press, 1999), 324 *et seq.*   [71] See Articles 225 and 225a EC.

[72] The Treaty establishing a Constitution for Europe was adopted by the Convention on the Future of Europe on 13 June and 10 July 2003 and submitted to the President of the European Council in Rome on 18 July 2004. It formed the basis of negotiations in the Inter Governmental Conference, which began under the Italian Presidency on 4 October 2003, but the European

rejection in the French and Dutch referenda, the future of the Constitution is highly uncertain but it is conducive to examine here its values as reflected in Article 2. These values have declaratory character and represent the EU legal order as it currently stands. They have also, to a great extent, been based on the case law of the ECJ on general principles.

Article 2 reflects the values of the Union as follows:

The Union is founded on the values of respect for human dignity, freedom, democracy, equality, the rule of law and respect for human rights, including the rights of persons belonging to minorities. These values are common to the Member States in a society in which pluralism, non-discrimination, tolerance, justice, solidarity and equality between women and men prevail.

Article I-2 is more comprehensive than the provision of Article 6(1) TEU currently in force.[73] It operates on three levels: moral, political and legal. It seeks to encapsulate the spirit of liberal democracy and, more generally, 'the cultural, religious and humanist inheritance of Europe'.[74] It provides ideological continuity with the constitutional traditions of the Member States and defines what the Union stands for.[75] In doing so, it seeks to forge a common political identity and also serves as a postulate: respect for the values enshrined therein becomes a political and legal imperative both for the Union institutions and the Member States. Article I-2 provides a declaration of nascent nationhood and lays down the underpinnings for the recognition of European citizenship in subsequent provisions of the Constitution. The values of Article I-2 are 'indivisible and universal'.[76]

Council held in Brussels on 12 December 2003 failed to reach agreement on the final text. The major stumbling block proved to be the provisions allocating voting rights in the Council of Ministers. Following some amendments, it was adopted by the European Council on 17/18 June 2004 under the Irish Presidency. Under Article III-447(1) the Constitution cannot come into force unless it is ratified by all Member States in accordance with their respective constitutional requirements. As of the end of June 2005, it has been ratified by ten Member States but France and Netherlands failed to ratify it as it was rejected in referenda held on 29 May and 1 June 2005 respectively. Both countries rejected the Constitution decisively (France by 54.68% and the Netherlands by 62.8%). The European Council of Luxembourg held on 16/17 June 2005 called for a period of reflection. Some Member States have declared their commitment to continue with the ratification process. It is however very difficult to imagine how the Constitutional Treaty could be adopted in its present form. For the text of the Constitutional Treaty, see OJ 2004 C 310 (16 December 2004). For a discussion, see *inter alia*, J. Ziller, *La nouvelle Constitution européenne* (Paris: Editions la Découverte, 2004); D. Triantafyllou, *La Constitution de l'Union européenne* (Brussels: Bruylant, 2005).

[73] Article 6(1) TEU states as follows: 'The Union is founded on the principles of liberty, democracy, respect for human rights and fundamental freedoms, and the rule of law, principles which are common to the Member States.'

[74] See Preamble to the Constitution, recital 1.

[75] Note also the grand and emotive language used in the Preamble to the Constitution and the Preamble to the EU Charter of Fundamental Rights which is included in Part II of the Constitution. The former at recital 1 refers to the 'universal values of the inviolable and inalienable rights of the human person, democracy, equality, freedom and the rule of law'. The Preamble to the EU Charter on Fundamental Rights, paragraph 2, states that 'the Union is founded on the indivisible, universal values of human dignity, freedom, equality and solidarity'.

[76] See Preambles, *ibid.*

The legal significance of the provision is twofold. Respect for these values is a condition for admission to membership of the European Union.[77] Also, Article I-2 occupies a distinct position in the Constitutional Treaty and features at the top tier of the hierarchy of norms of EU law. It thus provides a prime point of reference for the interpretation of other provisions of the Constitution and, in effect, enhances the constitutional jurisdiction of the ECJ. There is no doubt that the values listed therein are abstract. However, shared commitment to abstract ideals is a feature of all constitutions. The purpose of Article I-2 is precisely this, i.e. to function as a source of convergence, to lay down a set of parameters within which political conflict can be resolved and social unity achieved.[78] Whether such idealism will survive the test of time remains to be seen. There is however a clear intention to cultivate the emergence of a European demos by laying down the attributes of a moral identity and a political community. A concept which is of particular relevance in this context is the concept of 'solidarity'. This transcends the relations between the individual and the State and refers to a sense of community. According to Bogdandy, it embodies an aspiration to make life better, 'to create new bonds' and 'the social basis for a broader polity in which the individual acts as a responsible *social* being'.[79]

Article I-2 underwent several revisions in the process of the drafting of the Constitution and the final text is, overall, better than previous versions. It is noteworthy that the reference to the rights of minorities was included in the final text by the Inter Governmental Conference of June 2004. This follows the pattern of many Central and Eastern European constitutions which make express reference to the protection of minority rights separately and in addition to classic human rights.[80] The reference to human dignity as the first value in Article I-2 is not accidental. Human dignity 'constitutes the real basis of fundamental rights'.[81] It is granted prevalent position in the Constitutions of many Member States,[82] features in the very first Article of the EU Charter[83] and lies at the 'very essence' of the ECHR.[84] It has also been recognized by the ECJ[85] and underlies key judgments on

---

[77] See Article I-1(2).

[78] See here the discussion by Sunstein, *op. cit.*, n. 3 above p. 4 and pp. 35 *et seq.*

[79] A. von Bogdandy, 'The Preamble' in Bruno de Witte (ed), *Ten Reflections on the Constitutional Treaty for Europe* (EUI, 2003), 3–10, at 9.

[80] See e.g. the Slovakian Constitution of 1992, Articles 33–34.

[81] See Updated Explanations relating to the text of the Charter of Fundamental Rights issued by the Praesidium of the Convention, CONV 828/1/03, p. 4.

[82] See e.g. Article 2 of the Greek Constitution.

[83] See Article II-61 of the Constitution which declares that 'Human dignity is inviolable'. See also the preamble to the 1948 Universal Declaration of Human Rights which states that 'recognition of the inherent dignity and of the equal and inalienable rights of all members of the human family is the foundation of freedom, justice and peace in the world'.

[84] See *SW v United Kingdom* and *CR v United Kingdom* (1995) 21 EHRR 363, paras 44 and 42, quoted by S. Millns, 'Bio-Rights, Common Values and Constitutional Strategies' in Tridimas and Nebbia (eds), *EU Law for the 21st Century*, Vol II, (Oxford: Hart Publishing, 2004) 387–402, at 393, n. 20.

[85] See Case C-377/98 *Netherlands v European Parliament and Council* [2001] ECR I-7079, paras 70–77.

non-discrimination law.[86] Some of the values laid down in Article I-2, such as democracy and non-discrimination, are exemplified and elaborated upon by other provisions of the Constitution. In relation to democracy, suffice it here to say that Article I-2 defines the Union as 'a society of pluralism, tolerance, justice, solidarity and non-discrimination'. This statement, which is reminiscent of the case law of the European Court of Human Rights,[87] envisages a notion of democracy which extends beyond majoritarianism and incorporates a broad conception of human rights. A further change made by the 2004 Inter Governmental Conference was the express reference to the principle of equal treatment between men and women in the final sentence of Article I-2.

1.6. The general principles as a source of Community law

1.6.1. The gap-filling function of general principles

Recourse to general principles as a source of law may be made by a court either as a result of an express reference contained in a legal text (*renvoi obligatoire*) or spontaneously by the court itself in order to fill a gap in written law (*référence spontanée*).[88] An example of an express reference is provided by Article 38(1)(c) of the International Court of Justice which mandates that court to apply the general principles of law recognized by civilized nations.[89] The EC Treaty contains two such references, an express one in Article 288(2) and a more oblique one in Article 220. Further references to specific principles have now been included in Articles 6(1) and (2) of the TEU and the EU Constitution.[90] These provisions are examined elsewhere in this book. For the time being, it is worth looking more closely at the function of general principles in judicial reasoning.

In any system of law a situation may arise where a *lacuna* exists in that a given situation is not governed by a rule of law, statutory or judicial. In such a case, the court having jurisdiction will resolve the case by deducing from the existing rules a rule which is in conformity with the underlying premises on which the legal system is based. This process is by no means peculiar to the Community legal order. It is practised by national courts, including in particular the French Conseil d'État on

---

[86] *P v S, op. cit.,* n. 50; Case C-117/01 *K.B. v National Health Service Pensions Agency and Secretary for Health,* judgment of 7 January 2004.

[87] The Court of Human Rights has stressed that the hallmarks of a democratic society include 'pluralism, tolerance and broadmindedness': see e.g. *Smith and Grady v United Kingdom* (2000) 29 EHRR 493, judgment of 27 September 1999, para 87.

[88] See D. Simon, 'Y a-t-il des principes généraux du droit communautaire?', (1991) 14 *Droits,* 73.

[89] See below, 1.10.

[90] See Article 6 TEU, as amended by the Treaty of Amsterdam, and Article I-2 of the EU Constitution.

which the Court was modelled.[91] *Lacunae* are more likely to arise in Community law, especially in the early stages in its development, since it is a new legal order. Community law simply lacks the accumulated judicial experience, buttressed in case law, that national legal systems possess. The need to fill gaps is exacerbated by the distinct characteristics of the Community legal order. Community law is not only a new legal order but also a novel one in the sense that it has no historical precedent or indeed contemporary equivalent.[92] It represents a new development in the law of international organizations. Also, the EC Treaty is a *traité cadre*. It provides no more than a framework. It is rampant with provisions overpowering in their generality and uses vague terms and expressions which are not defined. It bestows the Court with very broad powers to develop Community law. Further, Community law seeks to supplement rather than to substitute the national legal systems. It is logical for the Court, in filling any gaps which arise, to resort to and gain inspiration from the laws of Member States. Finally, by its nature, the Community is a dynamic entity. The founding and amending treaties are moulded by teleology. The EC Treaty itself sets final objectives and intermediate goals, the notion of incremental integration being inherent in its provisions.[93] Recourse to general principles enables the Court to follow an evolutive interpretation and be responsive to changes in the economic and political order.

Those features peculiar to Community law might explain why the Court is more 'active' than some national courts, i.e. why, as it is often said, it engages in judicial law-making.[94] The need to fill *lacunae* by recourse to national laws was expressly referred to in *Algera*, one of the early cases, where, faced with the problem of revocation of administrative acts granting rights to individuals, the Court stated:[95]

The possibility of withdrawing such measures is a problem of administrative law, which is familiar in the case-law and learned writing of all the countries of the Community, but for the solution of which the Treaty does not contain any rules. Unless the Court is to deny justice it is therefore obliged to solve the problem by reference to the rules acknowledged by the legislation, the learned writing and the case-law of the member countries.

---

[91] See, for example, to this effect the comments of commissaire du gouvernement Letourneur, quoted in D. Simon, *op. cit.*, n. 88 above, p. 73: 'à côté des lois écrites existent de grands principes dont la reconnaissance comme règles de droit est indispensable pour compléter le cadre juridique dans lequel doit évoluer la Nation, étant donné les institutions politiques et économiques qui sont les siennes'.

[92] Even if it is true that specific aspects of the legal and political system of the Community are found in other organizations, no organization combines all those aspects in the way that they are combined in the European Community.

[93] In its reasoning the Court sometimes inserts the proviso 'in the present state of Community law'; see e.g. Case 81/87 *The Queen v Treasury and Commissioners of Inland Revenue, ex p Daily Mail and General Trust plc* [1988] ECR 5483. It will be noted, however, that the term 'integration' lacks a specific legal meaning. See further for a discussion of the term, G. Soulier, *L'Europe*, p. 271.

[94] See T. Tridimas, 'The European Court of Justice and Judicial Activism', (1996) 21 ELR 199.

[95] Joined Cases 7/56 and 3-7/57 *Algera v Common Assembly* [1957–58] ECR 39 at 55.

Two points may be made at this juncture. First, it must be emphasized that the significance of general principles is not exhausted in their gap-filling function. They express constitutional standards underlying the Community legal order so that recourse to them is an integral part of the Court's methodology. The second point follows from the first. Once it is accepted that the general principles embody constitutional values, they may bear determinative influence on the interpretation of written rules, irrespective of the existence of gaps. In fact, the rational sequence may be reversed. Legislative provisions may be interpreted in the light of the underlying premises of the legal system in such a way as to leave gaps which then need to be filled by recourse to general principles. That is in effect what happened in *Chernobyl* where the Court, in order to avoid an openly *contra legem* interpretation of Article 173 (now 230) EC, established the existence of a procedural gap which it then filled by recourse to the principles of institutional balance and effective judicial protection.[96]

1.6.2. Article 220

Article 220(1) EC gives to the Court responsibility 'to ensure that in the interpretation and application of this Treaty the law is observed'. At first sight, this appears to be a tautology. Is it not, after all, obvious that the function of a court is to uphold the law? In fact, this concise and seemingly innocuous provision is replete with values, and arguably the most important provision of the founding Treaties. It establishes that the Community is bound by the rule of law and recognizes the separation of powers. When the European Communities were established in the 1950s, they were a political experiment. They set in motion a dynamic process projecting economic integration as the best way of enhancing peace and prosperity, as 'the thin entering wedge necessary to begin to dismantle the state's monopoly on authority'.[97] The postulation of Article 220 EC gave a clear signal that the founders of the EEC intended it to be not simply an international organization but a nascent form of a supra-national order founded on solid liberal credentials. Article 220 grants the Court responsibility to oversee the Community institutions so as to ensure that they do not extend their mandate under the Treaty. At the same time, it requires the Court to supervise the Member States thus releasing the integrative potential of the new entity. Article 220 thus enables the Court to oversee both branches of political authority, i.e. the Community institutions and the Member States, and signals an early transition from 'power-oriented' to 'rule-oriented' politics.[98]

Article 220 however does not provide any substantive standards of review. As has been noted, it assumes the existence of a legal order but tells us nothing about

---

[96] *Chernobyl, op. cit.*, n. 18 above, discussed below' 1.7.2.

[97] See J. P. Trachtman, 'L'Etat, C'est Nous: Sovereignty, Economic Integration and Subsidiarity', (1992) 33 *Harvard International Law Journal* 459, p. 465.

[98] The terms paraphrase J. H. Jackson, *The World Trading System* (Boston: MIT Press, 1989), at 85 who uses them in the context of the WTO.

its substantive principles.[99] Its cardinal importance lies precisely in that it mandates the Court to work out a system of legal principles in accordance with which the legality of Community and Member State action must be determined. In assessing the compatibility of Member State action with the Treaty, the Court is guided by the objectives and scheme of the Treaty, giving preference to a teleological interpretation of Community norms. Where it exercises judicial review of Community measures, the Court has even less guidance. Article 220 establishes the principle of legality as a paramount and overriding principle of Community law. Also, since it contains no substantive principles of its own, it mandates the Court to have recourse to the legal traditions of the Member States and extrapolate principles of law found therein, with a view to developing a notion of the rule of law appropriate to the Community.[100] In effect, Article 220 does no less than grant the Court jurisdiction to create 'constitutional doctrine by the common law method',[101] drawing inspiration from the liberal constitutional tradition. According to this model, the general principles of law as applied by the Court can be said to represent a common constitutional heritage. As Dutheillet de Lamothe AG put it:[102]

The fundamental principles of national legal systems ... contribute to forming that philosophical, political and legal substratum common to the Member States from which through the case-law an unwritten Community law emerges, one of the essential aims of which is to ... ensure the respect for the fundamental rights of the individual.

In conclusion, the fundamental justification of judicial recourse to the general principles of law should be sought in the function which those principles fill in the Community legal order. They enable the Court to develop a notion of the rule of law appropriate to the Community polity and at the same time ensure conceptual and ideological continuity with the legal systems of the Member States.

1.6.3. The Court's evaluative approach

It has become obvious from the above that the search for principles in the legal systems of Member States is not a mechanical process. The Court does not make a comparative analysis of national laws with a view to identifying and applying a

---

[99] See T. Koopmans, 'The Birth of European Law at the Crossroads of Legal Traditions', (1991) 39 AJCL 493, at 495.

[100] The Court has certainly understood Article 220 as giving it jurisdiction to gain inspiration from the laws of the Member States: see e.g. Joined Cases C-46 and C-48/93 *Brasserie du Pêcheur v Germany* and *the Queen v Secretary of State for Transport, ex p Factortame Ltd* [1996] ECR I-1029, paras 27, 41.

[101] See R. Posner, *Law and Legal Theory in the UK and the USA*, (Oxford University Press, 1996) p. 14. The comparatist will find it difficult to resist the temptation to draw parallels with the US Supreme Court. See, *inter alia*, K. Lenaerts, *Le Juge et la Constitution aux États-Unis d'Amérique et dans l'Ordre Juridique Européen*, 1988 and H. Rasmussen, *On Law and Policy in the European Court of Justice*, (Martinus Nijhoff, 1986).

[102] *Internationale Handelsgesellschaft, op. cit.*, n. 24 above, at 1146.

common denominator. Such an exercise would be as impractical as it would be futile. Rather, it makes a synthesis seeking the most appropriate solution on the circumstances of the case. The essence of the Court's evaluative approach was expressed by Lagrange AG as follows:[103]

... the case law of the Court, in so far as it invokes national laws (as it does to a large extent) to define the rules of law relating to the application of the Treaty, is not content to draw on more or less arithmetical 'common denominators' between the different national solutions, but chooses from each of the Member States those solutions which, having regard to the objects of the Treaty, appear to be the best or, if one may use the expression, the most progressive. That is the spirit ... which had guided the Court hitherto.

In accordance with the tenor of the above quotation, it has been said that the Court seeks such elements from national laws as will enable it to build a system of rules which will provide 'an appropriate, fair and viable solution'[104] to the legal issues raised, and the judicial enquiry has been referred to as 'free-ranging'.[105] The Court's approach can be illustrated by reference to two cases decided in the 1970s concerning respectively the protection of legitimate expectations and the rights of defence.

In the *Staff Salaries* case,[106] a dispute arose between the Commission and the Council regarding the formula to be used for the increase in the salaries of Community employees. Article 65 of the Staff Regulations provides that the Council shall review annually the remuneration of Community servants taking into account the rise in the cost of living and the increase in the salaries of public servants in the Member States. Following negotiations, the Council, the Commission, and staff representatives agreed a formula for adjusting salaries and by a decision of 21 March 1972 the Council decided to apply it on an experimental basis for a period of three years. Nine months after the adoption of the decision however, when the next salary review occurred, the Council used a different formula. The Commission argued that the Council was bound by its undertaking to use the formula specified in the decision of 21 March. Warner AG made a comparative overview of the laws of the Member States and came to the conclusion that, in the national laws, a public authority may not fetter its discretion for the future where it exercises a legislative power. It may only, in exceptional circumstances, be bound in relation to an individual decision. The Advocate General concluded that, since the contested decision applied generally to all employees of the Communities, legitimate expectations could not arise. The Council's decision 'was, in law, no better than a rope of sand'.[107] The Court took the opposite view. It held that in adopting the decision of 21 March 1972, the Council had gone

---

[103] Case 14/61 *Hoogovens v High Authority* [1962] ECR 253, at pp. 283–284.

[104] P. J. G. Kapteyn and P. Verloren van Themaat, *Introduction to the Law of the European Communities*, Third Ed., (Kluwer, 1998) p. 161.

[105] L. Neville Brown & F. G. Jacobs, *The Court of Justice of the European Communities*, Fifth Ed., (by L. Neville Brown and T. Kennedy), Sweet & Maxwell, 2000, p. 175.

[106] Case 81/72 *Commission v Council (Staff Salaries)* [1973] ECR 575.   [107] *ibid.*, p. 595.

beyond the stage of preparatory consideration and had entered into the phase of decision-making.[108] The principle of protection of legitimate expectations required the Council to be bound by its undertaking. The judgment may not be as far reaching as it appears on first sight: the Council considered itself bound by the decision of 21 March 1972 and the decision was not incompatible with the Staff Regulations. It does illustrate however that the content of a general principle of law as recognized by the Court may differ from that recognized in the laws of the Member States. The *Staff Salaries* case established the principle of protection of legitimate expectations as a general principle of Community law which binds the Community not only in relation to administrative acts but also in relation to legislative measures.

In *AM & S v Commission*,[109] the Commission required the applicant company to produce certain documents in the course of its investigation into a suspected violation of competition law. The company raised the objection that the documents in issue were covered by legal professional privilege. The problem was that neither Regulation 17,[110] which provides the powers of the Commission to order inspections and carry out investigations, nor any other provision of Community law, recognized the confidentiality of communications between lawyer and client. The Court started by pointing out that Community law derives not only from the economic but also from the legal interpenetration of Member States and must take into account the principles and concepts common to their laws concerning the confidentiality of lawyer–client communications. The rationale for such confidentiality is to ensure that a person is not inhibited from consulting a lawyer and obtaining independent legal advice. The Court noted that, although the confidentiality of lawyer–client communications is protected in all Member States, the scope of protection varies. It identified two tendencies. In some Member States, the protection against disclosure is seen as deriving from the very nature of the legal profession and serving the interests of the rule of law, whilst in others, it is justified on the more specific ground that the rights of defence must be respected. Despite those differences, the Court found that all national laws protect legal professional privilege subject to two criteria, namely, that communications are made in the interests of the client's rights of defence and that they emanate from independent lawyers, that is to say, lawyers who are not bound to the client by a relationship of employment. It concluded that Regulation No 17 must be interpreted as protecting legal professional privilege subject to those conditions and, on the facts, annulled in part the Commission's request for disclosure.

AM & S, in contrast to the *Staff Salaries* case, suggests a minimalist approach. The Court identified common criteria in the national laws and recognized a principle of Community law subject to those criteria. By contrast, in *Staff Salaries* the Court provided a higher degree of protection for the individual than that recognized in

---

[108] Para 8.   [109] Case 155/79 [1982] ECR 1575.
[110] First Regulation implementing Articles 85 and 86 of the Treaty, OJ, English Special Ed., 1959–62, p. 87. This has now been superseded by Regulation 1/2003 (OJ 2003 L1/1).

national laws. Two points may be made in this context. It is evident that the Court's function is *par excellence* a creative one. It borrows elements from the laws of Member States and may have particular regard to 'the best elaborated national rules'[111] but principles and solutions suggested by national laws are conditioned by the Community objectives and polity. This is of particular importance in the area of human rights which are protected in Community law but, according to the standard formula used by the Court, may be subject to limits justified by the objectives of the Community provided that their substance is left untouched.[112] The second point refers to comparative law as an aid to interpretation. In both cases discussed above, the advocates general made ample references to the laws of Member States.[113] Although recourse to national laws was made more often at earlier stages in the development of Community law, it is by no means an exercise which has exhausted its usefulness.[114] More recent examples are provided by *van Schijndel* and *Peterbroeck*,[115] where Jacobs AG referred to the laws of the Member States concerning the powers of national courts to raise issues of national law *ex propriu motu*. In fact, a criticism which may be levelled against the Community judiciary is that it does not always take comparative law sufficiently seriously. For example, in the first generation of cases establishing the liability of Member States in damages,[116] the Court referred to the laws of the Member States with a view to articulating the conditions of liability, but did not make a serious attempt to derive truly common principles from the national legal systems regarding the right to reparation.[117]

1.6.4. The influence of national laws

No doubt, the Court's approach is eclectic but the raw material is found, inevitably, in the laws of Member States. Have the laws of any particular State or States proved more influential? Since in most cases it is not possible to trace the origins of Community solutions directly to concepts of national laws, this question can

[111] Case 5/71 *Zuckerfabrik Schöppenstedt v Council* [1971] ECR 975, at 989 *per* Roemer AG.

[112] See e.g. *Nold, op. cit.*, n. 30 above, para 14.

[113] The Court incorporates a Research and Documentation Division which is staffed by experts in national laws. One of their tasks is to prepare at the request of the Court comparative accounts of the laws of Member States on specific topics. These are used for internal purposes and are not published. Occasionally, the Court may ask the Commission to produce information regarding the regulation of an economic activity in the Member States: see Joined Cases 60 and 61/84 *Cinéthèque v Fédération Nationale des Cinémas Français* [1985] ECR 2605, para 19.

[114] See T. Koopmans, 'Comparative Law and the Courts', (1996) 45 ICLQ 545.

[115] Joined Cases C-430 and C-431/93 *van Schijndel and van Veen v SPF* [1995] ECR I-4705 and Case C-312/93 *Peterbroeck v Belgian State* [1995] ECR I-4599.

[116] See Joined Cases *Brasserie du Pêcheur* and *Factortame, op. cit.*, n. 100 above, Case C-5/94; *The Queen v Ministry of Agriculture, Fisheries and Food ex p Hedley Lomas (Ireland) Ltd* [1996] ECR I-2553; Joined Cases C-178, C-179, C-188–190/94 *Dillenkofer and others v Federal Republic of Germany* [1996] ECR I-4845.

[117] See the criticism of W. van Gerven, 'Taking Article 215 EC Seriously' in J. Beatson and T. Tridimas (eds), *New Directions in European Public Law*, (Hart Publishing, 1998), p. 47.

only be answered in more general terms by reference to principles, trends, and methodology. It may be said that two legal traditions have proved particularly influential in forming Community administrative law: the German and the French tradition. The reasons are, more than anything, historical.

The German influence is prominent in the development of the general principles, such as proportionality, legitimate expectations and protection of fundamental rights.[118] Why has German law proved so influential? The analysis of Nolte is here instructive.[119] It is arguable that, in the formative years of the Community, the Court of Justice found itself in a position similar to that of the German judiciary in post-war years. In the aftermath of the Second World War, German legal thought experienced a resurgence of natural law thinking. The abuses of the Nazi regime had as a consequence the distrust of executive power and the search for constitutional principles constraining administrative discretion. Prevailing doctrine sought to give the concept of 'Rechtsstaat' a minimum substantive content. The principles of equality, proportionality and protection of legitimate expectations which, in the pre-war era were recognized only in embryonic form and played only a limited scope in judicial reasoning, were developed in the 1950s by the judiciary as constitutionally mandated principles forming part of a wider substantive 'Rechtsstaat'. Those principles, together with the doctrine of limited administrative discretion, gradually led to the establishment of a body of administrative law founded on the new constitutional order. A parallel has been drawn between the emergence of general principles of administrative law in post-war Germany and the elaboration of general principles in the case law of the Court of Justice. In both cases, recourse to general principles has been in search of legitimacy. In the case of post-war Germany, it was imbued by considerations of substantive justice and was the result of a crisis of legitimacy. In Community law, recourse to general principles has been in an effort to assert the legitimacy and supremacy of Community law over conflicting national traditions.[120]

The French tradition has influenced Community law both directly and indirectly. Its direct influence is particularly prominent in the system of legal protection established by the Treaties. It has been decisive as regards the action for annulment, e.g. Articles 33 ECSC and 173 (now 230) EC, and as regards the organization of the Court of Justice which was modelled on the French Conseil d'État. French law also influenced Community law indirectly through its impact on the national laws of other Member States. The French public law tradition is the strongest in Europe and French administrative law provided a model for other continental countries from the nineteenth century onwards.

It should also not be overlooked that the French and the German traditions were represented by the first two Advocates General of the Court, Lagrange AG and

---

[118] See Schwarze, *European Administrative Law*, n. 6 above, esp. Chapters 1, 2 and 8.

[119] See G. Nolte, 'General Principles of German and European Administrative law—A Comparison in Historical Perspective', (1994) 57 MLR 191.

[120] Nolte, *op. cit.*, 200, 205–6.

Roemer AG. They served during the most formative years of Community law fulfilling in effect the role of pathfinders. Their influence has been particularly instrumental in establishing the principles of Community administrative law, and in distilling, through a comparative method of interpretation, the elements of national laws most suitable for transposition in the Community legal order. Notable examples include *ASSIDER v High Authority*,[121] where Lagrange AG made a comparative analysis of the notion of misuse of powers, and *Algera v Common Assembly*[122] where he considered the national rules governing the revocation of beneficial administrative acts.

English law, by contrast, has had comparatively less influence at least on the development of substantive principles of law. The reasons are not difficult to understand. The United Kingdom and Ireland being late entries, the common law tradition was absent in the early formative years of Community law. More importantly, English administrative law does not share the theoretical under-pinnings of its continental counterparts. Bred in a Diceyan tradition, it developed subject to the constraints of Parliamentary supremacy and the *ultra vires* doctrine. But its weakness has also been its strength: preoccupied as it has traditionally been with issues of procedure, it influenced decisively the development of procedural safeguards in the case law of the Court of Justice.[123]

If any conclusion may be drawn from this short survey it is that no national law can claim overriding influence on the development of Community public law. More importantly, perhaps, one must not be left with the impression that the flow of ideas has been only one way. Even legal systems which have proved particularly influential on the case law, such as the German and the French systems, have themselves been profoundly influenced by jurisprudential developments for which they provided the raw material in the first place.[124] Rather than dividing the national legal systems in to 'borrowers' and 'lenders', one should celebrate the dialectical development of Community and national laws through which a *jus communae* is steadily and increasingly evolving.

1.6.5. Attributes of general principles

What attributes must a legal proposition present in order to be recognized as a general principle of Community law? The Court will first seek guidance from the text, the aims, and the objectives of the Treaty and the provisions of Community

---

[121] Case 3/54 [1954–56] ECR 63.   [122] *Op. cit.*, n. 95 above.

[123] See n. 109 above *AM & S* and below Chapter 7.

[124] For the influence of the Court's case law on general principles on French law, see Y.Galmot, 'L'apport des principes généraux du droit communautaire à la garantie des droits dans l'ordre juridique français', (1997) 33 CDE 67. For its influence on German law, see Nolte, *op. cit.*, n. 119, 206–211. For the inter-relationship between Community law and English law, see D.Wyatt, 'European Community Law and Public law in the United Kingdom', in B. S. Markezinis, *The Gradual Convergence: Foreign Ideas, Foreign Influences and English Law on the Eve of the 21st Century*, (Oxford University Press, 1994) 188–201.

law. It will also look at the laws of the Member States and international agreements to which the Community or the Member States are parties. As a general guidance, the principle must incorporate a minimum ascertainable legally binding content. In the absence of guidance by Community written law, it must be widely accepted in one way or another by the Member States. As already stated, the approach of the ECJ is selective and creative. It does not look for a common denominator.[125] Nonetheless, to be elevated to the status of a general principle, a proposition must enjoy a degree of wide acceptance, i.e. represent 'conventional morality'.[126] In *D and Sweden v Council* the ECJ felt unable to equate a same sex relation sanctioned by national law to a marriage but hinted that it would have been more adventurous if there had been support in the laws of the Member States.[127] In *Hautala*,[128] Léger AG identified three sources of fundamental rights and general principles. First, international instruments, such as the ECHR to which Member States gave access. Second 'the convergence of the constitutional traditions of the Member States' noting that such convergence suffices in itself to establish the existence of a general principle in the absence of its express recognition in the ECHR or another international convention. Further, the Advocate General stated that a general principle may be recognized without first establishing the existence of either constitutional rules common to the Member States or rules laid down in international instruments. It may be sufficient that Member States have a common approach to the right in issue 'demonstrating the same desire to provide protection, even when the level of that protection and the procedure for affording it are provided for differently in the various Member States'. On that basis, the Advocate General concluded that the right of access to documents is a fundamental right in Community law.[129]

A principle may be derived from specific rules of Community law only if it is in accordance with the objectives of the Treaty. Thus, the Court will be reluctant to

---

[125] If a principle is common to the laws of most Member States it will be recognized as a general principle of Community law although, as already pointed out, its specific content and limits may be different in Community law. There is an example of a case where the ECJ refused to adopt a solution common to the laws of the Member States. In C-321/95 P *Greenpeace Council and Others v Commission* [1998] ECR I-1651, it refused *locus standi* under Article 230(4) EC to an environmental association despite the fact that, arguably, the applicants would have enjoyed standing in an equivalent case in the national courts of most, if not all, Member States. The judgment was justified by the strict interpretation of the concept of individual concern and the perception that the restricted *locus standi* of individuals under Article 230(4) is compensated by the availability of indirect challenge before national courts. The Court stressed that the environmental rights invoked by Greenpeace 'are fully protected by national courts'. This reasoning however is unconvincing.

[126] See John Hart Ely, *Democracy and Distrust* (Boston: Harvard University Press, 1980) p. 63, n. 97 and references provided therein.   [127] *Op. cit.*, n. 67 above, paras 50–51.

[128] Case C-353/99 P *Council v Hautala* [2001] ECR I-9565 at 9582–3.

[129] The Advocate General noted that thirteen out of the fifteen countries which were then Member States recognized as a general rule that the public has a right of access to documents held by the administration. In nine of them it was a principle of a constitutional nature or a right founded in the constitution but of a legislative nature. In the remaining four, the right derived from specific laws.

derive a principle from a provision derogating from fundamental rules even if such derogations are contained in many provisions.[130]

In *Jippes*[131] the Court declined the invitation to recognize animal welfare as a general principle of law. It reasoned as follows. It held that ensuring the welfare of animals does not form part of the objectives of the Treaty as defined in Article 2 EC nor is it mentioned as one of the objectives of the common agricultural policy in Article 33 EC. It then referred to the Protocol on the protection and welfare of animals annexed to the EC Treaty by the Treaty of Amsterdam and held that the Protocol does not lay down a well-defined principle which is binding on the Community institutions.[132] The Court held further that it was not possible to infer a general principle of animal welfare from the European Convention on the Protection of Animals kept for Farming Purposes[133] since it does not impose any clear, precise and unqualified obligation. Nor could a general principle be inferred from any other provision of EU law.

The Court's approach was reactive rather than pro-active. It examined Treaty and legislative texts with a view to establishing the existence of a general principle thus employing a deductive reasoning which is in sharp contrast with its approach in the 1960s and 1970s when it recognized general principles of law despite the lack of statutory guidance. It will be noted however that neither the laws of the Member States nor Community law provided the basis for recognizing a general principle of animal welfare. In any event, it is doubtful whether recognition of a principle of animal welfare would have made any difference to the outcome in the circumstances of the case. The Court accepted that the public interest of the Community includes the health and protection of animals and found that the contested measures did take animal welfare into account.

Although the case law makes references to concepts such as equity or fairness and the ECJ has accepted that considerations of fairness may underlie certain Community provisions,[134] it has held that there is no general principle of fairness in EC

---

[130] In Case T-18/97 *Atlantic Container Line and Others v Commission* [2002] ECR II-1125, it was held that there is no general principle in Community law that undertakings which notify anti-competitive agreements enjoy immunity from fines. The fact that Regulations No 17, No 4056/86 (maritime transport) and No 3975/87 (air transport) all contain provisions for immunity from fines in the event of notification does not imply the existence of a general principle. It follows that, since Regulation No 1017/68 (applying rules of competition to transport by rail, road and inland waterway) contains no provision granting immunity from fines, notification of agreements falling within the scope of that regulation does not confer immunity.

[131] Case C-189/01 *Jippes and Others* [2001] ECR I-5689.

[132] The Court pointed out that although the Protocol provides that full regard must be had to the welfare requirements of animals in the formulation and implementation of Community policy, this obligation is limited to specific spheres of Community activity and is qualified by the need to respect the laws and customs of Member States as regards, in particular, religious rites, cultural traditions and regional heritage.

[133] The Convention was adopted within the framework of the Council of Europe on 10 March 1976 and approved by the EC by Council Decision 78/923, OJ 1978, L 323/12.

[134] See e.g. C-61/98 *de Haan v Inspecteur der Invoerrechten en Accijnzen te Rotterdam* [1999] ECR I-5003; Case C-290/91 *Peter v Hauptzollamt Regensburg* [1993] ECR I-2981, para 11; Case C-366/95

law.[135] What lies behind those rulings are, to a great extent, considerations of efficiency. The meaning of fairness is so vague that it lacks objective determination. Recognizing such a general principle might encourage undue litigation and hamper legislative discretion. What appears fair to one person may appear unfair to another and, as Jacobs AG pointed out, the individual conception of fairness must be balanced with what appears from the point of view of the Community.[136] In short, the principle is too abstract to have any autonomous normative concept outside the bounds of other principles such as equality, legitimate expectations, or proportionality.[137]

Despite early cases which may suggest otherwise,[138] Community preference, according to which preference must be given to Community agricultural products over products from third countries, is not a general principle of Community law. Preference in favour of Community production underlies aspects of the common agricultural policy but there is no general principle of Community preference which transcends written law and on the basis of which the ECJ may invalidate Community legislation.[139] In any event, such a principle would nowadays run a serious risk of being contrary to the Community's international obligations under the WTO and other international agreements.

By contrast, the ECJ and the CFI have made reference and endorsed in various contexts and for various purposes the principles of democracy,[140] transparency, institutional balance,[141] good administration, good faith,[142] and abuse of rights.

Landbrugsministeriet v Steff-Houlberg Export and Others [1998] ECR I-2661. For the distinction drawn in some national laws between subjective and objective equity, see the Opinion of Jacobs AG in *Peter*, at 2993, also Case 5/73 *Balkan Import-Export v Hauptzollamt Berlin-Packhof* [1973] ECR 1091, at 1192.

[135] See C-174/89 *Hoche v BALM* [1990] ECR I-2681, at 31; Case 299/84 *Newmann v BALM* [1985] ECR I-3663, para 23.   [136] *De Haan, op. cit.*, 5025.

[137] The ECJ has also rejected the suggestion that there is a general principle of administrative law requiring continuity in the composition of an administrative body handling a procedure which may lead to a fine: Joined Cases T-305- 307, 313–318, 325, 328, 329 & 335/94 *Limburgse Vinyl Maatschappij NV and Others v Commission (Polypropylene cases)* [1999] ECR I-931.

[138] Case 5/67 *Beus v HZA München* [1968] ECR 83 at 98.

[139] Case C-353/92 *Greece v Council* [1994] ECR I-3411, para 50. The ECJ however has recognized that, in some circumstances, it may not be unlawful to give preference to Community production: see e.g. *Balkan Import-Export, op. cit.*, n. 134 above, para 15; Case 58/86 *Coopérative Agricole d'Approvisionnement des Avirons v Receveur des Douanes* [1987] ECR 1525, para 9. For further discussion of this principle, see the Opinion of Jacobs AG in *Greece v Council, op. cit.*, at 3432 and Usher, *General principles, op. cit.*, n. 6, pp.13–16. Community preference may be, in certain contexts or at certain times, a political objective. See e.g. a reference in relation to the labour market, Council Resolution of 27 June 1980 on guidelines for a Community labour market policy, OJ 1980, C 168/1.

[140] See e.g. Joined Cases T-222/99, T-327/99 and T-329/99 *Jean Claude Martinez et al v European Parliament* [2001] ECR II-2823; Case T-135/96 *UEAPME v Council and Commission* [1998] ECR II-2335. For a discussion of the notion of democracy in the case law, see K. Lenaerts and T. Corthaut, 'Judicial Review as a Contribution to the Development of European Constitutionalism', in Tridimas and Nebbia, *European Union Law for the Twenty-first century, op. cit.*, Volume 1, pp. 17–64.

[141] See *Chernobyl, op. cit.*, n. 18 above; Case C-282/90 *Vreugdenhil v Commission* [1992] ECR I-1937; Case C-58/94 *Netherlands v Council* [1996] ECR I-2169.

[142] See e.g. Case T-115/94 *Opel Austria v Council* [1997] ECR II-39.

In some cases, instead of developing general principles of EU law, the ECJ has been content to allow national courts to rely on general principles recognized by the law of Member States. This has occurred in relation to the principle of protection of legitimate expectations[143] and the doctrine of abuse of rights[144] in the context of the adjudication of Community rights by national courts. Such selective deference to concepts of national law may be seen as an application of judicial subsidiarity in the field of remedies and legal protection.

1.7. The function of general principles in the Community legal order

In Community law, the general principles perform a threefold function. They operate as aids to interpretation, as grounds for review, and as rules of law breach of which may give rise to tortious liability. Each of those functions will now be examined in turn.

1.7.1. Aid to interpretation

Recourse to the general principles may be made as an aid to the interpretation of written law. According to a general rule of interpretation which derives from the principle of hierarchy of norms, where a Community measure falls to be interpreted, preference must be given as far as possible to the interpretation which renders it compatible with the Treaty and the general principles of law.[145] Thus, the Court has interpreted agricultural regulations and other measures so as to comply with the principle of equal treatment,[146] the principle of protection of legitimate expectations,[147] the freedom to pursue a trade or profession,[148] other fundamental rights,[149] and the principle of proportionality.[150] In the same vein, it has been held that the Staff Regulations must be interpreted in such a way as to ensure that there is no breach of a superior rule of law, such as the principle of equal treatment.[151] The rule of consistent interpretation applies of course not only to regulations but to all provisions of secondary Community law.[152] One of its specific expressions is the presumption against the retroactive application of laws.[153]

---

[143] See e.g. Joined cases 205–215/82 *Deutsche Milchkontor* v *Germany* [1983] ECR 2633.

[144] Case C-373/97 *Diamandis* v *Elliniko Domosio* [2000] ECR I-1705.

[145] See Case 218/82 *Commission* v *Council* [1983] ECR 4063, para 15; *Klensch, op. cit.*, n. 31 above, para 21; Case C-314/89 *Rauh* [1991] ECR I-1647, para 17.   [146] *Klensch, op. cit.*

[147] *Rauh, op. cit.* See also for legal certainty: Case C-1/94 *Cavarzere Produzioni Industriali* v *Ministero dell' Agricoltura e delle Foreste* [1995] ECR I-2363, para 30.

[148] Joined Cases C-90 and C-91/90 *Neu and Others* [1991] ECR I-3617.

[149] See e.g. in relation to the rights of defence, Joined Cases 46/87 and 227/88 *Hoechst* v *Commission* [1989] ECR 2859, para 12.   [150] Case C-206/94 *Brennet* v *Paletta* [1996] ECR I-2357.

[151] See e.g. Case T-93/94 *Becker* v *Court of Auditors* [1996] ECR II-141.

[152] See e.g. for directives Case C-392/93 *The Queen* v *HM Treasury ex p British Telecommunications plc* [1996] ECR I-1631, para 28, and for decisions, Case C-135/93 *Spain* v *Commission* [1995] ECR I-1651, para 37.   [153] See below 6.3.9.

A question which defies general answer is what are the limits of consistent interpretation. Clearly, general principles of law do not authorise a *contra legem* interpretation of Community measures[154] and there are dicta to the effect that the Court does not have a general power to supplement or amend legislation which otherwise would be invalid.[155] The provision in issue must be reasonably capable of being interpreted so as to comply with the general principles. However, what is a *contra legem* interpretation is itself an open question. A parallel may be drawn here with the duty of *interpretation conforme* laid down by the Court in *Marleasing*.[156] In both instances, the purpose of consistent interpretation is the same, namely to ensure that in a hierarchical system of norms rules of the lower tier are interpreted in the light of rules in the higher tier.[157] It will be noted that, at least in one case, the Court adopted in the light of general principles a more liberal interpretation of the Treaty itself than it is normally prepared to adopt in relation to measures of secondary Community law.[158]

The limits of what can be achieved by interpretation are illustrated by *Mulder I* and *von Deetzen*.[159] In those cases, the Court held that the contested regulation on milk quotas could not be interpreted in such a way as to guarantee a quota to producers who returned to the market after suspending production for a limited period, and found that the regulation was invalid for breach of the principle of protection of legitimate expectations. In borderline cases, there may be disagreement between the Court and the Advocate General. In *Diversinte*,[160] the Advocate General was prepared to follow a liberal interpretation of the provision in issue so as to ensure compliance with the principle of proportionality although he conceded that, in view of the text, such interpretation required 'goodwill'.[161] The Court took a different view and annulled the provision. In exceptional circumstances, the need to comply with the general principles may justify the analogical application of Community law.

---

[154] Case C-37/89 *Weiser* [1990] ECR I- 2395 at p. 2415 *per* Darmon AG.

[155] Case C-85/90 *Dowling* [1992] ECR I-5305 at p. 5319 *per* Jacobs AG.

[156] This view received judicial recognition in Case C-125/97 *Regeling* [1998] ECR I-4493 at 4503 *per* Cosmas AG. In Case C-106/89 *Marleasing* [1990] ECR I-4135, it was held that, in applying national law, a national court is required to interpret it 'as far as possible' in the light of the wording and the purpose of the directive in issue, whether the national law was adopted before or after the directive (para 8).

[157] In his Opinion in *Marleasing*, van Gerven AG emphasised the limits imposed on the duty of national courts to interpret national legislation so as to comply with Community law by the principles of legal certainty and non-retroactivity. Also, in his Opinion in *Barber, op. cit.*, n. 66 above, at p. 1937, he stated that Community law may set limits to certain methods of inter-pretation applied under national law but it may not compel the national court to give a *contra legem* interpretation. The imperfect character of the interpretative duty laid down in *Marleasing* was implicitly recognized by the Court in Case 334/92 *Wagner Miret* [1993] ECR I-6911. The potential scope and limitations of *Marleasing* are vividly illustrated by the following judgments: Case C-32/93 *Webb v EMO Cargo* [1994] ECR I-3567; Joined Cases C-240 to C-244/98 *Océano Grupo Editorial and Salvat Editores* [2000] ECR I-4941; Case C-168/95 *Arcaro* [1996] ECR I-4705.

[158] See *Chernobyl op. cit.*, discussed below 1.7.2.

[159] Case 120/86 *Mulder v Minister van Landbouw en Visserij* [1988] ECR 2321; Case 170/86 *von Deetzen v Hauptzollampt Hamburg-Jonas* [1988] ECR 2355. Discussed below 1.7.2.

[160] Joined Cases C-260 and C-261/91 *Diversinte et Iberlacta* [1993] ECR I-1885.

[161] *Op. cit.*, p. 1903 *per* Gulmann AG.

In *Krohn v BALM*[162] it was held that traders may be entitled to rely on the application by analogy of a regulation which is not intended to apply to them if two conditions are satisfied: (a) the rules to which they are subject contain an omission which is incompatible with a general principle of Community law, and (b) those rules are very similar to the rules whose application they seek by analogy.[163]

The general principles of law may be used also as an aid for the interpretation of national measures which implement Community law and, more generally, which fall within the scope of Community law. It follows that a national court must, as far as possible, interpret a provision of national law which falls within the ambit of Community law so as to comply with general principles and, if necessary, make a reference to the Court of Justice in order to ascertain the requirements of Community law in the case in issue.

1.7.2. Grounds for review

Most commonly, the general principles are invoked in order to obtain the annulment of a Community measure in proceedings under Article 230 or under Article 234. As far as the grounds of review are concerned, indirect challenge under Article 234 is equivalent to direct challenge under Article 230.[164] A Community measure which infringes a general principle will be annulled by the Court or the CFI, depending on which court has jurisdiction.[165] It will then be up to the institution concerned to take the measures necessary to comply with the judgment, as provided by Article 233(1) of the Treaty. The Court, or the CFI, does not have jurisdiction to order the institutions to take such measures and may not issue directions to that effect.[166] An interesting illustration of this is provided by *AssiDomän Kraft Products and Others v Commission (Woodpulp III)*.[167] It was held at first instance that where the CFI or the ECJ annuls a Commission decision addressed to several undertakings, the Commission may be required under Article 233 to take measures in relation not only to the successful parties but also to the addressees of the decision who did not bring an action for annulment. Although

---

[162] Case 165/84 [1985] ECR 3997.

[163] *Op. cit.*, para. 14. The omission of the regulation in issue infringed the principle of equal treatment. See for the same principle, Case 64/74 *Reich v Hauptzollamt Landau* [1975] ECR 261, Case 6/78 *Union Française de Céréales v Hauptzollamt Hamburg-Jonas* [1978] ECR 1675. Cf Case T-489/93 *Unifruit Hellas v Commission* [1994] ECR II-1201, paras 56 *et seq.*, where the CFI rejected an argument calling for the analogical application of a regulation in order to ensure the protection of legitimate expectations. Confirmed on appeal: Case C-51/95 P, [1997] ECR I-727.

[164] For a detailed discussion of these articles, see T. Hartley, *The Foundations of European Community Law* (Fifth Ed., 2003); Schermers and Waelbroeck, *op. cit*, Ch. 3.

[165] For the jurisdiction of the CFI, see above.

[166] See e.g. Case T-346/94 *France-Aviation v Commission* [1995] ECR II-2841, paras 41–43; Case T-5/94 *J v Commission* [1994] ECR II-391, para 17 and see further Joined Cases 97, 99, 193 and 215/86 *Asteris v Commission* [1988] ECR 2181 and Case T-224/95 *Tremblay v Commission* [1997] ECR II-2215.

[167] Case T-227/95 [1997] ECR II-1185. See also Joined Cases 42 and 59/59 *Snupat v High Authority* [1962] ECR 53.

the circumstances of the case were exceptional and the CFI made its ruling subject to strict conditions being met,[168] the ECJ reversed it on appeal.[169] It held that Article 233 requires the Commission to take the necessary measures to comply with the judgment annulling the measure. The scope of Article 233, however, is limited in two respects. First, in annulling a Community act, the Court may not pronounce further than what is sought by the applicant. Consequently, if an addressee of a decision decides to bring an action for annulment, the matter to be tried by the Court relates only to those aspects of the decision which concern the addressee. Unchallenged aspects concerning other addressees do not form part of the matter to be tried by the Court. Second, an annulling judgment applies *ergo omnes* but cannot go as far as to entail annulment of an act not challenged before the Court but alleged to be vitiated by the same illegality.

The Court also reiterated the principle that a decision which has not been challenged by the addressee within the time limit laid down by Article 230 becomes definitive against him.[170] Otherwise, an applicant would be able to circumvent the time limit provided for in Article 230. The Court concluded that, where a number of similar individual decisions imposing fines have been adopted pursuant to a common procedure and only some addressees have taken legal action against the decisions concerning them and obtained their annulment, the principle of legal certainty means that the institution which adopted the decision does not need to re-examine at the request of other addressees the legality of the unchallenged decisions in the light of the grounds of the annulling judgment.

The judgment of the ECJ in *Woodpulp III* embraces formalism and accepts that legality must give way to legal certainty. The case illustrates that the notion of illegality is relative and celebrates the voidable character of Community acts. It also enhances the risk character of litigation. Although economic considerations were not an express part of its reasoning, the Court accepted in effect the Commission's argument that, if the respondents succeeded, they would derive an unfair advantage by free riding on the success of competitor undertakings who incurred the financial risks of bringing the action for annulment.[171]

Article 231(2) provides that, in the case of a regulation, the Court shall, if it considers it necessary, state which of the effects of the regulation which it has

---

[168] In *AssiDomän*, the Court pointed out three material conditions: (a) the previous judgment in *Woodpulp* had annulled an act of the Commission which was made up of a number of individual decisions which were adopted on the completion of the same administrative procedure; (b) the applicants were addressees of the annulled act and had been fined for the alleged violation of Article 81 EC which the Court set aside in the *Woodpulp* judgment; and (c) the individual decisions adopted in relation to the applicants were based on the same findings of fact and the same economic and legal analyses as those declared invalid by that judgment (para 71).

[169] Case C-310/97 P *Commission v AssiDomän Kraft Products aB and Others* [1999] ECR I-5363.   [170] See Case C-188/92 *TWD v Germany* [1994] ECR I-833.

[171] The judgment in *Woodpulp III* has subsequently been extended to anti-dumping duties: Case C-239/99 *Nachi Europe GmbH v Hauptzollamt Krefeld* [2001] ECR I-1197; but distinguished by the CFI in relation to other aspects of the anti-dumping procedure: see *Medici Grimm, op. cit.*, n. 40 above.

declared void shall be considered as definitive. That provision applies not only to regulations but to any act of general application, including directives.[172] An example is provided by the *Staff Salaries* case.[173] It will be remembered that the Court annulled the contested decision laying down the method of calculating salary increases on the ground that the Council had not followed the formula which it had undertaken to use in subsequent adjustments. But to avoid a gap in the payment of salaries, the Court declared that the contested decision would continue to have effect until the measures taken to give effect to the judgment came into force. Article 231(2) is used in particular where a measure is annulled on procedural grounds. In the 1990s, the Parliament's tactical litigation policy, where successful, supplied fruitful ground for its application.[174]

A ruling in proceedings under Article 234 that a Community provision is invalid produces *vis-à-vis* national courts comparable effects to a declaration of invalidity under Article 230.[175] By analogy with Article 231(2), the effects of the ruling may be restricted in time so as not to affect past transactions.[176] In exceptional cases, a finding of illegality may not lead to a declaration of invalidity. In the *quellmehl* cases,[177] Community regulations granted a subsidy for the manufacture of quellmehl, a product derived from maize, and for the processing of starch. A subsequent regulation provided for the grant of subsidy for starch but not for quellmehl. The Court held that the abolition of the subsidy infringed the principle of non-discrimination on the ground that quellmehl was in a comparable position with starch. It stated however that the finding of illegality did not necessarily involve a declaration of invalidity of the contested regulation. Equal treatment could be restored in several ways and it was for the Community institutions responsible for

---

[172] Case C-295/90 *Parliament v Council (Students' right of residence)* [1992] ECR I-4193.

[173] *Op. cit.*, n. 106.

[174] Since the seminal judgment in *Chernobyl, op. cit.*, n. 18 above, the Parliament has tended to challenge measures of the other institutions if it considers that its prerogatives are infringed even where it agrees with the substantive provisions of the measure. In cases where the Parliament is successful, the Court usually declares that the annulled measure shall continue to produce effects until a new measure, following the correct procedure, is adopted. See e.g. Case C-65/90 *Parliament v Council (Cabotage)* [1992] ECR I-4593; Case C-271/94 *Parliament v Council (Telematic networks)* [1996] ECR I-1689. In recent years, the extension of the co-decision procedure and the elevation of the Parliament to co-legislature has led to fewer such actions.

[175] This follows from Case 66/80 *International Chemical Corporation v Amministrazione delle Finanze dello Stato* [1981] ECR 1191, para 13 where the Court held that, although a judgment given in proceedings for a preliminary ruling declaring a Community act to be void is directly addressed only to the national court which made the reference, it is sufficient reason for any other national court to regard the act as void for the purposes of a judgment which it has to give. However, the effects of a declaration of invalidity under Article 234 may be different from a finding of invalidity under Article 230 as regards national authorities: see Case C-127/94 *R v MAFF, ex p Ecroyd* [1996] ECR I-2731, per Léger AG at 2753 *et seq.*

[176] See Case 4/79 *Providence Agricole de la Campagne v Office National Interprofessionnel des Céréales* [1980] ECR 2823; Case 109/79 *Maiseries de Beauce v Office National Interprofessionnel des Céréales* [1980] ECR 2883; Case 145/79 *Roquette Frères v France* [1980] ECR 2917.

[177] See *Ruckdeschel, op. cit.*, n. 25 above; Joined Cases 124/76 and 20/77 *Moulin Pont-à-Mousson v Office Interprofessionnel des Céréales* [1977] ECR 1795.

administering the common agricultural policy to take into account economic and political considerations and to select the appropriate course of action.[178] The effect of the judgments was to maintain provisionally in force the subsidy but to apply it without discrimination to both products. By contrast, where the Court finds that a measure runs counter to the principle of non-discrimination because it imposes a financial burden on a product, rather than because it denies a financial benefit granted to another product, it will annul the measure even though it may subsequently be possible for the Council to restore equality by spreading the burden equally among all comparable products.[179]

An interesting question which arises in this context is this: what are the duties and powers of national authorities responsible for implementing Community law where a Community measure is annulled? In *R v Ministry of Agriculture, Fisheries and Food ex parte Ecroyd*[180] the Court held that the conclusions which may be drawn in the national legal system from a ruling of invalidity delivered under Article 234 depend directly on Community law as it stands in the light of the ruling. In some cases, such consequences will be obvious or arise by necessary implication from the judgment.[181] In other cases, the consequences may not be so obvious. As already stated, the Court has no power to order the Community institutions to take the necessary measures and it is for the institutions to do so without undue delay in accordance with the principle of good administration.[182] In *Ecroyd* it was argued that the national authorities were required to grant a milk quota to the applicants, following the previous judgment in *Wehrs*.[183] In that case, the Court had annulled a Community regulation on the ground that it denied unlawfully a milk quota to a category of producers to which the applicants in *Ecroyd* belonged. The claim of the applicants was that the national authorities should not have waited for the Council to adopt new rules to give effect to the judgment in *Wehrs* because the judgment annulled only a specific provision leaving intact the system governing the allocation of milk quotas. The Court rejected that claim. It held that the state of the law did not permit the allocation of a quota to a producer in the situation of the applicants before the adoption by the Council of measures to give effect to the ruling in *Wehrs*.[184] The Court was influenced by the particular complexity of the milk quota

---

[178] *Ruckdeschel, op. cit.*, paras 11–13; *Moulin Pont-à-Mousson, op. cit.*, paras 24–29.

[179] See Joined Cases 103 and 145/77 *Royal Scholten-Honig v Intervention Board for Agricultural Produce* [1978] ECR 2037, para 86. [180] *Op. cit.*, n. 175 above, para 58.

[181] Thus, national authorities must revoke measures adopted on the basis of, or to give effect to, the act declared invalid: *Ecroyd, op. cit.*, at I-2754 *per* Léger AG; see also Case 23/75 *Rey Soda* [1975] ECR 1279. On the powers of national authorities to reimburse sums unduly paid on the basis of Community acts declared invalid, see Case 130/79 *Express Dairy Foods v Intervention Board for Agricultural Trade* [1980] ECR 1887; Case C-228/92 *Roquette Frères* [1994] ECR I-1445.

[182] An analogy may be drawn here with the duties of Member States following a judgment in enforcement proceedings finding an infringement of Community law. Under the case law, the necessary action to comply with the judgment must be commenced immediately and be completed as soon as possible: Joined Cases 227–30/85 *Commission v Belgium* [1988] ECR 1.

[183] C-264/90 *Wehrs v Hauptzollamt Lüneburg* [1992] ECR I-6285.

[184] *Ecroyd, op. cit.*, n. 175 above, para 59 and para 65.

system. In other cases national authorities may find themselves in a precarious position. The consequences to be drawn from the illegality of a Community measure may be a matter for Community law but this is not to say that national authorities may not be required to draw them. This is a developing area of law where the case law has not yet laid down clear guidelines. It should be accepted that national authorities are under a duty, founded on Article 10 EC, to give, as far as possible, effect to a ruling of the Court declaring a Community act invalid, without prejudicing the powers of the Community institution which authored the act to take the necessary measures to comply with the ruling. Pursuant to that duty, they must uphold any legally complete rights which ensue from the Court's ruling. A more difficult issue is to what extent national authorities may intervene provisionally as trustees of the Community interest until the Community institution concerned takes the necessary measures.

An individual may attack, by way of incidental challenge, the validity of a Community measure before a national court on grounds of infringement of the general principles.[185] Under Article 234, the national court having jurisdiction may, and in certain circumstances must, make a reference for a preliminary ruling if it considers that such a ruling is necessary for it to give judgment. If the national court considers that the arguments put forward in support of invalidity are unfounded, it may reject them upholding the validity of the Community act. According to a well-established principle however a national court may not declare a Community act invalid.[186] If that were possible, divergences would occur between courts in the Member States as to the validity of Community acts and those divergences would be liable to jeopardize the unity and uniformity of Community law and detract from legal certainty.[187] A national court however may, under certain circumstances, order interim measures.[188]

1.7.3. Breach of general principles and liability in damages

The liability of the Community and the Member States is examined elsewhere in this book.[189] Suffice it to say here that breach of a general principle of law by a Community institution may give rise to liability in damages on the part of the Community. This applies in particular to breach of equal treatment, legitimate expectations, proportionality, and fundamental rights. Also, although no case law exists in this area, it should be accepted that a Member State may be liable in damages for failing to observe those principles where it implements or acts within the scope of Community law, provided that the conditions for state liability are met.[190]

---

[185] For an express declaration of this principle, see Case C-27/95 *Woodspring District Council v Bakers of Nailsea Ltd* [1997] ECR I-1847, para 17.
[186] Case 314/85 *Foto-Frost* [1987] ECR 4199.   [187] *Ibid.*, para 15.
[188] See below 9.11.   [189] See below Ch. 10.
[190] See *Brasserie du Pechêur* and *Factortame, op. cit.*, n 100 above; *Hedley Lomas, op. cit.*, n. 116 above.

1.8. The scope of application of general principles

The ECJ has jurisdiction to apply the general principles in every area where it exercises jurisdiction under Article 46 TEU, including the Third Pillar and the other provisions of the Treaty on European Union within the limits specified therein.[191] The general principles of law bind the Community institutions and the Member States. The issue whether they also bind individuals is more controversial.[192] The application of general principles to Community measures does not pose particular problems. Suffice it to say that, as a rule, any Community act which is susceptible to judicial review can be challenged on grounds of breach of a general principle. It is less settled what types of national measures may be so challenged. In recent years, the ECJ has expanded substantially the scope of application of general principles, especially fundamental rights, but the case law does not provide exacting criteria. The following categories may be distinguished:

- implementing measures;
- measures which restrict the fundamental freedoms but come within the ambit of an express derogation provided for in the Treaty;
- other measures falling within the scope of Community law.

Each of these categories will now be examined in turn. This section discusses in general the application of general principles to national measures. The application of fundamental rights to Member State action is examined in more detail in chapter 6.[193]

1.8.1. Implementing measures

Where national authorities implement Community law, they act as agents of the Community and must observe the general principles of law. A national measure must respect general principles whether it was adopted specifically in order to implement a Community act or whether it pre-existed the Community act but gives effect to it upon its coming into force. The application of general principles to national implementing measures was recognized in passing in *Eridania* in 1979,[194] but was expressly declared by the Court some years later in cases concerning the milk quota regime. In *Klensch*,[195] decided in 1986, Community regulations

---

[191] Note that most recently in Case C-105/03 *Pupino*, judgment of 16 June 2005, the ECJ understood its jurisdiction under the Third Pillar broadly holding that individuals may invoke a framework decision adopted under Article 34(2) TEU to procure a consistent interpretation of national law. For the application of general principles in the Third Pillar, see S. Peers, 'Who's Judging the Watchmen? The Judicial System of the "Area of Freedom Security and Justice" ', 18 (1998) YEL 337, at 376. [192] See below 1.8.6.
[193] See below, 7.3.
[194] Case 230/78 *Eridania v Minister for Agriculture and Forestry* [1979] ECR 2749, para 31. See also Case 77/81 *Zuckerfabrik Franken v Germany* [1982] ECR 681; *Deutsche Milchkontor, op. cit.,* n. 143 above. [195] *Klensch, op. cit.,* n. 31 above.

provided for the imposition of a levy on quantities of milk produced beyond quotas allocated to producers. Regulation No 857/84[196] provided that the quota was to be calculated on the basis of milk production in the calendar year 1981 but granted Member States the option to calculate it instead on the basis of production in the year 1982 or 1983. Luxembourg opted for the 1981 calendar year. The applicants argued that the adoption of that year favoured the largest dairy in Luxembourg which had links with the state to the detriment of other producers. The Court held that, where Community rules leave Member States free to choose among various methods of implementation, the Member States must comply with the principle of equal treatment. A Member State may not choose an option whose implementation in its territory would be liable to create, directly or indirectly, discrimination between producers, having regard to the specific conditions in its market and, in particular, the structure of agricultural activities.[197]

Subsequently, in its leading judgment in *Wachauf* the Court declared that, in implementing Community law, Member States must respect fundamental rights.[198] Although *Wachauf* concerned national measures implementing a regulation, recent case law has made it clear that fundamental rights and general principles bind the national authorities also where they implement directives.[199] The application of general principles to directives however gives rise to some problems which will be discussed below.[200] A Member State must respect the general principles of Community law not only as regards the content of the implementing measures but also as regards the procedure for their adoption.[201]

The overwhelming majority of cases relating to the application of general principles to national implementing measures concerns the principles of equality,[202] respect for fundamental rights,[203] and respect for legitimate expectations.[204]

---

[196] OJ 1984 L 90/13.

[197] *Klensch, op. cit.*, paras 10–11. The Court held that Article 40(3) (now 34(2)) covers all measures relating to the common organization of the market, irrespective of the authority which lays them down, and is therefore binding on Member States. Previous case law was not clear as to whether Article 40(3) itself bound national authorities: see e.g. Case 51/74 *van der Hulst* [1975] ECR 79, Case 52/76 *Benedetti v Munari* [1977] ECR 163 at 187 *per* Reischl AG; Case 139/77 *Denkavit v Finanzamt Warendorf* [1978] ECR 1317, at 1342 *per* Reischl AG. In *Klensch* Slynn AG took the view that Article 40(3) was directed to the law-making function of the Community institutions and not to implementing measures taken by Member States. He considered however that Member States were required to observe the general principle of non-discrimination: *op. cit.*, p. 3500.

[198] Case 5/88 *Wachauf v Bundesamt fur Ernahrung und Forstwirtschaft* [1989] ECR 2609. See also Case C-2/92 *Bostock* [1994] ECR I-955; Case C-186/96 *Demand* [1998] ECR I-8529.

[199] Joined Cases C-20 and C-64/00 *Booker Aquaculture Ltd and Hydro Seafood GSP Ltd v The Scottish Minister*, judgment of 10 July 2003.   [200] See below 7.3.1.

[201] Case C-313/99 *Mulligan and Others* [2002] ECR I-5719, para 48.

[202] See e.g. *Klensch, op. cit.*, n. 31 above; Case C-36/99 *Idéal Tourisme* [2000] ECR I-6049; Case C-292/97 *Karlsson and Others* [2000] ECR I-2737.

[203] See e.g. *Wachauf, op. cit., Bostock, op. cit., Booker Acquaculture, op. cit.* Discussed in detail below, 7.3.

[204] For cases concerning the protection of legitimate expectations, see e.g. Case C-459/02 *Gerekens and Association agricole pour la promotion de la commercialisation laitière Procola v Luxembourg,*

The principle of proportionality has also been litigated.[205] Suffice it here to give a few examples concerning the principle of equality. In one case,[206] the Court reiterated that implementing legislation must respect the principle of equality and held that the national authorities may treat differently different forms of associations formed by milk producers without infringing the principle where such different treatment is in accordance with the objectives of the milk quota regime. Also, the Court has accepted that the Member States may differentiate among milk producers using social criteria, for example, in order to accord some priority to small producers.[207]

Whether national implementing legislation leads to a breach of a general principle is a matter for the national court to decide on the basis of guidance given by the Court of Justice under Article 234 proceedings. Depending on the circumstances of the case, such guidance may be very specific, leaving effectively no discretion to the national court,[208] or more general.[209] It should be stressed however that the national court is bound to apply the general principles as their content is determined by Community law and not as they are recognized by national law.

1.8.2. Measures adopted under an express Treaty derogation

In its seminal judgment in *ERT*[210] the Court held that national measures which are adopted on the basis of an express derogation provided for in the Treaty must respect fundamental rights. The justification and ramifications of the judgment are examined elsewhere in this book.[211] For the purposes of the present discussion, it suffices to point out that the Court's finding applies not only to fundamental rights but, more widely, to all general principles of law.

In *ERT* the Greek Government sought to justify a State television monopoly by recourse to Articles 46 and 55 EC which permit derogations from the freedom to provide services on grounds of public policy, public security and public health. The issue was raised whether the monopoly, by prohibiting other broadcasters from entering the field, might contravene freedom of expression. The Court held that, where a Member State relies on Articles 46 and 55 EC in order to justify rules which are likely to obstruct the exercise of freedom to provide services, such justification must be interpreted in the light of the general principles of law and the fundamental rights. Thus the national rules in issue could fall within Articles 46 and

judgment of 15 July 2004; *Mulligan, op. cit.*, n. 201 above; Case C-16/89 *Spronk* [1990] ECR I-3185; Joined Cases 196–8/88 *Cornée and others v Copall and others* [1989] ECR 2309; and, earlier, *Zuckerfabrik Franken, op. cit.*, n. 194 above.

[205] See Joined Cases 41, 121 and 796/79 *Testa v Bundesanstalt für Arbeit* [1980] ECR I-1979, para 21.
[206] Case C-15/95 *EARL de Kerlast v Unicopa* [1997] ECR I-1961. See further Case C-351/92 *Graff* [1994] ECR I-3361.   [207] *Cornée op. cit.*, para 16. See also *Spronk, op. cit.*
[208] See e.g. *Booker Aquaculture, op. cit.*   [209] See e.g. *Mulligan, op. cit.*, paras 53–54.
[210] Case C-260/89 [1991] ECR I-2925.   [211] See below, 7.3.2.

55 only if they were compatible with the fundamental rights the observance of
which is guaranteed by the Court.[212] The Court held that it was for the national
court, and if necessary, for the Court itself to appraise the application of those
Articles having regard to the general principle of freedom of expression embodied
in Article 10 of the European Convention of Human Rights.[213]

Subsequent case law has extended the application of general principles beyond
national measures based on express derogations to cover measures which are based
on mandatory requirements and overriding requirements in the public interest and
even national measures which may potentially restrict free movement.[214]

1.8.3. Measures which fall within the scope of Community law

Although on the facts *ERT* concerned a measure which a Member State sought to
justify under an express derogation of the Treaty, the language used by the Court
was broader. It held that it has jurisdiction to determine the compatibility of
national rules with fundamental rights where such rules 'fall within the scope of
Community law'.[215] That begs the question what other national measures may be
covered. So far, the case law has not positively ascertained any other category of
such measures. There is however a clear and, indeed, remarkable tendency towards
the broad application of general principles, in particular, fundamental rights.[216]
Further, the case law has understood European citizenship as an autonomous
source of rights thus bringing within the scope of application of Community law
a range of situations not directly linked with free movement.[217] In addition to
those developments, which are examined elsewhere in this book, the following
comments may be made.

A purely hypothetical prospect of exercising the right to free movement does
not establish a sufficient connection with Community law to trigger the application of the general principles.[218] More recently, however, in *Karner*[219] the Court
seemed to accept that where a measure is likely to constitute a potential impediment to intra-Community trade and its compatibility falls to be examined under

---

[212] *Op. cit.*, para 43.   [213] *Op. cit.*, paras 44–45.
[214] See Case C-368/95 *Vereinigte Familiapress Zeitungsverlags- und Vertreibs GmbH v Bauer Verlag*
[1997] ECR I-3689 and Case C-71/02 *Herbert Karner Industrie-Auktionen GmbH v Troostwijk
GmbH*, judgment of 25 March 2004; discussed below 7.3.2 and 7.3.5.2 (respectively).
[215] *ERT, op. cit.*, para 42. See also Case 12/86 *Demirel v Stadt Schwäbisch Gmünd* [1987] ECR
3719, para 28; Case C-159/90 *Society for the Protection of Unborn Children Ireland Ltd v Grogan*
[1991] ECR I-4685.
[216] Note in particular: *Karner, op. cit*; Case C-112/00 *Schmidberger v Austria*, judgment of 12
June 2003; Case C-60/00 *Carpenter v Secretary of State for the Home Department, ECR* I-6279 2002;
Case C-101/01 *Lindqvist*, judgment of 6 November 2003; Joined Cases C-465/00, C-138/01 and
C-139/01 *Rechnungshof v Österreichischer Rundfunk*, judgment of 20 May 2003.
[217] See e.g. Case C-148/02 *Garcia Avello v Etat Belge*, judgment of 2 October 2003.
[218] Case C-361/97 *Nour* [1998] ECR I-3101, para 19; Case 180/83 *Moser* [1984] ECR 2539,
para 18; Case C-299/95 *Kremzow v Republik Österreich* [1997] ECR I-2629, para 16.
[219] *Op. cit.*

the provisions of the Treaty on free movement, the Court has jurisdiction to determine whether it respects fundamental rights, even if it falls neither within the scope of free movement of goods nor within the scope of the free movement of services. This is a significant, albeit unprincipled, expansion of the scope of application of general principles.

In the few areas where the Community enjoys exclusive competence by virtue of a Treaty provision, it is accepted that, in principle, Member States may not enact legislation on their own initiative even in the absence of Community measures. Community law occupies the field and pre-empts Member State action.[220] Member States may only intervene as trustees of the Community interest subject to strict conditions.[221] Therefore, national measures in such an area, where permitted, are subject to review on the grounds of breach of a general principle. This is however a fairly exceptional case which affects only a limited range of national measures.

The binding effect of general principles does not extend to national measures in areas which fall within the potential non-exclusive competence of the Community, i.e. areas where the Community has competence but has not exercised it. For example, the fact that the Community has competence to adopt measures relating to the environment does not mean that a national measure in that field, which does not affect Community legislation, must comply with the principle of proportionality. The application of general principles in such a case is not warranted by the authorities. In *Maurin*,[222] a trader who was charged with selling food products after the expiry of their use-by date contrary to French law, sought the assistance of Community law with a view to overturning the conviction on the ground that his rights of defence had been infringed. The Court referred to Directive 797/112 on the approximation of the laws of the Member States relating to the labelling, presentation and advertising of foodstuffs for sale to the ultimate consumer,[223] which was the applicable measure of Community law at the time. The Directive provides that the use-by date of a product must be indicated on the labelling and requires Member States to prohibit trade in products which do not comply with its provisions. The Court pointed out that the Directive imposed only labelling requirements and did not intend to regulate the sale of products which complied with those requirements but whose sell-by date had expired. It followed that the offence with which the accused was charged involved national legislation falling outside the scope of Community law.[224] The Court has also stated that the fact that a measure which pursues objectives laid down by national law might

---

[220] For the areas where the Community enjoys exclusive competence, see T. Tridimas and P. Eeckhout, 'The External Competence of the Community and the Case-Law of the Court of Justice: Principle versus Pragmatism', (1994) 14 YEL 143. See also at 1.5 above the discussion of the EU Constitution.   [221] Case 804/79 *Commission v United Kingdom* [1981] ECR 1045.
[222] Case C-144/95 [1996] ECR I-2909.
[223] OJ 1979, L 33/1 as amended by Council Directive 89/395, OJ 1989 L 186/17.
[224] See also *Kremzow, op. cit.*, n. 218 above, para 16; C-177/94 *Perfili* [1996] ECR I-161.

indirectly affect the common organization of an agricultural market is not sufficient to bring the measure within the scope of application of general principles.[225]

Where, however, national legislation affects interests protected by Community law or pertains to an area where there is Community legislation, the general principles apply. Thus, where Member States are required to give effect to a Community act, all national measures which are necessary for the application of that act fall within the scope of Community law even if they are not expressly required by it. Also, any national measure which is capable of undermining or affecting the objectives of the Community act in issue is reviewable on grounds of compatibility with the general principles.[226] Similarly, national legislation which affects interests whose protection falls within the ambit of Community legislation, e.g. a common organization of the market, comes within the scope of Community law.[227]

In *Booker Aquaculture Ltd v The Scottish Minister*[228] the ECJ reviewed the compatibility with fundamental rights of national legislation which went beyond the minimum requirements of a directive. The case suggests that national implementing legislation is reviewable on grounds of violation of general principles of law even if it imposes additional or more stringent provisions than those required by a directive. The ambit of the judgment in *Booker Aquaculture* is unclear and, potentially, far-reaching. It seems that, at the very least, a national measure is caught if (a) it has been adopted in order to give effect to a directive and (b) pursues the same objectives as the directive.

Further, it is submitted that a national measure falls within the scope of application of Community law if its legal basis is a Community measure. If that is correct, a national act may need to observe the general principles even though its adoption is not required by Community law.[229] That will be the case for example where a Member State chooses to implement by measures capable of producing legal effects a Community recommendation which in itself, under Article 249 EC, has no binding force. The duty of the national authorities to observe the general principles in such a case flows from Article 10 of the Treaty.

Penalties adopted by Member States for failure to respect requirements of Community law must respect the general principles even if the adoption of such penalties is not expressly required by the Community measures in issue. This is because Member States are under a general obligation to provide sufficient penalties for breach of Community law and therefore such penalties can be said to fall within the scope of its application.[230]

---

[225] Case C-309/96 *Annibaldi v Sindaco del Comune di Guidonia and Presidente Regione Lazio*, [1997] ECR I-7493.
[226] See Joined Cases C-286/94, C-340/95, C-401/95 and C-47/96 *Garage Molenheide BVBA and Others v Belgian State* [1997] ECR I-7281.
[227] Case 207/86 *Apesco v Commission* [1988] ECR 2151.
[228] *Op. cit.* See also Case C-28/99 *Verbonck and Others* [2001] ECR I-3399.
[229] See above, *Booker Aquaculture, op. cit.*, n. 199.
[230] See *Zuckerfabrik Franken, op. cit.*, n. 194 above.

Where Community legislation confers an option on Member States to introduce special provisions in order to take into account the specific interests of a certain class of persons, and a Member State chooses to exercise that option, it must do so in accordance with the general principles of Community law.[231] Is it however possible that those principles will require a Member State to exercise the option given to it by the Community rules, i.e. remove its discretion by imposing an obligation to act? In cases arising from the Community milk quota regime there are dicta to the effect that general principles bind the institutions and the Member States in exactly the same manner. Thus, where those principles do not impose an obligation on the Community legislature to allocate special quotas to producers who have implemented a development plan, they may not be relied upon to impose such an obligation on Member States.[232] Those dicta however must be read in the context in which they were made. They do not exclude the possibility that, in appropriate circumstances, the general principles may be relied upon not only to review the manner in which Member States exercise their discretion but also to review the failure to exercise that discretion.[233]

1.8.4. The reaction of English courts

The scope of application of general principles has given rise to litigation also at national level. The issue first arose in the High Court in *R v Ministry of Agriculture, Fisheries and Food, ex p First City Trading Limited*.[234] Following the BSE crisis and the imposition of a world-wide ban on the export of British beef by the Commission, the United Kingdom Government adopted the Beef Stock Transfer Scheme granting emergency aid to undertakings operating slaughterhouses and cutting premises. The applicants were exporters of beef who did not have their own slaughtering and cutting facilities and were therefore not entitled to aid. They argued that the aid scheme infringed the general principle of equal treatment as recognized in Community law. Laws J held that the aid scheme was not reviewable on grounds of compatibility with the principle of equality. In his view, the contextual scope of the general principles of law is narrower than that of the Treaty provisions. Laws J drew a distinction between, on the one hand, measures which a Member State adopts by virtue of domestic law and, on the other hand, measures which a Member State is authorised or required to take under Community law. The first type of measure is a matter for national law. It is constrained by Community law in that it must not conflict with the Treaty or other provisions of

---

[231] See *Klensch, op. cit.*; *Wachauf, op. cit.*

[232] See Case C-63/93 *Duff and Others v Minister for Agriculture and Food, Ireland, and the Attorney General* [1996] ECR I-569, *per* Cosmas AG at 583. See also *Corneé, op. cit.*, n. 204 above; *Spronk, op. cit.*, n. 204 above.

[233] But see below *The Queen v Ministry of Agriculture, Fisheries and Food ex p British Pig Industry* [2000] EuLR 724 where the High Court of England and Wales rejected such a claim.

[234] [1997] 1 CMLR 250.

written Community law but need not comply with unwritten principles developed by the Court of Justice since the Court does not enjoy original jurisdiction. The second type of measure, by contrast, is a creature of Community law and must comply not only with written Community norms but also with the general principles of law. In accordance with this distinction, Laws J concluded that the scope of the principle of equal treatment as an unwritten principle developed by the Court of Justice is narrower than the principle of non-discrimination enshrined in Article 12 EC.[235]

According to the test enunciated by Laws J, a national measure is not subject to the general principles of Community law unless either (a) it has been adopted in order to implement a Community provision or (b) in enacting it, the Member State must rely on a permission or derogation granted by Community legislation.[236] The applicants proposed a different, more extensive, test. They argued that the Beef Regulations were enacted as a direct consequence of the Commission's decision banning the export of British beef and thus fell within the scope of Community law because their *fons et origo* was a Community act. This test however was rejected by Laws J.[237]

First City Trading was followed in *R v Customs and Excise Commissioners, ex p Lunn Poly Limited*[238] but received a cold reception in *The Queen v Ministry of Agriculture, Fisheries and Food ex parte British Pig Industry*.[239] The applicants contended that the British authorities had provided substantial financial assistance to the beef and sheep industries to overcome the difficulties caused by the outbreak of BSE, but had failed to provide equivalent assistance to the pig industry despite the fact that it was in a comparable situation. They challenged the Minister's decision not to apply to the Commission for authorisation for aid and argued that the failure to do so was contrary to the general principle of equal treatment. Richards J expressed misgivings about the distinction drawn by Laws J between Community written law and Community common law as to their respective scope of application. He took the view that the grant of state aid by a Member State is a measure which falls within the scope of Community law and can be reviewed on grounds of compatibility with the general principle of non-discrimination but proceeded to dismiss the claim on other grounds.[240]

---

[235] *Ibid.*, at 267.   [236] *Ibid.*, at 271.

[237] His view finds support in the Opinion of Gulmann AG in *Bostock, op. cit.*, n. 198 above.

[238] [1998] 2 CMLR 560; [1998] EuLR 438. In that case, it was argued that the higher rate of tax applied by English law on travel insurance premiums was contrary to the principle of non-discrimination. The Divisional Court held that the general principles of law could not create a new jurisdiction and did not apply to a domestic measure which was neither required nor permitted by virtue of Community law. The Divisional Court found, however, that the differential rate of tax was state aid and unlawful for lack of notification under the state aid provisions of the Treaty. The latter part of the judgment was confirmed by the Court of Appeal: [1999] 1 CMLR 1357.   [239] *Op. cit.*

[240] Richards J held that pig producers were not in a comparable situation to cattle and sheep producers. He also held that, even if there was a breach of the principle of equal treatment, the applicant's challenge would fail. Their argument was not that the various measures giving aid to beef producers were unlawful but rather that, although they were lawful at the time, they had

In *ex p British Pig Industry*, the connecting factors which triggered the application of the principle of equality were that the government's support measures were in an area of regulation which was covered by a common organization of the market, they were liable to be state aid contrary to Community law, and, most importantly, the alleged discrimination arose as a result of the side-effects of both national and Community measures. The judgment in *British Pig Industry* suggests that the test laid down in *First City Trading* is no longer good law but does not clarify the wider picture nor does it propose a general test for ascertaining in what situations a national measure is reviewable on grounds of compatibility with general principles.[241]

The case however remains that the general principles of Community law are not by themselves capable of bringing a certain field of activity within the scope of Community law if that field is not otherwise so covered. If that were the case, all aspects of national law would be reviewable on grounds of compatibility with the general principles of the EU. This is not accepted by the case law of the ECJ[242] although the recent judgment in *Karner* has somewhat muddied the waters.[243]

1.8.5. Public authorities bound by the general principles

The general principles bind, first and foremost, public authorities. The issues which arise in this context are the following. First, which public authorities are so bound and, second, are there any circumstances under which general principles may also be said to bind private individuals?

Authorities which are considered as emanations of the State for the purposes of direct effect are bound to respect the general principles where they act within the scope of application of Community law. It is clear that the notion of the State includes central government, local and regional authorities,[244] and other

resulted in unlawful side-effects and the government was under a duty to remove those side-effects. Richards J did not accept that a series of lawful measures could produce by way of side-effects a state of affairs that was in breach of the principle of equal treatment. Even if that were the case, he took the view that, where incidental discrimination arises as a result of both national and Community support measures, the duty to rectify those measures cannot rest solely on the Member States but also on the Community institutions.

[241] Note that neither Laws J not Richards J thought it appropriate to make a reference for a preliminary ruling. Laws J decided not to make a reference since, in any event, he took the view that the scheme did not infringe the principle of equal treatment as provided for in Article 34(2) of the Treaty. His reasoning was that aid to undertakings operating their own slaughterhouses and premises was vital to maintain supply of fresh meat to the domestic market and meet consumer demand. Those aims did not justify granting aid to exporters. Similarly, Richards J thought it unnecessary since he found that the applicants' claim failed on the facts.

[242] Note *Kremzow, op. cit.*; *Annibaldi, op. cit.* Note also Case C-249/96 *Grant v South-West Trains Ltd* [1998] ECR I-621. The Court declared at para. 45 that, although respect for fundamental rights is a condition for the legality of Community acts, those rights cannot in themselves have the effect of extending the scope of Treaty provisions beyond the competences of the Community.

[243] See 1.8.3 above.

[244] Case 103/88 *Fratelli Constanzo* v *Commune di Milano* [1989] ECR 1839; Case 31/87 *Beentjes BV v Netherlands* [1988] ECR 4635.

constitutionally independent public authorities, such as a Chief Constable.[245] In *Foster v British Gas*,[246] the issue was whether the plaintiff female employees could invoke the Equal Treatment Directive against British Gas prior to privatization. The Court held, at paragraph 18 of the judgment, that unconditional and sufficiently precise provisions of directives may be relied on against organizations or bodies which are 'subject to the authority or control of the State *or* have special powers beyond those which result from the normal rules applicable to relations between individuals' (emphasis added). If one were to interpret this formula literally, it would seem that the tests laid down in that paragraph are not cumulative and it suffices for a body to be under the control of the State in order to be considered as a State authority for the purposes of direct effect.[247] In *Kampelmann* the Court reiterated the disjunctive 'or' and confirmed that directives may be invoked against bodies which, irrespective of their legal form, have been given responsibility, by the public authorities and under their supervision, for providing a public service.[248] In that case, Tesauro AG took the view that municipal undertakings providing utilities for provincial cities were under the control of the municipal authorities and, by virtue of that fact alone, subject to the direct effect of directives.[249]

The definition of State however has given rise to problems in English courts. Following the Court's ruling in *Foster*, the House of Lords held that British Gas was a State authority because it met all the criteria laid down in paragraph 18. It was based on a statutory footing, it provided services under the control of the State, and had a monopoly on the supply of gas.[250] Subsequently, in *Doughty v Rolls Royce*[251] the Court of Appeal took the view that the criterion of State control was not in itself sufficient. It held that the fact that the share capital of Rolls Royce was wholly owned by the Crown did not suffice to make it an emanation of the State since the company had not been made responsible for providing a public service nor did it have any special powers beyond those which result from the normal rules applicable to relations between individuals. Rolls Royce was merely a commercial undertaking competing in the open market.

More recent cases suggest that English courts are prepared to accept a more liberal, functional, definition of the State. In *Griffin v South West Water Services Ltd*,[252] the High Court held that a privatized water company is a State authority against which directives can be enforced directly. Blackburn J stated that the

---

[245] Case 222/84 *Johnston* v *Chief Constable of the Royal Ulster Constabulary* [1986] ECR 1651.

[246] Case C-188/89 *Foster and Others* [1990] ECR I-3313, para. 18. See also in this context the comments of van Gerven AG at 3339–40.

[247] Uncertainty arose because, although at paragraph 18 of the judgment the Court used the disjunctive 'or', at paragraph 22 it used 'and' thus giving the impression that the tests may be cumulative.

[248] Joined Cases C-253–8/96 *Kampelmann and Others v Landschaftsverband Westfalen-Lippe and Others* [1997] ECR I-6907, para 46.   [249] *Ibid.*, at 6918.

[250] See V. Kvjatkovski, 'What is an "Emanation of the State"? An Educated Guess', (1997) 3 EPL 329.   [251] *Rolls-Royce v Doughty* [1987] IRLR 447.

[252] [1995] IRLR 15.

material criterion for the purposes of direct effect is not whether the body in question is under the control of the State but whether the public service which it performs is under State control. In *NUT & Others v Governing Body of St Mary's Church of England (Aided) Junior School* [253] the Court of Appeal held that the governing body of a voluntary-aided school was an emanation of the State, and therefore subject to the provisions of the Acquired Rights Directive, because it was under the authority and control of the State even though it did not have any special powers beyond those applicable to relations between individuals. The judgment is important because the Court of Appeal departed from the cumulative test laid down in *Doughty* and also because it adopted a functional approach to State control. Shiemann LJ acknowledged that the criteria laid down by the Court of Justice in paragraph 22 of *Foster*, and applied literally by the House of Lords in that case, did not lay down an exclusive formula for the definition of the State. The Court of Appeal distinguished the case from *Foster* and *Doughty* on the ground that those cases involved commercial undertakings in which the government had a stake rather than the provision of a public service like education. On the issue of State control, it noted that, although voluntary schools chose, rather than were obliged, to come within the State system, they were subject to a considerable degree of State control and influence by the both the local education authorities and the Secretary of State for Education. They could therefore be considered to be under the control of the State.

It is submitted therefore that, in order to be regarded as an emanation of the State, it suffices for a body to have been made responsible, pursuant to a measure adopted by the State, for providing a public service under the control of the State. This definition seems sufficiently wide to encompass private bodies which have been entrusted with the performance of functions traditionally reserved to the State and over which the State retains residual control. It should also be accepted that self-regulatory bodies, namely authorities which exercise public power without being based on a statutory footing, are also bound by directives in so far as such bodies implement Community law [254] or their actions affect fundamental freedoms. The issue is of importance in sports [255] but also in other sectors where self-regulation plays a significant role, for example, the financial services industry in the United Kingdom.

The definition of State authority was recently revisited by the CFI in *Salamander*. [256] Una Film, a private company, argued that it should be considered as an emanation

---

[253] [1997] IRLR 242. Cf: *Turpie v University of Glasgow*, decision of the Scottish Industrial Tribunal of 23 September 1986, unreported (University not a public authority for the purposes of applying the Equal Treatment Directive). Following *NUT*, the decision is an unreliable authority.

[254] The possibility of self-regulatory bodies being responsible for the implementation of Community law was left open by the judgment in Case 29/84 *Commission v Germany* [1985] ECR 1661. In any event, self-regulatory bodies may be delegated powers by official bodies which are designated by national law as the competent authorities to implement Community obligations.

[255] See e.g. *Wilander and Novacek v Tobin and Jude*, [1997] 2 CMLR 346, judgment of Lightman J (Chancery Division), 13 June 1996; see also Case C-415/93 *Bosman* [1995] ECR I-4921.   [256] Case T-172/98, 27 June 2000.

of the State because it had a de facto monopoly in the market for the advertising of tobacco products in Austrian cinemas. It derived its monopoly from being the sole contractual partner of Austria Tabak. This latter company formerly had a statutory monopoly in the import and sale of tobacco products. Since Austria's accession to the EC, it had been privatized but operated under State control and continued to have a dominant position in the tobacco market. The CFI did not accept those submissions. It held that, even if, following its privatization, Austria Tabak could be regarded as a State authority within the meaning of the *Foster* judgment, that was not decisive. Una Film's commercial activity, i.e. the distribution of advertising films for tobacco products in cinemas, was not a public service, was carried on under private law contracts and not under measures adopted by the state, and Una Film did not have any special powers beyond those resulting from the normal rules applicable in relations between individuals.[257]

It follows from *Salamander* that a private company to whom exclusive rights have been transferred by a public undertaking or a state authority will not qualify as an emanation of the State if it does perform a public service and is bound only by a private law relationship to the public undertaking. However, one may need to approach *Salamander* with caution. It was a case where the definition of the emanation of the State was not examined in proceedings where an individual sought to rely on a directive against a public entity but in the context of annulment proceedings brought under Article 230(4), and the circumstances of the case may have led the CFI to take a more restrictive view.

1.8.6. The application of general principles against individuals

So far the case law has not pronounced on the issue whether the general principles of law may give rise to obligations against private parties. The issue acquires particular importance in relation to fundamental rights.[258] It may be argued that the historical origins and purpose of general principles, which is to protect the individual against public authorities, suggests a negative reply. But that argument is not conclusive. In the modern pluralist State, the traditional public–private dichotomy is no longer valid. It may be said that in certain cases fundamental rights deserve to be protected as much against private entities as against public authorities so that failure to protect them against the former may run counter to their objectives.

In general, where the case law establishes obligations going beyond the text of the founding Treaties, it does so against the State. In the absence of written provisions, the case law seems reluctant to impose obligations on individuals. An interesting example is provided by *Bostock*.[259] Under the Community milk quota regime, upon the termination of a farm tenancy, the milk quota is returned to the

---

[257] *Ibid.*, para 60.
[258] See in general A. Clapham, *Human Rights in the Private Sphere* (Oxford University Press, 1993); D. Spielmann, *L'effet potentiel de la Convention européenne des droits de l'homme entre personnes privées* (Brussels: Bruylant, 1995).   [259] *Op. cit.*, n. 198 above.

landlord.[260] In *Bostock*, it was argued that the general principles of Community law required Member States to introduce a scheme for payment of compensation by a landlord to the outgoing tenant or conferred directly on the tenant a right to compensation from the landlord. Earlier in *Wachauf*[261] the Court had accepted that the protection of fundamental rights may require that the departing tenant must be entitled to compensation where that is justified by the extent of his contribution to the building up of the milk production on the holding. But in *Bostock* the Court was not willing to disrupt relations between private parties by giving a right to the tenant against the landlord. The applicant argued that he was treated unequally *vis-à-vis* tenants whose leases had expired after a subsequent date in relation to which the UK had introduced a compensation scheme. After pointing out that the principle of equal treatment is a general principle of Community law, the Court held:[262]

However, the principle of equality of treatment cannot bring about retroactive modification of the relations between the parties to a lease to the detriment of the lessor by imposing on him an obligation to compensate the outgoing lessee, whether under national provisions which the Member State in question might be required to adopt, or by means of direct effect.

The applicant also argued that, since his labour and his investments had contributed to the acquisition or the increase of the quota which reverted to his landlord on the expiry of the lease, the landlord was under an obligation to pay compensation in respect of his unjust enrichment. The Court however rejected that argument stating that legal relations between lessees and lessors, in particular on the expiry of a lease, are, as Community law now stands, still governed by the law of the Member State in question. Any consequences of unjust enrichment of the lessor on the expiry of a lease are therefore not a matter for Community law.

The judgment in *Bostock* must be read in the light of the peculiarities of the milk quota regime and it is difficult to draw general conclusions. The existing authorities do suggest however that the Court is reluctant to accept that the general principles may by themselves impose obligations on individuals.[263]

Despite this, in some cases a horizontal or quasi-horizontal effect may be present. Thus, the obligation to respect the fundamental rights of an individual or a group may by reflection give rise to incidental obligations or the worsening of the legal position of another individual or group, such as for example where the freedoms of assembly and expression conflict with the freedom to inter-state trade.[264] Also, specific directives may protect fundamental rights not only against state authorities but also against individuals. This is for example the case with the Race Directive, the framework Directive on equal treatment, and the Directive on the processing

---

[260] The milk quota regime is discussed in more detail below at 6.4.2. and 7.3.1.

[261] *Op. cit.*, n. 198 above.   [262] *Bostock, op. cit.*, para 14.

[263] See also Case C-60/92 *Otto v Postbank NV* [1993] ECR I-5683.

[264] See e.g. *Schmidberger, op. cit.*, n. 216 above.

of personal data.[265] The wider such directives are interpreted, the wider the obligations imposed on individuals.[266] Such norms however will impose obligations on individuals only through national law, i.e. through implementing legislation or through the obligation of consistent interpretation, since directives may not by themselves produce horizontal effect.[267]

The case law accepts that certain provisions of the EC Treaty may produce horizontal effect. In *Defrenne v Sabena*[268] it was held that Article 119 (now 141), which provides for the principle of equal pay between men and women for equal work, establishes a right to equal pay which can be relied on in national courts against both public and private employees. In *Walrave and Koch v Association Union Cycliste Internationale*[269] it was held that the prohibition of discrimination on grounds of nationality, as incorporated in Articles 12, 34 and 49 of the Treaty, does not apply only to the actions of public authorities but extends also to rules of private organizations which aim at regulating in a collective manner gainful employment and the provision of services.

Subsequently, in *Bosman*[270] the Court reiterated that Article 39 EC, which provides for the free movement of workers, applied to the football transfer rules of the international football federations FIFA and UEFA. Both in *Walrave* and *Bosman*, however, the provisions of the Treaty on free movement were applied against private associations which exercised some type of regulatory action and had therefore a quasi-public law character. More recently, in *Angonese v Cassa di Risparmio di Bolzano SpA*,[271] the Court unequivocally held that Article 39 has horizontal direct effect and binds private employers also. It pointed out that the principle of non-discrimination in Article 39 is drafted in general terms and is not specifically addressed to the Member States. It then referred to its reasoning in *Defrenne* and held that it applied *a fortiori* in the case of Article 39 which lays down a fundamental freedom. The extension of Article 39 to cover fully-fledged horizontal situations has been criticised mainly on two grounds.[272] First, on the ground that the Court intervenes in the sphere of private autonomy and creates legal uncertainty, and second, on the ground that it upsets the balance of competence

---

[265] See respectively Council Directive 2000/43/EC of 29 June 2000 implementing the principle of equal treatment between persons irrespective of racial or ethnic origin, OJ 2000, L 180/22; Council Directive 2000/78/EC of 27 November 2000 establishing a general framework for equal treatment in employment and occupation, OJ L 303/16; Directive 95/46/EC of the European Parliament and of the Council of 24 October 1995 on the protection of individuals with regard to the processing of personal data and on the free movement of such data, OJ 1995, L 281/31.

[266] See e.g. in relation to the data processing Directive, *Lindqvist, op. cit.*, n. 216 above.

[267] Case C-91/92 *Faccini Dori v Recreb* [1994] ECR I-3325.

[268] Case 43/75 [1976] ECR 455.

[269] Case 36/74 [1974] ECR 1405. See also Case 13/76 *Doná v Mantero* [1976] ECR 1333.

[270] *Bosman, op. cit.*, n. 255 above; see also Case C-176/96 *Lehtonen and Castors Canada Dry Namur-Braine ASBL v FRBSB*, [2000] ECR I-2681, para 35.

[271] Case C-281/98 *Angonese v Cassa di Risparmio di Bolzano SpA*, [2000] ECR I-4139, para 36.

[272] See S. van den Bogaert, 'Horizontality: Rowing with Square or Feathered Blades?' paper delivered in the conference on 'Unpacking the Internal Market', organized in CELS, Cambridge, 2001.

between the Community and the Member States by intervening in the sphere of private law which falls within the remit of the latter. This however does not appear a persuasive criticism. The judicial arguments underlying the progressive extension of horizontality are the need to ensure the effectiveness of fundamental freedoms and, as the Court put it in *Angonese*, to avoid discrimination in the labour market.[273] Within the European polity, the prohibition of discrimination on grounds of nationality and the free movement of workers can best be viewed as norms of constitutional status whose value and effects are not exhausted in vertical situations. Also, the competence of the Community to harmonize key areas of national private law, such as contract law, is well settled. Against this background, it would be the denial of horizontal effect of Article 39 against a private employer that could be viewed as an aberration rather than its acceptance. This is not to say that horizontality is without problems. Once it is accepted that Article 39 binds private employers, it should also be accepted that the latter have available to them the derogations from the free movement of workers recognized in the Treaty and the case law.[274] These however have been designed as defences for public and not private action. Inevitably, those derogations will need be tailored to the defence of private parties and, in some contexts, interpreted more broadly.

The Court has not unequivocally pronounced on the horizontality of the other fundamental freedoms, but the reasoning of *Angonese* may apply also, at least in some respects, to the freedom to provide services and the right of establishment.[275] Notably, in a recent case, the Queen's Bench Division held that a maritime company could rely on the right of establishment, as guaranteed by Article 43 EC, to obtain an injunction against trade unions threatening strike action.[276] Such uncompromising application of Article 43 raises fundamental issues pertaining to the scope and objectives of free movement.

1.9. The general principles of law and the EC Treaty

1.9.1. The general principles in the hierarchy of Community rules

The Community legal order is based on a system of hierarchy of rules under which rules of a lower tier derive their validity from, and are bound to respect, the rules of the higher tiers. What is the position of the general principles of law in that order of hierarchy? It is clear that those principles which are accorded constitutional status

---

[273] *Angonese, op. cit.*, para 35.   [274] This was acknowledged in *Bosman, op. cit.*, para 86.
[275] For the free movement of goods, see the dicta in Case 58/80 *Dansk Supermarked v Imerco* [1981] ECR I-18, para 17.
[276] *Viking Line Abp v International Transport Workers' Federation and Finnish Seamen's Union*, The Times, 23 June 2005.

are superior to Community legislation since acts adopted by the institutions are subject to review on grounds of compatibility with them. Their position *vis-à-vis* primary Community law may be summarised as follows. Since their origins lie in the EC Treaty, they have equivalent status with the founding Treaties. Their equal ranking derives from their character as constitutional principles emanating from the rule of law. This applies in particular to the principles of respect for fundamental rights, equality, proportionality and legal certainty.

One of the consequences which flow from this is that those principles bind the Community in the exercise of its treaty-making power. They form part of the rules of law, compliance with which the Court ensures in the exercise of its jurisdiction under Article 300(6). It follows that a proposed international agreement which the Court has found to infringe a general principle of law may not enter into force unless the procedure for the amendment of the Union Treaties provided for in Article 48 of the Treaty on European Union is followed.[277] Furthermore, an international agreement already concluded by the Community which runs counter to a general principle is incompatible with Community law. In *Germany v Council*,[278] the Court found that an agreement on bananas concluded with countries of South and Central America infringed the principle of non-discrimination because it discriminated against certain categories of Community banana producers. As a consequence, the Court annulled the decision of the Council by which the latter approved the agreement on behalf of the Community.[279]

1.9.2. The general principles as rules of Treaty interpretation

The relationship between the general principles and primary Community law requires further analysis. Since the founding and the amending treaties are at the top of the Community law edifice, they are *ex hypothesi* valid. No provision in the founding treaties grants the Court jurisdiction to rule on their validity. Nor is it possible for the Community to be liable to an individual for loss arising from primary legislation.[280]

The Court however has jurisdiction to interpret Treaty provisions and may do so in the light of the general principles of law. The interpretative function of general principles acquires particular importance in this context precisely because it is the only function which they may fill. Where courts are called upon to interpret

---

[277] See Opinion 1/91 *on the Draft Agreement relating to the creation of the European Economic Area* [1991] ECR I-6079, paras 61–64. In its ruling, the Court found that the judicial system set up by the draft agreement was incompatible with the Treaty, *inter alia*, on grounds of incompatibility with the principle of legal certainty.

[278] Case C-122/95 *Germany v Council* [1998] ECR I-973. Cf. C-149/96 *Portugal v Council* [1999] ECR I-8395.

[279] The Court followed the same reasoning in Joined Cases C-364 and C-365/95 *T. Port* [1998] ECR I-1023. For the ensuing (unsuccessful) action in damages see Case T-1/99 *T. Port v Commission* [2001] ECR II-465, confirmed on appeal: C-122/01 P *T. Port v Commission*, judgment of 8 May 2003.

[280] Case T-113/96 *Dubois et Fils v Council and Commission* [1998] ECR II-125.

rules which they have no jurisdiction to annul, interpretation becomes the primary means by which they can influence their effectiveness. Interpretation in that context becomes particularly instructive as the expression of judicial policy: it tells us what the court perceives to be its function, what it considers to be the underpinnings of the legal system, and how it prioritizes its rules. Needless to say, interpretation is a creative exercise. Even where a court gives to the words of a statute what appears to be their literal or natural meaning, it does not apply the statute mechanically. What appears to be the natural meaning of a rule to one judge may not appear to be the natural meaning to another.[281] Also, the very fact that a court follows a literal interpretation as opposed to a more liberal one is in itself significant as an indication of judicial policy.

The case law suggests that, in the light of the general principles, the Court of Justice has interpreted Treaty provisions more liberally than acts of the institutions. In particular, it has understood its own jurisdiction widely in order to ensure respect for the fundamental right to judicial protection, which has a defining character in the Community legal order.[282] This approach is illustrated by the judgments in *les Verts* and *Chernobyl*.

In *les Verts*,[283] decided in 1986, the Court held that, although at that time the Parliament was not mentioned as a possible defendant in Article 173 (now 230 EC), binding measures adopted by it were subject to judicial review. The rationale of the judgment was as follows. First, the Court made a general declaration of the principle of legality. In the Court's peremptory language,[284]

It must be emphasised ... that the European Economic Community is a Community based on the rule of law, inasmuch as neither its Member States nor its institutions can avoid a review of the question whether the measures adopted by them are in conformity with the basic constitutional charter, the Treaty.

Then, the Court stated that by Articles 173, 184 and 177 (now 230, 241, and 234 EC respectively) the Treaty intended to establish a complete system of legal remedies. The Court justified the absence of an express reference to the Parliament as a possible defendant in Article 173 (now 230) on the ground that, under the original version of the Treaty, the Parliament only had powers of consultation and political control and no power to adopt acts intended to have legal effects *vis-à-vis* third parties. It referred to Article 38 of the ECSC Treaty, which expressly stated that the Court may declare an act of the Parliament void, as evidence that where the Parliament was given power to adopt binding measures *ab initio* by one of the founding Treaties,[285] such measures were subject to annulment. *Les Verts* is a prime example of dynamic interpretation, an approach typical of the interpretation

---

[281] See for a classic example the House of Lords in *Liversidge v Anderson* [1942] AC 206.

[282] See further A. Arnull, 'Does the Court of Justice have inherent jurisdiction?' (1990) 27 CML Rev 683.   [283] *Op. cit.*, n. 64 above.

[284] *Ibid.*, para 23.

[285] The Parliament had power to adopt binding acts under Article 95 ECSC. Note that the ECSC Treaty has now expired and is no longer in force.

of a constitutional text, by which the Court sought to meet the requirements of the rule of law.

In *Chernobyl*,[286] decided in 1990, the Court went one step further. It held that the Parliament may bring an action for annulment against acts of the Council or of the Commission in order to safeguard its prerogatives, although at that time Article 173 (now 230) did not mention the Parliament as a possible plaintiff.[287] The Court's reasoning stands on two pillars: the need to ensure that the provisions of the Treaty concerning the institutional balance are fully applied; and the need to ensure that the Parliament's prerogatives, like those of the other institutions, cannot be breached without it having available a legal remedy which may be exercised in a certain and effective manner.[288] The Court stated that the absence in the Treaties of any provision giving the Parliament the right to bring an action constitutes a procedural gap which cannot prevail 'over the fundamental interest in the maintenance and observance of the institutional balance laid down in the Treaties establishing the European Communities'.[289]

Those cases illustrate that, although unwritten general principles of law do not technically take priority over the Treaty, they may influence decisively its interpretation.[290] This is particularly evident in the judgment in *Chernobyl* where the Court adopted what was in effect a *contra legem* interpretation of Article 173 (now 230). It is important to point out that *les Verts* and *Chernobyl* concerned essentially the fundamental right to judicial protection. Both cases raised issues relating to the admissibility of the action and therefore pertaining to procedure. One may take the view that judicial activism can easier be justified in procedural matters, which fall *par excellence* in the judicial province, than in issues of substance. But that appears to be a false distinction. The boundaries between substance and procedure are not clear-cut and, in any event, procedural requirements may be as influential in forming political processes as substantive ones. There can be little doubt that in *Chernobyl* the Court intervened as a political actor. The judgments in *les Verts* and *Chernobyl* are based on the premise that access to judicial remedies is an integral part of the rule of law. Their rationale seems to be that the Community is by its nature a dynamic organization. As the Community develops, the ensuing increase in the powers of the institutions has to be accompanied by adequate control mechanisms, if the rule of law is to be observed.

---

[286] *Op. cit.*, n. 18 above, para 26. Cf the *Comitology* case, *op. cit.*, n. 63 above.

[287] See now Article 230(3) as amended by the TEU.

[288] *Chernobyl, op. cit.*, para 25.   [289] *Ibid.*, para 26.

[290] It has been argued that certain human rights may take priority even over primary Community legislation. See M. Dauses, 'The Protection of Human Rights in the Community Legal Order', (1985) ELR 398 at 412. The author draws a distinction between 'the substratum of suprapositive principles of law' incorporated in the ECHR and 'their substantive legal form'. The former are sources of law independent of the Treaties and take precedence even over primary Community law. The latter, by contrast, are superior to secondary Community law but take second place to the Treaties.

The same dynamism was illustrated by the seminal judgment in *Schmidberger*[291] where, for the first time, the ECJ held that the need to protect fundamental rights may justify derogations from the fundamental freedoms. The judgment is particularly important because the ECJ viewed fundamental rights as being at the top of the Community legal edifice and suggested by implication that they could justify even discriminatory restrictions on the free movement of goods.[292]

The judgments in *les Verts* and *Chernobyl* can be contrasted with *Laisa v Council*.[293] Spanish producers sought the annulment of certain provisions of the Act of Accession of Spain and Portugal which amended a previous agricultural regulation of the Council. They argued that the contested provisions were acts of the Council subject to review under Article 230. They relied on Article 8 of the Act of Accession which states that provisions of that Act the purpose or effect of which is to repeal or amend acts adopted by the Community institutions 'shall have the same status in law as the provisions which they repeal or amend and shall be subject to the same rules as those provisions'. The Court did not accept the submissions of the applicants. It held that provisions of the Act of Accession which amend existing Community measures are nonetheless rules of primary law, and cannot therefore be the subject of annulment proceedings under Article 230. The Court pointed out that Article 8 fulfils a different purpose. It enables the Community institutions to amend provisions of the Act of Accession amending acts of secondary Community legislation without the need to follow the procedure for the amendment of the Treaties which, under Article 6, is normally applicable for the amendment of provisions of the Act of Accession.

The judgment establishes that adaptations to secondary Community legislation deriving directly from the Act of Accession enjoy entrenched value in that they are not subject to review of legality. This results in a gap in judicial protection but the Court accepted it as an inevitable consequence of the status of the contested rules as primary law. The Court was guided by the intention of the authors of the Act of Accession who, by dealing with certain issues in the Act itself rather than leaving them to be dealt with by consequential Community acts, intended those issues not to be justiciable. The Act of Accession incorporated the outcome of political negotiations and as such it expressed a certain balance of powers which the Court was keen not to disturb. In the words of the judgment, the interpretation of the Act of Accession given by the Court 'is rendered all the more compelling by the fact that the provisions of the Act of Accession affirm the results of Accession negotiations which constitute a totality intended to resolve difficulties which accession entails either for the Community or for the applicant State'.[294]

---

[291] *Op. cit.*, n. 216 above.   [292] For a discussion, see below, Chapter 7.4.

[293] Joined Cases 31 and 35/86 *Laisa v Council* [1988] ECR 2285. See also Case 40/64 *Sgarlata and Others v Commission* [1965] ECR 215 and note, more recently, Case C-321/95 *Greenpeace and Others v Commission* [1998] ECR I-1651. Cf Case C-309/89 *Codorníu v Council* [1994] ECR I-1853.

[294] *Op. cit.*, para 15. Cf the Opinion of Lenz AG who held that the action was admissible.

A final issue which arises in this context is the following. Are all the provisions of the founding Treaties of equal rank in law? Can it be said that some of them take priority over others and, if so, what does such priority mean?[295] As a general rule, it is not unreasonable to consider that, in the light of the objectives of the Community, certain rules of the Treaty are more fundamental than others. If that is so, the higher value of the more fundamental rules may express itself in two ways: a rule which is considered to be more fundamental will be important for the interpretation of other rules which are not perceived to be as fundamental. Also, the more fundamental that a rule is, the clearer the expression that the Court may require before accepting that this rule is amended. The Court therefore may have difficulty in accepting that a fundamental rule is repealed or amended impliedly as a result of the express amendment of another, less important, rule. The ruling in Opinion 1/91 on the *Draft Agreement relating to the creation of the European Economic Area*[296] may provide some guidance as to the Court's views on the hierarchy of the provisions of the EC Treaty. In 1990 the Community entered into formal negotiations with the countries of the European Free Trade Area (EFTA) with a view to concluding an agreement on the establishment of a European Economic Area (EEA). The aim was to replace existing bilateral free trade agreements with the EEA agreement and to establish a homogeneous economic area subject to a legal framework substantially identical to that laid down by Community law. The Commission requested the opinion of the Court with regard to the compatibility of the judicial system provided for by the draft EEA Agreement with the Treaty under the procedure of Article 300(6) EC. In Opinion 1/91 the Court held that the judicial system of the draft EEA Agreement was not compatible with the Treaty.[297] In its request for an Opinion, the Commission also asked the Court whether Article 238 (now 310) of the Treaty, which deals with the conclusion by the Community of association agreements, authorized the establishment of a system of courts such as that provided in the draft EEA Agreement and if not whether Article 238 could be amended so as to permit such a system to be set up. The Court held as follows:[298]

... Article 238 of the EEC Treaty does not provide any basis for setting up a system of courts which conflicts with Article 164 [now Article 220] of the EEC Treaty and, more generally, with the very foundations of the Community.

[295] In his Opinion in *Laisa v Council* Lenz AG suggested that not all rules of primary Community law may be of the same rank: *Op. cit*, p. 2307.   [296] [1991] ECR I-6079.

[297] The Court gave the following reasons: (a) the jurisdiction of the EEA Court established under the draft Agreement affected adversely the autonomy of Community law (paras 35–36); (b) the judicial system established by the draft Agreement would condition the future interpretation of the Community rules on free movement and competition (paras 45–46); (c) the draft Agreement enabled courts of EFTA States to seek rulings from the Court of Justice on the interpretation of the draft Agreement but such rulings would be advisory and have no binding effect. That would change the nature of the Court's function (paras 61–64); (d) the Court expressed doubts regarding the compatibility with the Treaty of the composition of the EEA Court (paras 52–53).   [298] Paras 71–72.

For the same reasons, an amendment of Article 238 in the way indicated by the Commission could not cure the incompatibility with Community law of the system of courts to be set up by the agreement.

The brevity of the Court's reasoning has given rise to difficulties as to the exact meaning of the above statements. Some commentators have interpreted those dicta as meaning that the Community's judicial system may not be altered by an amendment of the Treaty and have criticized the Court for taking that view.[299] It is submitted that such reading of the judgment is not correct. The true meaning of the Court's statements must be ascertained in the light of the ruling as a whole. The Court took the view that the judicial system of the draft EEA Agreement would alter fundamentally the judicial system of the Community itself, which in turn would have far-reaching repercussions for the nature of the Community legal order. There can be no doubt that Member States remain free to make such fundamental changes to the nature of the Community by entering into an international agreement with third States but their intention to that effect must be expressed clearly and unequivocally. In declaring that an amendment of Article 310 of the Treaty could not cure the incompatibility of the draft Agreement with the Treaty, the Court employed, in effect, a presumption of legislative intention: a fundamental constitutional change will not be recognized by the Court unless it is supported by the clearest of expressions[300] The Opinion on the draft EEA Agreement illustrates the importance that the Court attaches to Article 220 and the judicial structure of the Community.[301]

1.10. The general principles as sources of international law

Article 38(1)(c) of the Statute of the International Court of Justice lists among the rules which that court applies 'the general principles of law recognized by civilized

---

[299] See Sir Patrick Neil QC, 'The European Court of Justice: a Case Study in Judicial Activism', Evidence submitted to the House of Lords Select Committee on the European Communities, Sub-committee on the 1996 Inter Governmental Conference, *1996 Inter Governmental Conference, Minutes of Evidence, House of Lords, Session 1994–95, 18th Report*, p. 218 at 238. See also T. Hartley, 'The European Court and the EEA', (1992) 41 ICLQ 841 at 846 who states that the Court's view is 'plainly wrong'.

[300] Hartley, *op. cit.*, at 846 states an adverse opinion by the Court under Article 300(6) [228(6)] can be overridden by an amendment to the Treaty and that 'it makes little difference which precise Article of the EEC Treaty is amended'. It should be recognized however that the provisions of the Treaty which the draft Agreement was found to infringe occupy a cardinal position in the Community legal order and their amendment cannot be the incidental result of amending Article 310 [238]. It is a different matter whether in Opinion 1/91 the Court was correct in concluding that the judicial system of the proposed EEA Agreement posed such a fundamental threat to the Community legal order. Arguably, the Court exaggerated the adverse repercussions of concluding the draft Agreement.

[301] As a result of the ruling the draft EEA agreement was amended and subsequently in Opinion 1/92 [1992] ECR I-2821 the Court held that, subject to certain conditions, the amended version was compatible with the Treaty.

nations'. The reference to general principles has been associated with concepts of natural law,[302] but objections have been expressed regarding the term 'civilized nations'.[303] It has been suggested that in terms of methodology, the mandate given to the International Court is similar to that of the European Court of Justice. It requires a synthesis of principles found in domestic legal systems rather than the mechanical application of the statistically predominant rules. As Professor Brownlie notes: 'An international tribunal chooses, edits and adapts elements from better developed systems: the result is a new element of international law the content of which is influenced historically and logically by domestic law'.[304] There are however significant differences between the application of general principles by the International Court and by the European Court. Although general principles are referred to by individual judges, it is notable that so far no majority decision of the International Court has been based expressly upon a general principle of law.[305] Such principles are rarely cited by the parties and, when they are, it is by way of supplementary argument.[306] A second difference is that in international law the general principles perform a gap-filling function, whereas in Community law their function goes further. They are, as already stated, an integral part of judicial methodology. A consequential difference is that the process of discovering general principles in European law is more eclectic: as shown in the *Staff Salaries* case the European Court may apply a principle creatively going significantly further than national laws. By contrast, a principle will not be recognized as a general principle of international law within the meaning of Article 38(1)(c) of the Statute unless it is adopted consistently as the solution to a specific legal problem by the various systems of municipal law.[307] It has to be specific and ubiquitous or near ubiquitous in municipal legal systems.[308] Those differences are accounted for by the different functions which the two courts perform in their respective legal orders. The International Court does not act as a constitutional court. It seems that the intention of the committee of jurists which prepared the Statute was to authorize the International Court of Justice to apply the general principles of law found in national, especially private, laws insofar as they could be transposed to relations between States.[309] This contrasts with the European Court of Justice which in its case law has developed primarily principles of public law.

The International Court of Justice has drawn on municipal systems of law, in particular, on issues of procedure. It has referred for example to the rules of *lis pendens*[310] and *res judicata*,[311] the rule that no one should be judge of his own

---

[302] E.g. by Judge Tanaka in the *South West Africa* cases, ICJ Reports (1966) 6 at 294–299.

[303] See the Opinion of Judge Ammoun in the *North Sea Continental Shelf* cases, ICJ Reports 1969, p. 132–133.

[304] I. Brownlie, *Principles of Public International Law*, Fourth Ed., Oxford University Press, 1990, p. 15.

[305] See H. Thirlway, 'The Law and Procedure of the International Court of Justice 1960–1989', (1990) 61 BYIL 1 at 110.   [306] *Ibid.*, 111.

[307] *Ibid.*, 114, 119.   [308] *Ibid.*, 119.

[309] Brownlie, *op. cit.*, p. 16 where further references are made.

[310] *German Interests in Polish Upper Silesia* case, PICJ, Series A, no.6, 1925, p. 20.

[311] *Administrative Tribunal* cases, ICJ Reports, 1954, p. 53.

cause[312] and to rules pertaining to the admission of evidence.[313] Among the principles relied on one also finds the principle of acquiescence,[314] the principle that breach of an engagement involves an obligation to make reparation,[315] abuse of right and good faith,[316] and the principle of equality of States. Certain principles, such as the principle of non-discrimination on grounds of race, religion and sex, are recognized as part of *jus cogens* and could, as a result, override the effect of ordinary rules.[317]

[312] *Mosul Boundary* case, PICJ, Series B, no.12, 1925, pp. 31–32.
[313] See the *Corfu Channel* case, ICJ Reports, 1949, pp. 4, 18.
[314] *Temple* case, ICJ Reports, 1962, pp. 6, 23, 31–32.
[315] *Chorzow Factory* case, PICJ, Series A, no. 17, 1928, p. 29.
[316] *German Interests in Polish Upper Silesia* case, PICJ, Series A, no. 7, 1926, p. 30; the *Free Zones* case, PICJ, Series A, no. 30, 1930, p. 12 and no. 46, 1932, p.167.
[317] See W. McKean, *Equality and Discrimination under International Law* (Oxford University Press, 1983), p. 283; Brownlie, *op. cit.*, p. 513. Most recently the CFI had the opportunity to consider the interaction among international law, EC law, and the protection of fundamental rights in Case T-315/01 *Kadi v Council and Commission* and Case T-306/01 *Yusuf v Council and Commission*, judgments delivered on 21 September 2005. The CFI held that the European Community is competent to adopt regulations imposing economic sanctions against private organizations in pursuance of UN Security Council Resolutions seeking to restrict terrorism; that although the EU is not bound directly by the UN Charter, it is bound pursuant to the EC Treaty to respect international law and give effect to Security Council Resolutions; and that the CFI has jurisdiction to examine the compatibility of UN Security Council Resolution with fundamental rights not as protected by the EU but by *jus cogens*. These are the most important judgments delivered so far on the relationship between EC law and international law and are currently under appeal to the ECJ.

2

The Principle of Equality

2.1. The principle of equality as a general principle of Community law

The notion of equality is closely linked to the idea of justice[1] and has perhaps greater resonance than any other legal concept.[2] The principle of equality operates at the moral, political and legal level. It was perceived as an attribute of human dignity and played a prominent role in the theories of leading political thinkers, such as Locke and Rousseau. As a legal principle, it is a product of the Enlightenment. It received express reference in the Declaration of Independence of the United States of 4 July 1776 and, subsequently, the Declaration of the Rights of Man of 1789.[3] Equality of citizens before the law was the normative illustration of the rise of the bourgeoisie and was understood as the rejection of the inequalities of the *ancien régime*.[4] In the late 18th and early 19th century, 'individualism, autonomy and equality before the law' were the leitmotifs of the nascent capitalist ideology which was founded on the twin principles of liberalism, namely, contractual

---

[1] Aristotle, who provided the first elaborate analysis of the notion, considered that equality and justice were synonymous: *Ethica Nicomachea* V.3. 1131a–1131b.

[2] For bibliography, see among others: G. Barrett, 'Re-examining the Concept and Principle of Equality in EC Law', 22 (2003) YEL 117; C. McCrudden, 'Equality and Discrimination' in D. Feldman (ed.), *English Public Law* (Oxford University Press, 2003); C. McCrudden, 'The New Concept of Equality', Conference Presentation in 'Fight Against Discrimination: The Race and Framework Employment Directives', Trier, 1 April 2003; M. Bell, *Anti-Discrimination Law and the EU* (Oxford University Press, 2002); S. Fredman (ed.), *Discrimination and Human Rights—The Case of Racism* (Oxford University Press, 2001); G. More, 'The Principle of Equal Treatment: From Market Unifier to Fundamental Right?' in P. Craig and G. de Burca (eds), *The Evolution of EU Law* (Oxford University Press, 1999), 517; A.Dashwood and S. O'Leary (eds), *The Principle of Equal Treatment in E.C. Law* (Sweet & Maxwell, 1997); J. Schwarze, *European Administrative Law* (Sweet & Maxwell, 1992) Ch. 4; K.Lenaerts, 'L'Égalité de Traitement en Droit Communautaire' (1991) 27 CDE 3; J.Jowell, 'Is Equality a Constitutional Principle?' (1994) 47 CLP 1; R. Plender, 'Equality and Non-discrimination in the Law of the European Union', (1995) 7 Pace Internl. LR57. For the principle of equality as a principle of international law, see Plender, *op. cit.*, and further W. McKean, *Equality and Discrimination under International Law* (Oxford University Press, 1983).

[3] See further Barrett, *op. cit.*, 118; C. Barnard, 'The Principle of Equality in the Community Context: P, Grant, Kalanke, and Marschall: Four Uneasy Bedfellows?' (1998) CLJ 352 at 362.

[4] The principle of equality before the law was included in many constitutional texts of the 19th century, including, among others, the Belgian Constitution of 1831, the Greek Constitution of 1844, and the German Constitution of 1871.

freedom and equality before the law.[5] The first underpinned freedom of trade and provided the foundations of private law whilst the second juxtaposed the liberty of the individual *vis-à-vis* the powers of the monarch and provided the basis of the rule of law.[6]

It is a truism to say that equality is a dynamic concept. Whilst in the 19th century it was seen as a complement to *laissez faire* philosophy, by the early 20th century it began to embrace the idea of social equality, calling for statutory intervention in many aspects of social and economic life and leading to a corresponding decrease in contractual freedom.[7] As a legal concept, equality fulfil a variety of functions and has multifarious meanings; so much so that, according to some leading political philosophers and scholars, it is devoid of any substantive content.[8]

In Community law, equality as a legal concept is omnipresent. It operates at a number of different levels and it may be said that, in contemporary EU law, equality is understood primarily as participation, integration, opportunity and empowerment.[9] Although these functions are inter-related and overlapping, they underlie different strands in the case law.

Firstly, as a general unwritten principle of law, equality functions as a ground for review of Community action. Although it binds the Community legislature and administration in all areas, it acquires particular importance in the field of economic law, especially agriculture. Equality is here understood as rationality and participation, its underlying objective being to ensure that public agencies do not discriminate against market actors on arbitrary grounds.

Secondly, it underpins the internal market. The prohibition of discrimination on grounds of nationality provides the starting point for, and is the most basic component of, the fundamental freedoms of movement. Equality as integration prohibits discrimination not only on grounds of nationality but also against free movers and restrains the nation state's power to regulate and tax.

Thirdly, equality is a fundamental right. In recent years, Community law has taken a large leap forward towards 'status-based equality'.[10] The prohibition of discrimination on grounds of sex, which has been a cornerstone of social law

---

[5] See S. Fredman, 'Combating Racism with Human Rights: the Right to Equality', in Fredman, *op. cit.*, 9 at 14; quoted by Barrett, *op. cit.*, 118.

[6] See for a discussion S. Manolkidis, *Granting Benefits through Constitutional Adjudication* (Thessaloniki: Sakkoulas Press, 1999), at 6–7.

[7] One of the first constitutions to deal directly with social discrimination was the Constitution of the Weimar Republic of 1919.

[8] See P. Westen, *Speaking of Equality: An Analysis of the Rhetorical Force of 'Equality' in Moral and Political Discourse* (Princeton University Press, 1990) and for previous contributions: Westen, 'The Empty Idea of Equality' (1982) 95 HLR 537; K. Greenawalt, 'How Empty is the Idea of Equality?' (1983) 83 Columbia Law Review. 1186; Westen, 'To Lure the Tarantula from its Hole: A Response', (1983) Columbia Law Review 1186; K. Karst, 'Why Equality Matters', (1983) Ga.L.Rev. 245.

[9] In his excellent analysis, McCrudden identifies four ideas of equality in Community law: equality as rationality, equality as a protection of rights, status-based equality, and equality of opportunity. See C. McCrudden, 'The New Concept of Equality', *op. cit.*, n. 2 above.

[10] I have borrowed this term from McCrudden, *op. cit.*

since the 1970s, has been supplemented by measures prohibiting discrimination on other specific grounds such as race or age.

Finally, the advent of Union citizenship has bred a new generation of rights and led the Court to re-assess the ambit of Article 12 which prohibits discrimination on grounds of nationality. This provision has slowly been transformed from a tool of economic integration to an instrument of citizen empowerment.[11]

A distinction is commonly drawn between formal and substantive equality. The first refers to enforcement and requires equality before the law. It does not pertain to the content of laws but simply mandates that public authorities must apply the law consistently and treat equally citizens who are in the same position. Substantive equality, on the other hand, refers to the content of laws and it is 'status-based'.[12] It requires that laws must not discriminate between citizens on certain prohibited grounds, such as sex, race, religion or nationality. In fact, the terms formal and substantive equality are relative and the distinction between them is less clear than it appears. The term formal equality may be understood differently in different legal systems. According to the Diceyan model, for example, formal equality required that the legality of government action must be assessed by ordinary courts applying the general law of the land. In sharp contrast with the French system, Dicey viewed a separate system of administrative courts as being incompatible with the rule of law.[13] Further, the fundamental premise of formal equality, that all citizens enjoy the equal protection of laws and should be subject to the same law, is not devoid of considerations of substance. Its logical consequence is that public bodies must not make distinctions on 'arbitrary' grounds which in turn sows the seeds of a substantive value-based analysis.

Community law protects not only formal but also substantive equality.[14] Although certain provisions of the Treaty provide for the principle of equal treatment with regard to specific matters,[15] the Court has held that the principle of equality is a general principle of law 'to be observed by any court'[16] of which those provisions are merely specific expressions. As a general principle, it precludes comparable situations from being treated differently unless the difference in

---

[11] See 2.9.1 below.   [12] See above.

[13] See A.V. Dicey, *The Law of the Constitution* (10th Ed, Macmillan, 1959), p. 193. For the historical reasons underlying this view and criticisms against it, see de Smith, Woolf and Jowell, *Judicial Review of Administrative Action*, (Sweet & Maxwell, 1995), pp. 5–8 and 156–158. See further J. Jowell, *op. cit.*, n. 2 above, at pp. 4 *et seq.*

[14] An aspect of formal equality distinct to Community law is the judicially elaborated rule that the enforcement of Community rights in national courts must be subject to national rules which are not less favourable than those applicable to comparable claims based on national law. See below Ch. 9.3.2.

[15] See e.g. Article 12 (prohibition of discrimination on the grounds of nationality), Article 34(2) (prohibition of discrimination between producers and between consumers in the common agricultural policy), Article 86(1) (equal treatment between public and private undertakings), Article 141 (equal pay for equal work for men and women). For a comprehensive list of the Treaty provisions which prohibit discrimination, see K. Lenaerts, 'L'Égalité de Traitement', *op. cit.*, n. 2 above, at pp. 39–40.   [16] Case 8/78 *Milac* [1978] ECR 1721, para 8.

treatment is objectively justified.[17] It also precludes different situations from being treated in the same way unless such treatment is objectively justified.[18]

The question arises why the Court has established a general principle of equality transcending the specific provisions of the Treaty. It may be that those provisions do not guarantee equal treatment in all cases so that the development of a general principle is necessary to cover the *lacunae* left in written law. The main reason for the development of a general principle, however, seems to be one of principle rather than one of practical necessity. In the light of the constitutions of the Member States, equality is viewed as 'a constitutive of democracy',[19] an integral part of the rule of law which underlies the political systems and the legal traditions of the Member States. The historical and ideological origins of the principle determine in turn its limits. In declaring equal treatment as a general principle of law the Court does not endorse any particular theory of equality.[20] It does not seek to advance a particular idea of the social good.[21] Rather, the principle is seen as a democratic guarantee which prevents Community and national authorities from imposing differential treatment without good reason. It requires, in other words, that 'distinctions between individuals or groups must be reasonably related to government's legitimate purposes'.[22] Viewed in that perspective, the function of equality can be defined better in negative than in affirmative terms. It does not seek to resolve the issues but rather to act as a check on the decision-makers.[23] The principle thus does not dictate a single result: more than one policy choice may be compatible with it. It can be said that, as a general principle of Community law, equality is consistency and rationality: it requires Community institutions to justify their policies; and it prohibits them from engaging in arbitrary conduct. What is arbitrary conduct, however, requires an evaluation which in turn is based on certain ideas which are not politically neutral. At its barest minimum, the principle of equal treatment as applied by the Court is based on models of egalitarianism and distributive justice and it is imbued by ideas of classic liberalism. In the sphere

---

[17] This is the standard formula used by the Court since 1977. See e.g. Joined Cases 117/76 and 16/77 *Ruckdeschel v Hauptzollamt Hamburg-St.Annen* [1977] ECR 1753, para 7; Case 810/79 *Überschär v Bundesversicherungsanstalt für Angestellte* [1980] ECR 2747, para 16; Joined Cases 201 and 202/85 *Klensch v Secrétaire d'État à l'Agriculture et à la Viticulture* [1986] ECR 3477, para 9; Case 84/87 *Erpelding v Secrétaire d'État à l'Agriculture at à la Viticulture* [1988] ECR 2647, para 29; Case C-56/94 *SCAC v Associazione dei Produttori Ortofrutticoli* [1995] ECR I-1769, para 27. For recent confirmation, see e.g. Case C-292/97 *Karlsson and Others* [2000] ECR I-2737, para 39; Joined Cases C-27 & C-122/00 *Omega Air and Others* [2002] ECR I-2569, para 79.

[18] See Case 106/83 *Sermide v Cassa Conguaglio Zucchero* [1984] ECR 4209, para 28; *Karlsson and Others, op. cit.*, para 39; *Omega Air and Others, op. cit.*, para 79.

[19] Jowell, *op. cit.*, n. 2 above, p. 7.

[20] For such theories see Jowell, *op. cit.*, p. 5; see further R. Dworkin, *Taking Rights Seriously* (London, Duckworth, 1978), Ch. 9; J. Rawls, *A Theory of Justice* (Clarendon Press, 1972); R.A. Posner, *The Problems of Jurisprudence*, Ch. 11, (Harvard University Press, 1990). See also T.R.S. Allan, *Law, Liberty and Justice* (Oxford University Press, 1993) Ch. 7.   [21] Jowell, *op. cit.*, p. 7.

[22] Jowell, *op. cit.*, p. 7.

[23] See Sir Robin Cooke, 'The Struggle for Simplicity in Administrative Law' in M. Taggart (ed), *Judicial Review of Administrative Action in the 1980s* (Oxford University Press, 1986) pp. 16–17.

of economic law, the Court favours what can be termed a traditional, pluralistic, conception of equality which accepts State intervention as necessary for the fair redistribution of resources rather than a market-oriented idea of equal treatment which subordinates State action to market forces and gives primacy to property rights.[24] In the sphere of social law, the Court has followed a pro-active approach, going sometimes beyond the concept of equality as accepted in national law and seeking to form rather than follow an underlying societal consensus.[25]

The principle of equality endorsed by the Court of Justice entails a stricter degree of judicial scrutiny than the concept of *Wednesbury*[26] unreasonableness traditionally endorsed by English courts. Nowadays, English law incorporates the principle of equal treatment as a result of the obligations flowing from Community law and the Human Rights Act 1988. Traditionally, in contrast with Community law, it did not recognize the existence of a general principle of non-discrimination. In many contexts, however, it accepted equality as a principle of lawful adminis-tration[27] and in some cases *Wednesbury* unreasonableness had been interpreted to include 'partial and unequal' treatment.[28] The prime difference between Community law and traditional English law lies in that the former requires the decision-maker to demonstrate a substantive justification or, in other words, to 'provide a fully reasoned case'.[29] The authority is not constrained merely by the requirement that the decision must be one which a reasonable authority might take.[30] It is submitted that the approach of the Court of Justice is better. If it is accepted that the purpose of the supervisory jurisdiction of the courts is to prohibit arbitrary conduct and control abuses by the administration, the principle of equality is an appropriate and necessary ground of review. By contrast, the greater deference to the decision-making authority inherent in the *Wednesbury* test finds its historical explanation in the Diceyan concept of unitary democracy and can be justified only within the confines of that model. Adoption of equality as a ground of review is advantageous also from the practical point of view. Increasing the burden of the administration to justify its actions is likely to lead to a more diligent assessment of the interests involved and, ultimately, to better decision-making.

---

[24] See the discussion by P. Craig, *Administrative Law* (Fifth Ed., Sweet & Maxwell, 2003) pp. 36–37 and C. Harlow, 'Back to Basics: Reinventing Administrative Law' (1997) PL 245.

[25] See Case C-13/91 *P v S and Cornwall County Council* [1996] ECR I-2143; Case C-117/01 *K.B. v National Health Service Pensions Agency and Secretary for Health*, judgment of 7 January 2004. Cf. Joined Cases C-122/99 P and C-125/99 P *D and Sweden v Council* [2001] ECR I-4319. The cases are discussed at 2.8.2 below.

[26] *Associated Provincial Picture Houses Limited v Wednesbury Corporation* [1948] 1 KB 223.

[27] See de Smith, Woolf and Jowell, *op. cit.*, n. 13 above, at 578 *et seq.*

[28] See *Kruse v Johnson* (1889) 2 QB 291; *R v Immigration Appeal Tribunal ex p Manshoora Begum* [1986] ImmAR 385. Judicial authorities in England, however, were not consistent and, in the absence of procedural unfairness, an applicant might have difficulties in establishing a substantive right to equal treatment. See e.g. *R v Special Adjudicator, ex p Kandasamy*, The Times 11 March 1994 in relation to unequal treatment of asylum applications.

[29] *R v Ministry of Agriculture, Fisheries and Food, ex p First City Trading Limited* [1997] 1 CMLR 250 at 279 *per* Laws J.   [30] *Ibid.*

A distinction is sometimes drawn between non-discrimination and equality.[31] The former emphasizes the negative aspect of the right to equal treatment as a Dworkinian 'tramp card' and requires abstention from discriminatory treatment. The second signifies more the notion of positive obligations on the part of the state and the transition towards status-based equality. Such a distinction is drawn in the EU Charter of Fundamental Rights[32] and also the EU Constitution[33] but is not clearly made in the case law of the Community judicature which seems to use the terms equality and non-discrimination as interchangeable.[34]

2.2. Formalizing equality: Article 13 EC and the Charter

2.2.1. Article 13 EC

As stated in the first chapter, one of the most prominent developments in Community law has been the proliferation of statute-based rights many of which expressly declare and supplement rights first recognized by the ECJ. This is not to be seen as a failure of the case law but as an assertion of competence and a statement of constitutional maturity. This tendency towards formalization is particularly evident in the wider field of fundamental rights and, more specifically, non-discrimination law. It is prominently illustrated by Article 13 EC, the directives adopted thereunder, the Charter, and the EU Constitution.

Article 13(1) EC, inserted by the Treaty of Amsterdam, provides an all-embracing legal basis for the adoption of measures to combat discrimination 'based on sex, racial or ethnic origin, religion or belief, disability, age or sexual orientation'. This is an important provision which has both symbolic and legal value. It increases the visibility of equality as a political aspiration and significantly enhances the Community's powers in the field of anti-discrimination law. Article 13 provides the basis for taking action to combat discrimination but does not in itself impose any specific legal obligations on Member States. It does not therefore have direct effect. Procedurally, the adoption of legislation is not easy since the Council is mandated to act unanimously on a proposal from the Commission and after consulting the European Parliament. The requirement of unanimity was the *quid pro quo* for allowing Community competence in the area[35] but the Treaty of Nice has since found a limited role for the cooperation procedure.[36]

---

[31] D. J. Harris, M. O'Boyle and C. Warbrick, *Law of the European Convention on Human Rights* (Butterworths, 1995), p. 463.   [32] See 2.2.2 below.
[33] See Article 2 of the EU Constitution.   [34] See e.g. *Überschär, op. cit.*, n. 17 above, at p. 2764.
[35] See F. van den Berghe, 'The European Union and the Protection of Minorities: How Real is the Alleged Double Standard?' (2003) 22 YEL 155 at 170.
[36] Under Article 13(2) EC, introduced by the Treaty of Nice, the cooperation procedure applies when the Council adopts Community incentive measures to support action by the Member States in order to contribute to the achievement of the objectives stated in Article 13(1). Measures adopted under Article 13(2) cannot pursue the harmonization of national laws.

Article 13(1) is subject to two provisos. It applies 'without prejudice to the other provisions of this Treaty'. This suggests that it does not detract from other provisions of the Treaty which provide more specific legal bases for the adoption of anti-discrimination legislation on specific grounds, e.g. Article 141(3) EC. This is of practical importance because other legal bases, such as Article 114(3), may enable the Council to act by qualified majority and the cooperation procedure. Article 13(1) cannot take priority over such provisions.[37]

Article 13(1) operates 'within the limits of the powers conferred by [the Treaty] to the Community'. This rider reiterates that, in taking action under this provision, the Council must respect the general conditions for the exercise of its competence, e.g. the principles of subsidiarity and proportionality. Also, more importantly, it means that the Council may act only within the objectives of the Treaty and not 'beyond the general framework created by the provisions of the Treaty as a whole'.[38] This is not to deny the autonomous character of Article 13 as a legal basis. It is not a requirement for the adoption of legislation that it must have a substantive link with another provision of the Treaty which may serve as the basis for Community action.[39] It is however a requirement that the field of action falls *ratione materiae* within the competence of the Community.

Under Article 13, the Council may adopt legislation applying not only to Union nationals but also to citizens from third states. This is because the text of the provision is not restricted to nationals of Member States and, more generally, social provisions of the Treaty tend to apply to all those residing within the EU.[40] Indeed, the Race Directive and the Framework Directive are all-embracing and cover also third-country nationals.[41]

Article 13 mandates the Council to 'take appropriate action to combat discrimination.' Appropriate action is sufficiently wide to cover not only legally binding measures but also *sui generis* soft measures such as guidelines or action programmes.[42] Finally, it has been said that 'combatting discrimination' goes beyond mere prohibition and may include affirmative action schemes.[43]

---

[37] See M. Bell, 'The New Article 13 EC Treaty: A Sound Basis for European Anti-Discrimination Law?' (1999) 6 Maastricht Journal of Eur. Comp. Law, 9; van Den Berghe, *op. cit.*, 172.

[38] Cf. the formula used by the ECJ in Opinion 2/94 *Accession to the ECHR* [1996] ECR I-1759, para 30.

[39] Article 13 corresponds to Article III-124 of the Constitution which provides that the Council acts unanimously after obtaining the consent of the European Parliament. In addition, Article III-118 of the Constitution makes the combating of discrimination on the same grounds a permeating objective which underlies the implementation of all policies and activities referred to in Part III of the Constitution.

[40] See Bell, *op. cit.*, at 20; van den Berghe, *op. cit.*, n. 35 above, at 170.

[41] See 2.2.3 below.

[42] L. Flynn, 'The Implications of Article 13—After Amsterdam, Will Some Forms of Discrimination Be More Equal than Others?' (1999) 36 CMLRev 1132, 1136.

[43] van den Berghe, *op. cit.*, 174.

2.2.2. The Charter of Fundamental Rights

The right to equal treatment finds its most comprehensive expression in the Charter of Fundamental Rights. Chapter III bears the title 'Equality' but its provisions are far-reaching, encompassing a number of positive and substantive rights whose normative content goes beyond the concept of equality. It covers the following: equality before the law (Article 20); non-discrimination (Article 21); cultural, religious and linguistic diversity (Article 22); equality between men and women (Article 23); the rights of a child (Article 24); the rights of the elderly (Article 25); and integration of persons with disabilities (Article 26). The underlying premises of these stipulations are to honour human dignity and provide for equality of opportunity.

Article 21(1) provides for an all-embracing prohibition of discrimination. It states as follows:

Any discrimination based on any ground such as sex, race, colour, ethnic or social origin, genetic features, language, religion or belief, political or any other opinion, membership of a national minority, property, birth, disability age or sexual orientation shall be prohibited.[44]

According to the non-binding Praesidium explanations accompanying the Charter, Article 21(1) draws on Article 13 EC, Article 14 ECHR and Article 11 of the Convention on Human Rights and Biomedicine as regards genetic heritage.[45] It is supplemented by Article 21(2) which prohibits discrimination on grounds of nationality within the scope of application of the EC and the TEU.

Article 21(1) of the Charter differs from Article 13 EC in a number of respects. The most fundamental difference is that, whilst Article 21(1) provides for a substantive prohibition of discrimination, Article 13 is solely an empowering provision. By contrast, Article 21(1) does not provide any legal basis for the adoption of legislation. In accordance with the general provisions which govern the Charter's scope of application, Article 21 applies only to Union institutions and bodies and Member States when they implement Community law.[46] Furthermore, it is not as such binding since the Charter itself is not, although it might be used as an indirect source of obligations. Thus, whilst Article 21 has in itself a normative substantive content, it is in fact of much more limited scope than the directives which have been adopted under Article 13 which bind the Member States and apply also to relations between individuals. A further difference is that, whilst Article 21 of the Charter contains an indicative list of prohibited grounds of discrimination, the list of grounds contained in Article 13 EC is exhaustive and narrower.

---

[44] Article 21 of the Charter corresponds to Article II–81(1) of the Constitutional Treaty.

[45] See Text of the Explanations relating to the Charter issued by the Praesidium, Document Charter 4473/00, 11 October 2000.

[46] This clarification was included in the Updated explanations relating to the text of the Charter of Fundamental Rights issued by the Praesidium of the Constitutional Convention, CONV 828/1/03 REV 1, Brussels, 18 July 2003.

A number of references to the principle of equality are also made in Part I of the EU Constitution. Equality and non-discrimination feature among the fundamental values of the Union in Article 2, whilst references, mostly express but some implicit, are made in other provisions.[47] Notably, Article 5(1) expressly requires the Union to respect the equality of Member States. This is an expression of formal equality and was inserted primarily as a reassurance to smaller Member States. As a legal declaration, however, it is of limited value. The representation of Member States in the political structures and processes of the Union is concretized by other provisions of the Constitution which are imbued with a loose concept of fairness rather than with a pre-existing, objective notion of equal treatment.[48] Finally, formal equality among citizens is expressly provided by Article 1–45 which, under the heading of democratic equality, states that 'in all its activities, the Union shall observe the principle of the equality of its citizens, who shall receive equal attention from its institutions, bodies, offices and agencies'.

2.2.3. The anti-discrimination directives

On the basis of Article 13 EC, the Council has adopted Directive 2000/43 implementing the principle of equal treatment between persons irrespective of racial or ethnic origin,[49] and Directive 2000/78 establishing a general framework for equal treatment in employment and occupation.[50] The detailed discussion of these directives is beyond the scope of this book. It is appropriate however to highlight some of their salient features.

The purpose of the Race Directive is to lay down a framework for combating discrimination on the grounds of 'racial or ethnic origin'.[51] It prohibits not only discrimination but also harassment and instruction to discriminate.[52] Race and ethnicity are not defined by the Directive. This poses the risk, evident in some national legal systems, that certain groups may not qualify as racial or ethnic ones and thus not benefit from the protection of its provisions.[53] The terms 'racial or ethnic origin', however, are concepts of Community law to be defined by the ECJ and are not left to national law to determine.

---

[47] See Article 2 (equality between men and women), Article I-3(3) (obligation to combat social exclusion and discrimination and promote social justice and protection, equality between women and men, solidarity between generations and protection of the rights of the child); Article I-4(2) (prohibition of discrimination on grounds of nationality), Article 52 (religious equality).

[48] See Article I-5(1) and, for specific illustrations, Article I-24(7) (equal rotation of Member States in the Presidency of the Council), and Article I-26(6) (equal rotation of Member States in the formation of the Commission).   [49] OJ 2000, L 180/22.

[50] OJ 2000, L 303/16. See also Directive 2002/73 on the implementation of the principle of equal treatment for men and women as regards access to employment, vocational training and promotion and working conditions, OJ 2002, L 269/15. This Directive amends Directive 76/207 on equal treatment and was adopted under Article 141(3) EC.

[51] For a discussion, see, among others, F. Brennan, 'The Race Directive: Recycling Racial Equality' (2004) Cambridge Yearbook of European Legal Studies 311; M. Bell, 'Beyond European Labour Law? Reflections on the EU Racial Equality Directive' (2002) 8 ELJ 384.

[52] See Articles 3(3) and 3(4).   [53] See the criticism by Brennan, *op. cit.*, at 320 *et seq.*

The scope of application of the Directive *ratione materiae* is wide. In accordance with its fundamental purpose to ensure democratic and tolerant societies,[54] it goes beyond access to employment and prohibits discrimination in the social sphere.[55] The Directive protects both Community nationals and nationals of third states. It does not however prohibit difference in treatment based on nationality and is without prejudice to provisions and conditions relating to the entry and residence of third-country nationals.[56] Although this limitation has attracted justifiable criticism[57] it should be seen in context. The introduction of an unqualified principle of equal treatment between Union nationals and nationals of third States would go beyond the political consensus which underlies the European social model. The Directive is not an instrument of immigration policy but of social inclusion. Two points may nonetheless be made in this context. First, the use of nationality as a differentiating criterion may in some circumstances amount to indirect discrimination on grounds of race or ethnic origin, in which case it must be objectively justified in order to be compatible with the Directive. To put it differently, the fact that difference in treatment based on nationality is not covered by the Directive does not foreclose the possibility of such a difference being caught by the Directive, at least if it is disguised discrimination on grounds of race or ethnic origin. In practice, however, it would be difficult to establish in any specific case that a difference in treatment has occurred on the basis of race rather than nationality.

Second, the limitation of the Directive may be mitigated by recourse to the general principle of non-discrimination. It may be argued that, in accordance with the general principle of equal treatment as observed by the case law of the ECJ, the use of nationality as a differentiating criterion may amount to discrimination unless it is objectively justified.

The Framework Directive seeks to combat discrimination on the grounds of religion or belief, disability, age or sexual orientation.[58] In line with the Race Directive, it prohibits discrimination as well as harassment and instruction to

---

[54] See Preamble, recital 12.

[55] Under Article 3(1), it applies to: (a) conditions for access to employment, to self-employment and to occupation, including selection criteria and recruitment conditions, whatever the branch of activity and at all levels of the professional hierarchy, including promotion; (b) access to all types and to all levels of vocational guidance, vocational training, advanced vocational training and retraining, including practical work experience; (c) employment and working conditions, including dismissals and pay; (d) membership of and involvement in an organization of workers or employers, or any organization whose members carry on a particular profession, including the benefits provided for by such organizations; (e) social protection, including social security and healthcare; (f) social advantages; (g) education; (h) access to and supply of goods and services which are available to the public, including housing.

[56] See Article 3(2). A similar limitation applies to the Framework Directive. See Directive 2000/78, Article 3(2).

[57] See F. Brennan, 'The Race Directive, Institutional Racism and Third Country Nationals', in Tridimas and Nebbia, *European Union Law for the Twenty-first century: Rethinking the New Legal Order*, Volume 2, (Oxford: Hart Publishing, 2004) 371–386 at 380–1.

[58] Directive 2000/78, Article 1. Note that, most recently, in an important judgment, the ECJ held that the principle of non-discrimination on grounds of age is a general principle of Community law: Case C-144/04 *Mangold*, judgment of 22 November 2005.

discriminate[59] but its scope of application is narrower as it applies only in relation to employment and occupation.[60]

A distinct feature of both Directives is their horizontal application. They mandate Member States to apply their provisions both to the public and private sectors and thus, within the scope of their application, make the principle of equal treatment as implemented by national law binding also on private entities.[61] Since directives may not produce horizontal effect, individuals may rely against other private entities not on the Directives themselves but on norms of national law which implement them or can be interpreted in conformity with them.[62]

Both the Race and the Framework Directive take a minimalist approach. They impose only minimum requirements and allow Member States to apply provisions which are more favourable to the protection of equal treatment.[63]

The Directives prohibit both direct and indirect discrimination. Under the Race Directive, direct discrimination occurs 'where one person is treated less favourably than another is, has been or would be treated in a comparable situation on grounds of racial or ethnic origin'.[64] A similar definition *mutatis mutandis* is given in the Framework Directive.[65]

Under Article 2(2)(a) of the Race Directive, indirect discrimination occurs:

where an apparently neutral provision, criterion or practice would put persons of a racial or ethnic origin at a particular disadvantage compared with other persons, unless that provision, criterion or practice is objectively justified by a legitimate aim and the means of achieving that aim are appropriate and necessary.

This definition of indirect discrimination is based on the criterion of particular disadvantage which is used also in the Framework Directive.[66] It contrasts with the classic definition of indirect discrimination adopted in the case law of the ECJ on sex discrimination which is based on a statistical criterion.[67] The statistical criterion was developed in the Court's case law and subsequently expressly endorsed by the Burden of Proof Directive.[68] Under this definition, indirect discrimination exists where an apparently neutral provision disadvantages a substantially higher proportion of the members of one sex unless it is proportionate and objectively

---

[59] *Ibid.*, Articles 2(1), 2(3) and 2(4).

[60] *Ibid.*, Article 1 and Article 3(1): the Directive applies to conditions for access to employment and self-employment, vocational training, employment and working conditions, including dismissal and pay, and membership of workers' or employers' organizations. It does not apply in relation to entitlements under social security or social protection schemes. See Article 3(4).

[61] Directive 2004/43, Article 3(1); Directive 2000/78, Article 3(1).

[62] See Case C-91/92 *Faccini Dori v Recreb* [1994] ECR I-3325; C-106/89 *Marleasing* [1990] ECR I-4135.

[63] Directive 2000/43, Article 6(1); Directive 2000/78, Article 8(1). Also, both Directives expressly state that their implementation may in no circumstances constitute grounds for a reduction in the level of protection against discrimination already afforded by Member States. See Articles 6(2) and 8(2) reespectively.   [64] Directive 2000/43, Article 2(2)(a).
[65] Directive 2000/78, Article 2(2)(a).   [66] See Article 2(2)(b).
[67] See Case C-237/94 *O'Flynn v Adjudication Officer* [1996] ECR I-2617, paras 18–19 and n. 70 below.   [68] Council Directive 97/80 of 15 December 1997 OJ 1998, L 14/6.

justified.[69] The criterion of particular disadvantage echoes, but is not identical to, the case law on free movement. Still, in that area also a quantitative criterion seems to be crucial in establishing indirect discrimination.[70] The adoption of a different definition of indirect discrimination from that adopted in cases of sex discrimination is liable to lead to confusion especially in cases of multiple discrimination.[71] This risk is particularly present in the case of the Framework Directive. One of the reasons why the Race Directive did not rely on a statistical criterion is that, under the legislation of some Member States, data protection legislation prohibits the collection of data concerning the ethnic origin of individuals.[72] As far as the Framework Directive is concerned, some Member States were unwilling to endorse the statistical criterion followed in the Burden of Proof Directive.[73] Also, whilst statistical evidence is readily available on the male/female balance, in other areas, such as sex orientation, it is difficult to gather.[74] The risk of confusion is lessened by the fact that Directive 2002/73 on equal treatment between men and women, which amends Directive 76/207, now adopts the test of particular disadvantage also in relation to indirect

[69] Ibid., Article 2(2). Under the case law, indirect discrimination exists when a rule affects a considerably smaller percentage, or a much lower proportion, or a much higher proportion of one sex than of the other. See e.g. Case 96/80 *Jenkins v Kingsgate* [1981] ECR 911, para 13; Case 170/84 *Bilka Kaufhaus v Weber von Hartz* [1986] ECR 1607, para 29; Case C-457/93 *Kuratorium fur Dialyse und Nierentransplantation v Lewark* [1996] ECR I-243, para 28; Case C-278/93 *Freers and Speckmann v Deutsche Bundespost* [1996] ECR I-1165, para 22. In any event, there must be a considerable difference in percentage for indirect discrimination to be established: See Case C-167/97 *R v Secretary of State for Employment, ex p Seymour-Smith and Perez* [1999] ECR I-623, paras 60–65. In that case, it was held that a difference between 77.4% of men and 68.9% of women was not considerable. The above case law is referred to by Jacobs AG in paras 30–44 of his Opinion in Case C-79/99 *Schnorbus v Land of Hessen*, judgment of 7 December 2000.

[70] According to established case law, the prohibition of discrimination on grounds of nationality covers not only direct but also indirect difference in treatment, namely, one which although based on a criterion other than nationality (for example residence in the national territory or years of service there, or linguistic competence) leads effectively to the same result. This case law underlies both Article 12 EC and the provisions of the Treaty on free movement of persons. See, for a recent reiteration, Case C-209/03 *The Queen on the application of Dany Bidar v London Borough of Ealing and Secretary of State for Education and Skills*, judgment of 15 March 2005, para 51. In *O'Flynn op. cit.*, n. 67 above, paras 18–19, the ECJ held: 'Conditions imposed by national law must be regarded as indirectly discriminatory where, although applicable irrespective of nationality, they affect essentially migrant workers . . . or the great majority of those affected are migrant workers, . . . where they are indistinctly applicable but can be more easily satisfied by national workers than by migrant workers . . . or where there is a risk that they may operate to the particular detriment of migrant workers . . . It is otherwise only if those provisions are justified by objective considerations independent of the nationality of the workers concerned, and if they are proportionate to the legitimate aim pursued by national law.' In *O'Flynn* the ECJ did not rely solely on a statistical criterion but used as an alternative the particular detriment test. Still, a quantitative criterion seems to be crucial. In *Angonese* the ECJ held that the fact that nationals of the host state may also be affected by a rule does not prevent it from being indirectly discriminatory provided that the majority of those affected are non-nationals: see Case C-281/98 *Angonese v Cassadi Risparmio di Bolzano* [2000] ECR I-4139, para 41.

[71] See House of Lords, Select Committee on European Union, Fourth Report, 19 December 2000, *The EU Framework Directive on Discrimination*, para 36.

[72] See McCrudden, *op. cit.*, n. 2 above, p. 16, n.71 and further references given therein.

[73] See House of Lords, *op. cit.*, para 35.   [74] Ibid.

discrimination on grounds of sex.[75] Also all Directives under discussion allow rules of national law or practice to provide that indirect discrimination may be established by any means including statistical evidence.[76]

The Race Directive allows Member States to introduce limited exceptions from the prohibition of discrimination. Member States may provide that a difference in treatment which is based on a characteristic related to racial or ethnic origin may not constitute discrimination if the following conditions are fulfilled:

(a) such a characteristic constitutes a genuine and determining occupational requirement;
(b) it does so by reason of the nature of the particular occupational activities concerned or the context in which they are carried out;
(c) the objective pursued is legitimate; and
(d) the difference in treatment is proportionate.[77]

A further synergy between the two Directives is in the treatment of positive or affirmative action. Article 5 of the Race Directive states that 'with a view to ensuring full equality in practice, the principle of equal treatment shall not prevent any Member State from maintaining or adopting specific measures to prevent or compensate for disadvantages linked to racial or ethnic origin'. Article 7(1) of the Framework Directive uses *mutatis mutandis* the same formulation. These provisions are somewhat narrower than Article 141(4) EC which provides for positive action to counterbalance sex discrimination but are imbued with the same reactive model of harmonization: they condone rather than mould policies, making Union law less than a protagonist. Such reticence conforms with a pluralist model of integration which defers to local political preferences and reaches, in effect, a higher degree of legitimacy.[78] The Framework Directive, however, is more prescriptive in relation to disabled persons.[79]

---

[75] Directive 2002/73, *op. cit.*, Article 1(2).
[76] See Framework Directive, Preamble, recital 15; Race Directive, Preamble, recital 15; Directive 2002/73, Preamble, recital 10.
[77] See Race Directive, Article 4. A similar exception is provided for in Article 4(1) of the Framework Directive. The latter provides for further exceptions. See Article 4(2) (difference of treatment based on religious beliefs in relation to occupational activities within churches), Article 5 (reasonable accommodation for disabled persons) and Article 6 (justification of differences of treatment on grounds of age).   [78] See further at 2.8 below.
[79] See Article 5, which provides for so-called 'reasonable accommodation' for disabled persons, and Article 7(2). Article 5 states that, in order to guarantee compliance with the principle of equal treatment in relation to persons with disabilities, reasonable accommodation must be provided. This means that employers must take appropriate measures, where needed in a particular case, to enable a person with a disability to have access to, participate in, or advance in employment, or to undergo training, unless such measures would impose a disproportionate burden on the employer. The burden is not considered to be disproportionate when it is sufficiently remedied by measures existing within the framework of the disability policy of the State concerned. Article 7(2) states further that, with regard to disabled persons, the principle of equal treatment is without prejudice to the right of Member States to adopt provisions on protection and safety at work or measures aimed at creating provisions for safeguarding or promoting their integration into the working environment.

Finally, both Directives are prescriptive in relation to remedies and enforcement. They require Member States to provide for effective judicial remedies,[80] bestow representative associations with *locus standi* to bring actions on behalf of individuals,[81] contain rules on the reversal of proof[82] and provide for sanctions.[83] Further, they require Member States to take a number of positive measures with a view to fostering a culture of equality in the workplace and promote social dialogue.[84]

2.3. The principle of non-discrimination in the ECHR

The right to non-discrimination is also provided for in the European Convention for the Protection of Human Rights and Fundamental Freedoms, Article 14 of which states as follows:[85]

The enjoyment of the rights and freedoms set forth in this Convention shall be secured without discrimination on any ground such as sex, race, colour, language, religion, political or other opinion, national or social origin, association with a national minority, property, birth or other status.

Article 14 does not confer a self-standing right to equal treatment but complements the rights established in the other provisions of the Convention by providing for the equal enjoyment of those rights. In the *Belgian Linguistic* case, however, the ECtHR made clear that Article 14 does not presuppose breach of another article in order to come into operation. Provided that the applicant's claim falls within the ambit of one of the rights guaranteed by the Convention, the applicant may establish violation of Article 14 even though violation of another article is not established.[86] To give an example, Article 6 of the Convention which provides for the right to a fair trial does not require States to institute a system of appeal courts. But if a Contracting State did so, it would violate Article 6 in conjunction with Article 14 if it debarred certain persons from the right to appellate proceedings without a legitimate reason whilst it granted that right to other persons in respect of the same type of actions.[87]

---

[80] Race Directive, Article 7(1); Framework Directive, Article 9(1).
[81] Race Directive, Article 7(2); Framework Directive, Article 9(2).
[82] Race Directive, Article 8; Framework Directive, Article 10.
[83] Race Directive, Article 14; Framework Directive, Articles 16–17.
[84] Race Directive, Articles 10–13; Framework Directive, Articles 12–14.
[85] See S. Livingstone' 'Article 14 and the Prevention of Discrimination in the ECHR' (1997) European Human Rights Law Review 25.
[86] See *Belgian Linguistic* (*No. 1*) case, judgment of 9 February 1967, Series A, No. 5 (1979–80) 1 EHRR 241; *Abdulaziz, Cabales and Balkandali v UK*, judgment of 28 May 1985, Series A, No 94(1985) 7 EHRR 471; *Inze v Austria*, Series A, No. 126 (1987).
[87] *Belgian Linguistic* case, *op. cit.*, Section I B, para 9 of the judgment. The ECtHR has held that, where a substantive article of the Convention has been invoked both on its own and together with Article 14 and a separate breach has been found of the substantive article, it is not necessary to consider the case also under Article 14 unless a clear inequality of treatment is a fundamental

Article 14 provides an open-ended list of grounds on which discrimination is prohibited. 'Other status' within the meaning of Article 14 has been interpreted to include, among others, marital status, illegitimacy, military status, professional status and conscientious objection.[88] There is no discrimination where there is objective and reasonable justification for the difference in treatment. Such justification is established where the provision in issue pursues a legitimate aim and, in addition, there is a reasonable relationship of proportionality between the means employed and the aim sought to be realized.[89] As the European Court of Human Rights has stated, the differences in treatment must 'strike a fair balance between the protection of the interests of the community and respect for the rights and freedoms safeguarded by the Convention'.[90] In a vein similar to that of the Court of Justice, the Court of Human Rights seeks to maintain a supervisory role rather than to substitute its own views for the views of the national authorities, although sometimes the distinction is difficult to draw. The European Court of Human Rights has acknowledged a margin of appreciation to States in deciding what means are reasonable to pursue a legitimate objective. The margin of appreciation differs depending on the ground on the basis of which the difference in treatment is practised. Thus, difference in treatment on grounds of race, sex or illegitimacy has been treated by the Court of Human Rights as particularly serious imposing a heavy burden on the State to provide justification.[91]

As in Community law, discrimination contrary to Article 14 occurs not only where a State treats similar situations differently but also where it treats situations which are objectively different in the same way.[92]

Where a right falls outside the scope of the Convention, a Contracting State is not required to observe the principle of non-discrimination. It follows that the principle does not apply to social and economic rights. It has been observed that this is a substantial restriction since, in practice, anti-discrimination law acquires particular importance precisely in those areas.[93]

The fundamental limitation of Article 14 which results from the absence of a self-standing right to non-discrimination is addressed by Protocol 12 which establishes a general right to equal treatment irrespective of any ground such as sex, race, colour, language, religion, political or other opinion, national or social origin, association with a national minority, property, birth or other status.[94] The Protocol

---

aspect of the case: See *Dudgeon v UK* Series A, No. 45 (1981) 4 EHRR 149; *Chassagnou and others v France*, judgment of 29 April 1999 (2000) 29 EHRR 615.

[88] Harris, O'Boyle and Warbrick, *op. cit.*, n. 31 above, p. 470.

[89] See the *Belgian Linguistic* case, *op. cit.*, Section I B, para 10 of the judgment.   [90] *Ibid.*

[91] Harris, O'Boyle and Warbrick, *op. cit.*, pp. 481–483. See e.g. in relation to discrimination on grounds of sex: *Abdulaziz, Cabales and Balkandali v UK op. cit.*, para 78.

[92] See e.g. in relation to Article 9 on freedom of thought, conscience and religion, *Thlimmenos v Greece*, Judgment of 6 April 2000, (2001) 31 EHRR 411.

[93] See Harris, O'Boyle and Warbrick, *op. cit.*, p. 464.

[94] Article 1 of the Protocol reads as follows:

1. 'The enjoyment of any right set forth by law shall be secured without discrimination on any ground such as sex, race, colour, language, religion, political or other opominon, national or social origin, association with a national minority, property, birth or other status.

signals the transition from equality before the law to a right to equal treatment irrespective of status and it has a wide scope of application. In accordance with the Official Explanatory Report accompanying the Protocol, the general right to equal treatment goes beyond Article 14 and its additional scope concerns cases where a person is discriminated against:

(1) in the enjoyment of any right specifically granted to an individual under national law;
(2) in the enjoyment of a right which may be inferred from a clear obligation of a public authority under national law, that is, where a public authority is under an obligation under national law to behave in a particular manner;
(3) by a public authority in the exercise of discretionary power (for example granting certain subsidies);
(4) by any other act or omission by a public authority (for example, the behaviour of law enforcement officers when controlling a riot).

The Protocol was adopted by the Committee of Ministers in June 2000 and was opened for signature on 4 November 2000. It will come into force once it is ratified by ten contracting parties.[95]

2.4. The application of equality in Community law: General observations

The principle of equality is applied in a number of diverse areas. Although the scope of the principle is wide, its precise content and effects depend on a series of factors, including the factual and legislative context in which it is applied, the objectives of the legislation in issue, the interests represented in the litigation, and economic, social and other considerations of policy which may influence the decision of the Court in the specific circumstances of the case. In short, far from being a mechanical process, the application of the principle entails an evaluation and involves striking a balance between conflicting interests. The following general points may be made.

The principle of equality binds the Community institutions and also the Member States, where they implement, or act within the scope of, Community law.[96] In certain circumstances, it may bind natural and legal persons. This occurs in particular in three areas: prohibition of discrimination on grounds of

---

2. No one shall be discriminated against by any public authority on any ground such as those mentioned in paragraph 1.'

[95] At the time of writing the Protocol has been ratified by seven Contracting Parties, namely Albania, Armenia, Bosnia and Herzegovina, Croatia, Cyprus, Finland, and Georgia.

[96] See *Klensch, op. cit.*, n. 17 above, and 1.8 above.

nationality,[97] prohibition of sex discrimination,[98] and prohibition of anti-competitive conduct.[99]

Equality of Member States is a general, unwritten, principle of Community law which has now received express reference in the EU Constitution.[100] It has been referred to by the Court especially in enforcement actions under Article 226 EC. In one case, the Court stated:[101]

In permitting Member States to profit from the advantages of the Community, the Treaty imposes on them also the obligation to respect its rules.

For a State unilaterally to break, according to its own conception of national interest, the equilibrium between advantages and obligations flowing from its adherence to the Community brings into question the equality of Member States before Community law and creates discriminations at the expense of their nationals . . .

A Member State however may not plead the principle of equality in order to justify its failure to comply with Community law. Thus, where the Commission institutes proceedings against a Member State, it is not a good defence to argue that the same breach has been committed by other Member States.[102] Nor may a State delay the coming into force of measures implementing a directive until other Member States adopt such measures, even though the prompt implementation of the directive in the first State may lead to discrimination against undertakings operating in its territory because they have to comply with the higher regulatory burdens imposed by the directive.[103] In such a case, the means of redressing any discrimination arising is by insisting on the timely implementation of Community law by all Member States and imposing penalties against the Member State in default.[104]

The principle of equality acquires particular importance in the field of economic law. The distinct function of the principle in that context was expressed by Tesauro AG as follows:[105]

. . . the principle of equal treatment is fundamental not only because it is a cornerstone of contemporary legal systems but also for a more specific reason: Community legislation

---

[97] See e.g. *Angonese, op. cit.*, n. 70 above; Case 36/74 *Walrave and Koch v Union Cycliste Internationale* [1974] ECR 1405; Case 13/76 *Doná v Mantero* [1976] ECR 1333.

[98] See 2.8.1. below.   [99] See, in particular, Article 81(1)(d) and Article 82(c) EC.

[100] See EU Constitution, Article 5(1) and 2.2.2. above.

[101] Case 39/72 *Commission v Italy* [1973] ECR 101, para 24.

[102] Case 52/75 *Commission v Italy* [1976] ECR 277, para 11; Case 78/76 *Steinike und Weinlig v Germany* [1977] ECR 595.   [103] See Case C-38/89 *Blanguernon* [1990] ECR I-83.

[104] See Article 228 EC, as amended by the Treaty on European Union. For the role of the principle of equal treatment in the determination of penalties imposed on Member States under Article 228, see the comments by Fennelly AG in Case C-197/98 *Commission v Greece*, [2000] ECR I-8609 at para 43 of the Opinion. The case did not reach judgment as the Commission withdrew its application: see Order of 6 October 2000. Note also that Member States may be held liable in damages for breach of Community law to persons who have suffered loss as result. It is doubtful however whether State liability in damages may compensate adequately for loss arising out of inequalities in the national regulatory regimes.

[105] Case C-63/89 *Assurances du Credit v Council and Commission* [1991] ECR I-1799, at p. 1829.

chiefly concerns economic situations and activities. If, in this field, different rules are laid down for similar situations, the result is not merely inequality before the law, but also, and inevitably, distortions of competition which are absolutely irreconcilable with the fundamental philosophy of the common market.

Equality therefore is not only a constitutional necessity but also a keystone of integration. The notion of distortions of competition is central to understanding its function in Community economic law. Article 3(g) of the Treaty provides as one of the activities of the Community the establishment of 'a system ensuring that competition in the internal market is not distorted'. This imposes obligations both on the Community institutions and on Member States.[106] It will be noted however that the objective of eliminating distortions of competition is subject to inherent limitations. First, in the absence of full harmonization of national laws, such distortions are bound to arise. The principle of non-discrimination does not go as far as to prohibit inequalities which arise from the fact that comparable legal relations are subject to different legal systems.[107] Second, the aim of ensuring equal conditions of competition is severely compromised in sectors where the Treaty itself substitutes public intervention for market forces as the primary mechanism of resource allocation. That is particularly the case in agricultural law.[108] Third, whether a competitive disadvantage exists such as to create an unacceptable distortion of competition between two products or two undertakings is in itself sometimes difficult to determine.[109] It will be noted that there are fundamental differences in the application of the principle of equality as a ground for review of Community measures and as a ground for review of national measures affecting the fundamental freedoms. In the first case, the application of the principle is qualified by the discretion of the Community legislature and the Court focuses more on the objectives of the measure in issue.[110] In the second case, the Court applies the principle of equality as an instrument of integration, and focuses more on the effects of the measure.[111]

Equality means consistency and rationality. A decision maker must treat similar cases consistently. Fruitful ground for the application of equality as consistency is found not only in the agricultural sphere but also in competition law. When the Commission undertakes administrative proceedings to establish possible infringements of competition law it is under an obligation to conduct the proceedings fairly and treat all undertakings involved equally. This stems from the general principle of equal treatment, the obligation to respect fundamental rights, and Article 14

---

[106] For an early case where the Court examined this notion, see Joined Cases 32–33/58 *SNUPAT v High Authority* [1959] ECR 127.   [107] See 2.6. below.

[108] See 2.5 below.

[109] See e.g. the disagreements between the Court and the Advocate General in Joined Cases C-267–8/91 *Keck* [1993] ECR I-6097; Case C-387/93 *Banchero* [1995] ECR I-4663; Case C-320/93 *Ortscheit* [1994] ECR I-5243.

[110] See especially below in relation to the common agricultural policy.

[111] See further the discussion in Ch. 5.2.

ECHR.[112] The principle of equality also applies in relation to the imposition of fines. Where the Commission imposes fines on undertakings for anti-competitive conduct, the fines must be calculated according to the same method for all undertakings unless the use of a different method in relation to specific undertakings is objectively justified.[113] This applies not only to fines in competition law but to all types of penalties.[114]

The principle however cannot be invoked where there is illegality. Thus, the fact that the Commission has not imposed a fine on the perpetrator of a breach of competition law cannot in itself prevent a fine from being imposed on the perpetrator of a similar infringement.[115] Nor can an undertaking use as a defence that no fine has been imposed on other undertakings which followed similar conduct in the market and against which no proceedings have been brought.[116]

Although the principle of equality requires that traders who are in the same situation must be treated in the same manner, it is logically and practically impossible to take into account every difference which may exist among the various groups of economic operators. In an early case, the Court stated:[117]

By reason of the varied and changing nature of economic life, clear and objective criteria of general application and presenting certain common fundamental characteristics must be used in the establishment and functioning of the financial arrangements for safeguarding the stability of the Common Market. It is thus impossible to take account of every difference that may exist in the organization of economic units subject to the action of the High Authority for fear of fettering that action and rendering it ineffective.

The same point was made by Jacobs AG in a later case:[118]

The principle of equality cannot preclude the legislature from adopting a criterion of general application—indeed that is inherent in the nature of legislation. It may affect different

[112] See however, Case T-21/99 *Dansk Rørindustri v Commission* [2002] ECR II-1681. In that case a claim that the applicant undertaking had been treated unequally because, in contrast to other undertakings, the Commission did not warn it not to continue the infringement failed because, in calculating the fine, the Commission did not attach any importance to whether the undertakings had or had not been warned.

[113] Case T-354/94 *Stora Kopparbergs Bergslags v Commission* [2002] ECR II-843, para 78; Case C-280/98 P *Weig v Commission* [2000] ECR I-9757, paras 63–68; Case C-291/98 *Sarrió v Commission* [2000] ECR I-9991, paras 97–99; Case T-308/94 *Cascades v Commission* [2003] ECR II-813, para 65.

[114] See e.g. in the context of penalties imposed on Member States under Article 228 for failure to comply with Community law, Case C-387/97 *Commission v Greece* [2000] ECR I-5047, para 84.

[115] Case T-86/95 *Compagnie Générale Maritime and Others v Commission* [2002] ECR II-1011, para 487. In the same case however the CFI, in the exercise of its unlimited jurisdiction, reduced the fine imposed by the Commission on the ground that in a decision adopted shortly before the contested decision and dealing with a similar infringement the Commission had not imposed a fine on the undertakings responsible for the breach.

[116] This is the standard case law: See Case T-17/99 *Ke Kelit v Commission* [2002] ECR II-1647, para 101; Joined Cases C-89, C-104, C-114, C-116, C-117 and C-125–9/85 *Ahlström Osakeyhtiö and Others v Commission* (*Woodpulp cases*) [1993] ECR I-1307, para 197; Case T-49/95 *van Megen Sports v Commission* [1996] ECR II-1799, para 56; Case T-77/92 *Parker Pen v Commission* [1994] ECR II-549, para 86; Case T-43/92 *Dunlop Slazenger v Commission* [1994] ECR II-441, para 176.

[117] Joined Cases 17 and 20/61 *Klockner v High Authority* [1962] ECR 325 at 340.

[118] Joined Cases C-13–16/92 *Driessen and others* [1993] ECR I-4751 at p. 4780. See also Case 147/79 *Hochstraas v Court of Justice* [1980] ECR 3005, para 14.

persons in different ways, but beyond certain limits any attempt to tailor the legislation to different circumstances is likely only to lead to new claims of unequal treatment.

The same observations apply also to the principle of proportionality.[119] They acquire particular importance in certain areas, for example, agro-monetary legislation, where in view of the objectives of the measures in that field any search for objective criteria becomes virtually impossible.[120]

Historically, the principle of equality as a ground for review of Community action was first applied in the 1950s to measures adopted under the European Coal and Steel Community Treaty.[121] That early case law already evinces the adoption of an economic analysis centering on the notion of distortions in competition.[122] It has since been applied primarily in the following areas: agricultural law; harmonization measures; and disputes between the Community and its employees. The application of the principle will be examined primarily by reference to the first two categories of case. A brief reference will also be made to staff cases. The final sections will examine the prohibition of discrimination on grounds of sex as a general principle of Community law, and the prohibition of discrimination on grounds of nationality under Article 12 EC.

2.5. Agricultural law

Article 34(2) of the Treaty provides that the common organization of agricultural markets shall exclude any discrimination between producers or consumers within the Community. As a general principle of law, the prohibition of discrimination applies not only to producers and consumers but also to other categories of economic operators who are subject to a common organization of the market, including *inter alios*, importers, exporters and the processing industry.[123] There is abundant case law concerning the application of the principle of equality.[124] As already stated, the principle requires that comparable situations must be treated in the same manner unless there are objective grounds which justify a difference in treatment. The constituent parts of the principle therefore are two: comparability

---

[119] See e.g. Case 5/73 *Balkan-Import-Export v Hauptzollamt Berlin-Packhof* [1973] ECR 1091, para 22.   [120] See 2.5 below.
[121] For more recent cases where the principle of equality was examined in the context of ECSC measures, see e.g. Case 250/83 *Findsider* [1985] ECR 131; Case C-99/92 *Terni SpA and Italsider SpA v Cassa Conguaglio per il Settore Elettrico* [1994] ECR I-541.
[122] See *SNUPAT, op. cit.*, n. 106 above, an early dispute arising from the scrap equalization scheme imposed under the ECSC Treaty. In that case, the Court held that a regulatory measure would be discriminatory if 'by substantially increasing differences in production costs otherwise than through changes in productivity it gave rise to an appreciable disequilibrium in the competitive position of comparable undertakings concerned'. For a detailed discussion of cases arising under the ECSC equalisation scheme, see Schwarze, *op. cit.*, n. 2 above, 574 *et seq.*
[123] Case C-280/93 *Germany v Council* [1994] ECR I-4973, para 68. See also *Ruckdeschel, op. cit.*, n. 17 above, para 7; *Milac, op. cit.*, n. 16 above, para 18.
[124] See R. Barents, *The Agricultural Law of the EC* (Kluwer, 1994) Ch. 17.

and objective justification. In some cases the Court does not distinguish clearly between the two and treats them both as parts of the same enquiry.[125] Before examining those notions in more detail, it is necessary to investigate the function of equality in the specific context of the common agricultural policy.[126] As stated above, in the sphere of economic law, the concept of equality is inextricably linked with the notion of competition. The requirement to treat comparable products alike is to ensure as far as possible neutrality, avoid distortions of competition, and enable market forces to allocate resources accordingly. This conception of equality, however, which under Article 3(g) of the Treaty is the cornerstone of the internal market, is incompatible with the special treatment reserved by the Treaty to the agricultural sector. Article 33 mandates the Community institutions to intervene to the extent necessary to attain the objectives provided therein and the Chapter on agriculture subordinates the application of the provisions on free movement and competition to the provisions on agriculture.[127] The formidable task assigned to the Community institutions is encapsulated in the case law according to which, in working out the common agricultural policy, the institutions must seek constantly to reconcile any possible conflict between those objectives when considered individually and must, from time to time, give one or other of those objectives such priority as appears necessary.[128] In short, the principle of equality cannot perform its function as a safeguard against distortions of competition since the very purpose of intervention is to modify the natural play of economic forces. The heavier the intervention, the less the margin for the application of equality. As Lagrange AG noted in an early case, the scope of the principle is necessarily narrower where intervention measures exist, in which case the principle is to be respected only within the sphere of the ends pursued.[129] This is of profound importance in determining the Court's supervisory function, for it means that in determining whether there is lack of objective justification particular importance must be attached to the objectives of the contested measure.

The discussion below is structured as follows. First the judgment in *Royal Scholten-Honig* will be examined. The case provides a prime example of how the Court applies the notion of substantive equality in economic law. Then, the notions of comparability and objective justification will be discussed with reference to examples from the case law.

---

[125] See e.g. Case 8/82 *Wagner v BALM* [1983] ECR 371, paras 22–22; Joined Cases C-248–9/95 *SAM Schiffahrt and Stapf v Germany* [1997] ECR I-4475, para 55–56. In *Royal Scholten-Honig*, discussed at 2.5.1. below, the real issue was not whether there was objective justification but whether there was a difference in treatment between sugar and isoglucose, despite the fact that the Court used language which suggests otherwise.   [126] See further Barents, *op. cit.*, p. 335.

[127] See Article 32(2) and Article 36.

[128] See e.g. Case 203/86 *Spain v Council* [1988] ECR 4563, para 10; Joined Cases 197 etc/80 *Ludwigshafener Walzmuhle v Council and Commission* [1981] ECR 3211, para 41.

[129] Case 13/63 *Commission v Italy* [1963] ECR 165 at 190.

2.5.1. The *Royal Scholten-Honig* case[130]

By Regulation No 1111/77,[131] the Council imposed a production levy on the manufacture of isoglucose, a sugar substitute, which was introduced into the Community market in 1976. The aim of the levy was to offset the economic advantage which isoglucose enjoyed over sugar which, in view of excessive surpluses, had been made subject to a quota system by previous Community regulations. In *Royal Scholten-Honig* it was argued that Regulation No 1111/77 put manufacturers of isoglucose in a disadvantageous position *vis-à-vis* sugar producers. The Court first established that isoglucose and liquid sugar were in competition with each other and therefore in a comparable situation. It then pointed out that the two products were treated differently. Whereas in the case of isoglucose the levy was applied to the whole of production, in the case of sugar a production levy was imposed only to quantities produced above a basic quota. The Court held that although the amount of levy was lower in the case of isoglucose than in the case of sugar, a difference in treatment nonetheless existed because isoglucose manufacturers did not enjoy the marketing guarantees given to sugar manufacturers by the quota system. The Court then turned to examine whether the difference in treatment was objectively justified. The most important argument submitted by the Council and the Commission was that the production levy on isoglucose was comparable to the charges borne by sugar. The Court dismissed that argument on the ground that 60 per cent of the charges imposed on sugar were borne not by sugar manufacturers but by sugar beet growers. Manufacturers of isoglucose therefore were discriminated against *vis-à-vis* manufacturers of sugar. The Court also identified the following difference in treatment: whereas sugar manufacturers were in a position to reduce production charges by limiting production, isoglucose manufacturers were unable to do so since a reduction in production had no effect on the amount of the production levy. In an attempt to justify the contested regulation, the Council and the Commission also argued that alternative solutions to ensure the sharing by isoglucose producers of the losses of the sugar industry encountered practical difficulties. The Court however rebutted that argument by stating that 'inconveniences of the type alleged cannot justify the imposition of a charge which is manifestly unequal'.[132]

Royal Scholten-Honig is one of the few cases where a measure of economic policy has been found to infringe the principle of equal treatment.[133] What conclusions can be drawn from the judgment? The first conclusion concerns the relationship between an existing product and a new product entering the market. Manufacturers of an existing product do not enjoy an unfettered right to be protected

---

[130] Joined Cases 103 and 145/77 *Royal Scholten-Honig v Intervention Board for Agricultural Produce* [1978] ECR 2037.　　　　　　　　　　　　　　　　[131] OJ 1977 L 134, p. 4.

[132] *Royal Scholten-Honig, op. cit.*, para 82.

[133] For a more recent English case which was distinguished from *Royal Scholten-Honig*, see *The Queen v Ministry of Agriculture, Fisheries and Food ex p British Pig Industry* [2000] EuLR 724.

from competition from a new product even where the relevant market suffers seriously from over-supply.[134] As the Advocate General pointed out:[135]

According to the basic system of the Treaty, which is liberal, access to the market must... be guaranteed on the same terms even if in certain circumstances this involves additional sacrifices for the general public.

The second conclusion relates to the objectives of production control measures. The underlying objective of the contested regulation was to provide for a fair allocation of burdens by requiring isoglucose producers to share the costs incurred by the sugar sector. That was clearly a legitimate objective. The judgment indicates however that the allocation of burdens among producers of competing products must be based on rational criteria and a coherent regulatory system which, in the Court's view, was not the case in the circumstances. The third conclusion is closely linked to the second. In order to determine whether a measure complies with the principle of substantive equality, the Court scrutinizes closely the justification asserted by the institutions and assesses the effects of the measure on the groups of persons under comparison.

It is notable that the Advocate General took a different view.[136] He started from the assumption that isoglucose manufacturers operated large modern factories which had lower labour costs than sugar factories and that they should be compared with similar sugar manufacturers. In contrast to the Court, he accepted the argument that the production levy on isoglucose corresponded to the average charges borne by sugar manufacturers and concluded that there was no discrimination.

2.5.2. Comparability

In order to determine whether products or undertakings are in a comparable situation, the Court will normally have recourse to the criterion of competition.[137] In the case of products, the Court will consider whether the products in question fulfil the same function and therefore can be substituted for one another. Where products are interchangeable, they are in a comparable competitive position and should, in principle, be treated in the same manner. In the case of undertakings, the Court may have regard to their production[138] or to their legal structure[139] with a view to determining whether their competitive positions are comparable. The

---

[134] The sugar surpluses were by all accounts not inconsiderable. For example, the 1976–77 marketing year produced sugar surpluses of 1.7 million tonnes.

[135] *Op. cit.*, at p. 2027 *per* Reischl AG.   [136] *Op. cit.*, esp. pp. 2028–30.

[137] *Royal Scholten-Honig, op. cit.*, paras 28–29. See also A.G. Toth, *The Oxford Encyclopaedia of European Community Law* (Oxford University Press, 1990), Vol I, pp. 191 *et seq*. Note however that a lot depends on the circumstances. The fact that two products are in a competitive situation does not mean that they must be treated equally in all respects: Case T–472/93 *Campo Ebro* [1995] ECR II–421, paras 85 *et seq*.

[138] Case 14/59 *Pont-à-Mousson v High Authority* [1959] ECR 215 at 232.

[139] *Klockner, op. cit.*, n. 117 above, at 345.

criterion of substitutability or competitiveness is used by the Court as the principal criterion throughout the field of economic law, for example, in relation to Article 28,[140] or Article 82.[141] For two products or two undertakings to be in a comparable situation it is sufficient, in principle, that they are potentially in competition.[142]

An example of the application of the criterion of comparability in agricultural law is provided by the *quellmehl* cases.[143] Community regulations granted a production refund for quellmehl, a product derived from maize, on the basis that this product was interchangeable with starch which benefited from such a refund. A subsequent regulation abolished the refund for quellmehl on the ground that experience had shown that the opportunity for substituting the two products was slight. The Court held that the Council and the Commission had not produced any new technical or economic data to establish that the two products were no longer in comparable situations.[144] The difference in their treatment amounted therefore to discrimination. The case establishes that two products are in a comparable situation where one can be substituted for the other in the traditional or usual use to which the latter is put.[145] By contrast, where a product is diverted from its normal use, it may cease to be in a comparable situation.[146] Similarly, products which have different applications are not in a comparable competitive situation and a difference in their treatment will not normally amount to discrimination.[147] The Court has held that, in order to determine whether products can be substituted for one another, reference may not normally be made exclusively to the customs of a specific region or even of a single Member State.[148]

A producer who benefits from the services of an organization the aim of which is to promote national production is not in a comparable situation to a producer who does not so benefit and therefore the first producer may be made subject to a charge to finance the activities of that organization.[149] Categories of producers which are not exposed to the same risks may not be in a comparable situation. In *Denkavit*,[150] a Council regulation enabled Germany to grant aid to German

---

[140] See e.g. Case C-391/92 *Commission v Greece* [1995] ECR I-1621.

[141] See e.g. Case 27/76 *United Brands v Commission* [1978] ECR 207. Cf the difference between Article 90(1) and 90(2) EC.

[142] See e.g. Case C-319/81 *Commission v Italy* [1983] ECR 601, para 16.

[143] *Ruckdeschel, op. cit.*, n. 17 above. See also the 'gritz' cases: Joined Cases 124/76 and 20/77 *Moulins Pont-à-Mousson v Office Interprofessionnel des Céréales* [1977] ECR 1795.

[144] *Ruckdeschel, op. cit.*, para 8. By contrast, given the aims of the common agricultural policy, intra-Community trade is not comparable to trade with third countries so that different refunds may be applicable in the two cases: Case 6/71 *Rheinmuhlen v Einfuhr- und Vorratsstelle Getreide* [1971] ECR 823.   [145] *Ruckdeschel, op. cit.*, para 8.

[146] Case 90/78 *Granaria v Council* [1979] ECR 1081, paras 9–10.

[147] See e.g. Case 125/77 *Koninklijke Scholten-Honig v Hoofdproduktschap voor Akkerbouwprodukten* [1978] ECR 1991, paras 30–31; Case C-18/89 *Maizena* [1990] ECR I-2587.

[148] Case 77/86 *The Queen v Customs and Excise, ex p National Dried Fruit Trade Association* [1988] ECR 757, para 14.

[149] Joined Cases C-332, C-333 and C-335/92 *Eurico Italia and Others* [1994] ECR I-711. See also Case 2/73 *Ente Nazionale Risi* [1973] ECR 865.

[150] Case 139/77 *Denkavit v Finanzamt Warendorf* [1978] ECR 1317.

producers to compensate for the losses suffered as a result of the revaluation of the German mark. The German law adopted to give effect to the regulation differentiated between agricultural livestock breeders and industrial breeders. The Court held that the first category used their own farm produce and were subject to the risks inherent in working the soil whereas the second category purchased produce in the national and international market and were not exposed to such risks. By contrast, where the national currency was revalued they were able to obtain produce abroad at advantageous prices. The two groups of breeders therefore were not in a comparable situation.

In *Accrington*,[151] Community regulations provided a tariff quota for the importation of beef from third countries and divided it between traditional importers and new importers. Companies arising from mergers of traditional importers could cumulate their rights to individual quotas whereas companies arising from mergers of new importers and wishing to obtain a share of the new importers' quota could not combine their past trading performance to meet the eligibility criteria for the allocation of a quota. The Court held that the two categories of importers were not in a comparable situation. Traditional importers were allocated quotas in proportion to their imports in previous years. Newcomers were allocated quotas in proportion to the quantities applied for. If they could obtain a quota by merging, that would enable merger to be used as a ploy to obtain maximum allocation of quotas. Commercial groups would be able to spread their activities artificially over a large number of separate companies in the knowledge that if the thresholds for eligibility to the quota were unexpectedly raised they could continue, by making the necessary mergers, to make multiple applications for a share of the newcomers' quota.

In *SAM Schiffahrt and Stapf v Germany*[152] it was argued that the imposition of a levy on owners of inland waterway vessels with a view to reducing overcapacity discriminated against inland waterway carriers in favour of road and rail carriers. The claim was rejected on the ground that the transport sectors were not in a comparable situation. Rail and road transport did not experience overcapacity comparable to that in the inland waterways and the Council was entitled to decide that responsibility for structural improvements in a given sector of the economy lay with operators in that sector.

2.5.3. Objective justification

Difference in treatment between comparable situations is not prohibited where it is objectively justified. The notion of objective justification is not easy to define in the abstract. Whether such justification exists depends on the particular circumstances of each case, account being taken of the objectives of the measure in issue.

---

[151] Case C-241/95 *The Queen v Intervention Board for Agricultural Produce ex p Accrington Beef and Others* [1996] ECR I-6699.   [152] *Op. cit.*, n. 125 above, paras 55–56.

On the basis of the case law, Toth lists the cases where different treatment of comparable products or undertakings is justified as follows:[153]

1) where it is justified by the aims which Community institutions lawfully pursue as part of Community policy;[154]
2) where its purpose is to obviate special difficulties in a sector of industry;
3) where it is not arbitrary in the sense that it does not exceed the broad discretion of the Community institutions;
4) where it is based on objective differences arising from the economic circumstances underlying the common organization of the market in the relevant products.

The guiding principle seems to be that the difference in treatment must not be arbitrary,[155] i.e. it must be based on rational and objective considerations.[156] It should be emphasised, however, that the Community institutions are conceded wide discretionary powers.

A difference in treatment will no longer be justified where the objective justification ceases to exist. In such a case, the measure will become unlawful not *ab initio* but as from the time when objective justification lapses. A person affected may then challenge the validity of the measure incidentally in the course of proceedings against individual acts adopted on its basis under Article 241 of the Treaty or in proceedings under Article 234.[157] In *Altmann and Casson v Commission* the CFI stated:[158]

Since any difference in treatment is ... in the nature of an exception, derogating from a fundamental principle of Community law, it is self-evident that it can no longer be regarded as remaining valid, even if the rule establishing it does not explicitly limit its duration, once the circumstances constituting the objective justification for its existence have ceased to obtain.

In such a case it will be for the Court of Justice, or the CFI, to establish the specific time as from which the measure becomes illegal.

2.5.3.1. Discretion of the Community institutions

The Court has held that, in matters concerning the common agricultural policy, the Community legislature has a broad discretion which corresponds to the

---

[153] Toth, *op. cit.*, n. 137 above, p. 193.

[154] See e.g. for a recent example, *Karlsson, op. cit.*, n. 17 above, para 39.

[155] See e.g. *Denkavit, op. cit.*, n. 150 above, para 15; Case 106/81 *Kind v EEC* [1982] ECR 2885, para 22.

[156] Note however that the term 'arbitrary' has been used also with a more specific meaning, namely to characterize action which is not merely illegal but also unlawful and gives rise to liability in damages. See the second generation of *isoglucose* cases, where the Court held that the Community was not liable in damages on the ground that the conduct of the defendant institutions was not 'verging on the arbitrary': Joined Cases 116 and 124/77 *Amylum v Council and Commission* [1979] ECR 3497, para 19; Case 143/77 *Koninklijke Scholten-Honig Council and Commission* [1979] ECR 3583, para 16.

[157] Joined Cases T-177 and T-377/94 *Altmann and Casson v Commission* [1996] ECR II-2041, para 119. See also Case 36/83 *Mabanaft v Hauptzollamt Emmerich* [1984] ECR 2497, para 34.

[158] *Altmann and Casson, op. cit.*, para 119.

political responsibilities imposed upon it by Articles 34 and 37 of the Treaty and which qualifies judicial review.[159]

The *Bananas* case[160] illustrates vividly the situation where the Court is called upon to apply the principle of non-discrimination in circumstances where the Community legislature seeks to balance diametrically opposed national interests. By Regulation No 404/93,[161] the Council introduced a common organization of the market in bananas replacing the existing diverse national markets. Before the introduction of that Regulation, there existed essentially two tendencies. Producer Member States imposed quantitative restrictions on imports from third countries with a view to ensuring an outlet for domestic production. Non-producer Member States favoured liberal importation rules. The Regulation granted preferential treatment to bananas produced in the Community and, in compliance with the provisions of the Fourth Lomé Convention, to those produced in the ACP States. An annual tariff quota was opened for imports of bananas from third countries other than ACP States. It was argued that the division of the tariff quota discriminated against traders traditionally trading in third country bananas because it reduced their existing market share. The Court stated that, before the introduction of Regulation No 404/93, the traders among whom the tariff quota was subdivided were subject to different national regimes and not in comparable situations. Since the Regulation came into force, traders were affected differently. Those who were traditionally supplied by third country bananas suffered, as a result of the regulation, restrictions in their imports. Those formerly required to market Community and ACP bananas could, as a result of the Regulation, import specified quantities of third country bananas. The Court continued:[162]

However, such a difference in treatment appears to be inherent in the objective of integrating previously compartmentalized markets, bearing in mind the different situations of the various categories of economic operators before the establishment of the common organization of the market. The Regulation is intended to ensure the disposal of Community production and traditional ACP production, which entails the striking of a balance between the two categories of economic operators in question.

The circumstances of the *Bananas* case were distinct because of the strongly opposing national interests and the need to draw a balance between two competing forces, namely, protectionism and free market.[163] The Court came to the conclusion that there was no breach of the principle of equal treatment because the

---

[159] See e.g. Case 179/84 *Bozzetti v Invernizzi* [1985] ECR 2301, para 30.

[160] Case C-280/93 *Germany v Council* [1994] ECR I-4973.

[161] OJ 1993 L 47, p. 1. Note the regulation has since been amended.   [162] *Op. cit.*, para 74.

[163] The Bananas Regulation and related measures have given rise to extensive litigation. See e.g. for other unsuccessful challenges on different grounds: Case C-466/93 *Atlanta Fruchthandelsgesellschaft v Bundesamt für Ernährung und Forstwirtschaft* [1995] ECR I-3799; Case C-104/97 P *Atlanta v Council and Commission*, [1999] ECR I-6983. Cf Case C-364/95 *T. Port GmbH v Hauptzollamt Hamburg-Jonas*, [1998] ECR I-1023 where the ECJ declared invalid Commission Regulation No 478/95 because it imposed only on certain categories of traders the obligation to obtain export licences for bananas; Case C-122/95 *Germany v Council* [1998] ECR I-973 where

common organization of the market provided for a reasonable allocation of risks and benefits among the various categories of traders. The case illustrates that, in the sphere of economic law, the principle of equality prohibits only measures imposing on traders risks beyond those which they can reasonably be expected to bear in the light of the underlying economic circumstances.[164]

A further example of how the discretion of the Council conditions the application of the principle of equality is provided by the judgment in *Wuidart*.[165] Community regulations imposed a levy on milk production in excess of the producer's quota and provided for two alternative formulae on the basis of which, at the option of the Member States, the levy was to be calculated. It was argued that producers subject to the first formula were subject to higher financial burdens than producers subject to the second formula. The Court held that where the Community legislature is required, in adopting rules, to assess their future effects and those effects cannot accurately be foreseen, its assessment is open to criticism only if it appears 'manifestly incorrect' in the light of the information available to it at the time of the adoption of the rules in question.[166] The Court found that the principle of non-discrimination had not been breached because, at the time when the Council introduced the rules, it could reasonably take the view that the higher rate of levy provided for under the second formula would neutralize the advantage which producers subject to that formula would derive.[167]

The above cases clearly illustrate that although the principle of equal treatment enables the Court to exercise more intense review than the test of *Wednesbury* unreasonableness, a range of options do remain available to the Community decision makers. As Laws J put it, it is highly unlikely that only one of the choices available to the legislature will pass the test of objective justification.[168] Of particular interest in this context is the Court's finding that, in taking policy decisions which require the assessment of a complex economic situation, the Community legislature enjoys wide discretion in the sense that the Court will only engage in marginal review. The Court cannot substitute its own assessment for that of the Community legislature but must confine itself to examining whether the assessment made contains a manifest error or constitutes a misuse of powers or exceeds

---

the ECJ annulled the Council decision concluding an international agreement on bananas as being contrary to the principle of equal treatment. For an example of a successful action in damages, see Joined Cases T-79/96, T-260/97 and T-117/98 *Camar and Tico v Commission and Council* [2000] ECR II-2193 and, on appeal, Case C-312/00 [2002] ECR I-11355.

[164] A claim that the introduction of a common organization to previously disparate markets led to discrimination has also been rejected in other cases, see e.g. 1 *Kind, op. cit.*, n. 155 above.

[165] Joined Cases C-267–85/88 *Wuidart and others* [1990] ECR I-435.

[166] *Ibid.*, para 14; see also Case 59/83 *Biovilac v EEC* [1984] ECR 4057, para 17. But note that in *SAM Schiffahrt, op. cit.*, n. 125 above, paras 32, 46, 47 the Court left open the possibility that in some cases the validity of a Community measure may need to be assessed *ex post facto*. See also the Opinion of Jacobs AG at 4489. See further *Altmann, op. cit.*

[167] See also Joined Cases C-133/93, C-300/93 and C-362/93 *Crispoltoni* [1994] ECR I-4863, discussed below 3.5.2.2.   [168] *First City Trading, op. cit.*, n. 29 above, p. 279.

clearly the bounds of the legislature's discretion. In such cases, the discretion of the institution which authored the act extends also 'to a certain extent, to the findings as to the basic facts, especially in the sense that it is free to base its assessment, if necessary, on findings of a general nature'.[169]

Another area where the Community institutions have been allowed a wide margin of discretion is in the field of monetary compensatory amounts. Disputes arose in the 1970s as a result of Community action to alleviate the adverse effects caused by the fluctuation of national currencies. Although nowadays these cases are largely of historical importance, they remain indicative of the Court's approach in agro-monetary matters and provide a guide of its likely reaction in comparable situations. In *Merkur*,[170] it was argued that by not fixing compensatory amounts for the export of products processed from barley, the Commission discriminated against German exporters *vis-à-vis* two other categories of traders: exporters from other Member States, and German exporters of other products in relation to which compensatory amounts had been fixed. With regard to exporters from other Member States, the Court stated that the system of compensatory amounts had been introduced because certain Member States, including Germany, had widened the margins of fluctuation for the exchange rates of their currencies. Although the Community institutions had the power to mitigate the effects of such national measures, they enjoyed wide powers of appraisal and they were not bound to compensate for all disadvantageous effects to traders in the Member States concerned. With regard to traders of other products, the Court held:[171]

As regards the comparison made with German exporters of goods which had the benefit of this compensatory system from the start, the different treatment of which the applicant complains would not be a violation of the principle of non-discrimination unless it appeared to be arbitrary.

... in applying the last sentence of Article 1(2) of Regulation No 974/71, the Commission has wide powers of appraisal in judging whether the monetary measures contemplated by the said regulation could lead to disturbances in trade in agricultural products.

After pointing out that the contested measures were emergency provisions, which had to be drawn within a short period of time and in relation to which the Commission had to assess whether disturbances in trade would occur in relation to specific products, the Court continued:[172]

Since the assessment which the Commission had to make was perforce an overall one, the possibility that some of the decisions it made might subsequently appear to be debatable on economic grounds or subject to modification would not in itself be sufficient to prove the existence of a violation of the principle of non-discrimination, once it was established that the considerations adopted by it for guidance were not manifestly erroneous.

---

[169] *SAM Schiffahrt, op. cit.*, paras 24–25.
[170] Case 43/72 *Merkur v Commission* [1973] ECR 1055.   [171] *Ibid.*, paras 22–23.
[172] *Ibid.*, para 24.

As a rule of thumb it may be said that, in the field of agro-monetary measures, it is virtually impossible that a claim that the principle of non-discrimination has been violated will succeed,[173] save in the case of misuse of powers or a particularly blatant disregard of discretionary powers.[174] Measures of general application taken in order to stabilize the market may give rise to difference in treatment among producers but the Court is prepared to give the Community institutions the benefit of the doubt in order to discourage litigation and facilitate their speedy intervention to a highly technical area. In some cases, however, the reasoning of the Court does not appear satisfactory.[175]

2.5.3.2. Different treatment of products of different Member States

Sometimes agricultural regulations provide for special provisions in relation to producers or goods in certain Member States. On a number of occasions the Court has been confronted with the question whether such provisions are compatible with the principle of non-discrimination. The Court has held that differences in treatment which are based on objective differences arising from the underlying economic situations of Member States cannot be considered discriminatory.[176] In one case, it was held that the fact that economic structures in Italy were unusually fragmented into small production units created considerable difficulties for the implementation of the Community milk quota system and therefore justified the temporary postponement of certain aspects of that system.[177] It has also been accepted that differential treatment among economic operators established in different Member States may be the inevitable consequence of the fact that Community harmonization measures provide only for minimum requirements.[178] Regional differentiations within the same Member State may also be objectively justified.[179]

Breach of the principle of non-discrimination was found in *Codorniu v Council*.[180] A Council regulation adopted in 1989 reserved the term 'crémant' to certain quality

---

[173] See e.g. Case 138/78 *Stölting* [1979] ECR 713; Case 49/79 *Pool v Council* [1980] ECR 569; Case 281/82 *Unifrex v Commission and Council* [1984] ECR 1969; Case 244/83 *Meggle* [1986] ECR 1101; Case 195/87 *Cehave v Hoofdproduktschap voor Akkerbouwprodukten* [1989] ECR 2199; Case C-244/95 *Moskof v EOK* [1997] ECR I-6441; and see Barents, *op. cit.*, n. 124 above, p. 170.

[174] See Case 29/77 *Roquette v France* [1977] ECR 1835, paras 20–21.

[175] See, e.g. *Cehave, op. cit.* and contrast the judgment with the more persuasive Opinion of Tesauro AG.

[176] See Case 230/78 *Eridania v Minister for Agriculture and Forestry* [1979] ECR 2749, para 19; Joined Cases C-181, C-182 and C-218/88 *Deschamps and others v Ofival* [1989] ECR 4381.

[177] *Wuidart, op. cit.*, n. 165 above, paras 28–30.

[178] Case C-128/94 *Hönig v Stadt Stockach* [1995] ECR I-3389.

[179] In Case C-189/01 *Jippes and Others* [2001] ECR I-5689, paras 130–132, it was held that the restriction of vaccination of animals against foot and mouth disease only to regions of a Member State where the virus was present was justified by the fact that vaccination in the affected areas sought to prevent the spread of the virus, whilst in areas where the virus was not present vaccination might in fact contribute to the spread of the virus and thus be counter-productive.

[180] Case C-309/89 [1994] ECR I-1853.

sparkling wines traditionally produced in France and Luxembourg. The applicant was a Spanish company which was the holder of the Spanish graphic trademark 'Gran Cremant de Codorniu'. It alleged that the regulation was discriminatory. The Court observed that, whereas the first national measures providing in France and Luxembourg for the use of the term 'crémant' as a traditional description were adopted in 1975, the applicant company had been using that term since 1924. The reservation of the term for wines produced in France and Luxembourg could not therefore be justified on the basis of traditional use. The Court also held that the term 'crémant' referred to the method of manufacture of the product rather than to its geographical origin. It followed that there was no objective reason justifying the difference in treatment and the regulation was void. The case provides an example of what constitutes arbitrary conduct. The contested regulation can be seen as a blatant disregard of acquired rights, indeed, as verging on expropriation. *Codorniu* is also important from the point of view of procedure. It is the first case where the Court expressly acknowledged, outside the limited field of anti-dumping, that an individual may challenge a true legislative measure under Article 230(4). The judgment shows that, where an applicant has a very strong case on the merits, the Court may be prepared to grant him *locus standi* to challenge a legislative measure despite the restrictive requirements of that provision.[181]

In a subsequent case, the Court held that producers who were entitled to use the registered designation 'champagne' were able to use the terms 'méthode champenoise' for the description of their products to the exclusion of other producers who traditionally used those terms, the restricted use of the terms being justified in the interests of protecting registered indications of the geographical origin of wines.[182]

Where, in applying a criterion laid down by Community legislation, a Community institution commits an error of assessment and as a result favours a Member State, the other Member States may challenge the preferential treatment granted to that State but may not claim that such treatment must be extended to them. This is illustrated by *Italy v Council*.[183] The common organization of the market in sugar guaranteed minimum prices to producers and enabled higher prices to be fixed for regions where a deficit in supply was foreseen. Regulation No 1361/98 fixed the intervention prices for the marketing year 1998/99. It classified as deficit areas the United Kingdom, Ireland, Portugal, Finland and Spain. Italy, by contrast, was not classified as a deficit area. As a result, the lower intervention price fixed by Regulation No 1360/98 in relation to all non-deficit areas applied to Italy by default. Italy argued that the Council had breached the principle of equal treatment

---

[181] The Court conceded that the contested provision was a legislative measure because it applied to traders in general. It held however that that did not prevent it from being of individual concern to some traders. The applicant was able to establish individual concern because the regulation prevented it from using a graphic trademark which it used traditionally, by reserving that trademark to other traders.

[182] Case C-306/93 *SMW Winzersekt* [1994] ECR I-5555.

[183] Case C-340/98 *Italy v Council* [2002] ECR I-2663.

because Ireland had been classified as a deficit area although in fact production exceeded consumption, and sought to annul Regulation No 1361/98 insofar as it omitted to fix a higher intervention price for Italy. The Court dismissed the claim, stating that even if Italy's argument was proven, it could not lead to the annulment of the regulation. The criterion for determining the existence of a deficit was whether the total available production falls short of consumption. Even if by classifying Ireland as a deficit area the Council had committed an error, that would affect the validity of the applicable regulations only insofar as they concerned Ireland. By contrast, Mischo AG took a different view. He opined that, if Italy's claim was proven, and the Council had applied to other Member States a different method for forecasting a deficit from the one applied to Italy, the application should be granted. It would then be for the Council pursuant to Article 233 EC to find the most judicious way of removing discrimination, i.e. either by applying to Italy the method used for other Member States or vice versa. In the circumstances, the Court's view appears more orthodox. Where an institution applies an objective test incorrectly thereby leading to favourable treatment of a group, other groups in a similar situation may challenge the preferential treatment granted to that State but may not claim that such treatment must be extended to them.

2.5.3.3. Similar treatment of dissimilar situations

As stated above, the principle of equal treatment prohibits not only comparable situations from being treated differently but also different situations from being treated in the same way unless such treatment is objectively justified.[184] In a number of cases, Community measures have been challenged on the ground that they fail to recognize material differences between products or producers.

2.5.3.3.1. Individual circumstances of producers

Clearly, it is not possible to tailor legislation so as take into account the individual circumstances of all traders.[185] In general, the Court's approach is to require the application of similar rules to groups of traders who are in similar situations notwithstanding that such rules may produce different effects. It has held that the introduction of general rules under the common organization of the market may affect producers in different ways depending on the nature of their production or on local conditions but that such differences cannot be regarded as discrimination, provided that the rules are based on objective criteria.[186] Thus in *Hierl*[187] it was argued that the temporary withdrawal of a uniform proportion of milk quota from all producers placed a heavier burden on small holdings than on large holdings, which operated on an industrial scale and were able to compensate for

---

[184] *Sermide, op. cit.*, n. 18 above; Case 13/63. *Commission v Italy* [1963] ECR 165, at p. 178; Case 8/82 *Wagner Bundesanstalt fur landwirtschaftliche Marktordnung* [1983] ECR 371.

[185] See above 2.3.

[186] *Bozzetti v Invernizzi, op. cit.*, n 159 above, para 34; *SCAC, op. cit.*, n. 17 above, para 28.

[187] Case C-311/90 *Hierl v Hauptzollamt Regensburg* [1992] ECR I-2061.

the withdrawal either by reducing purchases or by intensifying other production. The Court rejected that argument on the ground that the withdrawal was determined on the basis of objective criteria formulated to meet the needs of the general common organization of the market.

The principle of equal treatment has also been invoked together with the principle of proportionality to challenge measures which impose flat-rate reductions on all producers. In *SITPA*,[188] with a view to limiting production of tomato products, a Council regulation provided for a specified quantity as a guaranteed threshold for each marketing year. If the guaranteed threshold were exceeded, the aid payable to producers would be reduced for the following marketing year depending on the extent of the excess production. It was argued that the reduction in aid made by the Commission following a finding that the guaranteed threshold had been exceeded infringed the prohibition of discrimination. It applied uniformly throughout the Community so that French traders who were not responsible for the excess production were treated in the same way as traders in other Member States who were so responsible. Dismissing that argument, the Court held:[189]

In a common organization of markets with no system of national quotas all Community producers, regardless of the Member State in which they are based, must together, in an egalitarian manner, bear the consequences of the decisions which the Community institutions are led to adopt, in the exercise of their powers, in order to respond to the risk of an imbalance which may arise in the market between production and market outlets.

The Court has taken a similar view in other cases.[190] The possibility cannot be excluded that measures which require producers to bear the adverse consequences of an excess in production on a flat-rate basis may lead to unfair results in individual cases. The Court's approach is justified however because alternative policies, such as the introduction of individual quotas, are by their nature more restrictive of commercial freedom. Also, it is not practically possible to identify the producers who are responsible for excess production. By contrast, it is submitted that, where it is feasible for the Community administration to link excess production to a specific class of producers, the principles of equality and proportionality would require that class to bear commensurately the consequences of excessive production and a generally applicable measure penalising all producers may be challenged on those grounds.[191]

2.5.3.3.2. Similar treatment of products of different Member States

In general, agricultural regulations lay down uniform rules which are applicable to all Member States. The above discussion shows that, in reviewing the choices of

---

[188] Case C-27/90 *SITPA* [1991] ECR I-133.   [189] *Ibid.*, para 20.

[190] *Crispoltoni, op. cit.*, n. 167 above; Case 250/84 *Eridania v Cassa Conguaglio Zucchero* [1986] ECR 117, para 32; *SAM Schiffahrt, op. cit.*, n. 125 above, paras 32 *et seq.*

[191] Support for this view can be found in *Karlsson, op. cit.*, n. 17 above.

the Community legislature in areas where it exercises wide discretion, the Court is content to accept similarity of rules and does not look for similarity of effects. It has been held that the various elements in the common organization of the market, such as protective measures or subsidies, may not be differentiated according to region or according to other factors affecting production or consumption except by reference to objective criteria which ensure a proportionate division of the advantages and disadvantages for those concerned without distinction between the territories of Member States.[192] In *Sermide*[193] it was argued that the method of calculating the production levy on sugar adversely affected Italian producers *vis-à-vis* producers from northern Member States owing to the differences in the crop cycle for sugar beet in southern and northern Europe. The Court rejected that argument by stating that,[194]

That line of reasoning calls in question the Council's choice of dates for the commencement of the sugar marketing year and for the entry into force of the new intervention price, a choice which may be challenged only by contending that it constitutes a misuse of powers.

In some cases Community regulations make the granting of benefits conditional on the meeting of certain conditions by a specified date. It is possible that the setting of a uniform date throughout the Community may affect producers differently depending on soil and climatic conditions. In such cases the Court seems to focus on the following considerations: whether the fixing of a date is necessary for the common organization of the market; whether the specified date affects producers in a certain Member State disproportionately; and whether exceptions from the specified date are provided for deserving cases.[195]

Where a Community regulation leaves some freedom of action to Member States and requires implementing measures at the national level, divergences among the national implementing rules are not discrimination provided that those rules conform with the objectives of the Community regime and apply to all producers concerned in accordance with objective criteria.[196]

2.5.3.4. Other considerations

The Court has accepted that, among others, the following considerations provide objective grounds justifying a difference in treatment between comparable situations:

- *Costs and Burdens on the Administration.* The obligation on the administration to ensure so far as possible equal competitive conditions to all market participants is

---

[192] *Sermide, op. cit.,* n. 18 above, para 28; *Codorniu, op. cit.,* n. 180 above, para 26. See also *SAM Schiffahrt and Stapf v Germany, op. cit.,* n. 125 above, para 64.   [193] *Op. cit.*

[194] Para. 31. Cf the Opinion of Verloren van Themaat AG who found that the contested measure infringed the principle of proportionality.

[195] See e.g. Case C-353/92 *Greece v Council* [1994] ECR I-3411. See further Case 224/82 *Meiko-Konservenfabrik v Germany* [1983] ECR 2539; Case C-101/99 *British Sugar* [2002] ECR I-205, para 47; for the relevance on dates in a staff case, Joined Cases T-164/99, T-37/00 and T-38/00 *Leroy et al v Council* [2001] ECR, judgment of 27 June 2001, para 75.

[196] *Karlsson, op. cit.,* para 53.

conditioned by the need to implement structural objectives by means which are 'achievable and verifiable in practice'[197] and which do not give rise to undue administrative and supervisory difficulties. Thus the method of calculating a levy may work to the disadvantage of certain traders but, provided that it is based on objective criteria, it does not breach the principle of equal treatment.[198] Also, it has been held that the difference which arises from the fact that a regulation grants aid for a product in transit between warehouses situated in a single Member State but refuses such aid for the same product in transit between warehouses situated in different Member States is objectively justified on the ground that the supervisory measures which would be necessary if the aid were to be granted in the case of international transport would involve disproportionate administrative costs.[199]

- *Prevention of fraud.* The existence of a higher risk of fraud in relation to a category of products may justify the imposition of different rules to that category from those applicable to comparable products.[200] Similarly, the need to prevent speculative transactions may be an objective differentiating factor.[201]

- *Legal certainty.* The Court has held that where a producer's milk production has been significantly reduced by an exceptional event throughout the years which, according to Community law, may be taken as reference years and, as a result, that producer has been unable to obtain an individual quota based on a representative production, the Community rules treat him adversely in comparison with other producers who are able to rely on a representative production, but that such an effect is justified by the need to limit the number of years which may be taken as reference years in the interests of both legal certainty and the effectiveness of the quota system.[202]

- *Legitimate expectations.* A difference in treatment between two groups of traders or products may be justified if preferential treatment in favour of one group is necessary to protect their legitimate expectations.[203]

---

[197] *SAM Schiffahrt, op. cit.*, para 60.   [198] *Ibid.*

[199] *Wagner v BALM, op. cit.*, n. 125 above.

[200] *Wagner v BALM, op. cit.*; see also Case C-256/90 *Mignini* [1992] ECR I-2651, at p. 2674 per Jacobs AG.   [201] *Accrington, op. cit*, n. 151 above.

[202] *Erpelding, op. cit.*, n. 17 above, para 30; see also Case C-177/90 *Kühn v Landwirtschaftskammer Weser-Ems* [1992] ECR I-35, para 18 and Case C-85/90 *Dowling* [1992] ECR I-5305. For another case concerning the milk quota regime where the principle of equal treatment was held not to have been breached, see Case C-63/93 *Fintan Duff v Minister for Agriculture, Fisheries and Food* [1996] ECR I-569. Cf Case 120/86 *Mulder I* [1988] ECR 2321 and Case C-189/89 *Spagl* [1990] ECR I-4539.

[203] *Omega Air, op. cit.*, n. 17 above. In that case it was argued that a Council Regulation seeking to reduce aircraft noise discriminated between aeroplanes having identical engines on the basis of the date on which the engines were fitted. Re-engined aeroplanes with a by-pass ratio less than 3 were prohibited whilst aeroplanes originally designed with the same by-pass ratio were not. The Court held however that the distinction was justified by the concern to protect acquired rights. Manufacturers who have developed aeroplanes by reference to the standards of Chapter 3 of the Chicago Convention on International Civil Aviation and airlines which have bought such

- *Economic differences in the markets of different products.* Different treatment of comparable products is justified where it is based on objective differences arising from the economic circumstances underlying the common organization of the market in the products in issue. In *Biovilac*[204] it was argued that by subsidising skimmed milk powder the Commission discriminated against competing products made from whey which were not subsidised. The Court held that the granting of subsidies to skimmed milk powder was justified owing to the nature of the product and the market-supporting role it played in the common organization of the market in milk products. By contrast, whey did not present similar characteristics being a waste produce obtained in the making of cheese.

- *Third States.* Does the general principle of equality prohibit also discrimination against traders or products from third states? This question cannot be answered in general. Much will depend on the legal rules governing the specific situation. The following guidelines may be offered. Some provisions of the Treaty specifically restrict their application to Community nationals or products. Nationals of third states may therefore not necessarily enjoy comparable rights. The discretion of the Community institutions and the national authorities may be bound by international agreements which may require the granting of equal or national treatment. The EC Treaty itself does not incorporate any general principle enforceable by individuals which requires the Community to accord in its external relations equal treatment to third states.[205] According to the general principle of equality, however, similar situations must not be treated differently unless there is objective justification. Thus, if it is to be true to its intentions, the principle also covers situations from third states. In some cases, the fact that a product originates from a third country may provide an objective justification for differential treatment. It should be noted however that there is no legally binding general principle of Community preference in EU agricultural law. In *Omega Air*[206] one of the arguments submitted by the applicants was that the prohibition of the operation of re-engined aeroplanes with a low by-pass ratio imposed by a Council regulation seeking to reduce aircraft noise discriminated in favour of EU manufacturers against those established in the US and against aircraft owners whose aeroplanes had been re-engined with engines manufactured in the US. The ECJ however found that there was no evidence of any direct or indirect discrimination on the facts and thus dismissed the claim.

---

aeroplanes must enjoy, in principle, greater protection of their legitimate expectations of being able to operate them than manufacturers and owners of aeroplanes whose original construction did not comply with those standards.

[204] *Biovilac op. cit.*, n. 166 above, para 19. See also Joined Cases 279, 280, 285 and 286/84 *Rau v Commission* [1987] ECR 1069.

[205] Case 245/81 *Edeka v Germany* [1982] ECR 2745, para 19.

[206] See above and, for a detailed discussion of the case, see 3.4 below.

2.6. Equal treatment and harmonization of national laws

As a general principle of law, equal treatment binds the Community institutions in the exercise of their powers to coordinate national laws. In this context, as in the context of the common agricultural policy, the fact that Community rules may produce different effects in the various Member States does not in itself mean that they run counter to the principle of equal treatment. It has been held that a harmonization measure which is intended to standardize previously disparate national rules may produce different effects depending on the previous state of the national laws but that does not amount to discrimination, provided that the measure applies equally to all Member States.[207]

An interesting issue is to what extent the principle of equality imposes limitations on the Community legislature with regard to the choice of harmonization areas. The application of the principle in this context encounters certain fundamental obstacles. In coordinating national laws, partial, step-by-step, harmonization is the preferred, indeed the only feasible, Community policy. Incremental harmonization may lead to differences in treatment since certain legal relations may be subject to Community rules whereas other comparable relations remain subject to national laws. Such difference in treatment may be provisional, where the Community has not yet harmonized a certain area of law, or more permanent, where the Community does not intend or, for one reason or another, is unable to harmonize an area of law. The harmonization process is by its nature a complex exercise surrounded by legal and political difficulties which are determinative both of the order in time in which harmonization measures are adopted and the specific contents of those measures. The issue arises whether such obstacles, which are inherent in the harmonization process, can be considered as objective grounds justifying difference in treatment emanating from partial harmonization. In *Assurances du Crédit v Council and Commission*[208] the Court was concerned with the First Insurance Directive[209] as amended by Directive 87/343.[210] The amending Directive imposed additional financial requirements on private insurance companies but maintained the exclusion of public undertakings providing export credit insurance from the burdens of the first Directive. In an action for damages against the Community, the applicants argued that the Directive imposed discriminatory burdens on the private sector. The Court held that export credit insurance operations transacted for the account of the State were in an objectively different situation from other such operations. In relation to the former, the protection of insured persons was

---

[207] Case C-331/88 *Fedesa and others* [1991] ECR I-4023, para 20; see also *Germany v Council (Bananas case), op. cit.,* n. 160 above.   [208] *Op. cit.,* n. 105 above.
[209] Directive 73/239 on the coordination of laws, regulations and administrative provisions relating to the taking-up and pursuit of the business of direct insurance other than life assurance, OJ 1973 L 228, p. 3.   [210] OJ 1987 L 185, p. 72.

provided by the State itself so that the application of the financial guarantees provided by the Directive was not justified. In the light of the arguments submitted by the Advocate General, who took the opposite view, the laconic reasoning of the Court seems unpersuasive.[211] The Advocate General found that in the field of export credit insurance, private and public undertakings competed with each other and should be subject to equal burdens. In his view, the fact that public undertakings were supported by the financial backing of the State was not a good reason to exclude them from the financial guarantees provided for in the Directive. By contrast, he considered that financial intervention by the State was in itself discriminatory and questioned its legality under Articles 86 and 88 of the Treaty. The Advocate General also dismissed the argument that the difficulties surrounding harmonization in the area of export credit insurance justified the exclusion of public operations from the scope of the Directive.

Francovich II[212] concerned Directive 80/987 on the approximation of the laws of the Member States relating to the protection of employees in the event of the insolvency of their employer,[213] which was adopted by the Council on the basis of Article 100 (now 94) of the Treaty. The Court interpreted the Directive as applying only to employees whose employers may, under national law, be made subject to insolvency proceedings for the collective satisfaction of the creditors. It was argued that the Directive infringed the general principle of equality to the extent that it protected only those employees. In its judgment, the Court did not deny that the Directive resulted in a difference in treatment between two categories of employees.[214] Rather, it focused on whether the difference in treatment was objectively justified. It held that, in the exercise of the powers conferred upon them by Article 94, the institutions have a discretion in particular with regard to the possibility of pursuing harmonization in stages.[215] It also noted the difficulties surrounding the harmonization process given the complexity and divergence of national laws and the need to obtain unanimity in the Council under the procedure provided for in Article 94. The Court held that, given the difficulties in finding a concept of insolvency capable of unambiguous application in the divergent laws of the Member States, the distinction between employees according to whether their employer may be subject to proceedings to satisfy collectively the claims of creditors derived from a concept of insolvency which was objective and justified. The Directive therefore did not infringe the principle of equal treatment.

---

[211] See *Assurances du Crédit, op. cit*, esp. pp. 1832 *et seq. per* Tesauro AG.

[212] Case C-479/93 *Francovich v Italian Republic* [1995] ECR I-3843.

[213] OJ 1983 L283, p. 23.

[214] In his Opinion, Cosmas AG expressly rejected the argument that employees whose employers are subject to a collective procedure for the satisfaction of creditors deserve more protection than employees whose employers are not: see para 31 of the Opinion.

[215] See also on the same point Case 37/83 *Rewe-Zentrale v Landwirtschaftskammer Rheinland* [1984] ECR 1229, para 20; C-193/94 *Skanavi and Chryssanthakopoulos* [1996] ECR I-929, para 27.

It follows from *Assurances du Crédit* and *Francovich II* that difficulties surrounding harmonization may be objective reasons justifying a difference in treatment.[216] That seems to be the case whether such difficulties result from divergences in national laws or from policy disagreements which restrict the scope of application of a measure *ratione materiae*. A difference in treatment however will not be justified if it runs counter to the objectives of the Treaty provision on the basis of which the harmonization measure has been adopted. The judgments recognize that harmonization of national laws remains *par excellence* a political exercise. If in *Francovich II* the Court had reached the opposite result, it would have elevated the principle of non-discrimination to an autonomous source of harmonization. It is notable that in *Assurances du Crédit*, the Advocate General was not prepared to recognize a margin of discretion to the Community legislature as wide as that recognized by the Court. He stated:[217]

It is true . . . that different situations exist in the Member States. However, it is precisely such diversity which a harmonizing directive serves to eliminate and it cannot therefore in itself be regarded as an insuperable obstacle. The Council, when it decided to restrict harmonization to a single category of operators ought therefore to have justified that limitation— which . . . distorts competition—by adducing *additional, specific* difficulties other than those which normally exist when differing national rules are harmonized.

A final point may be made in relation to *Francovich II*. There, the difference in treatment resulted from the fact that the Directive pursued partial harmonization: one category of employees was subject to Community rules whereas another category of employees remained subject to the laws of the Member States. It would have been a different issue if the Directive applied *ratione materiae* to all categories of employees but introduced different standards of protection depending on the type of insolvency procedure to which their employer was subject. In such a case, the claim that the difference in treatment amounted to discrimination might be stronger. Legal relations which are covered by the same legal system must be subject to the same rules unless there is objective justification.[218] It is notable that, in a different context, the Court has accepted in exceptional circumstances the analogical application of Community measures in the interests of ensuring equal treatment.[219]

2.7. Staff cases

The principle of equality is a fundamental principle of the Community civil service.[220] It requires that Community officials who are in identical situations

---

[216] See further Case C-36/99 *Idéal Tourisme* [2000] ECR I-6049 where it was held that Belgian legislation which, in accordance with the Sixth VAT Directive, exempted international air transport from VAT but imposed VAT on international transport by coach was compatible with the principle of equal treatment (paras 37–38 of the judgment). See also Case C-28/99 *Verbonck and Others* [2001] ECR I-3399.   [217] *Op. cit.* n. 105, at 1837 (emphasis in the original).
[218] See e.g. *Omega Air, op. cit.*   [219] Case 165/84 *Krohn v BALM* [1985] ECR 3997.
[220] Since 1989, jurisdiction to hear staff cases at first instance lies with the CFI and, on appeal, the ECJ. First instance jurisdiction will be transferred to the European Union Civil Service

must be governed by the same rules.[221] In *Prais*[222] the Court recognized the principle of religious equality in Community law by stating that, in setting the date for a competition to fill a vacant post, the appointing authority is obliged to take reasonable steps to avoid dates which a candidate has informed it are unsuitable for religious reasons. In *Weiser*[223] the Court annulled a provision of the Staff Regulations which enabled a person upon joining the Community service to transfer pension rights from a national scheme to the Community scheme if he had acquired such rights as an employed person but not if he had acquired them as a self-employed person. But the refusal to grant to the ex-spouse of a Community official cover under the Community sickness insurance scheme was held not to infringe equality even though such cover was provided to members of the Community institutions. The differentiating factor was that members of the institutions, unlike officials, serve for a limited time. The purpose of the benefit is to ensure that they have sickness cover in the event that, at the end of their term of office, they do not engage in gainful employment enabling them to be covered by a public sickness insurance scheme.[224]

In *Scaramuzza*,[225] it was held that a Community official who serves in a third country is in an objectively different position from an official who performs his duties within the Community inasmuch as the accommodation and medical costs of the former are covered by the Community. Thus, it is not contrary to the principle of equal treatment to pay to an official serving in a third country only 80 per cent of his remuneration in local currency whereas in the case of officials serving within the Community the entire remuneration is paid in the currency of the place of employment.

The conditions of recruitment, appointment and promotion in the Community civil service are subject to the principle of equal treatment.[226] An interesting

---

Tribunal which is currently being set up: see Council Decision 2004/752 (2004 OJ L 333/7). The judgments of the Civil Service Tribunal are subject to appeal on points of law only before the CFI (see Annex to the Decision 2004/752, Article 11) and, exceptionally, subject to review by the ECJ at the instigation of the first Advocate General where there is a serious risk of the unity or consistency of Community law being affected: see Article 225(2) EC and Statute of the Court of Justice, Article 62.

[221] Joined Cases 152, 158, 162, 166, 170, 173, 175, 177–9, 182 and 186/81 *Ferrario v Commission* [1983] ECR 2357, para 7.

[222] Case 130/75 *Prais v Council* [1976] ECR 1589. For the principle of sex equality in staff cases, see e.g. Case 246/83 *de Angelis v Commission* [1985] ECR 1253 and the cases mentioned below.

[223] Case C-37/89 [1990] ECR I-2395. The case is one in a series of cases concerning the transfer of pension rights where the Court followed an approach favourable to Community officials: see further Case 130/87 *Retter v Caisse de Pension d'Employés Privés* [1989] ECR 865, Case C-137/88 *Schneemann and others v Commission* [1990] ECR I-369. Cf Joined cases 81, 81 and 146/79 *Sorasio v Commission* [1980] ECR 3557, where it was held that the principle of equality does not require account to be taken of possible inequalities which may ensue because the Community and national tax systems overlap.   [224] Case T-66/95 *Kuchlenz-Winter v Commission* [1997] ECR II-637.

[225] Case C-76/93 P *Scaramuzza v Commission* [1994] ECR I-5173.

[226] See Article 5(3) of the Staff Regulations. For a case where the CFI annulled a decision concerning the classification in grade of the applicant, see T-93/94 *Becker v Court of Auditors* [1996] ECR II-141.

example in relation to recruitment is provided by *Noonan*.[227] The Commission introduced a policy of restricting admission to certain secretarial posts to candidates who did not possess a university degree. The applicant was refused admission to a competition for such a post on the ground that she was a university graduate. The Court of First Instance held that the Commission's policy ran counter to the principle of equal treatment in conjunction with Article 27 of the Staff Regulations which requires the institutions to recruit the services of officials of the highest standard of ability, efficiency and integrity.

A further example is provided by *Gevaert v Commission*.[228] In its previous judgment in *Alexopoulou*[229] the CFI had held that, when it recruits officials, the Commission may not waive its discretion to make in exceptional circumstances an appointment to a grade higher than the starting grade. In compliance with this judgment, by a decision of 7 February 1996, the Commission changed its policy which had been in force since 1983. The effect of the decision was to allow officials appointed after 5 October 1995, the date of the *Alexopoulou* judgment, to request reclassification of their grade where the specific needs of the service so justified or where the person recruited had exceptional qualifications. The possibility of reclassification however was not open to officials who were appointed before the date of the *Alexopoulou* judgment. In *Gevaert*, reversing the CFI, the ECJ held that the latter category of officials was treated less favourably and that the difference in treatment was not objectively justified. The Court reasoned that it was not necessary for the Commission, in order to comply with *Alexopoulou*, to make its decision applicable to all officials who were appointed after the judgment and not just to the applicants in that case. Although the Commission had displayed regard for the welfare of officials who had been appointed after that date, there was nothing to justify or explain why it did not extend that concern to officials who had been appointed between 1983 and the date of the *Alexopoulou* judgment. Although *Gevaert* is only a three-member chamber judgment, it is interesting in terms of judicial policy because the ECJ followed a more pro-individual judgment than the CFI and the Advocate General. The case illustrates that, where the Community administration decides to offer a benefit going beyond what is required to comply with a judgment, it must respect the principle of equal treatment in determining the categories to which the benefit is available.[230]

---

[227] Case T-60/92 *Noonan v Commission* [1996] ECR II-215. See further on recruitment, Case T-132/89 *Gallone v Council* [1990] ECR II-549 and Case C-100/88 *Oyowe and Traore v Commission* [1989] ECR 4285.

[228] Case C-389/98 P *Gevaert v Commission* [2001] ECR I-65. See also Case C-459/98 P *Martinez del Peral Cagigal v Commission* [2001] ECR I-135.

[229] Case T-17/95 *Alexopoulou v Commission* [1995] ECR-SC I-A-227 and II-683.

[230] Note however that, where one of the EC institutions decides on its own initiative to adopt measures more favourable for its staff going beyond its obligations under the Staff Regulations, there is no obligation on the other institutions to adopt similar measures: Joined Cases C-193 & C-194/87 *Maurissen and European Public Service Union v Court of Auditors* [1990] ECR I-95; paras 26–27; Case C-315/97 P *Brigaldi v Commission*, [1999] ECR I-1287.

A prime example of the application of the principle of equal treatment in staff affairs is provided by the *JET* cases. In 1978 the Council set up the Joint European Torus (JET) undertaking to carry on research as part of the Community fusion programme. JET was based at the headquarters of the UK Atomic Energy Authority (UKAEA), its constituent members being Euratom, the UKAEA and the atomic agencies of the other Member States and of Switzerland. Under the Statutes of JET, staff made available to it by the UKAEA continued to be employed by that authority. By contrast, staff made available from the other national organizations had the status of temporary Community servants and received significantly higher remuneration. In *Ainsworth*[231] the Court held that the difference in treatment was objectively justified, reasoning as follows. JET was devoted entirely to research and its duration was limited in time. An undertaking of such a nature could work effectively only in close association with a national organization already in existence. Hence, its close links with UKAEA. The latter, being the host organization, was in a special position which distinguished it from the other national agencies. Its personnel was divided between staff working on its own projects and staff working on the JET project. The Court accepted that UKAEA was entitled to require that staff working on the JET project be subject to its own conditions of service so as to ensure equality of treatment among the two classes of its own staff.

The reasoning of the Court was flawed in two respects. First, it is surprising that the Court found no discrimination on grounds of nationality. Although each national organization member of JET was free to make available to it employees of any nationality, the Statutes of JET were clearly indirectly discriminatory against British nationals since they were much less likely to be employed by the national organizations of other Member States. Second, although it was inevitable that differential treatment between some groups of employees would arise, the appropriate comparator for UKAEA staff working for JET was staff of other organizations working on the same project rather than UKAEA staff working on other projects. The Court was clearly influenced by the fact that the UKAEA, which provided installations and technical support to JET and bore a much higher contribution to the expenses of the project than the other national authorities, was anxious not to disturb relations among its employees and the functioning of its own organization.

Subsequently, in *Altmann and Casson v Commission*[232] the CFI made history by effectively reversing the judgment of the Court of Justice in *Ainsworth*. The applicants were British nationals employed in the JET project as members of staff of the UKAEA. They challenged the Commission's refusal to appoint them as temporary Community servants on the grounds that it infringed the principle of equal treatment and the prohibition of discrimination on grounds of nationality.

---

[231] Joined Cases 271/83 and 15, 36, 113, 158 and 203/84 and 13/85 *Ainsworth v Commission and Council* [1987] ECR 167.   [232] *Altmann and Casson, op. cit.,* n. 157 above.

The CFI started by noting that all JET staff were in a comparable situation, irrespective of the national organization which made them available to the JET project. It found that staff made available by the UKAEA were treated less favourably in two respects: first, with regard to the conditions of employment, since they received lower salary than their colleagues employed by other national organizations, and second, with regard to security of employment because staff employed as temporary Community servants had a much better opportunity of obtaining permanent posts in the Community civil service. The CFI considered that, owing to factual developments since the judgment in *Ainsworth*, the justification for the difference in treatment had ceased to exist. It took into account the following factors: the extension of the duration of JET, the lesser role played by the UKAEA in its organization and functioning, the fact that the UKAEA no longer objected to staff employed by it in the JET project leaving its employment for that of the Commission, the disruption of the functioning of the JET undertaking as a result of industrial relations conflict, and the inability of the JET recruitment system to achieve the aims for which it was designed.

Having established that objective justification for the difference in treatment no longer existed, the CFI proceeded to determine the legal consequences thereof. In *Altmann and Casson*, as earlier in *Ainsworth*, the applicants challenged the validity of the JET Statutes incidentally under the plea of illegality,[233] the main challenge being against the Commission's refusal to recruit them. The CFI held that since the legality of the individual recruitment decisions must be assessed on the basis of the elements of fact and law existing at the time when they were adopted, the legality of the legislative measure which formed their legal basis must also be assessed at that time rather than the time of its own adoption.[234] The CFI held that its finding did not conflict with the principle of legality. The latter required the Commission to continue applying the JET Statutes even after they had, in the applicants' view, become illegal as a result of the supervening change in the circumstances. However the applicants should not be denied the right to bring a challenge before the Community judicature seeking a declaration that they are inapplicable, not *ab initio* but as from the date of a specific change in circumstances.[235]

The CFI declared the JET Statutes inapplicable in the cases of the applicants to the extent that they conflicted with the principle of equal treatment. It rejected however their claim for compensation on the ground that the breach of the principle of equal treatment did not amount to a manifest and grave disregard of discretionary powers by the Council and the Commission. Subsequently, however, in *Eagle v Commission*[236] the CFI held that, in the circumstances of that case, by failing to offer the applicants contracts as temporary servants in breach of

---

[233] See Article 241 EC, Article 156 EAEC. [234] *Altmann and Casson, op. cit.*, para 119.
[235] Para 123.
[236] Case T-144/02 *Eagle v Commission*, judgment of 5 October 2004. Cf T-177/97 *Simon v Commission* [2000] ECR-SC I-A-75 and II-319, upheld on appeal: C-274/00 P *Simon v Commission* [2002] ECR I-5999.

the JET statutes, the Commission had committed a serious misconduct in the exercise of its administrative duties.

Altmann and Casson is a well-argued judgment on a delicate and complex issue. The CFI was walking on a tightrope having to balance, on the one hand, respect for the authority of the Court of Justice and, on the other, the requirements of equal treatment. It succeeded in undoing injustice whilst carefully distinguishing precedent. It would be incorrect, however, to derive the impression from these cases that the CFI always follows a more pro-individual view. As we saw, the reverse occurred in *Gevaert*.

Finally, in *Connolly v Commission* the ECJ had the opportunity to reiterate that the principle of equal treatment does not justify illegal conduct. An official who has breached the Staff Regulations cannot challenge the penalty imposed on him on the ground that another official who has committed the same breach was not penalised.[237]

2.8. Prohibition of discrimination on grounds of sex and sexual orientation

2.8.1. Sex equality as a fundamental right

Sex equality is an area where Community law has had a profound influence on the laws of the Member States. The principle of equal pay for equal work was originally included in the Treaty of Rome not so much on social as on economic grounds. Its purpose was to ensure that employers in Member States, especially France, which promoted an active agenda on sex equality were not put at a competitive disadvantage *vis-à-vis* employers from other Member States in an integrated market. Be that as it may, Article 119 (now 141)[238] and the directives adopted by the Council on sex equality have had an enormous influence on the laws of Member States. Buttressed by an activist case law, they did much to promote a culture of sex equality and establish legal rights and remedies.[239] In view of the large number of cases raising issues of Community law, sex equality law acted, perhaps more than any other area, as a catalyst for the reception of Community law into the national legal orders.

The Court regards sex equality as a fundamental human right whose observance it has a duty to ensure and which transcends Article 141 and the provisions of

---

[237] Case C-273/99 P *Connolly v Commission* [2001] ECR I-1575, para 43.

[238] This is now Article III-214 of the EU Constitution.

[239] Among the most important cases decided by the ECJ have been Case 43/75 *Defrenne v Sabena* [1976] ECR 455 and C-262/88 *Barber v Guardian Royal Exchange* [1990] ECR I-1889. In *Defrenne* the ECJ held that Article 119 had direct effect, thus making it possible for a female employee to rely on that provision against her employer. In *Barber* the Court held that benefits paid under contracted out pension schemes were 'pay' within the meaning of Article 119. In both cases, the financial repercussions of the rulings were considerable and the ECJ made use of its power to restrict the retroactive effect of its rulings.

secondary Community law. In the *Third Defrenne* case[240] it declared that the elimination of sex discrimination forms part of the fundamental rights recognized and enforced by the Court. On the facts, that declaration proved of little assistance to Ms Defrenne. The Court refused to widen the scope of Article 119 (now 141) so as to require, apart from equality in pay, equality in respect of other working conditions. It stated that, as regards employment relationships governed by national law, the Community had not, at the time of the events giving rise to the litigation, assumed any responsibility for securing the observance of equal treatment in working conditions other than remuneration. The dispute therefore was governed by the provisions of national law.

The Court was more forthcoming in cases involving employment relationships governed by Community law. In *Razzouk and Beydoun v Commission*[241] the Staff Regulations discriminated against widowers of Community officials in relation to pension rights.[242] Referring to *Defrenne v Sabena*, the Court pointed out that sex equality is a fundamental right which must be ensured within the framework of the Staff Regulations. In relations between the institutions and their employees, therefore, the requirements of the principle of equal treatment 'are in no way limited to those resulting from Article 119 of the EEC Treaty or from the Community directives adopted in this field'.[243] On that basis, the Court annulled the Commission's decision refusing a pension to the applicants since it was based on provisions of the Staff Regulations violating the right to sex equality.

The purpose of this section is not to examine the Community law on sex discrimination but to evaluate how, by relying on sex equality as a general principle, the Court has dealt with issues which lie beyond sex discrimination.[244] The following areas will be discussed: discrimination against trans-sexuals, discrimination on grounds of sexual orientation,[245] and positive discrimination.

---

[240] Case 149/77 *Defrenne v Sabena* [1978] ECR 1365.

[241] Joined Cases 75 and 117/82 [1984] ECR 1509. See also Case 20/71 *Sabbatini v European Parliament* [1972] ECR 345; Case 21/74 *Airola v Commission* [1975] ECR 221; and more recently Case T-45/90 *Speybrouck v Parliament* [1992] ECR II-33.

[242] The regulations discriminated in more ways than one. The widow of an official or former official was entitled to a survivor's pension equal to 60% of the pension paid to her husband and her right to the pension was independent of her own resources. The husband of a deceased female official, by contrast, could only receive a pension if he had no income of his own and was unable for reasons of health to engage in gainful employment. The pension was paid to him at the lower rate of 50%. Also, although entitlement to pension ceased upon remarriage, the widow of an official could claim a capital sum up to twice the annual amount of her survivor's pension. No such right was extended to a widower.   [243] *Op. cit.*, para 17.

[244] For EU sex equality law, see among others: C. Barnard, *EC Employment Law* (Second Ed., Oxford University Press, 2000); E. Szyszczak, *EC Labour Law* (Longman, 2000); E. Ellis, *European Community Sex Equality Law* (Oxford University Press, Second Ed., 1998); S. Prechal and N. Burrows, *Gender Discrimination Law of The European Community* (Dartmouth, 1990); C. McCrudden (ed), *Women, Employment and European Equality Law* (Eclipse, 1987); B. Bercusson, *European Labour Law* (Butterworths, 1996), Part IV.

[245] See, as part of the growing bibliography on the issue, R. Wintemute and M. Andenas (eds), *Legal Recognition of Same-Sex Partnerships* (Hart Publishing, 2001). For an excellent comparative analysis, see N. Carey, 'From Obloquy to Equality: In the Shadow of Abnormal Situations' (2001)

2.8.2. Beyond discrimination on grounds of sex

The first case concerning discrimination against trans-sexuals was *P v S and Cornwall County Council*.[246] The applicant in the main proceedings was dismissed from his employment following his decision to undergo gender reassignment by surgical operation. The question referred was whether the Equal Treatment Directive[247] precludes dismissal of a trans-sexual for reasons related to gender reassignment. The Court held that, in view of sex equality as a fundamental human right, the scope of the Directive cannot be confined to discrimination based on the fact that a person is of one or other sex.[248] It stated that discrimination arising from gender reassignment is based essentially, if not exclusively, on the sex of the person concerned. Where a person is dismissed on the ground that he or she has undergone gender reassignment, he or she is treated unfavourably by comparison with persons of the sex to which he or she was deemed to belong before undergoing gender reassignment.[249] The Court concluded:[250]

> To tolerate such discrimination would be tantamount, as regards such a person, to a failure to respect the dignity and freedom to which he or she is entitled, and which the Court has a duty to safeguard.

The case provides a prime example of the way the Court views the principle of equality as a general principle of Community law transcending the provisions of Community legislation. In effect, it applied a general principle of unwritten human rights law, according to which discrimination on arbitrary criteria is prohibited, rather than the provisions of the Equal Treatment Directive, a literal interpretation of which does not support the Court's finding.

The importance of *P v S* can hardly be overstated. It is a sign that the Court takes rights seriously, endorses a substantive conception of equality, and, at least in some contexts, accords as much importance to social justice as to market integration.[251] One of the most crucial issues for establishing whether discrimination

---

20 YEL 79; for Community initiatives in this area, see L. Papadopoulou, 'Indivisible Citizenship: Same Sex Partners in European Unuion Immigration Law' (2002) 21 YEL 229. See further: R. Rains, (2005) 33 Ga. J. Intrn. Comp. Law, 333.

[246] *Op. cit.*, n. 25 above.

[247] Council Directive 76/207 on the implementation of the principle of equal treatment for men and women as regards access to employment, vocational training and promotion, and working conditions, OJ 1976 L 39, p. 40.

[248] *P v S, op. cit.*, para 20. The Court (at para 16) adopted the following definition of trans-sexual given by the European Court of Human Rights in its judgment of 17 October 1986 *Rees v United Kingdom*, Series A, No 106: 'the term "transsexual" is usually applied to those who, whilst belonging physically to one sex, feel convinced that they belong to the other; they often seek to achieve a more integrated, unambiguous identity by undergoing medical treatment and surgical operations to adapt their physical characteristics to their pychological nature. Transsexuals who have been operated upon thus form a fairly well-defined and identifiable group.'

[249] *Op. cit,* para 21.   [250] *Op. cit.*, para 22.

[251] See C. Barnard, '*P v S*: Kite Flying or a New Constitutional Approach?' in A. Dashwood and S. O'Leary, *The Principle of Equal Treatment in E.C. Law* (London: Sweet & Maxwell, 1997), pp. 59–79.

against trans-sexuals is sex discrimination is the identification of the appropriate comparator. The United Kingdom submitted that no discrimination was involved because a female to male trans-sexual would have been treated in exactly the same way as the applicant. The Court however had little sympathy for this argument adopting instead as the appropriate comparator the trans-sexual's previous persona. It was led by the highly influential Opinion of Tesauro AG who submitted that it was necessary to go beyond the traditional man/woman dichotomy and accept that there is a range of other characteristics, behaviour and roles shared by men and women 'so that sex *itself* ought rather to be thought of as a continuum'.[252] The Advocate General emphasised that, for the purposes of the case, sex was important as a convention, a social parameter. He pointed out that the reason why women are frequently the victims of sex discrimination is their social role, the image traditionally ascribed to them in societal terms. In the same way, the unfavourable treatment suffered by trans-sexuals is most often linked to a negative image, a moral judgment which has nothing to do with their abilities in the sphere of employment.[253]

One of the issues which is left open by the judgment is whether differential treatment on grounds of gender reassignment necessarily amounts to discrimination or whether it may be justified on grounds of objective justification. On the facts, the applicant was working as a manager in an educational establishment operated by the County Council and there was no suggestion that her suitability for the employment in issue was affected by her change of sex. One suspects that different considerations will apply, for example, to a person who is employed to perform bodily searches in airports or as an attendant of public restrooms. In such a case, a female-to-male trans-sexual who was dismissed from his job would not be discriminated against since no male person could be employed in that capacity. There is therefore no discrimination on grounds of sex. More difficulties however would arise in the case of certain occupations where a change of sex might be viewed as unacceptable, e.g. employment as a school teacher. *P v S* does not state clearly whether discrimination against a trans-sexual is direct or indirect discrimination. It has been observed that, if the appropriate comparator is the person's previous persona, discrimination against a trans-sexual should always be classified as direct discrimination.[254] Still, differential treatment against trans-sexuals may be justified in certain employment relationships where sex discrimination strictly understood is not.

P v S opened Pandora's Box. An important issue is whether the Equal Treatment Directive is broad enough to encompass discrimination against other groups, in particular, homosexuals. In *Grant v South West Trains Ltd* [255] the applicant, a female employee, argued that she was the victim of sex discrimination because she was refused by her employer certain travel concessions, which had been made available

---

[252] *P v S, op. cit.*, p. 2153.   [253] *Ibid.*, p. 2155.   [254] Barnard, *op. cit.*, p. 61, n. 10.
[255] Case C-249/96 [1998] ECR I-621.

to her predecessor for his cohabitee of the opposite sex, on the grounds that her cohabitee was of the same sex. The material contractual provision was Clause 8 of the British Railways Board Ticket Regulations which stated that a member of staff was entitled to privilege tickets for his or her 'common law opposite sex spouse' subject to a statutory declaration being made that a 'meaningful relationship' had existed for a minimum period of two years. Elmer AG referred to *P v S* and pointed out that the decisive criterion for the application of the Equal Treatment Directive is that the discrimination complained of is based essentially on gender. The same should therefore also apply to the interpretation of Article 119 (now 141). Then, the Advocate General stated that Clause 8 made no mention of the sexual orientation of the employee or the cohabitee and thus the question of sexual orientation was, under the objective content of the clause, irrelevant as far as entitlement to the concessions was concerned. Clause 8 made the concessions conditional on the cohabitee being of the opposite sex to the employee and therefore, in the view of the Advocate General, discriminated exclusively on grounds of gender.

This reasoning is not convincing. First, it is not correct to say that sexual orientation is irrelevant for the application of Clause 8. Clearly, the effect of the clause is to favour heterosexual *vis-à-vis* homosexual relations. Its effect therefore is to discriminate against the manifestation of sexual orientation. The crucial issue in the case was whether discrimination against a homosexual relationship can be classified as sex discrimination. Second, the Advocate General distinguished cohabitation from marriage stating that, if travel concessions were made conditional on the employee being married, that would not be contrary to Community law because, in such a case, the criterion would be defined by reference to a family law concept, the content of which is laid down by the laws of the Member States.[256] If however discrimination against homosexual cohabitation is discrimination on grounds of sex, the use of marriage as the decisive criterion might be viewed as indirect discrimination against homosexual couples. It would then be a matter of whether objective justification could be found.[257]

In its judgment the Court did not follow the Opinion of Elmer AG. The Court started by examining whether Clause 8 gave rise to direct discrimination on grounds of sex and gave a negative reply. The condition that the worker must live in a meaningful relationship with a person of the opposite sex in order to benefit from the travel concessions is applied regardless of the sex of the worker concerned. Travel concessions are refused to a male worker if he is living with a person of the same sex just as they are refused to a female worker if she is living with a person of the same sex.[258] Then the Court turned to examine whether persons who have a stable relationship with a partner of the opposite sex are in the same situation as persons who have such a relationship with a partner of the same sex. After referring to the laws of Member States, the European Convention on Human Rights and

---

[256] Para 28 of the Opinion.   [257] See below.   [258] *Grant, op. cit.*, para 27.

the fact that the Community has not yet adopted rules providing for such equivalence, it concluded that, in the present state of the law within the Community, stable relations between two persons of the same sex are not regarded as equivalent to marriages, or stable relationships outside marriage, between persons of opposite sex. In those circumstances, it was for the legislature to adopt, if appropriate, relevant measures.[259]

Finally, the Court held that differences in treatment based on sexual orientation are not discrimination based on sex within the meaning of Article 119 (now 141). It stated that its reasoning in *P v S* is confined to a worker's gender reassignment and cannot be extended to differences in treatment on grounds of sexual orientation. It is submitted that this distinction is correct. Discrimination on grounds of sex reassignment is effectively discrimination on grounds of sex. This becomes obvious if we view the difference in treatment from the point of view of the discriminator: an employer who discriminates against an employee on the ground that he has undergone a sex change operation draws a comparison between the sex of the employee before and after the operation. It practises discrimination between the sexes, albeit not the sexes of different persons but the different sexes of the same person existing sequentially at different points in time. Discrimination on grounds of sexual orientation, unacceptable as it may be, is a different concept.[260]

The issue of same sex partnerships re-emerged in *D and Sweden v Council*.[261] Swedish law allows couples of the same sex to register their partnership. Such registration has, subject to certain exceptions, the same legal effects as a marriage. D, the applicant, was a Community official of Swedish nationality who had registered a same sex partnership in Sweden. He applied to receive a household allowance which, according to the Staff Regulations, is only granted to married officials. His application having been refused, D brought an action seeking entitlement to the allowance. His claim was rejected by the CFI and, on appeal, by the ECJ. The reasoning of the ECJ was as follows. First, the Court rejected the argument that there was sex discrimination since, under the Staff Regulations, it was irrelevant for the purposes of granting the allowance whether the official was a man or a woman. Second, the Court held that there was no discrimination on grounds of sexual orientation. This is because the determining factor for granting the allowance was not the sex of the partner but the legal nature of the ties between the official and the partner.[262] The ECJ then carried on to examine whether there was an infringement of the general principle of equal treatment. The material question here was whether the situation of an official who had a registered partnership with a person of the same sex was comparable to that of a married official. The Court held that, in making such an assessment, the Community judicature cannot disregard the views prevailing within the Community as a whole. It stated

---

[259] *Ibid.*, paras 35–36.
[260] See now the Framework Directive, *op. cit.*, which prohibits discrimination on grounds of sexual orientation in employment and occupation. [261] *Op. cit.*, 25 above.
[262] *Ibid.*, para 47.

that the existing situation in the Member States as regards recognition of partnerships between persons of the same sex or of the opposite sex reflected a great
diversity of laws and the absence of any general assimilation of marriage and other
forms of statutory union.[263] In those circumstances, the situation of an official who
had registered a same sex partnership in a Member State could not be considered to
be comparable to that of a married official.

This reasoning is interesting in a number of respects. The implication of the
judgment is that the Court would be prepared to equate same sex relations with
marriage if there was a sufficient degree of political and social consensus at the
national level and this had crystallised in the laws of the Member States. In such a
case, the Court would be content to go beyond the language of the Staff Regulations and extend the award of the household allowance to officials in registered
same sex partnerships. It is not surprising that, before risking a ruling which would
affect the fundamental institution of marriage by questioning its exclusivity as a
source of certain rights, the Court sought inspiration from the laws of the Member
States. In interpreting the general principle of equal treatment, the Court allows
itself to be guided by 'conventional morality'.[264] This operates as a source of
legitimacy. However, to ensure objectivity, the Court does not seek to rely on
some kind of perceived social consensus but on concrete policy choices as they
are reflected in the laws of the Member States. The question here is what precise
degree of support from the laws of the Member States would the Court require
to take that step of equating same sex relations with marriage?

It is also interesting that this was not a one-man legal struggle. The government
of Sweden joined D as a co-appellant whilst two more governments, those of the
Netherlands and Denmark, intervened in support. By contrast, no government
intervened in support of the Council.

An interesting aspect of the judgment is that the Court rejected the existence of
discrimination on grounds of sexual orientation holding that the determining factor
for granting the allowance was not the sex of the partner but the legal nature of
the ties between the official and the partner.[265] This is correct in that the condition
for granting the allowance is the status of a married person. An official who is
married to a person of the opposite sex is entitled to the allowance irrespective of
his/her sexual orientation. Nevertheless, the requirement of marriage could be
viewed as indirectly discriminatory insofar as homosexual couples are excluded
from fulfilling it.

The Charter of Fundamental Rights, which is now part of the Constitutional
Treaty, expressly prohibits discrimination on grounds of sexual orientation.[266] As
things currently stand, the Charter is binding on the institutions of the EU but not on

---

[263] *Ibid.*, paras 50–51.

[264] See John Hart Ely, *Democracy and Distrust* (Harvard University Press, 1980) p. 63, n. 97 and
references provided therein.   [265] *D, op. cit.*, para 47.

[266] See Charter, Article 21 which corresponds to Article II-81(1) of the EU Constitution. See
also the Framework Directive, *op. cit.*

Member States. Would the result have been different, if the facts of *D v Council* had been decided under the Charter? As stated above, the Court rejected the argument that the differential treatment against D was discrimination on grounds of sexual orientation. The Court's reasoning on that point was brief and the issue clearly merits further investigation but the signs are that it is unlikely that the Court would accept such an argument. In terms of legislative practice, measures which seek to combat discrimination on grounds of sexual orientation tend to operate without prejudice to marital status.[267] More importantly, in the context of the European Convention for the Protection of Human Rights, the Commission and the Strasbourg Court allow distinctions to be made between a marriage and a same sex relationship.[268]

The ECJ had the opportunity to revisit differential treatment against trans-sexuals in *K.B. v National Health Service Pensions Agency and Secretary for Health*.[269] KB, a female nurse, was living with R, a female-to-male trans-sexual. Under English law it was impossible for KB and R to marry because s. 11(c) of the Matrimonial Causes Act 1973 did not allow a person to change his or her birth certificate except to correct a clerical error or errors of fact. Under the law therefore R remained female. The NHS Pensions Agency informed KB that if she pre-deceased, R would not be entitled to receive a widower's pension since pensions were only payable to a surviving spouse. In the ensuing litigation, the Court of Appeal sought a preliminary reference on whether the exclusion from pension benefits of the female-to-male trans-sexual partner of a female member of the NHS pension scheme runs counter to Article 141 EC and the Equal Treatment Directive.

Following *D v Council*, the Court accepted that the restriction of pension rights only to married couples could not be regarded as discriminatory on grounds of sex.

---

[267] See e.g. Article 1a of the Staff Regulations which was added by Council Regulation No 781/98 (OJ 1998 L 113/4). This Article gives officials entitlement to equal treatment irrespective of their sexual orientation but applies without prejudice to the provisions of the Staff Regulations requiring a particular marital status. The article came into force after the contested decision in *D v Council* was adopted and for that reason was not taken into account by the Court. In view, however, of the fact that it does not affect requirements pertaining to marital status, it would not have made any difference to the outcome of the case.

[268] See application No 9369/81, *X. and Y. v the United Kingdom*, 3 May 1983, *Decisions and Reports* 32, p. 220; application No 11716/85, *S. v the United Kingdom*, 14 May 1986, D.R. 47, p. 274, paragraph 2; and application No 15666/89, *Kerkhoven and Hinke v the Netherlands*, 19 May 1992, unpublished, para 1, where it was held that stable homosexual relationships do not fall within the scope of the right to respect for family life under Article 8 of the Convention. It has also been held that national provisions which, for the purpose of protecting the family, accord more favourable treatment to married persons and persons of opposite sex living together as man and wife than to persons of the same sex in a stable relationship are not contrary to Article 14 of the Convention (see the decisions in *S. v the United Kingdom*, paragraph 7; application No 14753/89; *C. and L.M. v the United Kingdom*, 9 October 1989, unpublished, paragraph 2; and application No 16106/90, *B. v the United Kingdom*, 10 February 1990, D.R. 64, p. 278, paragraph 2). Further, the ECtHR has interpreted Article 12 of the Convention as applying only to the traditional marriage between two persons of opposite biological sex (see the *Rees* judgment of 17 October 1986, Series A no. 106, p. 19, § 49, and the *Cossey* judgment of 27 September 1990, Series A no. 184, (1991) 13 EHRR 622, p. 17, § 43).

[269] Case C-117/01 *K.B. v National Health Service Pensions Agency and Secretary for Health*, judgment of 7 January 2004.

It held however that there was inequality of treatment which did not relate to the award of the widower's pension but to a necessary precondition for its grant, namely the capacity to marry.[270] KB and R were unable to satisfy the marriage requirement and were therefore discriminated against by comparison to a heterosexual couple of which neither party was a trans-sexual. The ECJ gained inspiration from the judgment in *Goodwin* where the European Court of Human Rights held that the fact that a trans-sexual could not marry a person of the sex to which he or she belonged prior to gender reassignment was a breach of Article 12 ECHR.[271] It concluded that the UK legislation which, in breach of the ECHR, prevented a couple such as KB and R from meeting the marriage requirement was incompatible with Article 141 EC.[272]

Notably, in *KB* the ECJ followed a more progressive approach than the Commission which distinguished the case from *P v S* on the ground that in *KB* the unfavourable treatment did not flow directly from gender reassignment. It seems that under *KB, Grant* and *D v Council* remain good law. The ECJ does not require Member States to equate a same sex relationship with marriage nor does it advocate that discrimination against homosexuals is sex discrimination. The reasoning of the judgment is based on the fact that this was not a homosexual but a heterosexual relationship. The judgment however takes *P v S* one step further. In that case, the discrimination was between the sex of a person before and after undergoing a gender reassignment operation. In *KB* the adverse treatment arose because of the refusal of national law to recognize the new sex. The new sex was not treated differently from the old one because if KB had remained a woman he would not be able to marry. The difference in treatment is between an 'ordinary' heterosexual couple and a heterosexual couple, one of the parties to which is a trans-sexual. It may be argued that this is not sex discrimination *stricto sensu* since a male-to-female trans-sexual would not be equated to a female person and therefore could not marry, either. In effect, the Court chose a comparator different from that which it chose in *Grant* and *D v Council* and one remains with the feeling that the Court does not follow a consistent approach in choosing the appropriate comparator. *KB* establishes the right of a person who has undergone a gender reassignment operation to have his new sex recognized by law. This may more appropriately be considered as a fundamental right to choose one's sex than as an aspect of the prohibition of discrimination on grounds of sex.

[270] *Ibid.*, para 30.

[271] See *Goodwin v United Kingdom*, judgment of 11 July 2002, paras 97–104; and *I v United Kingdom*, judgment of 11 July 2002, paras 77–84.

[272] The ECJ refused to apply the principle of direct effect. It held that it is for the Member States to determine the conditions under which legal recognition is given to the change of a person's gender and it was therefore up to the national court to determine whether in the case in issue a person in KB's situation could rely on Article 141 in order to gain recognition of her right to nominate her partner as the beneficiary of a survivor's pension. See para 35. This is different from other cases where even though Member States retain various options on how to redress unequal treatment between men and women, the ECJ has not viewed that as a reason to deny direct effect.

So far, the case law of the Court establishes a distinction between trans-sexuals and homosexuals. Difference in treatment against the latter is more difficult to be caught by the general principle of non-discrimination. The judgment in *KB* however may open the way for undermining previous judgments. If discrimination on grounds of sexual orientation is prohibited, as it is under the EU Charter and the Framework Directive, restricting certain benefits to married persons may be seen as indirectly discriminatory on the basis of the reasoning in *KB*: the inequality of treatment against homosexuals lies in that they are unable to meet a necessary precondition for the award of the benefit since they are excluded from marrying a person of the same sex.

2.8.3. Positive discrimination

Although the Court has traditionally interpreted the Equal Treatment Directive liberally, initially it took a cautious approach in relation to positive discrimination. The case law has now progressed substantially revealing a more liberal attitude. The issue first arose in *Kalanke v Freie Hansestadt Bremen*.[273] The Law of the State of Bremen governing sex equality in the public service provided that, in the case of appointment or promotion, women who had the same qualifications as men applying for the same post were to be given priority in sectors where women were under-represented. Under-representation was defined as existing in cases where women did not make up at least half of the staff in a salary bracket. Mr Kalanke was refused promotion on the ground that a female candidate was equally qualified to him and should therefore be given priority. The Bundesarbeitsgericht (Federal Labour Court) sought a preliminary ruling regarding the compatibility of the Bremen Law with Article 2(4) of the Equal Treatment Directive, which states that the Directive 'shall be without prejudice to measures to promote equal opportunity for men and women, in particular by removing existing inequalities which affect women's opportunities'.[274] Previously, that provision had been interpreted narrowly.[275]

---

[273] Case C-450/93 [1995] ECR I-3051.

[274] Note that Article 2(4) is now replaced by Article 2(8) following the amendments made by Directive 2002/73, OJ 2002, L269/15. For the text of Article 2(8), see n. 298 below. Note also Council Recommendation 84/635 on the promotion of positive action for women, OJ 1984 L 331/34.

[275] In Case 312/86 *Commission v France* [1988] ECR 6315, it was held that a French law which provided for the preservation of special rights for women in collective agreements was incompatible with the Equal Treatment Directive. The Court held that some of the special rights in issue related to the protection of women in their capacity as older workers or parents, categories to which both men and women may belong, so that the generalized preservation of special rights for women could not *en bloc* benefit from the exception of Article 2(4). In his Opinion in *Kalanke*, Tesauro AG (*op. cit.*, at p. 3063) considered that the judgment in *Commission v France* was excessively severe in rejecting the special rights provided for by French law. Nevertheless, the negative stance of the Court may be explained by the fact that the French Government had made no attempt to justify specific derogations but rather invoked Article 2(4) to maintain wholesale preferential treatment of women for an indefinite period.

In *Kalanke*, the Court started from the premise that national measures which automatically give priority to women involve discrimination contrary to Article 2(1) of the Directive. It proceeded to examine whether they were covered by the exception of Article 2(4). It held that Article 2(4) is exclusively designed to allow measures which, although discriminatory in appearance, are in fact intended to eliminate or reduce actual instances of inequality which may exist in social life. It thus permits national measures relating to access to employment, including promotion, which give a specific advantage to women with a view to improving their ability to compete on the labour market and pursue a career on an equal footing with men. The Court pointed out that, as a derogation from an individual right provided for in the Directive, Article 2(4) must be interpreted strictly. It continued:[276]

National rules which guarantee women absolute and unconditional priority for appointment or promotion go beyond promoting equal opportunities and overstep the limits of the exception in Article 2(4) of the Directive.

The Court also held that, insofar as it seeks to achieve equal representation of men and women in all grades and levels within a department, such a system substitutes for equality of opportunity as envisaged in Article 2(4) the result which is only to be arrived at by providing such equality of opportunity.

The Advocate General took a similar view. Starting from the text of Article 2(4), Tesauro AG stated that the provision authorizes measures which seek to guarantee equality of opportunity, that is to say place men and women in a position of equality as regards starting points. By contrast, the Bremen Law sought to achieve equality of results in the form of an equal distribution of posts in numerical terms.[277] He considered that, since the objective of the Directive is to achieve equality of opportunity, the only derogations from the principle of equal treatment which are permissible, and which are not genuine derogations, are those which seek to give women effective equality of opportunity by eliminating the obstacles which result from social structures. He stated:[278]

Positive action must therefore be directed at removing the obstacles preventing women from having equal opportunities by tackling, for example, educational guidance and vocational training. In contrast, positive action may not be directed towards guaranteeing women equal results from occupying a job, that is to say, at points of arrival, by way of compensation for historical discrimination. In sum, positive action may not be regarded, even less employed, as a means of remedying, through discriminatory measures, a situation of impaired inequality in the past.

The model of equal treatment which emerged from *Kalanke* seems to be as follows. It is permissible to assist women so as to give them equality of opportunity but it is not permissible to achieve equality of result by granting them preferential

---

[276] *Kalanke*, *op. cit.*, paras 22–23.   [277] *Ibid.*, p. 3060.   [278] *Ibid.*, p. 3063.

treatment. In other words, historical discrimination in fact cannot be undone by judicial interpretation.[279]

Kalanke is limited to national provisions 'which guarantee women *absolute and unconditional* priority'.[280] According to the Bremen Law in issue, where candidates were equally qualified, priority was to be given automatically to women.[281] The issue of affirmative action arose again in *Marschall v Land Nordrhein-Westfalen*,[282] this time in relation to the Law on Civil Servants of the Land of North Rhine-Westphalia. That law gave priority to women among equally qualified candidates in relation to promotion but provided a 'saving clause': the female candidate was to be given priority 'unless reasons specific to an individual [male] candidate tilt the balance in his favour'. The Court pointed out that, even where male and female candidates are equally qualified, male candidates tend to be promoted in preference to female ones. That is so particularly because of prejudices and stereotypes concerning the role and capacities of women in working life and the fear, for example, that women will interrupt their careers more frequently, that owing to household and family duties they will be less flexible in their working hours, or that they will be absent from work more frequently because of pregnancy, child birth and breastfeeding.[283] For those reasons, the mere fact that a male candidate and a female candidate are equally qualified does not mean that they have the same chances.[284] On that basis, the Court held that a national rule in terms of which, subject to the application of a saving clause, female candidates for promotion who are equally qualified to the male candidates are to be treated preferentially in sectors where they are under-represented may fall within the scope of Article 2(4) of the Directive if such a rule may counteract the prejudicial effects on female candidates of social attitudes.[285] The Court concluded that, unlike the rules in issue in *Kalanke*, a national rule which contains a saving clause comes within the exception of Article 2(4) if, in each individual case, it provides for male candidates who are equally qualified a guarantee that the candidatures will be the subject of an objective assessment which will take account of all the criteria specific to the individual candidates and will override the priority accorded to female candidates where one or more of those criteria tilts the balance in favour of the male candidate.

Marschall suggested a shift of emphasis from *Kalanke*. Despite the saving clause, the national law in issue in *Marschall* provided for equality of result rather than equality of opportunity at the starting points since it established a presumption in favour of female candidates. The Court therefore expanded the scope of application of the derogation of Article 2(4) to authorise some forms of equality of result.

---

[279] The judgment has been criticized: see S. Moore, 'Nothing Positive from the Court of Justice', (1996) 21 ELR 156.   [280] *Kalanke, op. cit.*, para 22, emphasis added.

[281] Notably, the referring court considered that the Bremen Law was compatible with the German Constitution. In particular, it held that Article 4 of the Law should be interpreted in accordance with the Basic Law to the effect that, even if priority for promotion was to be given in principle to women, exceptions should be made in appropriate cases.

[282] Case C-409/95 [1997] ECR I-6363.   [283] *Ibid.*, para 29.   [284] *Ibid.*, para 30.

[285] *Ibid.*, para 31.

Marschall starts from the factually correct premise that women are presumed to be disadvantaged in terms of employment prospects and puts the onus on the male candidates. The judgment evinces a pragmatic perception of justice.

Legislative changes occurred after *Marschall*. The Treaty of Amsterdam, which entered into force on 1 May 1999, inserted an express reference to affirmative action in the EC Treaty. The amendment is instructive of the cautious and incremental approach towards change. Article 114(4) EC provides for affirmative action not as a Community policy but as a concession to Member States, stressing its status as an exception to the principle of equal treatment.[286] Article 141(4) does not endorse any particular model of affirmative action but goes further than Article 2(4) of the Equal Treatment Directive in that it leaves the door open for the adoption of measures which go beyond equality of opportunity. It may be seen as an implicit endorsement of the Court's case law and is drafted in sufficiently abstract terms to let the Court 'get on with it'. The provision may come into play to rescue a national measure where it cannot take advantage of the exception of Article 2(4).[287] In fact, as we shall see, Article 141(4) has had little bearing in subsequent case law.

In *Badeck*[288] the Court summarised its general position as follows. A measure which is intended to give women priority in promotion in sectors where they are under-represented is compatible with Community law if it meets two conditions:

(a) it does not automatically and unconditionally give such priority when men and women are equally qualified;
(b) the candidates are the subject of an objective assessment which takes account of their specific personal situations.

In *Badeck* the Court was concerned with a law of the *Land* of Hesse which applied a 'flexible result quota' system in the public administration. Departments were required to draw up women's advancement plans containing binding targets on a two-year basis with a view to increasing the proportion of women in sectors where they were under-represented. In defining the targets, quotas were not determined uniformly but in accordance with the specific features of the sectors and departments concerned. The Law provided that, where male and female candidates for selection have equal qualifications, priority must be given to female candidates where that is necessary to comply with the binding targets, unless

---

[286] Article 141(4) states as follows: 'With a view to ensuring full equality in practice between men and women in working life, the principle of equal treatment shall not prevent any Member State from maintaining or adopting measures providing for specific advantages in order to make it easier for the under-represented sex to pursue a vocational activity or to prevent or compensate for disadvantages in professional careers'. Declaration 18 annexed to the Treaty of Amsterdam states that, when adopting measures referred to in Article 141(4), Member States 'should, in the first instance, aim at improving the situation of women in working life'. Article 141(4) corresponds to Article III-214(4) of the Constitution.

[287] This has been expressly stated by the Court: see Case C-158/97 *Badeck and Others* [2000] ECR I-1875, para 14.   [288] *Ibid.*, para 23.

reasons of greater legal weight require otherwise. The Court found that the last proviso rescued the measure. Reasons of greater legal weight referred to various laws which sought to give priority to social considerations and the protection of marriage and the family. There were, in particular, five groups which took priority over the advancement of women and included former public employees, part-time workers, former soldiers, seriously disabled persons, and long-term unemployed.

The judgment seems to suggest that it is acceptable to favour women over men among equally qualified candidates, if the law allows other deserving groups to be favoured over women. The insertion of additional factors into the equation removes the automatic occurrence of preferential treatment on grounds of sex. The judgment thus endorses the 'single-factor' model of discrimination according to which discrimination exists not where the dominant group is formally disadvantaged but where the decision maker is constrained to reach an outcome on the basis of a single factor, namely that a person belongs to the under-represented group. In formal terms, this reasoning is questionable. What the Court wishes to do is to allow Member States to engage in priority-setting and pursue their social agendas exercising residual control on grounds of arbitrariness. This approach may reveal a wider judicial choice going beyond discrimination on grounds of sex. In other words, the Court may view that, as a general rule, it would be contrary to the principle of equal treatment to provide for automatic preferential treatment of a specific group in areas where that group is under-represented whatever the basis on which that group is defined (e.g. social, ethnic or racial grounds). In a wider political context, the question is how the legislature defines 'deserving groups' and how it prioritizes social and economic objectives. This is a political choice but there is scope for judicial intervention at national, and sometimes at Community, level in ensuring, among other things, that each group has equal opportunity to express its views and have its interests taken into account in the decision-making process.[289]

In *Badeck* the Court also endorsed other aspects of the Hesse Law.[290] The law provided for a proportional quota. It stipulated that binding targets for certain academic posts must provide for a minimum percentage of women which is at least

---

[289] See, in a different context, the judgment in Case T-135/96 *UEAPME v Council and Commission* [1998] ECR II-2335.

[290] The Court also expanded further on the measures which are permissible under Article 2(4) of the Directive. It held that it is legitimate for the purposes of assessing the suitability of applicants, to take into account certain criteria which although formulated in neutral terms tend to favour women. For example, it may be decided that seniority, age and the date of last promotion are to be taken into account only insofar as they are of importance for the suitability, qualifications and professional capability of candidates. Similarly, it may be prescribed that the family status or income of the partner is immaterial and that part-time work, leave and delays in completing training as a result of looking after dependants must not have a negative effect. The aim of these criteria is to achieve substantive rather than formal equality by reducing *de facto* inequalities. However, the application of such criteria must be transparent and amenable to review in order to obviate any arbitrary assessment of the qualifications of the candidates. See *Badeck, op. cit.*, paras 31–32; confirmed in Case C-407/98 *Abrahamsson and Anderson* [2000] ECR I-5539, paras 47–49.

equal to the percentage of women among graduates in the respective discipline. The Court found this compatible with Community law on the ground that it did not fix an absolute ceiling but provided for a threshold by reference to the persons who received appropriate training and therefore amounted to using a 'fact as a quantitative criterion for giving preference to women'.[291]

The Court also endorsed a strict result quota in training. The Hesse Law provided that, in occupations where women were under-represented and for which the State did not have a monopoly in training, at least half of the training places were to be allocated to women. The applicants argued that the system sought to ensure a specified result as regards the proportions in which the sexes were represented and, as such, was contrary to *Kalanke*. The ECJ held however that the training system formed part of a restricted concept of equality of opportunity because it reserved for women not places in employment but places in training. Also, the quota applied to training places for which the State did not have a monopoly. As such, it concerned training for which places were also available in the private sector so that 'no male candidate is definitively excluded from training'.[292]

Further the ECJ cleared the following provisions: a rule under which, where male and female candidates have equal qualifications, women who satisfy all the conditions laid down by law must be called to interview or, if not all qualified female candidates are called for interview, the number of male candidates called cannot exceed that of female candidates; and a rule under which when appointments are made to employees' representative bodies at least half the number must be women.[293]

It is clear that *Badeck* goes far beyond equality of opportunity. It accepts qualified equality of result as being compatible with the principle of equal treatment thereby emasculating, and to a good extent reversing, *Kalanke*. Notably, the Court found the provisions of the Hesse Law to be compatible with Article 2(4) so that it did not even need to examine the possible application of Article 141(4).

The ECJ lends a helping hand to national affirmative action policies but employs the mechanism of proportionality to control their harsher effects. In *Lommers*[294] the Dutch Ministry of Agriculture made available to its staff a limited number of subsidized nursery places. To tackle the under-representation of women in the Ministry, these were reserved for female officials whilst male officials could access them only in cases of emergency. The Court accepted that the policy was designed to eliminate the causes of women's reduced opportunities for access to employment and thus improve their competitive position in the labour market. It noted however that a measure whose purported aim is to abolish a *de facto* inequality might also help to perpetuate a traditional division of roles between men and women. Thus, if the aim of promoting equality of opportunity between men and

---

[291] *Badeck, op. cit.,* para 42.   [292] *Ibid.,* para 53.

[293] Note that Saggio AG disagreed with the Court on this point opining that the provision was contrary to Article 2(1) and (4) of the Equal Treatment Directive but the ECJ cleared it on the ground that it was not mandatory.   [294] Case C-476/99 *Lommers* [2002] ECR I-2891.

women could still be achieved by extending the scope of the measure to include working fathers, their exclusion would run counter to the principle of proportionality. Thus, the Ministry scheme was acceptable provided that male officials who brought up their children by themselves had access to the nursery scheme.[295] *Lommers* adopts a functional view of affirmative action.

In *Abrahamsson and Anderson*,[296] the ECJ refused to endorse a rule of the Swedish law governing universities which provided that a candidate belonging to an under-represented sex and possessing sufficient qualifications may be chosen in preference to a candidate of the opposite sex who would otherwise have been chosen, subject to the condition that the difference in their respective qualifications is not so great that it would make such appointment contrary to the requirement of objectivity. The Court held that the scope and effect of that condition cannot be precisely determined. The method of selection was thus ultimately based on the mere fact of belonging to the under-represented sex even if the merits of that candidate were inferior to those of the candidate of the opposite sex. It held that such a method of selection was not permitted by Article 2(4) of the Directive nor could it be rescued by Article 141(4). The Court read into the latter provision a requirement of proportionality stating that the method of selection provided for by Swedish law was disproportionate to the aim pursued but provided no further guidance on the distinction between the two provisions.

The ECJ's attitude can be summarised as follows. It has moved forward from insisting on equality of opportunity to allowing qualified equality of result. As the boundaries of equality fall, it relies more on proportionality to outlaw clear or inflexible systems which rely on a single factor (*Badeck*) or strike at the hard core of equality, e.g., in relation to appointments (*Abrahamsson and Anderson*). The ECJ sees affirmative action as part of the wider social agenda which Member States are free to pursue. Just as the case law on free movement used the concepts of non-discrimination and proportionality to undermine entrenched consumer habits, the case law on affirmative action uses the same concepts to challenge social assumptions and stereotypes.

The above cases do not provide clear guidelines as to the interaction between Article 2(4) of the Equal Treatment Directive and Article 141(4) EC. Although Article 141(4) is broader than the first and, as a rule of primary law, may justify national measures not covered by it, so far the ECJ has not specified the normative content of the extra leverage and has, effectively, treated the two provisions as being coterminous. In any event, following the amendments made by Directive

---

[295] It held (para 47): 'A measure which would exclude male officials who take care of their children by themselves from access to a nursery scheme subsidised by their employer would go beyond the permissible derogation provided for in Article 2(4), by interfering excessively with the individual right to equal treatment which that provision guarantees. Moreover, in relation to those officials, the argument that women are more likely to interrupt their career in order to take care of their young children no longer has the same relevance.'

[296] *Op. cit.*, n. 290 above.

2002/73,[297] Article 2(4) is now replaced by new Article 2(8) which clearly aligns the scope of the Directive with the scope of Article 141(4).[298]

Provisions on positive action have been included also in the general Framework Directive[299] and the Directive prohibiting discrimination on grounds of ethnic or racial origin.[300] These, similarly to Article 141(4), do not provide the basis for the adoption of Community legislation but allow Member States to pursue their social agendas. They differ from affirmative action to counteract sex discrimination in the following respects. They are provided for in secondary law and not in the Treaty. They are also formulated in somewhat narrower terms than Article 141(4). They authorise the adoption of specific 'measures' rather than 'advantages' and refer to measures which prevent or compensate inequalities rather than facilitate access to employment and professional advancement.[301] The legal consequences of these textual differences remain to be seen.

2.9. Article 12 EC: The prohibition of discrimination on grounds of nationality

2.9.1. The content of the prohibition

The first paragraph of Article 12 EC states as follows:[302]

Within the scope of application of this Treaty, and without prejudice to any special provisions contained therein, any discrimination on grounds of nationality shall be prohibited.

Viewed in historical perspective, the right to equal treatment irrespective of nationality is the most important right conferred by substantive Community law. Traditionally, the laws of the Member States imposed restrictions on foreign

[297] Directive 2002/73 on the implementation of the principle of equal treatment for men and women as regards access to employment, vocational training and promotion, and working conditions, OJ 2002, L 269/15.

[298] Article 2(8) reads as follows: 'Member States may maintain or adopt measures within the meaning of Article 141(4) of the Treaty with a view to ensuring full equality in practice between men and women'. Member States must implement Directive 2002/73 by 5 October 2005: see Article 2 of the Directive.

[299] Directive 2000/78 establishing a general framework for equal treatment in employment and occupation, OJ 2000, L 303/16, Article 7.

[300] Directive 2000/43 implementing the principle of equal treatment between persons irrespective of racial or ethnic origin, OJ 2000, L 180/22, Article 5.

[301] See Article 5 of the Race Directive and Article 7(1) of the Framework Directive, above, n. 68. A common provision in the preambles of both directives, as well as directive 2002/73, is that national laws may permit the establishment of organizations of persons of a particular sex, religion, race etc where their main object is the promotion of the special needs of those persons. It is however questionable whether that gives a carte blanche to exclude persons who do not belong to the relevant group but nonetheless support its causes.

[302] In the original Treaty of Rome the prohibition of discrimination on grounds of nationality was provided for in Article 7. Article 7 was renumbered Article 6 by the TEU and became Article 12 by the TA. It corresponds to Article I-4(2) of the EU Constitution.

citizens in most aspects of economic and social life. The prohibition of discrimination on grounds of nationality, and the cognate right to national treatment, was the first essential step to promote integration. The function of Article 12 was explained by Jacobs AG in *Phil Collins* as follows:[303]

... The fundamental purpose of the Treaty is to achieve an integrated economy in which the factors of production, as well as the fruits of production, may move freely and without distortion, thus bringing about a more efficient allocation of resources and a more perfect division of labour. The greatest obstacle to the realization of that objective was the host of discriminatory rules and practices whereby the national governments traditionally protected their own producers and workers from foreign competition. Although the abolition of discriminatory rules and practices may not be sufficient in itself to achieve the high level of economic integration envisaged by the Treaty, it is clearly an essential prerequisite.

The prohibition of discrimination on grounds of nationality is also of great symbolic importance, inasmuch as it demonstrates that the Community is not just a commercial arrangement between the governments of the Member States but is a common enterprise in which all the citizens of Europe are able to participate as individuals ... No other aspect of Community law touches the individual more directly or does more to foster that sense of common identity and shared destiny without which the 'ever closer union among the peoples of Europe', proclaimed by the preamble to the Treaty, would be an empty slogan.

Article 12 has direct effect.[304] According to the case law it produces both vertical and, at least in some cases, horizontal direct effect so that national courts must enforce rights deriving from that provision not only against public authorities but also against individuals.[305] The prohibition of discrimination on grounds of nationality is implemented in specific spheres of Community law by a number of Treaty provisions, e.g. Article 39 (free movement of workers), Article 43 (right of establishment), Article 49 (free movement of services) and Article 249 (participation of non-nationals to the capital companies). Article 12 has a residual character. It is of autonomous application only in situations governed by Community law in relation to which the Treaty does not lay down a specific prohibition of discrimination.[306] It performs therefore a 'gap-filling' function. The Court has held that, since Article 12 is implemented in specific domains by separate provisions of the Treaty, where national rules are compatible with those provisions,

---

[303] Joined Cases C-92 and C-326/92 [1993] ECR I-5145 at 5163.
[304] See e.g. Case 24/86 *Blaizot v University of Liège* [1988] ECR 379, para 35; *Phil Collins, op. cit.,* para 35.
[305] *Angonese, op. cit.,* n. 70 above, para 36; Case C-415/93 *Union Royale Belge des Sociétés de Football Association and Others v Bosman* [1995] ECR I-4921; *Walrave, op. cit.,* n. 97 above, paras 15–18; *Doná v Mantero op. cit.,* n. 97 above, paras 17–19.
[306] See e.g. Case C-176/96 *Lehtonen and Castors Canada Dry Namur-Braine ASBL v Fédération Royale Belge des Sociétés de Basket-ball ASBL* [2000] ECR I-2681, para 37; Case 9/73 *Schlüter* [1973] ECR 1135; Case 305/87 *Commission v Greece* [1989] ECR 1461, para 13; Case C-10/90 *Masgio v Bundesknappschaft* [1991] ECR I-1119, para 12; Case C-20/92 *Hubbard* [1993] ECR I-3777.

they are also compatible with Article 12.[307] Strictly speaking, that statement is inaccurate.[308] It is correct to say that where a specific article of the Treaty permits derogations from the principle of non-discrimination, such derogations are also permitted by Article 12.[309] It is wrong to say however that a national provision which discriminates against nationals of other Member States cannot be contrary to Article 12 simply because it is not caught by the specific provisions of the Treaty. If that were the case, Article 12 would lose its independent character.[310] As we shall see, the case law has understood Article 12 as being an autonomous source of rights and obligations outside the sphere of free movement.

The Court has interpreted the provisions of the Treaty on free movement of persons as prohibiting not only discrimination on grounds of nationality but also discrimination against free movers irrespective of nationality.[311] Furthermore, it is now well established that those provisions, namely Articles 39, 43 and 49 EC, prohibit not only discriminatory but also indistinctly applicable restrictions.[312] In parallel, the case law has gradually broadened the scope of application of Article 12. Thus, the provisions of the Treaty on free movement and Article 12 have operated as complementary forces to expand the scope of EC law and restrict the discretion of Member States in two ways. On the one hand, the right to free movement has expanded beyond the concept of discrimination and the concept of nationality, whilst the right to national treatment has colonized fields hitherto occupied wholly by national law.

Article 12 requires a Member State to provide 'perfect' or 'absolute' equality of treatment between its own nationals and those of other Member States.[313] It must be applied 'in every respect and in all circumstances governed by Community law to any person established in a Member State'.[314] The prohibition of discrimination on grounds of nationality binds also the Community institutions,[315] and, as already stated, individuals.[316]

---

[307] See e.g. Case 305/87 *Commission v Greece* [1989] ECR 1461, para 12; Case C-41/90 *Hofner and Elser v Macrotron* [1991] ECR I-1979, para 36.

[308] *Phil Collins, op. cit., per* Jacobs AG, pp. 5163–5164.   [309] See below, *Rutili*, n. 320.

[310] *Phil Collins, op. cit.*

[311] See e.g. Case C-224/01 *Köbler v Austria*, judgment of 30 September 2003; Case C-419/92 *Scholz* [1994] ECR I-505; C-18/93 *Corsica Ferries* [1994] ECR I-1783; Case C-224/98 *D'Hoop* [2002] ECR I-6191, paras 30–31.

[312] For the application of this *in extremis*, see Case C-60/00 *Carpenter v Secretary of State for the Home Department*, judgment of 11 July 2002; see further C-76/90 *Säger* [1991] ECR I-4221; Case C-384/93 *Alpine Investments BV* [1995] ECR I-1141; *Bosman op. cit.*, n. 305 above; Case C-55/94 *Gebhard* [1995] ECR I-4165. See further C. Barnard, 'Fitting the Remaining Pieces into the Goods and Services Jigsaw?' (2001) 26 ELR 35; C.Hilson, 'Discrimination in Community Free Movement', (1999) 24 ELR 445; L. Daniele, 'Non-Discriminatory Restrictions to the Free Movement of Persons', (1997) 22 ELR 191; N.Bernard, 'Discrimination and Free Movement in EC Law', (1996) 45 ICLQ 82. For Article 28 see below, Ch. 5.2.

[313] Case C-323/95 *Hayes v Kronenberger* [1997] ECR I-1711, para 18; Case C-43/95 *Data Delecta and Forsberg* [1996] ECR I-4661, para 16.

[314] Case 137/84 *Ministère Public v Mutsch* [1985] ECR 2681, para 12.

[315] *Hochstraas op. cit.*, n. 118 above.   [316] See the cases cited in n. 305 above.

Article 12 covers not only direct but also indirect difference in treatment, namely, one which although based on a criterion other than nationality (for example residence in the national territory) leads effectively to the same results.[317] Indirect difference in treatment will be compatible with Article 12 if there is objective justification. In many cases the Court has examined, and in most cases has rejected,[318] arguments of the defendant government that the less favourable treatment of nationals from other Member States is objectively justified. An interesting example is provided by *Pastoors and Trans-Cap*.[319] There, the Court accepted that difference in treatment between Belgian nationals and nationals of other Member States with regard to penalties for breach of Community transport legislation was objectively justified although on the facts it found the Belgian measures disproportionate.

An interesting question is whether direct discrimination on grounds of nationality may be justified. Article 12 does not provide for any express derogations. This is not to say, however, that no derogations are permitted. If that were the case, it would follow that the residual content of Article 12 would be wider than the specific provisions of the Treaty prohibiting discrimination on grounds of nationality, since those provisions do recognize express derogations.[320] Such a difference is not justified by the intrinsic importance of the rights protected. To give an example, it would be incongruous if the right of a Community national to take up employment in the host Member State provided for in Article 39 was subject to derogations on the grounds of public policy or public health whereas the right to access to education in the host State, which has been based by the Court on Article 12, was not. The very notion of discrimination in Article 12 suggests difference in treatment without good justification. Consequently, it should be accepted that where Article 12 applies autonomously, it is at the very least subject to derogations analogous to those specified in the provisions of the Treaty on free movement. In fact, the range of situations covered by the residual content of Article 12 is so diverse that sometimes it may be difficult to pigeon-hole a national measure into the neat categories of direct and indirect discrimination and it may be appropriate to accept a wider objective justification test.[321]

---

[317] Case C-29/95 *Pastoors and Trans-Cap* [1997] ECR I-285; Case C-212/99 *Commission v Italy* [2001] ECR I-4923, para 24; *Dany Bidar op. cit.*, n. 70 above, para 51.

[318] But see for a successful claim: Case C-138/02 *Collins v Secretary of State for Work and Pensions*, judgment of 23 March 2004.

[319] *Op. cit.*, n. 317 above; see further Case C-224/00 *Commission v Italy* [2002] ECR I-2965; *Dany Bidar, op. cit.*; Case C-28/04 *Tod's SpA and Tod's France SARL v Heyraud SA*, judgment of 30 June 2005; Case C-411/98 *Ferlini* [2000] ECR I-8081; *Blaizot, op. cit.*, n. 304 above, paras 22–23; and in the context of staff cases: *Hochstraas*, op. cit., para 7.

[320] See Article 39(3) and (4), Article 46 and Article 55. As already stated, derogations from specific Treaty articles implementing the principle of non-discrimination on grounds of nationality are also derogations from Article 12. See e.g. Case 36/75 *Rutili v Minister for the Interior* [1975] ECR 1219, paras 12–13.

[321] Thus, in Case C-148/02 *Garcia Avello v Etat Belge*, judgment of 2 October 2003, the ECJ held that reverse direct discrimination, i.e. treating different nationals in the same way although they were in different situations, was subject to the defence of objective justification.

The Court has held that the rule of non-discrimination applies to all legal relationships insofar as these relationships, by reason either of the place where they are entered into or of the place where they take effect, can be located within the territory of he Community.[322] Thus, the fact that an artistic performance takes place outside the Community does not prevent the artist from invoking Article 12 with a view to prohibiting the unauthorised marketing of a reproduction of the performance in a Member State.[323]

Where national law discriminates in general against nationals of other Member States, the fact that it treats certain categories of nationals of those States equally to its own nationals does not deny the existence of discrimination. Thus, in *Gravier*, where Belgian law required from foreign but not from Belgian citizens a registration fee in relation to vocational training courses, it was no defence that Luxembourg nationals and foreign nationals paying taxes in Belgium were exempted from payment of the fee.[324]

In *Costa v ENEL*[325] the Court referred to Article 12 as an argument to support the primacy of Community law. The reasoning of the judgment was that, if national law adopted after the Treaty came into force was capable of taking precedence over Community law, that would prejudice the uniform application of Community law and give rise to discrimination on grounds of nationality. In other words, the Court viewed Article 6 as an instrument contributing to the elimination of distortions of competition in the common market.[326] However, distortions of competition which ensue from the fact that citizens are subject to the laws of different Member States cannot be undone by Article 12. The Court has held that Article 12 does not cover disparities in treatment or distortions which may result from divergences existing between the laws of the various Member States, so long as the latter affect all persons subject to them, in accordance with objective criteria and without regard to their nationality.[327] Similarly, in the absence of harmonization measures, the fact that the rules applied by one Member State are stricter than those applied by other Member States does not constitute a breach of Article 12, as long as those rules are applied equally to every person under the jurisdiction of that State.[328] Nor does Article 12 prohibit differences in treatment on the basis of

---

[322] *Walrave, op. cit.*, n. 97 above, para 28.   [323] *Phil Collins, op. cit.*, n. 303 above.

[324] Case 293/89 *Gravier v City of Liège* [1985] ECR 593, para 14.

[325] Case 6/64 [1964] ECR 585, at 594.

[326] Employing similar reasoning, the Court sometimes has recourse to the general principle of equal treatment to support the proposition that terms used in directives must be given an autonomous and uniform interpretation throughout the Community and must not be determined by reference to national laws. See e.g. in relation to Directive 85/337 (Environmental Impact Assessment), Case C-287/98 *Luxembourg v Linster*, judgment of 19 September 2000, para 43.

[327] Case 14/68 *Wilhelm v Bundeskartellamt* [1969] ECR 1.

[328] Case 223/86 *Pesca Valentia v Minister for Fisheries and Forestry* [1988] ECR 83, para 18, Joined Cases 185–204/78 *Van Dam* [1979] ECR 2345, para 10. See also Case C-379/92 *Criminal proceedings against Peralta* [1994] ECR I-3453, para 48. The absence of harmonization of national laws in a certain area however does not necessarily remove that area from the scope of application of the Treaty for the purposes of Article 12. As the Advocate General stated in *Phil Collins op. cit.*,

the place where traders are established. In *Oebel*,[329] the Court found that German rules which prohibited night work in bakeries did not infringe Article 12 since this applied to all persons subject to them irrespective of nationality. It held that national rules which make no distinction, directly or indirectly, on the ground of nationality do not infringe Article 12, even if they affect the competitiveness of the traders subject to them.[330] Similarly, in another case, the Court held that Luxembourg rules which prohibited exporters from obtaining payment for their exports in banknotes and required foreign currency payable to them to be paid through a bank and to be exchanged on the regulated foreign exchange market were not in breach of Article 12 even though they might place exporters subject to them at a disadvantage *vis-à-vis* their competitors established in other Member States where different rules applied.[331] Also, Article 12 does not apply where the legislation of a Member State favours certain national undertakings in relation to other national undertakings,[332] unless that difference in treatment amounts to indirect discrimination on grounds of nationality.

The prohibition of discrimination on grounds of nationality is reiterated by Article 21(2) of the Charter of Fundamental Rights which, in terms of substance, does not add anything to Article 12 EC.[333]

2.9.2. Scope of application

Article 12 prohibits discrimination only 'within the scope of application of this Treaty'. The case law has interpreted those terms particularly broadly and, according to one view, the scope of Article 12 is wider than the scope of the general principle of equality as an unwritten principle of law.[334] In areas which fall outside the scope of application of the Treaty, a Member State may discriminate against nationals of other Member States. It may also discriminate between nationals from other Member States, i.e. grant more favourable treatment to citizens from Member State A than to citizens from Member State B. In view, however, of the wide scope of Article 12 the circumstances where a Member State retains such discretion are limited.[335]

The trend towards the broad interpretation of Article 12 began in the 1980s. In *Cowan*,[336] it was held that a Community national who travels to another Member

---

p. 5166, it is precisely where no harmonization has been achieved that the principle of national treatment assumes special importance.

[329] Case 155/80 [1981] ECR 1993. See also Case 31/78 *Bussone v Italian Ministry for Agriculture and Forestry* [1978] ECR 2429, paragraph 38. [330] *Oebel, op. cit.*, para 8.

[331] Case 308/86 *Criminal proceedings against Lambert* [1988] ECR 4369.

[332] *Pesca Valentia, op. cit.*, para 20.

[333] This corresponds to Article II-81(2) of the EU Constitution.

[334] See *First City Trading, op. cit.*, n. 29 above, *per* Laws J and the discussion above in Ch. 1. Note that this view has now been overtaken by *British Pig Industry, op. cit.*, n. 133 above.

[335] For a situation falling outside the scope of Article 12, see Case C-430/97 *Johannes*, judgment of 10 June 1999 (national rules determining the consequences of divorce between an official and his spouse). [336] Case 186/87 *Cowan v Trésor Public* [1989] ECR 195.

State as a tourist may benefit in his capacity as a recipient of services from a scheme to grant compensation to the victims of violent crime. Such a scheme could not be restricted to domestic nationals but must also be extended to nationals from other Member States. The Court stated as follows:[337]

When Community law guarantees a natural person the freedom to go to another Member State the protection of that person from harm in the Member State in question, on the same basis as that of nationals and persons residing there, is a corollary of the freedom of movement. It follows that the prohibition of discrimination is applicable to recipients of services within the meaning of the Treaty as regards protection against the risk of assault and the right to obtain financial compensation provided for by national law when that risk materializes. The fact that the compensation at issue is financed by the Public Treasury cannot alter the rules regarding the protection of the rights guaranteed by the Treaty.

The rationale which underlies *Cowan* is that the prohibition of discrimination on grounds of nationality extends to situations which are not related to the exercise of economic rights strictly understood. The evolution in the interpretation of Article 12 can be traced by reference to cases pertaining to access to education, intellectual property rights, the right to judicial protection, and social rights emanating from Union citizenship. Examples from these categories will now be examined in turn.

2.9.2.1. Access to education

The evolutive interpretation of Article 12 is vividly illustrated by a line of cases pertaining to access to education. In *Gravier v City of Liège*,[338] Belgian law required students who did not possess Belgian nationality to pay a registration fee ('*minerval*') as a condition of attending vocational training courses. The Court held that, although educational organization and training was a matter for the Member States, access to vocational training fell within the scope of the Treaty. Consequently, the imposition on students who are nationals of other Member States of a registration fee as a condition of access to vocational training, where the same fee is not imposed on students who are nationals of the host Member State, constitutes discrimination prohibited by Article 12. The judgment is important because it extended the application of the principle of non-discrimination to education, a sensitive area which until then was thought not to be affected directly by Community law. Indeed, various governments argued in their submissions to the Court that Member States have special responsibilities towards their own nationals in the field of education which may justify more favourable treatment. The judgment had considerable financial repercussions as it forced Member States to rethink the educational budget.[339]

Subsequently, in *Blaizot*,[340] the Court took a broad view of what is vocational training holding that it includes university studies. In view of the serious economic

---

[337] Para 17.   [338] *Op. cit.*, n. 324 above.
[339] For the aftermath of *Gravier*, see Case 309/85 *Barra v Belgium and another* [1988] ECR 355.
[340] *Op. cit.*, n. 304 above.

implications of the ruling and the fact that until then it had generally been assumed that vocational training did not include university studies, the Court limited the retroactive effect of its judgment.[341]

In *Lair v Universität Hannover*,[342] the Court drew a distinction between tuition fees and maintenance grants. In accordance with the judgment in *Gravier*, assistance granted by the host State to cover tuition fees was held to fall within the scope of Article 12. By contrast, assistance granted for maintenance was held to fall outside the scope of the Treaty. The Court reasoned that maintenance grants were a matter of educational policy, which was not included in the spheres entrusted to the Community institutions, and also a matter of social policy, which fell within the competence of the Member States insofar as it was not covered by specific provisions of the Treaty.[343]

Lair was reiterated in *Brown*.[344] The distinction between tuition fees and maintenance grants drew a balance between, on the one hand, the desire to broaden the scope of Article 12 with a view to extending the protection afforded to non-nationals and, on the other hand, the concern to provide workable solutions which did not cause major upheaval to the educational policies of Member States.[345] Since maintenance grants fell outside the scope of the Treaty for the purposes of Article 12, it followed that a Community national could claim a maintenance grant for university training in the host State only in his capacity as a worker or as a member of the family of a worker. Those rights are provided for in Article 7(2) and Article 12 of Regulation No 1612/68[346] respectively, which have been interpreted generously by the Court.[347] In *Brown*, however, the Court held that a person who has acquired the status of a worker in the host State exclusively as a result of his being admitted to university to undertake studies may not rely on his status as worker in order to claim a maintenance grant. That would be an abusive exercise of rights guaranteed by Community law since his employment relationship is merely ancillary to the studies to be financed by the grant.[348]

---

[341] In *Blaizot* the Court held that vocational training includes university studies whether such studies lead directly to a professional qualification or provide the academic knowledge for the pursuit of a profession. It excluded only courses of study which, because of their particular nature, were intended for persons wishing to improve their general knowledge rather than prepare themselves for an occupation. See also Case 263/86 *Belgian State v Humbel* [1988] ECR 5365; cf the notion of 'vocational school' in Article 7(3) of Regulation No 1612/68 which was held not to cover universities: see Case 39/86 *Lair v Universität Hannover* [1988] ECR 3161, para 26 and, further, Case 242/87 *Commission v Council* [1989] ECR 1425.   [342] *Op. cit.*, n. 341 above.
[343] *Lair, op. cit.*, para 15. Where a Member State provides a general student grant, it is for the national court to determine what proportion of the grant is intended to cover the cost of access to vocational training: Case C-357/89 *Raulin* [1992] ECR I-1027, para 28.
[344] Case 197/86 *Brown v Secretary of State for Scotland* [1988] ECR 3205.
[345] In *Brown, op. cit.*, at p. 3230, Slynn AG explained the distinction on the ground that allowances covering maintenance costs do not have a sufficiently direct link with access to the course of study itself.   [346] OJ English Special Ed. 1968 II, p. 475.
[347] On Article 7(2), see *Lair, op. cit.*; on Article 12, see Joined Cases 389 and 390/87 *Echternach and Moritz v Netherlands Minister for Education and Science* [1989] ECR 723; Case C-308/89 *Di Leo v Land Berlin* [1990] ECR I-4185; Case C-7/94 *Gaal* [1995] ECR I-1031.
[348] *Brown, op. cit.*, para 27.

Somewhat prophetically, the Court expressly stated in *Lair* that maintenance grants fell outside the scope of the Treaty for the purposes of Article 12 'at the present stage of development of Community law'.[349] A number of developments occurred after *Lair* and *Brown*. The TEU introduced the status of Union citizenship. It also gave to the Community some competence on matters of education and vocational training.[350] Furthermore, the Council adopted a number of directives extending rights of residence beyond economically active citizens, including Directive 93/96 on the right of residence for students.[351] The rights of students were revisited in *Grzelczyk* in the light of those developments.[352] The Court reiterated that Directive 93/96 does not establish any right to payment of maintenance grants by the host Member State. Under Article 1 of the Directive, the authorities may require students who are Community nationals to have sufficient resources to avoid becoming a burden on the social assistance system of the host State. It held however that a student may be entitled under Articles 12 and 17 EC[353] to a non-contributory social benefit. In that case, the Belgian authorities had refused the *minimex*, a minimum subsistence allowance paid to residents, to a French student studying in a Belgian university. Under Belgian law, the *minimex* was available to Belgian nationals or non-Belgians who came within the scope of Regulation No 1612/68. Mr Grzelczyk, as student, was not covered by the Regulation. The Court held however, that Articles 6 (now 12) and 8 (now 17) of the Treaty preclude entitlement to a non-contributory social benefit, such as the *minimex*, from being made conditional, in the case of nationals of Member States other than the host State where they are legally resident, on their falling within the scope of Regulation No 1612/68 when no such condition applies to nationals of the host State.[354] The Court added that the authorities are not prevented from taking the view that a student who has recourse to social assistance no longer meets the conditions of his right of residence or from taking measures, within the limits imposed by Community law, either to withdraw his residence permit or not to

---

[349] See *Lair, op. cit.*, para 15.   [350] See Articles 149–150 EC.

[351] OJ 1993, L 317/59. The other measures were Directive 90/365 on the right of residence for employees and self-employed persons who have ceased their occupational activity (OJ 1990, L 180/28) and Directive 90/364 on the right of residence (OJ 1990 L 180/26). The latter extends the right of residence in the host Member State to Union citizens who do not enjoy it under any other provision of Community law and members of their families provided that they are covered by sickness insurance and have sufficient resources to avoid becoming a burden on the social assistance system of the host State. Note that Directive 93/96 on students together with Directive 90/364 were repealed and replaced with effect from 30 April 2006 by Directive 2004/38 on the right of citizens of the Union and their family members to move and reside freely within the territory of the Member States, OJ 2004 L 158/77.

[352] Case C-184/99 *Grzelczyk* [2001] ECR I-6193. See also *D'Hoop op. cit.*, n. 311 above: the Court held that Belgian law which granted the tideover allowance (a social security benefit available to young people who had completed their studies and were seeking their first employment), only to those who had completed their secondary education in Belgium and excluded Belgian citizens who had completed their education in another Member State was incompatible with Community law.

[353] Article 17 establishes European Citizenship. For the text of the article, see n. 380 below.

[354] *Op. cit.*, see paras 42–43.

renew it. Such measures however cannot be the automatic consequence of the student having recourse to the host State's social assistance system.

More recently, in *Bidar*[355] the ECJ took a step further and reconsidered its view that maintenance grants fall outside the scope of EU law. The Court identified two developments since the judgments in *Lair* and *Brown*: the establishment of Union citizenship and the addition to the EC Treaty by the TEU of the Chapter on education and vocational training. In view of those developments, the ECJ held that the situation of a Union citizen who is lawfully resident in another Member State falls within the scope of Article 12 for the purposes of obtaining a student maintenance grant or a subsidized loan. In terms of judicial policy, this is a remarkable judgment as the ECJ reverses precedent on the basis of an evolutive interpretation of Community law recapturing the spirit of *les Verts*[356] and *Chernobyl*,[357] only this time in the social field. The applicant in the main proceedings was a French national who had completed his secondary education in the UK living with his grandmother but whose application for a student loan to study in the UK had been rejected on the ground that he did not fall within the scope of Regulation No 1612/68. The argument submitted by several governments and endorsed by the Commission was that, in accordance with Article 18(1) EC, the situation of EU citizens falls within the scope of application of the Treaty, only subject to the limitations and conditions laid down in the Treaty and by the measures adopted to give it effect. This is after all stated expressly in Article 18(1).[358] These measures include Directive 93/96 on the right of residence of students, Article 3 of which excludes the right to payment of maintenance grants. The Court held however that Article 3 of the Directive does not preclude a national of a Member State who, by virtue of Article 18 EC and Directive 90/364 on the right of residence,[359] is lawfully resident in the territory of another Member State where he intends to start or pursue higher education, from relying during that residence on the fundamental principle of equal treatment enshrined in Article 12(1).[360]

The Court then proceeded to examine whether UK law was discriminatory on grounds of nationality. Under the UK regulations, persons who were not covered by Regulation No 1612/68 could claim student loans only if they satisfied the following conditions: they were settled in the UK for the purposes of national law, they resided in England on the first day of the first academic year, and had been so resident for the preceding three years. The Court held that the first and the third of those conditions were likely to be more easily satisfied by UK nationals and thus risked placing at a disadvantage primarily nationals from other Member States. It

---

[355] *Dany Bidar, op. cit.*, n. 70 above.

[356] Case 294/83 *Partie Ecologiste 'Les Verts' v European Parliament* [1986] ECR 1339.

[357] Case C-70/88 *Parliament v Council (Chernobyl case)* [1990] ECR I-2041.

[358] Article 18(1) states: 'Every citizen of the Union shall have the right to move and reside freely within the territory of the Member States, subject to the limitations and conditions laid down in this Treaty and by the measures adopted to give it effect.'   [359] *Op. cit.*

[360] *Bidar, op. cit.*, para 46.

then examined whether these conditions could be objectively justified and reached a negative conclusion. The Court accepted that it is permissible for a Member State to grant assistance to students from other Member States subject to the requirement that they have demonstrated 'a certain degree of integration into the society of that State'.[361] This was justified to ensure that support for students did not impose an unreasonable burden on the host State which could upset the overall level of assistance available to students.

The guarantee of sufficient integration was ensured by the requirement of three-year residence. The Court however took issue with the additional requirement that non-nationals are entitled to assistance only if they are settled in the United Kingdom. This requirement, as applied in UK law, precluded any possibility of a national of another Member State obtaining settled status as a student. Its effect was thus to prevent a Community national who is lawfully resident and has received a substantial part of his secondary education in the host Member State, and has consequently established a genuine link with its society, from being able to pursue his studies under the same conditions as nationals of that State.[362]

Grzelczyk and *Bidar* aptly illustrate the impact of European citizenship on the interpretation of Article 12. The judgments leave open a number of issues. An interesting question is whether, and if so under what circumstances, a Member State may provide financial assistance for the payment of tuition fees to non-resident nationals without extending it to nationals of other Member States. The issue also arises as to what obligations Article 12 imposes on the Member State of origin. The cases discussed so far concern obligations imposed on the State of destination. Since financial assistance to cover tuition fees falls within the scope of Article 12, could it be said that a Community national has a right to receive such assistance from his Member State of origin to study in another Member State where such assistance is available to him to study in the State of origin? The answer seems to be in the negative. Where a Member State refuses financial assistance to one of its nationals in order to enable him to study in another Member State, it does not discriminate on grounds of nationality. It would be otherwise if the national intended to pursue studies in a private institution, namely one which is not financed mainly by public funds. In such a case, the prospective student would be a recipient of services and might be entitled to take advantage of Article 49.[363] Such a right however would be subject to proportionate and non-discriminatory restrictions objectively justified in the public interest.[364]

2.9.2.2. Intellectual property rights

In *Phil Collins*,[365] the Court held that copyright and related rights fall within the scope of application of the Treaty for the purposes of Article 12. German law

---

[361] *Ibid.*, para 57.   [362] *Ibid.*, para 62.
[363] See Case C-109/92 *Wirth* [1993] ECR I-6447, esp. at pp. 6460–63 *per* Darmon AG.
[364] See the medical services cases: Case C-157/99 *Geraets-Smits and Peerbooms* [2001] ECR I-5473; Case C-368/98 *Vanbraekel and Others* [2001] ECR I-5363.   [365] *Op. cit.*, n. 303 above.

enabled German nationals to oppose the unauthorised reproduction of their musical performances irrespective of the territory where the performance took place but limited such protection of foreign artists to performances given in Germany. Referring to its previous case law, the Court held that exclusive rights conferred by literary and artistic property affect trade in goods and services as well as competition in the Community. It followed that such rights, although governed by national law, are subject to the requirements of the Treaty and fall within the scope of its application. The Court held that, giving effect to the principle of non-discrimination, German courts must enable performing artists of other Member States to prohibit the marketing in Germany of unauthorised performances given outside German soil. The principle of non-discrimination can be relied on by an artist of a Member State or his successor in title.[366] As the Advocate General pointed out, even in the case of an outright assignment without any provision for the payment of royalties, it would be wrong to discriminate on the basis of the nationality of the performer, who is the original right-holder, since the indirect victim of discrimination remains the performer himself.[367] Although *Phil Collins* referred only to copyright and related rights, there can be no doubt that intellectual property rights in general fall within the scope of application of the Treaty and, where they are not covered by any specific provision, are subject to Article 12.

In *Tod's SpA and Tod's France Sarl v Heyraud SA*,[368] it was held that the provision of the Berne Convention[369] under which works protected in their Member State of origin solely as designs and models are entitled in another Member State only to such protection as is granted there to designs and models and may thus not claim the higher protection offered by copyright law in that State runs counter to Article 12. The Court viewed this as a case of indirect discrimination. It held that by adopting a distinguishing criterion based on the country of origin of the work, the Berne Convention created a difference in treatment based on nationality. According to the Convention, in the case of unpublished work, the country of origin is the State of which the author is a national. In the case of published work, the country of origin is essentially the country where the work was first published. The Court pointed out that the author of a work first published in a Member State will, in the majority of cases, be a national of that State, whereas the author of a work published in another Member State will generally be a person who is not a national of the first Member State. There was therefore an indirect difference in treatment based on nationality. Such difference in treatment was not justified for

---

[366] In Case C-360/00 *Ricordi* [2002] ECR I-5089, the ECJ held that the fact that the author has died when the EEC Treaty entered into force in the Member State of which he was a national does not preclude the application of Article 12(1) EC.   [367] *Op. cit.*, at p. 5170.

[368] *Op. cit.*, n. 319 above. See also *Ricordi, op. cit.* In that case the ECJ held that Article 12 precludes the term of protection granted by the legislation of a Member State to the works of an author who is a national of another Member State from being shorter than the term granted to the works of its own nationals.

[369] See Berne Convention for the Protection of Literary and Artistic Works (Paris Act of 24 July 1971), as amended on 28 September 1979.

the following reason. Article 2(7) of the Convention contained a rule of reciprocity under which a country of the Union grants national treatment, that is to say, protection based on designs and models and copyright, only if the country of origin of the work also does so. However, the implementation of the obligations imposed on Member States by Community law cannot be made subject to a condition of reciprocity. It followed that, in the absence of any objective justification, there was a breach of Article 12 EC.

2.9.2.3. Judicial proceedings

In a number of cases the Court has had the opportunity to examine the compatibility with Article 12 of national rules pertaining to judicial proceedings. In *Data Delecta and Forsberg*[370] in issue was a rule of Swedish law which required a foreign plaintiff not resident in Sweden to furnish security to guarantee payment of the costs of the judicial proceedings which the plaintiff might be ordered to pay. The Court held that the Swedish rule was liable to affect the economic activities of traders from other Member States. Although it was not, as such, intended to regulate an activity of commercial nature, its effect was to place such traders in a less advantageous position than Swedish nationals as regards access to domestic courts. The Court pointed out that a corollary of the free movement of goods and services is that traders from other Member States must be able, in order to resolve any disputes arising from their economic activities, to bring actions in the courts of a Member State in the same way as nationals of that State. It held that Article 12 prohibits a Member State from requiring a person established in another Member State, who has brought before one of its own courts an action against one of its own nationals, to lodge security for the costs of those proceedings where no such requirement is imposed on persons established in the first Member State and where the action is concerned with the exercise of fundamental freedoms guaranteed by Community law.

It follows from *Data Delecta* that any rule of national law, whether substantive or procedural, which bears even an indirect effect on trade in goods and services between Member States falls within the scope of Community law for the purposes of the application of Article 12.[371] *Data Delecta* goes further than the previous judgment in *Mund & Fester*[372] where the Court had found incompatible with Community law a German rule which authorized the seizure of assets of a foreign plaintiff as a precautionary measure. In that case the German provision was held to be incompatible with Articles 12 and 293 of the Treaty in combination with the Brussels Convention. In *Data Delecta* the Court held, following *Cowan* and *Phil Collins*, that the right to equal treatment cannot be made subject to the existence of international agreements concluded by the Member States.

Subsequently, however, in *Hayes v Kronenberger GmbH*[373] the Court hinted that the Brussels and the Lugano Conventions may be relevant in this respect. Germany

---

[370] *Op. cit.*, n. 313 above.   [371] *Ibid.*, para 15.
[372] Case C-398/92 *Mund & Fester* [1994] ECR I-467; see also *Hubbard, op. cit.*, n. 306 above.
[373] *Op. cit.*, n. 313 above.

argued that the requirement that the plaintiff must lodge security for judicial costs is justified where an order for judicial costs cannot be enforced in the country of the plaintiff's domicile. In such a case, the requirement to lodge security is designed to avoid a foreign plaintiff being able to bring proceedings without running any financial risk should he lose his case. The Court pointed out that not all Member States are parties to the Brussels and Lugano Conventions and that, as a result, as between some Member States, it will be more difficult to enforce an order for costs made in a Member State against non-residents. It held, however, that it was not necessary for the purposes of the proceedings to consider whether that situation might warrant the imposition of security for costs on non-residents. It focused on the German rule of procedure in a question which applied to foreign nationals. It held that, insofar as that rule imposed different treatment depending on the plaintiff's nationality, it ran counter to the principle of proportionality. On the one hand, it could not secure payment of judicial costs in every trans-frontier case since security could not be required from a German plaintiff not residing in Germany and having no assets there. On the other hand, it was excessive because a non-German plaintiff who resided and had assets in Germany could also be required to furnish security. Notably, in *Chequepoint SARL v McClelland and another*[374] the English Court of Appeal held that a court order requiring an impecunious foreign company ordinarily resident in another Member State to provide security for costs was not discriminatory contrary to Community law since an English company in a similar position would be treated in the same manner and might be required to provide security for costs under the Companies Act 1985.

The application of Article 12 to criminal proceedings was examined in *Pastoors and Trans-Cap*.[375] Belgian law provided for criminal penalties for breach of Community regulations in the field of road transport. Under the Belgian rules, a person found in breach of Regulation No 3820/85 or 3821/85 had the option to pay immediately a fine of 10,000 francs per breach or face criminal proceedings. A person who did not have a permanent residence in Belgium, however, could not choose the second option unless he lodged a deposit of 15,000 francs per breach to cover the amount of any possible fine and ensuing legal costs. Failure to do so led to the impounding of his vehicle at his risk and expense. The Court started by pointing out that, although Belgian law established differential treatment on the basis of residence and not on nationality, it was liable to operate mainly to the detriment of foreign nationals and was therefore indirectly discriminatory. The Court accepted that it was objectively justified to require non-resident offenders to lodge a security. That requirement would prevent them from avoiding an effective penalty simply by declaring that they do not consent to the immediate levying of the fine and opting for criminal proceedings. It found the Belgian rules however contrary to the principle of proportionality. It pointed out that the sum of the deposit was 50 per cent higher than the fine payable immediately to extinguish prosecution. Also,

---

[374] [1997] 2 All ER 384.   [375] *Op. cit.*, n. 317 above.

a deposit was demanded separately in relation to each infringement with which the offender was charged. However, where various infringements are simultaneously found to exist, they give rise to a single set of proceedings. In a subsequent case the ECJ held that Article 207 of the Italian Highway Code which imposed a disproportionate difference in treatment between offenders based on the place of registration of their vehicles runs counter to Article 12.[376]

Finally, in *Bickel and Franz*[377] the Court held that Article 12 requires a Member State which grants residents in part of its territory the right to use a language other than its official language in criminal proceedings against them to extend that right to nationals of other Member States visiting that territory, if they have that language as their mother tongue.

2.9.2.4. European citizenship

The conclusion to be drawn from the above cases is that by creative case law the Court of Justice has developed Article 12 to an autonomous source of rights and obligations beyond the sphere of the internal market strictly understood, which encompasses a diverse range of situations and whose outer limits remain elusive. In some areas, such as education, the normative prohibition of discrimination on grounds of nationality has been used as a vehicle to extend the scope of Community law to areas traditionally considered immune from Community obligations and has acted as the precursor to future Community legislation. In other cases, such as *Phil Collins* and the cases on judicial costs, Article 12 has become an instrument for attaining equal standards of judicial protection in the host State.

In more recent case law, Article 12 has been used to complement European citizenship and co-found a new generation of equal treatment rights. The case law has proclaimed that citizenship of the Union 'is destined to be the fundamental status of nationals of the Member States'[378] and viewed it as an autonomous source of rights. The link between Article 12 and Union citizenship was made for the first time in *Martinez Sala*.[379] Mrs Sala, a Spanish national resident in Germany, had been denied a child raising allowance because she did not have a formal residence permit. Her presence in Germany was lawful in that she could not be deported. She had held residence permits in the past and, at the material time, a certificate that she had applied for one. The important issue in *Martinez Sala* was not the existence of discrimination, which the German Government did not deny, but whether the situation fell *ratione personae* within the scope of the Treaty. The Court's response

---

[376] *Commission v Italy, op. cit.*, n. 319 above. The Italian legislation provided that where a breach of the highway code was committed with a vehicle registered in Italy, the offender had 60 days in which to pay the penalty or bring an appeal whilst, if a breach was committed with a vehicle registered in another State, the offender either had to pay the penalty immediately or, if he wished to contest the infringement, provide security equal to twice the minimum amount on pain of having his driving licence confiscated or his vehicle impounded.

[377] Case C-274/96 *Bickel and Franz* [1998] ECR I-7637.

[378] See Case C-413/99 *Baumbast and R* [2002] ECR I-7091, para 82; *Grzelczyk, op. cit.*, n. 352 above, para 31.   [379] Case C-85/96 *Martinez Sala* [1998] ECR I-2691.

was that, even if Mrs Sala was not a worker within the meaning of Article 34 EC, she came within the scope *ratione personae* of the provisions on European citizenship as a national of a Member State lawfully residing in the territory of another Member State. She could therefore rely on the rights deriving from European citizenship, including Article 12 EC.

Martinez Sala signalled the importance of Union citizenship as a new legal status from which autonomous rights could be derived beyond the rights flowing from free movement. The ECJ performed a quantum leap making the transition from Article 12 as a tool of integration to Article 12 as an instrument of citizen empowerment and solidarity. We saw above that this was trend was followed in cases such as *Grzelczyk* and *Bidar*.

A further example of the interaction between Article 12 and Article 17 EC[380] is provided by *Garcia Avello v Etat Belge*.[381] The case involved Mr Garcia Avello, a Spanish national, and Mrs Weber, a Belgian national, who were living in Belgium. In accordance with Belgian law, which provides that a child bears the surname of his father, their children were given the surname Garcia Avello. When their parents sought to have their surname changed to Garcia Weber, to comply with Spanish usage, their request was rejected on the ground that in Belgium requests to add the mother's name are habitually denied. The ECJ held that, although citizenship of the Union does not bring within the scope of Community law situations purely internal to a Member State, there was a link with Community law since the children had dual nationality. They could therefore rely on Article 12 so as not to suffer discrimination on grounds of nationality with regard to the rules governing their surname. The Court understood Article 12 as prohibiting the similar treatment of dissimilar situations. It pointed out that Belgian nationals who also have Spanish nationality are in a different situation from persons who have only Belgian nationality since the former have different surnames under the two legal systems. The children had been refused the right to bear the surname which resulted from the application of Spanish law. The Court stated that discrepancy in surnames is liable to cause serious inconvenience at both professional and private levels resulting, for example, from the legal effects of diplomas and documents drawn up in the surname recognized in another Member State of which they are also nationals.

Thus, the Court established that Belgian law discriminated potentially against the children by treating them in the same way as children having only Belgian nationality although their circumstances were different. It then proceeded to determine whether there was objective justification for such differential treatment

---

[380] Article 17 states as follows: '1. Citizenship of the Union is hereby established. Every person holding the nationality of a Member State shall be a citizen of the Union. Citizenship of the Union shall complement and not replace national citizenship.
'2. Citizens of the Union shall enjoy the rights conferred by this Treaty and shall be subject to the duties imposed thereby.'
[381] Case C-148/02 *Garcia Avello v Etat Belge*, judgment of 2 October 2003. For other cases, see e.g. *Grzelczyk, op. cit.*

and came to the conclusion that there was none. Neither the principle of immutability of surnames nor the argument that Belgian law in fact facilitated integration of foreign nationals into domestic social life provided sufficient justification for the difference in treatment.

The case is important for two reasons. First, in the name of EU citizenship, it makes great intrusion into the national laws governing surnames contrary to what previous cases had suggested.[382] Second, it departs from the customary rule of international law that, in relations with its nationals who also have the nationality of another country, a State is permitted to give precedence to its own nationality. The judgment is motivated partly by the need to avoid obstacles to free movement arising from discrepancies in the national laws governing surnames. It does not however remove such discrepancies. It is not clear why Spanish law should take priority over Belgian law. One wonders if children in the same circumstances living in Spain could claim against the Spanish authorities the right to have only the surname of their father and not both the paternal and maternal surnames to ensure compliance with Belgian law. In effect, the judgment does not promote uniformity of surnames within the EU but the freedom of the individual to choose a surname.

The use of Article 12 as an instrument of social solidarity was evident in *Trojani*.[383] The Court reiterated that the right of residence conferred by Article 18(1) EC[384] to all EU nationals is not unconditional and that a Member State may make residence in its territory of a Union citizen who is not economically active conditional on his having sufficient resources. It added however that a Union citizen who is not economically active may rely on Article 12 EC if he has been lawfully resident in the host Member State for a certain time or possesses a residence permit. Thus national legislation which refuses a social assistance benefit to citizens of other Member States even though they satisfy the conditions required by nationals of that State constitutes discrimination on grounds of nationality. This is potentially a far-reaching judgment which illustrates the effect of Union citizenship and the prohibition of discrimination on grounds of nationality as a double-edged sword.[385] Union citizenship gives rise to autonomous rights, thus bringing certain situations which would not otherwise be covered within the scope of the Treaty. Although these rights may be limited, any limitations imposed must comply with the fundamental principle of Article 12.[386]

---

[382] See Case C-168/91 *Konstantinidis* [1993] ECR I-1191.

[383] Case C-456/02 *Trojani v CPAS*, judgment of 7 September 2004.

[384] For the text of Article 18(1) EC, see above n. 358.

[385] The ECJ reiterated its caveat in *Grzelczyk* that it is open to the host Member State to take the view that a national of another Member State who has recourse to social assistance no longer fulfils the conditions for his right of residence and may thus be removed: see para 45 of the judgment and *Grzelczyk, op. cit.*, paras 42 and 43.

[386] *Collins v Secretary of State for Work and Pensions, op. cit.*, n. 318 above. In that case, it was held that the host State may make a social security benefit, such as a job seeker's allowance, conditional on the person concerned establishing a genuine link with the employment market of the host State, which may be determined by establishing that the person has for a reasonable period resided

2.9.3. Article 12, second paragraph

The second paragraph of Article 12 mandates the Council to adopt rules designed to prohibit discrimination on grounds of nationality.[387] Article 7(2), the predecessor to Article 12(2), was considered by the Court in the *Students' right of residence Directive* case.[388] The Parliament sought annulment of Directive 90/366 on the right of residence for students,[389] which had been adopted by the Council on the basis of Article 235 (now 308), on the ground that it should have been adopted on the basis of the second paragraph of Article 7.[390] The Directive sought to provide students from other Member States with a right of residence in the host Member State for the duration of their studies. The Council argued that because the Directive extended the right of residence to the student's spouse and dependent children it conferred upon students a freedom of movement which was similar to that of migrant workers and went beyond a right of residence for the purposes of vocational training. Consequently, the Council claimed that Article 7 (now 12) provided an insufficient basis for the adoption of the Directive. The Court held that measures adopted under the second paragraph of Article 7 (now 12) need not be limited to the implementation of the right of non-discrimination strictly understood but may also cover aspects which are necessary for the effective exercise of that right. It pointed out that the right of residence conferred upon the spouse and dependent children was an essential element for the genuine exercise of the student's right to residence. On that basis, the Court held that the Council should have adopted the Directive on the basis of Article 7 (now 12). In compliance with the ruling, the Council subsequently adopted another directive containing identical provisions on the correct legal basis.[391]

---

in the host State and genuinely sought work there. However, the residence requirement can be justified only if it is founded on the basis of objective criteria which are laid down in advance, independent of the nationality of the persons concerned, and proportionate to the legitimate aim of the national provisions.

[387] The corresponding provision of the EU Constitution is Article III-123 which states that European laws or framework laws may lay down rules to prohibit discrimination on grounds of nationality as referred to in Article 1–4(2) of the Constitution.

[388] Case C-295/90 *Parliament v Council* [1992] ECR I-4193.

[389] OJ 1990 L 180, p. 30. Until that Directive was adopted, the second paragraph of Article 7 had never been used as the only legal basis for a Community act although it had occasionally been used in combination with other provisions. See e.g. Regulation No 2001/76 laying down a common structural policy for the fishing industry, OJ 1976 L 20/19.

[390] At that time, Article 7(2) provided for the adoption of measures via the cooperation procedure. Note that, following the Treaty of Amsterdam, measures under Article 12(2) are now adopted by the co-decision procedure which gives the Parliament an enhanced role in the decision-making process.

[391] Directive 93/96, OJ 1993 L 317, p. 59. See now Directive 2004/38 on the right of citizens of the Union and their family members to move and reside freely within the territory of the Member States (OJ 2004 L 229/35) which replaces Directive 93/96 on students together with Directive 90/364 with effect from 30 April 2006.

3

The Principle of Proportionality: Review of Community Measures

3.1. The principle of proportionality and its function in Community law

At its most abstract level, the principle of proportionality requires that action undertaken must be proportionate to its objectives. The notion of proportionality goes back to ancient times[1] but as a general principle of law in modern legal systems it is inspired by ideas underpinning liberal democracy, in particular, the concern to protect the individual *vis-à-vis* the State and the premise that regulatory intervention must be suitable to achieve its aims.[2] The principle was developed in continental legal systems, especially in Germany and France, in the 20th century. Its development as a ground for review can be seen as the judiciary's response to the growth of administrative powers and the augmentation of administrative discretion.[3] The principle found only limited expression in the Treaty of Rome[4] but has been developed by the Court as a fundamental principle deriving from the rule of law[5] and requiring in particular that 'the individual should not have his freedom of action limited beyond the degree necessary in the public interest'.[6] Although the

---

[1] The spirit of the principle is encapsulated in the ancient Greek dictum '*pan metron ariston*'.

[2] J. Schwarze, *European Administrative Law* (Sweet & Maxwell, 1992), p. 679.

[3] In German law it is known as *Verhältnismassigkeit* and, according to the case law of the Federal Constitutional Court, it underlies certain provisions of the Basic Law. For a review of the principle in Community law and the laws of the Member States, see N. Emiliou, *The Principle of Proportionality in European Law* (Kluwer, 1996); Schwarze, *op. cit.*, pp. 680 *et seq*. See further Tridimas, 'The Principle of Proportionality in Community Law: From the Rule of Law to Market Integration', (1996) 31 The Irish Jurist, 83; G. de Bùrca, 'The Principle of Proportionality and its Application in EC Law' (1993) 13 YEL 105. For the application of the principle in the European Convention on Human Rights, see, *inter alia*, Schwarze, *op. cit.*, pp. 704 *et seq*.; C. Picheral and A.D. Olinga, 'La théorie de la marge d'appréciation dans la jurisprudence récente de la Cour européenne des droits de l'homme', (1995) RTrim Dr Homme, 567; L. Adamovich, 'Marge d'appréciation du législateur et principe de proportionnalité dans l'appréciation des "restrictions prévues par la loi" au regard de la Convention européenne des droits de l'homme', (1991) Rtrim Dr Homme, 291.

[4] See now Article 5(3) EC. The case law has held that, among others, the following provisions incorporate a proportionality standard: Articles 34(2), 134, 284 and those providing for derogations to the fundamental freedoms, i.e. Articles 30, 39(3), 46, 55 EC.

[5] Case 4/73 *Nold v Commission* [1974] ECR 491, at pp. 513–514 *per* Trabbucchi AG.

[6] Case 11/70 *Internationale Handelsgesellschaft v Einfuhr- und Vorratsstelle Getreide* [1970] ECR 1125 at 1147 *per* de Lamothe AG.

principle is particularly important in the field of economic law, in its case law the Court has applied it in diverse areas including, for example, remedies and interim measures,[7] and external trade,[8] so that it now permeates the whole of the Community legal system. As Jacobs AG stated 'there are few areas of Community law, if any at all, where [the principle of proportionality] is not relevant'.[9] The only cases where the Court appears reluctant to apply the principle are where it is invoked in an attempt to justify a failure to comply with Community law.[10] In addition, the application of the principle is severely restricted in the following cases. First, where the jurisdiction of the ECJ itself is excluded under the founding Treaties, for example under Article 68(2) EC on matters of visas, asylum and immigration. Second, where the Treaty excludes specifically the application of the principle of proportionality by the ECJ. This occurs in Article 35(5) TEU which pertains to Third Pillar matters. Even in such cases, however, it may be argued that what is precluded is the application of proportionality by the ECJ and not its application by the national courts which may, and indeed must, apply the principle within the limits of their jurisdiction insofar as they are called upon to apply provisions which fall within the scope of Community law. More generally, a rule which does not in itself interfere with the interests of the individual is not capable of breaching the principle of proportionality.[11]

The principle of proportionality applies both to Community and to national measures and covers both legislative and administrative action. It can be said that in Community law, it fulfils three primary functions:

- it is used as a ground for review of Community measures;
- it is used as a ground for review of national measures affecting one of the fundamental freedoms;
- by virtue of Article 5(3) of the Treaty, it governs the exercise by the Community of its legislative competence.

It should be emphasised that the underlying interests which proportionality seeks to protect in each of the above cases are different. As a result, the intensity of review exercised by the Court varies considerably. Where proportionality is invoked as a ground for review of Community policy measures, the Court is called upon to

---

[7] See e.g. Case C-12/95 P *Transactiones Maritimas and Others v Commission* [1995] ECR I-467; C-149/95 P(R) *Commission v Atlantic Container Line and Others* [1995] ECR I-2165.

[8] See e.g. Case C-367/89 *Aime Richardt* [1991] ECR I-4621; Case C-111/92 *Lange* [1993] I-4677; Case C-26/90 *Wünsche II* [1991] ECR I-4961; Case 112/80 *Durbeck v Hauptzollamt Frankfurt am Main-Flughafen* [1981] ECR 1095.

[9] Case C-120/94 *Commission v Greece (FYROM Case)* [1996] ECR I-1513, p. 1533.

[10] Thus, in relation to State aids, the Court has held that the obligation to recover unlawful State aid with interest cannot in principle be regarded as disproportionate to the objectives of the provisions of the EC Treaty: Case 142/87 *Belgium v Commission (Tubemeuse case)* [1990] ECR I-959, para. 66; Case C-305/89 *Italy v Commission (Alfa Romeo case)*, [1991] ECR I-1603, para. 41; Case C-169/95 *Spain v Commission* [1997] ECR I-135, para 47.

[11] Case C-329/01 *The Queen on the application of British Sugar plc v Intervention Board for Agricultural Produce*, judgment of 19 February 2004, paras 59–60.

balance a private *vis-à-vis* a public interest. The underlying interest which the principle seeks to protect is the rights of the individual but, given the discretion of the legislature, review of policy measures is based on the so-called 'manifestly inappropriate' test. The Court will not strike down a measure unless it considers that it is manifestly inappropriate to achieve its objectives.[12] By contrast, where proportionality is invoked in order to challenge the compatibility with Community law of national measures affecting one of the fundamental freedoms, the Court is called upon to balance a Community *vis-à-vis* a national interest. The principle is applied as a market integration mechanism and the intensity of review is much stronger. It is based, at least in most cases, on the notion of 'necessity' exemplified by the 'less restrictive alternative' test. A national measure which affects the fundamental freedoms of the Treaty will be found incompatible with Community law unless it is necessary to achieve a legitimate aim and provided that that aim cannot be achieved by other measures which restrict less intra-Community trade.[13]

A distinct feature of recent case law is that the Court has expanded significantly its human rights jurisdiction. Thus, in assessing the compatibility of national measures with the Treaty freedoms, it concentrates not only on whether the measure in issue interferes excessively with inter-state trade but also on whether it imposes a disproportionate restriction on a fundamental right, such as for example, the right to family life or freedom of expression.[14]

By virtue of Article 5(3) of the EC Treaty, added by the Treaty on European Union, proportionality has been elevated to a fundamental principle underpinning the constitutional order of the Community. Article 5(3) was included in the Treaty primarily with a view to protecting the interests of Member States rather than the interests of the individual but has not added much to the case law. The intensity of review is, in general, no different from when the principle is applied as a ground for review of Community measures for the protection of the individual. The Court applies a soft proportionality test.[15]

As a ground for review of Community measures, proportionality has traditionally been applied in the case law mainly in the following areas: agricultural law, measures concerning the external trade of the Community, and measures imposing charges, penalties and sanctions. In recent years, its application has been particularly evident in relation to Community measures in the broader fields of health and consumer protection and harmonization measures for the establishment of the internal market. The present chapter discusses the application of the principle to

---

[12] The same test applies, as a general rule, where national authorities implement Community law. see Case C-120/97 *Upjohn v Licensing Authority* [1999] ECR I-223.   [13] See 5.3 below.

[14] See e.g. Case C-60/00 *Carpenter v Secretary of State for the Home Department*, judgment of 11 July 2002; Case C-413/99 *Baumbast and R v Secretary of State for the Home Department* [2002] ECR I-7091; Case C-109/01 *Secretary of State for the Home Department v Akrich*, judgment of 23 September 2003; C-112/00 *Schmidberger*, judgment of 12 June 2003; Case C-71/02 *Herbert Karner Industrie-Auktionen GmbH v Troostwijk GmbH*, judgment of 25 March 2004.

[15] See 4.1 below.

Community measures. Its application to national measures is examined in the next chapter. There is no attempt to deal exhaustively with the case law. The application of the principle in diverse areas is illustrated selectively.

3.2. What does proportionality entail?

The principle of proportionality requires that a measure must be appropriate and necessary to achieve its objectives. According to the standard formula used by the Court, in order to establish whether a provision of Community law is consonant with the principle of proportionality, it is necessary to establish whether the means it employs to achieve the aim correspond to the importance of the aim and whether they are necessary for its achievement.[16] Thus, the principle comprises two tests: a test of suitability and a test of necessity. The first refers to the relationship between the means and the end. The means employed by the measure must be suitable, namely reasonably likely, to achieve its objectives. The second is one of weighing competing interests. The Court assesses the adverse consequences that the measure has on an interest worthy of legal protection and determines whether those consequences are justified in view of the importance of the objective pursued. It has been said that the application of the principle of proportionality entails in effect a three-part test.[17] First, it must be established whether the measure is suitable to achieve a legitimate aim (test of suitability). Second, it must be established whether the measure is necessary to achieve that aim, namely, whether there are other less restrictive means capable of producing the same result (the least restrictive alternative test). Third, even if there are no less restrictive means, it must be established that the measure does not have an excessive effect on the applicant's interests (proportionality *stricto sensu*). The tripartite test has received some judicial support[18] but in practice the Court does not distinguish in its analysis between the second and the third test. Also, as it will be shown, in some cases the Court finds that a measure is compatible with proportionality without searching for less restrictive alternatives or even where such alternatives seem to exist. The essential characteristic of the principle is that the Court performs a balancing exercise between the objectives pursued by the measure in issue and its adverse effects on individual freedom.

[16] See e.g. Case 66/82 *Fromançais v Forma* [1983] ECR 395, para 8; Case 15/83 *Denkavit Nederland v Hoofdproduktschap voor Akkerbouwprodukten* [1984] ECR 2171, para. 25; Case 47/86 *Roquette Frères v ONIC* [1987] ECR 2889, para 19; Case 56/86 *Société pour l'exportation des sucres* [1987] ECR 1423, para 28; Case 281/84 *Zuckerfabrik Bedburg v Council* [1987] ECR 49, para 36; Case C-358/88 *Oberhausener Kraftfutterwerk Wilhelm Hopermann GmbH v Bundesanstalt für landwirtschaftliche Marktordnung* [1990] ECR I-1687, para 13.

[17] G. de Burca, *op. cit.*, n. 3 above, at 113. See also C. Tomuschat, 'Le principe de proportionnalité: *Quis iudicabit?*' (1977) 13 CDE 97.

[18] See the Opinion of van Gerven AG in Case C-159/90 *SPUC v Grogan* [1991] ECR I-4685 and the Opinion of Mischo AG in Case C-331/88 *Fedesa and Others* [1990] ECR I-4023, at 4051; see 3.4 and 3.6 below.

The principle of proportionality requires that the burdens imposed on an individual must not exceed what is necessary to achieve the objectives pursued. In assessing what is necessary, account must be taken of the specific circumstances of the case. In the context of an agricultural policy measure, Capotorti AG stated that whether a measure exceeds what is necessary must be appraised in the light of the economic and social conditions, having regard to the means available.[19] Clearly, however, that does not prevent the Community legislature from adopting rules of general application. The Court has held that although, in exercising their powers, the Community institutions must ensure that the amounts which commercial operators are charged are no greater than is required to achieve the desired objective, it does not necessarily follow that that obligation must be measured in relation to the individual situation of any one particular group of operators. Given the multiplicity and complexity of economic circumstances, such an evaluation would not only be impossible to achieve but would also create perpetual uncertainty in the law.[20]

Proportionality as a ground for review differs from misuse of powers in that it involves an objective rather than a subjective test. In applying proportionality, the Court performs a balancing exercise guided by the tests of suitability and necessity. By contrast, in order to establish that an act is vitiated by misuse of powers the applicant must prove that the institution which adopted the act did so in order to pursue a purpose other than that which it is lawfully entitled to pursue. The allegation of misuse of powers therefore, unlike proportionality, involves an enquiry as to the motives of the author of the act.[21]

The application of the tests of suitability and necessity enable the Court to review not only the legality but also, to some extent, the merits of legislative and administrative measures. Because of that distinct characteristic, proportionality is often perceived to be the most far-reaching ground for review, the most potent weapon in the arsenal of the public law judge. It will be noted however that much depends on how strictly a court applies the tests of suitability and necessity and how far it is prepared to defer to the choices of the authority which has adopted the measure in issue. As already stated, in Community law, far from dictating a uniform test, proportionality is a flexible principle which is used in different contexts to protect different interests and entails varying degrees of judicial scrutiny. Subject to this *caveat*, it is correct to say that in general the principle of proportionality goes further than *Wednesbury* unreasonableness and facilitates the

---

[19] Case 114/76 *Bela-Muhle v Grows-Farm* [1977] ECR 1211, at p. 1232 *per* Capotorti AG.

[20] See e.g. Case 5/73 *Balkan-Import-Export v Hauptzollamt Berlin-Packhof* [1973] ECR 1091, para. 22; Case 9/73 *Schlüter v Hauptzollamt Lorrach* [1973] ECR 1135, para. 22; Joined Cases 154/78 etc. *Valsabbia v Commission* [1980] ECR 907, para. 118. For similar limitations on the principle of equal treatment, see above, Ch. 2.

[21] See T. Hartley, *The Foundations of European Community Law*, 5th Ed, (Oxford University Press, 2003) pp. 420–1. Hartley's view received judicial endorsement in Joined Cases C-133, C-300 and C-362/93 *Crispoltoni* [1994] ECR I-4863, by Jacobs AG at p. 4874, and implicitly by the Court at paras 23–29 of the judgment.

application of higher standards of judicial scrutiny than those traditionally followed by English courts.[22]

3.3. The development of the principle in Community law

As a ground for review, the principle of proportionality was first developed by the Court to counter-balance the effects of market-regulation measures restricting economic freedom adopted under the ECSC Treaty. In *Fédéchar v High Authority*[23] decided in 1956, the Court referred to 'a generally-accepted rule of law' according to which the 'reaction by the High Authority to illegal action must be in proportion to the scale of that action'. An indirect reference to the principle was made in *Mannesmann*, where the Court held that,[24]

the High Authority, in working out and applying the financial arrangements which it has established to safeguard the stability of the market, has . . . a duty to take account of the actual economic circumstances in which these arrangements have to be applied, so that the aims pursued may be attained under the most favourable conditions and with the smallest possible sacrifices by the undertakings affected.

The principle was applied in early years also in staff cases.[25] It was not until 1971, however, that proportionality was expressly relied on by the Court. The opportunity became available in the field of agriculture. In *Internationale Handelsgesellschaft*,[26] it was argued that the system of deposits accompanying import and export licences[27] infringed the principle of proportionality. Although on the facts the Court found that no breach had occurred, the judgment firmly established the

---

[22] Traditionally, English courts did not accept proportionality as a ground for review. For an express rejection of the principle by the House of Lords, see *R v Home Secretary, ex p Brind* [1991] 1 AC 696. In recent years, however, proportionality has been applied by domestic courts as an integral part of the judicial enquiry where Community rights are at stake or where rights under the Human Rights Act 1988 are invoked. See, e.g. *Commissioners of Customs and Excise v Newbury* [2003] EuR 476; *R (Hoverspeed) v Commissioners of Customs and Excise* [2002] EuLR 668; *International Transport Roth v Secretary of State for the Home Department* [2002] EWCA Civ 158. In effect, the principle seems to have percolated through English administrative law and been applied, to a greater or lesser extent, by English courts. For a discussion of the role of the principle in English law, see P. Craig, *Administrative Law*, Fifth Ed., 2003, pp. 411 *et seq.* and pp. 617 *et seq.* See further S. de Smith, H. Woolf and J. Jowell, *Judicial Review of Administrative Action*, Fifth Ed. (Sweet & Maxwell), pp. 593 *et seq.* See also J. Jowell and A. Lester, 'Proportionality: neither novel nor dangerous' in (1988) CLP Special Issue, *New Directions in Judicial Review*, 51; S. Boyron, 'Proportionality in English Administrative Law: A Faulty Translation?' (1992) 12 OJLS 237.

[23] Case 8/55 *Fédération Charbonnière Belgique v High Authority* [1954–56] ECR 292 at 299.

[24] Case 19/61 *Mannesmann AG v High Authority* [1962] ECR 357 at 370–371. See also Case 15/57 *Hauts Fourneaux de Chasse v High Authority* [1957–58] ECR 211 at 228.

[25] See e.g. Case 18/63 *Wollast v EEC* [1964] ECR 97 at 99.

[26] *Op. cit.*, n. 6 above. See also Case 25/70 *Einfuhr- und Vorratsstelle v Koster* [1970] ECR 1161; Case 26/70 *Einfuhr- und Vorratsstelle v Henck* [1970] ECR 1183.

[27] For the system of deposits, see 3.5.5. below.

principle as a ground for review. Dutheillet de Lamothe AG stated that 'citizens may only have imposed on them, for the purposes of the public interest, obligations which are strictly necessary for those purposes to be attained'.[28] He took the view that the principle forms part of Community law in the field of agriculture by virtue of Article 40(3) (now 34(2)) EC and more widely by virtue of the general principles of Community law which derive from the national legal systems.[29] The distinctive characteristics of proportionality, which the Court elaborated in subsequent cases, were laid down in the judgment in that case. After *Internationale Handelsgesellschaft*, the application of the principle as a ground for review gradually expanded beyond administrative and executive discretion to cover policy measures of general application.

The development of the principle as a ground for review of national measures followed a somewhat different pattern. At an early stage the case law made it clear that a national measure could not take advantage of a derogation from the fundamental freedoms unless it was strictly necessary to achieve the objectives in view.[30] Proportionality however began to acquire particular importance in the early 1980s. Two reasons account for that development. The first relates to the increase in litigation. As national jurisdictions became more familiar with Community law, litigation before the Court of Justice increased and so correspondingly did reliance on proportionality as a ground for challenging national measures. The second reason relates to a fundamental shift in judicial policy. The extension of Article 28 to encompass non-discriminatory national measures, firmly established in the seminal *Cassis de Dijon*,[31] brought a vast range of national provisions within the scope of that Article, which hitherto were considered 'safe' from the point of view of Community law. The emancipation of Article 28 from the notion of discrimination elevated proportionality to the determining criterion of compatibility with Community law. Similar developments followed in the context of the free movement of services and persons.[32]

3.4. Review of policy measures: The 'manifestly inappropriate' test

Although the Court is prepared to assess whether a measure is appropriate and necessary in view of all relevant circumstances and to scrutinize the way the institution concerned has exercised its discretion, where it comes to the adoption of legislative measures involving economic policy choices, it will defer to the

---

[28] *Internationale Handelsgesellschaft, op. cit.*, p.1146.   [29] *Ibid.*, p.1147.
[30] See e.g. Case 41/74 *Van Duyn v Home Office* [1974] ECR 1337.
[31] Case 120/78 *Rewe-Zentrale AG v Bundesmonopolverwaltung für Branntwein* [1979] ECR 649.
[32] See e.g. Case C-76/90 *Säger v Société Dennemeyer & Co. Ltd* [1991] ECR I-4221, Case C-415/93 *Union Royale Belge des Sociétés de Football Association and Others v Bosman and Others* [1995] ECR I-4921. See below, Chapter 5.

expertise and the responsibility of the adopting institution exercising only 'marginal review'.[33] In *Fedesa*,[34] it held that the lawfulness of the prohibition of an economic activity is subject to the condition that the prohibitory measures are appropriate and necessary in order to achieve the objectives legitimately pursued by the legislation. Where there is a choice between several appropriate measures, recourse must be had to the least onerous and the disadvantages caused must not be disproportionate to the aims pursued. The Court qualified that principle, however, by stating:[35]

with regard to judicial review of compliance with those conditions it must be stated that in matters concerning the common agricultural policy the Community legislature has a discretionary power which corresponds to the political responsibilities given to it by Articles 40 and 43 of the Treaty. Consequently, the legality of a measure adopted in that sphere can be affected only if the measure is manifestly inappropriate having regard to the objective which the competent institution is seeking to pursue . . . .

The expression 'manifestly inappropriate'[36] delineates what the Court perceives to be the limits of judicial function with regard to review of measures involving choices of economic policy. In fact, the test is rather reminiscent of that which the Court was directed to follow under Article 33(1) of the ECSC Treaty.[37] The test grants to the Community institutions ample discretion and applies to both aspects of proportionality, i.e. suitability and necessity. Although in a number of cases the suitability and effectiveness of a measure has been contested,[38] argument concentrates usually on the requirement of necessity. Necessity is more important because, in applying the principle of proportionality, the Court does not act as an appellate body exercising review of the merits but is concerned primarily with the restrictive effects of the measure on the freedom of the individual. The enquiry

---

[33] See H.G. Schermers and D. Waelbroeck, *Judicial Protection in the European Communities*, Sixth Ed., (Kluwer, 2001) p. 397, paras 806 *et seq.*   [34] *Op. cit.*, n. 18 above, para 13.

[35] *Ibid.*, para 14. See also Case 265/87 *Schräder v Hauptzollamt Gronau* [1989] ECR 2237, paras 21–22; Case 179/84 *Bozzetti v Invernizzi* [1985] ECR 2301, para 30.

[36] In other cases the Court has stated that the measure must not be 'patently' or 'manifestly unsuitable' to achieve its objectives. See Case 138/78 *Stölting v Hauptzollamt Hamburg-Jonas* [1979] ECR 713, para. 7; Case 59/83 *Biovilac v EEC* [1984] ECR 4057, para 17.

[37] The ECSC Treaty expired on 24 July 2002. Article 33(1) defined the jurisdiction of the Court in actions for judicial review against acts of the High Authority (the predecessor to the Commission). It provided that 'the Court may not . . . examine the evaluation of the situation, resulting from economic facts or circumstances, in the light of which the High Authority took its decision or made its recommendations, save where the High Authority is alleged to have misused its powers or to have manifestly failed to observe the provisions of this Treaty or any rule of law relating to its application'. For the historical background to this provision, see Schermers and Waelbroeck, *op. cit.*, para 806. In Case 6/54 *Netherlands v High Authority* [1954–56] ECR 103, at 115, the Court held that 'the term "manifest" within the meaning of Article 33 presupposes that a certain degree is reached in the failure to observe legal provisions so that the failure to observe the ECSC Treaty appears to derive from an obvious error in the evaluation . . . of the situation in respect of which the decision was taken'.

[38] See e.g. *Stölting, op. cit; Schräder, op. cit.; Crispoltoni, op. cit.*, n. 21 above; note also Case C-11/00 *Commission v ECB*, [2003] ECR I-7147, where the ECB unsuccessfully questioned the suitability of OLAF to investigate its activities.

whether such restrictive effects are justified centres on their necessity to achieve the objective in view. In practice, review of suitability is closely linked to review of necessity and a measure which is clearly unsuitable to achieve its objectives cannot be justified and will be struck down by the Court.[39] In assessing whether a measure is suitable to achieve its objectives, it is relevant to consider the actual effects of the measure. But the fact that a measure has failed to attain its objectives in practice does not mean that it is manifestly inappropriate. The Court has held that the legality of a Community act cannot depend on retrospective considerations of its efficacy.[40] Where the Community legislature is obliged to assess the future effects of rules to be adopted and these effects cannot be foreseen with accuracy, its assessment is open to criticism only if it appears manifestly incorrect in the light of the information available to it at the time of the adoption of the rules in question.[41]

The manifestly inappropriate test applies not only in relation to agricultural measures but in any area involving decision of economic or social policy where the Community legislature enjoys wide discretion. According to standard case law,[42]

Where the evaluation of a complex economic situation is involved, the Community institutions enjoy a wide measure of discretion. In reviewing the legality of the exercise of such discretion, the Court must confine itself to examining whether that exercise discloses manifest error or constitutes a misuse of powers or a clear disregard of the limits of its discretion.

The test has been applied, *inter alia*, in the following areas: agricultural policy,[43] fisheries policy,[44] transport policy,[45] social policy,[46] health protection,[47] and

[39] See e.g. Case C-368/89 *Crispoltoni I* [1991] ECR I-3695. In that case the Court held that a measure which retroactively fixed maximum quantities was incapable of achieving its objective of limiting production since production decisions had already been taken by producers before its adoption. See also Joined Cases C-27/00 and C-122/00 *Omega Air and Others* [2002] ECR I-2569, discussed later in this Section.

[40] Case 40/72 *Schroeder v Germany* [1973] ECR 125, para 14. See also *Crispoltoni II, op. cit.*, n. 21 above, discussed below; Joined Cases C-267–85/88 *Wuidart and Others* [1990] ECR I-435, para 14.

[41] See the cases referred in the previous footnotes and, for more recent confirmation, Case C-189/01 *Jippes and Others* [2001] ECR I-5689, para 84; Case C-150/94 *United Kingdom v Council* [1998] ECR I-7235, para 49. Note however that the Community institutions may be under an obligation to adapt existing measures following a fundamental change of circumstances: see, in relation to currency fluctuations, Case 248/80 *Glunz v Hauptzollamt Hamburg-Waltershof* [1982] ECR 197, para 23, and Joined Cases T-177 and T-377/94 *Altmann and Casson v Commission* [1996] ECR II-2041, discussed in Ch.1 above.

[42] Case T-180/00 *Astipesca v Commission* [2002] ECR II-3985, para 79; *Omega Air, op. cit.*, para 64; Joined Cases C-248–9/95 *SAM Schiffahrt and Stapf v Germany* [1997] ECR I-4475, para 23.

[43] *Fedesa, op. cit.*

[44] *Astipesca, op. cit.*, para 79; Case C-179/95 *Spain v Council* [1999] ECR I-6475, para 29; Case C-120/99 *Italy v Council* [2001] ECR I-7997, para 44; Joined Cases C-296/93 and C-307/93 *France and Ireland v Commission* [1996] ECR I-795, para 31.

[45] *SAM Schiffahrt, op. cit. Omega Air, op. cit.*

[46] Case C-84/94 *United Kingdom v Council* [1996] ECR I-5755, para 58.

[47] See e.g. *Jippes, op. cit.*; Case C-419/01 *The Queen v Secretary of State for Health ex p British American Tobacco Ltd* [2002] ECR I-11453; *Upjohn op. cit.*, n. 12 above.

measures to combat fraud against Community finances.[48] In those areas, the test applies both to internal Community measures and the conclusion of international agreements.[49] A similar test has also been applied in relation to the Commission's discretion whether to follow a complaint and conduct investigations for breach of competition law,[50] whether to exempt agreements under Article 81(3) EC,[51] and whether to find that State aid is compatible with the common market under Article 87(3) EC.[52] Although the language used by the Court in some of the above areas may be different, the emphasis remains on the discretion of the decision maker.

It would be incorrect, however, to give the impression that the Court's examination is one-sided. In fact, there seems to be an inherent contradiction between the Court's emphasis on the concept of 'manifest error', on the one hand, and the general posture of the case law that 'as a general rule the Community judicature undertakes a comprehensive review' of the case, on the other hand.[53] The above equivocation reflects the delicate nature of judicial intervention and strives to ensure that the judicature remains 'master of its tasks' keeping control of the degree of scrutiny that it exercises in each case.[54] As a general rule, it may be said that, in recent years, the CFI has been more willing to enter into the merits of economic assessments made by the Commission in the field of competition law[55] and the ECJ has, to some extent, been more critical of the exercise of Community competence.[56] This however has not been achieved through a more rigorous application of the principle of proportionality but rather through an exhaustive examination of the institutions' reasoning, a re-creation of the decision-making

---

[48] *Commission v ECB, op. cit.,* n. 38 above para 157.

[49] See Case T-572/93 *Odigitria v Council and Commission* [1995] ECR II-2025, para 36–38; confirmed on appeal: C-293/95 P [1996] ECR I-6129.

[50] Case T-7/92 *Asia Motor France v Commission* [1993] ECR II-669.

[51] See e.g. Case T-395/94 *Atlantic Container Line and Others v Commission* [2002] ECR II-875, para 257: Case T-86/95 *Compagnie Générale Maritime and Others v Commission* [2002] ECR II-1011, paras 339–340.

[52] The manifest error test also applies in relation to decisions pertaining to the Community civil service in areas where the Community administration enjoys wide discretion, e.g. recruitment and promotion. See Schermers and Waelbroeck, *op. cit.,* pp. 399–400, and for recent confirmation: Case T-144/02 *Eagle v Commission,* judgment of 5 October 2004, para 113.

[53] See e.g., on competition law, Case C-7/95 *Deere v Commission* [1998] ECR I-3111, para 34.

[54] Case C-83/98 P *France v Ladbroke Racing and Commission* [2000] ECR I-3271, at 3278 *per* Cosmas AG at n. 3.

[55] This is illustrated, in particular, by the 2002 merger cases where the CFI annulled decisions prohibiting mergers finding that the Commission had committed manifest errors of assessment in its economic analysis. See the CFI judgments in Case T-342/99 *Airtours plc v Commission* [2002] ECR II-2585; Case T-310/01 *Schneider Electric SA v Commission* [2002] ECR II-4071; and Cases T-5/02 *Tetra Laval BV v Commission* [2002] ECR II-4381.

[56] See the annulment of the Tobacco Advertisement Directive in Case C-376/98 *Germany v Parliament and Council (Tobacco case)* [2000] ECR I-8419. Note however that in subsequent cases the ECJ has refused to extend the application of its reasoning in that case and has cleared important harmonization measures: see C-377/98 *Netherlands v Parliament and Council* [2001] ECR I-7079 and *British American Tobacco Ltd,* n. 47 above; for a discussion of the case law, see below, Chapter 4.

process and, in the case of competence, a stricter interpretation of Treaty provisions that empower Community legislative intervention.

In order to determine whether a measure is necessary, the Court is receptive to argument that the same objective may be attained by less restrictive means. The case law suggests however that, in relation to policy measures, the Court does not apply the less restrictive alternative test scrupulously relying instead on some notion of reasonableness or arbitrary conduct. In *Fedesa*[57] it was claimed that the prohibition of certain hormones on health protection grounds was not necessary. The Court stressed that the Council enjoyed discretion and held that since it had made no manifest error in considering that the prohibition was appropriate, it was also entitled to take the view that the objectives pursued could not be achieved by less onerous means. The less restrictive alternative argument has been unsuccessfully submitted in a number of other cases[58] and recent case law suggests that, in fact, the Court pays lip service to it.[59]

The application of proportionality undoubtedly involves a subjective element. An interesting divergence of view between the Court and the Advocate General occurred in *Omega Air*.[60] With a view to reducing aircraft noise, the Council adopted Regulation No 925/1999 which imposed more stringent controls on noise levels than those provided by previous Community directives and those laid down in the Chicago Convention of 7 December 1944 on International Civil Aviation. In particular, the Regulation prohibited the registration and operation in the European Union of recertificated aeroplanes with a by-pass ratio of less than 3. Recertificated aeroplanes are essentially older models which had initially received authorization as complying with the lower noise levels prescribed in Chapter 2 of the Chicago Convention and which were subsequently modified to meet the higher Chapter 3 standards of the Convention. The Regulation came into force in 2000. In 1996, Omega Air had announced a programme to replace the engines in a number of its aircraft with new engines having a by-pass ratio of 1.74. By the time the Community institutions took the decision to prohibit re-engined aircraft with a by-pass ratio less than 3, it was too late for Omega to change its plans.

Omega argued that reliance on the by-pass ratio was inappropriate since aircraft noise may originate from sources other than the engine. Alternative measures could have been taken which would have been less damaging to its economic interests. In particular, the fixing of separate thresholds for noise, gaseous emissions, and fuel burn would have been less onerous but equally effective.

Applying the manifestly inappropriate test, the ECJ reiterated that, where implementation of a policy requires assessment of a complex economic situation,

---

[57] *Op. cit.*, n. 18 above.

[58] See e.g. the cases referred to above in n. 39 [*Crispoltoni, Wuidart*, etc] and also Case C-280/93 *Germany v Council (Bananas case)* [1994] ECR I-4973; Case C-8/89 *Zardi* [1990] ECR I-2515; Case 138/79 *Roquette Frères v Council* [1980] ECR 3333, *per* Reischl AG at pp. 3380 *et seq.*

[59] See *Omega Air, op. cit.; BAT Case, op. cit., Jippes, op. cit.*   [60] *Op. cit.*, n. 39 above.

the Council has discretion not only in relation to the nature and scope of the legislation but also, to a certain extent, in relation to the findings as to the basic facts, in the sense that it is free to base its assessment, if necessary, on findings of a general nature.[61] It came to the conclusion that the Council had not exceeded its margin of appreciation. Nor had Omega shown that the criterion relating to by-pass ratio was inappropriate. The Court found the Commission's data more persuasive and more representative since they were of general application and showed the development of noise pollution over three decades whilst Omega's data referred exclusively to a particular type of aircraft and were only forecasts.

As regards the less restrictive alternatives argument, the ECJ held that even if such measures could make a sufficient contribution to reducing environmental damage caused by air traffic, the Council could reasonably take into consideration that the application of separate criteria relating to the reduction of noise, fuel burn, and gaseous emissions would have represented a highly complex operation which was not justified by the limited number of aeroplanes such as those re-engined by Omega. In the same way, it could reasonably consider that reference to a single technical criterion could remove the uncertainties which specific standards might allow to persist.[62]

The Opinion of the Advocate General differs from the judgment in two respects. He favoured a higher standard of scrutiny and took more seriously the less restrictive alternative test. Borrowing from the case law on anti-dumping, Alber AG stated that, in assessing whether there is a manifest error, account must be taken of the following considerations: (a) whether the institution considered with the necessary care all the information contained in the file and assessed the relevant evidence; and (b) whether it neglected to take into account essential factors.[63] In the context of anti-dumping proceedings, if interested parties submit specific facts which contradict the view taken by the legislature during the legislative procedure leading to the adoption of a regulation, the Council may be obliged to take them into account.[64] The same considerations should apply more widely in assessing the validity of Community policy measures. Applying this test, the Advocate General came to the conclusion that reliance on the by-pass ratio was based on a manifest error of assessment and that the adoption of separate standards for noise, fuel burn, and emission, as suggested by the applicants would have been appropriate.

Although both the Advocate General and the Court reasoned seemingly on the basis of the same test, namely that of manifest error, *Omega Air* reveals a classic difference of view as to the applicable standard of scrutiny. Whilst the ECJ focused on whether the measure was appropriate with less emphasis on whether it was necessary, the Advocate General did exactly the opposite.

Overall, the 'manifestly inappropriate' test means that the onus on the applicant to prove that there is an equally effective, less restrictive alternative is particularly

---

[61] *Ibid.* para 65; *SAM Schiffahrt, op. cit.*, n. 42 above.   [62] *Ibid.*, para 72.
[63] See, in relation to anti-dumping regulations: Case C-16/90 *Nölle* [1991] ECR I-5163, para 13.   [64] *Omega Air op. cit.*, n. 39 above, at 2589.

high. In the absence of hard empirical or scientific evidence, the applicant faces an uphill struggle.

Omega Air may be seen as indicative of a trend to empower intervention of the Community *qua* regulator contrary to what the ECJ appeared to suggest in the *Tobacco Advertising* case where much hinged on the distinction between measures to facilitate the establishment and functioning of the internal market, which the Community was given power to adopt, and measures pertaining to the regulation of the internal market, which were held to fall within the province of the nation State.[65]

A further example of this trend may be found in the *Vitamins* case, where the Court again diverged from the Advocate General.[66] Private parties challenged Directive 2002/46 which introduced a positive list of food supplements.[67] The Directive provides essentially that only vitamins and supplements listed in its annexes may be used and, from 1 August 2005, trade in substances not listed therein is prohibited. The Advocate General found the Directive deficient in three respects:[68] first, it made no mention of the substantive criteria which the Commission must follow in deciding to permit the inclusion of new substances in the positive lists. Second, it did not make clear whether the Directive allows private parties to submit substances for evaluation with a view to having them included. Third, on the assumption that private parties were able to do so, there was no clear procedure for that purpose which provided minimum guarantees for protecting their interests. Geelhoed AG viewed the first shortcoming as a particularly serious one. Given the restrictive effects of the positive list on commercial freedom, he considered it indispensable that the Directive must itself prescribe the substantive parameters governing the Commission's power to make additions. Although the Advocate General structured his reasoning on the basis of the principle of proportionality, he read it as incorporating elements of legal certainty, good administration, and the right to judicial protection. The ECJ, by contrast, rescued the validity of the Directive by employing the following technique: it shifted the obligation to observe the above requirements to the Community administration, and read implied administrative duties in the Directive. It unequivocally recognized the importance of process rights. The introduction of a positive list must be accompanied by a procedure designed to allow a substance to be added and that procedure must respect the general principles of Community law, in particular, the principle of sound administration and legal certainty. The Court laid down the following substantive requirements:[69]

- the procedure must be accessible in the sense that it must be expressly mentioned in a measure of general application which is binding on the authorities concerned;

---

[65] *Op. cit.*, n. 56 above.

[66] Joined Cases C-154 and C-155/04, *The Queen on the application of Alliance for Natural Health v Secretary of State for Health*, judgment of 12 July 2005. For a further example, see *BAT, op. cit.*, discussed below.

[67] Dirrective 2002/46 on the approximation of the laws of the Member States relating to food supplements, OJ 2002, L 183/51.   [68] Opinion of Geelhoed AG, paras 68–69.

[69] *Op. cit.*, para 73.

- it must be capable of being completed within a reasonable time;
- an application to have a substance included in the list may be refused only on the basis of a full assessment of the risks posed to public health;
- that assessment must be made on the basis of the most reliable scientific data available and the most recent results of international research;
- finally, if the procedure results in a refusal, the refusal must be open to challenge.

The ECJ pointed out that Article 4(5) in combination with Article 13(2) of the Directive made applicable for the purposes of adding vitamins or minerals to the positive lists the comitology procedure provided for in Council Decision 1999/468.[70] The Court viewed that procedure as satisfying the above requirements although it criticized the Directive as being less than perfect in terms of transparency and completeness and charged the Commission with ensuring transparency and prompt action.[71]

The Court also took the view that the Commission had power to modify the positive lists only on the basis of objective criteria connected exclusively with public health. This derived from statements in the preamble to the Directive, which 'ideally' should have been included in the provisions of the Directive, in combination with their concrete expression through the positive lists.[72]

Thus the Court concluded that the legislature had done just enough to pass the threshold of validity but only at the expense of shifting the standards of good governance to the Community administration and leaving the door wide open to a second round of litigation against concrete administrative decisions refusing addition of substances.[73]

The judgment may be seen as an acknowledgment, and the natural consequence, of the maturity of Community government. Ample discretion for the legislature to roam in the field of public health and restrict economic freedom must be accompanied, as a *quid pro quo*, by high standards of administrative competence.

3.5. Agricultural law

The reason why proportionality has exerted particular influence in the field of agricultural law is not difficult to establish.[74] The common organization of the market consists typically of market regulation measures which inevitably entail restrictions on economic freedom. The principle of proportionality has been developed by the Court in order to counter-balance the restrictive effects of such measures. In effect, the fundamental difficulty which the Community's political

---

[70] OJ 1999, L 184/23.   [71] *Alliance for Natural Health, op. cit.*, paras 81–82.
[72] *Ibid.*, para 92.   [73] *Ibid.*, para 88.
[74] See further R. Barents, *The Agricultural Law of the EC*, (Kluwer, 1994) Ch. 18; Emiliou, *op. cit.*, n. 3 above, Ch. 6 ; S. Neri, 'Le principe de proportionnalité dans la jurisprudence de la Court relative au droit communautaire agricole', (1981) 17 RTDE 652.

institutions, and reflectively the Court, have encountered in the sphere of the common agricultural policy is how to allocate burdens in declining and over-supplied markets. Proportionality has been applied primarily to the following types of measures:

- market regulation measures involving choices of economic policy;
- the Community deposit system;
- measures imposing charges, sanctions and penalties.

Selected cases in those areas will now be examined.

3.5.1. Market regulation measures

The 'manifestly inappropriate test' has been applied in particular to measures seeking to control production, measures setting up a common organization of the market, and monetary compensatory amounts.

3.5.2. Production control measures

Article 33 provides that one of the objectives of the common agricultural policy is to increase agricultural productivity.[75] As a result of technological and legal factors, the Community moved into surplus production at a relative early stage in the development of the common agricultural policy. Excessive growth had adverse consequences for everyone concerned, in particular, the producers, the agricultural markets, the economies of the Member States and, not least, the Community budget. Faced with such difficulties, the Council and the Commission took measures with a view to controlling production. Since the mid-1970s various means have been employed, among which were the introduction of a co-responsibility levy, maximum guaranteed quantities, and individual quotas allocated to producers.[76] Such measures have been challenged, mostly unsuccessfully, on grounds of proportionality.

---

[75] See Article 33(1)(a). Notably, this provision has remained intact in the EU Constitution, see Article III-227(1)(a).

[76] Note that, since its inception in July 1958, the common agricultural policy has undergone a number of reforms. A major redirection of the policy occurred in the 1990s. See the outline of new policy objectives by the Commission in 'The Development and Future of the Common Agricultural Policy', EC Bulletin, Suppl. 5/91. That reform was based essentially on a cutback of agricultural prices with a view to making them more competitive in the Community and the world markets and countervailing measures to compensate farmers for loss of income. The most far-reaching reform of the CAP occurred in 2000 as part of the so-called 'Agenda 2000'. This marked a shift of emphasis towards rural development, integrating environmental considerations into the CAP, and sought to balance increased competitiveness of agricultural products with the promotion of fair and decent standards of living for the farming community. A further reform occurred in 2003. This is currently phased in and its basic tenet is 'decoupling', i.e. the separation of aid from production with a view to eliminating surpluses and balancing supply and demand. Decoupling is accompanied by modulation, i.e. the gradual reduction of direct payments to

3.5.2.1. Co-responsibility levy

A so-called co-responsibility levy was introduced by various Community regulations in an attempt to reduce surpluses in agricultural produce.[77] Between 1975 and 1977 there was a considerable increase in surpluses of milk and milk products in the Community. With a view to reducing those surpluses, the Council adopted Regulation No 1079/77[78] introducing a co-responsibility levy payable by producers. The amount of the levy was calculated by reference to the target price for milk. In *Stölting v Hauptzollamt Hamburg-Jonas*[79] it was argued that the levy was inadequate to remedy the difficulties of disposal and to achieve a structural balance in the market. After examining the characteristics of the levy, the Advocate General stated that the adoption of Regulation No 1079/77 indicated 'a choice of economic policy which [was] in certain respects regrettable' adding that his criticism concerned only the expediency of the measure and did not affect its validity.[80] The Court stated that the Regulation was directed towards restraining production and therefore, given the surpluses, it contributed to the attainment of the objective of stabilizing the market. It added that the rate of the levy did not appear to be disproportionate. In *Schräder v Hauptzollamt Gronau*,[81] it was argued that the co-responsibility levy on cereals imposed by Council Regulation No 1579/86[82] and Commission Regulation No 2040/86[83] was neither appropriate nor necessary to stabilize the market on the ground that it affected less than half of the agricultural produce concerned and that it caused a rise in the price of processed cereals, which did not encourage reduction of surpluses. In dismissing those arguments, the Court held:[84]

When the Community legislature introduced the levy … and fixed the rules for its application, it selected from the various possibilities open to it the one which seemed most appropriate for reducing the structural surpluses on the cereals market by exerting direct but moderate pressure on the prices paid to cereals producers. Such a measure, which seeks to limit supply by reducing prices for producers, must in principle be regarded as appropriate to the objective of stabilizing agricultural markets, referred to in Article 39(1)(c) of the Treaty, even if, because of certain exemptions, the measure does not affect all the products in question.

On that basis, the Court concluded that the contested measure did not infringe the principle of proportionality.

---

producers, and making remaining direct aid subject to food safety and environmental requirements. Special rules apply to the new Member States which acceded in 2003. For a concise history of reforms and policy initiatives, see the website of the EU: *http://www.europa.eu.int/scadplus/leg/en/lvb/lo4000.htm.*

[77] The co-responsibility levy was challenged also on the ground of the infringement of the principle of non-discrimination. See 2.5 above.   [78] OJ 1977 L 131, p. 6.
[79] *Op. cit.*, n. 36 above.   [80] *Ibid.*, at p. 728 *per* Mayras AG.
[81] *Op. cit.*, n. 35 above.   [82] OJ 1986 L 139, p. 29.   [83] OJ 1986, L 173, p. 65.
[84] *Ibid.*, para 23.

3.5.2.2. Maximum guaranteed quantities

The legality of the maximum guaranteed quantities system was put in issue in *Crispoltoni II*[85] which concerned the Community regime governing the common organization of the market in tobacco. With a view to controlling the increase in Community production, Council Regulation No 1114/88[86] provided for the annual fixing of a maximum guaranteed quantity for each variety of tobacco. For each percentage point by which the maximum quantity was exceeded, there would be a corresponding reduction in the intervention prices and the premiums up to a maximum reduction of 15 per cent. Some years after the Regulation came into force, it was argued that the system was unsuitable to achieve its objectives since it had not in reality ensured compliance with the maximum guaranteed quantities. Italian producers argued that, in order to ensure that the guaranteed quantities were not exceeded, a system of individual quotas should have been instituted similar to that which was subsequently introduced by Council Regulation No 2075/92.[87] The Court held that the mere fact that the system had proved ineffective was not sufficient to invalidate the Regulation. When the Council adopted the Regulation, it was entitled to consider, without making any manifest error of assessment, that a system based on maximum guaranteed quantities was less onerous for tobacco growers than a system based on individual quotas. Under the former, the production of growers was not limited since they could always sell their products to the intervention agencies, albeit at a reduced price or premium. Under the latter system, growers received no support for that part of their production which exceeded their individual quota.

An unsuccessful claim was also made in *Zardi*.[88] Community law provided for the collection of a levy from cereal producers as a condition for the placing of cereals on the market. The levy would be reimbursed in full only if production in the marketing year did not exceed the maximum guaranteed quantity. It was argued that it was not necessary to require payment of the levy in advance since less restrictive means existed. The Court held, however, that advance collection of the levy was likely, by reducing the price paid to producers, to persuade them not to increase production during the marketing year and that the Community legislature had not committed any manifest error of assessment in rejecting other options.

3.5.2.3. Individual quotas

The system of quotas imposed on the production of isoglucose was challenged in the second generation of the isoglucose cases.[89] It will be remembered that in the first isoglucose case, the Court annulled the production levy on isoglucose on the

---

[85] *Op. cit.*, n. 21 above.   [86] OJ 1988, L 110/35.   [87] OJ 1992 L 215/70.
[88] Case C-8/89 [1990] ECR I-2515.
[89] For unsuccessful challenges on export quotas, see e.g. *Germany v Council*, *op. cit.*, n. 58 above, discussed at 3.5.3 below; Case C-241/95 *The Queen v Intervention Board for Agricultural Produce ex p Accrington Beef and Others* [1996] ECR I-6699.

ground that it ran counter to the principle of equal treatment.[90] Following the annulment of the levy, the Council introduced a system of individual quotas. In *Roquette Frères v Council*[91] it was unsuccessfully argued that the system of quotas infringed the principle of proportionality in that it was excessively onerous. In a concisely reasoned judgment, the Court relied mainly on three arguments. First, it held that the introduction of a quota system was a usual procedure in Community law appropriate when necessary to control production. Second, in adopting measures of general interest, the Council could not have regard to the commercial choices and the internal policy of individual undertakings. Third, the applicant had not used the quota allocated to it for the marketing year and was therefore unable to show that the introduction of the quota system had limited its production.[92]

3.5.2.4. *The* Skimmed Milk *cases*

The principle of proportionality was successfully invoked to challenge production control measures in the skimmed milk powder cases.[93] In an attempt to reduce stocks of skimmed milk powder, accumulated as a result of over-production, Council Regulation No 563/76[94] provided for the compulsory purchase of powder by producers for use in feedstuffs. The compulsory purchase of powder was imposed at a price equal to about three times its value as animal feed. The Court annulled the Regulation on two grounds. It stated that the obligation to purchase at such a disproportionate price was discriminatory. It also held that such an obligation was not necessary in order to attain the disposal of stocks of skimmed milk powder.[95] The cases illustrate that the Court is prepared to engage in a cost-benefit analysis even in areas where the Community institutions enjoy a wide discretion. It is also instructive as regards the test of necessity. The Council argued that Regulation No 563/76 was essential in order to reduce the accumulated 'mountain' of powder since, if it had not been for the obligation to purchase, it would have been impossible for the surplus to be absorbed. The Court rejected that argument. Although it did not refer to any less restrictive alternatives, it came to the conclusion that the obligation to purchase at such a disproportionate price was not necessary. The judgment implies that the imposition of an obligation to purchase at a lower price might have met the test of proportionality.[96]

Although the skimmed milk powder cases can be taken as an indication that the Court is prepared to review the merits of economic policy decisions taken by the

---

[90] Joined Cases 103 and 145/77 *Royal Scholten Honig (Holdings) Ltd v Intervention Board for Agricultural Produce* [1978] ECR 2037, discussed at 2.5.1 above.

[91] *Op. cit.*, n. 58 above. See also Case 139/79 *Maizena v Council* [1980] ECR 3393. Note that in those cases, although the Court rejected the substantive grounds for review, it annulled the contested regulation on procedural grounds, namely, failure by the Council to consult the Parliament.

[92] *Roquette Frères, op. cit.*, paras 29–31. In *Maizena, op. cit.*, para 26, the Court relied more directly on the discretionary powers of the Council to reject the arguments for annulment.

[93] *Bela-Mühle, op. cit.*, n. 19 above, Case 116/76 *Granaria* [1977] ECR 1247, Joined Cases 119 and 120/76 *Ölmühle and Becher* [1977] ECR 1269.   [94] OJ 1976 L 67, p. 18.

[95] See *Bela-Mühle, op. cit.*, para 7.   [96] de Burca, *op. cit.*, n. 3 above, p. 121.

Community legislature, it should be acknowledged that the facts were exceptional, the contested Regulation being an example of a legislative conundrum. The cases are not an exception to the manifestly inappropriate test but rather an illustration of its application. As stated above, under the contested Regulation, the purchase price of the powder was three times higher than that of the substances which it replaced. Furthermore, the breach of the principle of proportionality was closely linked to the breach of the principle of equality. The aim of the scheme being to sustain milk prices, its beneficiaries were milk producers who, in effect, were given preferential treatment at the expense of feedstuff producers and livestock owners. The Court did not balance only the Community interest in reducing stocks *vis-à-vis* the interest of feedstuff producers to use cheaper substances. It also balanced the interests of two separate categories of economic traders. It held that, in imposing on feedstuff producers the obligation to purchase skimmed milk powder, the Council treated unfairly those producers *vis-à-vis* milk producers, stating that the 'obligation to purchase at such a disproportionate price constituted a discriminatory distribution of the burden of costs between the various agricultural sectors'.[97]

3.5.3. Establishment of a common organization of the market

Review is limited where, in establishing a common organization of the market, the Council has to reconcile divergent interests and thus select options 'within the context of the policy choices which are its own responsibility'.[98] Thus in *Germany v Council*,[99] where the German Government sought the annulment of Council Regulation No 404/93[100] setting up a common organization of the market in bananas, the Court refuted the argument that the regulation imposed a disproportionate burden on traders who traditionally marketed third country bananas by reducing their share of the market. It held that, in adopting the Regulation, the Council had to reconcile the conflicting interests of producer and non-producer Member States. The first category was concerned to ensure that its agricultural populations living in economically less-favoured areas were able to dispose of produce at acceptable prices and thus avoid social problems. The second category was primarily concerned to ensure that its consumers were supplied with produce at the best possible price.[101] In response to the argument that less onerous measures could achieve the desired result, the Court stated that it could not 'substitute its assessment for that of the Council as to the appropriateness or otherwise of the measures adopted by the Community legislature if those measures have not been proved to be manifestly inappropriate for achieving the objective pursued'.[102] Where the adoption of a measure involves striking a balance between strongly

---

[97] *Bela-Mühle, op. cit.*, para 7.   [98] *Bananas case, op. cit.*, n. 58 above, para 91.
[99] *Op. cit.* The case is also discussed above, p. 85. See also Case C-466/93 *Atlanta Fruchthandelsgesellschaft (II) v Bundesamt für Ernährung und Forstwirtschaft* [1995] ECR I-3799.
[100] OJ 1993 L 47, p. 1.   [101] *Germany v Council, op. cit.*, para 92.   [102] *Ibid.*, para 94.

conflicting national interests, the Court is prepared to defer to the choices made by the Council especially if, as in that case, the choice made expresses a hard-fought compromise between considerations of free market and considerations of protectionism.

3.5.4. Monetary compensatory amounts

One of the earlier cases where the Court applied the 'manifestly inappropriate' test concerned monetary compensatory amounts, the system of which was introduced by Council Regulation No 974/71[103] to counterbalance the collapse of fixed exchange rates. In order to avoid inflationary effects caused by an abnormal influx of short-term speculative capital in early 1971, Germany and the Netherlands widened the margins of fluctuation for the exchange rates of their currencies in relation to their official parities. This *de facto* revaluation was bound to create disturbances in agricultural trade which is based on a system of uniform prices. The prices of products continued to be determined by reference to the official parity of currencies but, following revaluation, transactions could take place according to the actual rate of exchange below the fixed prices laid down by Community regulations. To avoid distortion of prices, Regulation No 974/71 authorized Member States to charge compensatory amounts on imports. In *Balkan Import-Export*,[104] amounts were charged on the importation into Germany of cheese from Bulgaria. It was argued that Regulation No 974/71 ran counter to the principle of proportionality because the compensatory amounts were not based on any profit made by the importer on the rate of exchange but on the relationship between the official parity of the Deutschmark and the dollar and its true parity, independently of the country of origin of the products. The Court accepted that since a general criterion was selected, it was possible that imports into Germany from countries whose currencies were fluctuating in relation to the Deutschmark to an extent different from that of the dollar might be affected adversely. It rejected however the alternative methods of calculation put forward by the applicant and came to the conclusion that, in opting for the system which was adopted by Regulation No 974/71, the Council did not impose on traders burdens which were manifestly out of proportion to the object in view. The same reasoning was followed by the Court in other cases concerning monetary compensatory amounts decided at that time.[105]

It is interesting that in *Balkan Import-Export*, the Court applied the test of proportionality loosely. The preamble to Regulation No 974/71 expressly stated that the compensatory amounts adopted should be limited to those strictly necessary to compensate the incidence of the monetary measures, namely the freeing of

---

[103] OJ 1971 L 106, p. 1.   [104] *op. cit.*, n. 20 above.
[105] See e.g. Case 9/73 *Schlüter v Hauptzollampt Lörrach* [1973] ECR 1135; Case 10/73 *Rewe-Zentral v Hauptzollamt Kehl* [1973] ECR 1175.

currencies from fixed exchange rates. However, the compensatory amounts imposed were based solely on the relationship between the official parity and the true parity of the Deutschmark to the dollar. The result was that imports into Germany from countries the rate of exchange of whose currencies remained stable *vis-à-vis* the Deutschmark were subjected to higher compensatory rates which could not be said to be 'strictly necessary'. Nonetheless, the Court refused to annul the Regulation.[106] It seems that three considerations led the Court to that conclusion. The impracticality of the alternative methods of calculation suggested by the applicants; the pressing need to adopt corrective measures within a short period; and the assessment, implicit in the judgment of the Court, that although the system adopted could have adverse financial consequences on certain traders, those consequences were not beyond the sphere of commercial risks that economic operators could reasonably be expected to bear.

3.5.5. Administrative measures: Forfeiture of deposits and securities

In the case of administrative measures, the intensity of review is determined by criteria more exacting than the 'manifestly inappropriate' test. This is because, understandably, the Court is more willing to review the discretion of the administration than to question the policy choices made by the Community legislature. As a principle of administrative law, proportionality requires that, where entitlement to a benefit is conditional upon the meeting of certain administrative requirements, failure to abide strictly by those requirements does not necessarily lead to the loss of benefit. Much depends on the specific circumstances of the case and the objectives of the requirements in issue. In one case where the granting of an export subsidy was conditional on the exportation of the total quantities of produce placed under supervision, it was held that, in the absence of bad faith, the fact that a negligible part of that quantity was missing was not material.[107] In other cases, however, the Court has taken a stricter view especially in relation to time-limits.[108]

In the field of administrative law, the system of deposits has provided a fruitful area for the application of proportionality.[109] The purpose of a deposit is to ensure that a trader who gives an undertaking to the Commission in order to secure a benefit complies with that undertaking. Agricultural regulations typically make the issue of import and export licences subject to the lodging of a deposit the purpose

---

[106] In a different respect, the Court saw the system of monetary compensatory amounts as the least restrictive. It accepted that compensatory amounts constituted a partitioning of the market but held that, in the light of the aims of the common agricultural policy, diversions of trade which would otherwise be caused by the freeing of exchange rates could be considered more damaging: *Balkan Import-Export, op. cit.,* para 29.

[107] Case C-101/88 *Gausepohl* [1990] ECR I-23.   [108] See below.

[109] On the application of the principle to deposits and securities, see Schwartze, *op. cit.,* n. 3 above, pp. 727 *et seq.*; Emiliou, *op. cit.,* n. 3 above, pp. 206–223; W. Alexander, 'Perte de la caution en droit agricole communautaire', (1988) CDE 384.

of which is to ensure that the export or import transaction will be completed within the period of validity of the licence. Save in cases of *force majeure*, failure to carry out the transaction leads to forfeiture of the deposit.[110] *Internationale Handelsgesellschaft*[111] put in issue the compatibility of the deposits system with the principle of proportionality. After explaining the objectives of the deposit system, the Court held that it was both necessary and appropriate to achieve its objectives and compared favourably with alternative systems. The Court stated that a system of fines imposed *a posteriori*, as suggested by the applicant, would involve considerable administrative and legal complications both at the stage of decision and execution, which were aggravated by the fact that the traders concerned may be beyond the reach of the national competent authorities by reason of their residence in another Member State.[112]

The Community administration is under a duty to take into account the specific circumstances of the persons affected by its decisions, and the indiscriminate character of a measure may infringe proportionality. In *Atalanta*,[113] Commission Regulation No 1889/76[114] laying down detailed rules for granting storage aid for pigmeat provided that the security would be wholly forfeit if the obligations imposed by the storage contract were not fulfilled. The Court held that the absolute nature of that provision ran counter to the principle of proportionality because it did not enable the penalty to be made commensurate with the degree of failure to implement the contractual obligations or with the seriousness of the breach of those obligations. *Maas*[115] concerned the validity of Article 20(1) of Commission Regulation (EEC) No 1974/80[116] laying down implementing rules in respect of certain food aid operations involving cereals and rice. Maas, a Belgian undertaking, had been declared successful tenderer for the supply of food aid to Ethiopia. It transported the goods to the intended destination but the intervention agency declared the security furnished forfeit recording two violations. The undertaking had not shipped the goods within the period laid down by Community law and, contrary to Community rules, it had used vessels which were more than 15 years old. The Court held that forfeiture of the security was not justified since the shipment period had been exceeded by only a short time. It also held that Article 20(1) infringed the principle of proportionality insofar as it required that the security had to be wholly forfeit where the goods were transported in vessels which were more than 15 years old. The

---

[110] The notion of *force majeure* incorporates an element of proportionality; see Case 4/68 *Schwarzwaldmilch v Einfuhr- und Vorratsstelle* [1968] ECR 377 at pp. 385–386. It is understood narrowly by the Court however and covers only unusual circumstances beyond the control of the trader. An exporter's mistake as to classification of the goods is not *force majeure:* Case C-101/99 *British Sugar* [2002] ECR I-205, para 69.   [111] *Op. cit.*, n. 6 above.

[112] *Ibid.*, para 11, and see the analysis of the Advocate General, at pp. 1147–1152.

[113] Case 240/78 *Atalanta v Produktschap voor Vee en Vlees* [1979] ECR 2137.

[114] OJ 1976, L 206, p. 82.

[115] Case 21/85 *Maas v Bundesanstalt für Landwirtschaftliche Marktordnung* [1986] ECR 3537.

[116] OJ 1980, L 192, p. 11.

Court considered that this requirement was not of such importance as to justify total forfeiture.[117]

By contrast, the Court required strict compliance with the applicable requirements in *Beste Boter and Hoche*.[118] At issue was a Commission regulation which provided for the sale by tender of butter at reduced prices to processing undertakings. To ensure performance of the obligation to process, the regulation imposed the obligation to provide a deposit. The deposit would be forfeit even where the failure of the successful tenderer to fulfil his undertakings was not due to his own fault but to the fault of a subsequent purchaser of the product. The Court held that forfeiture was not a penalty. Its effect rather was to make the successful tenderer pay a total amount equivalent to the market price of the butter in accordance with the contractual obligation freely entered into, where the obligation to process was not met. On that basis, it concluded that forfeiture did not infringe the principle of proportionality.

Where Community rules impose a primary and a secondary obligation, the penalty for failing to meet the latter should in principle be less onerous than the penalty for failure to fulfil the former. In *Buitoni*,[119] Commission Regulation No 193/75 made the issue of import and export licences for agricultural products conditional upon the giving of a security, release of which was subject to production of proof of completion of the customs formalities. The security would be released in proportion to the quantities of products in respect of which the requisite proof was furnished. Regulation No 499/76 provided for the total forfeiture of the security where the requisite proof had not been furnished within the six months following the expiry of the licence. That provision was said to be prompted by 'administrative reasons'. The Court held that it was invalid. It pointed out the inequality of treatment between the failure to meet the obligation to import or export imposed by the licence, which was the primary obligation and whose fulfilment the security was intended to guarantee, and the failure to furnish proof within the specified period, which was an ancillary obligation. Failure to perform the first carried a proportionate penalty. By contrast, failure to perform the second carried a fixed penalty, even though the obligation was considerably less serious. On that ground, the Court held that the fixed penalty was excessively severe in relation to the objectives of administrative efficiency. The Court held that the Commission should have sanctioned failure to furnish proof within the specified period with a penalty considerably less onerous and more closely allied to the practical effects of that failure.[120]

---

[117] But where a trader receives advance payment of export aid and owing to *force majeure* he is unable to export the goods to the agreed destination and exports them instead to different destinations which qualify for a lower export aid or none at all, it is not contrary to the principle of proportionality to require that the security forfeited must be equal to the difference between the amount of the aid paid in advance and the amount actually due: Case C-299/94 *Anglo-Irish Beef Processors International v MAFF* [1996] ECR I-1925.

[118] Joined Cases 99 and 100/76 *Beste Boter and Hoche v Bundesanstalt für Landwirtschaftliche Marktordnung* [1977] ECR 861.   [119] Case 122/78 *Buitoni v Forma* [1979] ECR 677.

[120] See also *Atalanta, op. cit.* In Case 181/84 *Man (Sugar) v IBAP*, [1985] ECR 2889 the Court held that the obligation of the successful tenderer to obtain an export licence performs a useful

In assessing what is a primary obligation regard must be had to the objectives of the measure in issue.[121] Particular importance attaches to the need to prevent fraud. In *Cereol Italia v Azienda Agricola Castello*[122] the Court found that penalties which went as far as forfeiture of entitlement to aid for two marketing years, where a producer deliberately or by reason of serious negligence failed to notify the Commission of changes in the area sown, were proportionate in view of the importance of the obligation of notification for the operation of the aid system. It rejected the submission that the obligation of notification was merely a secondary obligation breach of which could only have limited consequences.

In a number of cases, breach of the principle of proportionality has been pleaded against penalties imposed as a result of failure to observe time limits. We saw above that in *Buitoni* the failure to submit proof within the specified time limit was judged not to justify total forfeiture of the security lodged.[123] Similarly, in *Man (Sugar) v IBAP*[124] where the security was declared wholly forfeit although an application for an export licence was made only a few hours after the expiry of the requisite time limit, the Court held that forfeiture infringed proportionality. Much depends on the objectives that the time limit is designed to serve. Where Community law requires a transaction to take place within a specified time limit, failure to observe it may justify forfeiture where its strict observance is to prevent speculative transactions. In *Fromançais v Forma*,[125] Commission regulations provided for the sale of butter by tender for processing. The purpose of the tenders was to sell at reduced prices excess butter held by intervention agencies which could not be sold under market conditions. The regulations in issue provided for the lodging of a security and excluded its release if processing took place after the expiry of a specified period. It was argued that by totally excluding the release of the security in the event of late processing, the provisions infringed proportionality. The essence of the argument was that failure to carry out the processing in time should not carry the same penalty as failure to carry out the processing at all. The Court held that forfeiture was proportionate in order to avoid speculative transactions. It pointed out that if no processing period was imposed, or if the processing period could be extended for long periods, the successful tenderer might be tempted to accumulate stocks with a view to avoiding the effect of a subsequent increase in the purchase price. Such speculation would conflict with the purposes of the regulations which was to remove surplus quantities from the market and would also encourage the accumulation of stocks at reduced prices to the detriment of the Community budget. Less convincingly, Reischl AG considered that the regulations were invalid inasmuch as they imposed the same penalty for a complete failure to carry out the

---

administrative function but it is not as important as the obligation to export and, consequently, the automatic forfeiture of the entire security for failure to obtain an export licence within the specified period was too drastic a penalty.

[121] See Case C-161/96 *Südzucker Mannheim/Ochsenfurt* [1998] ECR I-281.
[122] Case C-104/94 *Cereol Italia v Azienda Agricola Castello* [1995] ECR I-2983.
[123] See also above, *Maas, op. cit.*   [124] *Op. cit.*   [125] *Op. cit.*, n. 16. above.

processing of butter and for the carrying out of the processing after the expiry of the prescribed period.

The Court took a strict view of time limits also in *Denkavit v Forma*.[126] A Commission regulation provided for a time limit of six months within which a claim for the payment of monetary compensatory amounts should be made. The Court held that according to prevailing practice the necessary documents were submitted within a short period, and that the time limit of six months was not out of proportion to the aim of ensuring sound administration. Nor could the applicant claim that the loss of the relevant documents was due to *force majeure* since it had not availed itself of other opportunities to prove the completion of customs formalities. Notably, relying on *Buitoni*, Lenz AG took a different view holding that complete forfeiture of monetary compensatory amounts was unreasonable.[127] It is not without interest that in both *Fromançais v Forma* and *Denkavit v Forma* the Court disagreed with the Advocate General. Such disagreement is inevitable given that the application of the principle of proportionality involves in effect subjective judgments.

The strict approach of the Court is evident also in other cases, especially where the purpose of the time limit is to avoid speculation. In *Hopermann*,[128] the Court was concerned with the Community system of aid for certain agricultural products. Council Regulation No 1431/82 provided for the granting of aid to operators who purchased peas and field beans produced in the Community to use for the manufacture of animal feed. A Commission implementing regulation provided, as a condition for the granting of the aid, that the operator must lodge an application not later than one working day after the application for placing the products under supervision.[129] The Court held that strict adherence to the time limit was essential to the proper functioning of the aid system. Under the applicable Community rules, the amount of the aid to be granted was that in force on the date on which the application for aid was lodged. If the period laid down for the submission of the obligation was not mandatory, operators might wait for a more favourable moment for doing so, thereby obtaining an unjustified advantage.

Time limits may need to observed not only by traders but also by the administration. An example is provided by *British Sugar*.[130] Under the common organization of the market in sugar, producers are liable to a charge for quantities produced in excess of the allowable quotas which are disposed of within the Community. The applicable rules provide that the national competent authority must notify manufacturers who are liable to the charge of the total amount to be paid before 1 May following the end of the marketing year. The ECJ held[131] that a

---

[126] Case 266/84 *Denkavit France v Forma* [1986] ECR 149.   [127] *Ibid.*, p. 161.
[128] *Op. cit.*, n. 16 above. See also Case C-357/88 *Hopermann* [1990] ECR I-1669.
[129] Placing the products under supervision signifies the operation whereby the competent authority determines in the premises of the operator the quantity and quality of the products to be used.   [130] *Op. cit.*, n. 110 above, para 63.
[131] *Ibid.*, para 63.

national agency is in principle not authorised to demand payment where it has not informed the undertaking concerned by the due date. Exceeding of the time limit may be permitted only where the authority without negligence on its part did not know the details of the undertaking's sugar production and where such lack of knowledge may reasonably be attributed to the undertaking because it has not acted in good faith and has not complied with the relevant provisions.

3.6. Health and consumer protection measures

In a number of cases proportionality has been invoked to challenge Community measures in the field of health and consumer protection. This is an area where judicial intervention is characterised by a tendency to defer to the choices of the policy makers and where, in recent years, the requirements of proportionality have paid heed to the application of the precautionary principle.[132]

In *Fedesa*[133] the Court was called upon to balance the financial interests of the traders concerned *vis-à-vis* considerations of health protection. The case concerned the validity of a Council directive which prohibited the use of certain hormones in livestock farming in the interests of public health. It was argued that the directive infringed the principle of proportionality in three respects. First, the outright prohibition of the hormones in question was inappropriate in order to attain the objectives of the directive, since it was impossible to apply in practice and led to the creation of a black market. Second, the prohibition was not necessary since consumer anxieties could be allayed by less restrictive measures such as information campaigns and labelling requirements. Third, the prohibition entailed excessive disadvantages, in particular considerable financial losses on the part of the traders concerned. After emphasising that in the sphere of agricultural policy the legality of a measure can be affected only if it is manifestly inappropriate, the Court came to the conclusion that the prohibition satisfied the test of proportionality. In response to the argument that it was not possible to apply the prohibition in practice, because the presence of natural hormones in all meat prevented the detection of the presence of the hormones prohibited by the directive, the Court held that adequate control methods existed to detect the presence of the prohibited hormones. Also, it was not obvious that the authorization of only one type of hormones, as suggested by the applicants, would be likely to prevent the emergence of a black market for dangerous but less expensive substances. Moreover, the Court

---

[132] See *Alliance for Natural Health, op. cit.*, n. 66 above, para 68 and *British American Tobacco op. cit.*, n. 56 above, *per* Geelhoed AG at para 229 of the Opinion. For the importance of the precautionary principle, see Case C-157/96 *National Farmers' Union and Others* [1998] ECRF I-2211, para 64; Case C-180/96 *United Kingdom v Commission* [1998] ECR I-2265, para 100; Case C-41/02 *Commission v Netherlands* judgment of 2 December 2004, para 45. For a discussion of the case law, see J. L. da Cruz Vilaca, 'The Precautionary Principle in EC Law', (2004) 10 EPL 369.

[133] *Op. cit.*, n. 18 above. See also de Burca, *op. cit.*, n. 3 above, pp. 117–120.

stated that any system of partial authorization would require costly control measures whose effectiveness would not be guaranteed. With regard to the claim that the prohibition was not necessary, the Court attached particular importance to health protection, stating that 'the importance of the objectives pursued is such as to justify even substantial negative financial consequences for certain traders'.[134] It is clear that in *Fedesa* the Court attributed particular importance to the fact that the objective of the directive in issue was to protect public health. That also influenced Mischo AG who stated:[135]

As regards proportionality in the narrow sense, that is to say the weighing of damage caused to individual rights against the benefits accruing to the general interest, it should be stated that the maintenance of public health must take precedence over any other consideration. Once the Council had taken the view, in the context of its discretionary power, that it could not ignore the doubts felt by many Member States, and a large proportion of public opinion, as to the harmlessness of these substances, it was entitled to impose financial sacrifices on the persons concerned.

The Advocate General's Opinion illustrates not only the importance of public health but also the influence of the public's perception of risk in policy making.

The issue was revisited in *Jippes* where the Court held that, in assessing the proportionality of a health protection measure, the criterion to be applied is not whether the measure in question was 'the only one or the best one possible' but whether it was manifestly inappropriate.[136] The case put in issue the Community's preferred method to eliminate foot-and-mouth disease. The Community decided to fight the disease by a policy of non-vaccination accompanied by sanitary slaughter and not by systematic preventive vaccination. As a result, Directive 85/511, as amended by Directive 90/423,[137] banned the vaccination of animals against the disease. It was argued that the ban was contrary to the principles of proportionality and animal welfare. The Court found that the Council's policy choice was well-reasoned. The Council had decided to ban vaccination on the basis of a study submitted by the Commission which considered that a policy of non-vaccination and sanitary slaughter would be more effective, less expensive, and less restrictive as regards movement of animals and animal products than a policy of preventive vaccination. The Court was satisfied that the Council had engaged in sound priority setting: it had carried out a global assessment of the advantages and drawbacks of the system to be established taking into account health considerations, the adverse economic repercussions of vaccination for Community trade, and the likely effectiveness of the alternative systems to contain the disease.

In *Jippes* the Court held that, in choosing among alternative health protection measures, the Council is entitled to take into account not only health but also economic considerations and is expected to take a global approach in the

---

[134] At para 16.   [135] [1990] ECR I-4023, at 4051.
[136] *Op. cit.*, n. 41 above, para 83.
[137] Directive 85/511, OJ 1985 L 315/11; Directive 90/423, OJ 1990 L 224/13.

public interest as a whole: although the effect of the Directive was to preclude the possibility of preventive vaccination of animals belonging to a specific group of farmers, the Council was obliged to have regard to the general state of health of all livestock rather than that of certain individual animals.[138]

The above cases suggest that, where issues of public health are involved, the Court concedes ample discretion to the Community institutions.[139] This contrasts with the Court's strict approach in cases under Article 30 where claims of public health are made.[140] The reason for this variation in standards is to be found in the different functions that judicial review serves in either case. In reviewing policy measures adopted by the Community institutions, the Court seeks to safeguard the economic freedom of the individual but within the confines of the broad discretionary powers of the institutions inherent in the exercise of legislative power. The Community institutions have the benefit of the doubt. That is not the case with national measures restricting freedom of movement which, by the very reason of their effects on market integration, have traditionally been viewed as suspect. There is evidence that this dichotomy is less marked in recent cases.[141] This is the result of a series of interlocking factors. As the internal market matured, the Community institutions saw national health measures as less of a threat to free movement. Health protection is an area where the Community enjoys supplementary rather than primary competence and thus national administrations continue to be the main policy actors. The absence of a comprehensive Community policy in conjunction with recent health scares on a mass scale, such as BSE, revealed a regulatory gap and highlighted the importance of coordinated intervention by Community and national authorities.

A further illustration of the application of proportionality on public health is provided by *British American Tobacco*.[142] The case put in issue the validity of Directive 2001/37[143] which reduced the maximum levels of tar, nicotine, and carbon monoxide permitted in cigarettes and provided for the health warnings which must appear on cigarette packets. An aspect of the Directive which was challenged

---

[138] *Jippes, op. cit.*, para 99.

[139] The same approach was followed in the politically sensitive *BSE* case, where the Court upheld emergency measures taken by the Community on health grounds giving priority to the protection of public health *vis-à-vis* economic and social interests. See Case C-180/96 R *United Kingdom v Commission* [1996] ECR I-3903, esp. paras 89–94. See also Case T-76/96 R *National Farmers' Union and Others v Commission* [1996] II-815. In Case C-365/99 *Portugal v Commission* [2001] ECR I-5645, the Court rejected Portugal's argument that the Commission's refusal to lift a previously imposed export ban on Portuguese products to protect against BSE was disproportionate. The case is unusual in that the Court rejected all the arguments of the applicant although the Commission did not lodge a defence.

[140] See e.g. Case 104/75 *De Peijper* [1976] ECR 613; Case 124/81 *Commission v United Kingdom (UHT milk)* [1983] ECR 203, discussed at 5.2.3 below.

[141] This is evident in the judicial approach to national derogations from harmonization measures adopted under Article 95(4). See especially Case C-3/00 *Denmark v Commission* [2003] ECR I-2643, paras 63–64.

[142] *British American Tobacco, op. cit.*, n. 56 above. For another example, see *Alliance for Natural Health, op. cit.*, n. 66 above.   [143] OJ 2001, L 194/26.

as being contrary to proportionality was the prohibition on the use of descriptors. Article 7 prohibited the use of signs, such as 'low tar' or 'mild', on the packaging suggesting that a particular tobacco product is less harmful than others. The Court held however that the use of such terms was liable to mislead consumers and therefore the provision was appropriate for attaining a high level of health protection on the harmonization of the provisions applicable to the description of tobacco products. As Geelhoed AG put it, the protection of public health carries such great value that in the legislature's assessment other matters of interest, such as the freedom of market participants, must be made subsidiary to it.[144] The Advocate General paid lip service to the argument that Spanish law provided a model of a less restrictive alternative. He opined that the less restrictive alternative test should not be examined in detail. Since the Community legislature enjoys freedom of appraisal in choosing the most appropriate instrument, the Court rules simply on whether the Community legislature could reasonably have come to the conclusion that the Spanish version did not provide equivalent protection to public health.

3.7. Protective measures in trade with third States

Regulations setting up a common organization of the market often contain provisions which enable the Community institutions to introduce appropriate measures in the event that imports from, or exports to, third States threaten to cause serious disturbances to the Community market.[145] The power to take protective measures is entrusted to the Commission which, in general, enjoys wide discretion. It is for the Commission to assess whether there is a risk of serious disturbance to the market and the Court will intervene only if the Commission has committed a manifest error of assessment.[146] In practice, a challenge to the Commission's evaluation of the market conditions is extremely unlikely to succeed. Also, it is for the Commission to choose the appropriate protective measures. Such measures may include the temporary suspension of imports, the imposition of levies, or the

---

[144] See para 229 of the Advocate General's Opinion.

[145] See e.g. Council Regulation No 1035/72 on the common organisation of the market in fruit and vegetables (OJ , English Special Ed. 1972 (II) p. 437) and its implementing Council Regulation No 2707/72 (OJ, English Special Ed. 1972 (28–30 December), p. 3); Council Regulation No 516/77 on the common organization of the market in products processed from fruit and vegetables (OJ 1977 L 73, p. 1) and its implementing Council Regulation No 521/77 (OJ 1977 L 73, p. 28). Regulation No 516/77 was replaced by Council Regulation No 426/86 (OJ 1986 L 49, p. 1). Regulation 521/77 was repealed, with effect from 1 July 1995, by Council Regulation N 3290/94 on the adjustments and transitional arrangements required in the agriculture sector in order to implement the agreements concluded during the Uruguay Round of multilateral trade negotiations (OJ 1994 L 349, p. 105).

[146] See e.g. Case C-205/94 *Binder v Hauptzollamt Stuttgart-West* [1996] ECR I-2871, para 17.

imposition of countervailing charges.[147] Such measures inevitably impose restrictions on the economic freedom of traders and are subject to the principle of proportionality.[148] The Court has held that a countervailing charge is not unlawful merely because it is set at a fixed rate, its legality being dependent on a whole range of factors, such as the prices charged for imports and the requirement of achieving the desired aim effectively.[149] The general principle however is that a charge may not be levied at a higher level than is necessary to achieve its objectives, and in a number of cases fixed-rate charges have been annulled. In *National Dried Fruit Trade Association*[150] Commission Regulation No 2742/82[151] introduced a minimum import price for dried grapes from third countries together with a fixed-rate countervailing charge applicable if the minimum price was exceeded. The Court stated that the aim of the countervailing charge was to enforce the minimum price so as to ensure Community preference in the market for dried grapes and not to inflict an economic penalty on traders who had imported below the minimum price. It followed that the introduction of a single, fixed-rate countervailing charge, imposed even where the difference between the import price and the minimum price was very small, amounted to an economic penalty and infringed the principle of proportionality.[152]

The Court's approach towards fixed-rate charges is best illustrated by reference to the mushroom cases. In 1980 the Community market in mushrooms was threatened by imports from third countries at prices well below the cost prices prevailing in the Community. In order to protect the Community industry, Commission Regulation No 3429/80 made the importation of preserved mushrooms above certain quantities subject to a levy referred to as an additional amount. The levy was imposed initially for a period of three months and had a fixed rate.

---

[147] In Case 345/82 *Wünsche v Germany* [1984] ECR 1995 it was argued that a Commission regulation imposing a levy on the importation of preserved mushrooms was invalid on the ground that the enabling regulation of the Council provided for an exhaustive list of protective measures which did not include the imposition of an additional levy. The Court rejected that argument stating that, since the enabling regulation authorised the Commission to take protective measures leading to a complete suspension of imports, the Commission was, *a fortiori*, entitled to adopt less restrictive rules. This has been confirmed in subsequent cases: see e.g. Case 291/86 *Central-Import Münster v Hauptzollamt Münster* [1988] ECR 3679; Case C-64/95 *Lubella v Hauptzollamt Cottbus* [1996] ECR I-5105.

[148] Examples are given in the text. See further Case 52/81 *Faust v Commission* [1982] ECR 3745, where the Court held that suspension of imports of mushrooms from certain third States was proportionate to achieve the dual objectives of stabilization of the market and the implementation of a Community policy relating to external trade. Cf Case 62/70 *Bock v Commission* [1971] ECR 897. In *Lubella v Hauptzollampt Cottbus, op. cit.*, the Court found compatible with the principle of proportionality protective measures consisting in the introduction of a minimum import price and a countervailing duty on the import of sour cherries.

[149] Case 77/86 *The Queen v Customs and Excise, ex p National Dried Fruit Trade Association* [1988] ECR 757, para 29.   [150] *Ibid.*

[151] OJ 1982 L 290, p. 28.

[152] *Op. cit.*, para. 32 and see also the reasoning of Slynn AG at p. 775. For the calculation of the countervailing duty following the partial annulment of the Regulation by the Court see Joined Cases C-351, 352 and 353/93 *Van der Linde and Tracotex* [1995] ECR I-85.

It was set at approximately 150 per cent of the cost price of top quality mushrooms. In *Werner Faust*[153] and *Wünsche I*[154] the Court held that the Regulation infringed the principle of proportionality. It penalized particularly imported mushrooms of lower quality, since it was calculated on the basis of the price of top quality mushrooms.[155] Also, it did not enable the levy to be set at different levels according to the quality of the products and the circumstances in which they were imported. The Court pointed out that the objective of the Regulation was not to penalize imports without a licence but to protect the Community market from serious disturbance. It came to the conclusion that the levy was set at such a high level as to constitute a considerable financial charge for importers and was therefore disproportionate in relation to the objective of the Regulation.[156]

Werner Faust and *Wünsche* illustrate a strict application of the principle of proportionality. They establish that, in applying protective measures, the Commission must choose the alternative which is least restrictive of commercial freedom. Whereas in *National Dried Fruit Trade Association* the fixed-rate charge was annulled because it was excessive in relation to its objectives, in *Werner Faust* and *Wünsche* the levy was annulled because it imposed an excessive burden on the traders concerned. An interesting argument submitted by the Commission was that the levy satisfied the test of proportionality because it was less restrictive of trade than a complete prohibition of imports which the Commission was authorized to impose under the enabling Council regulations. The Court dismissed that argument stating that the contested regulation was not intended to prohibit imports in excess of certain quantities. Rather, it left open the possibility of issuing import licences against payment of a levy even where those quantities were exceeded. Having opted for that solution, the Commission was required to comply with the principle of proportionality.[157] This reasoning evinces that whether a charge is proportionate is to be determined within the confines of the policy option chosen by the Commission. A charge imposed on the individual may not go beyond what

---

[153] Case C-24/90 [1991] ECR I-4905.   [154] Case C-25/90 [1991] ECR I-4939.

[155] Cf *Binder, op. cit,* n. 146 above; in that case, the Commission imposed a minimum price and a countervailing charge on the importation of strawberries from Poland. It was argued that the protective measures breached the principle of proportionality because the minimum price was the same irrespective of the quality of the imported strawberries. The Court held that there was no breach of proportionality because, before the entry into force of the protective measures, the Polish authorities had agreed to ensure that their exporters would comply with a mean export price applicable to all products irrespective of quality. Also, the Polish authorities were not able to ensure that the quality of exported strawberries was checked and therefore Community customs authorities were unable to monitor that minimum prices linked to the quality of imported strawberries were respected.

[156] The Court followed identical reasoning in the third mushroom case: *Wünsche II, op. cit.,* n. 8 above. See also Case 95/75 *Effem v Hauptzollamt Luneburg* [1976] ECR 361 where the Court held that the fixing of a standard export levy applicable irrespective of the quantity, whether negligible or substantial, of cereals in certain products used for animal feed infringed Community law. Although the judgment made no reference to the principle of proportionality, Reischl AG expressly referred to the principle: see p. 373.

[157] *Werner Faust, op. cit.,* para 21. See also Case C-295/94 *Hüpeden v Hauptzollamt Hamburg-Jonas* [1996] ECR I-3375, para 30.

is necessary to achieve the specific, avowed, objectives of the measure in issue. The fact that the institution which authored the measure might have chosen a different measure, more restrictive of commercial freedom, does not justify the charge. As Jacobs AG vividly put it: 'The use of a cannonball to kill a fly cannot be defended on the ground that a nuclear missile might have been used instead'.[158] The mushrooms judgments also highlight a second function performed by the principle of proportionality. Not only does it protect the individual but it also requires the Community administration to ensure consistency between the objectives sought and the means chosen. It thus contributes to the rationalization and coherence of the policy-making process.

It may be thought that in *Werner Faust* and *Wünsche* the Court applied the principle of proportionality strictly because the enabling Council regulation on the basis of which the Commission imposed the levy expressly provided that the Commission could take protective measures only to such extent and for such length of time as was strictly necessary. That however was not of paramount importance. Subsequently, in *Hüpeden v Hauptzollamt Hamburg-Jonas*[159] the Court applied the same reasoning and annulled a fixed charge on imports of mushrooms applying the general principle of proportionality even though the enabling regulation did not incorporate a specific proportionality requirement.

Following the judgments in the mushrooms cases, the Commission reduced the levy with retroactive effect but maintained it at a fixed rate. Under the new rules, the levy was no longer calculated on the basis of top quality mushrooms but on the basis of grade 3 mushrooms which were of lower quality. The levy was reduced from 150 per cent to 90 per cent of the value of the mushrooms. But the new regulation had no better fortune. In *Pietsch v Hauptzollamt Hamburg-Waltershof*[160] it was annulled as being contrary to the principle of proportionality. The starting point of the Court's reasoning was that the aim of the regulation was not to prohibit all imports beyond the quantities specified but to protect the Community market from disruption owing to excessive imports. Even though the level of the levy was reduced, it still amounted to two-thirds of the cost price of top quality Community mushrooms. The levy substantially increased the cost of imported mushrooms and was thus equivalent to a substantive prohibition of imports. It exceeded clearly what was necessary to attain its objective and was therefore contrary to the principle of proportionality.

In the above cases the Court exercised review of high intensity scrutinizing closely the Commission's means and objectives. An interesting aspect of *Pietsch* and *Hüpeden* is that they were decided by a three-member chamber, the lowest formation in which the ECJ may sit. It is rare for a three-member chamber to annul a Community measure and it is arguable that the cases deserved a higher court formation.

---

[158] *Werner Faust, op. cit.*, at p. 4926.   [159] *Op. cit.*, n. 157 above.
[160] Case C-296/94 [1996] ECR I-3409.

A final point is that in cases where the Court annulled protective measures against imports from third States, it was motivated primarily by the concern to ensure the protection of the traders involved rather than the concern to liberalize free trade with third States. Given the protectionist objectives of Community measures in the field of agriculture, it could hardly be otherwise. It is notable however that in one case the Court held that preference for Community products was not a legal requirement breach of which would result in the invalidity of a Community measure despite the fact that earlier authorities suggested that such a principle exists.[161]

3.8. Flat-rate reductions

It was seen in the previous sections that in a number of cases the Court has annulled measures which impose a fixed-rate charge.[162] The imposition of a fixed-rate charge, however, is not necessarily incompatible with the principle of proportionality. Much depends on the objectives of the measure. Cases like *Werner Faust* and *Wünsche* contrast with the Court's approach to economic policy measures of general application imposing flat-rate reductions with a view to controlling production. An example is provided by *Crispoltoni*.[163] We saw above[164] that at issue in *Crispoltoni* was the system of maximum guaranteed quantities introduced point by point by the Council in order to curtail production of tobacco. For each percentage point by which the maximum guaranteed quantity was exceeded, there was to be a corresponding reduction in the intervention prices and the premiums up to a maximum reduction of 15 per cent. It was argued that the regulation was contrary to the principle of proportionality and the principle of equal treatment because it penalized indiscriminately all producers for the excess production irrespective of whether, and if so the degree by which, they contributed to the maximum guaranteed quantities being exceeded. The Court held that in a common organization of the markets where no national quotas have been introduced, all Community producers, regardless of the Member State in which they are based, must bear together in an egalitarian manner the consequences of the decisions which the Community institutions are led to adopt in order to respond to the risk of imbalance which may arise in the market between production and market outlets.[165] The approach of the Court is not incompatible with its rulings in *Werner Faust* and *Wünsche*. As the Advocate General noted in *Crispoltoni*, there is a clear difference between the imposition of a flat-rate economic penalty on traders

---

[161] C-353/92 *Greece v Council* [1994] ECR I-3411, para 50. The Court stated that the institutions may take Community preference into account as an element in the common agricultural policy but it cannot affect their decision until all the economic factors influencing world trade have been taken into account. Cf Case 5/67 *Beus v Hauptzollamt München* [1968] ECR 83 at 89.

[162] See above, sections 6 and 7.

[163] *Op. cit.*, n. 21 above. See also *Bozzetti v Invernizzi, op. cit.*, n. 35 above; Case C-27/90 *SITPA* [1991] ECR I-133; *Wuidart* discussed in Chapter 2 above.   [164] See 3.5.2.2. above.

[165] *Crispoltoni, op. cit.*, n. 21 above, para 52.

and a sharing in the reduction of subsidies once the maximum guaranteed quantity is exceeded.[166]

3.9. Sanctions

Given that the primary objective of the principle of proportionality is to protect the citizen *vis-à-vis* public power, an area where its application is of particular importance is that of sanctions. The term 'sanction' may be understood broadly, as encompassing both compensatory and punitive penalties, whether or not of a criminal character. Lenaerts[167] defines as compensatory sanctions those imposed in order to remove the injury illegally caused by an individual or undertaking to competitors or the Community finances. Such sanctions include orders of restitution[168] or the levy of duties.[169] Punitive penalties are imposed because an individual or undertaking has engaged in conduct wrongful under Community law. Punitive sanctions may include the temporary exclusion from future benefits[170] or the imposition of pecuniary penalties. As a general principle of Community law, proportionality applies both to compensatory[171] and punitive sanctions but acquires particular importance in relation to the latter. The Community has limited competence to impose sanctions for breach of Community law so that in this context Community law has to rely on national law. Traditionally the emphasis has been on ensuring that penalties imposed by national law are not excessive. According to standard case law, such penalties must not go beyond what is strictly necessary for the objectives pursued and the control procedures must not be accompanied by a penalty which is so disproportionate to the gravity of the infringement that it becomes an obstacle to the freedoms enshrined in the Treaty.[172] In recent years, however, emphasis has been placed also on the need to ensure that the sanctions provided by national law for breach of Community obligations are adequate. This has been, at least partly, the result of greater awareness of fraud

---

[166] *Ibid.*, p. 4880 *per* Jacobs AG.

[167] See K. Lenaerts, 'General Report', in 'Procedures and Sanctions in Economic Administrative Law' 17th FIDE Congress, Vol. III, Berlin 1996, p. 506 at 533.

[168] E.g. repayment of unduly paid or misused aid: see Joined Cases T-231/94 R, T-232/94 R and T-234/94 R *Transacciones Maritimas v Commission* [1994] ECR II-885 and on appeal: C-12/95 P [1995] ECR I-467.

[169] E.g, anti-dumping or countervailing duties. For countervailing duties, see e.g. *National Dried Fruit Trade Association, op. cit.* For anti-dumping, see below.

[170] See e.g. Case C-135/92 *Fiskano v Commission* [1994] ECR I-2885 (temporary exclusion from fishing rights).

[171] As Lenaerts observes, although a compensatory sanction must in principle correspond to the injury to be eliminated, the extent of the sanction may often depend on assessing the importance of that injury. Such assessment entails a discretionary power of appraisal which is subject to the requirements of proportionality: *op. cit.*, p. 536, n.150.

[172] See e.g. Case C-210/91 *Commission v Greece* [1992] ECR I-6735, para 19 and Chapter 5.5 below.

against the Community budget.[173] When pronounced judicially, the need to ensure the adequacy of penalties has not been based on the principle of proportionality but on the need to provide for the effective protection of Community interests in conjunction with the duty of cooperation laid down in Article 10 EC, and the principle of equal treatment: Member States must pursue violations against Community law with the same diligence as violations against national law.[174] Thus, according to standard case law, where Community law does not specifically provide any penalty for an infringement or refers for that purpose to national law, Article 10 EC requires Member States to take all measures necessary to guarantee the application and effectiveness of Community law. While the choice of penalties remains within the discretion of the Member States, they are under the following specific obligations: first, they must ensure that infringements of Community law are penalised in conditions, both procedural and substantive, which are analogous to those applicable to infringements of national law of a similar nature and importance; second, they must provide penalties which are effective, proportionate and dissuasive.[175] In one case, where the Commission brought enforcement proceedings against Greece, the Court went so far as to say that Greece breached Community law by failing to institute criminal or disciplinary proceedings against civil servants responsible for fraud against the Community.[176]

Where the Commission imposes a compensatory sanction, it must take into account, *inter alia*, the duration of the infringement, its seriousness, and whether the applicant was liable for misconduct or negligence. Thus where the Commission reduces the amount of financial aid originally granted on the ground that the recipient has breached the conditions accompanying the granting of aid, it must take into account whether the condition breached was an essential or a secondary one.[177] In general, the CFI requires strict adherence to the conditions attaching to the granting of Community aid in order to ensure the proper management of structural funds and avoid fraud.[178] Proportionality here is understood

---

[173] In the mid-1990s, it was estimated that 10% to 20% of the Community budget was abused for fraudulent purposes every year. See Lenaerts, *op. cit.*, p. 534, n.140, where further references are given.

[174] Case 68/88 *Commission v Greece* [1989] ECR 2965, para 25. Article 280(2) EC, added by the Treaty on European Union, states that 'Member States shall take the same measures to counter fraud affecting the financial interests of the Community as they take to counter fraud affecting their own financial interests'. See also Council Regulation No 2988/95 on the protection of the European Communities' financial interests, OJ 1995 L 312, p. 1.

[175] This was recently reiterated in Joined Cases C-378, C-391 and C-403/02 *Criminal Proceedings against Berlusconi, Adelchi, Dell'Utri and Others*, judgment of 3 May 2005, para 65. For previous cases, see *Commission v Greece, op. cit.*, paras 23–24; Case C-326/88 *Hansen* [1990] ECR I-2911, para 17; Case C-177/95 *Ebony Maritime and Loten Navigation* [1997] ECR I-1111, para 35; Case C-167/01 *Inspire Art* [2003] ECR I-10155, para 62.

[176] *Commission v Greece, op. cit*; see also the comments of the Advocate General in Case C-56/91 *Greece v Commission* [1993] ECR I-3433, at 3453.   [177] *Astipesca, op. cit.*, n. 42 above.

[178] See e.g. *Astipeca, op. cit.* where the Court rejected the applicant's argument that the reduction of the aid should be merely symbolic. See further: Joined Cases T-551/93, T-231/94, T-233/94 and T-234/94 *Industrias Pesqueras Campos and Others v Commission* [1996] ECR II-247.

as reasonableness. It has been held, for example, that the penalty imposed by the Commission in the case of an irregularity may, without infringing the principle of proportionality, be greater than the amount which corresponds to that irregularity in order to have a deterrent effect and ensure proper management of financial resources.[179]

An interesting illustration of the application of proportionality on punitive sanctions is provided by *Advanced Nuclear Fuels v Commission*.[180] The case raised for the first time the question of sanctions for breach of the provisions of the Euratom Treaty on safeguards (Articles 77 to 85) the purpose of which is to ensure the security of nuclear materials. Under Article 83(1) of the Euratom Treaty, in case of infringement of the requirements imposed by the provisions on safeguards, the Commission may impose the following sanctions in order of severity: a warning; the withdrawal of special benefits such as financial or technical assistance; the placing of the undertaking responsible for the infringement under administration for a period not exceeding four months; total or partial withdrawal of source materials or special fissile materials. In *Advanced Nuclear Fuels*, radioactive material was exported inadvertently from Germany to the United States, as a result of a mistake in transportation. The Commission placed the applicant company under administration for a period of four months. The company alleged that the penalty was disproportionate, the appropriate one being a warning. The Court held that failure to observe the provisions of the Euratom Treaty, which seek to ensure that nuclear materials are not diverted to purposes other than those for which they are intended, is in itself a serious violation. It came to the conclusion that the sanction of administration was necessary in order to ensure that a similar incident would not occur in the future. The Court considered that the less severe option open to the Commission of appointing inspectors was not adequate because, unlike administrators, inspectors did not have the power to instruct the company to issue or modify its internal operating instructions. It is not surprising that in the area of nuclear safety, as in the area of external security,[181] the Court follows a loose application of the principle of proportionality, being prepared to err on the side of the enforcement agency. That does not mean however that the Court considers those areas as non-justiciable. By contrast, it assesses carefully all the arguments submitted and is prepared to scrutinize the conduct of the administration.

Anti-dumping duties and fines imposed by the Commission are also subject to the principle of proportionality. In the area of anti-dumping the Court is, in general, reluctant to intervene on the ground that the finding of dumping and the determination of injury involve the appraisal of complex economic and technical issues. The Court's reluctance to intervene has been criticized.[182]

---

[179] Case C-500/99 P *Conserve Italia v Commission* [1999] ECR II-3139, para 101.
[180] Case C-308/90 [1993] ECR I-309.   [181] For public security, see, 5.4.2 below.
[182] See A. Egger, 'The Principle of Proportionality in Community Anti-Dumping Law', (1993) 18 ELR 367. Note however that in Joined Cases T-163 and T-165/94 *Koyo Seiko v*

In the area of penalties and fines imposed under competition law, the Community judicature exercises unlimited jurisdiction.[183] This differs fundamentally from judicial review in that the ECJ and, since its establishment, the CFI act as appellate bodies with power to change the level of fine. Thus, the CFI may reduce a fine even when it appears that the Commission's decision finding an infringement of Articles 81 and 82 or of the Merger Regulation is not vitiated by any illegality.[184] The same applies where the Court exercises its jurisdiction under Article 36 ECSC which provides that the Court has unlimited jurisdiction in appeals against pecuniary sanctions and periodic penalty payments imposed under the ECSC Treaty.[185] In a number of cases under the ECSC Treaty the Court has refused to annul decisions imposing fines on the ground that they infringe general principles of law but, acting as an appellate body, it has reduced the fine imposed by the Commission primarily on the ground that the Commission's conduct was such as to leave the undertaking concerned in a state of uncertainty. In one case,[186] the Court reduced the standard fine imposed on the ground that the undertaking by its own initiative took steps to minimise the excess production whereas the Commission had acted in breach of the rules of good administration leaving the applicant in doubt as to its intentions. In another case[187] the Court reduced the fine imposed on the ground that the Commission did not notify the applicant in good time of the quota to which it was entitled and it was therefore unable to produce the quantity which it was entitled to produce.

In *Estel*,[188] the Court found that the Commission had not informed the undertaking concerned of the method which it intended to apply for the calculation of the quota and that, as a result, the Commission erred as to the gravity of the infringement. In *Bertoli*,[189] the fine was reduced *inter alia* on the ground that in previous cases where it had uncovered infringements, the Commission had not

Council [1995] ECR II-1381 the CFI annulled an anti-dumping regulation of the Council. Confirmed on appeal: Case C-245/95 P [1998] ECR I-401.

[183] See Article 229 EC and, specifically for Articles 81 and 82 EC, Regulation 1/2003 on the implementation of the rules on competition law laid down in Articles 81 and 82 of the Treaty (OJ 2003 L 1/1), Article 31 (replacing Regulation 17, Article 17).

[184] See Lenaerts, *op. cit.*, p. 577 and see e.g. Case T-13/89 *ICI v Commission* [1992] ECR II-1021, Case T-77/92 *Parker Pen v Commission* [1994] ECR II-549; Case T-142/89 *Böel v Commission* [1995] ECR II-867. Cf. T-83/91 *Tetra-Pak v Commission* [1994] ECR II-755. By contrast, the Court of Justice adjudicating on appeal from the CFI may not reduce the fine imposed by the CFI on grounds of fairness since the appeal is on points of law only: Case C-359/01 P *British Sugar plc v Commission*, judgment of 29 April 2004, para 48; Case C-219/95 P *Ferriere Nord v Commission* [1997] ECR I-4411, para 11; Case C-310/93 P *BPB Industries and British Gypsum v Commission* [1994] ECR I-865. Note also that the CFI may, if the circumstances so justify, confirm the fine even if it annuls a part of the Commission's decision finding an infringement: Case T-21/99 *Dansk Rørindustri v Commission* [2002] ECR II-1681.

[185] Note that the ECSC Treaty has now expired: see above, n. 37.

[186] Case 179/82 *Lucchini v Commission* [1983] ECR 3083.

[187] Case 188/82 *Thyssen v Commission* [1983] ECR 3721.

[188] Case 270/82 *Estel v Commission* [1983] ECR 1195, para 12.

[189] Case 8/83 *Bertoli v Commission* [1984] ECR 1649. See further Case 9/83 *Eisen und Metall Aktiengesellschaft v Commission* [1983] ECR 2071.

imposed any fines. The Court and the CFI however have not been particularly receptive to the same argument in relation to fines in the field of competition law.[190]

Finally, the principle of proportionality also applies to penalties imposed on Member States under Article 228 EC for failure to comply with Community law. Here again the ECJ exercises unlimited jurisdiction and is not bound by the fine or periodic penalty payment proposed by the Commission.[191] The ECJ has held that a penalty payment imposed under Article 228 must be appropriate to the circumstances and proportionate both to the breach and to the ability of the Member State to pay. On that basis, the basic criteria to be taken into account are, in principle, the duration of the infringement, its degree of seriousness, and the ability of the State to pay. In applying those criteria, account should be taken, in particular, of the effects of failure to comply on private and public interests and the urgency of effecting compliance.[192]

3.10. Overview of factors to be taken into account

It has become clear from the above analysis that, far from dictating a uniform test, proportionality is a flexible principle which is used in different contexts to protect different interests and entails varying degrees of judicial scrutiny. It is by its nature flexible and open-textured. The case law on proportionality may be seen as a celebration of judicial relativism. The application of the principle is best encapsulated in the dictum 'in law, context is everything'.[193] The Court applies the test of suitability and the test of necessity with varying degrees of strictness depending on a number of factors. It may be helpful here to recapitulate by listing some of them:

- *Power of appraisal.* The nature of the contested act and, in particular, the degree of discretion required is of decisive importance. The broader the power of appraisal

---

[190] See e.g. Joined Cases 100–103/80 *Musique Diffusion Française v Commission* [1983] ECR 1825; *ICI v Commission , op. cit.*, n. 184 above.

[191] Case C-387/97 *Commission v Greece* [2000] ECR I-5047.

[192] *Ibid.*, paras 92–93; in that case the ECJ imposed on Greece a penalty of € 20,000 for each day of delay in implementing the measures necessary to comply with a previous judgment finding Greece to be in violation of Directive 75/442 on waste (OJ 1975, L 194/39) and Directive 78/319 on toxic and dangerous waste (OJ 1978, L84/43). For the method of calculating the fine, see the EC Commission's Memorandum on applying Article 171 of the EC Treaty, OJ C [1996] 242/6 and Method for calculating the penalty payments provided for pursuant to Article 171 of the EC treaty OJ [1997] C 63/2. In his Opinion on Case C-304/02 *Commission v France* (Second Opinion delivered on 18 November 2004), Geelhoed AG opined that, since the ECJ enjoys full jurisdiction under Article 228(2), it may impose a lump sum payment even if the Commission only asked for a periodic penalty payment subject to the requirement that, in compliance with the rights of defence, if the Court contemplates imposing a more severe sanction that that suggested by the Commission, it must give the parties the right to be heard. Also, depending on the circumstances, the principle of proportionality may not preclude the Court from imposing both a lump sum and a penalty payment: see para 46 of the Opinion.

[193] See *Daly* [2001] 2 WLR 1622 per Lord Steyn at 1636.

that the adopting institution has, the less comprehensive the review exercised by the Court. In general, it can be said that the Court undertakes only marginal review in relation to legislative measures of economic policy and measures the adoption of which requires complex economic and technical evaluations.

- *The restrictive effect of the measure and the type of interest adversely affected.* The more severely a measure affects private interests, the more difficult it is to establish its necessity. For example, a charge or a penalty entails a greater restriction on commercial freedom than the refusal of a subsidy or a benefit and imposes a higher burden on the authorities to justify it. By contrast, it seems that limited importance is attributed to whether the provision under which the contested measure was adopted incorporates a test of necessity, e.g. requires action only where it is strictly necessary.[194]

- *The objective of the measure and the type of interest which the measure seeks to protect.* Thus, public health considerations may be accorded priority over economic interests[195] as may nuclear safety[196] and public security considerations.[197]

- *Whether the same objective can be achieved by less restrictive measures.* The Court is open to argument that the same objective can be achieved by less restrictive means. But where policy measures are involved, the less restrictive alternative test gives way to the manifestly inappropriate test.

- *The treatment of comparable products or producers.* With a view to determining whether a measure is necessary, regard may be had to the way comparable situations are treated.[198] The principle of proportionality is closely linked to the principle of equal treatment and incorporates an element of participation.[199]

- *Whether the individual has suffered actual hardship as a result of the measure.*[200]

- *The temporary effect of the measure.* Measures restricting economic freedom may be easier to justify if they are only of limited temporal application.[201]

- *The urgency of the situation.* A pressing need to regulate the market may give wider discretion to the institution which authors the act. The same applies to transitional measures urgently drawn to deal with an emergency.[202]

- *The technicality of the subject matter and the degree of expertise required.* The Court is more reluctant to intervene in areas where legislative intervention requires a degree of technical expertise such as anti-dumping.

---

[194] See *Hüpeden v Hauptzollamt Hamburg-Jonas, op. cit.,* n. 157 above; *Balkan-Import-Export, op. cit.,* n. 20 above.   [195] *Fedesa, op. cit.,* n. 18 above.

[196] *Advanced Nuclear Fuels, op. cit.,* n. 180 above.

[197] Case C-120/94 *Commission v Greece (FYROM Case)* [1996] ECR 1513, *per* Jacobs AG.

[198] See e.g. Case C-256/90 *Mignini* [1992] ECR I-2651.

[199] See e.g. *Bela Muhle, op. cit.,* n. 19 above, *Mignini* and see Cf *Portugal v Commission, op. cit.,* n. 139 above, para 57.

[200] *Roquette Frères, op. cit.,* n. 58 above, paras 29, 31. Case 106/83 *Sermide v Cassa Conguaglio Zucchero* [1984] ECR 4209.   [201] But see *Bela Muhle.*

[202] *Balkan-Import-Export, op. cit., Roquette Frères.*

4

The Principle of Proportionality: Relationship with Competence and Subsidiarity

The previous chapter traced the development of proportionality in Community law, explained its multiple functions, and examined the degree of scrutiny exercised by the Court by reference to the case law in selected areas. This chapter focuses on proportionality as a principle governing the exercise of Community competence. It examines Article 5(3) EC and looks selectively at the case law on proportionality, competence and subsidiarity. It concludes by examining the protocol on proportionality and subsidiarity accompanying the EU Constitutional Treaty. Although the adoption of the Treaty, at least in its current form, is no longer a possibility, the Protocol remains important. A consensus appears to be emerging that, in any future constitutional model, national Parliaments should be given a greater say in Community affairs and, as an attempt to promote bicameralism, the Protocol may provide inspiration for future arrangements. Indeed, some of its provisions, or a version of the control mechanism envisaged therein, could be introduced by Community and national legislation without need for Treaty amendment.

4.1. Proportionality as a principle governing the exercise of Community competence

Article 5(3) EC, added by the Treaty on European Union, states that 'Any action by the Community shall not go beyond what is necessary to achieve the objectives of this Treaty'.[1] According to the prevailing view, Article 5(3) does not add to the existing case law. It merely reiterates the importance of the principle of proportionality and expressly grants it constitutional status.[2] The only difference seems to be one of emphasis. As a general principle of law, proportionality has been

---

[1] This corresponds to Article I-11(4) of the Constitution which states that, 'under the principle of proportionality, the content and form of Union action shall not exceed what is necessary to achieve the objectives of the Constitution'.

[2] See K. Lenaerts and P. Van Ypersele, 'Le principe de subsidiarité et son contexte: Étude de l'article 3B du traité CE' (1994) 30 CDE 3, at p. 61; T.C. Hartley, *The Foundations of European*

developed by the Court primarily with a view to protecting the individual from action by the Community institutions and by the Member States. By contrast, Article 5(3) forms part of a system of provisions whose aim is to control the expansion of Community legislative action and seeks to limit burdens on Member States rather than burdens on individuals. This is not to say that the protection of rights of the individual is excluded from the scope of Article 5(3). The provision is understood to mean that 'any burdens, whether financial or administrative, falling upon the Community, national governments, local authorities, economic operators and citizens, should be minimized and should be proportionate to the objectives to be achieved'.[3]

Proportionality is also incorporated by implication in the principle of subsidiarity. Article 5(2) requires that the Community take action 'only if and in so far as' the objectives of the proposed action cannot sufficiently be achieved by the Member States. This is in turn exemplified by the dual test of scale and effectiveness. There are however differences between the two principles. First, subsidiarity comes into play at an earlier stage than proportionality.[4] It defines whether or not action must be taken at Community level. Proportionality, by contrast, comes into play only once it is decided that Community action is necessary and seeks to define its scope. The second difference is this. Under Article 5(2), subsidiarity applies only in cases where the competence of the Community is not exclusive whereas, under Article 5(3), proportionality applies also where the Community enjoys exclusive competence. Indeed, it seems that the reason why Article 5(3) was added by the Treaty of European Union was to ensure that the Community respects the interests of Member States not only where it exercises concurrent competence but also where it exercises its exclusive competence.[5]

Article 5(3) refers both to the extent and the intensity of Community action. It requires that such action does not exceed what is necessary to achieve the objectives of the Treaty but does not itself limit those objectives nor does it require their restrictive interpretation. It lays down a principle which, like the principle of subsidiarity, is directed primarily, although not exclusively, at the political institutions of the Community and is designed to influence the legislative process *ex ante* i.e. at the stage of preparation of legislation. The Conclusions of the Presidency of the European Council held in Edinburgh in December 1992 laid down guidelines for the adoption of Community legislation in the light of Article 5(3). These formed the basis for the Protocol on the application of the principles of

---

Community Law (5th Ed, Oxford 1994) p. 152; N. Emiliou, *The Principle of Proportionality in European Law* (Kluwer, 1996) at p. 401. But see V. Constantinesco, R. Kovar, D. Simon, *Traité sur l'Union Européenne*, Economica, 1995, p. 113.

[3] European Council of Edinburgh, 11–12 December 1992, Presidency Conclusions, Annex 1 to Part I A, (Agence Europe, Special Ed., No. 5878BIS, 13/14 December 1992).

[4] See Lenaerts and van Ypersele, *op. cit.*, para 100; G. Strozzi, 'Le principe de subsidiarité dans la perspective de l'intégration européenne: une énigme et beaucoup d'attentes', (1994) 30 RTDE 373, at 379. Those texts received judicial recognition by Léger AG in Case C-84/94 *United Kingdom v Council* [1996] ECR I-5755 at 5783.   [5] Lenaerts and van Ypersele, *op. cit.*, p. 62.

subsidiarity and proportionality annexed to the EC Treaty by the Treaty of Amsterdam.[6] The EU Constitution envisages the repeal of the Amsterdam Protocol and its replacement by another enhancing the role of national parliaments in monitoring observance of the principles of subsidiarity and proportionality.[7]

The guidelines included in the Amsterdam Protocol state *inter alia* that Community measures should leave as much scope for national decision as possible and that, while respecting Community law, care should be taken to respect well-established national arrangements and the organization and working of Member States' legal systems. Where appropriate, and subject to the need for proper enforcement, Community measures should provide Member States with alternative ways to achieve the objectives of the measures.[8] The Community should legislate only to the extent necessary. Other things being equal, directives should be preferred to regulations and framework directives to detailed measures.[9]

The Guidelines of the Edinburgh Council are more detailed that those of the Amsterdam Protocol. An interesting guideline posited by the former is that, where difficulties are localized and only certain Member States are affected, any necessary Community action should not be extended to other Member States unless this is necessary to achieve an objective of the Treaty.[10] This brings to the surface the relationship between proportionality and equality of Member States. In its case law the Court has accepted that it is compatible with the principle of equal treatment for the Community to adopt rules which apply only to certain Member States, where that is objectively justified.[11] The European Council conclusions recognize that differences in infrastructure or the underlying conditions of Member States in specific sectors where Community action is envisaged may make intervention by the Community proportionate in relation to some Member States but disproportionate in relation to others.[12]

4.2. Case law on proportionality

Before the Treaty on European Union came into force, the case law accepted that the principle of proportionality can be invoked not only by individuals but also by Member States.[13] In one case, the Court rejected the argument that proportionality amounted to a 'principle of minimum intervention' according to which, in interpreting Community measures, preference should be given to the interpretation which restricted Community intervention on Member States' sovereignty to

---

[6] Protocol No 30.   [7] See 4.5 below.   [8] Protocol, *op. cit.*, para 7.

[9] *Ibid.*, para 6.   [10] *Ibid.*, para (vii).

[11] See e.g. Case 13/63 *Italy v Commission* [1963] ECR 165; Joined Cases C-181, 182 and C-218/88 *Deschamps v Ofival* [1989] ECR I-4381 and see further above, p. 88.

[12] Lenaerts and van Ypersele, *op. cit.*, p. 67.

[13] See e.g. Case 116/82 *Commission v Germany* [1986] ECR 2519; see also Case 37/83 *Rewe-Zentrale v Landwirtschaftskammer Rheinland* [1984] ECR 1229.

the minimum.[14] Proportionality as a principle governing the exercise of Community competence came to the fore in *Germany v Council*.[15] By Regulation No 2186/93,[16] adopted under Article 284 EC, the Council required Member States to establish registers for statistical purposes containing information on commercial enterprises. The purpose of registers was to provide the Commission with reliable information so as to enable it to perform its various tasks. The German Government argued that the regulation infringed the principle of proportionality in two respects. First, it required the registration of certain data which were not necessary to achieve its objectives. Second, the financial and administrative costs in establishing and periodically updating the national registers were disproportionate by comparison to the potential benefits. The Court rejected both arguments. With regard to the first, it held that the information required to be included was statistically relevant. With regard to the second, it stated that the German Government had not shown that the costs were manifestly disproportionate to the advantages resulting for the Community from the availability of reliable data regarding the structure of the economy throughout the Community.

The case was introduced before the Treaty on European Union came into force so that Article 5(3) was not directly relevant. However, the test employed by the ECJ under Article 5(3) remains the same. The Court will be reluctant to intervene unless it is shown that a measure manifestly goes beyond the objectives of the Treaty. The intensity of review is no different from when proportionality is applied for the protection of the individual to control the legality of policy measures.[17] This was confirmed by the *Organisation of the Working Time Directive* case[18] where the Court rejected the challenge of the United Kingdom against Council Directive 93/104[19] on grounds of breach of the principle of proportionality. The Court stated that, in making social policy choices, the Community legislature is required to make complex assessments and must be allowed wide discretion. Consequently, review is limited to examining whether the exercise of discretion has been vitiated by manifest error or misuse of powers or whether the institution concerned has manifestly exceeded the limits of its discretion.[20]

In the *Organisation of Working Time Directive* case, the United Kingdom objected to what it saw as the introduction of broad social policy measures by the back door, namely on the basis of Article 118a (now 138) which deals with health and safety at work and authorizes the adoption of directives by qualified majority as opposed to unanimity in the Council. One of the arguments submitted by the Government was that the measures for the organization of working time provided in Directive

---

[14] Case 28/84 *Commission v Germany* [1985] ECR 3097.
[15] Case C-426/93 [1995] ECR I-3723.
[16] Regulation No 2186/93 on Community coordination in drawing up business registers for statistical purposes, OJ 1993 L 196, p. 1.
[17] See also Case C-206/94 *Brennet v Paletta* [1996] ECR I-2357.
[18] *United Kingdom v Council, op. cit.*, n. 4 above.
[19] Directive 93/104/EC of 23 November 1993 concerning certain aspects of the organization of working time, OJ 1993 L 307, p. 18.   [20] *United Kingdom v Council, op. cit.*, para 58.

93/104, including minimum rest periods and maximum weekly working time, were disproportionate. The desired level of protection could have been achieved by less restrictive measures such as the use of risk assessments where working hours exceeded particular norms. The Court held that the measures of the Directive contributed directly to the improvement of health and safety of workers and were therefore suitable to attain their objectives. With regard to the test of necessity, it held that the Council had not committed a manifest error in considering that the objectives of Article 118a could not be achieved by less restrictive measures. In reaching that conclusion, it placed particular emphasis on the flexibility of the Directive. Its provisions were subject to several derogations thus leaving scope for adjustments at national level.

A further example of the use of the principle is provided by *Germany v Parliament and Council (deposit guarantee case)*.[21] The German Government challenged the 'export prohibition' contained in Directive 94/19 on deposit guarantee schemes[22] *inter alia* on the ground that it went beyond what was necessary to achieve its objectives. The Directive provides that branches of credit institutions located in other Member States are covered by the deposit guarantee scheme of the State where the credit institution has its registered office. Article 4(1) however states that, until the end of 1999, the cover provided for depositors in branches located in other Member States could not exceed the cover offered by the corresponding guarantee scheme of the host Member State. The rationale of this provision was to avoid disturbances which might be caused if branches of foreign banks offered higher levels of cover than those offered by domestic banks in Member States with less developed financial markets. The German Government took issue on the ground that the underlying objective could be met with less restrictive measures, for example, a system authorizing intervention only where a disturbance in the market of a Member State was imminent. The Court rejected the claim holding that it was not its task to substitute its own assessment for that of the legislature. It can, at most, find fault with the legislative choice of the institutions 'only if it appears manifestly incorrect or if the resultant disadvantages for certain economic operators were wholly disproportionate to the advantages otherwise offered'.[23] The finding is hardly surprising. The German Government invoked proportionality to procure a solution which it had supported unsuccessfully in the Council negotiations leading to the adoption of the Directive. Its submissions, however sensible, were alternative legislative choices rather than grounds of illegality. The dispute encapsulates the complexities of the harmonization process in areas where wide variations exist in the economic sector in question. The Directive spelt a compromise. On the one hand, it brought about some degree of coordination of national laws thus facilitating the right of establishment. On the other hand, it

---

[21] Case C-233/94 [1997] ECR I-2405.   [22] OJ 1994 L 135, p. 5.

[23] *Germany v Parliament and Council, op. cit.*, para 56. The German Government also challenged unsuccessfully on grounds of proportionality the provisions of the Directive on supplementary cover. See paras 66–74.

sought to avoid, at least for an initial period, the level of guarantee cover becoming an instrument of competition. Its net effect was that credit institutions established in Member States providing for a high degree of consumer protection lost out in that they were unable to exploit commercially the advantages of consumer protection legislation. But the solution of the Community legislature seems compatible with the underlying perception of regulation as a public good.

The above cases decided in the 1990s suggest that proportionality is an unreliable ground on the basis of which to question economic and social policies and tame Community competence. However, to assess where the ECJ stands in the division of powers between the Community and the Member States, Article 5(3) should not be examined in isolation but in the context of Article 5 as a whole. The ECJ might decide that Community legislation interferes excessively with the sovereign rights of Member States but address the issue not in terms of proportionality but in terms of competence or, even, subsidiarity. In fact, the three paragraphs of Article 5 are closely intertwined so that their separate examination risks giving a misleading impression. The sections below examine briefly recent case law on competence and subsidiarity.

4.3. Community competence

One of the main ways in which the Court has traditionally influenced the development of the Community legal order and contributed towards the constitutionalization of the Treaties has been through an expansive interpretation of Community competence.[24] There are signs that, in recent years, the Court is prepared to adopt a more critical stance. In Opinion 2/94,[25] the ECJ interpreted narrowly Article 235 (now Article 308) EC, holding that the Community did not have competence to accede to the European Convention of Human Rights. In the *Tobacco Advertisement Directive* case,[26] it went a step further, challenging the powers of the Community legislature in the core area of the internal market. The Court annulled Directive 98/43 prohibiting the advertisement and sponsorship of tobacco products[27] on the ground that it provided for excessive regulation and fell beyond the scope of Article 100(a) (now Article 95) EC. For the first time the Court gave a narrow interpretation to that provision. It held that the Community legislature has power to adopt measures which are intended to improve the

---

[24] For a detailed discussion, see e.g., S. Weatherill, 'Competence Creep and Competence Control' (2004) YEL; G. Bermann, 'Competences of the Union' in Tridimas and Nebbia (eds)' '*EU Law for the 21st Century: Rethinking the New Legal Order*', (Oxford, Hart Publishing 2004) Vol. 1; A. von Bogdandy and J. Bast, 'The European Union's Vertical Order of Competences: The Current Law and Proposals for its Reform', (2002) 39 CMLR 227.

[25] Opinion 2/94 *Accession to the ECHR* [1996] ECR I-1759, discussed in 7.5.5 below.

[26] C-376/98 *Germany v Parliament and Council* [2000] ECR I-8419.

[27] OJ 1998, L 213/9.

conditions for the establishment and functioning of the internal market but is not vested with a general power to regulate it.[28]

The judgment reverses a long trend towards the expansive interpretation of Community competence and makes clear that the powers of the Community institutions are finite: Community legislation may supplement but not replace State regulatory intervention. By drawing the distinction between the Community as a facilitator of free trade and as a regulator, the judgment circumscribed the limits of supra-national intervention and asserted the regulatory power of the nation state.

The comparatist may hear in the *Tobacco Advertisement* case echoes of the US Supreme Court judgments in *Lopez*[29] and *Morrison*.[30] But why did the ECJ appear to favour a deceleration of integration and greater deference to nation states? The judgment may be seen as a response to a discernible sentiment of Euro-scepticism and criticisms that the Community polity lacks legitimacy, a feeling that had already been evident in *Keck*.[31] Having seen their sovereignty diluted by the rulings of the Court from the mid 1960s to the mid 1990s, the national governments clipped its powers by keeping it out of the Common Foreign and Security Policy and restricting its engagement in Justice and Home Affairs. The more cautious approach of the Court was perhaps a recognition of this uneasiness on the part of national governments.

The *Tobacco Advertisement* judgment endorsed a more 'nation state-friendly' theory of integration but did not set an uncompromising trend towards the dilution of Community powers. Far from it. In subsequent cases, the Court refused to annul directives at the instigation of state and private actors on the ground that they were

---

[28] See para 83 of the judgment. For a detailed analysis, see G. Tridimas and T. Tridimas, 'The European Court of Justice and the Annulment of the Tobacco Advertisement Directive: Friend of National Sovereignty or Foe of Public Health?' (2002) 14 European Journal of Law and Economics, 171–183. The Court's reasoning was as follows: it concluded that the need to ensure the free movement of goods did not justify the adoption of the Tobacco Directive. First, the prohibition imposed by the Directive was too general. It extended to all forms of advertising even though in relation to some of them, there was no risk of obstacles to trade. This was true, in particular, with regard to the so-called static advertising media (i.e. advertising on posters, parasols, ashtrays and other articles used in hotels, restaurants and cafes) and advertising spots in cinemas. Second, the Directive did not in fact ensure free movement of products which were in conformity with its provision because Member States retained power to lay down stricter requirements concerning the advertising and sponsorship of tobacco products. The Court also held that the Community legislature could not rely on the need to eliminate distortions of competition either in the advertising sector or in the sale of tobacco products in order to adopt the Directive. It held that, in determining the lawfulness of a directive adopted on the basis of Article 100a, it is required to verify whether the distortions of competition which the measure purports to eliminate are appreciable. It accepted that advertising agencies and producers of advertising media established in Member States which impose fewer restrictions are at an advantage in terms of economies of scale and profitability. It held however that the effects of such advantages on competition are remote and indirect and do not constitute appreciable distortions. The Court identified some appreciable distortions in that the prohibition of tobacco sponsorship in some Member States led to the relocation of some sporting events (e.g. Formula One racing). It conceded that such distortions could be a basis for recourse to Article 100a in order to prohibit certain forms of sponsorship but held that they could not justify an outright prohibition.
[29] 514 U.S. 549.
[30] 529 U.S. 598.   [31] Joined Cases C-267–8/91 [1993] ECR I-6097.

ultra vires the Community and sought to empower rather than curtail Community regulatory intervention.[32] In *Netherlands v Parliament and Council*[33] the Court rejected the argument of the Dutch Government that Directive 98/44 on the legal protection of biotechnological inventions[34] could not be adopted under Article 95 EC.[35] In the *BAT Industries* case,[36] the Court refused to annul Directive 2001/37 on the approximation of national laws concerning the manufacture, presentation and sale of tobacco products.[37] The Directive reduced the maximum levels of tar, nicotine, and carbon monoxide permitted in cigarettes and provided for the health warnings which must appear on cigarette packets. The Court reiterated that recourse to Article 95 is possible even if the aim is to prevent the emergence of future obstacles to trade resulting from multifarious development of national laws provided that the emergence of such obstacles is likely and the measure in question is designed to prevent them.[38] It also recalled that, if the conditions for recourse to Article 95 as a legal basis are met, the Community legislature cannot be prevented from relying on that legal basis on the ground that public health protection is a decisive factor in the choices to be made.

The Court pointed out that the market for cigarettes in the Community is one where trade between Member States represents a relatively large part. It also stated that, despite previous harmonization measures in this area, differences in the national laws had already emerged or were likely to emerge by the time the Directive came into force. This is because the previous measures only provided for minimal requirements and covered only certain aspects of the manufacture and presentation of tobacco products.

BAT Industries can be distinguished from the *Tobacco Advertisement* case. The Tobacco Advertising Directive over-regulated whilst Directive 2001/37 did not. Also, the first Directive concerned selling arrangements whilst the second concerned product-related requirements which are more pernicious to free movement. In that respect, the Court's differential approach finds support in

---

[32] Apart from the judgments discussed in the text, see on Article 95 EC: Joined Cases C-154–5/04, *The Queen on the application of Alliance for Natural Health v Secretary of State for Health (Vitamins case)*, judgment of 12 July 2005, discussed in the previous chapter; Case C-210/03 *The Queen on the application of Swedish Match AB v Secretary of State for Health*, judgment of 14 December 2004; Case C-434/02 *Arnold André GmbH & Co KG v Landrat des Kreises Herford*, judgment of 14 December 2004; In Case C-222/02 *Paul and Others v Bundesrepublik Deutschland*, judgment of 12 October 2004, the ECJ appeared to suggest that it would be beyond the powers of the Community under Article 95 EC to harmonize the rules governing the liability of banking regulators in the EU stating that intervention must be restricted to 'the essential harmonisation necessary and sufficient' to secure mutual recognition. This however was an *obiter dictum*. The Court did not intend to make a general pronouncement on Community competence in the field. For other aspects of Community competence, see Case C-93/00 *Parliament v Council* [2001] ECR I-10119 (annulment of a Council regulation adopted on the wrong legal basis); Case C-11/00 *Commission v ECB*, [2003] ECR I-7147 (annulment of ECB decision on fraud investigations as being *ultra vires*).   [33] Case C-377/98 *Netherlands v Parliament and Council* [2001] ECR I-7079.

[34] OJ 1988 L 213/13.   [35] For its reasoning, see 4.4 below.

[36] Case C-491/01 *The Queen v Secretary of State for Health ex p British American Tobacco Ltd* [2002] ECR I-11453.   [37] OJ L 2001, L 194/26.

[38] *BAT, op. cit.*, n. 55, para 61.

Keck.[39] Finally, unlikely the Tobacco Advertisement Directive, Directive 2001/37 contained a provision which guaranteed the free movement of products which complied with its requirements. As the Court pointed out, by forbidding Member States to prevent the import, sale or consumption of tobacco products which complied with the requirements of the Directive, Article 13 of the Directive 'gave the Directive its full effect'.[40] By contrast the Tobacco Advertisement Directive permitted Member States to lay down stricter requirements concerning the advertising and sponsorship of tobacco products and did not take any measures to ensure the free movement of products which conformed with its provisions.

In *BAT Industries* the Court was keen to safeguard the prerogative of the Community legislature to amend existing harmonization measures. It declared that, even where a provision of Community law guarantees the removal of all obstacles to trade in the area that it harmonizes, that cannot make it impossible for the Community legislature to adapt that provision in step with other considerations. It also held that progress in scientific facts is not the only ground on which the Community legislature can decide to adapt Community legislation since it must, in exercising its discretion, also take into account other considerations such as the increased importance given to the social and political aspects of the anti-smoking campaign.

4.4. Subsidiarity and the ECJ

Since its introduction, the principle of subsidiarity has had virtually no impact as a ground for review or as a rule of interpretation in the case law of the ECJ or the CFI. This contrasts with the judicial application of proportionality. It is true that, where it applies proportionality, the Court leaves ample discretion to the legislature and the chances of success are limited. Nonetheless, it pursues a robust and structured enquiry. This is not the case in relation to subsidiarity which in no case so far has been a pillar of the Court's reasoning. What accounts for this difference? Proportionality is a well-established instrument of judicial review and owes its origins to the protection of human rights. Subsidiarity, by contrast, does not share a human rights ancestry. It is perceived by the judiciary as being *par excellence* a political principle which seeks to influence the legislative process *ex ante*. It pertains to the allocation of power among different levels of government and, as such, it is less susceptible to judicial determination.

The case law contains only a handful of references to subsidiarity. The principle may function as a rule of interpretation or as a ground for review but there has been no spill-over effect in its judicial application. Thus, the ECJ has resisted attempts to restrict the scope of application of the fundamental freedoms on the

---

[39] *Op. cit.*, n. 31 above, n. 52.   [40] *BAT, op. cit.*, n. 55, para 74.

basis of subsidiarity.[41] The principle has not prevented the Court from following an activist case law in the field of European citizenship or expanding its human rights jurisdiction.[42] Nor has it had much impact on the field of national remedies, recent developments in which suggest that there is a resurgence of interventionism.[43] This is not intended to be a criticism. Both the perception of subsidiarity as primarily a political principle and its restriction to the exercise of Community legislative powers are fully in conformity with the intended use of the principle.

In some cases, the ECJ has used subsidiarity as an aid to interpretation. An example is provided by *AvestaPolarit Chrome Oy*.[44] The case concerned the interpretation of Directive 75/442 on waste,[45] Article 2(1)(b) of which, as amended by Directive 91/156,[46] excludes from the scope of its application certain types of waste 'where they are already covered by other legislation'. The question arose whether Article 2(1)(b) covers only national legislation which entered into force before 1 April 1993, the date of entry into force of Directive 91/156, or extends to national legislation that has entered into force after that date. The Court referred to the principle of subsidiarity and held that, since the Community legislature provisionally allowed Member States to entrust the management of certain categories of waste to the national authorities and since Article 2(1)(b) did not expressly provide otherwise, it should be interpreted as including national legislation in force before or after that date.[47]

In most cases subsidiarity is used as a supporting argument to strengthen the Court's reasoning or because the measure which the Court is called upon to interpret itself refers to the principle[48] or because one of the parties has expressly relied on it. An interesting example is provided by *Commission v Germany*.[49] The Commission brought an enforcement action seeking a declaration that Germany had breached the provisions of Directive 89/686 on the harmonization of national laws relating to personal protective equipment,[50] because the legislation of certain *Länder* made firefighters' equipment subject to additional requirements not provided for in the Directive. The Court rejected the argument that the Directive

---

[41] See Case C-415/93 *Bosman* [1995] ECR I-4921, para 8, where, in response to an argument by the German Government, the ECJ held that the principle of subsidiarity cannot lead to a situation where the freedom of private associations to adopt sporting rules restricts the exercise of rights derived from Article 48 (now 34) of the Treaty.

[42] See e.g. Case C-413/99 *Baumbast and R v Secretary of State for the Home Department*, [2002] ECR I-7091; Case C-109/01 *Secretary of State for the Home Department v Akrich*, judgment of 23 September 2003; C-112/00 *Schmidberger*, [2003] ECR I-5559.

[43] See e.g. C-224/01 *Köbler v Austria*, judgment of 30 September 2003; Case C-129/00 *Commission v Italy*, judgment of 9 December 2003; Case C-453/00 *Kühne & Heitz NV v Productschap voor Pluimvee en Eieren*, judgment of 13 January 2004.

[44] Case C-114/01 *AvestaPolarit Chrome Oy*, judgment of 11 September 2003.

[45] OJ 1975, L 194/39.   [46] OJ 1991, L 78/32.   [47] *Op. cit.*, para 57.

[48] See e.g. Case C-271/01 *Ministero delle Politiche Agricole e Forestali v COPPI*, judgment of 22 January 2004, para 39 *et seq.* (power of national authorities to manage structural funds and revoke the granting of financial assistance from Community funds in case of irregularities).

[49] Case C-103/01 *Commission v Germany*, judgment of 22 May 2003.

[50] OJ 1989, L 399/18.

should be interpreted in accordance with the principles of subsidiarity and pro-portionality as allowing the imposition of additional requirements. The German Government submitted that the organization of fire brigades came within the legislative competence of the *Länder* and it was up to them to decide whether fire brigades were bodies responsible for 'securing public safety or order', and could therefore take advantage of the exception provided in Annex I, point 1, to the Directive.

The Court pointed out that the ordinary tasks of the fire brigade differed from those of forces whose main responsibility was the maintenance of law and order. Since the national provisions relating to protective equipment differed significantly from one Member State to another, they might constitute a barrier to trade with direct consequences for the creation and operation of the common market. The harmonization of such divergent provisions could, by reason of its scope and effects, be undertaken only by the Community legislature. The Court added that the Directive did not encroach on the competence of the States to define the tasks and powers of fire brigades nor on the organization of the forces responsible for the maintenance of law and order.[51]

The Court has also rejected subsidiarity as an argument against the exercise of the Commission's powers to enforce competition law. In *van den Bergh Foods v Commission*, it held that the existence of parallel proceedings before national courts did not prevent the Commission from initiating proceedings under Articles 81 and 82 if inter-state trade was potentially affected, even if all the facts of the case were confined to the same Member State.[52]

Subsidiarity is a legally binding rule compliance with which is subject to review by the Court. A Member State or a person who considers that a Community measure has been adopted contrary to it may seek its annulment by the Court of Justice. Given, however, that the principle is political in nature and gives much scope for subjective judgment, the Court cannot employ a high level of scrutiny. As we have seen, where the Community legislature is called upon to make complex assessments, it must be allowed wide discretion corresponding to its political responsibilities. The Amsterdam Protocol, and the Edinburgh Council Guidelines on which it was based, opened the door to judicial control by laying down certain parameters within which the institutions must exercise their discretion.[53]

Subsidiarity has greater potential as a procedural ground than as a ground of substance. Much will depend on how far the ECJ is prepared to press the Community institutions to justify their belief that the tests of comparative efficiency and

---

[51] Paras 47–48 of the judgment.

[52] T-65/98 *Van den Bergh Foods v Commission*, judgment of 23 October 2003, paras 197–199. See also the *Cements* cases: Case T-25/95 (etc.) *SA Cimenteries CBR v Commission*, [2000] ECR II-491 paras 752–754. Note now the new Council Regulation 1/2003 of 16 December 2002 on the implementation of the rules on competition laid down in Articles 81 and 82 of the Treaty, OJ 2003, L1/1.   [53] See 4.1 above, *op. cit.*

scale are met. The statement of reasons must explain in substance why the Community legislature considers that the measure is necessary and satisfies the tests. Failure to do so will render the reasoning deficient and may lead to annulment. It is not necessary however for the statement of reasons to refer expressly to the principle of subsidiarity. It suffices if the reasoning of the legislature can be derived by implication from the preamble of the measure.[54]

Notably, the Amsterdam Protocol states that the reasons for concluding that a Community objective can be better achieved by the Community must be substantiated by qualitative or, wherever possible, quantitative indicators.[55] It will therefore be open to the Court to assess whether the view of the Community legislature that the tests of comparative efficiency and scale have been met in relation to a given measure is correct.[56] The Court however has not applied the principle vigorously. So far, in no case has it annulled a measure on the ground that it contravenes the principle. Where it has annulled measures, it has preferred to do so on grounds of competence or proportionality rather than on grounds of subsidiarity even though the principle may have influenced the judgment.[57] The cases which illustrate most clearly the judicial approach to subsidiarity are *Netherlands v Parliament and Council* and *BAT*.

In *Netherlands v Parliament and Council*[58] the Dutch Government sought the annulment of Directive 98/44 on the legal protection of biotechnological inventions.[59] The objective of the Directive, which had been adopted under Article 95 EC, was to require Member States to protect biotechnological inventions through their patent laws and, to that end, it determined which inventions involving plants, animals or the human body could be patented. The Dutch Government argued, *inter alia*, that the Directive could not be adopted under Article 95 and was in breach of the principle of subsidiarity. It claimed that harmonization in that area was not warranted as the laws of the Member States were based on international conventions and were therefore, to a fair degree, similar. To the extent that any divergences of national laws gave rise to uncertainty, reform should be pursued through renegotiation of the applicable international law conventions.

The ECJ placed emphasis on the risk of distortions in competition arising in the future. It reiterated that recourse to Article 95 EC as a legal basis is possible to prevent the emergence of future obstacles to trade provided that the emergence of such obstacles was likely. It held that, even though the national laws pre-existing

---

[54] *Germany v Parliament and Council, op. cit.*, n. 21 above, para 28. Note also that the preamble to a measure need not refer expressly to proportionality: Case C-150/94 *United Kingdom v Council* [1998] ECR I-7235, para 37.   [55] Amsterdam Protocol, *Op. cit.*, para 4.

[56] Wyatt takes the view that failure to take into account the guidelines laid down in the Amsterdam Protocol may lead to annulment. See D.F. Wyatt, 'Subsidiarity and Judicial Review', in D. O'Keeffe and A. Bavasso (eds.), *Judicial Review in European Union Law, Liber Amicorum in Honour of Lord Slynn* (Kluwer, 2000), 505–519 at 518.

[57] See e.g. *Tobacco case, Op. cit.*, n. 26 above.

[58] *Netherlands v Parliament and Council, op. cit.*, n. 33 above.   [59] OJ 1988 L 213/13.

the Directive were based primarily on the Convention on the Grant of European Patents, the differing interpretations to which these laws were open were liable to give rise to divergences of practice and case law prejudicial to the proper operation of the internal market. The Court also safeguarded the internal legislative autonomy of the Community by stating that, in relation to matters affecting the internal market, the Community legislature was free to pursue law reform on the basis of harmonization directives rather than through renegotiation of international agreements.

On subsidiarity, the ECJ provided only a rudimentary reasoning. It held that the objective pursued by the Directive, namely to ensure smooth operation of the internal market by eliminating differences between national laws on the protection of biotechnological inventions, could not be achieved by action taken by the Member States alone. It continued as follows: 'As the scope of that protection has immediate effects on trade, and, accordingly, on intra-Community trade, it is clear that, given the scale and effects of the proposed action, the objective in question could be better achieved by the Community.'[60]

This reasoning is problematic. First, it does not address the issue whether the very objective of harmonizing national laws on the protection of biotechnological inventions satisfies the test of subsidiarity. Why should this objective be pursued at Community rather than the national level? The fact that the Community has competence to pursue it under the terms of Article 95 does not necessarily mean that the Directive in issue satisfies the test of subsidiarity. The Court effectively equates the test of subsidiarity with the test of competence thus removing all independent legal value from the former. Second, the Court readily seemed to accept that the fact that the protection of biotechnological inventions had an effect on trade automatically meant that it had an immediate effect on intra-Community trade, thus denying any role for subsidiarity, whose function is precisely this, namely, to provide a threshold for Community action based, *inter alia*, on whether 'the issue under consideration has transnational aspects.'[61]

The argument of subsidiarity re-emerged in *British American Tobacco*.[62] The ECJ held that the principle of subsidiarity applies to measures adopted under Article 95 inasmuch as that Article does not give to the Community 'exclusive competence to regulate economic activity on the internal market but only a certain competence for the purpose of improving the conditions for its establishment and functioning'.[63] The Court thus reiterated that regulatory functions lie in principle with the nation state as it had first stated in the *Tobacco Advertisement* case.[64]

It then proceeded to assess the contested Directive *vis-à-vis* the test of Article 5(2). It held that the objective of the Directive, which was to eliminate barriers to trade raised by disparities in national laws whilst ensuring a high level of health protection, could not be sufficiently achieved individually by the Member States.

[60] *Netherlands v Parliament and Council, op. cit.*, para 32.
[61] See the Amsterdam Protocol, *op. cit.*, para 5.
[62] *Op. cit.*, n. 36 above.   [63] *Ibid.*, para 179.   [64] *Op. cit.*, n. 26 above.

The multifarious development of national laws made harmonization necessary. In fact, the ECJ did not employ distinct reasoning to deal with the argument of subsidarity. The issue whether Community action was justified had already been resolved by deciding that the Directive could be adopted under Article 95 EC. As regards the intensity of the harmonization action undertaken, the ECJ assimilated subsidiarity to proportionality and cross-referred to its reasoning in relation to the latter.

The case law thus suggests that the Court treats subsidiarity as a secondary part of its reasoning. The test of subsidiarity tends to be subsumed under the more general enquiries of legal basis and competence and the assessment of proportionality.[65]

4.5. Subsidiarity and proportionality under the EU Constitution: An assessment of the Protocol

Both subsidiarity and proportionality are expressly provided for in Article I-11 of the EU Constitution which corresponds to Article 5 EC. A novel feature of the Constitution is that it strengthens the role of national Parliaments in monitoring compliance with subsidiarity. This accords with one of the key objectives of the Constitutional Convention which was to increase democracy by enhancing 'the contribution of national Parliaments to the legitimacy of the European design'.[66] Article I-11(3) of the Constitution corresponds to Article 3(2) of the EC Treaty and with minor textual improvements incorporates the tests of scale and effectiveness. It also contains a new sub-paragraph which confers on national Parliaments responsibility to ensure compliance with the principle. The procedure for doing so is set out in the Protocol on the application of the principles of subsidiarity and proportionality annexed to the Constitution.[67]

The Protocol was based on proposals made by Working Group I set up by the Convention specifically for the purpose of examining subsidiarity.[68] The Working Group considered that both the application and the monitoring of the principle should be improved but advised against the establishment of an ad hoc body responsible for monitoring its application so as to avoid making the decision-making procedure more cumbersome or lengthier. It also rejected the appointment of an interlocutor within the Commission who would be responsible for ensuring respect for subsidiarity on the ground that each Commissioner should be responsible for compliance with the principle within the area of his or her competence. The Working Group envisaged instead the exercise of *ex ante* political

[65] See further the Court's reasoning in the *Vitamins* case, *op. cit.*, n. 32 above, paras 104–105.
[66] See the Preface to Parts I and II of the draft Treaty establishing a Constitution for Europe as submitted to the President of the European Council meeting in Rome on 18 July 2003, CONV 850/03.   [67] See Protocol 2 of the Treaty establishing a Constitution for Europe.
[68] See Conclusions of Working Group I on the Principle of Subsidiarity, CONV 286/02, 23 September 2002.

control and *ex post* judicial control by the national Parliaments. This model was endorsed by the Convention and incorporated in the Protocol. Thus, the Protocol establishes an 'early warning system' enabling national Parliaments to monitor compliance with subsidiarity before legislative measures are adopted. The core elements of this system are consultation, reasoning and voting.

Before proposing legislative acts, the Commission must consult widely. Such consultation must take into account the regional and local dimensions of the actions envisaged.[69] The Commission must forward its proposals for legislative acts and any amended proposals to national Parliaments at the same time as it transmits them to the Union legislator. The same obligation applies to the European Parliament as regards its draft legislative acts and amended drafts. It also applies to the Council as regards draft legislative acts originating from a group of Member States, the Court of Justice, the European Central Bank and the European Investment Bank.[70]

Article 5 of the Protocol subjects draft measures to a thorough cost-benefit analysis. Proposals should contain a detailed statement making it possible to appraise compliance with subsidiarity and proportionality. The statement should include some assessment of the proposal's financial impact and, in the case of a European framework law,[71] of its implications for the rules to be put in place by Member States, including, where necessary, the regional legislation.

Under Article 5, the assessment of subsidiarity must be effected, in particular, by reference to two considerations:[72] the reasons for concluding that a Union objective can be better achieved at Union level must be substantiated by qualitative and, wherever possible, quantitative indicators. Also, proposals must take account of the need for any burden, whether financial or administrative, falling upon the Union, national Governments, regional or local authorities, economic operators and citizens, to be minimised and be commensurate with the objective to be achieved.

Political control is exercised collectively by all national Parliaments acting through a novel voting system. Any national Parliament, or any Parliamentary chamber in the case of countries which have a bicameral system, may object to a legislative proposal by submitting a reasoned opinion stating why it considers that the proposal does not comply with subsidiarity.[73] National Parliaments may submit their reasoned opinions within six weeks from the date of transmission. The

---

[69] Protocol, Article I-2. See also the Protocol on the Role of National Parliaments in the European Union (Protocol 1) attached to the Constitutional Treaty.

[70] Protocol, Article 4.

[71] European framework laws correspond to Directives under Article I-33 of the Constitutional Treaty.

[72] Notably, Article 5 retains only these two considerations from the guidelines provided for in the Amsterdam Protocol, which is repealed by the Constitution.

[73] Protocol, Article 6. Note that, under Article 6, it is for each national Parliament or each chamber to consult, where appropriate, regional Parliaments with legislative powers before deciding to submit a reasoned opinion.

six-week time limit however seems short and may pose a challenge even to the best-organized national assemblies.

Each national Parliament has two votes shared out on the basis of the national parliamentary system. In the case of a bicameral Parliament, each of the two chambers has one vote.[74] Where reasoned opinions against a proposal represent at least one-third of the total number of votes allocated to national Parliaments and their chambers, the Commission is required to review its proposal.[75] After such a review, the Commission may decide to maintain, amend or withdraw it, giving reasons for its decision.[76]

Political control is supplemented by reinforced judicial control as provided in Article 8 of the Protocol. This grants the Court jurisdiction to hear actions for judicial review on grounds of infringement of the principle of subsidiarity brought 'by Member States, or notified by them in accordance with their legal order on behalf of their national Parliament or a chamber of it'. Such actions can be brought against legislative acts of the Union in accordance with the rules of Article III-365 (currently Article 230 EC). A similar right of action is granted to the Committee of the Regions as regards legislative acts for the adoption of which it must be consulted.

Although the language of Article 8 does not make this clear, it is arguable that the provision requires Member States to make available the right of action to national Parliaments and does not simply allow them to do so. The Praesidium notes attached to the Protocol suggest that the national Parliaments are given the right to challenge measures before the ECJ.[77] What is left to the Member States is to determine the arrangements for the exercise of that right, including the question whether it will be granted to each parliamentary chamber in States with a bicameral system. These arrangements can be made by ordinary law and need not have the status of constitutional rules.[78]

The Protocol does not specify the way in which the national Parliaments may take the decision to object to a Commission proposal or to initiate a judicial challenge against a measure. Thus, it is for each Member State to decide the proportion of votes by which the Parliament needs to act. Many models are conceivable here. A Member State may, for example, require the Parliament to act by majority. In such a case, if the Government controls the majority, it is unlikely that the Parliament will vote to submit an objection or initiate litigation if the Government itself does not consider it appropriate.[79] At the other extreme, national law may enable, say, a percentage of parliamentarians or a cross-party

---

[74] Article 7(2).

[75] Article 7(3). The threshold of one third is lowered to a one quarter in the case of a Commission proposal or an initiative emanating from a group of Member States under the provisions of Article III-264 of the Constitution on the area of freedom, security and justice.

[76] Article 7(4). This applies, as appropriate, to a group of Member States, the European Parliament, the Court of Justice, the ECB or the EIB if the draft legislative act originates from them.   [77] CONV 724/1/03 REV 1, p. 144.

[78] Ibid.

[79] Unless the Government allows the issue to be put to Parliament on a free vote or a sufficient majority of the ruling party considers the issue to be worth a rebellion.

parliamentary committee to take the initiative. Such arrangements would enhance the power of the Parliament to question Union legislation, acting independently of the Government's interests. National laws may well make the power of the Parliament to ask for a judicial challenge subject to the requirement that the Parliament must have first decided, by whatever procedures applicable, to submit a reasoned opinion objecting to the proposal.

Granting to national Parliaments their own political and judicial means to monitor compliance with subsidiarity may be seen as an indication of respect to representative democracy. The Protocol seeks to promote national Parliaments as centres of political power with a say in the exercise of Community competence independent of their national Governments. These newly founded rights may in some cases bring national Parliaments on a collision course with their respective Governments. But they also juxtapose the national Parliaments with the European Parliament. Now that the latter is elevated, at least in most areas, to a co-legislator with the Council, an objection on grounds of subsidiarity initiated by a national Parliament is as much a denial of Community competence as a refusal to heed the supremacy of the European Parliament.[80] These provisions of the Constitution may be seen as enhancing dialogue, democracy, and decentralization. They view Community competence not as a bipolar exchange between the Union institutions, on the one hand, and the Member States, on the other hand, but as a pluralistic dialogue among various political actors at national and Union level. It is however strange that, whilst the Protocol requires legislative proposals to be justified both with regard to subsidiarity and proportionality, it provides for the early warning system and judicial control only in relation to subsidiarity.

A final point relates to the scope of the action. It appears that, where an application for judicial review is made pursuant to the Protocol, the only ground that can be invoked is breach of the principle of subsidiarity. A national Parliament may not ask its Member State to challenge a Community measure on any other ground. This may give rise to problems since, in practice, some grounds for review may be closely intertwined. In the *Tobacco Directive* case[81] the Court annulled the contested Directive on the ground of lack of competence and formally, at least, did not address the argument of the German Government based on subsidiarity. Would the Court have reached the same result if it examined the issue on the basis of subsidiarity? Also, since the existence of Community competence is a condition precedent to its valid exercise, and therefore to the application of the principle of subsidiarity, can the ECJ examine arguments based on competence in actions brought under the Protocol? Given the demise of the Constitution, these problems remain theoretical. Suffice it to say that the EU Constitution enhances the role of national Parliaments in ensuring compliance with subsidiarity. In doing so, it strengthens democracy, accountability and transparency and contributes to the

---

[80] Note that in the *Biotechnological Inventions* case the action was brought at the express request of the Dutch Parliament. See *Netherlands v Parliament and Council*, *op. cit.*, para 4.

[81] *Op. cit.*

dispersal of political power. By increasing the number of potential plaintiffs, the Protocol increases the justiciability of subsidiarity and brings the Court of Justice closer to the political game. By transferring to the courtroom what are essentially political issues, it risks the politicization of the judiciary, not in the sense of making the Court a partisan institution but of involving it more directly in issues of European governance.

5

The Principle of Proportionality: Review of National Measures

5.1. From the rule of law to economic integration

We saw in the previous chapters that, where proportionality is applied as a ground for review of Community acts, the Court balances a private *vis-à-vis* a public interest. In that context, the principle operates in the traditional sphere of public law seeking to provide a check on public power and to protect the individual. Under Article 5(3) EC, it also seeks to protect the nation state from undue interference by the Community institutions. In Community law, the principle performs an additional distinct, but related, function. It is applied to determine the compatibility with the Treaty of national measures which interfere with the fundamental freedoms. The function of the principle in this context is to promote market integration. For that reason, the degree of scrutiny employed by the Court is much stricter and the 'manifestly inappropriate' test gives way to a test of necessity.[1] To state the obvious, the standard of deference to national policy choices is not determined by the principle itself but by the underlying objectives of the Community provisions whose interpretation it is recruited to assist. In the law of free movement, proportionality can be seen as the normative expression of negative integration and principle of free access to the market of the importing State. The importance of proportionality as an instrument of market integration is illustrated by contrasting the approach of the Court to restrictions on free movement imposed by national measures and such restrictions imposed by Community measures. Where Community measures restrict fundamental freedoms, the Court is more readily prepared to defer to the discretion of the Community institutions.[2] Also, provisions of agreements between the Community and third States which employ identical language to provisions of the EC Treaty are

[1] See above, Ch. 3. This distinction in the use of proportionality is not always made by national courts. See e.g. *R v Chief Constable of Sussex, ex p International Trader's Ferry Ltd* [1997] 2 All ER 65 *per* Kennedy LJ at 80–81.

[2] See Joined Cases C-154 and C-155/04, *The Queen on the application of Alliance for Natural Health v Secretary of State for Health*, judgment of 12 July 2005; Case C-51/93 *Meyhui v Schott Zwiesel Glaswerke* [1994] ECR I-3879; Cf. Case 27/80 *Fietje* [1980] ECR 3839 and Case C-369/89 *Piageme v Peeters* [1991] ECR I-2971, and below p. 218; Case C-284/95 *Safety Hi-Tech Srl v S & T Srl*, [1998] ECR I-4301, para 62.

subject to a less stringent test of proportionality, the reason being that their underlying objective is merely to facilitate free trade rather than to promote an economic constitutional order.[3]

The distinction drawn above between proportionality as the guardian of individual rights and proportionality as an instrument for economic integration does not mean that the two concepts are unrelated. In fact, the second incorporates the first. In *Kraus*,[4] as earlier in the *Beer* case,[5] the Court was adamant that, to be proportionate, a restriction on the exercise of a fundamental freedom must comply with essential procedural guarantees enabling the person concerned to assert his Community rights. In other words, freedom to trade and the rule of law are closely intertwined aspects of the same constitutional order.[6] In particular, the case law provides that, in order to meet the requirements of proportionality, a restriction on a fundamental freedom must be adequately reasoned and be subject to judicial review.[7] In fact, this public law element of proportionality has become much more prevalent in recent years as the ECJ has intensified judicial review of national measures on grounds of compatibility with human rights. The Court appears to engage in what can be termed collateral review on grounds of proportionality. It assesses the proportionality of a national measure not *vis-à-vis* its adverse impact on the primary Community interest (i.e. free movement), which is what brings the measure within the scope of Community law in the first instance, but on an incidental Community objective (i.e. human rights) with which the measure must conform.[8] Thus, in some ways, free movement has been transformed to the gateway for the Court to assert its human rights jurisdiction, a development which is examined in Chapter 7.

---

[3] See Case 299/86 *Drexl v Italian Republic* [1988] ECR 1213, Case C-312/91 *Metalsa v Italian Republic* [1993] ECR I-3751 and see also Opinion 1/91 *Draft Agreement relating to the creation of the European Economic Area* [1991] ECR I-6079. In those cases, the Court acknowledged that the internal market is not an end in itself but a means to achieving the ultimate objectives of the Community.   [4] Case 19/92 *Kraus v Land Baden-Württemberg* [1993] ECR I-1663.
[5] Case 178/84 *Commission v Germany* [1987] ECR 1227.
[6] On the Treaty as an economic constitution, see W. Sauter, *Competition Law and Industrial Policy in the EU* (Oxford University Press, 1997), p. 26; Miguel Poiares Maduro, *We, the Court: The European Court of Justice and the European Economic Constitution* (Oxford: Hart Publishing, 1998); and see by the same author, 'Reforming the Market and the State? Article 30 and the European Constitution: Economic Freedom and Political Rights', (1997) 3 ELJ 55.
[7] See Case 222/86 *UNECTEF v Heylens* [1987] ECR 4097; Case C-340/89 *Vlassopoulou* [1991] ECR I-2357; Case C-104/91 *Borrell and Others* [1992] ECR I-3003; Joined Cases C-65/95 and C-111/95 *The Queen v Secretary of State for the Home Department, ex p Mann Singh Shingara and Abbas Radiom* [1997] ECR I-3343; see also Case C-189/95 *Franzén* [1997] ECR I-5909, paras 50–51 and in relation to the 6th VAT Directive, Joined Cases C-286/94, C-340/95, C-401/95 and C-47/96 *Molenheide and Others v Belgian State* [1997] ECR I-7281.
[8] See e.g. Case C-60/00 *Carpenter v Secretary of State for the Home Department*, [2002] ECR I-8279; Case C-413/99 *Baumbast and R v Secretary of State for the Home Department* [2002] ECR I-7091; Case C-109/01 *Secretary of State for the Home Department v Akrich*, judgment of 23 September 2003; C-112/00 *Schmidberger*, judgment of 12 June 2003; Case C-71/02 *Herbert Karner Industrie-Auktionen GmbH v Troostwijk GmbH*, judgment of 25 March 2004.

This chapter will illustrate the application of proportionality primarily by reference to the free movement of goods. Before embarking on that discussion, it may be helpful to recount briefly the most important types of national measures to which the principle applies.

(1) *Escape clauses.* The Treaty provides for a number of express derogations from the principles established therein, the so-called 'exception' or 'escape' clauses.[9] Some of these clauses enable Member States to take action on well-defined, non-economic grounds.[10] Others include economic grounds.[11] In certain cases, Member States may act only after authorization by a Community institution[12] whereas in others they may act alone. Whatever their substantive or procedural requirements, escape clauses are governed by the following fundamental principles. First, they are exclusive in character. Member States have no power to derogate from the provisions of the Treaty except by virtue of express derogation.[13] Second, escape clauses must be interpreted strictly.[14] Third, measures taken pursuant to them may not be more restrictive than is necessary to realise the legitimate objective in view. The principle of proportionality is often incorporated in the text of escape clauses which use expressions such as that the measure in issue must be 'justified',[15] or be 'strictly necessary'[16] or 'cause the least disturbance of the functioning of the common market'.[17]

(2) *Proportionality and indirect discrimination.* Community law prohibits both direct and indirect discrimination. Where difference in treatment is indirect, namely based on a criterion other than the prohibited one, such difference does not amount to discrimination if it is objectively justified. The notion of objective justification incorporates that of proportionality in that a difference in treatment will not be objectively justified unless it is necessary to achieve its objectives. The issue acquires particular importance in relation to indirect discrimination on grounds of nationality[18] and also in relation to indirect sex discrimination.[19] In both areas the Court applies proportionality as a stringent test of necessity.

[9] For a discussion of escape clauses, see P. Oliver and M. Jarvis, *Free Movement of Goods in the European Community*, Fourth Ed. Sweet & Maxwell, 2002.

[10] See e.g. Articles 30, 46, 55.

[11] See e.g. Articles 119 and 120 which authorize a Member State to take measures to overcome difficulties relating to its balance of payments.

[12] See e.g. Article 134. See also Articles 297 and 298.

[13] Case 222/84 *Johnston v Chief Constable of the Royal Ulster Constabulary* [1986] ECR I-1651, para 26; Joined Cases C-19 and C-20/90 *Karella and Karellas* [1991] ECR I-2691 para 31.

[14] See e.g. in relation to Article 134, Case 41/76 *Donckerwolcke v Procureur de la République* [1976] ECR 1921, para 29; Case 62/70 *Bock v Commission* [1971] ECR 897, para 14.

[15] See e.g. Article 30.   [16] Article 120.   [17] Article 134, third paragraph.

[18] See e.g. Case C-330/90 *R v Inland Revenue Commissioners, ex p Commerzbank* [1993] ECR I-4017; Case C-237/94 *O'Flynn v Adjudication Officer* [1996] ECR I-2617 and above, the discussion of Article 12.

[19] See e.g. Case C-167/97 *R v Secretary of State for Employment ex p Seymour Smith and Perez* [1999] ECR I-623; Case C-328/91 *Secretary of State for Social Security v Thomas and Others* [1993] ECR I-1247; cf Case C-317/93 *Nolte v Landesversicherungsanstalt Hannover* [1995] ECR I-4625

(3) *Measures falling within the scope of Community law.* As a general principle of law, proportionality applies more widely to all national measures which implement or otherwise fall within the scope of Community law.[20] In particular, where Member States act as agents of the Community implementing Community policies, they must respect proportionality. In this context, the principle operates in the sphere of public law rather than as an instrument of market integration.

5.2. Equality and proportionality: Complementary or alternative patterns of integration?

5.2.1. Patterns of integration and the judgment in *Keck*

The notions of non-discrimination and proportionality have been used by the Court as conceptual tools for drawing the demarcation line between lawful and unlawful impediments to free movement. In that respect, the two notions complement each other and can be seen as forces centripetal to the establishment of the internal market. There is however an underlying tension between the two as they evince alternative patterns of integration. If it is accepted that free movement is exhausted in the obligation of Member States to treat imported products or services on an equal footing with domestic ones, discrimination is the touchstone of integration. But if it is accepted that free movement goes beyond equal treatment and requires freedom of access to the market, then any obstacle to free access becomes an unlawful impediment unless objectively justified. Under the second model, proportionality is elevated to the principal criterion for determining the dividing line between lawful and unlawful barriers to trade. It may be said then that equality and proportionality are in an inverse relationship: the less one relies on the first, the more it has to rely on the latter in order to determine what is a permissible restriction on trade. As an instrument for determining the legality of restrictions on trade, proportionality is the most flexible instrument that the European judicature possesses. It certainly broadens the scope of the judicial enquiry and increases the power of the Court. But in economic terms it is not necessarily the most efficient. It inserts a degree of uncertainty, encourages litigation and, in that respect, it is

---

and Case C-444/93 *Megner and Scheffel v Innungskrankenkasse Rheinhessen-Pfalz* [1995] ECR I-4743 where the Court found that the exclusion of persons working less than 15 hours a week from the statutory sickness and old age insurance schemes did not amount to indirect discrimination on grounds of sex as it was necessary to achieve social policy aims. See also C-400/93 *Royal Copenhagen* [1995] ECR I-1275. For indirect discrimination under the Race Directive, the Framework Directive and Directive 2002/73 on equal treatment, see above, Ch. 2.

[20] See above p. 36.

liable to increase transaction costs. It also raises issues of judicial legitimacy. Where does the Court derive its power to make choices of regulatory, economic or social policy? Indeed, the judgment in *Keck and Mithouard*[21] may be seen as an effort by the Court to infuse a higher degree of certainty into the interpretation of Article 28 and stop unmeritorious claims at an earlier stage.

It may be interesting to examine at this juncture the co-relation between equality and proportionality in the context of the free movement of goods by reference to the judgment in *Keck* and its aftermath.[22]

In *Keck* the Court redefined the scope of Article 28 by drawing a distinction between rules concerning 'product-related requirements' and those concerning selling arrangements.[23] With regard to the former, the principle enunciated in *Cassis de Dijon*[24] continues to apply. With regard to selling arrangements, the Court elevated discrimination to become the determining criterion.[25] At paragraph 16 of the judgment, it held that rules of the importing State pertaining to selling arrangements do not fall within the scope of Article 28 provided that they apply to all affected traders operating in the national territory and that they affect in the same manner, in law and in fact, the marketing of domestic products and those from other Member States. The judgment in *Keck* represents one of the most spectacular departures from precedent in the Court's history. To justify it, the Court referred to 'the increasing tendency of traders to invoke Article 30 (now 28) of the Treaty as a means of challenging any rule whose effect is to limit their commercial freedom even where such rules are not aimed at products from other Member States'.[26]

But what are the specific reasons which necessitated such a change in judicial policy? *Keck* can only be understood in historical perspective. In previous case law, the Court had interpreted the notion of measures having equivalent effect to quantitative restrictions very broadly. In *Dassonville* it was held that all national trading rules which are capable of hindering intra-Community trade, directly or

---

[21] Joined Cases C-267 and C-268/91 [1993] ECR I-6097.

[22] There is no intention here to examine Article 28 in detail, for a discussion of which the reader is referred to the general works of EC law. See e.g. C. Barnard, *The Substantive Law of the EU: The Four Freedoms* (Oxford University Press, 2004) Ch. 5.

[23] For influential contributions before the judgment, see E. White, 'In Search of the Limits of Article 30 of the EEC Treaty' (1989) 26 CMLRev 235; K. Mortelmans, 'Article 30 of the EEC Treaty and Legislation relating to Market Circumstances: Time to Consider a New Definition' (1991) 28 CMLRev 115. For a discussion of the judgment and initial reactions, see N. Reich, 'The "November Revolution" of the European Court of Justice', (1994) 31 CMLRev 459; D. Chalmers, 'Repackaging the internal market: the ramifications of the *Keck* judgment' (1994) 19 ELR 385; L. Gormley, 'Reasoning renounced? The remarkable judgment in *Keck and Mithouard*' [1994] Eur Bus L Rev 63; M. Poiares Maduro, '*Keck*: the end? Or just the end of the beginning?' (1994) Irish Journal of European Law 33.

[24] Case 120/78 *Rewe-Zentrale AG v Bundesmonopolverwaltung für Branntwein* [1979] ECR 649.

[25] Product-related rules are those which affect the physical characteristics of goods such as designation, form, size, weight, composition, presentation, labelling and packaging. See *Keck*, *op. cit.*, para 15. Selling arrangements are rules pertaining to marketing, e.g. regulating where, when, by whom and how products may be sold.   [26] *Ibid.*, para 15.

indirectly, actually or potentially, come within the scope of Article 28.[27] Subsequently, the seminal *Cassis de Dijon*[28] effectively introduced the 'home country control' principle to the free movement of goods and expanded the scope of Article 28 firmly beyond the notion of discrimination. As a result of *Cassis de Dijon*, the importing State was no longer able to impose restrictions applicable to goods produced in its territory on goods lawfully produced in other Member States unless that was justified. The concept of mandatory requirements was invented to counter-balance the expansion of Article 28. The emphasis shifted from the criterion of equal treatment between national and imported products to the criterion of justification on grounds of mandatory requirements bringing with it a corresponding increase in the powers of the Court. The *Dassonville* formula, as applied in *Cassis de Dijon*, brought within the ambit of Article 28 a host of national market-regulation measures many of which were by no means designed to affect imports, were dictated by non-economic considerations, and had evolved over the ages crystallizing local preferences.[29] Such measures were suddenly put under scrutiny in the light of a new pan-European economic constitutional order exemplified by the broad scope of Article 28. As *Dassonville* and *Cassis de Dijon* liberated Article 28 from the notion of discrimination, the Court had no option but to rely on the principle of proportionality in order to draw the demarcation line between lawful and unlawful impediments to trade. That, in effect, led the Court to make choices of a broadly political nature which many of its members thought exceeded the judicial province. Whence could the Court derive legitimacy to give priority to the liberal view of undistorted competition favoured by German law as opposed to the more protectionist view favoured in the French tradition?[30] As the late Judge Joliet vividly put it: 'Pouvions-nous, à nous treize, prétendre détenir plus de sagesse et d'intelligence que tous les gouvernements et les parlements nationaux de la Communauté?'[31]

There is a second reason which led the Court to revise the interpretation of Article 28. The previous case law was not devoid of inconsistencies. The uncertain state of the law combined with the broad scope attributed to Article 28 encouraged unmeritorious claims and led to an increase in litigation. In short, following *Dassonville* and *Cassis de Dijon* the scope of Article 28 seemed to become over-ambitious: questionable in conceptual terms and counterproductive in its practical

---

[27] Case 8/74 *Procureur du Roi v Dassonville* [1974] ECR 837, para 5.

[28] *Op. cit.*, n. 24 above.

[29] See S. Weatherill, *Law and Integration in the European Union*, Oxford University Press, 1995, Ch. 7.

[30] R. Joliet, 'La Libre Circulation des Merchandises: L'arrêt *Keck et Mithouard* et les nouvelles orientations de la jurisprudence', (1994) Journal des tribunaux, *Droit Européen*, 145 at 149.

[31] *Ibid.*

application. In the light of those problems, *Keck* sought to increase legal certainty by offering a more predictable filtering mechanism.

5.2.2. Post-*Keck* developments and initial reactions

In the first years after *Keck*, faithful to the newly-established distinction, the ECJ found a number of national measures to be selling arrangements and concluded that they fell outside the scope of Article 28. These included rules governing the opening hours of shops,[32] Sunday trading[33] and advertising.[34] The *Keck* formula became a contentious point and was received with scepticism. In *Leclerc-Siplec*,[35] Jacobs AG expressed misgivings about the distinction between physical characteristics and selling arrangements. He considered that a measure which restricts selling arrangements may create extremely serious obstacles to inter-State trade. That could be the case in particular with rules restricting advertising.[36] But his objection was more fundamental. He considered that the notion of discrimination, adopted by *Keck* in relation to selling arrangements, is not an appropriate criterion on which to base the establishment of the internal market. In his view, all undertakings which engage in a legitimate economic activity in a Member State should have unfettered access to the whole of the Community market, unless there is a valid reason for denying them full access to a part of it. The appropriate test therefore is whether the rules of the importing State constitute a substantial restriction on access. This amounts in effect to introducing a *de minimis* test into Article 28, contrary to previous case law.[37] But the Advocate General considered that a *de minimis* test was the best way to achieve the desired objective, namely to limit the scope of Article 28 in order to prevent excessive interference in the regulatory powers of the Member States.[38]

Although in *Leclerc-Siplec* Jacobs AG seemed in effect to favour proportionality over non-discrimination as the determining criterion of lawful impediments to trade, his test is not as different from *Keck* as it appears on first reading. In *Keck* the Court removed from the ambit of Article 28 non-discriminatory selling arrangements on the ground that the application of such rules to the sale of products from other Member States 'is not by nature such as to prevent their access to the market or to impede access any more than it impedes the access of domestic products'.[39]

---

[32] Joined Cases C-401 and 402/92 *Tankstation 'T Heukske and Boermans* [1994] ECR I-2199.
[33] Joined Cases C-69 and 258/93 *Punto Casa* [1994] ECR I-2355; Joined Cases C-418 etc/93 *Semeraro Casa Uno v Sindaco del Commune di Erbusco* [1996] ECR I-2975.
[34] C-412/93 *Leclerc-Siplec v TFI Publicité and M6 Publicité* [1995] ECR I-179.
[35] *Ibid.*   [36] *Ibid.*, p. 194.
[37] See Joined Cases 177/82 and 178/82 *van de Haar and Kaveka de Meern* [1984] ECR 1797.
[38] In the view of the Advocate General, a *de minimis* test should apply only to non-discriminatory restrictions and would perform a particularly useful function in relation to selling arrangements which, contrary to rules prohibiting the marketing of products, cannot be presumed to have a substantial impact on access to the market. *Leclerc-Siplec, op. cit.*, pp. 196–197.
[39] *Keck, op. cit.*, para 16.

A negative approach towards *Keck* was also adopted by Lenz AG in *Commission v Greece*.[40] There the Commission challenged the compatibility with Article 28 of a Greek law which prohibited the sale outside pharmacies of formula milk for infants. The Advocate General opined that *Keck* did not intend to exclude *a priori* all selling arrangements from the scope of application of Article 28.[41] He pointed out that rules governing the marketing of products are generally more intensive in their effects than rules governing general conditions of sale. In his view, the judgment in *Keck* did not apply to monopolies at the marketing level. This is because a sales monopoly established by law, although a selling arrangement, excludes perforce other sales channels and therefore makes imports more difficult. Although Lenz AG attempted to restrict *Keck's* scope of application rather than to criticize it openly, his views are hardly compatible with the judgment in that case.

The Advocate General also failed to persuade the Court in *Banchero*.[42] The case concerned the Italian state monopoly on tobacco products. One of the issues raised was whether the distribution system provided for by Italian law, which reserved the retail sale of tobacco products to outlets authorised by the State, was compatible with Article 28. The Commission had argued that, by channelling tobacco sales, the Italian distribution system was liable to affect marketing possibilities for imported products. The Court rejected that argument stating that the monopoly had been reorganized in such a way that the State no longer directly managed tobacco outlets and authorized retailers were guaranteed direct access to wholesalers. The Court found no evidence of discriminatory treatment against Community producers. Elmer AG reached the opposite conclusion. He drew a distinction between the Italian legislation at issue and the kind of provisions examined by the Court in *Keck* and in subsequent cases where the judgment had been applied. He considered that the latter concerned provisions limiting specific forms of marketing in such a general and non-restrictive way that they could not be presumed to have a serious effect on the marketing of imported goods.[43] By contrast, he found that the Italian rules governing the sale of tobacco did more than merely restrict certain selling arrangements: they were, as a whole, liable to affect marketing opportunities for imported goods and should therefore be regarded as constituting a measure having equivalent effect within the meaning of Article 28 of the Treaty.[44]

It seems then that in *Banchero* the Advocate General did not question the *Keck* formula but considered that the selling arrangements of the importing State were discriminatory in fact because they adversely affected marketing opportunities. *Banchero* may be contrasted with *Franzén*.[45] Swedish law made the production and the wholesale trade in alcoholic beverages subject to holding a licence and granted to a state company the monopoly for the retail sale of such products. The Court held that the monopoly was compatible with Article 31 because it did not

---

[40] C-391/92 [1995] ECR I-1621.   [41] *Ibid.*, pp. 1628, *et seq.*
[42] C-387/93 [1995] ECR I-4663.   [43] *Ibid.*, n. 112, p. 4677.
[44] *Ibid.*, pp. 4677–8.   [45] *Op. cit.*, n. 7 above.

discriminate against products from other Member States. It held however that the requirement to possess a production licence or a wholesale licence in order to be able to import alcoholic drinks infringed Article 28. It constituted an obstacle to imports from other Member States in that it imposed additional costs on imported products, such as intermediary costs, payment of charges and fees for the grant of a licence, and costs arising from the obligation to maintain storage capacity in Sweden.[46] The Court did not refer to *Keck* nor did it explain whether the licensing requirements were selling arrangements. But in the circumstances it was not necessary to do so since it found the licensing system discriminatory. Both in *Banchero* and in *Franzén* the Court engaged in an analysis of market structure, even though in the first case the analysis does not seem wholly convincing in the light of the Opinion of the Advocate General.

5.2.3. Refining *Keck:* The rediscovery of 'the access to the market' spirit?

Despite the initial scepticism with which *Keck* was greeted and the defensive attitude initially taken by the Court, subsequent case law suggests a more nuanced and flexible approach.[47] Thus the Court has adopted a relatively broad view of what is a product-related requirement and enters into a detailed analysis with a view to establishing whether a measure is discriminatory in fact as regards market access.

The first point is illustrated by *Familiapress*.[48] Austrian law prohibited publishers from including prize crosswords and competitions in newspapers and periodicals. Familiapress, an Austrian newspaper publisher, brought an action against the German publisher of a weekly magazine distributed in Austria for violating the

---

[46] *Ibid.*, para 71.

[47] For a discussion of *Keck* and post-*Keck* case law, see, among others, the analysis of C. Barnard, *op. cit.*, Ch. 5, and S. Enchelmaier, 'The Awkward Selling of a New Idea', (2003) YEL; N. Shiubhne, 'The Free Movement of Goods and Article 28 EC: An Evolving Framework' (2002) 27 ELR 35; J. Snell, *Goods and Services in EC Law* (Oxford University Press, 2002); A. Dashwood, 'Non-Discriminatory Restrictions After *Keck*' (2002) 61 CLJ 35; C. Barnard, 'Fitting the Remaining Pieces into the Goods and Services Jigsaw,' (2001) 26 ELR 35; P. Koutrakos, 'On Groceries, Alcohol and Olive Oil; More on Free Movement of Goods after *Keck*' (2001) 26 ELR 391; P. Oliver, 'Some Further Reflections on the Scope of Articles 28–30 (ex 30–36) EC' (1999) 36 CML Rev 783; S. Weatherill, 'Recent Case law concerning the free movement of goods' (1999) 36 CML Rev 51; J. Weiler, 'Text and Context in the Free Movement of Goods', in Craig and de Burca (eds), *The Evolution of EU Law* (Oxford University Press, 1998); M Jarvis, *The Application of EC Law by National Courts: The Free Movement of Goods* (Oxford University Press, 1998); S. Weatherill, 'After *Keck*: Some thoughts on How to Clarify the Clarification', (1996) 33 CML Rev 885.

[48] C-368/95 *Vereinigte Familiapress Zeitungsverlags- und Vertriebs GmbH v Bauer Verlag* [1997] ECR I-3689. For other examples of product-related requirements, see C-315/92 *Verband Sozialer Wettbewerb v Clinique Laboratories and Estée Lauder* [1994] ECR I-317; Case C-470/93 *Mars* [1995] ECR I-1923; Case C-383/97 *van der Laan*, [1999] ECR I-731; Case C-448/98 *Guimont*, [2000] ECR I-10663.

prohibition. The Austrian Government submitted that offering the readers the possibility of taking part in a crossword competition was a selling arrangement and therefore fell within the scope of *Keck*. The ECJ took a different view. It held that, even though the Austrian legislation was directed against a method of sales promotion, it bore on the actual content of products since the competitions in question formed an integral part of the magazine in which they appeared. More recently, it was held that the requirement to register imposed by Spanish law on undertakings wishing to market decoders and digital transmission and reception systems was not a selling arrangement because of the need 'in certain cases' to adapt the products to the rules in force in the Member State in which they are marketed.[49] Also, a measure which prohibits the importation of a product into the whole or part of the national territory is not treated as a selling arrangement but as a product-related requirement.[50] The case law suggests that the Court has not understood widely the notion of selling arrangements and anything which affects the product itself will be classified as a provision pertaining to physical characteristics.

The most crucial issue under *Keck* is to determine in what circumstances it may be said that a selling arrangement affects differently in law *or in fact* the marketing of domestic products and the marketing of imported products. A selling arrangement which has given rise to particular problems is advertising.[51] This is because the opportunities for marketing a product are so closely related to trading that a restriction on advertising could be viewed as a restriction on the trading of the product itself. To start with, the Court gave the impression that it was unwilling to differentiate between advertising and other selling arrangements. In *Leclerc- Siplec*,[52] a French supermarket chain wished to advertise the sale of petrol in its outlets but was prohibited from doing so by French law which precluded the distribution sector from advertising on television. The Court pointed out that the French law was not designed to regulate inter-State trade in goods nor did it prevent distributors from using other forms of advertising. The Court accepted that the prohibition restricted the volume of sales but, applying *Keck*, concluded that it imposed an equal burden on domestic and imported products.[53]

---

[49] Case C-390/99 *Canal Satélite Digital SL v Administration General del Estado* [2002] ECR I-607, para 30.

[50] See Case C-473/98 *Kemikalieinspektionen v Toolex Alpha AB* [2000] ECR I-5681 (general ban on the use of a chemical substance); Case C-67/97 *Ditlev Bluhme* [1998] ECR I-8033 (exlcusion of certain species of bees from part of the national territory).

[51] R. Greaves, 'Advertising Restrictions and the Free Movement of Goods and Services' (1998) 23 ELR 305.   [52] *Leclerc-Siplec, op. cit.*, n. 34 above.

[53] A similar finding was made in relation to a rule which prohibited pharmacies from advertising: see Case C-292/92 *Hünermund and others v Landesapothekerkammer Baden-Württemberg* [1993] ECR I-6787; see further Case C-337/95 *Parfums Christian Dior v Erora* [1997] ECR I-6013; Case C-6/98 *ARD v PRO Sieben & SAT 1*, [1999] ECR I-7599. For pre-*Keck* cases on advertising, see Joined Cases C-1/90 and C-176/90 *Aragonesa de Publicidad Exterior and Publivia* [1991] ECR I-4151; Case 152/78 *Commission v France* [1980] ECR 2299.

The turning point came in *KO v de Agostini and TV Shop*.[54] A British toy manufacturer challenged Swedish law which prohibited the broadcasting of television advertisements designed to attract the attention of children. The Court accepted that an outright ban on a method of promotion might have a greater impact on products from other Member States.[55] The difference between *Leclerc-Siplec* and *de Agostini* is that in the former French law prohibited a particular form of advertising (television advertising) of a particular form of marketing (i.e. distribution) of products[56] whereas in *de Agostini* Swedish law prohibited television advertising of the product itself.

In *de Agostini*, the Court stated that the efficacy of the various types of promotion is a question of fact to be determined in principle by the national court but took notice of the defendant's arguments that television advertising was the only effective form of promotion enabling it to penetrate the Swedish market. The Court concluded that it was for the national court to decide whether the ban disadvantaged in law or in fact the marketing of products from other Member States and, if so, to determine whether it was justified.

In *KO v Gourmet International Products AB (GIP)*,[57] Swedish law prohibited the advertisement of alcoholic drinks in magazines, on radio and on television. Such advertisement was also prohibited on the public highway and by direct mailing of advertising material to consumers. The Consumer Ombudsman sought to restrain the publication of a magazine which contained advertisements for wine and whisky. The magazine was sold by subscription, 90 per cent of its subscribers being traders and 10 per cent being individual consumers. The issue was raised whether the prohibition was contrary to Article 28. Referring to *de Agostini*, the Court held that the general ban imposed by Swedish law not only prohibited a form of marketing of products but in reality prohibited producers and importers from directing any advertising messages to consumers. It noted that in the case of products such as alcoholic beverages, the consumption of which is linked to traditional social practices and local habits, a prohibition of all advertising directed at consumers is liable to impede access to the market by products from other Member States more than it impedes access by domestic products with which consumers are instantly more familiar.[58] The prohibition therefore affected the marketing of products from other Member States more heavily and was caught by Article 28. The Court accepted that the rules restricting advertising in order to combat alcohol abuse reflect legitimate concerns of public health and could be justified under Article 30 but left it to the national court to decide whether the prohibition was proportionate in the circumstances.

---

[54] Joined Cases C-34-6/95 *KO v de Agostini and TV Shop* [1997] ECR I-3843.

[55] Para 42.

[56] The French law in issue prohibited advertising by the distribution sector but not the advertisement of petrol itself so that oil companies were free to advertise their fuel.

[57] Case C-405/98 *KO v Gourmet International Products AB (GIP)* [2001] ECR I-1795.

[58] *Ibid.*, para 21.

In selling arrangements other than advertising, the more nuanced approach of the Court is illustrated in *Schutzverband gegen unlauteren Wettbewerb v TK-Heimdienst Sass GmbH*.[59] Austrian law provided that bakers, grocers and butchers could offer their products for sale on rounds only within the municipality where their permanent establishment was located or in adjacent municipalities. The Court held that this rule related to selling arrangements because it laid down the geographical areas in which traders could sell their goods. It did not however affect in the same manner the marketing of domestic products and that of imported ones. Traders from other Member States who wished to sell their goods on rounds in an Austrian district were obliged to set up a permanent establishment in that district or in an adjacent municipality. Consequently, they had to bear additional costs. The Court pointed out that this conclusion was not affected by the fact that the Austrian legislation affected both the sale of products from other parts of the national territory and the sale of imported products. For a national measure to be categorised as discriminatory or protective, it is not necessary for it to have the effect of favouring national products as a whole or of placing only imported products at a disadvantage.[60] The Austrian Government argued that the legislation was justified because its purpose was to protect the supply of foods at short distance to the advantage of local businesses. The Court reiterated that aims of a purely economic nature cannot justify a barrier to the free movement of goods. It accepted however that, in certain circumstances, it may be possible to justify a restriction on the basis that it is necessary to avoid deterioration in the conditions under which goods are supplied at short distance in relatively isolated areas of a Member State. It found however that the measure was, in any event, disproportionate.

In *Deutscher Apothekerverband eV v DocMorris and Watervel*,[61] it was held that German rules which prohibited the sale of medical products via the internet and by mail order were discriminatory in fact because they posed a greater obstacle to pharmacies outside Germany. For German drugstores, internet and mail order sales provided an *additional* form of reaching the consumer whilst for drugstores based in other Member States they were the *only* form of direct access to the German market. In *Douwe Egberts*[62] it was held that Belgian provisions which prohibited advertisements of food products from making any references to their slimming or medical qualities were liable to affect access to the market of imported products more severely, extending its reasoning in *Gourmet*.[63]

---

[59] Case C-254/98 *Schutzverband gegen unlauteren Wettbewerb v TK-Heimdienst Sass GmbH* [2000] ECR I-151.   [60] Para 27; see also *Aragonesa op. cit.*, n. 53 above, para 24.

[61] Case C-322/01, judgment of 11 December 2003.

[62] Case C-239/02 *Douwe Egberts v Westrom Pharma NV and Christophe Souranis*, judgment of 15 July 2004.

[63] The Court held (para 53) that 'an absolute prohibition of advertising *the characteristics of a product* is liable to impede access to the market by products from other Member States more than it impedes access by domestic products, with which consumers are more familiar' (emphasis added). The judgment goes further than *Gourmet* in that, in the latter, the Court linked the discrimination in fact with the distinct character of alcohol as a product, whose consumption is associated with

What conclusions can be drawn from the case law? The ECJ seems to be rediscovering the access to market spirit thus making the *Keck* test increasingly pregnable. The ECJ has not embraced 'a pure and explicit' market access test.[64] Contrary however to the first generation of post-*Keck* case law, where the ECJ was understandably preoccupied with establishing the new formula and was impervious to nuances, recent cases suggest that it attributes particular importance to market access and is prepared to take the concept of discrimination *in fact* seriously.

It is now well established that the provisions of the Treaty on free movement of persons cover not only directly and indirectly discriminatory measures but also indistinctly applicable ones which hinder access to the market of the host state.[65] Although it is not always easy to distinguish between indirectly discriminatory and indistinctly applicable measures, the Court does not require discrimination as a condition for triggering the application of Articles 34, 43 and 47 EC. This is aptly illustrated by cases such as *Bosman* (free movement of workers), *Alpine Investments* (freedom to provide services) and *Gebhard* (freedom of establishment). In *Alpine Investments*[66] it was held that the prohibition of cold-calling imposed by Dutch law on providers of financial services established in the Netherlands 'directly affected access' to the market in services in other Member States and was thus capable of hindering inter-State trade in services. In *Bosman*[67] the Court took the view that the FIFA transfer rules applicable to footballers, although they applied both to transfers between clubs within the same Member State and in different Member States, affected directly players' access to the employment market in other Member States and were thus capable of impeding freedom of movement for workers. In *Gebhard*[68] the Court held that rules of the host State regulating a professional activity which pose an obstacle to free movement are compatible with the Treaty only if they meet the following requirements: they must be applied in a non-discriminatory manner; they must be justified by imperative requirements in the general interest; they must be suitable for securing the attainment of their objective; and they must not go beyond what is necessary to achieve it.

traditional social practices and habits. This accounted for the fact that lack of advertising disadvantaged imported beverages *vis-à-vis* local ones with which consumers are 'instantly more familiar'. *Douwe Egberts* suggests that the reasoning of *Gourmet* is of more general application so that any rule which prohibits the advertisement of the qualities of a product is likely to disadvantage imported products *vis-à-vis* domestic ones.

[64] H. Toner, 'Non-Discriminatory Obstacles to the Exercise of Treaty-rights: Articles 39, 43, 49 and 18' (2004) YEL.

[65] For bibliography on the convergence of freedoms, see Toner, *ibid.*; J. Snell, 'Who's got the Power? Free Movement and Allocation of Competences in EC Law', (2003) YEL; D. O'Keeffe and A. Bavasso, 'Four Freedoms, One Market and National Competence: In search of a Dividing Line', in O'Keeffe and Bavasso (eds), *Judicial Review in European Union Law, Liber Amicorum in Honour of Lord Slynn* (The Hague, Kluwer, 2000), 554; L. Daniele, 'Non-Discriminatory Restrictions to the Free Movement of Persons' (1997) 22 ELR 191.

[66] Case C-384/93 [1995] ECR I-1141. For the more recent example taking an even broader view of the freedom to provide services, see *Carpenter, op. cit.,* n. 8 above.

[67] Case C-415/93 *Bosman* [1995] ECR I-4921.

[68] Case C-55/94 *Gebhard* [1995] ECR I-4165.

Two points may be made at this juncture. First, the case law does not assimilate in all respects the free movement of workers, the right of establishment and the freedom to provide services. Differences among them remain but all of them are based on an access to the market rather than a discrimination criterion. Second, in relation to the free movement of persons, there is no safety mechanism to avoid the over-extension of Community presence. There is no *Keck* valve to filter out unmeritorious claims. It may thus be said that *Keck* corresponds to a model where more State autonomy is granted within a federal structure whilst the free movement of persons case law appears to correspond to a more interventionist model.[69] The reason for this differentiation appears to be based partly on historical happenstance and partly on principle. First, in the 1980s and the beginning of the 1990s, the free movement of persons did not receive as wide an interpretation as the free movement of goods. The need therefore for a *Keck*-type control mechanism was not present. Second, the distinction between selling arrangements and product-related requirements is not easily transposable to the free movement of persons. This may well have influenced the Court in *Alpine Investments* which was the first case where it had the opportunity to extend *Keck* to services and the appropriate timing to do so. Third, the Court may have felt that inter-State trade in goods and services was at different stages of development. Whilst the former had come of age through *Cassis de Dijon* and had all the attributes of a mature supranational polity, free movement of persons had still to reach that stage. An access to market test in relation to free movement of persons would be compatible with cultivating a sense of European demos and open the way for an enhanced fundamental rights jurisdiction.

The question which arises is this: in the absence of a discrimination-based test, what determines the scope of application of the free movement of persons? The ECJ in fact has not followed a systematic approach. It excludes measures whose impact on free movement is too tenuous, remote, and uncertain[70] but the articulation of positive, consistently applied, criteria is more difficult to establish. The Court uses somewhat varying formulas.[71] Toner suggests that, to be caught, a measure must pose a direct or substantial obstacle to the free movement of persons,[72] and this approach is supported by much, if not all, of the case law. Notably, in a recent case, the ECJ held that a measure, whose only effect is to create additional costs for a service and which affects in the same way the provision of

---

[69] See Snell, *op. cit.*

[70] See e.g. Case C-412/97 *ED v Italo Fenocchio* [1999] ECR I-3845, para 11; Case C-379/92 *Peralta* [1994] ECR I-3453, para 24.

[71] In some cases the case law refers to measures 'liable to prohibit or otherwise impede the activities of a provider of services'; see e.g. Case C-76/90 *Säger* [1991] ECR I-4221, para 12; Case C-429/02 *Bacardi France SAS v Télévision française 1 SA*, judgment of 13 July 2004, para 31; and in other cases to 'measures liable to hinder or make less attractive the exercise of fundamental freedoms'; see e.g. *Gebhard*, para 37; *Kraus, op. cit.*, n. 4 above, para 32. Yet in other cases, the ECJ does not even use the access to the market test, see e.g. *Carpenter, op. cit.* where the Court placed emphasis on the need to ensure that free movement must be 'fully effective': see para 39.

[72] See Toner, *op. cit.*, n. 64 and accompanying text.

services between Member States and within a Member State does not fall within the scope of Article 49 EC.[73] The measure in issue was a local tax imposed on mobile telephone masts. The Court reiterated the all-embracing nature of Article 49 as a provision which covers both discriminatory and indistinctly applicable restrictions on trade but the judgment does not sit easily with the over-ambitious interpretation of Article 49 in *Carpenter*.[74]

The danger here is that failure to articulate criteria defining the scope of application of the fundamental freedoms breeds the risk of over-reliance on the principle of proportionality which may lack objectivity, certainty and transparency, a risk highlighted by *Carpenter*. As has been pointed out, the decision of a court as to whether a national measure is or is not compatible with free movement is not politically neutral.[75] In fact, it allocates competence at three different levels. Firstly, it passes a judgment as to whether a piece of regulation may stand or be removed giving way to market forces. It thus allocates competences between regulation and the market. It also passes a judgment as to the respective powers of the supra-national authority and the nation state since, where a national measure fails for incompatibility with free movement, the Community effectively trumps a national choice. Finally, it allocates powers between the Court of Justice itself and the other branches of government, i.e. the executive and the legislature at the Community and national level. Thus, proportionality is a Procrustean concept which allows the Court to retain residual but potentially extensive control. This judicial power can be mitigated by the Court itself in two ways: by applying a soft proportionality test, i.e. a mild degree of scrunity over national choices and/or by leaving to the national court the task of applying the principle and reaching an outcome on the facts thus internalising within the national polity the balance of Community and national interests.

There is thus no denying that proportionality remains the most important judicial tool for drawing the distinction between lawful and unlawful impediments to free movement. The pattern which emerges from the case law is as follows. National laws which obstruct trade are permissible only if they are shown to be justified. The means of justification differ depending on the discriminatory or non-discriminatory character of the measure. Measures which are discriminatory can be justified only by the grounds of derogation expressly stated in the Treaty. Measures which are non-discriminatory may also be justified by recourse to mandatory requirements, or imperative reasons in the public interest, the list of which is open.[76] It includes, *inter alia*, the prevention of tax evasion, consumer protection,

---

[73] Joined Cases C-544/03 and C-545/03 *Mobistar v Commune de Fléron*, judgment of 8 September 2005, para 31.   [74] *Op. cit.*

[75] Snell, *Op. cit.*

[76] In *de Agostini* the Court accepted that a selling arrangement which disadvantages the marketing of products from other Member States and therefore falls foul of paragraph 16 of *Keck*, may be justified not only by reference to Article 30 but also by reference to overriding requirements of general public importance. See: paras 45–47 of the judgment.

and unfair trading;[77] the protection of the environment,[78] the improvement of working conditions,[79] and the promotion of national and regional culture.[80] It should be emphasised that it is open to Member States to plead new mandatory requirements provided that the interest whose protection is sought is of a non-economic nature.[81]

An obstacle to trade cannot be justified, whether under the grounds of derogation provided for in Article 30 or under mandatory requirements, unless it is proportionate. In determining the compatibility with Community law of national rules imposing obstacles to inter-State trade, the Court performs a balancing exercise.[82] In *Stoke-on-Trent* it held:[83]

Appraising the proportionality of national rules which pursue a legitimate aim under Community law involves weighing the national interest in attaining that aim against the Community interest in ensuring the free movement of goods. In that regard, in order to verify that the restrictive effects on intra-Community trade of the rules at issue do not exceed what is necessary to achieve the aim in view, it must be considered whether those effects are direct, indirect or purely speculative and whether those effects do not impede the marketing of imported products more than the marketing of national products.

Although *Stoke-on-Trent* has been overtaken by *Keck* in that the prohibition of Sunday trading now falls outside the scope of Article 28 as a non-discriminatory selling arrangement, the above quotation still captures the essence of the proportionality test where the principle applies.

Recent case law in fact suggests that the Court places less emphasis on the concept of discrimination. Thus, it appears that, in certain exceptional circumstances, discriminatory restrictions may be justified even by mandatory requirements such as environmental protection[84] or the need to ensure the balance of the social security system.[85] These developments suggest that what matters is not so much the discriminatory or non-discriminatory character of the measure but its

---

[77] Those three mandatory requirements were mentioned in *Cassis de Dijon*.

[78] Case 302/86 *Commission v Denmark* [1988] ECR 4607.

[79] Case 155/80 *Oebel* [1981] ECR 1993.

[80] Joined Cases 60 and 61/84 *Cinéthèque v Fédération Nationale des Cinémas Français* [1985] ECR 2605; and see also in the area of services the *tourist guides* cases, e.g. Case C-154/89 *Commission v France* [1991] ECR I-649; Case C-288/89 *Collectieve Anntenevoorziening Gouda v Commissariaat voor de Media* [1991] ECR I-1709; Case C-353/89 *Commission v Netherlands* [1991] ECR I-4069; Case C-17/92 *Federacion de Distribuidores Cinematograficos v Spain* [1993] ECR I-2239.

[81] See Case 7/61 *Commission v Italy* [1961] ECR 317 at 329 and P. Oliver, *Free Movement of Goods in the European Community*, Fourth Ed., Sweet & Maxwell, 2002, p. 247. Oliver takes the view that in Case C-18/88 *RTT v GB-Inno* [1991] ECR I-5941, which concerned standards for telephone equipment to be connected to the public network, the Court intended to create a new mandatory requirement, namely, 'the protection of the public network and its proper functioning'.

[82] Part of that exercise is sometimes performed by national courts; see 5.6 below.

[83] Case C-169/91 *Council of the City of Stoke-on-Trent and Another v B & Q* [1992] ECR I-6635, para 15.

[84] See Case C-379/98 *PreussenElektra v Schleswag*, [2001] ECR I-2099.

[85] Case C-120/95 *Decker v Caisse de maladie des Employés Privés*, [1998] ECR I-1831.

restrictive effect on free movement. They also evince a rearrangement of priorities of the Community polity and the embracing of a more pluralist pattern of integration which places fundamental rights and environmental causes on a par with economic interests and makes the test of proportionality more open-ended. The importance of fundamental rights in this context is illustrated by the judgment in *Schmidberger* which places the protection of fundamental rights on a par with the fundamental freedoms.[86]

5.3. The 'less restrictive alternative' test

In applying the principle of proportionality in relation to restrictions on fundamental freedoms, the Court has been guided by the less restrictive alternative test. This means that national measures will be justified only if the interest which they seek to protect cannot be protected as effectively by measures which restrict less intra-Community trade. This test will now be examined in more detail.

5.3.1. Article 30

The free movement of goods is subject to the derogation of Article 30 which states as follows:

The provisions of Articles 30 to 34 shall not preclude prohibitions or restrictions on imports, exports or goods in transit justified on grounds of public morality, public policy or public security; the protection of health and life of humans, animals or plants; the protection of national treasures possessing artistic, historic or archaeological value; or the protection of industrial and commercial property. Such prohibitions or restrictions shall not, however, constitute a means of arbitrary discrimination or a disguised restriction on trade between Member States.

As an exception to a fundamental freedom, Article 30 must be interpreted strictly.[87] According to consistent case law, the purpose of Article 30 is not to reserve certain matters to the exclusive jurisdiction of Member States, but merely to allow national legislation to derogate from the free movement of goods to the extent to which that is justified in order to achieve the objectives provided for in that Article.[88] A measure adopted on the basis of Article 30 can be justified only if it does not restrict intra-Community trade more than is absolutely necessary.[89] The Article has

---

[86] *Op. cit.*, n. 8 above, discussed at 7.4 below.
[87] Case 124/81 *Commission v United Kingdom* [1983] ECR 203, para 13.
[88] Case 153/78 *Commission v Germany* [1979] ECR 2555, para 5; Case 72/83 *Campus Oil Limited v Minister for Industry and Energy* [1984] ECR 2727, para 32; Case C-367/89 *Richardt and 'Les Accessoires Scientifiques'* [1991] ECR I-4621, para 19.
[89] *Campus Oil, op. cit.*, para 37; *Richardt, op. cit.*, para 20. See also Case 12/78 *Eggers* [1978] ECR 1935; Case 42/82 *Commission v France* [1983] ECR 1013.

a 'provisional character' in that it applies only insofar as the Community has not adopted harmonization measures protecting the interest in issue.[90] Similar principles govern the express derogations from the right of establishment and the freedom to provide services which enable Member States to derogate on grounds of public security, public policy and public health.[91]

The application of the less restrictive alternative test in the context of Article 30 is vividly illustrated by the judgment in *de Peijper*.[92] Netherlands law made the importation of medicinal products conditional upon the production of certain documents which could be obtained only from the manufacturer. The effect of that requirement was to favour importers associated with the manufacturer to the detriment of parallel importers. It was claimed that the purpose of the requirement to produce the documents, which concerned the composition and method of preparation of the medicinal products, was to protect public health. The Court held that, within the limits imposed by the Treaty, it is for the Member States to decide what degree of protection to grant to the health and life of humans. National provisions do not fall within the exception of Article 30, however, if the health and life of humans can be protected as effectively by measures which restrict less intra-Community trade. In particular, the Court held that Article 30 cannot be relied on to justify rules or practices which, even though they are beneficial, contain restrictions which are explained primarily by a concern to lighten the administration's burden or reduce public expenditure, unless, in the absence of the said rules or practices, that burden or expenditure would clearly exceed the limits of what can reasonably be required.[93] On the basis of those considerations, the Court drew a distinction between, on the one hand, documents relating to a medicinal product in general and, on the other hand, documents relating to a specific batch of that product. With regard to the former, where the authorities of the importing Member State had in their possession, as a result of a previous importation, all the particulars relating to the product in order to be able to ascertain whether it was harmful to health, it was unnecessary to require a subsequent importer to produce the same particulars. With regard to documents relating to a specific batch, the Court accepted that the national authorities must be in a position to satisfy themselves that the batch imported complies with the particulars of the product. It continued:[94]

Nevertheless, having regard to the nature of the market for the pharmaceutical product in question, it is necessary to ask whether this objective cannot be equally well achieved if the

[90] See e.g. Case 5/77 *Tedeschi v Denkavit* [1977] ECR 1555; Case 251/78 *Denkavit Futtermittel v Minister für Ernährung, Landwirtschaft und Forsten* [1979] ECR 3369; Case 73/84 *Denkavit Futtermittel v Land Nordrhein-Westfalen* [1985] ECR 1013; Case 190/87 *Oberkreisdirektor des Kreises Borken and Another v Moormann* [1988] ECR 4689. Adoption of a harmonization measure may preclude reliance on Article 36 even if the measure is not exhaustive: Case C-5/94 *The Queen v Ministry of Agriculture, Fisheries and Food, ex p Hedley Lomas (Ireland) Ltd* [1996] ECR I-2553. Cf Case C-347/89 *Freistaat Bayern v Eurim-Pharm* [1991] ECR I-1747, para 26.

[91] See Articles 56 and 66.   [92] Case 104/75 [1976] ECR 613.
[93] *Ibid.*, paras 17–18.   [94] *Ibid.*, paras 24–25.

national administrations, instead of waiting passively for the desired evidence to be produced to them—and in a form calculated to give the manufacturer of the product and his duly appointed representatives an advantage—were to admit, where appropriate similar evidence and, in particular, to adopt a more active policy which could enable every trader to obtain the necessary evidence.

This question is all the more important because parallel importers are very often in a position to offer the goods at a price lower than the one applied by the duly appointed importer for the same product, a fact which, where medicinal preparations are concerned, should, where appropriate, encourage the public health authorities not to place parallel imports at a dis-advantage, since the effective protection of health and life of humans also demands that medicinal preparations should be sold at reasonable prices.

The Court pointed out two less restrictive alternatives. First, national authorities possessed the powers necessary to compel the manufacturer or his duly appointed representatives to supply particulars making it possible to ascertain the qualities of the medicinal product imported by the parallel importer. Second, cooperation between the authorities of the Member States would enable them to obtain on a reciprocal basis the documents necessary for checking largely standardized and widely distributed products. The Court concluded that, taking into account the possible ways of obtaining information, national authorities must consider whether the effective protection of health justifies a presumption of the non-conformity of an imported batch, or whether on the contrary it is sufficient to lay down a presumption of conformity placing on the administration the onus of rebutting it.[95]

The less restrictive alternative test was also applied in *Commission v United Kingdom (UHT milk case)*.[96] UK legislation made the importation of UHT milk subject to an import licence on the ground that licences were necessary to enable the authorities to identify consignments of imported milk and, upon receiving information from the exporting country, to trace infected consignments and destroy them before reaching the market. The Court had little sympathy for this argument, dismissing it as follows:[97]

... the issue of an administrative authorization ... results in an impediment to intra-Community trade which, in the present case, could be eliminated without prejudice to the effectiveness of the protection of animal health and without increasing the administrative or financial burden imposed by the pursuit of that objective. That result could be achieved if the United Kingdom authorities abandoned the practice of issuing licences and confined themselves to obtaining the information which is of use to them, for example, by means of declarations signed by the importers, accompanied if necessary by the appropriate certificates.

---

[95] *Ibid.*, paras 26–28. In any event, the Court held that a parallel importer could not be compelled to prove the conformity of his products with the requisite standards on the basis of documents to which he had no access, where such conformity can be provided by alternative means. Cf Case 188/84 *Commission v France (Woodworking machines case)* [1986] ECR 419, para 39.

[96] *Op. cit.*, n. 88 above. See further Case C-62/90 *Commission v Germany* [1992] ECR I-2575, below p. 221.   [97] *Op. cit.*, para 18.

In addition to the requirement of import licences, UK legislation required that imported UHT milk was packed on premises within the United Kingdom. That requirement was said to be indispensable in order to ensure that the milk was not infected. The Court held however that health protection could be ensured by requiring importers to produce certificates issued by the competent authorities of the exporting Member State.[98] Where cooperation between national authorities makes it possible to facilitate and simplify frontier checks, the authorities responsible for health inspection must ascertain whether the substantiating documents issued within the framework of that cooperation raise a presumption that the imported goods comply with the requirements of domestic health legislation thus enabling the checks carried out upon importation to be simplified. The Court came to the conclusion that in the case of the UHT milk the conditions were satisfied for there to be a presumption of accuracy in favour of the statements contained in such documents. It added that the necessary cooperation did not preclude the authorities of the importing Member State from carrying out controls by means of samples to ensure observance of the requisite standards.[99]

5.3.2. Mandatory requirements

The case law suggests that, as a general rule, the degree of scrutiny exercised by the Court does not differ depending on whether a restriction is imposed in the interests of one of the express derogations provided in the Treaty or of a mandatory requirement. In relation to the latter, the Court has expressly stated that where a Member State has a choice between various measures to attain the same objective it is under an obligation to choose the means which least restrict the free movement of goods.[100]

In application of the less restrictive alternative test, the Court has laid down the principle that the sale of a product must not be prohibited where consumers may sufficiently be protected by adequate labelling requirements.[101] In *Commission v Italy*[102] Italian law restricted the designation 'aceto' to vinegar produced from wine and prohibited the marketing of vinegar produced from other agricultural products under that designation. The Italian Government argued that the purpose of the prohibition was to protect the Italian consumer who was accustomed to treat all vinegars as wine vinegars and would otherwise run the risk of being misled as to the essential characteristics of the product. The Court held that the need for consumer protection could be satisfied by the 'compulsory affixing of suitable labels' indicating the nature of the product. Such a course would enable the consumer to

---

[98] *Ibid.*, para 29.   [99] Paras 30–31.
[100] Case 261/81 *Rau v De Smedt* [1982] ECR 3961, para 12; Case 25/88 *Criminal Proceedings against Wurmser and others* [1989] ECR 1105, para 13; Case 407/85 *Glocken and Kritzinger v USL Centro-Sud and Provincia autonoma di Bolzano* [1988] ECR 4233, para 10.
[101] This is referred to by Oliver as the 'golden rule'. See, *op. cit.*, n. 9 above, p. 227.
[102] Case 193/80 *Commission v Italy* [1981] ECR 3019. See also Case 788/79 *Grilli and Andres* [1980] ECR I-2071.

make his choice in full knowledge of the facts and would guarantee transparency.[103] In the *German Beer* case,[104] German law provided that beer may be manufactured only from certain ingredients and prohibited the marketing as beer of drinks made by other methods. The German Government sought to justify the prohibition arguing that in the minds of German consumers the designation 'Bier' was inseparably linked to the beverage manufactured solely from the ingredients specified in German laws. The Court rejected that argument. It held that it is legitimate for national law to enable consumers who attribute specific qualities to beers manufactured from particular ingredients to make their choice on the basis of that consideration. That however could be ensured by a less restrictive means, namely by indicating the raw materials used in the manufacture of beer. The Court added that such a system of consumer information could operate in practice even in relation to products, like beer, which are not necessarily supplied in bottles or cans. Where beer is sold on draught, the requisite information may appear on casks or the beer taps.[105] Labelling requirements have been considered as sufficient alternatives in other cases. In *Rau*[106] the requirement that margarine can only be sold in cube-shaped packs so as to enable the consumer to distinguish it from butter was struck down on the ground that consumers could be protected by labelling requirements. Notably, in the *German Beer* case the Court stated that a system of mandatory consumer information must not entail negative assessments for products not complying with the requirements of national law.[107] It is arguable then that, depending on the circumstances, a requirement to indicate on the label of a product that it is produced by methods banned in the Member State of marketing may not meet the test of proportionality.

It is clear that, in assessing the compatibility with Community law of national measures which pursue a legitimate aim but restrict inter-State trade, the Court performs a weighing exercise. It juxtaposes the national interest in attaining that aim against the Community interest in ensuring the free movement of goods.[108] In performing that exercise, the Court follows a pro-active rather than a reactive approach. Thus in examining restrictions allegedly justified for the protection of consumers the Court has seen the internal market as one of the factors set to influence consumer choices and has held that the legislation of a Member State must not 'crystallize given consumer habits so as to consolidate an advantage acquired by national industries concerned to comply with them'.[109] The case law

---

[103] *Op. cit.*, para 27. Cf the Opinion of Slynn AG.

[104] *Commission v Germany, Op. cit.*, n. 5 above.

[105] *Ibid.*, paras 35–36. A similar reasoning was followed in *Glocken and Kritzinger, op. cit.*, n. 101 above. The Court found the prohibition of Italian law on the sale of pasta made from common wheat incompatible with Article 28 insofar as it applied to imported products. It considered labelling requirements as a sufficient alternative and indicated that Italian law could also require information to be given to the consumer as to the composition of pasta in restaurants.

[106] *Rau v de Smedt, op. cit.*, n. 101 above.   [107] Para 35.

[108] *Stoke-on-Trent, op. cit.*, n. 83 above.

[109] Case 170/78 *Commission v United Kingdom* [1980] ECR 417; *German Beer* case, para 32.

evinces a tendency towards interpreting the fundamental freedoms not merely as exponents of free trade but as the normative expressions of a European economic constitution.

Finally, it should be noted that where a national measure is found incompatible with the Treaty provisions on free movement, the national authorities must cease to apply it in relation to imported products. Whether a domestic producer can take advantage of the rights granted by Community law to a producer from another Member State is a matter for national law to decide.[110]

5.3.3. The limits of the less restrictive alternative test

The less restrictive alternative test entails a strict application of proportionality but by no means a mechanical one. The principle is by its nature open-textured and the degree of scrutiny remains far from uniform. Thus, the less restrictive alternative test does not necessarily mean that a restriction imposed by a Member State will fail if another Member State imposes a less restrictive requirement. In *Alpine Investments*,[111] the Dutch authorities prohibited financial intermediaries operating in the commodities futures market from making unsolicited contact with prospective clients by telephone (cold-calling). The Court held that the objectives of the prohibition, which was to protect investors and to safeguard the integrity of the Dutch financial services industry, were imperative reasons of public interest capable of justifying a restriction on the freedom to provide services. It was argued, however, that the total ban on cold-calling infringed proportionality. Alpine Investments referred to less stringent requirements applicable in the United Kingdom where financial intermediaries were under the obligation to keep records of telephone conversations. The Advocate General, whose view on this point was fully endorsed by the Court, stated that harmonization directives in the field of consumer protection usually permit Member States to impose additional or more stringent requirements. *A fortiori*, where no harmonization measures have been introduced, the rules of a Member State cannot be held disproportionate merely because another Member State applies less restrictive rules. If that were so, Member States would need to align their legislation with the Member State which imposed the least onerous requirements.[112] The obvious concern was to avoid a 'race to the bottom'.

Alpine Investments shows that whether a restriction on a marketing technique passes the test of proportionality should be assessed *inter alia* by reference to the conditions prevailing in the national market and the reasons which led to its adoption. Although in this case there was clearly a less restrictive alternative

---

[110] *Guimont, op. cit.,* n. 48 above, para 23; *Douwe Egberts, op. cit.,* n. 62 above, para 58.
[111] *Op. cit.,* n. 66 above.
[112] *Ibid.,* at p. 1165 *per* Jacobs AG and para 51 of the judgment. The point was confirmed in Case C-3/95 *Reisebüro Broede v Gerd Sandker* [1996] ECR I-6511, para 42; Case C-262/02 *Commission v France (Loi Evin),* judgment of 13 July 2004, para 37; Case C-36/02 *Omega Spielhallen-und Automatenaufstellungs v Oberbürgermeisterin der Bundesstadt Bonn,* judgment of 14 October 2004, para 38; Cf Case 40/82 *Commission v United Kingdom* [1982] ECR 2793.

operative in another Member State, the Court focused on the effects of the restriction rather than on a comparison between the laws of different Member States. A similar approach has been followed in other cases. Accordingly, the Court has held that, in assessing the proportionality of measures taken on grounds of public health, account may be taken of 'national consumption habits'.[113]

In *Oosthoek*,[114] Netherlands law prohibited the giving of free gifts as a means of sales promotion unless the consumption or use of the free gift was related to the product in respect of the purchase of which it was given. The Court found that, although the requirement of related consumption or use had not been incorporated in the laws of other Member States, it did not exceed what was necessary for the attainment of the objectives pursued. In *Aragonesa de Publicidad*,[115] it was held that national legislation which prohibited the advertising in certain places of beverages having an alcoholic strength of more than 23 degrees was proportionate on the ground that it was not manifestly unreasonable as part of a campaign against alcoholism.[116] The Court concentrated on the notion of reasonableness rather than on the existence of less stringent alternatives. In that case however the national measure at issue restricted freedom of trade only to a limited extent as it applied to a limited range of products. The more tenuous the restriction on free movement, the more lax the standard of proportionality.[117] In *Buet*[118] French law prohibited canvassing for the purpose of selling educational material. The Court confirmed that rules seeking to protect the consumer must be proportionate and that Member States must make use of the least restrictive means at their disposal capable of attaining the objective pursued. It then stated that canvassing at private dwellings exposed potential customers to the risk of making an ill-considered purchase. Although, to guard against that risk, it was normally sufficient to ensure that purchasers had the right to cancel a contract, special considerations applied where the canvassing related to educational causes. That was because the potential purchaser often belonged to a group of person who were behind with their education and were seeking to catch up, which made them particularly vulnerable to salesmen. Also, the Court took into account the fact that the prohibition of canvassing had been introduced as a result of numerous complaints caused by abuses. Finally, it noted that the consequences of an ill-considered purchase were not only financial since the purchase of unsuitable material could compromise the consumer's chances of obtaining further training and thus consolidating his position in the

---

[113] Case 97/83 *Melkunie* [1984] ECR 2367, para 19.

[114] Case 286/81 *Oosthoek's Uitgeversmaatschappij* [1982] ECR 4575. See also *Commission v France, op. cit.*, n. 96 above, discussed at 5.3.4 below.

[115] *Op. cit.*, n. 93 above. Cf Case C-362/88 *GB-INNO-MB* [1990] ECR I- 667.

[116] As Weatherill remarks, the approach of the Court in *Aragonesa* is compatible with that in *Cassis de Dijon* where the Court rejected the argument of the German Government that controlling the supply of *weak* alcoholic drinks was part of a policy for the protection of public health. See S. Weatherill, *Law and Integration in the European Union*, Oxford University Press, 1995, p. 238.

[117] *Cinéthèque, op. cit.*, n. 80 above.

[118] Case 382/87 *Buet and another v Ministère public* [1989] ECR 1235.

labour market. In conclusion, it held that a Member State could legitimately consider that giving consumers a right of cancellation was not sufficient protection and that it was necessary to ban canvassing in private dwellings.[119]

Oosthoek, Aragonesa and *Buet* concerned selling arrangements which will now fall outside the scope of Article 28 unless it can be shown that they do not meet the *Keck* conditions. They remain however good illustrations of the fact that, inevitably, the notion of proportionality has a close affinity to that of reasonableness. In effect, the underlying judicial policy is to invite Member States to a dialogue. Member States are called upon to justify measures which cause obstacles to trade and to search for less restrictive solutions, but the application of the principle does not remove all discretion from national authorities. The model which emerges from the case law is one of selective judicial deference to the choices of national administrations. *Cinéthèque* and, more recently, *Alpine Investments* show that the wider the Court understands the scope of fundamental freedoms the less vigorously it is prepared to apply proportionality. Viewed in that light, a soft proportionality test may be the *quid pro quo* for extending the scope of free movement.[120]

In some cases, it may be difficult, or even impossible, to ascertain on the basis of objective factors that a less restrictive rule is sufficiently effective to pursue the objective in view. The procedure before the Court of Justice does not lend itself to fact-finding missions and, inevitably, heavy reliance is placed on the submissions of the parties. In references for preliminary rulings, this is compensated by leaving the precise determination of the issue to the national court although that raises other concerns.[121] Overall, the Court pursues only a limited economic analysis of market conditions. The subjective evaluation required in applying the principle of proportionality explains why disagreements between the Court and advocates general are not infrequent in this area.

The difficulties in applying the less restrictive alternative test are illustrated by *Meyhui v Schott Zwiesel Glaswerke*.[122] The case concerned the compatibility with Article 28 of Directive 69/493 on the approximation of the laws of the Member States on crystal glass.[123] The Directive classifies crystal glass products into four categories. In relation to high quality products belonging to categories 1 and 2, the descriptions specified in the Directive may be used freely whatever the country of destination. By contrast, in relation to lower quality products belonging in categories 3 and 4, the Directive provides that only the description in the language or languages of the country in which the goods are marketed may be used. Litigation arose as a result of the refusal of a German glass producer to affix to products belonging to categories 3 and 4 their description in Belgium's official languages. The Court pointed out that the purpose of the requirement pertaining to

---

[119] *Ibid.*, paras 12–15.   [120] This view is countenanced also by *de Agostini, op. cit.*
[121] See 5.6 below.   [122] *Op. cit.*, n. 2 above.
[123] OJ, English Special Ed., 1969 (II), p. 599.

description is to protect both the consumer against fraud and the manufacturer who complies with the standards laid down in the Directive. It then held:[124]

It may . . . be considered that, in the case of the first two categories, consumers are adequately protected by the fact that in all the descriptions adopted by the directive (cristal supérieur 30%, cristallo superiore 30%, hochbleikristall 30%, volloodkristal 30%, full lead crystal 30%, krystal 30% . . .) the word 'crystal' is easily recognizable and, moreover, is always accompanied by an indication of the percentage of lead.

In the case of the lower two categories, on the other hand (crystallin, vetro sonoro superiore, kristallglass, kristallynglas, sonoorglas, crystal glass, crystallin, vidrio sonoro superior, vidro sonoro superior, verre sonore, vetro sonoro, vidrio sonoro, vidro sonoro . . .) the difference in the quality of the glass used is not easily discernible to the average consumer for whom the purchase of crystal glass products is not a frequent occurrence. It is therefore necessary for him to be given the clearest information possible as to what he is buying so that he does not confuse a product in categories 3 and 4 with a product in the higher categories and consequently that he does not pay too much.

The fact that consumers in a Member State in which the products are marketed are to be informed in the language or languages of that country is therefore an appropriate means of protection. In this regard it should be held that the hypothesis referred to by the national court that another language may be easily comprehensible to the purchaser is of only marginal importance.

Finally, the measure chosen by the Community legislature in order to protect consumers does not appear disproportionate to the goal pursued. There is nothing in the file to suggest that there might conceivably be some different measure which could achieve the same goal while being less constrictive for producers.

The Court's reasoning contrasts with the approach of the Advocate General, who identified two limbs of the description requirement: the requirement to use the language of the country of marketing; and the prohibition against using any other languages in addition. The Advocate General found that the first requirement was justified in some cases but not in others. For example, it is reasonable to require that French products belonging to category 3 (*crystallin*) must be marketed in the Netherlands under the description applying in that country (*sonooorglas*). However, it may be unnecessarily restrictive to require a French producer of category 4 products (*verre sonore*) to use, when marketing them in Italy, Spain or Portugal, the descriptions applicable in those countries (*vetro sonoro*, *vidrio sonoro* and *vidro sonoro*). The Advocate General found the prohibition of using additional languages particularly onerous on traders. On balance, he came to the conclusion that both aspects of the requirement were invalid. He stated that corresponding requirements laid down by national law would be in breach of Article 28 and concluded that it was possible for the Community legislature to find an alternative rule which would take better account of the requirements inherent in the establishment of the internal market.[125] The case illustrates how difficult it is to apply the principle of proportionality which, in some cases, entails in effect a subjective test. The difference

---

[124] *Op. cit.*, paras 17–20.   [125] *Ibid.*, pp. 3891–3892.

between the Opinion of the Advocate General and the Court is striking, but the answer may lie somewhere between the two. The Court seems to have authorised the most restrictive measure, that is to say, a prohibition on the use of other languages in addition to that of the State of marketing, without good reason.[126] On the other hand, the Advocate General gave no concrete examples of measures less restrictive of the compulsory use of the language of the State of destination which would guarantee effective protection of consumers in all cases. The judgment contrasts sharply with other cases concerning the compulsory use of certain languages where the Court took a more critical view of such requirements,[127] but the distinction may lie in the fact that in *Meyhui* at issue was the validity of a Community measure and not of a national one. Article 28 binds not only Member States but also the Community institutions but the Court tends to allow the latter more latitude with regard to justification for restrictions on trade[128] and implied as much in *Meyhui*.[129]

5.3.4. Equivalence and duplication

The Court has derived from the principle of proportionality two specific, inter-related, requirements: the requirement of equivalence and the requirement of cooperation between national authorities. Regulatory restrictions imposed on goods or services by the host State must not duplicate requirements imposed by the State of origin. In the context of the free movement of goods[130] this applies in particular to health inspections. The Court has held that health inspections carried out by Member States in accordance with Article 30 are justified provided that the measures adopted are in reasonable proportion to the aim pursued and that the protection of health cannot be achieved as effectively by measures which restrict intra-Community trade to a lesser extent. According to the same line of cases, the free movement of goods is served by the carrying out of health inspections in the country of production and the health authorities of the Member States concerned should cooperate in order to avoid the repetition, in the importing country, of checks which have already been carried out in the country of production.[131] In

---

[126] See the criticism by Oliver, *op. cit.*, n. 9 above, pp. 231–232.

[127] See e.g. Case 27/80 *Fietje* [1980] ECR 3839; *Piageme v Peeters, op. cit.*, n. 2 above.

[128] See Oliver, *op. cit.*, pp. 45 *et seq.*, p. 232.

[129] At para 21 of the judgment the Court stated that by adopting the contested requirement the Council has not exceeded the limits of its discretion, implying a more lax application of the proportionality test. However, as Oliver notes, *op. cit.*, p. 232, there is nothing to suggest that the ruling does not apply equally to national measures. See further *Alliance for Natural Health, op. cit.*, n. 2 above.　　　　[130] For services, see e.g. Case C-76/90 *Säger* [1991] ECR I-4221, para 15.

[131] See Case 73/84 *Denkavit Futtermittel v Land Nordrhein-Westfalen* [1985] ECR 1013, para 14 and also Case 35/76 *Simmenthal v Italian Minister for Finance* [1976] ECR 1871, Case 46/76 *Bauhuis v The Netherlands State* [1977] ECR 5; Case 251/78 *Denkavit Futtermittel v Minister für Ernährung, Landwirtschaft und Forsten* [1979] ECR 3369; *Commission v United Kingdom (UHT milk), op. cit.* n. 88 above; Case 42/82 *Commission v France* [1983] ECR 1013.

Frans-Nederlandse Maatschappij voor Biologische Producten[132] the Court held, in relation to plant protection products containing toxic substances, that the national authorities are not entitled to require without good reason laboratory tests which have already been carried out in another Member State, the results of which are available to those authorities or may at their request be placed at their disposal. The principle of cooperation however does not impair the right of each Member State to apply its own legislation to protect public health, provided that the requirements of Article 30 are fulfilled.[133]

The principle of equivalence is a powerful tool of negative integration but its application is restricted where Member States espouse conflicting regulatory philosophies. In the *French Woodworking machines* case[134] the Commission took issue with the safety standards imposed by French law on woodworking machines which severely inhibited imports by requiring prior technical inspection and, in the case of more dangerous equipment, approval by the Ministry of Labour. The safety requirements were the expression of the risk prevention philosophy underlying the French system. The legislation was based on the idea that users of machines must be protected from their own mistakes and that the machines must be designed so that the user's intervention is limited to the minimum. In other Member States, in particular Germany, the underlying idea was that the worker should receive thorough and continuing training. The Court held that a Member State is not entitled to prevent the marketing of a product originating in another Member State which provides a level of protection equivalent to that which the national rules are intended to ensure. It is therefore contrary to proportionality for national rules to require that such imported products must comply strictly and exactly with the provisions or technical requirements laid down for domestic products. The Court however dismissed the Commission's claim on the ground that it had not been proved that machines in free circulation in other Member States provided the same level of protection as French ones. The requirement of equivalence is effectively a requirement of non-discrimination and fundamental differences in the philosophy of control existing in the various Member States may make it impossible to carry out a meaningful comparison of the national requirements with a view to establishing comparability.

The principle of the less restrictive alternative applies in relation to the other fundamental freedoms. According to the case law, requirements imposed on providers of services must be such as to guarantee the achievement of the intended objective and must not go beyond what is necessary in order to achieve that objective. In other words, it must not be possible to obtain the same result by less restrictive rules.[135] The Court has accepted that Article 49 also covers non-discriminatory restrictions on the freedom to provide services.[136] Such restrictions

---

[132] Case 272/80 [1981] ECR 3277, paras 14–15.
[133] *Melkunie, op. cit.*, n. 114 above, para 14.   [134] *Op. cit.*, n. 96 above.
[135] *Gouda, op. cit.*, n. 80 above, para 15 of the judgment; Case C-154/89 *Commission v France* [1991] ECR I-659, para 15; Case C-198/89 *Commission v Greece* [1991] ECR I-727, para 19.
[136] See *Säger, op. cit.*, at 4234 *per* Jacobs AG.

however may be justified not only by reference to the express derogation of Article 56 but also by imperative reasons of public interest insofar as that interest is not protected by the rules to which the person providing the services is subject in the Member State in which he is established. In particular, those requirements must be objectively necessary in order to ensure compliance with the professional rules and to guarantee the protection of the recipient of services and they must not exceed what is necessary to attain those objectives.[137] Thus in *Säger*, the Court accepted that the requirement to possess a professional qualification in order to be entitled to give legal advice was necessary to protect the public. However, it came to the conclusion that the requirement to possess a professional qualification in order to offer patent renewal services of the type at issue in that case was not necessary for the protection of the public. The services at issue were of a straightforward nature and did not require any specific professional aptitudes. The provider of the patent renewal services did not advise his clients. He simply alerted them when renewal fees had to be paid and paid the fees on their behalf. Also, failure to renew the patent had only limited consequences for the patent holder.[138]

An example in relation to the right of establishment is provided by *Kraus v Land Baden-Württemberg*.[139] The question raised was whether a German national could use in Germany a postgraduate law degree obtained in Scotland without prior authorization from the German authorities. The Court held that the requirement of authorization was not in itself incompatible with Community law. However, the Court derived from the principle of proportionality the following requirements: the procedure for authorization must have as its sole purpose to verify that the degree has been correctly awarded, the procedure must be readily available and not dependent on payment of excessive charges, any refusal of authorization must be subject to judicial review, the person concerned must be able to find out the reasons for a refusal, and the sanctions provided for disregard of the authorization procedure must not be disproportionate to the seriousness of the offence.

5.4. Specific grounds

We turn now to examine in more detail the application of the principle of proportionality on measures taken in the interests of public health, consumer protection and public security. Public security and public health are among the grounds of derogation expressly stated in the Treaty.[140] The principle of proportionality will be examined here by reference especially to Article 30. Consumer protection is one of the mandatory requirements recognized by the Court under the *Cassis de Dijon* formula and also one of the imperative reasons of public interest which may justify national measures restricting the free movement of services.

---

[137] *Ibid.*, para 15 and see cases referred to therein.
[138] See further *Gebhard, op. cit.,* n. 68 above.   [139] Case 19/92 [1993] ECR I-1663.
[140] See Articles 30, 39(3), 46 and 55.

5.4.1. Public health

The Court has held that human health and life rank first among the interests protected by Article 30 and that, in the absence of Community legislation, it is in principle for the Member States to decide on the degree to which they wish to protect human health and life and how that degree of protection is to be achieved.[141] Nevertheless, measures taken to protect public health may not go beyond what is necessary to protect the objective in view. We saw above that in *de Peijper* and in the *UHT* case the Court was prepared to apply the test of proportionality strictly.[142] Clearly, measures taken on grounds of health protection must not constitute a disguised restriction on imports.[143] In *Commission v United Kingdom*,[144] the Court held that the imposition of an import ban on poultry products from other Member States constituted a quantitative restriction on imports, which was not justified on the ground of preventing the spreading of the Newcastle disease, since there were other less stringent measures for attaining the same result. The Court found that on the facts the real aim of the ban was to protect the British producers and, it 'did not form part of a seriously considered health policy'.[145]

In *Commission v Germany*[146] German law prohibited the importation for personal use of medicinal products lawfully prescribed by a doctor and purchased in another Member State where such products were available in Germany only on prescription. The German Government argued that the foreign language on the label and the fact that the doctor who prescribed the product and the pharmacist who dispensed it were far away posed the danger that the imported product might be incorrectly used. The Court held that the purchase of a medicinal product in a pharmacy in another Member State provides a guarantee equivalent to that which would be provided if the product was purchased in the importing State. That finding was all the more compelling given that the provisions for access to, and the exercise of, the profession of pharmacist and the profession of doctor had been made subject to harmonization directives. It added that the fact that the doctor who prescribed the medicinal product or the pharmacist who sold it are established in another Member State does not prevent them from supervising the use of the product, if necessary, with the aid of a colleague established in the importing State. Also the doctor or the pharmacist supplying the product could make up for any problems arising from the foreign language of the label by giving oral instructions.

---

[141] Joined Cases 266 and 267/87 *R v Royal Pharmaceutical Society of Great Britain, ex p Association of Pharmaceutical Importers* [1989] ECR I-1295, para 21. For recent confirmation, see e.g. *Deutscher Apothekerverband eV, op. cit.*, n. 61 above, paras 104–105.

[142] *de Peijper, op. cit.*, n. 93 above; *UHT* case, *op. cit.*, n. 88 above.

[143] On restrictions on exports on grounds of public health, see e.g. Case 118/86 *Openbaar Ministerie v Nertsvoederfabriek Nederland* [1987] ECR 3883.

[144] Case 40/82 [1982] ECR 2793.   [145] *Ibid.*, para. 38.

[146] Case C-62/90 *Commission v Germany* [1992] ECR I-2575. See also Case 215/87 *Schumacher v Hauptzollamt Frankfurt am Main-Ost* [1989] ECR 617.

More recently, in *DocMorris* it was held that Article 30 can be relied on to justify a national prohibition on the sale by mail order of medicinal products which may be sold only in pharmacies insofar as it refers to products sold on prescription. It cannot be relied on, however, to justify an absolute prohibition on the sale on the internet and delivery by mail order of products which are not subject to prescription.[147] The judgment gives the green light to virtual pharmacies for the cross-border sale of non prescription medicines.

An over-restrictive approach was followed in *Commission v France*[148] where the ECJ upheld the compatibility of the French *Loi Evin* with the freedom to provide services. The *Loi Evin* prohibits the television advertisement of alcoholic beverages. The prohibition includes indirect advertising resulting from the appearance on the television screen of hoardings visible during the re-transmission of bi-national sporting events taking place in other Member States. The Court accepted that the prohibition was a restriction on the freedom to provide services but found that it was proportionate. It confined its reasoning to the general observations that the prohibition was appropriate to achieve the objective of public health and did not go beyond what was necessary to achieve its objectives. The judgment appears to apply a soft proportionality test given that the restriction on freedom to provide services was both direct and substantial whilst the violation of the French law was indirect. Similar advertising restrictions were not imposed on tobacco. More importantly, the Court paid lip service to the argument that indirect television advertising was allowed in multinational sporting events where the French audience was very high but not in bi-national events which tended to attract lower audience numbers. It pointed out that bi-national events targeted specifically a French audience and therefore the restriction of the prohibition to such events made it proportionate. It is submitted that this reasoning is not persuasive. The Court was preoccupied not so much with upholding a consistent health policy but with national choice.

In *Freistaat Bayern v Eurim-Pharm*[149] it was held that a requirement on a parallel importer to repackage medicinal products lawfully marketed in another Member State before they enter the national territory so as to comply with the packaging requirements of the importing State was not necessary for the protection of public health. The products were subject to a marketing authorization in the importing State and the importer held a permit for the purpose of labelling and packaging them in accordance with the legislation of that State. It was therefore disproportionate to require that the products be repackaged before they entered the national territory. The contested measure clearly prevented the importer from operating an integrated sales strategy. If the measure were upheld, parallel importers would be required to move their packaging process to each of the States into which they import proprietary medicinal products.

---

[147] *Deutscher Apothekerverband eV, op. cit.*
[148] *Commission v France, op. cit.*, n. 113 above. Confirmed also in *Bacardi France SA, op. cit.*, n. 71 above.   [149] *Eurim-Pharm, op. cit.*, n. 91 above.

It has further been held that an absolute prohibition on references to slimming and to 'medical recommendations, attestations, declarations or statements of approval' in the labelling and advertising of foodstuffs goes beyond what is necessary to protect public health and consumers.[150] A less restrictive alternative would be to require the manufacturer or distributor to furnish proof of the accuracy of the facts mentioned in the label.[151]

In assessing whether a national measure meets the test of proportionality, the degree to which it restricts freedom of movement is obviously of crucial importance. A general ban is more likely to infringe the principle than one which is targeted to a certain category of products chosen on the basis of objective criteria. The intensity of risk is also of importance. In the *Newcastle disease* case the Court considered that, taking into account the situation prevailing in the UK and in the Community as a whole, 'the possibility of infection by imported poultry products would be so much due to sheer hazard that it cannot justify a complete prohibition of imports from Member States which admit the use of vaccine'.[152] Similarly, the costs which importers have to meet in order to comply with the requirements imposed will be taken into account. In *Franzén*[153] it was held that the requirement to possess a licence in order to carry out wholesale trade in alcoholic beverages in Sweden was not justified on grounds of public health because the conditions for obtaining the licence were too onerous. The Court singled out in particular two such conditions: the requirement to provide storage capacity within Sweden and the imposition of high fees and charges on licence holders.

It is submitted that in none of the cases discussed above did the Court jeopardize health protection as in all of them it could objectively be said that there existed less restrictive alternatives which were equally effective to attain the objective in view. By contrast, the Court erred on the side of safety in *R v Royal Pharmaceutical Society of Great Britain, ex parte Association of Pharmaceutical Importers*.[154] Professional rules prohibited a pharmacist from substituting, except in an emergency, another product for a product specifically named in the prescription even if the therapeutic effect and quality of the two products were identical. The prohibition severely affected parallel imports but was upheld as proportionate. The Court stated that the prohibition did not go beyond what was necessary to achieve its objective which was to leave the entire responsibility for the treatment of patients in the hands of the doctor responsible for treatment. The Court found itself unable to discount reasons based on 'psychosomatic phenomena', for which a specific proprietary medicinal product might be prescribed rather than another product having the same therapeutic effect.[155] The judgment has been criticized on the ground that

---

[150] *Douwe Egberts, op. cit.*, n. 68 above.
[151] Case C-77/97 *Unilever* [1999] ECR I-431, para 42.
[152] *Op. cit.*, n. 146 above, para 44.
[153] *Op. cit.*, n. 7 above. Cf *Aragonesa, op. cit.*, n. 54 above.   [154] *Op. cit.*, n. 143 above.
[155] *Ibid.*, para 22.

it is based more on psychological than objective considerations[156] and sits uncomfortably with the German medicinal products case.[157]

A common regulatory tool used to pursue health protection policies is the requirement to approve or inspect products before they can be marketed. The Court has held that health inspections carried out by Member States in accordance with Article 30 are justified provided that the measures adopted are proportionate and that the protection of health cannot be achieved as effectively by measures which restrict intra-Community trade to a lesser extent.[158] The discretion of the importing State is restricted by the requirement of non-duplication.[159] But a lot depends on the circumstances in issue and in *Melkunie*[160] the Court upheld national legislation the purpose of which was to ensure that milk products did not contain micro-organisms in a quantity which may constitute a risk 'merely to the health of some, particularly sensitive consumers'.[161]

In a number of cases, issues pertaining to public health have arisen in connection with restrictions placed on food additives.[162] According to standard case law, where there are scientific uncertainties, it is for the Member States to decide what degree of protection is needed on health grounds subject to the requirements of the free movement of goods.[163] A Member State may in principle make the importation of products containing additives lawfully marketed in the Member State of production subject to the requirement of authorization on grounds of public health. Proportionality, however, provides a number of substantive and procedural guarantees. In *Sandoz*[164] Dutch law made the importation of products to which vitamins had been added subject to prior authorization. The Court held that, in view of the difficulty in assessing the harmful consequences of excessive intake of vitamins and the lack of harmonization, Member States enjoyed wide discretion. According to the principle of proportionality, however, Member States must authorize vitamins lawfully marketed in the Member State of production where the addition of vitamins to foodstuffs 'meets a real need, especially a technical or nutritional one'.[165] In *Motte*[166] it was held that, in deciding whether to permit the importation of products containing additives, the national authorities must take into consideration the results of international scientific research and must grant authorization where there is a

---

[156] See Oliver, *op. cit.*, p. 215.   [157] See above *Commission v Germany, op. cit.*

[158] See e.g. Case 73/84 *Denkavit Futtermittel v Land Nordrhein-Westfalen* [1985] ECR 1013, para 14.   [159] See above p. 218.

[160] *Op. cit.*, n. 114 above.   [161] *Ibid.*, para 18.

[162] Note that now much of this area has been harmonized by the use of positive lists at Community level: Directive 2002/46 on the approximation of the laws of the Member States relating to food supplements, OJ 2002 L 183/51, whose validity was upheld in the *Vitamins* case: see above, Ch. 3.

[163] See e.g. *de Peijper, op. cit.*, Case 272/80 *Frans-Nederlandse Maatschappij voor Biologische Producten* [1981] ECR 3277, para. 12; Case 174/82 *Sandoz BV* [1983] ECR 2445, para 16.

[164] *Op. cit.*, previous note.   [165] Para 19.

[166] Case 247/84 [1985] ECR 3887. See also Case 304/84 *Ministère Public v Muller* [1986] ECR 1511; Case 53/80 *Officier van Justitie v Kaasfabriek Eyssen* [1981] ECR I-409; Case 94/83 *Heijn* [1984] ECR 3263.

real need taking into account the eating habits in the State of importation. In the *German Beer* case, the Court found the ban on the use of additives applicable to beer disproportionate in view of its generality as it excluded all additives authorized in other Member States.[167] But the *German Beer* case does not provide authority for the proposition that a potential risk to public health is in itself insufficient to justify the prohibition of an additive. The Court stated that mere references to the potential risks of the ingestion of additives did not suffice to justify the imposition of *stricter* rules in the case of beer than those applicable to other beverages.[168] A Member State nonetheless must be in a position to defend the prohibition of an additive and a general ban on all products of a certain category on the ground that they may contain an additive harmful to health will be struck down.[169]

The onus of proving that a substance is harmful to health rests with the national authorities. They may require the importer to produce information regarding the product but it is for them to assess whether authorization must be granted in accordance with Community law.[170] Recent cases stress in this respect the importance of the precautionary principle. Thus a decision to prohibit a food substance, which is lawfully marketed in another Member State, can be introduced only if the risk to public health is real and sufficiently established on the basis of the latest scientific data available. If the assessment carried out reveals that there is scientific uncertainty, the Member State may in accordance with the precautionary principle take protective measures without having to wait until the existence and gravity of the risks involved are fully demonstrated. The risk assessment however cannot be based on purely hypothetical considerations.[171] Finally, Member States must make available to traders an effective procedure by which they can apply for the authorization to use a specific additive. It must also be open to traders to challenge before the courts an unjustified failure to grant authorization.[172]

The conclusion to be drawn from the above cases is that, although, understandably, in matters of public health the Court has followed a cautious approach, the application of the principle of proportionality remains strict.

5.4.2. Public security

Article 30 does not provide for an order of priority among the grounds of derogation provided therein. All of them are equivalent in law in that they can

---

[167] *Op. cit.*, n. 5 above.   [168] Para 49.

[169] See *Glocken and Kritzinger, op. cit.*, n. 101 above, para 13. Unless, one assumes, detection of the existence of the additive is impossible.   [170] *Sandoz*, paras 22–24.

[171] See Case C-24/00 *Commission v France*, judgment of 5 February 2004, paras 55–56; Case C-192/01 *Commission v Denmark* [2003] ECR I-9693 para 49; Case C-236/01 *Monsanto Agricoltura Italia and Others* [2003] ECR I-8105; para 106; Case C-157/96 *National Farmers' Union and Others* [1998] ECR I-2211, para 63.

[172] *Ministère Public v Muller op. cit.*, para 26; *Commission v Germany, op. cit.*, paras 45–47. In that case German law did not provide for a procedure by virtue of which traders could obtain authorization of a specific additive.

justify a restriction on free movement. Public security, nonetheless, presents certain distinct characteristics. The safeguarding of public security is a core state function. The issues involved may be more difficult to define objectively and thus less susceptible to judicial determination. Within the context of a national polity, courts may be more willing to defer to executive choices on matters connected with the defence of the realm. *A fortiori*, a supra-national court may be even more reticent to intervene in issues which are closely linked to State sovereignty for fear that rigorous judicial intervention may raise concerns of legitimacy. This is not to say that such issues fall, or should fall, outside the judicial province. That would run counter to the rule of law. Clearly, each case should be judged on its merits. It is reasonable to suggest, however that within the context of Article 30 EC, once a genuine risk to public security is established, a Member State can exercise relatively wide discretion with regard to the measures which are appropriate to safeguard it.

In *Campus Oil*,[173] Irish law required importers of petroleum products to purchase a certain proportion of their requirements from a State refinery at fixed prices. It was argued that the operation of the State refinery, which was the only one in the national territory, was essential in order to guarantee the supply of petroleum products in Ireland and that, in turn, the purchasing obligation was necessary to guarantee that the refinery could dispose of its products. The Court pointed out that, because of the fundamental importance of petroleum products as an energy source in modern economy, the aim of ensuring a minimum supply transcended purely economic considerations and was covered by the objective of public security. It then examined whether the Irish rules could be justified on the basis of Article 30. It accepted that the installation of a refinery in the national territory contributed to improving the security of supply of petroleum products. It was argued, however, that the purchasing obligation was disproportionate. The Court held that this obligation would be justified only if the major distributors refused to purchase from the State refinery despite the fact that it charged market prices. In addition, it specified, *inter alia*, the condition that the quantities of petroleum products which may be covered by the purchasing obligations must not exceed the minimum supply requirements of the State concerned 'without which the operation of essential public services and the survival of its inhabitants would be affected'. The application of the principle of proportionality in *Campus Oil* appears to be relatively strict. In a carefully balanced judgment, the Court gave detailed guidelines to be applied by the national court. It is clear from the judgment that the purchasing obligation was considered compatible with Community law only insofar as it satisfied non-economic interests.[174] The Opinion of the Advocate General differs from the judgment in two respects. Slynn AG expressed doubts as to whether the purchasing obligation was necessary in view of Community measures which required Member States to maintain minimum stocks. By contrast, the Court took the view that the existing Community legislation fell short of providing

[173] *Op. cit.*, n. 89 above.   [174] *Ibid.*, para 35.

'an unconditional assurance' that sufficient supplies could be maintained. Also, applying the principle of the less restrictive alternative, Slynn AG considered that the holding of stocks of petroleum products may be a sufficient safeguard in the eventuality of shortages.[175]

Subsequently, in *Commission v Greece*[176] the Court found that special rights reserved to the Greek State with regard to the importation and marketing of petroleum products were not justified on grounds of public security. One of the requirements imposed by Greek law was that distribution companies had to submit annually to the Greek authorities a procurement programme setting out their projected sales and their sources of supply for the following year. The procurement programme was subject to approval by the Greek authorities. The Court held that the requirement of approval was not essential in order to ensure a minimum supply of petroleum products for the country at all times. It pointed out that Greece had two public sector refineries whose production capacity exceeded the country's minimum requirements in a period of crisis. It was therefore sufficient to require distribution companies merely to notify the authorities in due time of their procurement programmes and any significant amendments thereto.

In *Cullet v Leclerc*[177] the French Government sought to justify the imposition of minimum prices for the retail sale of petrol on grounds of public policy and public security. It argued that an unrestricted price war for the sale of fuel would result in social unrest, even violence, by disaffected retailers. This far-fetched submission was rejected by the Court on the ground that the Government had failed to show that it would be unable to deal with any public disorder using the powers at its disposal. Verloren van Themaat AG took a more stern view and was reluctant to accept that civil disorder could provide justification for restrictions on the free movement of goods.[178]

Issues concerning public security have arisen in relation to dual-use goods, i.e. goods that can be used for both military and civil purposes.[179] In *Richardt*,[180] the Court held that the concept of public security within the meaning of Article 30 covers both the internal and the external security of a State.[181] It also held that the importation, exportation and transit of goods capable of being used for strategic purposes may affect the public security of a State, and therefore that Member States are entitled to make the transit of such goods subject to the grant of a special authorization. The judgment in *Richardt* was followed in *Werner*[182] and in *Leifer*,[183]

---

[175] *Ibid.*, p. 2765.   [176] Case C-347/88 [1990] ECR I-4747.
[177] Case 231/83 [1985] ECR 305.
[178] *Ibid.*, at 312–313. See further Case C-265/95 *Commission v France* [1997] ECR I-6959 and *Schmidberger, op. cit.*, n. 8 above, discussed at 7.4 below.
[179] For Community measures on the issue, see Council Decision 2000/243/CFSP of 20 March 2000 amending Decision 94/942/CFSP on the Joint Action concerning the control of exports of dual-use goods, OJ 2000 L 82/1.
[180] *Richardt and 'Les Accessoires Scientifiques', op. cit.*, n. 89 above.
[181] Para 22. Confirmed: Case C-423/98 *Alfredo Albore*, judgment of 13 July 2000, para 18.
[182] Case C-70/94 *Werner Industrie-Ausrushungen v Germany* [1995] ECR I-3189.
[183] Case C-83/94 *Leifer* [1995] ECR I-3231.

both of which arose from preliminary references from German courts. In *Werner*, the applicant in the main proceedings was refused a licence to export a vacuum-induction oven to Libya on the ground that it was capable of being used for military purposes. In *Leifer*, the German authorities instituted criminal proceedings against traders on the ground that they had delivered certain chemical products to Iraq without export licences. In both cases, a broad interpretation of the common commercial policy was followed by an equally broad interpretation of the notion of public security and, in *Leifer*, by a relatively lax application of the principle of proportionality.[184] The Court held that a national measure whose effect is to restrict the export of certain products to third countries cannot be treated as falling outside the scope of the common commercial policy on the ground that it pursues foreign and security policy objectives. If that were so, a Member State could unilaterally restrict the scope of the common commercial policy in the light of its own foreign policy requirements.[185] The Court also made clear that dual-use goods fall within the scope of the common commercial policy.[186]

With regard to public security, the Court held that this notion comprises national measures seeking to avoid the risk of a serious disturbance to foreign relations or to peaceful coexistence of nations. It held that the notion of public security cannot be interpreted more restrictively in Article 11 of the Export Regulation[187] than in Article 30 of the Treaty for that would be tantamount to authorizing Member States to restrict the movement of goods within the internal market more than movement between themselves and third countries. In *Leifer*, the Court held that the exportation of goods capable of being used for military purposes to a country at war with another country may affect the public security of a Member State and that, in such cases, the national authorities have a certain degree of discretion when adopting measures which they consider to be necessary in order to guarantee their public security. Thus, where the export of dual-use goods involves a threat to public security, a Member State may require an applicant for an export licence to show that the goods are for civil use. Also, having regard to specific circumstances, such as the political situation in the country of destination, it is proportionate for a Member State to provide that the export licence shall be refused if the goods are objectively suitable for military use.[188]

Leifer can be contrasted with cases such as *UHT* and *de Peijer*. In the former, the application of proportionality is more lax in that a greater margin of discretion is left to the Member States and more power is delegated to the national courts to make the final determination whether the national provision is compatible with proportionality.[189] A distinction could be drawn, however, between measures

---

[184] The issue of proportionality did not arise in *Werner*.   [185] *Werner*, paras 10–11.
[186] *Leifer*, para 11.
[187] Council Regulation No 2603/69 establishing common rules for exports (OJ, English Sp.Ed. 1969 (II), p. 590), as amended by Council Regulation No 3918/91 (OJ L 372, p. 31). Article 11 authorizes Member States to impose quantitative restrictions on exports to third countries on grounds similar to those specified in Article 30.   [188] *Leifer*, paras 35–36.
[189] *Op. cit.*, paras 34–36.

restricting exports of strategic goods on grounds of public security and criminal penalties imposed for breach of such restrictions. With regard to the former, as the Advocate General stated in *Leifer*, the scope for judicial review is necessarily limited as it is not easy for a court to assess the threat posed to the security of a State by the exportation of strategic goods.[190] By contrast, the Court may feel able to give more specific guidance with regard to the proportionality of penalties imposed for breaches of restrictions since the severity of criminal sanctions is a matter susceptible to judicial determination.

Although the standard of scrutiny is less rigorous, it is notable that even where issues of national security are at stake the Court is prepared to hold an enquiry on grounds of proportionality. The need for judicial vigilance was underlined by Slynn AG in *Campus Oil* where he stated that, if the standards adopted are not sufficiently vigorous, the derogations of public security and public policy may be used in such a way as to diminish the basic concept of the common market.[191] An example from the freedom of capital is provided by *Albore*.[192] Italian law made the purchase of real property in areas designated as being of military importance subject to prior authorization. The requirement was discriminatory in that it applied only to non-Italian nationals. The Court held that a general reference to the defence interests of the State was not sufficient. The authorization requirement would survive only if it could be demonstrated, for each area to which the restriction applies, that non-discriminatory treatment of all Community nationals would expose the military interests of Italy to 'real, specific, and serious risks which could not be countered by less restrictive procedures'.[193] In that case, the standard of proportionality applied by the Court was strict but a degree of deference to the national interests was ensured by leaving the test to be applied by the national court and thus internalising within the national polity the balance of interests.

Issues pertaining to public security arose also in cases concerning the imposition of sanctions against Serbia and Montenegro following the Yugoslav conflict. In *The Queen, ex parte Centro-Com v HM Treasury and Bank of England*[194] the United Kingdom decided not to permit the release of funds from Yugoslav accounts held in British banks in order to pay for medical products sent to Serbia or Montenegro unless the export of the products concerned was authorised by the United Kingdom competent authorities. The decision was taken in the light of suspected abuses of the authorization procedure established by the UN Sanctions Committee and was aimed at ensuring that no funds were released for payments unconnected with medical or humanitarian purposes. As a result of that policy, Barclays Bank was refused authorization to transfer from a Yugoslav account sums needed to pay for medical products exported from Italy to Montenegro despite the fact that the exportation had been approved by the UN Sanctions Committee and authorized by

---

[190] *Op. cit., per* Jacobs AG, para 42.   [191] *Campus Oil, op. cit.*, p. 2767.
[192] *Alfredo Albore, op. cit.*   [193] *Op. cit.*, para 22.
[194] Case C-124/95 [1997] ECR I-81.

the Italian authorities. The United Kingdom argued that the measures were justified on grounds of public security and were therefore covered by Article 11 of the Export Regulation which permits derogations from the freedom of export on the grounds referred to in Article 30. The Court held that measures intended to apply sanctions imposed by the United Nations fell within the scope of public security but that recourse to Article 11 could not be made if Community rules provided for the necessary measures to ensure protection of the interests enumerated therein. That was so in the circumstances as the Sanctions Regulation[195] laid down the conditions on which exports of medical products to Serbia and Montenegro were to be authorized. The effective application of the sanctions could be ensured by the authorization procedures of the other Member States, as provided for in the Sanctions Regulation. A Member State could secure the effectiveness of such sanctions by less restrictive measures than those adopted by the UK. Thus, where it had particular doubts about the accuracy of descriptions of goods appearing in the export authorization issued by another Member State, before releasing funds from accounts held in its territory it could have resort to the collaboration established by Council Regulation No 1468/81.[196] That measure contains provisions to facilitate mutual assistance between the administrative authorities of the Member States and cooperation between the latter and the Commission in order to ensure the correct application of the law on customs and agricultural matters.

Centro-Com contrasts with *Bosphorus Airways*[197] and *Ebony Maritime*[198] where the Court upheld measures very restrictive of commercial freedom in order to ensure the effectiveness of sanctions against Serbia and Montenegro. The difference is that in the latter cases the measures in issue had been adopted by the Community whereas in *Centro-Com* they had been adopted by a Member State and the Court was concerned to safeguard the exclusive nature of commercial policy.

The protection of national security interests is also provided for in Articles 297 and 298 (formerly 224 and 225 respectively) of the Treaty. Article 297 states that Member States must consult each other with a view to taking together the steps needed to prevent the functioning of the common market being affected by measures which a Member State may be called upon to take in the event of serious internal disturbances affecting the maintenance of law and order, in the event of war, serious international tension constituting a threat of war, or in order to carry out obligations it has accepted for the purpose of maintaining peace and international security. Article 298 provides for an expedited procedure, in derogation of Articles 226 and 227, by virtue of which the Commission or a Member State may

---

[195] Council Regulation (EEC) No 1432/92 of 1 June 1992 prohibiting trade between the European Economic Community and the Republic of Serbia and Montenegro, OJ 1992 L 151, p. 4.   [196] OJ 1981 L 144, p. 1.
[197] Case C-84/95 *Bosphorus Hava Yollari Turizm ve Ticaret AS v Minister for Transport and the Attorney General* [1996] ECR I-3953.
[198] Case C-177/95 *Ebony Maritime and Loten Navigation v Prefetto della Provincia di Brindisi and Others* [1997] ECR I-1111.

bring enforcement proceedings directly before the Court if it considers that another Member State is making improper use of the powers provided for in Articles 296 and 297. Article 297 concerns 'a wholly exceptional situation'.[199] It is distinct in that it enables a Member State to derogate not only from a specific freedom but from the rules of the common market in general. In *Commission v Greece (FYROM case)*[200] Jacobs AG held that the issue whether there is international tension constituting a threat of war within the meaning of Article 297 is justiciable. He accepted however that the scope and intensity of judicial review is severely limited on account of the nature of the issues raised. He pointed out the paucity of judicially applicable criteria on the basis of which an objective determination may be made as to whether there is a threat of war and held that issues of national security are primarily a matter for the appraisal of the State concerned. Similarly, the Advocate General accepted that the intensity of review under Article 298 is extremely limited. He considered that a Member State would be making improper use of its powers under Article 297 if the real purpose of the measures adopted was to protect its own economy, thus drawing a parallel between 'improper use' within the meaning of Article 298 and the concept of misuse of powers. Beyond that, the Advocate General stated, it was difficult to see how a Member State would be making improper use of its powers by imposing economic sanctions on a third State. But the Advocate General did not refuse to review the embargo imposed by Greece on the Former Yugoslav Republic of Macedonia on grounds of proportionality.

He held that in determining whether the measures taken by a Member State under Article 297 were excessive, one would have to assess the damage caused by the measures taken on the Community interest in the functioning of the common market and the maintenance of undistorted competition. In the circumstances, the damage caused to those interests by the embargo was only slight since the embargo affected only a tiny percentage of the total volume of Community trade and was unlikely to have any perceptible impact on the competitive situation in the Community. Greece therefore could not be said to have breached Article 297 on grounds of proportionality.[201]

5.4.3. Consumer protection

Consumer protection is a mandatory requirement under the *Cassis de Dijon* formula and an imperative requirement of public interest which may justify restrictions to the free movement of services. As such, it may justify only non-discriminatory restrictions.[202] It is the most oft-invoked mandatory requirement and in many cases it

---

[199] *Johnston v Chief Constable, RUC, op. cit.,* n. 13 above, para 27.
[200] Case C-120/94 [1996] ECR I-1513.   [201] *Ibid.* 1533.
[202] The Court has expressly held that consumer protection as such is not covered by the derogations of Article 36: Case 177/83 *Kohl v Ringelhan & Rennett* [1984] ECR 3651, para 19; *Criminal Proceedings against Wurmser and others, op. cit.,* n. 101 above.

is pleaded in combination with the protection of public health or the defence of fair trading or both of those defences.[203] For example, in *Clinique*[204] proceedings were brought against European subsidiaries of Estée Lauder to stop the marketing in Germany of cosmetic products under the name 'Clinique' on the ground that the name could mislead consumers into believing that the products in question had medicinal properties. The Court held that the prohibition was not justified either on grounds of consumer protection and prevention of unfair competition or on grounds of public health. The products in question were not available in pharmacies but were sold exclusively in perfumeries and department stores, they were not presented as medicinal products, and were ordinarily marketed in other countries under the name 'Clinique' without that name misleading consumers. The degree of protection which must be afforded to consumers depends on the products and the market in issue. In *Alpine Investments* the Court recognized that investors in financial investments require particular protection due to the intangible nature of securities and the inability of investors to exercise control over their value.[205] The defence of consumer protection is often relied upon to justify controls of marketing techniques and selling arrangements. A number of cases where the principle of proportionality has been applied to such measures have already been examined in the context of the less restrictive alternative test.[206] In assessing the necessity and suitability of restrictions, the Court sometimes uses as a yardstick the concept of 'an average consumer who is reasonably well informed and reasonably observant and circumspect'.[207] It may be interesting to examine here some cases concerning language requirements.[208] This is a particularly sensitive area since the Court has to balance commercial freedom and inter-State trade on the one hand with national concerns pertaining to cultural and regional identity on the other.

In *Piageme I*[209] a company marketed in Flanders bottled water labelled in French or in German in contravention of a Belgian law which required that food products marketed in the Flemish speaking region of Belgium must be labelled in Dutch. The issue arose whether the law was compatible with Article 28 and Directive 79/112 on the approximation of national laws relating to the labelling, presentation and advertising of foodstuffs for sale to the ultimate consumer.[210] Article 14 of the Directive provides that particulars must be in a language easily understood by

---

[203] See e.g. *Commission v Germany (Beer Case), op. cit.; Criminal Proceedings against Wurmser, op. cit.,* In Case 12/74 *Commission v Germany* [1975] ECR 181, the Court appeared to take the view that a measure may be justified only if it is necessary *both* on grounds of consumer protection *and* unfair trading. Following *Cassis de Dijon* that view is no longer valid. See also Oliver, *op. cit.,* p. 226.

[204] C-315/92 *Verband Sozialer Wettbewerb v Clinique Laboratories and Estée Lauder* [1994] ECR I-317.

[205] *Alpine Investments, op. cit.,* n. 66 above, paras 42, 46 and *per* Jacobs AG at 1161.

[206] See 5.2.3 above.

[207] See e.g. *Douwe Egberts, op. cit.,* para 46; Case C-465/98 *Darbo* [2000] ECR I-2297, para 20; Joined Cases C-421/00, C-426/00 and C-16/01 *Sterbenzand Haug* [2003] ECR I-1065, para 28.

[208] For a detailed examination, see Oliver, *op. cit.,* pp. 226 *et seq.*

[209] *Op. cit.,* n. 2 above.   [210] OJ 1979 L 33, p. 1.

purchasers, unless other measures have been taken to ensure that the purchaser is informed. The Court held that the purpose of the Directive is to prohibit the sale of products whose labelling is not easily understood by the purchaser rather than to require the use of a specific language. On that basis, it found that the obligation to use exclusively the language of the linguistic region where the goods are sold exceeded the requirements of the Directive. It also held that the requirement of exclusive use constituted a measure having equivalent effect to a quantitative restriction on imports prohibited by Article 28. Surprisingly, the Court did not give guidance on whether a non-exclusive language requirement would infringe Article 28 although in fact the Belgian law in issue imposed a non-exclusive requirement.[211] On appeal by the plaintiffs, the Court of Appeal of Brussels made a second reference and in *Piageme II*[212] the Court held that the obligation to use a specific language for the labelling of food products, even if the use of additional languages is not precluded, also exceeds the requirements of Directive 79/112. Since incompatibility with the Directive was established, the Court did not examine whether the non-exclusive language requirement would be incompatible also with Article 28.[213]

In *Piageme II* the Court held that it is for the national court to determine in each case whether labelling given in a language other than the language mainly used in the Member State or region concerned can easily be understood by consumers in that region. Various factors may be relevant in that respect, for example, the possible similarity of words in different languages, the widespread knowledge among the population concerned of more than one language, or the existence of special circumstances such as a wide-ranging advertising campaign or widespread distribution of the product.[214] The Belgian Court of Appeal also referred the question whether, in order to determine if the labelling is in a language easily understood by consumers, regard must be had only to the information provided on the packaging or account may also be taken of other circumstances which indicate that the consumer is familiar with the product, for example, its widespread distribution or a wide-ranging advertising campaign. The Court held that in order to provide adequate consumer protection, it is necessary for consumers to have access to the compulsory particulars specified in the Directive not only at the time of purchase but also at the time of consumption. That is particularly so as regards the date of minimum durability and any special storage conditions or conditions of the use of the product. The Court also pointed out that the ultimate consumer is not

---

[211] Belgian law required that the labelling must appear at least in the language or languages of the linguistic region where the products are offered for sale. See Article 10 of the Royal Degree of 2 October 1980, replaced by Article 11 of the Royal Degree of 13 November 1986.

[212] Case C-385/94 *Piageme and Others v Peeters* [1995] ECR I-2955.

[213] Oliver (*op. cit.*, p. 230) takes the view that such a requirement would also fall foul of Article 28, on the basis of the judgment in *Fietje, op. cit.*, n. 128 above. In *Piageme II*, Cosmas AG also came to the view that Article 28 precludes a non-exclusive language requirement but the Opinion does not discuss how that view can be compromised with *Meyhui* discussed above.

[214] *Piageme II, op. cit.*, para 30.

necessarily the person who purchased the products. It concluded that consumer protection is not ensured by measures other than labelling such as information supplied at the sales point or as part of a wide-ranging advertising campaign. All the compulsory particulars specified in the Directive must appear on the labelling in a language easily understood by purchasers or by means of other measures such as designs, symbols or pictograms. The approach of the Court in *Piageme II* contrasts sharply with its approach in the *German Medicinal products* case.[215] If one were to transpose to the latter the reasoning of *Piageme II*, the inevitable conclusion would be that the German law did not infringe the principle of proportionality.

5.5. Criminal penalties

Penalties of whatever nature imposed for breach of national provisions which restrict the fundamental freedoms are subject to a strict test of proportionality. In *Casati* the Court stated:[216]

In principle, criminal legislation and the rules of criminal procedure are matters for which the Member States are still responsible. However, it is clear from a consistent line of cases decided by the Court, that Community law also sets certain limits in that area as regards the control measures which it permits the Member States to maintain in connection with the free movement of goods and persons. The administrative measures or penalties must not go beyond what is strictly necessary, the control procedures must not be conceived in such a way as to restrict the freedom required by the Treaty and they must not be accompanied by a penalty *which is so disproportionate to the gravity of the infringement that it becomes an obstacle to the exercise of that freedom.*

In a number of cases the Court has examined the proportionality of penalties imposed by the host State on Community nationals exercising their freedom of movement for failure to comply with formalities or other restrictions provided for by national law. The Court approaches the legality of such penalties in two stages. First, it considers the nature of the requirement for breach of which the penalty is imposed and then it assesses the penalty itself. Clearly, a penalty is incompatible with Community law where it is imposed for failure to comply with a provision which is itself contrary to Community law. In such a case, the penalty becomes inapplicable and it is not even necessary to examine whether it is proportionate.[217] Where restrictions on fundamental freedoms are justified under Community law,

---

[215] Discussed above p. 221.

[216] Case 203/80 [1981] ECR 2595, para 27, emphasis added. For subsequent confirmation, see Case C-210/91 *Commission v Greece* [1992] ECR I-6735, para 19; Case C-36/94 *Siesse* [1995] ECR I-3573, para 21; Case C-213/99 *de Andrade* [2000] ECR I-11083; Case C-262/99 *Louloudakis* [2001] ECR I-5547, para 67.

[217] Joined Cases C-338/00 and C-429/00 *Radiosistemi* [2002] ECR I-5845, paras 79–80; Case C-13/01 *Safalero Srl v Prefetto di Genova*, judgment of 11 September 2003, paras 45–46; Case C-12/02 *Grilli*, judgment of 2 October 2003; para 49.

penalties or coercive measures imposed for their breach must be proportionate. In *Messner*[218] Italian law required nationals of other Member States who entered Italy as employed persons or as persons supplying or receiving services to make a declaration of residence within a period of three days of their arrival. Failure to make a declaration was punishable by imprisonment of up to three months or a fine. The Court held that the period of three days was not 'absolutely necessary' in order to protect the host State's interest in obtaining exact knowledge of population movements. That was confirmed by the fact that the majority of Member States imposing a similar obligation allowed appreciably longer periods.[219] The Court indicated that, in any event, imprisonment would be an excessive penalty for the offence in issue.[220] In *Pieck*[221] it was held that national authorities may impose penalties for failure to comply with requirements relating to residence permits but, given that residence permits issued to Community nationals only have a declaratory effect, such penalties must be comparable to those attaching to minor offences committed by nationals. Imprisonment would be a disproportionate penalty. In *Sagulo*[222] the Court held that a Community national who fails to obtain in the host Member State the identity documents required according to Community law may be made subject to reasonable penalties although such penalties are not imposed on nationals of the host State for comparable offences. It may not be permissible however to equate a Community national with an alien in that regard and, where national law does not provide penalties appropriate to the requirements of Community law, it is the task of the national court by using its judicial discretion to impose a penalty appropriate to the character and objectives of the Community provisions in issue. In any event, penalties imposed on nationals of other Member States resident in the national territory for failure to hold the necessary identification documents must not be disproportionately different from those imposed on the nationals of the host State for comparable offences.[223]

The strictness with which the Court applies the principle of proportionality in this context is illustrated by the judgment in *Skanavi*.[224] The German authorities fined two Greek nationals who had failed to exchange their driving licences within a year after taking up residence in Germany as required by German law pursuant to Directive 80/1263.[225] The Court held that the issue of a driving licence by the host State in exchange for a licence issued by another Member State does not constitute

---

[218] Case C-265/88 *Criminal Proceedings against Messner* [1989] ECR I-4209. See also Case 118/75 *Watson and Belmann* [1976] ECR 1185; Case 8/77 *Sagulo, Brenca and Bakhouche* [1977] ECR 1495, paras 6–7.   [219] *Messner, op. cit.*, para 11.

[220] Deportation is also a disproportionate penalty for such an infraction: *Watson and Belmann, op. cit.*, para 20.   [221] Case 157/79 *Regina v Pieck* [1980] ECR 2171.

[222] *Sagulo, op. cit.*, n. 220 above.

[223] Case C-24/97 *Commission v Germany* [1998] ECR I-2133.

[224] Case C-193/94 *Skanavi and Chryssanthakopoulos* [1996] ECR I-929. See also Case C-29/95 *Pastoors and Trans-Cap* [1997] ECR I-285.

[225] Council Directive 80/1263 on the introduction of a Community driving licence (OJ 1980 L 375, p. 1).

the basis of the right to drive in the territory of the host State but evidence of the existence of such right. The obligation to exchange driving licences meets administrative requirements and a Community national who has failed to exchange his licence should not be assimilated to a person driving without one. The Court concluded that criminal penalties even of a financial nature for failure to exchange a licence are disproportionate since a criminal conviction may have adverse consequences for the exercise of a trade or profession in particular as regards access to certain offices or activities.[226]

In relation to the free movement of goods, the Court has held that any penalties imposed must be restricted to what is strictly necessary. Confiscation of goods or pecuniary penalties calculated on the basis of the value of goods have been held to be excessive where imposed for administrative offences, such as failure by an importer to disclose the origin of goods in free circulation in the Community.[227] Where under Community law an importer does not need to disclose the origin of goods, a false declaration of origin may not be punished by the indiscriminate application of penalties provided against false declarations made in order to effect prohibited imports.[228] The Court has also held that seizure or confiscation of a product imported illegally could be considered disproportionate, and therefore incompatible with Article 30, to the extent to which the return of the product to the Member State of origin would be sufficient.[229]

Proportionality has also been applied in relation to tax offences. In *Drexl*[230] the Court held that national legislation which penalizes offences concerning the payment of value added tax on importation from another Member State more severely than those concerning the payment of value added tax on domestic transactions is incompatible with Article 90 of the Treaty insofar as the difference is disproportionate to the dissimilarity between the two categories of offences.[231] The Court found that such lack of proportion exists where the penalty provided for in the case of importation involves imprisonment and the confiscation of goods whereas comparable penalties are not imposed in the case of offences concerning the payment of value added tax on domestic transactions. In a subsequent case, the Court found that such disproportion also exists where failure to pay value added tax upon importation gives rise to the penalty of confiscation and in addition to the imposition of a fine up to twice the value of the goods, whereas failure to pay value added tax on a domestic transaction gives rise only to a fine which is calculated by

---

[226] As a result of Directive 91/439 on driving licences (OJ 1991 L 237, p. 1) which became effective on 1 July 1996, Member States may no longer require the exchange of driving licences. The impending liberalization of the law may have influenced the Court in taking such a strict view in *Skanavi*.

[227] *Donckerwolcke, op. cit.*, n. 14 above; Case 52/77 *Cayrol v Rivoira* [1977] ECR 2261.

[228] Case 179/78 *Procureur de la République v Rivoira* [1979] ECR 1147.

[229] *Aimé Richardt op. cit.*, n. 89 above, para 24.   [230] Case 299/86 [1988] ECR 1213.

[231] The Court held that the two categories of offence were distinguishable both with regard to their constituent elements and with regard to their enforcement and therefore Member States were not required to have the same system of rules for the two. Cf the Opinion of Darmon AG.

reference to a percentage of the tax due.[232] In *Metalsa*,[233] however, the Court refused to apply a similar rule of equivalence of penalties in relation to offences concerning the importation of goods from Austria (at a time when Austria was not a Member State) although Article 18 of the Agreement on Free Trade between the Community and Austria contained a provision similar to that of Article 90 EC. It held that Article 18 should be interpreted in the light of the Agreement the objectives of which were more limited than those of the Treaty and came to the conclusion that Article 18 did not require any comparison to be made between penalties imposed by Member States for tax offences on imports from Austria and penalties imposed for tax offences on domestic transactions or on imports from other Member States. The Advocate General, by contrast, went further stating that, although the ruling in *Drexl* could not be transposed to the Agreement on Free Trade with Austria, Member States were nonetheless bound by the principle of proportionality in imposing penalties in relation to offences arising from imports from third countries with which the Community has concluded free trade agreements.

The above line of tax cases illustrate that, with a view to assessing whether a penalty infringes proportionality, regard may be had to the penalties imposed on comparable offences.[234] It is submitted that the argument of equivalent treatment of comparable offences carries less force where a penalty is imposed for breach of national measures restricting freedom of movement, in particular freedom of movement of persons. In such cases, the material test is whether the penalty is so grave as to become an obstacle to the exercise of free movement. If so, it is likely to infringe the principle of proportionality even though similar penalties are imposed for comparable offences of a purely domestic nature.

In *Louloudakis*[235] the Court was concerned with Directive 83/182[236] which provides for tax exemptions in relation to the temporary importation of motor cars into one Member State from another. The Greek implementing legislation imposed severe penalties in the event of infringement of the temporary importation arrangements laid down by the Directive. The penalties included increased duty which could be up to ten times the taxes in question and a fine set at a flat rate calculated solely on the basis of the cubic capacity of the vehicle and without taking into account its age.

The ECJ left the issue of proportionality to the national court to decide. It stated that, although overriding requirements of enforcement and prevention may justify national legislation setting penalties at a certain level of severity, it is nevertheless possible that penalties determined in accordance with rules such as those applicable under Greek law may prove to be disproportionate and constitute an obstacle to free movement. A penalty based on the sole criterion of cubic capacity, without

---

[232] Case C-276/91 *Commission v France* [1993] ECR I-4413.
[233] Case C-312/91 [1993] ECR I-3751.   [234] Cf *Metalsa, op. cit., per* Jacobs AG at p. 3763.
[235] *Op. cit.,* n. 218 above.   [236] OJ 1983, L 105/59.

account being taken of the vehicle's age, could be disproportionate to the gravity of the infringement, in particular where it is associated with another heavy penalty imposed in respect of the same infringement. The same could be true of a penalty amounting to a multiple of the charge at issue, for example ten times the applicable charges. The Court concluded that it is for the national court to assess whether, in view of the overriding requirement of enforcement and prevention, as well as of the amount of the taxes in question and the level of the penalties actually imposed, those penalties are proportionate.[237]

In *Louloudakis* the Court also held that the issue whether, in determining the proportionality of a tax penalty, the national authorities must take into account the good faith of the offender is in principle a matter for national law to decide. Thus, Community law does not preclude the application of a general principle of national penal law according to which everyone is presumed to know the law. Given, however, the purpose of the Directive which is to promote the freedoms guaranteed by the Treaty, account must be taken of the good faith of the offender, where the determination of the complex arrangements applicable under the Directive has given rise to difficulties on the facts of the case.[238]

5.6. The role of national courts

Where the principle of proportionality is invoked to challenge the validity of a Community act, it is for the Court of Justice to apply the principle and determine whether it is infringed by the contested act. But where the principle is invoked in preliminary reference proceedings to assess the compatibility with Community law of a national measure, the final determination of the issue may be left to the national courts.[239] More specifically, where proportionality is an issue in proceedings under Article 234, the Court has the following options:

- It may decide that the national measure does not interfere excessively with a fundamental freedom.[240]
- It may decide that the national measure interferes excessively with a fundamental freedom and is therefore in breach of the principle of proportionality.[241]

---

[237] *Louloudakis, op. cit.*, paras 69–70. Alber AG took the view that, in relation to an intentional breach, a fine amounting to ten times the applicable charges was compatible with proportionality: *op. cit.*, p. 5569.   [238] *Ibid.* para 76.

[239] In enforcement proceedings, it will be for the Court of Justice to determine conclusively whether the national law or practice in issue infringes Community law in the light of proportionality. See e.g. *UHT milk* case; Case 193/80 *Commission v Italy (Italian Vinegar case)* [1981] ECR 3019; *German Beer* case *op. cit.*, n. 5 above.

[240] See e.g. *Ditlev Blume, op. cit.; Alpine Investments; op. cit.; R v Royal Pharmaceutical Society of Great Britain, ex p Association of Pharmaceutical Importers, op. cit.; Clinique op. cit.; Mars op. cit.; Sass GmbH, op. cit.* For a case where the Court endorsed a national measure exercising virtually no proportionality control, see Case C-275/92 *Schindler* [1994] ECR I-1039.

[241] See e.g. *Schumacher, op. cit.; Eurim-Pharm, op. cit.; Deutscher Apothekerverband eV, op. cit.*

- It may give detailed guidelines as to what the principle of proportionality requires leaving it to the national court to apply the principle in the circumstances of the case.[242]
- It may provide only minimal guidelines leaving it in effect totally to the national court to decide the issue.[243]

Whether the principle of proportionality should be left to the national court to apply depends on the nature of the issue involved and the specific circumstances of the case. In some cases, because of the nature of the dispute, it will simply not be possible for the Court of Justice to apply the principle conclusively. Thus, the ECJ may leave the matter to the national court because the latter is better able to make an economic assessment of the effects of the measure on free movement.[244] Also, the national court usually has the final say when the issue is the severity of criminal penalties. Whether a penalty is proportionate may depend on factors such as the good faith of the accused which the Court of Justice, because of the limits of its jurisdiction, is not in a position to determine.[245] As we saw above in *Louloudakis*[246] the Court confined itself to some general observations and left the proportionality of the fine to the national court to decide. This however led to problems in Greece as Greek courts do not engage in a rigorous proportionality review assessing all the facts of the case and instead confine themselves to ensuring that the penalty imposed is within the range of possible penalties provided by the legislation.[247]

One area where the Court has left considerable discretion to national courts is measures restricting free trade in the interests of national security.[248] In other cases, the issue may not be straightforward and opinions may differ. In *Clinique*[249] the Court found that the prohibition imposed by German law on the marketing of products under the name 'Clinique' was not justified on grounds of consumer protection, leaving no discretion to the national court. Gulmann AG, however, took the view that such a conclusive answer by the Court would overstep the limits of its jurisdiction under Article 234 and urged the Court to leave the issue to the national court to decide giving only general guidelines.[250] The specificity of guidance given by the Court may also be influenced by the amount of information given by the national court in the order for reference and the way it has phrased the questions referred. The better the quality of reference the more helpful the reply given by the Court is likely to be.

In some cases, because of the discretion left to it, the national court will have a creative role to play in applying the principle. In *Piageme II*,[251] the Court held that

---

[242] See e.g. *Familiapress, op. cit.*
[243] See e.g. *Louloudakis, op. cit.; de Agostini, op. cit; Gourmet, op. cit.*
[244] See e.g. *Grilli op. cit.*   [245] See, e.g. *Richardt, op. cit.*, para 25.   [246] *Op. cit.*
[247] See e.g. Judgment No 990/2004 of the Greek *Conseil d'Etat* in case *Mamidakis v Minister of Finance* (2 April 2004) and note there the views of the dissenting minority which submitted that failure of the administrative authorities to take into account the principle of proportionality amounted to a breach of Article 6 ECHR.   [248] See, e.g. *Richardt, op. cit., Leifer, op. cit.*
[249] *Op. cit.*   [250] *Clinique, op. cit.*, pp. 326–328 *per* Gulmann AG.
[251] *Op. cit.* See also *Fietje, op. cit.*; Case 220/81 *Robertson* [1982] ECR 2349.

it is for the national court to determine in each individual case whether labelling given in other than the language mainly used in the Member State or region where the goods are marketed can easily be understood by consumers. Considerable discretion was also left to the national court in *de Peijper*,[252] where the Court held that the national rule in issue, which had the effect of impeding parallel imports, could not be maintained unless it was clearly proved that any other rule or practice less restrictive of trade between Member States would be beyond the means which could reasonably be expected of the national administration. Similarly, in *Wurmser* the Court stated that, where a Member State requires an importer to ensure that the composition of imported products complies with health and safety regulations, the importer may discharge that obligation by producing a certificate concerning composition issued by the authorities of the Member State of production or by a laboratory approved by those authorities. Where the Member State of production does not require official certificates concerning composition of the product, the importer must be entitled to supply other attestations providing a similar degree of assurance. The Court concluded that it is for the national court to determine whether, having regard to all the circumstances of the case, the attestations provided by the importer are sufficient to establish that the latter has met his obligation to verify.[253] In some cases, leaving ample discretion to the national court may be seen as deference to local social or cultural preferences. In *de Agostini*[254] the Court left the issue whether Swedish rules restricting television advertising satisfied the test of proportionality entirely to the national court, making little effort to develop a Community standard. Arguably, the Court should have gone further.

The approach of leaving considerable discretion to the national courts is not without drawbacks. The national court which made the reference may not get an answer to the question referred. Lengthy and costly litigation before the Court of Justice may prove inconclusive or even of little help for the solution of the dispute. This was clearly illustrated in the protracted Sunday trading litigation.[255] Also, leaving the application of proportionality to the national court inevitably gives rise to differences in the application of Community law in the various Member States. Despite those problems, entrusting national courts, where appropriate, with the application of the principle is the correct policy. In determining the demarcation line between lawful and unlawful impediments to fundamental freedoms, national jurisdictions cannot be denied a role and this is so for two reasons. The first is a practical one. As already stated, in some cases, national courts are better placed to perform the balancing exercise which is the essence of proportionality. The second reason is one of principle. The underlying objective of the case law is to achieve a balance between the need for uniform application of Community law and the need to respect the autonomy of Member States in areas where there is no Community harmonization. That is best served by leaving discretion to the

---

[252] *De Peijper, op. cit.*   [253] *Wurmser, op. cit.*, para 19.   [254] *Op. cit.*, paras 46, 52.
[255] See especially *Stoke-on-Trent C.C. and Norwich C.C. v B & Q* [1991] Ch. 48.

national jurisdictions, within certain limits. Drawing the appropriate balance is not an easy exercise. It is submitted that overall the Court of Justice has not followed an inconsistent approach, leaving the issue to national courts to decide only where the latter is by virtue of objective criteria better placed to do so.[256] It will be noted that, even where the Court of Justice does not give to the referring court a conclusive answer for the solution of the dispute, its reference to the principle of proportionality by no means lacks relevance. However large the discretion left to the national court in a specific case, it is under an overriding obligation to perform a balancing exercise paying due regard to the requirements of the fundamental freedoms. It is with this consideration in mind that the case law should be assessed. In effect, the Court infuses certain standards of judicial control and cultivates a propensity on the part of the national courts to 'think federal'. That is particularly important for legal systems like English law, where proportionality is not traditionally recognized as a ground for review.

[256] There are, however, exceptions. See e.g. *de Agostini, op. cit.* A case in the area of sex discrimination where it is submitted the issue should have been left to the national court to decide as suggested by the Advocate General is Case C-457/93 *Kuratorium für Dialyse und Nierentransplantation e. V. v Johanna Lewark* [1996] ECR I-243.

6

Legal Certainty and Protection of Legitimate Expectations

6.1. Legal certainty

The principle of legal certainty expresses the fundamental premise that those subject to the law must know what the law is so as to be able to plan their actions accordingly. The affinity of the principle with the rule of law is evident. In *Black Clawson Ltd v Papierwerke AG*, Lord Diplock stated that 'the acceptance of the rule of law as a constitutional principle requires that a citizen, before committing himself to any course of action, should be able to know in advance what are the legal consequences that will flow from it'.[1] In some ways, legal certainty is even more important than equality. A group of persons which knows that it will be discriminated against by public authorities can plan its actions accordingly so as to alleviate the adverse effects of such discrimination. The principle acquires particular importance, *inter alia*, in economic law. Economic and commercial life is based on advance planning so that clear and precise legal provisions reduce transaction costs and promote efficient business. Legal certainty may thus be seen as contributing to the production of economically consistent results.[2]

A specific expression of legal certainty is the protection of legitimate expectations. The Court of Justice does not always distinguish between the two.[3] Respect for legitimate expectations as a principle of law is particularly developed in French and German jurisprudence.[4] In English law, it has given rise to a thriving academic discussion.[5] English courts have traditionally been reluctant to accept the protection

---

[1] [1975] AC 591 at 638.

[2] See the analysis of E. Sharpston, 'Legitimate Expectations and Economic Reality', (1990) 15 ELR 103. For recent bibliography, see J. Raitio, *The Principle of Legal Certainty in EC Law* (Kluwer, 2003); G. Barrett, 'Protecting Legitimate Expectations in European Community Law and in Domestic Irish Law' (2001) 20 YEL 191; S. Schonberg, 'Legal Certainty and Revocation of Administrative Decisions: A Comparative Study of English, French, and EC Law' (1999–00) 19 YEL 257.

[3] See e.g. Joined Cases 212–217/80 *Salumi* [1981] ECR 2735, para 10; Case 120/86 *Mulder v Minister van Landbonw en Vissenji, (Mulder I)* [1988] ECR 2321, discussed at 6.4.2 below.

[4] For a discussion of the principle in the laws of the Member States, see J. Schwarze, *European Administrative Law*, (Sweet & Maxwell, 1992) Ch 6, Section 2.

[5] See S. de Smith, H. Woolf and J. Jowell, *Judicial Review of Administrative Action* (Sweet & Maxwell, 1995), pp. 417 *et seq.*; C. Forsyth, '*Wednesbury* Protection of Substantive Legitimate Expectations', [1997] PL 375; P. Craig, 'Substantive Legitimate Expectations in Domestic and Community Law', (1996) 55 CLJ 289; P. Craig, 'Legitimate Expectations: A Conceptual Analysis',

of substantive legitimate expectations as an independent ground for review[6] but, as a result of the judgment in *Coughlan* it is now part of English law.[7] In Community law, legal certainty and legitimate expectations, like all other general principles of law, bind not only the administration but also the legislature.

Legal certainty is by its nature diffuse, perhaps more so than any other general principle, and its precise content is difficult to pin down. The case law has used it with creativity, invoking it in diverse contexts to found a variety of propositions both in the substantive and the procedural plain. For example, in *Automec* the CFI invoked legal certainty to depart from the normal rule that the losing party must pay the costs of litigation.[8] Legal certainty has also been a consideration in determining the jurisdiction of national courts to apply Article 81 of the Treaty.[9] It is clearly a relative principle and may have to give way to other competing considerations. In *Kühne & Heitz NV*,[10] for example, it was held that the national authorities may be under an obligation to review a final administrative act in order to take account of the interpretation of Community law provided by the ECJ even though this may have adverse effects on legal certainty. The cynic may argue that the principle is devoid of legal content because it can be used to support contradictory results. In the seminal *van Duyn*, for example, the Court invoked legal certainty to support the direct effect of directives.[11] That principle however can also be invoked to support the opposite conclusion. It may be argued that, since Article 249 EC makes a clear distinction between regulations and directives, legal certainty prevents directives from producing direct effect. It is not submitted here that the reasoning of the Court in *van Duyn* was unpersuasive. Rather, the case is used to show that legal certainty rarely dictates a specific result in itself. It is a

---

(1992) 108 LQR 79; C. Forsyth, 'The Provenance and Protection of Legitimate Expectations' (1988) 47 CLJ 238; P. Elias, 'Legitimate Expectation and Judicial Review' in Jowell and Oliver (eds) *New Directions on Judicial Review*, CLP Special Issue, 1988, pp. 37–50.

[6] See in particular, the judgment of the Court of Appeal in *R v Secretary of State for the Home Department ex p Hargreaves* [1997] 1 All ER. Cf *R v Ministry for Agriculture, Fisheries and Food, ex p Hamble (Offshore) Fisheries Limited* [1995] 2 All ER 714 and *R v Secretary of State for Transport, ex p Richmond upon Thames London BC* [1994] 1 WLR 74; *R v Home Secretary ex p Khan* [1984] 1 WLR 1337.

[7] *R v North and East Devon Health Authority ex p Coughlan* [2001] QB 213. For analysis, see P. Craig, *Administrative Law*, Fifth Ed., Sweet & Maxwell, 2003, pp. 649 *et seq.*; P. Craig and S. Schonberg, 'Substantive Legitimate Expectations after *Coughlan*' [2000] PL 684. See also more recently *R v Secretary of State for the Home Department ex p Zeqiri* [2002] UKHL 3. In *R (Theophilus) v London Borough of Lewisham* [2002] EuLR 563, Silber J held that a legitimate expectation is created where a student relies on specific and unambiguous promises given to her by the administration that her fees will be paid. The tenet of the judgment is that the protection of legitimate expectations may restrict the discretion that an administrative authority lawfully possesses but does not enable it to act beyond its statutory powers.

[8] Case T-64/89 *Automec v Commission* [1990] ECR II-367, para 64.

[9] Case C-234/89 *Delimitis v Henninger Bräu AG* [1991] ECR I-935, para 47. See also in relation to the provisions of the Treaty on State aids, Case C-39/94 *SFEI and Others* [1996] ECR I-3547.

[10] Case C-453/00 *Kühne & Heitz NV v Productschap voor Pluimvee en Eieren*, judgment of 13 January 2004.   [11] Case 41/74 *Van Duyn v Home Office* [1974] ECR 1337, para 13.

conceptual tool which must not be viewed in isolation but in the context of judicial reasoning taken as a whole.

Continental public lawyers are more receptive to arguments based on legal certainty than English lawyers. This point may be illustrated by the divergent views expressed by Jacobs AG in *Vaneetveld*[12] and Lenz AG in *Faccini Dori*.[13] Both advocates general argued in favour of horizontal effect of directives despite the earlier judgment in *Marshall I*[14] which appeared to have settled the issue.[15] Their views however differed on a crucial point. A classic argument against horizontal effect of directives was that, until the Treaty of European Union came into force, there was no obligation to publish directives.[16] Jacobs AG attributed little importance to that consideration. He pointed out that, according to established practice, all legislative directives were published in the Official Journal and was content to accept that failure to publish in a specific case might prevent the directive in issue from producing legal effects.[17] Lenz AG, by contrast, considered that the absence of a legal obligation to publish made horizontal effect extremely problematic.[18] In his view, a *sine qua non* condition for a measure to take effect was its 'constitutive publication' in an official organ. The consistent practice of publishing directives in the Official Journal had no effect since it was purely declaratory in character. He concluded that directives adopted on the basis of the EEC Treaty, before the Treaty on European Union came into force, were not capable of producing horizontal effect.[19]

Legal certainty is invoked more commonly as a rule of interpretation than as a ground for review. But a Community measure which breaches legal certainty will be held inapplicable by the Court. The case law suggests that the principle entails, in general, the following requirements.

Clarity of Community measures. Legal certainty requires that the effect of Community legislation must be clear and predictable.[20] The aim of the principle is 'to ensure that situations and legal relationships governed by Community law remain foreseeable'.[21] Obligations imposed on individuals must be clear and understandable and ambiguities arising from the language of the law should be resolved in favour of the individual.[22] The Court has held, in particular, that rules imposing charges on a taxpayer must be clear and precise so that he may be able to ascertain unequivocally

---

[12] Case C-316/93 *Vaneetveld v SA Le Foyer* [1994] ECR I-763.

[13] Case C-91/92 *Faccini Dori v Recreb* [1994] ECR I-3325.

[14] Case 152/84 *Marshall v Southampton and South-West Hampshire Area Health Authority* [1986] ECR 723.

[15] In *Faccini Dori* the Court confirmed that directives may not give rise to rights against individuals. See also Case C-192/94 *El Corte Inglés v Blázquez Rivero* [1996] ECR I-1281.

[16] See now Article 254 EC, as amended by the Treaty on European Union.

[17] *Vaneetveld, op. cit.*, n. 98, p. 772.   [18] *Faccini Dori, op. cit.*, n. 99, p. 3342.

[19] *Ibid.*, p. 3343.   [20] *Salumi, op. cit.*, n. 3 above, para 10.

[21] Case C-63/93 *Duff and Others v Minister for Agriculture and Food, Ireland, and the Attorney General* [1996] ECR I-569, para 20.

[22] Case 169/80 *Administration des Douanes v Gondrand Frères* [1981] ECR 1931, paras 17–18.

his rights and obligations.[23] The principle has found fruitful ground for its application in customs law. In relation to the Common Customs Tariff, for example, it has consistently been held that, in the interests of legal certainty and ease of verification, the decisive criterion for the classification of goods for customs purposes is to be sought in their objective characteristics and properties, as defined in the Common Customs Tariff.[24]

An interesting example in customs law is provided by *Van eS Douane Agenten*.[25] The issue arose whether a Commission regulation classifying goods under the old Common Customs Tariff nomenclature lapsed when the Council regulation which provided its legal basis was repealed and the new nomenclature was adopted. The Court held that the Commission was under an obligation to amend classification regulations issued under the previous nomenclature so as to enable individuals to ascertain unequivocally their rights and obligations. Since there were significant differences between the subheadings of the old and the new nomenclature, individuals were unable to determine the precise scope of the contested regulation. It followed that the regulation could not be applied to imports which took place after the new nomenclature came into force.

To state the obvious, the use of abstract terms in Community legislation does not render the provision in question incompatible with the principle of legal certainty. In *Netherlands v Parliament and Council*[26] the Dutch Government challenged the validity of Directive 98/44 on the legal protection of biotechnological inventions, *inter alia*, on the ground that the Directive exacerbated existing ambiguities resulting from national laws because it relied on terms such as 'ordre public' or 'morality' as grounds to rule out the patentability of certain inventions. This argument was bound to fail. The Court held that these terms allowed a scope for manoeuvre to national authorities which was necessary to take account of the social and cultural context of each Member State. The terms were well-known in patent law and furthermore the Directive provided some guidelines for their application.

Examples of situations which might be held to be contrary to legal certainty are the following: where a provision is wholly meaningless or manifestly irreconcilable

[23] *Administration des Douanes v Gondrand Frères, op. cit.*; Case T-115/94 *Opel Austria v Council* [1997] ECR II-39, para 124; see also Case C-110/94 *Inzo v Belgian State* [1996] ECR I-857, para 21 (principle of legal certainty prevents the status of taxable person under the Sixth VAT Directive from being withdrawn retroactively); Case 78/77 *Lührs v Hauptzollamt Hamburg-Jonas* [1978] ECR 169 (in calculating tax on exports, the exchange rate which is less onerous for the taxpayer concerned should be applied). Not every difficulty in interpretation however leads to breach of legal certainty: Case C-354/95 *The Queen v Minister for Agriculture, Fisheries and Food ex p National Farmers' Union and Others* [1997] ECR I-455, para 58.

[24] See e.g. Joined Cases C-59 and C-64/94 *Ministre des Finances v Société Pardo & Fils and Camicas* [1995] ECR I-3159, para 10.

[25] Case C-143/93 *Van eS Douane Agenten v Inspecteur der Invoerrechten en Accijnzen* [1996] ECR I-431. Cf Case C-103/96 *Directeur Général des Douanes et Droits Indirects v Eridania Beghin-Say SA* [1997] ECR I-1453; Case C-315/96 *Lopex Export GmbH v Hauptzollamt Hamburg-Jonas* [1998] ECR I-317.

[26] Case C-377/98 *Netherlands v European Parliament and Council* [2001] ECR I-7079.

with other provisions of the same measure;[27] where a situation is governed by a thicket of successive inter-related rules of primary, secondary and judge-made law so as to make it manifestly impossible for the citizen to know the rules and the courts to apply them; or where a provision is repealed or amended, or burdens are imposed on citizens, by a provision included in a measure dealing with a wholly different area of law.

Full enforcement of Community law. Legal certainty has been used to reinforce the binding character of Community law and the obligations which ensue for Member States, in particular, in relation to directives. According to established case law, in areas covered by Community law, national rules should be worded unequivocally so as to give the persons concerned a clear and precise understanding of their rights and obligations and enable national courts to ensure that those rights and obligations are observed.[28]

The Court has accepted that it may not be necessary for a Member State to take implementing measures if existing legislation already meets the requirements of a directive.[29] But it has laid down a number of specific obligations.[30] First, it is essential for national law to guarantee that the national authorities will effectively apply the directive in full; second, the legal position under national law should be sufficiently precise and clear; and third, individuals must be made fully aware of all their rights and, where appropriate, be able to rely on them before the national courts.

A requirement to which the case law attaches particular importance is that rights flowing from directives must be unequivocally stated so that citizens have a clear and precise understanding of them.[31] In general, the standard of legal certainty applied by the ECJ in this context is high and has been raised since the 1990s.[32] In *Commission v Greece*,[33] the Commission brought enforcement proceedings claiming

---

[27] *Opel Austria, op. cit.*, para 125; *Netherlands v European Parliament and Council, op. cit.*, per Jacobs AG at 7110.

[28] See e.g. Case 29/84 *Commission v Germany* [1985] ECR 1661; Case 143/83 *Commission v Denmark* [1985] ECR 427; Case 363/85 *Commission v Italy* [1987] ECR 1733; Case C-120/88 *Commission v Italy* [1991] ECR I-621; Case C-119/92 *Commission v Italy* [1994] ECR I-393.

[29] Case 29/84 *Commission v Germany, op. cit.*, para 23; Case C-365/93 *Commission v Greece* [1995] ECR I-499, para 9.

[30] See for a recent exposition, Case C-63/01 *Evans v Secretary of State for the Environment, Transport and the Regions and the Motor Insurers' Bureau*, judgment of 4 December 2003, para 35; Case C-144/99 *Commission v Netherlands* [2001] ECR I-3541, para 17.

[31] See the cases referred above in n. 28.

[32] Contrast Case 248/83 *Commission v Germany* [1985] ECR 1459, where the Court accepted that Germany did not need to adopt new legislation to comply with the Equal Treatment Directive in view of the categorical and express guarantees provided by the German Basic Law and the existing system of judicial remedies, with Case C-187/98 *Commission v Greece* [1999] ECR I-7713, where it was held that the Government could not escape its obligation to incorporate sex equality directives by relying on the direct effect of the relevant provisions of the Greek Constitution: see para 54.

[33] Case C-236/95 [1996] ECR I-4459. See also Case C-220/94 *Commission v Luxembourg* [1995] ECR I-1589.

that Greece had failed to implement Directive 89/665[34] which requires Member States to ensure that decisions taken by contracting authorities as regards the award of public procurement contracts may be reviewed effectively. Greece conceded that it had not formally transposed the Directive but argued that existing provisions of administrative and civil law, as interpreted by the Greek *Conseil d'Etat*, afforded sufficient judicial protection. The Court considered that the provisions of national law were of a general character and insufficient in themselves to comply with the Directive. It acknowledged that the Greek *Conseil d'Etat* applied those provisions in conformity with the Directive but held that, having regard to the wording of the provisions which confined the capacity to bring proceedings only to certain categories of persons, the case law of the *Conseil d'Etat* could not satisfy the requirements of legal certainty. Greece therefore had failed to comply with the Directive.[35] In *Commission v Italy*[36] the Court found that Italy failed to fulfil its obligations by not amending a provision governing repayment of duties collected in breach of Community law. Although the provision in itself was not incompatible with Community law, it was interpreted by the national authorities and a substantial proportion of the national courts, including the Corte suprema di cassazione, in breach of Community requirements. The Court held that, where national legislation has been the subject of different relevant judicial constructions, some leading to the application of that legislation in compliance with Community law, others leading to the opposite application, it must be held that, at the very least, such legislation is not sufficiently clear to ensure its application in compliance with Community law.[37]

The requirement of legal certainty applies *a fortiori* in areas where it is particularly important to ensure that directives are transposed by binding measures as for example where non-implementation could endanger public health.[38]

Legal certainty not only reduces the implementation options available to Member States but may also render inapplicable time limits provided for by national law. In *Emmott*[39] it was held that, as long as a directive has not been properly transposed into national law, individuals are unable to ascertain the full extent of their rights and that, until proper transposition takes place, a Member State may not rely on an individual's delay in instituting proceedings to protect

---

[34] Directive 89/665 on the coordination of laws relating to the application of review procedures to the award of public supply and public works contracts, OJ 1989 L 395, p. 33.

[35] Clearly, the fact that a Member State simply informs the competent administrative authorities of the implications of directives does not in itself satisfy the requirements of publicity, clarity and certainty. Individuals must be able to ascertain clearly their rights under Community law: Case C-96/95 *Commission v Germany* [1997] ECR I-1653. Note however that, for an enforcement action to succeed, the Commission must demonstrate that the general legal context of the implementing legislation fails to effectively secure full application of the directive: Case C-300/95 *Commission v United Kingdom* [1997] ECR I-2649.

[36] Case C-129/00, judgment of 9 December 2003.   [37] Para 33.

[38] Case C-298/95 *Commission v Germany* [1996] ECR I-6747, para 16; Case C-58/89 *Commission v Germany* [1991] ECR I-4983, para 14.

[39] Case C-208/90 *Emmott* [1991] ECR I-4269, paras 21–23.

rights conferred upon him by the directive. Subsequent case law however has restricted severely the scope of *Emmott* which now applies only where national law forecloses any opportunity to seek judicial protection of Community rights.[40]

Finally, a national measure which is non-transparent and gives rise to uncertainty in its judicial application may be considered to be an unjustifiable restriction on free movement.[41]

Unity and coherence of the Community legal order. Recourse to the principle of legal certainty has been made in order to safeguard the integrity of the Community legal order. In *Foto-Frost*, it was held that national courts do not have the power to declare Community acts invalid *inter alia* because divergences between national courts as to the validity of a Community act would pose a threat to legal certainty.[42] In a different context, in the *First Opinion on the EEA Agreement*[43] it was held that the system of preliminary references by courts of the EFTA States to the Court of Justice, set up by the draft EEA Agreement, was incompatible with Community law. According to the draft Agreement, rulings delivered by the Court of Justice were to be purely advisory without any binding effect. The Court considered that this would be incompatible with its judicial function and have an adverse impact on legal certainty as it would give rise to doubt as to the legal value of such rulings for the courts of Member States.

Further, the principle of legal certainty may prevent the Community institutions by their conduct from anticipating planned Treaty amendments. Thus, Community measures must be adopted in accordance with the Treaty rules in force at the time of their adoption. It would be contrary to legal certainty if, in determining the legal basis of a measure, account was taken of an alleged development in relations between institutions which does not yet find confirmation in any provision of the Treaty or finds confirmation in the provisions of a treaty which has not yet entered into force.[44]

Protection of Member States. Legal certainty may be invoked not only by individuals but also by Member States.[45] The principle is claimed in particular in the law relating to public finance. According to the system for the financing of the common agricultural policy, Member States effect the expenditure necessary to finance intervention and the Commission verifies on an annual basis the accounts of national authorities. Under established case law, a Member State has a legitimate

---

[40] Case C-188/95 *Fantask A/S and Others v Industriministeriet (Erhvervsministeriet)* [1997] ECR I-6783. For a discussion of the case, see 9.4. below.

[41] See Case C-118/96 *Safir* [1998] ECR I-1897.

[42] Case 314/85 *Foto-Frost v Hauptzollamt Lübeck-Ost* [1987] ECR 4199, para 15.

[43] Opinion 1/91 *Draft Agreement relating to the creation of a European Economic Area* [1991] ECR I-6079, paras 61–64.   [44] Case C-269/97 *Commission v Council* [2000] ECR I-2257, para 45.

[45] See e.g. Case 44/81 *Germany v Commission* [1982] ECR 1855. Case 26/69 *Commission v France* [1970] ECR 565 suggests that the equivocal state of Community law may be a valid defence in enforcement proceedings brought by the Commission. The reasoning of the Court however is unclear. Cf the Opinion of Roemer AG.

expectation that expenditure will be charged to Community funds if it has been incurred as a result of an erroneous interpretation of Community law attributable to a Community institution, but not if the incorrect application of the Community rules is attributable to national authorities.[46] The Court has also held that the fact that the Commission did not call into question an expenditure incurred by a Member State in previous financial years does not give rise to an expectation that it will not be called into question in the future. Thus, where the Commission has tolerated irregularities on grounds of fairness, the Member State concerned does not acquire any right to demand that the same position be taken with regard to irregularities committed in the following financial year.[47]

Procedural exclusivity. Rules providing for procedural exclusivity are often said to be justified on grounds of legal certainty. In *TWD*[48] the Court held that the recipient of State aid who has failed to challenge a Commission decision declaring the aid unlawful within the requisite time limit under Article 230 is time-barred from challenging it under Article 234. The Court stated that the time limit within which a direct action for annulment must be brought safeguards legal certainty by preventing Community measures from being called into question indefinitely. Once the time limit has passed, the Commission decision becomes definitive *vis-à-vis* the undertaking in receipt of the aid. Its definitive nature binds the national court by virtue of the principle of legal certainty and precludes it from questioning its validity in proceedings under Article 234.[49]

Since legal certainty is the underlying rationale of the judgment, it must also determine the scope of its application. It is submitted that *TWD* is correctly decided but should be interpreted restrictively to the effect that proceedings under Article 234 are barred only where it is manifestly clear that a private individual has *locus standi* to bring proceedings under Article 230. Two reasons countenance such a restrictive interpretation, the first being a reason of law, the other a reason of policy. If the *TWD* principle were extended to other cases, it would lead to the following paradox. In order to prove that it can challenge a measure under Article 234, an undertaking would have to establish that it could reasonably take the view that it did not have *locus standi* under Article 230. This, in turn, would lead to argument being heard before the national court on whether the undertaking had direct and individual concern.[50] Far from serving the requirements of legal certainty, such a solution would insert the ambiguity of Article 230(4) into Article 234. Also an undertaking might find itself in a position where all procedural rules

---

[46] See e.g. Case 820/79 *Belgium v Commission* [1980] ECR 3537, para 11; Case 1251/79 *Italy v Commission* [1981] ECR 205; Case C-49/94 *Ireland v Commission* [1995] ECR I-2683. For a successful claim, see C-56/91 *Greece v Commission* [1993] ECR I-3433, paras 33 *et seq.*

[47] Case C-339/00 *Ireland v Commission*, judgment of 16 October 2003, para 81; Case C-54/95 *Germany v Commission* [1999] ECR I-35, para 12.

[48] Case C-188/92 *TWD Textilwerke Deggendorf* [1994] ECR I-833.

[49] *Ibid.*, paras, 16, 17 and 25.

[50] See e.g. *IKEA Wholesale Ltd v Customs and Excise Commissioners* [2004] EWHC 1758.

were closed. It may have decided not to bring a direct action under Article 230 on the understanding that it has no *locus standi* only to find that it is precluded from challenging the validity of the measure under Article 234 because in such proceedings the Court decides that it had *locus standi* under Article 230. It is submitted therefore that the principles of effective judicial protection and access to justice require a restrictive application of *TWD*.

The second reason justifying a restrictive interpretation is that rules of exclusivity tend to favour affluent litigants. By their nature, they require swift action to take advantage of the only procedural route available and therefore expert legal advice. It should not however be taken for granted that small and medium-sized undertakings in Europe whose economic operations are affected by Community law can afford such advice. In short, the *TWD* principle should be restricted only to those cases where it is patently obvious that the undertaking concerned has *locus standi* under Article 230. There are signs that the case law is favourably disposed towards such a view. In *The Queen v Intervention Board for Agricultural Produce ex p Accrington Beef and Others*[51] the Court refused to apply the *TWD* principle in relation to a regulation and in *Eurotunnel SA v SeaFrance* it refused to apply it in relation to a directive.[52] By contrast, the Court has applied *TWD* in the context of anti-dumping proceedings. In *Nachi Europe GmbH v Hauptzollamt Krefeld*,[53] it held that an importer of products on which anti-dumping duty has been imposed and who undoubtedly had a right to seek annulment of the duty before the CFI but did not exercise it, cannot subsequently plead the invalidity of the duty before a national court.[54]

Legal certainty was also the underlying principle behind the appeal judgment in *AssiDomän*.[55] In that case the ECJ held, reversing the CFI, that where a number of similar individual decisions imposing fines have been adopted pursuant to a common procedure and only some addressees have taken legal action against the decisions concerning them and obtained their annulment, the institution which adopted the decision does not need to re-examine at the request of other addressees the legality of the unchallenged decisions in the light of the grounds of the annulling judgment. *AssiDomän* favours finality and legal certainty at the expense of substantive legality and may be seen as an indication of undue formalism.[56] More recently, in a different context, the CFI has taken a narrow view of the demands of legal certainty. It has held that a rule of procedural exclusivity does not apply where

---

[51] Case C-241/95 *The Queen v Intervention Board for Agricultural Produce ex p Accrington Beef and Others* [1996] ECR I-6699.   [52] Case C-408/95 [1997] ECR I-6315.

[53] C-239/99 *Nachi Europe GmbH v Hauptzollamt Krefeld* [2001] ECR I-1197.

[54] *TWD* applies *a fortiori* where a Commission decision is addressed to the applicant: see Case 178/95 *Wiljo NV v Belgian State* [1997] ECR I-585. Also, a Member State which has not challenged a Commission decision addressed to it within the time limit laid down in Article 230(5) cannot subsequently invoke its unlawfulness before a national court in order to dispute the merits of an action brought against it: C-241/01 *National Farmers' Union* [2002] ECR I-9079.

[55] Case C-310/97 P *Commission v AssiDomän Kraft Products aB and Others* [1999] ECR I-5363.

[56] See the discussion above, chapter 1.

two actions arise as a result of different acts or conduct of the Community administration, even if the financial outcome of the actions is the same.[57]

An interesting illustration of the application of *TWD* in national proceedings is provided by *IKEA Wholesale Ltd v Customs and Excise Commissioners*.[58] The applicant company sought repayment of anti-dumping duties paid on the importation of bed linen from Pakistan and India. The duties had been imposed pursuant to Council Regulation 2398/97 which was subsequently found by the WTO Appellate Body to be in breach of WTO law. The applicants contested the validity of Regulation 2398/97 and subsequent related regulations but the VAT and Duties Tribunal held that it was precluded from making a reference to the European Court of Justice because the applicant had not proved that it did not have direct and individual concern to challenge them before the CFI. On appeal, Lightman J overruled the Tribunal's decision and decided to make a reference to the ECJ. He held that the onus of proving that a litigant may not challenge the validity of a Community provision before a national court lies with the party who raises the objection. He also held that the Tribunal had followed the wrong test to establish the *locus standi* of the applicant relying on the liberal test laid down by the CFI in *Jégo-Quéré*[59] and not the more stringent test subsequently adopted by the ECJ in *UPA*.[60] Prior to the appeal, Customs had received a letter from the Commission stating that, as an importer not related to the manufacturers, the applicant did not meet the conditions of *locus standi* under Article 230(4) as laid down in *Extramet Industrie SA v Council*.[61] Lightman J held that the Tribunal should not have discounted the Commission's letter as being merely persuasive and not binding and, if it had decided to discount the letter on that ground, it should have explained its reason for doing so.

6.2. Protection of legitimate expectations

Respect for legitimate expectations is one of the most oft-invoked general principles of Community law. It has found fertile ground for its application particularly in agriculture and staff cases. Although the overwhelming majority of claims based on breach of the principle have been rejected, in some cases such actions have succeeded in leading to the annulment of the measure concerned[62] or liability in damages on the part of the Community.[63] The principle acquires particular importance in the context of retroactive application of laws. It may also be invoked in other contexts but only to the extent that the Community itself has previously

---

[57] See Case T-7/99 *Medici Grimm v Council* [2000] ECR II-2671, discussed at 6.3.7 below.

[58] *Op. cit.*, n. 50 above, judgment of 22 July 2004.

[59] Case T-177/01 *Jégo-Quéré v Commission* [2002] ECR II-2365; subsequently reversed on appeal: C-263/02 P *Commission v Jégo-Quéré*, judgment of 1 April 2004.

[60] Case C-50/00 P *Unión de Pequeños Agricultores v Council* [2002] ECR I-6677.

[61] Case C-358/89 [1991] ECR I-2501.

[62] See e.g. Case C-152/88 *Sofrimport v Commission* [1990] ECR I-2477, Case *Crispoltoni II* and the milk quota cases discussed at 6.3.10 and 6.4.2 below.   [63] See e.g. *Mulder II*, at 6.4.2 below.

created a situation which can give rise to a legitimate expectation.[64] Such expectations may arise out of previous legislation[65] or out of conduct of the Community institutions.[66] The principle may be invoked only where the legislation or conduct of the institution concerned is the proximate cause of the legitimate expectation. Also, breach of the principle may be pleaded only where the legitimate expectations in issue have been frustrated by the Community or its agents. In one case,[67] traders received advance payment of export aid to export goods to Iraq but, following the invasion of Kuwait, the goods were stopped in Turkey and never reached the agreed destination. The result was that the security lodged by the traders was forfeited. It was argued that the security should be reimbursed because the goods failed to reach their destination as a result of a Community measure, namely Regulation No 2340/90 preventing trade by the Community as regards Iraq and Kuwait. But the Court held that the Turkish authorities refused transit because of the trade embargo imposed by the UN and therefore the failure to perform the agreed transaction was not attributable to the Community.

Protection of legitimate expectations may be said to differ from legal certainty with regard to 'the time factor'.[68] Legal certainty requires the rules which apply at a given time to be clear and precise for the benefit of the individual. Protection of legitimate expectations, on the other hand, requires public authorities to exercise their powers over a period of time in such a way as to ensure that 'situations and relationships lawfully created under Community law are not affected in a manner which could not have been foreseen by a diligent person'.[69] Legal certainty therefore has a static character whereas legitimate expectations are enjoyed for the future. This explains the different function of the principles. Legitimate expectations may be a source of substantive rights whereas legal certainty has a more general character and is usually invoked as a rule of interpretation. The various aspects of the principle of protection of legitimate expectations will now be examined.

6.3. Non-retroactivity

6.3.1. Criminal measures

The principle of respect for legitimate expectations imposes strict limitations on the retroactive application of Community law. A distinction should be drawn here between criminal and other measures. With regard to criminal measures, the

---

[64] Case C-177/90 *Kühn v Landwirtschaftskammer Weser-Ems* [1992] ECR I-35, para 14.
[65] See e.g. Case 74/74 *CNTA* [1975] ECR 533; Case C-152/88 *Sofrimport v Commission* [1990] ECR I-2477, and the milk quota cases, at 6.4.2 below.
[66] See e.g. Case 127/80 *Grogan v Commission* [1982] ECR 869; Case 289/81 *Mavridis v Parliament* [1983] ECR 1731, para 21.
[67] Case C-299/94 *Anglo-Irish Beef Processors International v MAFF* [1996] ECR I-1925.
[68] See *Duff v Minister for Agriculture and Food, op. cit.,* n. 21 above *per* Cosmas AG at 582.
[69] *Ibid.*

prohibition of retroactivity is absolute. In this respect, Community law abides fully by the general principle of Article 7 ECHR, which incorporates the general principle *nullum crimen, nulla poena sine lege*. Article 7 prohibits the retroactive application of criminal measures and the retroactive increase of criminal penalties. It also requires that offences must be clearly defined by law. This latter condition is satisfied where individuals can know from the wording of the relevant provision and, if need be, with the assistance of judicial interpretation what acts and omissions will make them liable.[70] Further, according to the case law of the Strasbourg court, Article 7 prohibits the extensive application of criminal law by judicial interpretation. This prohibition however is relative. National courts are inevitably allowed a margin of discretion since, as the Strasbourg court has observed, 'the progressive development of criminal law through judicial law-making is a well-entrenched and necessary part of legal tradition'.[71] Thus, Article 7 does not outlaw the gradual clarification of criminal rules, provided that the resulting development is consistent with the essence of the offence and could reasonably be foreseen.[72]

In *R v Kirk*, the ECJ referred to Article 7 of the ECHR as incorporating a principle common to the laws of the Member States.[73] In fact, the need to refer to Article 7 has rarely arisen in Community law. A more interesting issue is the definition of a 'criminal' measure for the purposes of Article 7. According to Strasbourg case law, this issue is not left to the laws of the contracting states but is determined objectively in accordance with the following criteria: the legal classification of the offence under national law, the nature of the offence, and the nature and severity of the applicable penalty.[74] It would appear that the same criteria should apply also in relation to Community provisions. The issue has not been examined systematically by the Luxembourg courts. In *Gerekens* the ECJ held that the additional levy imposed on quantities of milk produced above the quota allocated to producers under Community regulations was not a criminal penalty for the purposes of Article 7.[75] In *Orkem* the ECJ took the view that competition law investigations do not involve criminal charges.[76] The CFI has held that, although competition law fines are not classified as criminal in nature,[77] the prohibition of

---

[70] *Kokkinakis v Greece*, judgment of 25 May 1993, Series A, No. 260-A; (1994) 17 EHRR, para 52.

[71] *CR v United Kingdom*, judgment of 2 November 1995, Series A, No 335-C; (1996) 21 EHRR 363, para 34.

[72] *Ibid*. See in this context the East German cases: *Streletz, Kessler and Krenz v Germany*, judgment of 22 March 2001, (2001) 33 EHRR 751, and *K-HW v Germany*, judgment of 22 March 2001 (Appl. 32701/97); see also the earlier case of *X v Austria* (1970) 13 YB 789.

[73] Case 63/83 *R v Kirk* [1984] ECR 2689, paras 21–22. See also Case C-331/88 *Fedesa* [1990] ECR I-4023, paras 41–42.

[74] *Engel v Netherlands (No 1)* (1976) 1 EHRR 647, para 81; *Öztürk v Germany*, judgment of 21 February 1984, Series A, No 73, p. 18, para 50; *Lauko and Kadubec v Slovakia*, judgment of 2 September 1998, Reports of Judgments and Decisions 1998-VI, p. 2504, para 56.

[75] Case C-459/02 *Gerekens and Association agricole pour la promotion de la commercialisation laitière Procola v Luxembourg*, judgment of 15 July 2004, para 36.

[76] Case C-374/87 *Orkem SA v Commission* [1989] ECR I-3283, para 31.

[77] See Regulation 17, Article 15(4), which has now been replaced by Regulation No 1/2003 (OJ 2003 L1/1), Article 23(5).

retroactivity applies fully to them. Thus, a fine imposed on an undertaking must correspond to the penalties provided by law at the time when the infringement was committed. This however does not prohibit the Commission from introducing new guidelines for the calculation of fines which may in some cases lead to their increase as long as the maximum level provided for in Article 15 of Regulation 17 (now Article 23 of Regulation No 1/2003) is not exceeded.[78] Still, the assumption that competition law fines are not criminal in nature is not beyond dispute.[79]

6.3.2. Non-criminal measures

With regard to non-criminal measures, retroactivity is not prohibited but is subject to strict conditions. According to established case law, a measure may exceptionally produce retroactive effect provided that two conditions are fulfilled:[80] (a) the purpose of the measure so requires; and (b) the legitimate expectations of those affected are duly respected. Those conditions must be satisfied whether retro-activity is expressly stated in the measure itself or it results from its contents.[81] Retroactive application is not subject to the above conditions where its purpose is to protect rather than to prejudice the interests of the individual. In such a case retroactivity may be permitted, and in certain cases it may even be required subject to any vested rights of third parties.[82] A measure whose retroactive effect is incompatible with Community law will normally be declared invalid or, where appropriate, non-binding insofar as it has retroactive effect.[83]

A measure must indicate in its statement of reasons why retroactivity is neces-sary.[84] In *Diversinte*[85] the Court took a particularly strict view of the requirement of reasoning. A Commission Regulation imposing a levy on the export of milk powder from Spain to other Member States was published on 17 March 1987

---

[78] Case T-23/99 *LR AF 1988 A/S v Commission* [2002] ECR II-1705, paras 220–221 and para 235.

[79] In *Société Stenuit v France*, Series A No 232-A (1992) 14 EHRR 509, the European Commission of Human Rights held that fines imposed under French competition law were criminal charges for the purposes of the Convention. But in *OOO Nestle St Petersburg and Others v Russia*, Application 69042, decision of 3 June 2004, the ECtHR dismissed the argument of the applicants that penalties imposed for breach of the Russian law on competition and restriction of monopolies in the commodities market involved the determination of criminal charges. This case, however, because of its specific circumstances does not provide conclusive evidence that fines under EU competition law are not criminal in nature.

[80] See e.g. Case 98/78 *Racke v Hauptzollampt Mainz* [1979] ECR 69, para 20; Case 99/78 *Decker* [1979] ECR 101, para 8; *Fedesa, op. cit.*, n. 73 above, para 45; Case C-110/97 *Netherlands v Council* [2001] ECR I-8763, para 151.

[81] Case C-368/89 *Crispoltoni I* [1991] ECR I-3695, para 17.   [82] See 6.3.7 below.

[83] See e.g. *Van eS Douane Agenten, op. cit.* n. 25 above; Case 158/78 *Biegi v Hauptzollamt Bochum* [1979] ECR 1103.

[84] Case 1/84 R *Ilford v Commission* [1984] ECR 423, para 19. By contrast, where there is no retroactivity, a regulation need not provide reasons why it did not include transitional measures for producers who might be affected indirectly by its provisions: see Case T-472/93 *Campo Ebro and Others v Council* [1995] ECR II-421, para 81.

[85] Joined Cases C-260 and C-261/91 *Diversinte and Iberlacta* [1993] ECR I-1885.

and applied retroactively from 12 February 1987. The preamble to the Regulation provided that it should be applied as a matter of urgency with a view to avoiding speculative transactions. The Court held that that statement did not provide adequate reasoning and annulled the Regulation to the extent that it was retro-active.[86] The judgment shows that the statement of reasons must include specific justification for retroactivity. It also suggests that failure to provide adequate reasons is in itself a ground of annulment even if retroactive application can objectively be justified. If so, where a measure fails to provide adequate reasons, it is not open to the institution which authored the measure to defend retroactivity *ex post facto* in case where litigation arises. In this respect however the case law is not consistent. The procedural issue whether adequate reason for retro-activity is given is intertwined with the substantive issue whether retroactivity is objectively justified. In *Moskof*[87] the Court held that a Commission regulation which applied retroactively met the substantive conditions of retroactivity and refused to annul it despite the fact that its preamble provided scant reasoning to justify retroactivity.[88]

In determining whether a legislative measure has retroactive effect account must be taken of the time of its publication rather than its adoption. A measure which takes effect from a date subsequent to the date of its publication cannot, in prin-ciple, be regarded as having retroactive application.[89] Following continental legal doctrine, publication of a measure has a 'constitutive' character[90] so that failure to publish bars the measure from producing legal effects. Article 254 of the Treaty requires measures of general application to be published in the Official Journal. It provides that such measures enter into force on the date specified in them or, in the absence thereof, on the twentieth day following their publication. A regulation is regarded as published throughout the Community on the date borne by the issue of the Official Journal where it is published. Where it is proved, however, that the

---

[86] Cf the Opinion of Gulmann AG. The Advocate General favoured a different interpretation of the contested Regulation according to which it applied to a well-defined category of products already subject to the levy under a previous regulation, its sole objective being to prevent traders from fraudulently avoiding payment. In his view the traders concerned could not invoke a 'legitimate' expectation as they abused the levy system. With regard to the requirement of rea-soning, the Advocate General considered that those traders were in a position to understand the reasons which led the Commission to adopt the contested Regulation on the basis of its preamble, their knowledge of the previous regulation, and the reasons which led to the adoption of the latter. *Op. cit.*, pp. 1906–1907.

[87] Case C-244/95 *Moskof v Ethnikos Organismos Kapnou* [1997] ECR I-6441.

[88] In the context of competition law, the case law accepts that in principle the reasons for a Commission decision must appear in the actual body of the decision and explanations given *ex post facto* cannot be taken into account: Case T-61/89 *Dansk Pelsdyravlerforening v Commission* [1992] ECR II-1931; Case T-30/89 *Hilti v Commission* [1991] ECR II-1439; but in exceptional cir-cumstances it may be otherwise: Case T-352/94 *Mo och Domsjö AB v Commission*, judgment of 14 May 1998, paras 276–279.

[89] By contrast, the fact that a measure makes eligibility to a future benefit subject to events that occurred in the past is not in itself sufficient to give it retroactive effect: see Joined Cases C-37 and C-38/02 *di Lenardo Adriano and Dilexport v Ministero del Commercio con l'Estero*, judgment of 15 July 2004, paras 67–69. [90] *Faccini Dori, op. cit.*, n. 13 above, *per* Lenz AG at 3342; see 6.1 above.

date when an issue was in fact available does not correspond to the date which appears on that issue, regard must be had to the date of actual publication.[91]

6.3.3. The conditions of retroactivity

As stated, retroactivity is subject to two conditions. Retroactive effect must be necessary to achieve the objectives of the measure, and the legitimate expectations of those affected must be respected.[92] The case law refers to those conditions as separate requirements which must be met cumulatively. In reality, they are inextricably linked and represent the conflicting interests which are involved. The Court weighs, on the one hand, the public interest which retroactivity is purported to serve and, on the other hand, the requirement that the legitimate expectations of those affected must be respected. It performs *par excellence* a balancing exercise, in the context of which a variety of factors are taken into account, in order to determine whether the expectation 'in fairness outtops the policy choice'.[93] As Trabbuchi AG stated in *Deuka*,[94]

the existence of legitimate expectations worthy of protection can be established only on the merits of each case ... By its very nature the principle does not lend itself to mechanical application, which might lead to unjustified generalizations and would accord neither with its specific equitable function nor with the day-to-day requirements of Community rules governing the economy.

In determining which interest takes priority the Court will consider the objective which retroactivity seeks to attain. Clearly, not every objective would be capable of taking priority over the legitimate expectations of those affected. In *Amylum v Council*, Reischl AG considered that there must be an imperative reason of public interest and the Court referred to an objective to be achieved 'in the general interest'.[95] In general, a claim that a retroactive measure is incompatible with Community law will not succeed easily. In the majority of cases, the Court has rejected such claims. Thus, to give but few examples, it has been held that the retroactive effect of transitional measures concerning the Accession of Greece was necessary to prevent speculative movements of agricultural products.[96] Also, the need to maintain the stability of prices of agricultural products, threatened as a

---

[91] *Opel Austria, op. cit.*, n. 23 above, para 127; *Racke v Hauptzollamt Mainz, op. cit.*, n. 80 above; *Decker, op. cit.*, n. 80 above; Case C-337/88 *SAFA* [1990] ECR I-1, para 12.

[92] In an early case, Case 37/70 *Rewe-Zentrale v Hauptzollamt Emmerich* [1971] ECR 23, the Court considered a retroactive decision of the Commission to be compatible with Community law solely on the ground that retroactive effect was necessary to maintain the level of agricultural prices in Germany without examining the protection of legitimate expectations. That case, however, is not a reliable authority as it has been superseded by subsequent judgments defining the conditions of retroactivity. See *Racke, op. cit*, and *Decker, op. cit.* See also the *milk quota* cases, discussed at 6.4.2 below.   [93] *Hamble (Offshore) Fisheries, op. cit.*, n. 6 above, *per* Sedley J.

[94] Case 5/75 *Deuka v Einfuhr- und Vorratsstelle Getreide* [1975] ECR 759, at 777.

[95] Case 108/81 *Amylum v Council* [1982] ECR 3107, paras 6, 8 and *per* Reischl AG at 3144.

[96] *SAFA, op. cit.*

result of the revaluation of the German mark, was held to justify retroactive imposition of countervailing duties.[97] In a more recent case, the Court accepted that the uniform application of the *acquis communautaire* throughout the Union may be a reason justifying the retroactive application of measures adapting existing Community acts following the accession of new Member States.[98] Also, it has been held that public health considerations may justify the immediate application of protective measures on products imported from third countries.[99] More generally, the need to prevent speculation, or disturbances in the Community market have been held to provide overriding reasons in the general interest.[100]

6.3.4. Cases where the Court has annulled retroactive measures

A classic example of invalid retroactivity is provided by *Crispoltoni I*.[101] With a view to limiting production in tobacco, Council regulations fixed maximum guaranteed quantities, excess of which would lead to a reduction in subsidies payable to producers and tobacco processors. The regulations were adopted and became applicable after producers had made their production decisions for the current year. The Court held that retroactive effect was not capable of limiting production as decisions regarding cultivation had already been taken and, indeed, the harvest had begun before the publication of the measures. It added that, although the measures were foreseeable, producers were entitled to expect that they would be notified in good time of any measures having effects on their investments. *Crispoltoni* may be seen as a case of a legislative conundrum, a policy hastily arranged and implemented which entailed not only a quantitative but also a qualitative regulatory change.

In *Agricola Commerciale Olio*[102] and *Savma*[103] the Court struck down the retroactive revocation of previous measures. By a regulation adopted in January 1981, the Commission offered for sale by tender consignments of olive oil held by the Italian intervention agency. After the applicants were declared successful purchasers, the Commission by new regulations adopted on 3 August 1981 decided to cancel the sale and reopen the tender procedure. The Commission's rationale was that, during the period which elapsed between the adoption of the first regulation and the adoption of the subsequent ones, the conditions of the market had radically altered. The 1980/81 harvest was much below what had been predicted causing an unexpected increase in prices. In these circumstances, the conditions of sale under the initial regulation became unreasonably favourable and would have permitted a limited number of traders to make enormous profits at the expense of the taxpayer

---

[97] *Rewe-Zentrale*, op. cit., n. 92 above.
[98] Case C-259/95 *Parliament v Council* [1997] ECR I-5303.
[99] Case C-183/95 *Affish BV v Rijksdienst voor de Keuring van Vee en Vlees* [1997] ECR I-4315.
[100] See e.g. *Netherlands v Council*, op. cit., n. 80 above, para 155.
[101] Op. cit., n. 81 above. Cf C-324/96 *Odette and Simou* [1998] ECR I-1333.
[102] Case 232/81 *Agricola Commerciale Olio v Commission* [1984] ECR 3881.
[103] Case 264/81 *Savma v Commission* [1984] ECR 3915.

and to dominate the market in Italy. The Court found that the Commission's assessment was vitiated by factual errors. With the assistance of an independent witness, it was satisfied that no radical change in market conditions had taken place. The Commission's change of mind was not the result of supervening developments but of its own failure of appreciation. The Court pointed out that the means of observing market conditions at the disposal of the Commission should have permitted it to revise its forecasts regarding the 1980/81 harvest long before the contested regulations were adopted. The fact that the terms of the initial sale may have led to the successful tenderers deriving a windfall benefit was not sufficient to annul the sale retroactively:[104]

The mere fact that the conditions on which the Commission permitted the national agency to put the products up for sale proved to be favourable, and even extremely favourable, to the purchasers, does not entitle the Commission to prevent that agency from carrying out the contract which had been concluded in accordance with the said conditions.

It should be noted that the regulations were annulled as being vitiated by errors of fact. The Commission failed to show that a change in market conditions, or abuse by the successful purchasers, had taken place. The Court expressly left open the questions whether in other circumstances the Commission would have been entitled to cancel the initial sale retroactively and what would have been the consequences of such cancellation with regard to the right of successful purchasers to compensation.

Meiko-Konservenfabrik v Germany[105] arose from the Community system of aid for processing fruit and vegetables. Under the applicable Community rules for the marketing year 1980/81, fruit processors were entitled to aid provided that two conditions were met. A processing contract had to be concluded by 31 July 1980 and a copy of the contract had to be forwarded to the competent national agency before the contract took effect, that is to say, before the first delivery of fruit. As a result of weather conditions, the cherry harvest in 1980 was late and processors were unable to comply with the second condition. In recognition of those exceptional circumstances, the Commission by a regulation adopted on October 1980 provided that contracts concluded for cherries could be forwarded to agencies even after the date on which they took effect but not later than 31 July 1980. Meiko, an undertaking which had entered into processing contracts with producers of cherries, was refused aid as it notified the competent authority of the contracts after the time limit of 31 July. The Court found that the time limit ran counter to the principle of protection of legitimate expectations and the principle of equality. On the former, it stated:[106]

... by retroactively subjecting the payment of aid to the forwarding of the contracts by 31 July 1980 the Commission acted in breach of the legitimate expectations of the persons

[104] *Agricola Commerciale Olio, op. cit.,* para 18; *Savma, op. cit.,* 18.
[105] Case 224/82 [1983] ECR 2539.   [106] *Ibid.,* para 14.

concerned, who, having regard to the provisions in force at the time the contracts were concluded, could not reasonably have anticipated the retroactive imposition of a time-limit for forwarding contracts which coincided with the time-limit for their conclusion.

It has been suggested that in *Meiko* the Court reached 'an eminently sound economic result'.[107] The reasoning of the judgment however is not entirely satisfactory. It is hard to see how there could be a breach of legitimate expectations since, when they entered into processing contracts, processors were not entitled to expect that they would be granted aid if they failed to meet the second condition stated above. Indeed, the Court accepted that the Commission was under no obligation to alter the conditions applicable retroactively.[108] Although the judgment is couched in terms of breach of legitimate expectations, the real basis of the claim was breach of equal treatment.[109] The Court accepted that the date of 31 July gave rise to discrimination among processors. It stated that, once the Commission decided to take into account the processor's difficulties, it was under a duty, in adopting the appropriate measures 'to have regard to the legitimate expectations of the persons concerned and to ensure that they were accorded equal treatment'.[110] In the circumstances of the case, it is clear that the applicants did not suffer as a result of reposing their trust in the Commission, their 'legitimate expectation' being no more than that they would be treated equally with other processors.

6.3.5. Monetary compensatory amounts

The Court has had the opportunity to examine the conditions governing retroactivity in a number of cases involving monetary compensatory amounts. In *Racke*[111] a regulation provided for the levying of monetary compensatory amounts on imports of wine from Yugoslavia from a date earlier than the date of its adoption. The Court found that the levying of the amounts was necessary and that the legitimate expectations of the traders concerned had been met. In view of the nature and the objectives of the system of monetary compensatory amounts, traders ought to expect that any appreciable change in the monetary situation may entail the extension of the system to new categories of products and the fixing of new amounts. The tenet of the judgment is that the nature of monetary compensatory amounts made the retroactive effect of the measures imposing them unavoidable.[112]

---

[107] Sharpston, *op. cit.*, n. 2 above, p. 143.   [108] *Meiko, op. cit.*, para 16.

[109] Rozès AG considered that the contested regulation was invalid as being in breach of the principle of proportionality and, in the alternative, as being in breach of the principle of equal treatment.   [110] *Op. cit.*, para 17.

[111] *Op. cit.*, n. 6 above. See also *Decker, op. cit.*, n. 80 above.

[112] See also Case 7/76 IRCA v Amministrazione delle Finanze dello Stato [1976] ECR 1213. On the other hand, a trader may not have a legitimate expectation that the Commission will respond immediately to the devaluation of national currency since monetary compensatory amounts do not provide traders with absolute guarantees against risks of changes in the rates of exchange: Case 281/82 *Unifrex v Commission and Council* [1984] ECR 1969.

The balancing exercise performed by the Court in determining whether legitimate expectations have been respected is illustrated by *Staple Dairy Products*.[113] A Council regulation adopted in 1979 introduced a new system for the calculation of monetary compensatory amounts providing for a deduction ('franchise') at a set rate from the sum calculated. The regulation expired on 31 March 1980. On 26 April 1980 another Council regulation entered into force which extended retrospectively the application of the previous regulation 'without the individual rights acquired by operators being thereby affected'. The applicants, who exported dairy products between 1 April and 26 April, argued that the monetary compensatory amounts applicable to them should be calculated without the deduction. This was because the first regulation had expired and the second regulation could not validly produce retroactive effect since it expressly protected acquired rights. The Court rejected their claim. It stated that the retroactive effect was necessary to prevent an interruption in the maintenance of agricultural prices. Also, the situation at the time when the applicants entered into the transactions in issue gave them no cause to expect that the deduction would be abolished. On the contrary,

the history of the rules in question, as well as their scope and purpose, were such as to lead traders to conclude that the franchise, which for years had constituted a well-established feature of the system of monetary compensatory amounts, would be maintained for some time.[114]

On the basis of the above considerations, the Court interpreted the protection of acquired rights in the second regulation narrowly as referring only to rights definitely conferred on traders by individual decisions of the competent authorities. Neither the principle of legitimate expectations nor the express recognition of acquired rights excluded retroactive effect in the circumstances of the case.[115]

By contrast, in *CNTA* the Court considered that the withdrawal with immediate effect of monetary compensatory amounts without prior warning required the Commission to compensate traders who suffered loss as a result since the withdrawal was not necessitated by any overriding reasons of public interest. The Court held that the Commission should have adopted transitional measures which would have enabled the traders concerned to avoid loss in the performance of export contracts.[116]

6.3.6. Reinstatement of effects of a measure declared void

Retroactive application of a measure may be permitted where its purpose is to reinstate the effects of a previous measure declared void on procedural grounds.

---

[113] Case 84/81 *Staple Dairy Products v Intervention Board for Agricultural Produce* [1982] ECR 1763.
[114] *Ibid.*, para 15.   [115] Cf *Sofrimport*, discussed at 6.4.1 below.
[116] Case 74/74 *CNTA v Commission* [1975] ECR 533. Cf the Opinion of Trabucchi AG. The applicant's action for compensation failed in subsequent proceedings as it was unable to prove loss: [1976] ECR 797.

This principle is illustrated by the last generation of the *isoglucose* cases.[117] By Regulation No 1293/79,[118] the Council introduced a system of quotas and levies in relation to the production of isoglucose. In *Roquette* and *Maizena*,[119] the Court declared that Regulation void because it was adopted without prior consultation with the Parliament. Subsequently, after duly following the consultation procedure, the Council adopted Regulation No 387/81,[120] which reintroduced with retroactive effect the same provisions. In *Amylum*[121] it was held that the retroactive application of Regulation No 387/81 did not infringe Community law. Such application was necessary to ensure the stabilization of the sugar market. Also, the traders affected were limited in number and well aware of the need to restrict isoglucose production and of the intention of the Community institutions to take measures to that effect. Retroactivity was therefore foreseeable.

In *Amylum* the Court upheld for the first time a long period of retroactivity.[122] Although the judgment has been criticized,[123] retroactivity in that case can hardly be said to be in breach of legal certainty. Whilst in *Roquette* and *Maizena* the Court annulled Regulation No 1293/79 on procedural grounds, it rejected the substantive grounds of review submitted by the applicants and expressly stated that nullity was without prejudice to the Council's power to take all appropriate measures pursuant to Article 233(1) of the Treaty. The effect of Regulation No 387/81 was to comply with, rather than to nullify, the effects of the judgments in *Roquette* and *Maizena*. In that respect, Regulation No 387/81 is to be distinguished from the War Damage Act 1965 which nullified the effect of the earlier judgment of the House of Lords in *Burmah Oil Co Ltd v Lord Advocate*.[124] In that case, the House of Lords upheld the claim of the applicant company to receive compensation for the wartime destruction of its installations which had been ordered by the British authorities to prevent their falling into the hands of the advancing Japanese army. The difference is that by the War Damage Act, the Westminster Parliament retroactively nullified rights recognized by a judicial decision. Arguably, this runs counter to the separation of powers and raises questions of constitutionality. By contrast, the judgments in *Roquette* and *Maizena* did not create any rights in favour of isoglucose producers. The equivalent situation in Community law would be if, by amending the Treaties or adopting an act of primary Community law, the Member States undid substantive rights recognized by a judgment of the Court of Justice.[125]

---

[117] *Amylum v Council, op. cit.,* n. 95 above; Case 110/81 *Roquette Frères v Council* [1982] ECR 3159; Case 114/81 *Tunnel Refineries v Council* [1982] ECR 3189.

[118] OJ 1979 L 162, p. 10.

[119] Case 138/79 *Roquette Frères SA v Council* [1980] ECR 3333, Case 139/79 *Maizena GmbH v Council* [1980] ECR 3393.   [120] OJ 1981, L 44, p. 1.

[121] *Op. cit.*

[122] See *per* Reischl, AG *op. cit.*, p. 3144 and Lamoureux, *op. cit.*, p. 283.

[123] T. C. Hartley, *The Foundations of European Community Law* (Fifth Ed, Oxford, 2003), p. 149, n. 70.   [124] [1965] AC 75.

[125] See in this context, the Protocol concerning Article 119 annexed to the EC Treaty by the Treaty on European Union. The Protocol was introduced following the judgment in Case

Amylum was confirmed in *Fedesa*.[126] In that case the applicants challenged the validity of a directive by which the Council introduced with retroactive effect the provisions of a previous directive which had been annulled on procedural grounds. The Court pointed out that the period between the annulment of the first directive and the publication of the second was short, being less than a month, and that the first directive had been annulled on procedural grounds. In those circumstances, the persons concerned could not expect the Council to change its attitude on the issues involved.

6.3.7. Obligation to provide for retroactive effect

In some cases, far from being prohibited, retroactivity may be permitted[127] or even in fact be a legal obligation of the Community administration. Thus in one case the Court held that, where a measure infringes the principle of protection of legitimate expectations because it does not provide for adequate transitional arrangements, such arrangements must be introduced with retroactive effect.[128]

An interesting illustration is provided by *Medici Grimm v Council*.[129] The applicant was a German importer of Chinese leather handbags on which the Council had imposed a definitive anti-dumping duty by a regulation adopted in 1997. The applicant had not taken part in the initial investigations. Subsequently, following a review investigation carried out by the Commission in relation to the same period, the Council adopted Regulation No 2380/98[130] which found that no dumping had taken place and abolished prospectively the anti-dumping duty imposed on the applicant. The latter sought annulment of Regulation No 2380/98 insofar as it had not abolished the anti-dumping duty retroactively.

The case raised two issues. The first was an issue of procedure. The Council and the Commission argued that the action for annulment was an abuse of process since the applicant had failed to apply for a refund of the duty as provided by Article 11(8) of the basic anti-dumping regulation.[131] Under Article 11(8), an importer may apply to the Commission for reimbursement of duties collected where it is shown that the dumping margin on the basis of which the duties were paid has been eliminated or reduced to a level which is below the level of the duty in force. The application for reimbursement must be made within six months of the

C-262/88 *Barber* [1990] ECR I-1889 with a view to limiting claims arising under it. In subsequent cases, the Court interpreted its unclear judgment in *Barber* in such a way as to comply with the Protocol: see Case C-109/91 *Ten Oever* [1993] ECR I-4879; Case C-200/91 *Coloroll* [1994] ECR I-4389.

[126] *Op. cit.*, n. 73 above, para 47.
[127] See e.g. Case C-345/88 *Butterabsatz Osnabrück-Emsland* [1990] ECR I-159. In that case, the Court attributed retroactive effect to a regulation so as to ensure that a previous regulation complied with the principle of proportionality.
[128] See *Grogan v Commission op. cit.*, n. 66 above, para 37, discussed at 6.7 below.
[129] *Op. cit.*, n. 57 above. See also Case C-310/95 *Road Air* [1997] ECR I-2229, para 47.
[130] OJ 1998 L 296/1.   [131] Regulation No 384/96, OJ 1996 L 56/1, as amended.

determination of the duties. The applicant had not availed itself of that procedure. The CFI held however that the two procedures had different objectives. The purpose of a refund application under Article 11(8) was to request the Commission to exempt an undertaking from application of the original regulation imposing anti-dumping duties. By contrast, the applicant sought the annulment of the new regulation which resulted from the Commission's review procedure. Even if the two procedures had the same financial outcome, they were different in nature and related to different acts of the institutions. The CFI distinguished the judgment of the ECJ on *AssiDomän*.[132] It held that a second action is precluded only where the applicant has already had an opportunity to submit for review the act which is effectively the subject of the second claim. It does not apply where the two actions arise as a result of different acts or conduct on the part of the administration, even if the financial outcome is the same.

The second issue raised in the case was an issue of substance, i.e. whether the Council should abolish the duty retroactively. The Court held that when, in a review investigation, the institutions found that one of the factors on the basis of which the definitive anti-dumping duties had been imposed was missing, it was no longer possible to consider the conditions for imposing anti-dumping duties were satisfied at the time when the original regulation was adopted. The institutions were bound to abide by all the consequences flowing from their choice of investigation period and give to their findings retroactive effect. The CFI rejected the argument that retroactive application of the contested regulation would be an unjustified reward for the applicant's failure to cooperate in the initial investigation. It held that the power of the Commission to fix anti-dumping duties on the basis of available information in the event of failure to cooperate in the investigation was to ensure that anti-dumping duties were imposed in a non-discriminatory manner on all imports of goods from a particular country. It was not to penalize traders for their failure to participate in an anti-dumping investigation.

The judgment is vehemently pro-individual and takes a strong stance against the Community institutions. Although the CFI did enough to distinguish it in normative terms from the judgment of the ECJ in *AssiDomän*, it is clear that its approach is imbued by different considerations: the CFI placed emphasis on the principle of legality rather than legal certainty and applied a high standard of scrutiny to the conduct of the Community institutions.[133]

[132] *AssiDomän (Woodpulp III), op. cit.,* n. 55 above, reversing on appeal Case T-227/95 [1997] ECR II-1185. Discussed above p. 31.

[133] Note that, subsequently, the applicant brought an action for damages against the Council seeking to obtain compensation in the form of interest on the duty which was initially paid and later refunded and in the form of the legal expenses it incurred in the course of administrative proceedings before the Commission and the German customs authorities. Case T-363/03 pending. *Medici Grimm* can be contrasted with Case T-89/00 *Europe Chemi-Con (Deutschland) v Council* [2002] ECR II-3651 where a plea to abolish retroactively definitive anti-dumping duties so as to comply with the principle of equal treatment was rejected.

In accordance with principles common to the laws of Member States, Community law requires the retroactive effect of the most favourable criminal provision.[134] Given however that competence to introduce criminal penalties lies with the Member States and not the Community legislature, the above principle may come into conflict with the obligation to provide for effective, proportionate and dissuasive penalties for breach of requirements laid down by Community law. This obligation may flow from a specific provision of Community law requiring Member States to introduce penalties or, in the absence thereof, from the duty of cooperation laid down in Article 10 EC.[135] The question which arises is this: what happens if national law introduces a penalty for violation of an obligation provided for by Community law but subsequently this penalty is reduced or nullified by an amendment to the national law in question and the new penalty is not sufficiently dissuasive under Community law? Would the obligation to provide effective penalties outrank the principle of retroactive effect of the most lenient provision? An important consideration would be whether the obligation to impose penalties derives from a directive or a regulation. The issue was touched upon in *Berlusconi*.[136] The Court reiterated that the principle of the retroactive application of the more lenient penalty emanates from the constitutional traditions common to the Member States. It forms part of the general principles of Community law which national courts must respect when applying the national legislation adopted for the purpose of implementing Community law. The Court however left open the question whether that principle applies where the new criminal provision is at variance with other rules of Community law, e.g. the obligation to provide for effective penalties. On the facts of the case, the ECJ did not have to examine that question because the effectiveness of the penalties provided for by an Italian law was to be judged *vis-à-vis* Article 6 of the First Company Law Directive which requires Member States to provide appropriate penalties for failure to disclose the corporate accounts. The Court held that it was not possible for the Italian authorities to rely on the Directive to establish or aggravate the criminal liability of individuals.[137]

The implication of the judgment is that, if the requirement to impose penalties is laid down not in a directive but in a regulation and the national penalty subsequently introduced is not sufficiently severe in the light of the objectives of the regulation, then the national court might be under an obligation to set it aside in accordance with *Simmenthal*[138] in order to guarantee the effectiveness of Community law. This takes the principle of primacy to its extreme and, at least as regards remedies, conveys an understanding of Community law as a fully fledged

---

[134] For the retroactive application of administrative penalties, see *MAFF ex p National Farmers' Union, op. cit.*, n. 23 above.

[135] See above, Case 68/88 *Commission v Greece* [1989] ECR I-2965, paras 23–24; Case C-167/01 *Inspire Art* [2003] ECR I-10155, para 62; and see above 3.9.

[136] Joined Cases C-378, C-391 and C-403/02 *Criminal Proceedings against Berlusconi, Adelchi, dell'Utri and Others*, judgment of 3 May 2005.   [137] *Ibid.*, paras 65 *et seq.*

[138] Case 106/77 *Simmenthal* [1978] ECR 629.

federal system. The implicit assumption of the Court is that in such a case national law simply lacks authority to make a new less stringent penalty applicable.

The same would apply if the obligation to provide for a penalty is borne not by a specific regulation but by Article 10 EC. This however leads to a paradox: it means that Member States are under more stringent obligations where the duty to provide effective penalties results from the general imposition of Article 10 rather than a specific provision of a directive.

6.3.8. The criterion of foreseeability

It has become clear from the above analysis that, in assessing whether a measure frustrates legitimate expectations, the Court places reliance on the criterion of foreseeability. If it is reasonably foreseeable that a forthcoming measure is likely to have retroactive or immediate application, affected traders may not be able to claim breach of a legitimate expectation.[139] The requisite degree of foreseeability is far from fixed. Depending on the circumstances, the advance warning given to traders must be express, sufficiently specific, and given in good time,[140] or general and even presumed.[141] Thus a qualitative, as opposed to merely a quantitative, change in the regulatory system requires specific advance warning to the economic operators affected.[142] In assessing whether the advance warning given is sufficient, account must also be taken of how easy it would be for the traders concerned to protect themselves against the possibility of a change in the law.

In applying the test of foreseeability, the Court pursues the enquiry whether a prudent and well-informed trader would have been able to foresee the change in the law.[143] In *Accrington*[144] it was held that in a system which provides for the allocation of import quotas on an annual basis, a prudent and diligent trader must know that the conditions of eligibility may be subject to a quantitative change whenever a new annual quota is adopted. Articles in specialized press, or widely publicized correspondence between professional bodies and the Community authorities, may be taken into account in assessing whether impending changes in the law were foreseeable.[145] Proposals for legislation submitted by the Commission or communications published by the Commission in the Official Journal may also

---

[139] *Amylum, op. cit.*, para 21.

[140] *Sofrimport v Commission, op. cit.*, n. 62 above, para 18; Joined Cases C-133, C-300 and C-362/93 *Crispoltoni II* [1994] ECR I-4863.

[141] See e.g. *Decker, op. cit.; IRCA, op. cit.*, Thus in *Campo Ebro, op. cit.*, n. 84 above, para 63, the CFI held that prudent and well-informed traders ought to have realised that the completion of the single market might lead to an early realignment of the intervention prices for Spanish sugar and thus lower prices for Spanish producers although the Council had previously extended the period for the alignment of prices initially provided by the Act of Accession.

[142] *Crispoltoni I, op. cit.*, n. 81 above.

[143] Case C-350/88 *Delacre and Others v Commission* [1990] ECR I-395, para 37. Case 78/77 *Lührs v Hauptzollamt Hamburg-Jonas* [1978] ECR 169, para 6; Case 265/85 *van den Bergh en Jurgen v Commission* [1987] ECR 1155, para 44.   [144] *Op. cit.*, n. 51 above.

[145] Joined Cases C-13–16/92 *Driessen* [1993] ECR I-4751.

be relevant.[146] The participation of the undertaking concerned in Community committees and even the size and 'substantial economic importance' of the undertaking may be relevant factors.[147] The framework of applicable rules seen in historical perspective may alert traders to impeding changes.[148] Another consideration to be taken into account is whether the transaction in issue falls within an area where changes in the law occur frequently.[149] Thus, in areas of market regulation where constant adjustments are needed to reflect changes in the economic situation, and where the regime has already been amended many times, foreseeability is disincarnated from any subjective element. A legitimate expectation is precluded from arising because a prudent and circumspect trader ought to have foreseen the possibility of changes.[150] In order for legitimate expectations to be honoured it is not necessary that a discerning trader must be able to predict every detail of the new rules.[151] It is sufficient that the likely possibility of a change in the law is foreseeable. Even where retroactive effect cannot be said to be foreseeable, a trader cannot have a legitimate expectation to derive a benefit which runs counter to the objectives of the legislation applicable at the time when he entered into the material act or transaction.[152]

6.3.9. Immediate application of the law

A distinction is sometimes drawn between retroactivity and immediate application of the law.[153] The first occurs where a rule applies to acts or transactions already completed at the time of its adoption. The second occurs where a rule applies to an act or transaction in progress.[154] It seems that the immediate application of the law is subject to less stringent rules than those applicable to true retroactivity. However, no hard and fast rules can be drawn. Sometimes, it may be difficult to establish whether there is immediate application or true retroactivity and the Court does not necessarily distinguish between the two. In any event, the case law makes it clear that any legitimate expectation of those affected must be protected also in case of immediate application.[155] Lamoureux argues that it is not a

---

[146] See e.g. *Netherlands v Council op. cit.*, n. 80 above, para 156; *Staple Dairy Products, op. cit.*, n. 113 above, para 15; *Driessen, op. cit.* Case C-22/94 *Irish Farmers Association and Others v Ministry for Agriculture, Food and Forestry, Ireland, and the Attorney General* [1997] ECR I-1809, para 23.

[147] See the *ECSC Steel Aid* cases: Case T-243/94 *British Steel v Commission* [1997] ECR II-1887, para 78.; Case T-244/94 *Wirtschaftsvereiningung Stahl and Others v Commission* [1997] ECR II-1963, para 60.   [148] *Staple Dairy Products, op. cit.*,

[149] Case T-489/93 *Unifruit Hellas v Commission* [1994] ECR II-1201.

[150] *Dilexport, op. cit.*, n. 89 above, paras 70–71 (quotas for the importation of bananas).

[151] *Driessen, op. cit., per* Jacobs AG, p. 4775.

[152] See e.g. *SAFA, op. cit.*, n. 91 above; *Moskof, op. cit.*, n. 87 above.

[153] See e.g. *Rewe-Zentrale v Hauptzollamt Emmerich, op. cit.*, n. 92 above, at 45 *per* de Lamothe AG; Case 1/73 *Westzucker v Einfuhr- und Vorratsstelle für Zucker* [1973] ECR 723 at 739 *per* Roemer AG. See also Case 74/74 *CNTA v Commission* [1975] ECR 533, paras 32–33.

[154] Immediate application is also referred to as 'material' or 'quasi-retroactivity'.

[155] *Driessen, op. cit.* at 4773 *per* Jacobs AG.

specific condition of validity that immediate application must be justified by overriding considerations.[156] The case law seems to suggest that, in general, an overriding consideration must exist although the Community judicature does not always search for such a justification. In *Campo Ebro and Others v Council*, the CFI held that there is a breach of legitimate expectations in the sphere of economic law where 'in the absence of an overriding matter of public interest, a Community institution abolishes with immediate effect and without warning a specific advantage, worthy of protection, for the undertaking concerned without adopting appropriate transitional measures'.[157] In reality, in determining whether legitimate expectations have been infringed, the Court performs a balancing exercise part of which is an assessment of the importance of the objectives which immediate application seeks to achieve. The existence of legitimate expectations however may be more difficult to establish in the case of immediate application than in the case of true retroactivity.

The majority of cases concerning immediate application have arisen in the sphere of agricultural law.[158] In *Westzucker*,[159] a change in the law took place after export licences had been issued but before the actual exports had taken place as a result of which exporters could no longer benefit from an increase in the intervention price. The Court held that, according to a generally accepted principle, the laws amending a legislative provision apply in principle to the future effects of situations which arose under the former law. It added that the former law did not confer on the persons concerned the certainty of profiting from an increase in the intervention price.[160] In *Tomadini*,[161] the issue was whether a regulation introducing monetary compensatory amounts was applicable to exports made pursuant to contracts concluded before its adoption. It was argued that the failure to provide for transitional measures ran counter to the principle of protection of legitimate expectations. The Court held that this principle cannot be extended to the point of generally preventing new rules from applying to the future effects of situations which arose under earlier rules. It added that the position is different where the Community institutions have laid down specific rules enabling traders to protect themselves with regard to transactions definitely undertaken from the effects of the frequent variations in the detailed agricultural measures in return for entering into specific obligations with the public authorities. Such rules cannot be amended without laying down transitional arrangements unless the adoption of transitional measures is contrary to an overriding public interest.[162] In *Delacre*[163] the applicants were manufacturers of pastry products who applied to receive aid for butter in

---

[156] F. Lamoureux, 'The Retroactivity of Community Acts in the Case Law of the Court of Justice', (1983) 20 CML Rev 269, p. 290.   [157] *Op. cit.*, n. 84 above, para 52.
[158] See further R. Barents, *The Agricultural Law of the EC* (Kluwer, 1994), Ch. 16.
[159] *Westzucker, op. cit.*   [160] Cf Roemer AG, *ibid.*, p. 741.
[161] Case 84/78 *Tomadini* [1979] ECR 1801.
[162] *Ibid.*, para 20. The judgment in *Tomadini* has been followed in subsequent cases. See e.g. Case 278/84 *Germany v Commission* [1987] ECR 1, paras 35 *et seq.*; Case 203/86 *Spain v Council* [1988] ECR 4563.   [163] *Delacre, op. cit.*, n. 143 above.

response to an invitation to tender. Their application was rejected on the ground that the amount of aid for which they applied was higher than the maximum amount of aid fixed by the Commission after their application was submitted. The reason for reducing the maximum amount in comparison with previous invitations to tender was the fall in the Community butter stock, the disposal of which the aid system was designed to achieve. The Court held that the adjustment of the amount of aid to the state of the market was inherent in the system set up to promote the disposal of surplus butter. The applicants could not claim a vested right to the maintenance of advantages which they had derived over a certain period from that system. The Court also held that the applicants, as prudent and well-informed traders, ought to have foreseen the progressive increase in the selling price of butter and the concomitant reduction of the amount of aid, which was the inevitable consequence of a fall in stock levels.

The theme underlying the above case law is that, in agricultural law, the possibility of changes in the rules governing pending transactions forms an integral part of the commercial risks to which economic operators are subject. They may not therefore have a legitimate expectation that a given system of market regulation will be maintained in force. Since changes in the applicable rules fall within the sphere of ordinary commercial risk, the issue of foreseeability becomes less important and it may not be necessary to examine whether the change in the law could have been foreseen in the specific circumstances of the case.[164]

An interesting example of immediate application is provided by *Driessen*.[165] A regulation aimed at reducing the structural overcapacity in the fleets operating in the Community inland waterways introduced a premium for scrapping existing vessels. It also provided that a new vessel could be brought into service only if the owner scrapped a tonnage equivalent to the new vessel. The applicants had entered into shipbuilding contracts before the regulation came into force. They claimed that they concluded the shipbuilding contracts after the Commission had published a proposal for a regulation and that on the basis of that proposal they expected to be able to bring new vessels into service without being subject to conditions which made the exploitation of the new vessels uneconomic. The Court rejected their claim on two grounds. It held that a legitimate expectation could not be founded on a Commission proposal. It also held that the applicants ought to have known that the provisions of the proposal were not perceived as adequate to reduce overcapacity, given the view taken by the professional associations concerned and articles published in specialized professional press.

A different outcome was reached in *Bock*[166] where the Commission, acting under Article 134, authorized Germany to prohibit the importation of Chinese mushrooms, including those in respect of which applications for import licences were pending at the time of the authorization. The Court held that the authorization

---

[164] See e.g. *Tomadini, op. cit.*, where the Court did not examine the issue of foreseeability.
[165] *Op. cit.*, n. 145 above.   [166] Case 62/70 *Bock v Commission* [1971] ECR 897.

was invalid insofar as it extended to such products. They represented an insignificant percentage of the annual quantity of mushrooms imported into Germany and therefore their importation would not affect the effectiveness of the protective measure. The Commission had therefore exceeded what was necessary within the meaning of Article 134. The immediate application of the law, and *a fortiori* its retroactive application, may only be permitted to the extent that it is necessary.[167]

6.3.10. Maintenance of existing advantages and benefits

It is clear that producers and traders have no vested right that the existing common organization of the market or the current regulatory system will be maintained unchanged. It could hardly be otherwise since the Community institutions must be able to respond to changes in the underlying economic situations. According to the established case law, traders cannot have a legitimate expectation that an existing situation which is capable of being altered by the Community institutions in the exercise of their discretionary power will be maintained. That is particularly so in an area such as the common organization of the markets whose purpose involves constant adjustments to meet changes in the economic situation. Traders therefore cannot claim a vested right to the maintenance of an advantage which they derive from the establishment of the common organization of the markets and which they enjoyed at a given time.[168] In *Eridania*[169] the applicants challenged the validity of a Council regulation which reduced their production quota for sugar. They claimed that undertakings had the right to produce the quantities of sugar corresponding to the basic quotas granted to them by Community legislation and that this right was inherent in the carrying on of economic activity. In rejecting the challenge, the Court pointed out that the basic quotas laid down by Community rules aimed at protecting and assisting the production of sugar in the Community. An essential feature of the common organization of the market in sugar was that,[170]

it is variable in terms of the economic factors which affect the development of the market and in terms of the general direction of the common agricultural policy. It follows that an undertaking cannot claim a vested right to the maintenance of an advantage which it obtained from the establishment of the common organization of the market and which it enjoyed at a given time.

---

[167] See the Opinion of Dutheillet de Lamothe AG [1971] ECR 897 at 915–6.

[168] See Case T-113/96 *Dubois et Fils v Council and Commission* [1998] ECR II-125, para 66; *Delacre, op. cit.*, n. 143 above, paras 34–35; Case 245/81 *Edeka v Germany* [1982] ECR 2745, para 27; *Tomadini, op. cit.*, n. 163 above, para 22; Case 230/78 *Eridania v Minister of Agriculture and Forestry* [1979] ECR 2749; Case 52/81 *Offene Handelsgesellschaft in Firma Werner Faust v Commission* [1982] ECR 3745; Joined Cases 424 and 425/85 *Frico* [1987] ECR 2755; Case 112/80 *Firma Anton Dürbeck v Hauptzollamt Frankfurt am Main/Flughafen* [1981] ECR 1095; Joined Cases 133 to 136/85 *Walter Rau Lebensmittelwerke v Bundesanstalt für Landwirtschaftliche Marktordnung* [1987] ECR 2289.   [169] *Eridania, op. cit.*

[170] *Ibid.*, paras 21–22.

In subsequent cases the Court has confirmed that where a quota system is in force, the Commission is under no obligation to consult or notify the traders concerned before changing for the future the criteria of eligibility for the allocation of a quota.[171] In *Crispoltoni II*,[172] it was argued that the introduction of maximum guaranteed quantities in relation to the production of tobacco, excess of which would result in a reduction in subsidies, frustrated the legitimate expectations of producers. The Court held that producers could not claim a vested right to the maintenance of a certain market system. A possible reduction in their earnings could not be contrary to the principle of legitimate expectations. The contested regulation respected that principle since the maximum guaranteed quantities were known in advance. Similar considerations apply to the bananas regime. The Commission may change the criteria on the basis of which quotas for the importation of bananas are allocated to producers. The fact that the new criteria result in the exclusion of some producers from quotas or in the reduction of their quota is not a breach of the principle of legitimate expectations since there can be no legitimate expectation that an existing regulatory regime will be maintained.[173]

A similar approach has been taken by the Court in the external trade of the Community. A trader has no legitimate expectation that an established pattern of trade with a non-member country will be maintained. In *Edeka*[174] and *Faust*[175] importers challenged the imposition by the Commission of protective measures which virtually prohibited the importation of mushrooms from Taiwan. The protective measures were the result of a reorientation in the Community's trade policy which favoured trade with China. In rejecting the applicants' claim that their legitimate expectations had been breached, the Court emphasized the wide margin of discretion enjoyed by the Community institutions:[176]

In the present case, there can be no question of a breach of the principle of the protection of legitimate expectation, particularly since the commercial agreement entered into on 3 April 1978 between the Community and the People's Republic of China ... was of such a nature as to alert traders to an imminent change of direction in the Community's commercial policy and, in the absence of an obligation on the part of the Community to accord equal treatment to non-member countries, no informed trader was entitled to expect that patterns of trade existing when the protective measures were adopted would be respected.

The protective measures in issue in those cases were exceptional in that a total prohibition of imports from Taiwan was imposed within an unusually short period.[177] Yet it is difficult to see how, in the absence of retroactivity, the claim of

---

[171] *Accrington Beef, op. cit.*, n. 51 above.

[172] *Op. cit.*, n. 140 above, para 61. See also Case C-280/93 *Germany v Council (Bananas case)* [1994] ECR I-4973.

[173] *Dilexport, op. cit.*, n. 89 above; Case C-104/97 P *Atlanta v European Community* [1999] ECR I-6983.   [174] *Op. cit.*, n. 168 above.

[175] *Op. cit.*, n. 168 above.   [176] *Faust, op. cit.*, para 27; *Edeka, op. cit.*, para 27.

[177] The agreement with China was entered into on 3 April 1978 and was published in the Official Journal on 11 May 1978. The protective measures against Taiwan came into effect in late May and June 1978.

the applicants could have succeeded.[178] Although the existence of a commercial agreement may be sufficient to impute to traders knowledge that a change of direction in the Community's trade policy is imminent, the existence of an international agreement does not necessarily establish a legitimate expectation that the Community will not take unilateral measures. In *Unifruit Hellas v Commission*,[179] it was argued that the conclusion of a Framework Cooperation Agreement established a climate of confidence between the Community and Chile such as to preclude the introduction of a countervailing charge on imports from Chile. The Court held however that the agreement did not intend to amend the provisions of a previous Council Regulation on the basis of which countervailing charges were adopted after the conclusion of the Agreement.

6.3.11. The presumption against retroactivity

The principle of non-retroactivity is not only a rule of substantive law but also a rule of interpretation according to which, in the absence of a clear indication to the contrary, a Community measure is presumed not to be retroactive.[180] In *Salumi*[181] the Court held that rules of substantive law, as opposed to rules of procedure, apply to situations existing before their entry into force only if that clearly follows from their terms, objectives, or general scheme.[182] Thus, in one case[183] where a regulation was published in the issue of the Official Journal dated 1 July 1976 and expressly stated that it would come into force on 1 July but because of a strike the issue appeared on 2 July, the Court interpreted the regulation as not being in force until the date of its actual publication.

[178] See further on protective measures, *Anton Dürbeck, op. cit.*, n. 168 above; see also *Sofrimport, op. cit.*, n. 62 above and *Unifruit Hellas, op. cit.*, n. 149 above.

[179] Case C-51/95 [1997] ECR I-727. CFI, Case T-489/93 [1994] ECR II-1201.

[180] *Staple Dairy Products, op. cit.*, n. 113 above at 1783 *per* Slynn AG. See also *IRCA, op. cit., per* Warner AG at pp. 1237–1239 for a comparative analysis of the laws of Member States.

[181] *Salumi, op. cit.*, n. 3 above, para 9. For recent confirmations, see Case C-61/98 *de Haan v Inspecteur der Invoerrechten en Accijnzen te Rotterdam* [1999] ECR I-5003, para 22; Case C-251/00 *Ilumitronica* [2002] ECR I-10433, para 29; Case C-28/00 *Kauer* [2002] ECR I-1343, para 20.

[182] Procedural rules, by contrast, are presumed to apply to all pending situations: see e.g. for a recent confirmation: Joined Cases C-361 and C-362/02 *Elliniko Dimosio v Tsapalos*, judgment of 1 July 2004. A good illustration is provided by Case T-366/00 *Scott SA v Commission*, judgment of 10 April 2003, where the CFI held that Regulation No 659/1999 (OJ 1999 L 83/1), which establishes the procedural rules applicable in state aid, applies to all administrative procedures pending before the Commission at the time of its entry into force. The Regulation provides that the Commission's power to recover state aid is subject to a limitation period of 10 years which begins to run on the day on which the unlawful aid is awarded. The CFI held that the limitation period applied to aid granted by France in August 1987 and therefore the initiation of the procedure by the Commission in January 1997 had the effect of interrupting the limitation period and enabled the Commission validly to order the recovery of unlawful aid. Note however that, prior to Regulation No 659/1999, Community law did not provide for any specific limitation period so the undertaking concerned could not derive any legitimate expectation that any such period would apply. Cf Case T-308/00 *Salzgitter AG v Germany*, judgment of 1 July 2004.

[183] Case 88/76 *Société pour l'exportation des sucres SA v Commission* [1977] ECR 709. See also above, n. 182 and accompanying text.

The presumption against retroactivity does not apply to immediate application. By contrast, the presumption is reversed and lies with immediate application so that a legislative provision applies in principle to the future effects of situations which arose in the past.[184] Where respect for legitimate expectations so requires, however, a measure may be interpreted as not having immediate application. In *Deuka*[185] two successive Commission regulations reduced and abolished respectively a denaturing premium payable to producers with a view to maintaining stability in the market in cereals. On grounds of legal certainty, the Court interpreted the regulations as not applying to denaturing operations irrevocably undertaken before the regulations came into force even if the actual denaturing was not to take place until after that date. The judgment is particularly laconic as to why in the circumstances legal certainty required the protection of pending transactions. It is notable that the Advocate General took the opposite view submitting persuasive arguments.

The same principles apply in relation to primary law. Provisions of primary Community law which grant rights or benefits to individuals are, in general, immediately applicable from the time of their entry into force. This applies, for example, to the provisions of the TEU. A national of a Member State may derive rights from the provisions on the citizenship of the Union as soon as they enter into force.[186] It applies also to international agreements.[187] Further, in accordance with a standard clause in the Treaties of Accession, provisions of the EC Treaty are immediately applicable from the date of accession and capable of applying to the present effects of situations which arose prior to accession.[188] In *Duchon*,[189] it was held that the situation of a national of a Member State who, before the accession of that State to the EU, was employed in another Member State where he was the victim of an accident at work and who, after the accession of his home State, applied to its authorities for an incapacity pension, falls within the scope of Regulation 1408/71. Note however that Community law rights cannot be acquired before accession and therefore cannot be recognized after accession when the conditions for their acquisition are no longer in place.[190]

In general, the case law concerning retroactivity and immediate application does not offer the consistency one may have wished for although that seems to be due

---

[184] See *Westzucker, op. cit; Tomadini, op. cit.*; for recent confirmation, see Case C-290/00 *Duchon* [2002] ECR I-3567, para 21; Case C-162/00 *Porkzeptowicz-Meyer* [2002] ECR I-1049, paras 49–50.   [185] *Op. cit.*, n.94 above.
[186] Case C-224/98 *D'Hoop* [2002] ECR I-6191, para 25.
[187] *Porkzeptowicz-Meyer, op. cit.*, paras 49–50: the prohibition of discrimination on grounds of nationality in favour of Polish citizens provided for in the Europe Agreement with Poland applies to a fixed-term contract of employment which was concluded before the entry into force of the Agreement for a term expiring after that date.
[188] See e.g. *Duchon, op. cit.*, para 21; Case C-195/98 *Österreichischer Gewerkschaftsbund* [2000] ECR I-10497, para 55; Case C-122/96 *Saldanha and MTS* [1997] ECR I-5325, para 14; see further Case C-464/98 *Stefan* [2001] ECR I-173, para 21; Case C-35/98 *Verkooijen* [2000] ECR I-4071, para 42.   [189] *Op. cit.*
[190] see Case C-443/93 *Vougioukas* [1995] ECR I-4033; Case C-131/96 *Mora Romero* [1997] ECR I-3659 and *Duchon, op. cit. per* Jacobs AG at 3584.

largely to the distinct nature of agricultural policy measures which require frequent regulatory interventions to meet the demands of changing markets.

6.4. Legitimate expectations arising from legislation

6.4.1. Protection of specific interests

A legitimate expectation may be founded on previous[191] legislation where the legislation directs a Community institution to take into account a specific, well defined, interest. In *Sofrimport v Commission*,[192] by two regulations adopted on 12 and 14 April 1988 respectively the Commission suspended, as a protective measure, the import of dessert apples originating in Chile. On 31 March, Sofrimport had shipped a cargo of apples from Chile for import into the Community. While the goods were still in transit, it lodged an application for import licences which was refused by the French authorities pursuant to the regulations. Article 3(3) of Council Regulation No 2702/72[193] required the Commission, in adopting protective measures, to take into account the 'special position of products in transit to the Community'. The Court held that Article 3(3) enabled an importer whose goods were in transit to rely on a legitimate expectation that no suspensory measures would be applied against him unless an overriding public interest required otherwise. The Commission argued that a reasonably careful trader should have envisaged the possibility that measures might be taken because in a previous regulation it had expressly reserved the power to do so. The Court held that simply informing traders of the possibility that protective measures might be taken was not sufficient. In order to meet the requirement of 'special protection', the Commission ought to have indicated the situations in which the public interest might justify the application of protective measures with regard to goods in transit. The Court added that the Commission had not demonstrated the existence of any overriding public interest.

Subsequently, in *Unifruit Hellas v Commission*[194] the CFI, and on appeal the Court of Justice, took a restrictive view of *Sofrimport* and refused to extend Article 3(3) of Regulation 2702/72 so as to protect goods in transit from the imposition of countervailing charges. The Court of Justice distinguished between countervailing charges and protective measures on the ground that the purpose of the first is to protect the level of Community prices whilst the second seek essentially to suspend imports where the Community market is threatened by serious disturbances. It stated that the effect of Article 3(3) is to allow traders to rely on a legitimate expectation that

---

[191] Clearly, a legitimate expectation may only be derived from an act or omission prior to the measure which is alleged to have infringed it: Joined Cases T-466, T-469 etc 193 *O'Dwyer and Others v Council* [1995] ECR II-2071, para 57.   [192] *Op. cit.*, n. 62 above.

[193] Council Regulation (EEC) No 2707/72 of 19 December 1972 laying down the conditions for applying protective measures for fruit and vegetables, OJ English Special Ed, 1972 (28 to 30 December), p. 3.   [194] *Op. cit.*, n. 179 above.

products already in transit will not be refused entry on arrival in the Community. It does not necessarily require the Commission to exempt goods in transit from other protective measures, such as countervailing charges, since such charges affect traders less severely. The Court added that, in any event, the system seeking to maintain the level of Community prices would be rendered completely ineffective if goods in transit were exempted from the levying of the countervailing charge in issue.[195]

Where legislation does not require specific interests to be taken into account it is very difficult for a legitimate expectation to arise. The starting point of any judicial analysis has to be that the legislature enjoys ample discretion. In *Campo Ebro*[196] the Act of Accession of Spain and Portugal of 1985 provided that, where the price of an agricultural product in Spain at the time of accession was higher than the Community intervention price, the price in Spain was to be frozen and that alignment of prices was to be achieved during the seven years following accession. In 1991 the Council decided to prolong the period of alignment of sugar prices and carry it out in two stages, the second stage being completed in the 1995/1996 marketing year. Subsequently, however, by Regulation No 3814/92, the Council provided for full alignment of prices from 1 January 1993. The CFI held that no legitimate expectation arose from the 1991 legislation. The decision to discontinue the alignment period was a legitimate choice of economic policy. Prudent and well-informed traders ought to have realised that the achievement of the single market might lead to an early realignment of the intervention prices.

A legitimate expectation may not arise out of proposed legislation. If it were otherwise, the discretion of the Commission to amend the proposal and the powers of the other institutions in the decision-making process would be prejudiced.[197] Also, an expectation will not be protected unless it is reasonable.[198] A person may not rely on the principle to derive a speculative benefit which the legislation was not intended to confer.[199]

An expectation however may arise from the Community's declared intention to abide by a rule of international law. The leading case is *Opel Austria v Council*.[200] The dispute arose from the legal regime governing the relations between the Community and Austria before the latter acceded to the Community. An Austrian company challenged a Council Regulation which withdrew tariff concessions granted to Austria under the Free Trade Agreement between Austria and the EC and reintroduced import duties on products manufactured by the applicant imported to the Community. The reason for the imposition of the import duty was that Austria had granted state subsidies to the applicant. The Regulation was adopted on 20 December 1993 seven days after the Council and the Commission approved the EEA Agreement and shortly before that Agreement was due to come into force. The

---

[195] Case C-51/95 P, *Unifruit Hellas*, para 27.   [196] *Op. cit.*, n. 84 above.
[197] *Driessen, op. cit.*, n. 145 above, para 33 and *per* Jacobs AG, p. 4774.
[198] Hartley, *op. cit.*, p. 149.
[199] See e.g. Case 2/75 *EVGF v Mackprang* [1975] ECR 607.
[200] *Op. cit.*, n. 23 above.

applicant company argued that the import duty was contrary to Article 10 of the EEA Agreement which prohibits import duties and measures having equivalent effect. The Court held that the legality of the Regulation must be assessed on the basis of law as it stood at the time when it was adopted, i.e. before the EEA came into force. It held however that, where the Community has deposited the instruments of approval of an international agreement and the date of entry into force of that agreement is known, traders may rely on the principle of protection of legitimate expectations in order to challenge the adoption by the institutions, during the period preceding the entry into force of that agreement, of any measure contrary to the provisions of that agreement which will have direct effect after it has entered into force. The Court saw the principle of good faith, as a rule of customary international law under which, pending the entry into force of an international agreement, the signatories may not introduce measures which will defeat its object and purpose, as a corollary of the principle of protection of legitimate expectations. The CFI annulled the Regulation on three grounds: first, because by adopting it, the Council infringed the legitimate expectations of the applicants; second, because by adopting it, the Council created a situation where two contradictory rules were in force, namely the Regulation and Article of the EEA Agreement; and third, because by deliberately backdating the issue of the Official Journal in which the Regulation was published, the Council committed a further breach of the principle of legal certainty.

No legitimate expectation however may arise from recommendations or rulings of the WTO Dispute Settlement Body.[201]

6.4.2. Milk quotas

Perhaps the best illustration of the application of the principle of protection of legitimate expectations is provided by the milk quota cases. With a view to limiting surplus production in milk, Council Regulation No 1078/77[202] offered to producers incentives to leave the market temporarily. A non-marketing premium was granted to producers who undertook not to market milk for a period of five years. A conversion premium was granted to producers who undertook to convert their dairy herds to meat production for a period of four years. It soon became clear that these measures were not sufficient and, in a further attempt to curb milk production, Council Regulation No 856/84[203] introduced an additional levy payable on quantities of milk delivered beyond a guaranteed threshold, known as reference quantity (quota). The procedure for calculating the quota was provided for in Council Regulation No 857/84.[204] According to this Regulation, the Member States could provide for the quota to be calculated on the basis of the quantity of milk delivered by the producer during 1981, 1982 or 1983. Regulation No 857/84 did not provide for the allocation of a quota to returning producers, namely those

---

[201] Case T-19/01 *Chiquita Brands International Inc v Commission*, judgment of 3 February 2005, para 256.   [202] OJ 1977, L 131, p. 1.
[203] OJ 1984, L 90, p. 10.   [204] OJ 1984, L 90, p. 13.

who pursuant to a non-marketing or conversion undertaking did not deliver milk during the reference year adopted by the Member State concerned and who, upon the termination of their undertaking, were willing to restart milk production. In *Mulder v Minister van Landbouw en Visserij (Mulder I)*[205] the Court held that Regulation No 857/84 was invalid insofar as it did not provide for the allocation of a reference quantity to returning producers on the ground that it infringed their legitimate expectations. The Court stated that a producer who has voluntarily ceased production for a certain period cannot legitimately expect to be able to resume production under the same conditions as those which applied previously. Nor can he expect not to be subject to any rules of market or structural policy adopted in the meantime.[206] However, it continued:[207]

The fact remains that where such a producer, as in the present case, has been encouraged by a Community measure to suspend marketing for a limited period in the general interest and against payment of a premium he may legitimately expect not to be subject, upon the expiry of his undertaking, to restrictions which specifically affect him precisely because he availed himself of the possibilities offered by the Community provisions . . .

Contrary to the Commission's contention, total and continuous exclusion of that kind for the entire period of application of the regulations on the additional levy, preventing the producers concerned from resuming the marketing of milk at the end of the five-year period, was not an occurrence which those producers could have foreseen when they entered into an undertaking, for a limited period, not to deliver milk. There is nothing in the provisions of Regulation No 1078/77 or in its preamble to show that the non-marketing undertaking entered into under that regulation might, upon its expiry, entail a bar to resumption of the activity in question. Such an effect therefore frustrates those producers' legitimate expectation that the effects of the system to which they had rendered themselves subject would be limited.

The reason, therefore, why the Court annulled the contested regulation was that returning producers had a legitimate expectation not to be excluded permanently from the market. They had agreed to suspend rather than to terminate production. As Slynn AG put it, to substitute a quota system for a non-marketing undertaking 'crosses the line between what is merely "hard luck" and what is unreasonable treatment'.[208]

In order to comply with the judgment in *Mulder I*, the Council provided for the allocation of a quota to returning producers. Article 3a, inserted into Regulation No 857/84 by Regulation No 764/89,[209] provided essentially that returning producers who, pursuant to their undertaking, had not delivered milk during the reference year adopted by the Member State concerned, were to receive a special reference quantity equal to 60 per cent of their milk production during the 12 months preceding the month in which the application for the non-marketing or

---

[205] *Op. cit.*, n. 3 above. See also Case 170/86 *von Deetzen v Hauptzollamt Hamburg-Jonas* [1988] ECR 2355.   [206] *Mulder I*, para 23; *von Deetzen*, para 12.
[207] *Mulder I*, paras 24, 26; *von Deetzen*, paras 13, 15.   [208] *Mulder I*, p. 2341.
[209] OJ 1989 L 84, p. 2.

conversion premium was made. Article 3a was also found to infringe the principle of protection of legitimate expectations. In *Spagl*[210] the Court held that, in calculating the quota to be allocated to returning producers, the Community legislature was entitled to apply a reduction coefficient designed to ensure that returning producers were not accorded an undue advantage by comparison with continuing producers.[211] However, it added:[212]

the principle of the protection of legitimate expectations precludes the rate of reduction from being fixed at such a high level, by comparison with those applicable to [continuing producers], that its application amounts to a restriction which specifically affects them by very reason of the undertaking given by them under Regulation No 1078/77.

The Court held that the reduction of 40 per cent specifically affected returning producers by reason of their undertaking since it was much higher than the rates of reduction applicable to continuing producers which did not exceed 17.5 per cent.

In *Spagl*, the Court saw legitimate expectations as a principle of participation, namely, as requiring proportionate allocation of burdens and benefits among comparable groups of producers.[213] In their attempt to justify the 60 per cent rule, the Council and the Commission argued that the allocation to returning producers of a quota based on more than 60 per cent of their production would entail an increase in the Community's overall quantities and would thus undermine the objective of the additional levy scheme which was to reduce structural surpluses. In response, the Court stated:[214]

Even if an increase larger than the Community reserve could not be contemplated without the risk of disturbing the balance of the milk market, the fact remains that it would have been sufficient to reduce the reference quantities of the other producers proportionately by a corresponding amount, so as to be able to allocate larger reference quantities to the producers who gave an undertaking under Regulation No 1078/77.

The link between legitimate expectations and equal treatment is even more evident in the Opinion of Jacobs AG who reached a different conclusion. The Advocate General took the view that returning producers had no expectation to resume full production. Rather they had an expectation not to be treated less favourably than continuing producers. He considered that there was a difference in treatment but that it was objectively justified on the following grounds:[215]

- continuing producers were dependent for their livelihood on continuing production, whereas returning producers had been able to make use of their farms for other reasons;

---

[210] Case C-189/89 [1990] ECR I-4539.
[211] Continuing producers were not entitled to 100 per cent of their production in the reference year but were subject to deductions imposed by the Community and to variable deductions imposed by Member States under Article 2(1) of Regulation No 857/84.
[212] *Spagl*, para 22; see also Case C-217/89 *Pastatter* [1990] ECR I-4585, para 13.
[213] This is also evident from the later judgment in *Duff*, *op. cit.*, n. 21 above.
[214] *Spagl*, para 28; *Pastatter*, para 19.   [215] *Spagl*, pp. 4568–9.

- no exact comparison was possible between continuing and returning producers because the base figures on which their quotas were to be calculated were by their nature different;
- continuing producers would be adversely affected by any reduction in their existing production levels; that was not necessarily true of returning producers since they were returning to production from a nil base;
- unlike continuing producers who were a relatively homogeneous group, returning producers were not in a comparable position among themselves. Assessed by reference to all diverse cases, the 60 per cent rule was not discriminatory.

It will be noted that, in view of the nature of the scheme and the Community's initial error, no solution would be wholly satisfactory. Both the Court and the Advocate General sought a fair solution attempting to remedy the most obvious shortcomings of a fundamentally flawed system.[216] The cases illustrate the Court's general approach in the field of the common agricultural policy: the case law can be seen as a search for fairness in declining markets, inspired primarily by considerations of participation, namely the fair allocation of burdens among different groups of producers.

In *Mulder I* and *Spagl* the Court held that returning producers had a legitimate expectation as a class. The underlying rationale of the judgments is that those who repose faith on the authorities must not suffer as a result. This is the material criterion which distinguishes them from other cases where the Court refused to intervene to remedy hardship suffered by individual milk producers. In *Dowling*,[217] a returning producer was unable to resume milk production after the expiry of his non-marketing undertaking owing to ill health and made no deliveries during 1983, the year adopted as reference year by the Member State where he was established. The Court held that he had no legitimate expectation to receive a reference quantity as his failure to produce was unconnected with his undertaking. The applicant also argued that he was discriminated against *vis-à-vis* continuing producers on the following ground. Continuing producers whose milk production during the reference year chosen by the Member State concerned had been affected by exceptional events, such as occupational incapacity, had the right to obtain a reference quantity on the basis of their production in another year within the 1981 to 1983 period. He was unable to do so since, as a result of his undertaking, he had produced no milk in 1981 and 1982. He claimed therefore that he should obtain a reference quantity by reference to his production in another year. The Court held that the Community rules did not allow account to be taken of a reference year outside the period 1981 to 1983. The resulting difference in

---

[216] In order to comply with the judgment in *Spagl*, the Council adopted Regulation No 1639/91 which provided for a new method for the calculation of reference quantities to returning producers. That method of calculation was also challenged but this time the challenge was unsuccessful: C-21/92 *Kamp* [1994] ECR I-1619.　　　[217] C-85/90 [1992] ECR I-5305.

treatment between continuing and returning producers was objectively justified by the need to limit the number of years which may be taken as reference years in the interests of legal certainty and of the effectiveness of the additional levy system.

Clearly, the principle of legitimate expectations may not be relied upon to derive an advantage which the relevant legislation was not intended to grant. In *von Deetzen II*[218] the Court held that the legitimate expectations of returning producers were not frustrated by a Community provision which provided that if they sold or leased their holding the special quota allocated to them would be returned to the Community reserve and would not be passed on to the transferee. The Court's rationale was that special reference quantities had been allocated to returning producers in order to enable them to resume their occupational activity and not to derive a profit by realising the market value of the quota.

Overall, the cases on milk quotas indicate that the principle of protection of legitimate expectations imposes more severe restraints on the discretion of Community institutions than the principle of equal treatment, and a trader who is able to establish that somehow he has a legitimate expectation is more likely to succeed in his claim.[219]

Following *Mulder I* and *Spagl* the Community institutions were faced with claims for compensation. In *Mulder II*,[220] returning producers brought actions under Article 288(2) EC with a view to recovering the loss which they had allegedly suffered as a result of the regulations which were annulled in *Mulder I* and *Spagl*. The Court recalled its established case law according to which in areas where the Community institutions enjoy wide discretion, the Community does not incur liability unless the institution concerned has manifestly and gravely disregarded the limits on the exercise of its powers. It then made a distinction. It found that the conditions of liability were met in relation to Regulation No 857/87, which totally excluded returning producers from the market, but that they were not met in relation to the 60 per cent rule. In relation to the total exclusion of returning producers, the Court held that the Community institutions failed completely to take into account their specific situation without invoking any higher public interest. It pointed out that returning producers constituted a clearly defined group of economic operators. Their total and permanent exclusion from the allocation of a quota could not be regarded as falling within the bounds of the normal economic risks inherent in the activities of a milk producer. The Community was therefore bound to make good the damage suffered by the applicants as a result of Regulation No 857/84. By contrast, the 60 per cent rule was not a sufficiently serious violation. It represented a choice of economic policy made by the institutions

---

[218] Case C-44/89 *von Deetzen* [1991] ECR I-5119, para 21.

[219] For other cases on milk quotas where claims based on breach of legitimate expectations were rejected see e.g. Case C-177/90 *Kühn v Landwirtschaftskammer Weser-Ems* [1992] ECR I-35; *Duff, op. cit.*, n. 21 above; Case C-22/94 *Irish Farmers Association and Others v Minister for Agriculture, Food and Forestry, Ireland, and the Attorney General* [1997] ECR I-1809.

[220] Joined Cases C-104/89 and C-37/90 *Mulder v Council and Commission* [1992] ECR I-3061.

which sought to draw a balance between the interests of returning producers and the interests of continuing producers in the light of the objectives of the milk quota scheme. The institutions took account of a higher public interest without gravely and manifestly disregarding the limits of their discretionary powers.[221] The material difference seems to be that, in the first case, the Community legislature totally failed to take into account the interests of returning producers whereas, in the second case, those interests featured in the balancing exercise performed by the legislature. The definitive effects of the regulation annulled in *Mulder I* were also crucial. The Court pointed out that producers were totally and permanently excluded from the market.

With regard to the extent of compensation, the Court held in *Mulder II* that it should cover the loss of earnings consisting in the difference between, on the one hand, the income which the applicants would have obtained in the normal course of events from the milk deliveries which they would have made if they had obtained a quota during the material period and, on the other hand, the income which they actually obtained from milk deliveries made during the same period in the absence of a quota plus any income which they obtained, or could have obtained, from any replacement activities. The Court laid down detailed guidelines in order to calculate the quota to which the applicants would have been entitled so as to ensure, as much as possible, equal treatment between them and continuing producers.[222]

6.5. Legitimate expectations arising from conduct of the Community institutions

A legitimate expectation may arise from the conduct of the Community administration but only as a result of precise assurances given by the administration.[223] Thus where an official requests confirmation of an entitlement and the Commission fails to answer, a legitimate expectation may not be founded on the Commission's silence.[224] Even where the Commission confirms the existence of an

---

[221] *Ibid.*, paras 15–22.

[222] In a subsequent case it was held that the calculation of a hypothetical quota which a producer should have been granted in the past made by the Court in order to assess the quantum of damages is not binding on the Council where it calculates the quotas to be allocated to returning producers for the future. See Case C-21/92 *Kamp* [1994] ECR I-1619. Compensation was offered by Regulation No 2187/93, OJ 1993 L 196/6. The amount of compensation in *Mulder* was determined in *Mulder II, op. cit.* For claims for compensation brought by individual producers following *Mulder II*, see Case T-554/93 *Saint and Murray v Council and Commission* [1997] ECR II-563; Case T-541/93 *Connaughton and Others v Council* [1997] ECR II-549; Case T-20/94 *Hartmann v Council and Commission* [1997] ECR II-595. For consequential issues arising concerning limitation periods, see T-201/94 *Kustermann v Council and Commission*, [2002] ECR II-415.

[223] *Dubois et Fils, op. cit.*, n. 168 above, para 68; Case T-123/89 *Chomel v Commission* [1990] ECR II-131, para 26.   [224] *Ibid.*

entitlement, such an undertaking cannot give rise to a legitimate expectation, since no official of a Community institution can give a valid undertaking not to apply Community law.[225] For the same reason, promises which do not take account of the provisions of the Staff Regulations cannot give rise to legitimate expectations on the part of those concerned.[226] The Court has also consistently held that the communication of an incorrect interpretation of Community rules cannot give rise to liability on the part of the Community administration, although there is an obligation to correct incorrect information previously circulated.[227] The principle of legitimate expectations may not be relied upon by an undertaking which has committed a manifest error of the rules in force.[228]

In applying the principle, the Court understands its jurisdiction equitably. In *Mavridis v Parliament*[229] the applicant's candidature for a post in the Community civil service was rejected on the ground that he had passed the requisite age limit. The age requirement had not been included in the vacancy notice published in the Official Journal but was introduced subsequently by the selection committee. Rozès AG opined that refusal to accept candidatures on the basis of a condition which did not appear in the vacancy notice disregarded the candidates' legitimate expectation that the information laid down in the notice was complete. In the circumstances of the case, she took the view that it was not necessary to annul the recruitment procedure since, even if the Parliament were to commence a new procedure following the correct form, the applicant would still be excluded. The Court considered that the submission based on the breach of legitimate expectations was unfounded but its reasoning is far from clear. It pointed out that an infringement of legitimate expectations would not automatically lead to the annulment of the contested measure but it might justify the award of damages, if the person concerned had suffered injury as a result. The applicant in the case had not submitted a claim in damages so the issue did not arise. The case suggests that in certain circumstances, failure to disclose relevant information may infringe legitimate expectations.

An incorrect calculation of benefits by the Commission does not give rise to a legitimate expectation, at least not where the benefits are of a commercial nature and the Commission has discovered the error promptly. In *Töpfer v Commission*,[230] a sugar exporter received lower compensation than in previous exports as a result of changes in the method of calculation. The compensation was provided to alleviate

---

[225] Case 188/82 *Thyssen AG v Commission* [1983] ECR 3721, para 11.

[226] Case 162/84 *Vlachou v Court of Auditors* [1986] ECR 459, para 6.

[227] Joined Cases 19, 20, 25 and 30/69 *Richez-Parise and Others v Commission* [1970] ECR 325; Case 23/69 *Fiehn v Commission* [1970] ECR 547; Case 137/79 *Kohll v Commission* [1980] ECR 2601; Case C-255/90 P *Burban v Parliament* [1992] ECR I-2253, paras 10–12. Cf T-203/96 *Embassy Limousines & Services v Parliament* [1998] ECR II-4239, para 56.

[228] Case 67/84 *Sideradria SpA v Commission* [1985] ECR 3983; Case C-96/89 *Commission v Netherlands* [1991] ECR I-461, para 30.

[229] Case 289/81 *Mavridis v Parliament* [1983] ECR 1731.

[230] Case 112/77 [1978] ECR 1019.

the adverse consequences of alterations in the unit of account. The Court stated that in previous transactions the Commission had calculated the compensation on bases which were more favourable but went beyond the objectives of the relevant regulations. The applicant had no right to the continuance of the incorrect calculations. On the contrary, as soon as the inaccuracy of these calculations was discovered the Commission was under a duty to correct it in the financial interest of the Community and in order to 'prevent privileged positions from becoming established'.[231]

The principle of legitimate expectations has also been pleaded in the context of financial aid granted by the Community to undertakings to carry out various projects as provided by Community legislation. It is a strict condition that the beneficiary of the aid must observe the conditions on which the aid was granted. If it fails to do so, it cannot legitimately expect payment of the aid initially awarded.[232]

An interesting example in the area of the European Social Fund is provided by *Interhotel*.[233] According to the applicable Community rules, applications for financial assistance from the Fund are submitted to the Commission by Member States on behalf of undertakings. The approval of an application is followed by the payment of an advance. Once the project is completed, the Commission pays the balance after receiving a report by the undertaking detailing the results and financial aspects of the project. In *Interhotel*, the CFI held that the Commission may not consider as ineligible certain expenditure on the ground that it does not meet the conditions laid down in the decision approving the granting of assistance, where those conditions were not communicated to the undertaking concerned.

Interhotel puts the onus firmly on the Commission and evinces a strict application of the principle of legitimate expectations. Two points may be made in relation to the judgment. The first concerns its reasoning, the second the scope of its application.

The Commission's decision approving the assistance had been communicated to the undertaking, albeit not by the Commission itself but by the national competent authority. But the CFI took the view that such communication was not sufficient. It stated that where the Commission does not take the necessary precautions to satisfy itself that the beneficiary of assistance is informed of the conditions imposed by the decision of approval, it cannot reasonably expect it to observe those conditions. That reasoning may be questioned. Where, according to the applicable procedure, the national authorities act as intermediaries between the Commission and the individual, the Commission's duty is to notify duly the details of the decision approving assistance to the national authority. Provided that the Commission has done so, the individual's inability to ascertain the conditions specified in the decision cannot be attributed to the Commission but only to the national

---

[231] *Ibid.*, para 20.
[232] See e.g. Case T-331/94 *IPK v Commission* [1997] II-1665, para 46; Case C-181/90 *Consorgan v Commission* [1992] ECR I-3557, para 17.
[233] Case T-81/95 *Interhotel v Commission* [1997] ECR II-1265.

authority. *Interhotel* seems to accept that, in dealing with disbursements from the European Social Fund, the Commission is 'vicariously' responsible for the conduct of the national authorities. The CFI may have taken that view because otherwise it would be difficult for the undertaking concerned to obtain a remedy against the national authority.

Second, it is noteworthy that the applicant undertaking did not seek clarification from the Commission regarding the expenditure declared ineligible by the decision approving the assistance. It is submitted however that the judgment must be read on its facts. In other cases, failure to seek clarification from the public authority may prevent a legitimate expectation from arising.

Failure of the Commission to bring enforcement proceedings against a Member State under Article 226 EC promptly does not give rise to a legitimate expectation that proceedings will not be brought. The Commission is under no obligation to bring enforcement proceedings within a specified period.[234] It has discretion as to when to commence the pre-litigation procedure and also as to when to bring proceedings. In exceptional cases, the excessive duration of the pre-contentious procedure may make it more difficult for the defendant Member State to refute the Commission's arguments and might thus infringe the rights of defence but, in practice it would be difficult for such an argument to succeed. The defendant State will have to show in what way the unusual delay has prevented it from organising its defence. In *Commission v Netherlands* the Commission brought proceedings more than five years after its first letter to the Dutch Government but the Court held that this did not amount to abuse of discretion nor had it prejudiced the defence of the Dutch Government.[235]

The principle of protection of legitimate expectations binds the Community institutions also when they act in the context of a tendering procedure for the award of public procurement contracts. In *Embassy Limousines*[236] the European Parliament invited tenders for the supply of transport services to parliamentarians. After the completion of the tendering procedure, a Parliament official contacted the applicant company to inform it that the Parliament's Advisory Committee on Procurement and Contracts had delivered an opinion in favour of the authorizing officer's proposal to award the contract to the company. In view of the fact that the services had to be provided urgently and the applicant was a new company, it took steps to prepare entering into contracts for leasing vehicles and engaging drivers. Subsequently, the Parliament had doubts about the qualifications and experience of the applicant's drivers and, eventually, decided to annul the invitation to tender and reopen the tendering procedure. The CFI found a breach of the principle of protection of legitimate expectations. It held that, if before a public procurement contract is awarded, a tenderer is encouraged by the contracting institution to make

---

[234] Case 324/82 *Commission v Belgium* [1984] ECR 1861.
[235] *Commission v Netherlands, op. cit.*, n. 228 above, para 16; *Commission v Greece, op. cit.*, n. 32 above, para 39; Case C-207/97 *Commission v Belgium* [1999] ECR I-275. For proceedings to recover state aid, see 6.9 below.   [236] *Op. cit.*, n. 227 above, para 56.

irreversible investments in advance and thereby go beyond the risks inherent in making a bid, non-contractual liability may ensue. In this case, the establishment of a legitimate expectation was the result of two factors. First, the fact that the Parliament had implied to the applicant company the certainty of winning the contract and encouraged it to make irreversible investments, and, second, the fact that it had failed to inform the applicant of important changes in the conduct of the tendering procedure.

6.6. Revocation of beneficial administrative acts

The protection of legitimate expectations imposes limitations on the powers of the institutions to revoke favourable administrative acts retroactively. Revocation may take place where the beneficiary has procured the adoption of the act by means of false or incomplete information.[237] But where the beneficiary has acted in good faith, revocation is subject to strict conditions: it may take place only within a reasonable period and provided that the legitimate expectations of the beneficiary are respected.[238] There must also be a public policy interest which overrides the beneficiary's interest in the maintenance of a situation which he was entitled to regard as stable.[239] An interesting example is provided by *de Compte v Parliament*.[240] The Parliament revoked with retroactive effect a decision recognizing that the appellant suffered from an occupational disease. The decision was revoked on the ground that the Parliament had erred in law. The justification put forward was that an illness may be justified as occupational only where it arises in connection with the lawful performance of an official's duties. In the circumstances, the appellant's illness was the result of stress brought about by disciplinary proceedings initiated against him because he had been found guilty of serious irregularities. The CFI considered the revocation lawful on the ground that it was made within a period of three months, which was reasonable, and the appellant had no legitimate expectations: after Parliament took the initial favourable decision, the appellant was informed that its implementation was in jeopardy because it might be vitiated by illegality. According to the CFI, therefore, reliance on the decision had been swiftly undermined in such a way that by the time the Parliament issued the revocation the appellant was no longer entitled to entertain any legitimate expectation as to the legality of the decision revoked. The Court of Justice overturned the decision of the CFI, reasoning as follows. It pointed out that the appellant had not provoked the favourable decision by means of false or incomplete

---

[237] Joined Cases 42/59 and 49/59 *SNUPAT v High Authority* [1961] ECR 53.

[238] See e.g. Case 14/81 *Alpha Steel v Commission* [1982] ECR 749; Case 15/85 *Consorzio Cooperative d'Abruzzo v Commission* [1987] ECR 1005; Case C-24/89 *Cargill v Commission* [1991] ECR I-2987; Case C-365/89 *Cargill v Produktschap voor Margarine, Vetten en Oliën* [1991] ECR I-3045. [239] Case 14/61 *Hoogovens v High Authority* [1962] ECR 253.

[240] Case C-90/95 P *de Compte v Parliament* [1997] ECR I-1999.

information. When the decision was notified to the appellant and he took cognizance of it, he was entitled to rely on its apparent legality. The Court held that legitimate expectations as to the legality of a favourable administrative act, once acquired, may not subsequently be undermined. In the circumstances, there was no overriding public policy interest which overrode the appellant's expectation.

6.7. Expectations of a non-commercial nature

In a number of staff cases, successful claims have been based on expectations of a non-commercial nature. We saw above that in the *Staff Salaries* case,[241] one of the first cases on legitimate expectations, the Council was held to be bound by its previous undertaking to use a certain formula for the revision of Community salaries. The Court was generous to the applicants in a series of cases decided in 1982 concerning the calculation of pension benefits payable to former Community employees.[242] In *Grogan v Commission*[243] the applicant, an Irish national, was a former official of the Commission. Upon retirement, he took up residence in his country of origin and chose, as he was entitled to do under the Staff Regulations, to have his pension paid in Belgian francs. The Community rules applicable at the time gave rise to unequal treatment among different categories of pensioners. Under the Staff Regulations, pensions paid in a currency other than Belgian francs were calculated on the basis of the exchange rates in force on 1 January 1965. Although in subsequent years the currencies of certain Member States devalued substantially, the Council continued to apply the fixed exchange rates of 1965 and, in order to maintain the purchasing power of pensions paid in weak currencies, it applied corrective weightings. Strictly speaking, the application of those weightings was unlawful since, under the Staff Regulations, they could be used only to alleviate the effects of differences in the costs of living rather than to compensate for currency fluctuations. In the case of pensioners residing in Ireland who had opted to have their pension paid in Irish pounds, the reduction in the purchasing power resulting from the application of fixed exchange rates was offset by the increase in the weighting applicable to Ireland. However, the weighting was of general application and benefited also those pensioners who had chosen to have their pension paid in Belgian francs and who therefore did not suffer a reduction in their purchasing power. In 1978 the Council adopted two regulations which introduced updated rates of exchange and reduced the weighting applicable to Ireland. The effect of those regulations was to reduce the amount of pension benefits payable to the applicant, who argued that the regulations infringed the principle of protection of legitimate expectations. The Court held that the new system was lawful since

---

[241] Case 81/72 *Commission v Council* [1973] ECR 575. See above Chapter 1.
[242] *Grogan, op. cit.*, n. 66 above, Case 164/80 *de Pascale v Commission* [1982] ECR 909, Case 167/80 *Curtis v Parliament* [1982] ECR 931.   [243] *Op. cit.*

it was introduced in order to restore equality of treatment between various categories of pensioners residing in countries with weak currencies. However, the lack of adequate transitional measures infringed the principle of protection of legitimate expectations. The Court held that the inequality of treatment which occurred before the introduction of the new system was not in any way attributable to the conduct of pensioners but rather to the inaction of the Council which failed to rectify exchange rates which no longer bore any relation to economic reality. Pensioners benefiting from that inaction were entitled to expect the Council to take account of the situation in which they had been placed by the prolonged application of the system temporarily used.[244]

The Court erred on the side of generosity. On the facts of the case, an expectation effectively arose from past preferential treatment without the Community administration having given any specific assurance to the applicants that the system relating to the payment of pensions would remain unalterable. Also, some transitional arrangements had in fact been made.[245] The decisive criteria seem to have been the fact that the weighting system had been applied for many years and the nature of the benefit involved. Understandably, the Court is more susceptible to a claim pertaining to pension benefits than to commercial claims.[246] In recent years, it seems that the CFI has adopted a more sceptical approach to claims based on legitimate expectations in staff cases.[247]

6.8. Legitimate expectations and national measures

As general principles of law, legal certainty and legitimate expectations bind not only the Community institutions but also the Member States when they act within the scope of application of Community law. Their application is broad and occurs in many contexts. The following, non-exhaustive areas, may be highlighted:

- the principle of legal certainty imposes certain conditions as to the manner and form of implementing legislation;
- the protection of legitimate expectations may restrict the retroactive application of implementing measures;
- the same principle also applies to national rules which govern the protection of Community rights in national courts;

---

[244] *Grogan, op. cit.*, para 33. Capotorti AG considered that there was no infringement of legitimate expectations and advised the Court to dismiss the action.

[245] The contested regulations were adopted in December 1978 and applied to the applicants from 1 October 1979, providing for a progressive reduction of benefits over a period of ten months. The Court held, however, that a period at least twice that length should have been envisaged: see para 34 of the judgment.

[246] Compare the pension cases with *Töpfer, op. cit.*, n. 230 above.

[247] See e.g. *Chomel, op. cit.*; cf *de Compte v Parliament, op. cit.*

- the same principle may restrict the recovery of monies paid out by national authorities in breach of Community law.

In fact, the ECJ has not treated the above situations consistently. Whilst in the first three it has applied legal certainty and protection of legitimate expectations as principles of Community law, in the last one it suggests that there is some scope for reliance on the same principles as recognized by national law.

The first situation is illustrated by *Mulligan v Minister for Agriculture and Food*.[248] As part of the implementation of the Community milk quota regime, Irish law authorized the competent Minister to adopt a clawback mechanism by means of an administrative notice published in a national newspaper. The applicants argued that such an administrative notice infringed the principle of legal certainty because it did not specify the limits of the powers of the competent authorities nor did it enable individuals to have full knowledge of the extent of their rights and obligations. The Court held that Member States must respect the general principles of Community law not only as regards the content of the implementing measures but also as regards the procedure for their adoption.[249] It recalled its case law pertaining to the implementation of Community directives according to which Member States must implement Community obligations by binding rules which are clear, specific and precise. It held that the mere fact that a national legislative instrument has delegated to a minister authority to adopt implementing measures does not in itself infringe the principle of legal certainty. As regards the issue of publication, the ECJ provided some guidelines leaving it to the national court to make an assessment on the facts. It pointed out that, whilst the principle of legal certainty requires appropriate publicity of national implementing measures, it does not prescribe any specific form of publicity such as publication in the official journal of the Member State concerned. What matters is that the measure must inform those subject to it of their rights and obligations.[250]

The second situation outlined above, i.e. the application of legitimate expectations on implementing measures, was examined in *Gerekens*.[251] Following the judgment in *Klensch*,[252] where the ECJ held that the Luxembourg legislation which implemented the Community milk quota regime was contrary to the principle of non-discrimination, the Government repealed that legislation and introduced new measures with retroactive effect. It was argued that the new measures were contrary to the principle of protection of legitimate expectations. To assess the legality of retroactivity, the ECJ applied the same test that it applies in relation to Community measures, namely, whether retroactivity is required by the objectives pursued and the legitimate expectations of those affected are respected.[253] Both

---

[248] Case C-313/99 *Mulligan and Others* [2002] ECR I-5719.   [249] *Ibid.*, para 48.

[250] According to Geelhoed AG publication in a government website might also suffice: see para 97 of the Opinion. On publicity of implementing measures, see also Case C-336/00 *Republic Austria v Huber*, [2002] ECR I-7699.   [251] *Op. cit.*, n. 75 above, paras 21–22.

[252] Joined Cases 201 and 202/85 *Klensch and Others* [1986] ECR 3477.

[253] *Gerekens, op. cit.*, para 24.

conditions were found to be met. Where national measures implementing a Community regulation are declared invalid because they infringe rules of higher ranking, a Member State is under an obligation to adopt new implementing measures with retroactive effect so as to ensure that the regulation is properly and effectively applied from the time of its entry into force. Retroactivity therefore was justified by the objectives of the measure. Also, the applicants were unable to establish any legitimate expectation on the facts. There was nothing in the history of the national legislation from which it might be concluded that the period between the entry into force of the Community milk quota regime and the date on which the new implementing measures entered into force would not be covered by national rules designed to implement the regime.

In *Gerekens*, the initial implementing measures were annulled by the Luxembourg Conseil d'Etat because they violated the principle of non-discrimination as a principle of Community law. It is possible that implementing legislation may be annulled not because it infringes a higher-ranking rule of EC law but because it was adopted contrary to a rule of national law, e.g. without the correct procedure being followed. In such a case the Member State has an obligation to reinstate its effects retroactively so as to ensure compliance with the regulation from the date of its entry into force. This is no different from the *isoglucose* cases discussed above.[254] It would be difficult to establish a legitimate expectation as, in principle, it would be foreseeable that the national authorities would adopt measures to comply with Community law.

More difficult issues arise where, in a similar situation, a Member State adopts retroactive measures to implement a directive. It is well established that a public authority may not rely on an unimplemented directive to create or aggravate the criminal liability of individuals.[255] More generally, a state may rely neither on the doctrine of direct effect of directives nor on the *Marleasing* principle of consistent interpretation against an individual.[256] The reason for this is that it is incumbent upon Member States to implement directives and a State may not rely on its own failure to transpose a directive correctly into national law. On the basis of those principles, it could be argued that, if the initial implementing measures prove to be invalid, the national authorities should not have the power to adopt new implementing measures retroactively. An alternative reasoning is possible. It may be argued that the validity of retroactivity should be assessed by reference to the same conditions as those applied in *Gerekens* to regulations. The condition of foreseeability is important here. It may well be foreseeable that the national government intends to comply with a Community directive as soon as the time limit for its implementation expires, just as it may be foreseeable that it intends to take steps, where necessary, to comply with regulations from the time of their entry into force. Much will depend on the factual and legal background to the dispute and the interests involved.

---

[254] *Op. cit.*   [255] Case 80/86 *Kolpinghuis Nijmegen* [1987] ECR 3969.
[256] Case C-168/95 *Arcaro* [1996] ECR I-4705.

The situation is different in the case of criminal measures. The prohibition of retroactivity is absolute here so a Member State may not introduce retroactively criminal measures in order to comply with Community law.[257]

A further area where the protection of legitimate expectations applies is national rules of procedures and remedies which govern the protection of Community rights in the national legal orders. This is the third situation outlined above. In *Marks & Spencer*[258] the ECJ held that the principle of legitimate expectations precludes a national legislative amendment which retroactively curtails the limitation period within which repayment of unduly paid VAT may be sought.

6.9. Recovery of unduly paid Community monies

Legitimate expectations may arise against national authorities responsible for the enforcement of Community law. Their protection acquires particular importance where national authorities seek to recover Community monies paid by mistake. According to established case law, to the extent that there are no Community rules, the recovery of such monies is governed by national law provided that two conditions are fulfilled: (a) the rules and procedures laid down by national law must not render the system for collecting Community charges less effective than that for collecting similar national charges (requirement of equivalence); and (b) national law must not render virtually impossible or excessively difficult the implementation of Community rules (requirement of effectiveness).[259]

The *locus classicus* of this approach is *Deutsche Milchkontor.*[260] The German authorities sought to recover Community aid granted in relation to an agricultural product on the ground that it did not satisfy the conditions laid down by Community law. The applicants relied on Article 48 of the German law on Administrative Procedure, according to which an unlawful administrative act granting a pecuniary advantage may not be revoked insofar as the beneficiary has relied upon it and his expectation, weighed against the public interest in revoking the decision, merits protection. The Court pointed out that, in principle, national authorities are under a strict obligation to demand repayment of Community sums unduly granted. The exercise of any discretion on whether to demand repayment would compromise the effectiveness of Community law. But it held that Community law did not prevent national law from having regard, in excluding the recovery of unduly paid aid, to the protection of legitimate expectations provided that the

---

[257] See above, *Criminal Proceedings against Berlusconi, op. cit.*, n. 136 above.

[258] Case C-62/00 *Marks & Spencer v Commissioners of Customs and Excise* [2002] ECR I-6325; See also Case C-396/98 *Schlossstrasse* [2000] ECR I-4279.

[259] Case 265/78 *Ferwerda v Produktschap voor Vee en Vlees* [1980] ECR 617.

[260] Joined cases 205 to 215/82 *Deutsche Milchkontor v Germany* [1983] ECR 2633. For subsequent confirmations, see e.g. Joined Cases C-31 to C-44/91 *Lageder and Others* [1993] ECR I-1761; Case C-366/95 *Landbrugsministeriet v Steff-Houlberg Export and Others* [1998] ECR I-2661, para 15; *Republic Österreich v Huber, op. cit.*, n. 250 above.

recovery of Community financial benefits was placed on an equal footing with the recovery of purely national ones and that the interests of the Community were taken fully into account.

Deutsche Milchkontor opened the way for the application of protection of legitimate expectations, as a principle recognized in national administrative laws, against the enforcement of Community claims. The ECJ justified its approach on two grounds: legal certainty is recognized as a general principle in the Community legal order, and is also, albeit in different forms and degrees, common to the laws of the Member States.[261] The Court applies in effect a double-agency principle: it allows national laws to protect legitimate expectations and also entrusts national courts with the task of weighing the Community interest. This may be seen as an invitation to diversity but, as a matter of judicial policy, makes good sense. In the absence of Community harmonization measures, reliance on doctrines of national law is the most efficient and, indeed, the only pragmatic approach. By relying on national rules of procedure and remedies, the ECJ gains legitimacy. It heeds classic doctrines of national administrative laws whilst, at the same, time extending its franchise by entrusting national courts to act as its agents and infusing Community-wide standards through the preliminary reference dialogue. It is however important to recall that the Court's deference to the national legal systems is measured and selective. It is measured because it places particular importance on the Community interest. It is selective because it does not apply to all areas: as we shall see, the tenor of the case law on the recovery of unlawful state aid is markedly different.

The basic principles of the case law, as it evolved after *Deutsche Milchkontor*, may be summarized as follows.

Where domestic law requires a balance to be drawn between, on the one hand, the public interest in the revocation of an unlawful administrative measure and, on the other hand, the protection of the legitimate expectation of the individual concerned, the key imposition on the national court is to take fully into account the interests of the Community.[262] Subject to this requirement, the ECJ entrusts the national court with the task of drawing the balance and reaching an outcome on the facts.[263] In *Oelmühle and Schmidt Söhne*,[264] it held that the national authorities may be barred from seeking the recovery of Community agricultural subsidies paid to traders by mistake if the traders have passed on the pecuniary advantage derived to their suppliers and have thus lost any unjust enrichment. The defence of passing on is available only if (a) the recipient of the subsidy has acted in good faith; (b) it has passed on the resulting financial benefit to its suppliers by paying the target price prescribed by Community law; and (c) any right of recourse against the suppliers is worthless.

---

[261] *Op. cit.*, para 30.
[262] *Deutsche Milchkontor*, *op. cit.*, para 32; Case C-298/96 *Oelmühle and Schmidt Söhne v Bundesanstalt für Landwirtschaft und Ernährung* [1998] ECR I-4767, para 24.
[263] See e.g. *Hüber, op. cit.*   [264] *Op. cit.*

Provided that the dual requirements of equivalence and effectiveness are respected and that the interests of the Community are fully taken into account, Community law does not preclude a national rule from allowing non-recovery of Community aid paid incorrectly taking into account the fact that a considerable period of time has elapsed since the payment of the aid.[265] Nor does it prevent the national law from taking into account negligence on the part of the national authorities.[266] A national court may also take into account the principle of legitimate expectations as provided in national law in determining whether the national authorities may annul a contract concluded with a milk producer on behalf of the Council and the Commission.[267]

The ECJ requires that the person who relies on legitimate expectations must come with clean hands, i.e. he must have acted in good faith in his dealings with the authorities. In *Landbrugsministeriet v Steff-Houlberg Export and Others*,[268] the Danish authorities took steps to recover subsidies incorrectly paid to the applicants for the exportation of beef to third countries. The subsidies had been paid for a number of years but, following an investigation, it transpired that the composition of the products exported was substantially different from that declared to the authorities. In their defence the applicants argued that, as trading undertakings, they were not involved in the manufacturing of the products and were not in a position to check their composition. They should not therefore be held liable for the fraudulent conduct of their suppliers. The Commission and the Danish authorities counter-argued that the applicants could not plead good faith since they had themselves drafted the official declarations certifying the composition of the products. The ECJ held that the exporters were practically unable to inspect the composition of the goods. The only way of doing so would be by supervising production which would be technically difficult and expensive. In those circumstances, it accepted that failure to inspect their composition did not preclude the applicants from pleading good faith.

In *Steff-Houlberg Export* the ECJ interpreted good faith in a pragmatic way. Notably, it refused to endorse a general system of strict liability in relation to subsidies, although such a system is provided by other Community regulations, and took a restrictive view of its judgment in *Boterlux*[269] where it had held that fraudulent behaviour by a third party should be considered to be an ordinary commercial risk for the recipient of the aid.

The above judgments may be seen as being pro-national law and also pro-individual In that respect, they contrast sharply with the case law on state aid where, as we shall see below, the ECJ is much more interventionist. The question which

---

[265] *Op. cit.*, n. 260 above.   [266] *Ibid.*

[267] Joined Cases C-80 to C-82/99 *Flemmer and Others* [2002] ECR I-7211. In a different context, however, the Court has held that a trader who has benefited from decisions of a national authority that do not comply with Community law is not entitled to expect that the same authority will adopt a further decision in breach of Community law: Case C-325/96 *Fábrica de Queijo Eru Portugesa Ltd v Subdirector-General das Alfândegas* [1997] ECR I-7249, para 22.

[268] *Op. cit.* See also *Flemmer, op. cit.*   [269] Case C-347/93 [1994] ECR I-3933.

arises in this context is the following: if in a situation similar to that in *Deutsche Milchkontor* or *Steff-Houlberg Export* the national rules applicable did not protect the legitimate expectations of the individual, could an applicant rely on legal certainty as a principle of Community law to achieve such protection? It is submitted that in the light of the judgment in *Gerekens* there is no reason why the applicant should be unable to do so. Individuals may derive rights directly from the protection of legitimate expectations as a Community law principle which can be used to fill not only the gaps of Community law but also the gaps in the national legal systems.

Where the recovery of sums due is governed by Community provisions, such provisions may specifically incorporate the protection of legitimate expectations. An example is provided by the Community Customs Code,[270] Article 220 of which governs the post-clearance recovery of import or export duties where such duties have not been required of the person liable for payment. Article 220(2)(b) authorises the national authorities to waive post-clearance recovery where three conditions are cumulatively met: (a) the non-collection of the duties must have been due to an error by the authorities; (b) the error must be of such a kind that it could not reasonably have been detected by a person acting in good faith; and (c) he must have observed all the rules in force so far as his customs declarations are concerned. Where those conditions are satisfied, the person liable is entitled to waiver of recovery.[271] Whether an error of the authorities is detectable must be assessed having regard to the nature of the error, the professional experience of the operators concerned and the care which they exercised.[272] The nature of the error is assessed in the light of the complexity of the applicable rules and the period of time during which the authorities persisted in their error.[273] In *Biegi Nahrungsmittel and Commonfood*[274] the ECJ held, reversing the CFI, that, in the circumstances of the case, the error committed by the German customs authorities could not have been detected by an experienced importer. The Community rules governing the granting of WTO tariff quotas were ambiguous and complex, the error had been committed by the highest national custom authorities, and had not been corrected for several weeks.

6.10. Recovery of unlawful State aid

The defence of legitimate expectations has also been pleaded to prevent the recovery of unlawful state aid. Two separate issues arise here. The first is whether

---

[270] Council Regulation No 2913/92 establishing the Community Customs Code, OJ L 302/1.
[271] Case 292/91 *Weis v Hauptzollamt Würzburg* [1993] ECR I-2219; Case C-348/89 *Mecanarte* [1991] ECR I-3299.
[272] Joined Cases C-153 and C-204/94 *Faroe Seafood and Others* [1996] ECR I-2465, para 99; *Ilumitronica, op. cit.*, n. 181 above, para 54.
[273] Case C-499/03 P *Biegi Nahrungsmittel GmbH and Commonfood Handelsgesellschaft für Agrar-Produkte mbH v Commission*, judgment of 3 March 2005, para 48; Case C-187/91 *Belovo* [1992] ECR I-4937, para 18; Case C-38/95 *Foods Import* [1996] ECR I-6543, para 30.   [274] *Op. cit.*

the Commission itself may be prevented from ordering the recovery of unlawful aid. The second is whether legitimate expectations may be raised against the national authorities seeking recovery. The two situations are different in that, in the first, reliance is placed on protection of legitimate expectations as a principle of Community law whilst, in the second, reliance on it is placed as a principle recognized by national law. This dual character of the principle has been criticized[275] but flows from the fact that the decision to order recovery is taken by the Commission but is executed at the national level. It is thus the inevitable consequence of the decentralised enforcement of Community law. The basic principles of the case law may be summarized as follows.

A distinction is drawn between Member States and recipient undertakings. As a general rule, a Member State which has granted unlawful aid may not rely on the legitimate expectations of the recipient in order to justify its failure to comply with a Commission decision ordering recovery. If that were possible, national authorities would be able to rely on their own unlawful conduct in order to avoid their Community obligations.[276] Since the Member State concerned may not invoke the legitimate expectations of the recipient undertaking, it follows that the Commission itself may not decide to refrain from ordering recovery, relying merely on the submission of the national authorities that the legitimate expectations of the recipient undertakings would be prejudiced. In *Ladbroke Racing Ltd v Commission*[277] the Commission found that France had granted unlawful state aid to PMU, a French association of racecourse undertakings, by exempting it from payment of a social housing levy. It took the view however that it could not order repayment of the aid granted prior to the initiation of proceedings because in 1962 the Conseil d'Etat had held that horse racing was an agricultural activity and therefore exempt from the levy. The CFI annulled the Commission's decision holding that it was not for the Commission or the Member State concerned but for the recipient undertaking, in the context of proceedings before the public authorities or before the national courts, to invoke the existence of exceptional circumstances on the basis of which it had entertained legitimate expectations.[278] On appeal, the ECJ did not express a view on that proposition but confirmed the decision of the CFI on the ground that the Commission had not explained why the case law of the Conseil d'Etat amounted to an exceptional circumstance giving rise to a legitimate expectation.[279]

Overall, it appears that, although the case law does not totally foreclose the possibility of reliance by a Member State, the chances of success of such an

---

[275] See the Opinion of Cosmas AG in Case C-83/98 P *France v Ladbroke Racing and Commission* [2000] ECR I-3271 at 3290.

[276] Case C-5/89 *Commission v Germany* [1990] ECR I-3437, Case C-303/88 *Italy v Commission (Lanerossi case)* [1991] ECR I-1433.

[277] Case T-67/94 *Ladbroke Racing Ltd v Commission* [1998] ECR II-1.

[278] *Ibid.*, para 183.   [279] *France v Ladbroke Racing and Commission, op. cit.*, para 59–60.

argument are rather slim.[280] The better view is that the protection of legitimate expectations is an equitable principle and should be invoked by the person or entity who claims that its expectations have been frustrated and not by a proxy. A Member State therefore might be able to invoke the principle only if the Commission by its conduct created an expectation on the part of the State that the aid is lawful.

The defence of legitimate expectations may be available to the recipient undertaking. The scope for application of the principle in this context, however, is also limited. The Court has held that a recipient of unlawful State aid may rely only on exceptional circumstances on the basis of which it has legitimately assumed the aid to be lawful.[281] An undertaking to which State aid has been granted may not entertain a legitimate expectation that the aid is lawful unless it has been granted in compliance with the procedure laid down in Article 88 EC. The Court attaches particular importance to this requirement as is evident from *Spain v Commission*.[282] The Commission had adopted a decision finding that aid granted by Spain to a steel foundry in Aragon was compatible with the common market. Following an action by an English company, the Court annulled the Commission decision.[283] In compliance with the Court's judgment, the Commission initiated the procedure under Article 88(2) and, by a new decision, it declared the aid unlawful and ordered recovery. The Spanish Government argued that the decision ordering recovery frustrated the legitimate expectations of the recipient undertaking. The Court confirmed that undertakings to which aid has been granted cannot, in principle, entertain a legitimate expectation that the aid is lawful unless it has been granted in compliance with Article 88. A diligent operator should normally be able to determine whether that procedure has been followed. In the case in issue the aid had been granted without first being notified. The fact that the Commission initially decided not to raise any objections could not be regarded as capable of having caused the recipient undertaking to entertain any legitimate expectation since that decision was challenged in due time before the Court which annulled it.

However, in *RSV v Commission*[284] the Court accepted that the Commission's unreasonable delay in requiring the recovery of State aid gave rise to a legitimate expectation on the part of the recipient undertaking which prevented the Commission from requiring the national authorities to order recovery. In that case, the Commission adopted the contested decision more than two years after opening the Article 88(2) procedure. The delay was unjustifiable and wholly due

---

[280] See also Case C-169/95 *Spain v Commission* [1997] ECR I-135, discussed below, where the ECJ allowed a State to invoke the legitimate expectations of the undertaking concerned but rejected the argument on the facts.

[281] See e.g. Case 94/87 *Commission v Germany (Alcan I)* [1989] ECR 175, para 12; *Commission v Germany, op. cit.*, n. 276 above, paras 13–16; Case T-459/93 *Siemens v Commission* [1995] ECR II-1675, para 104.   [282] Case C-169/95 [1997] ECR I-135.

[283] Case C-198/91 *Cook v Commission* [1993] ECR I-2487.

[284] Case 223/85 *RSV v Commission* [1987] ECR 4617. Cf *Scott SA v Commission, op. cit.*, n. 182 above, discussed at 6.3.11 above.

to the Commission;[285] and the aid in issue was intended to meet additional costs of an operation which had received aid authorised by the Commission. The applicant therefore had reasonable grounds for believing that no objection would be raised. Similarly, in *Salzgitter AG v Germany*,[286] the CFI held that recovery of aid granted in the steel sector ran counter to legal certainty as a result of the combination of three factors. The Commission had withdrawn its initial non-objection to the aid scheme but the withdrawal was implicit and insufficiently clear; the withdrawal was also partial and there was ambiguity as to its scope; the Commission did not express objections for a prolonged period although it was aware that the applicant had received aid. These factors led to an equivocal situation which the Commission was under a duty to clarify before ordering recovery.

The defence of legitimate expectations may be available to the recipient undertaking against the national authorities effecting recovery if it is provided by national law in relation to domestic claims of a similar nature. This follows from the general principle that recovery of State aid is subject to the national rules of procedure, subject to the requirements of equivalence and effectiveness.[287] The starting point is the criteria laid down in *Deutsche Milchkontor*.[288] The Court however allows much less scope for reliance on legitimate expectations in the recovery of unlawful State aid than in the case of unlawfully paid Community aid. The reason for this is that the recovery of State aid is dictated by an imperative Community interest, namely the need to remove the competitive advantage enjoyed by the recipient undertaking and avoid distortions on free trade. Community aid, on the other hand, has different objectives, such as support for certain products or an economic sector. A finding that Community aid is unlawful means that the preconditions for its grant were not met but the infringement does not prejudice the fundamental Treaty provisions governing competition.[289]

In *Land Rheinland-Pfalz v Alcan Deutschland GmbH (Alcan II)*,[290] it was held that the competent national authority must revoke a decision granting unlawful aid even if the time limit laid down under national law for the revocation of unlawful administrative acts has elapsed. Where aid is found to be incompatible with the common market by the Commission, the national authorities do not have any discretion, their role being merely to give effect to the Commission's decision. Thus, the recipient of unlawfully granted State aid ceases to be in a state of uncertainty once the Commission has adopted a decision finding the aid incompatible with the common market and requiring recovery. The principle of legal certainty cannot therefore preclude repayment of the aid on the ground that

---

[285] Cf Case C-301/87 *France v Commission* [1990] ECR I-307, para 28 and p. 333 *per* Jacobs AG.   [286] *Op. cit.*, n. 182 above, paras 174 and 180.
[287] Case C-142/87 *Belgium v Commission* [1990] ECR I-959; *Siemens v Commission, op. cit.*
[288] *Op. cit.*
[289] See the Opinion of Cosmas AG in *France v Ladbroke Racing and Commission, op. cit.*, at 3291.
[290] Case C-24/95 [1997] ECR I-1591.

the national authorities were late in complying with the decision requiring repayment.[291] The Court also held that the competent authority must revoke a decision granting unlawful aid even if the authority itself is responsible for the illegality of the decision and revocation appears to be a breach of good faith towards the recipient.[292] The obligation to recover subsists even where such recovery is excluded by national law because the gain no longer exists, e.g. because it has been passed on to other parties.[293]

The strict approach taken by the Court in *Alcan II* contrasts with cases concerning the recovery of unduly paid Community aid where the ECJ has been content to leave more scope for the application of legitimate expectations as applied in national law and allow the national court to weigh the Community interest.[294] The judgment in *Alcan II* vividly illustrates the application of selective deference: where the Community interest so demands, the ECJ is prescriptive, shrinking the autonomy of national legal orders 'to almost nothing'.[295]

Detailed procedural rules for the review of State aids have now been laid down by Council Regulation No 659/1999.[296] Article 14 of the Regulation states that 'the Commission shall not require recovery of the aid if this would be contrary to a general principle of Community law'.[297] It also provides that recovery must be effected without delay and in accordance with the procedures of national law 'provided that they allow the immediate and effective execution of the Commission's decision'.[298] This suggests that the margins of reliance on national law are very narrow and that it would be possible for an undertaking to rely on the principle of legitimate expectations as provided by national law but only within the confines recognized by Community law. The provision serves in effect as a mandate to the ECJ to colonize this field fully.[299]

Finally, it should be noted that the principle of protection of legitimate expectations has played a role also in other aspects of the law of State aid. Policy statements or guidelines issues by the Commission may give rise to legitimate expectations and thus restrict the Commission's discretion, provided that they are in accordance with Treaty provisions. In *Deufil v Commission*,[300] the Commission had issued guidelines stating that, in view of the conditions prevailing in the industry, aid in relation to certain synthetic fibres and yarns would not benefit from the exemption provided for in Article 87(3)(c). The Court held that the guidelines did not give rise to a legitimate expectation that aid in relation to a product not contained in the guidelines could be granted without first being notified in accordance with Article 88(3). In *CIRFS v Commission*[301] the Court decided that a

---

[291] *Ibid.*, para 37.   [292] *Ibid.*, para 41.   [293] *Ibid.*, para 50.
[294] See e.g. *Oelmühle and Schmidt Söhne, op. cit.*
[295] *France v Ladbroke Racing and Commission, op. cit.*, per Cosmas AG at para 66 of the Opinion.
[296] Regulation No. 659/1999 laying down detailed rules for the application of Article 93 (now 88) of the Treaty OJ 1999, L 83/1.   [297] Article 14(1).
[298] Article 14(2).   [299] For other aspects of the Regulation, see above, n. 182.
[300] Case 310/85 *Deufil v Commission* [1987] ECR 901.
[301] Case C-313/90 [1993] ECR I-1125.

subsequent version of the same guidelines bound the Commission in a different way: the Commission was under an obligation to treat aid in relation to the products mentioned therein as new aid and require its notification. Enterprises competing with an undertaking to which such aid had been granted entertained a legitimate expectation that the Commission would open the procedure provided in Article 88(2).[302] The judgments in the two cases are fully compatible: a policy statement issued by the Commission may restrict its discretion for the future but may not derogate from the provisions of Articles 87 and 88.[303]

---

[302] But the adoption by the Commission of an Aid Code authorizing by way of exception certain categories of aid does not create a legitimate expectation that other categories will not be authorized: Case T-243/94 *British Steel v Commission* [1997] ECR II-1887, paras 74 *et seq.*; Case T-244/94 *Wirtschaftsvereiningung Stahl and Others v Commission* [1997] ECR II-1963, paras 56 *et seq.*

[303] According to standard case law, the Commission may lay down guidelines for the exercise of its discretionary powers in the field of State aid, provided that they contain directions on the approach to be followed by it and do not depart from Treaty rules: *CIRFS, op. cit.*; Case T-380/94 *AIUFFASS and AKT v Commission* [1996] ECR II-2169; para 57; Case T-149/95 *Établisssements Richard Ducros v Commission* [1997] ECR II-2031, para 61; Case C-288/96 *Germany v Commission* [2000] ECR I-8237, para 62.

7

Fundamental Rights

7.1. Introduction

The protection of fundamental rights in the Community legal order has been almost entirely the product of case law.[1] This still remains the case despite the fact that there are now express references to their protection in the TEU and the Union has acquired its own catalogue of fundamental rights in the form of the Charter. The Court's creative jurisprudence has not been without its critics. Coppel and O'Neill argued at earlier times that the high rhetoric of human rights is not based on a genuine concern to take them seriously but on a desire to extend the scope and impact of Community law which lacks legitimacy.[2] A more balanced assessment suggests that the gradual elaboration of judicial standards has been well founded and that the impact of the Court's jurisprudence has been positive.[3] There is no doubt that in recent years the importance of fundamental rights in the

---

[1] For extensive references, see the bibliography at the end of this book. A selective bibliography in English includes *inter alia*: A. von Bogdandy, 'The European Union as a Human Rights Organisation? Human Rights and the Core of the European Union', (2000) 37 CML Rev 1307; K. Lenaerts, 'Respect for Fundamental Rights as a Constitutional Principle of the European Union', 6 (2000) Columbia Journal of European Law, 1; P. Alston (ed.), *The EU and Human Rights* (Oxford University Press, 1999); N. Neuwahl and A. Rosas (eds), *The European Union and Human Rights* (Martinus Nijhoff, 1995); A. Cassese, A. Clapham and J. Weiler (eds), *Human Rights and the European Community*, Vos II–III, Nomos, 1991; A. Clapham, 'A Human Rights Policy for the European Community' (1990) 10 YEL 309; D. Curtin and T. Heukels (eds) *Institutional Dynamics of European Integration, Essays in Honour of H.G. Schermers* (Vols I–III) (Kluwer 1998); F.G. Jacobs, 'Human Rights in Europe: New Dimensions' (1992) 3 King's College Law Journal 49; F.G. Jacobs (ed), *European Law and the Individual* (Oxford University Press, 1976); S. Hall, 'Loss of Union Citizenship in Breach of Fundamental Rights' (1996) 21 ELR 129; L.B. Krogsgaard, 'Fundamental Rights in the European Community after Maastricht' (1993) LIEI 99; K. Lenaerts, 'Fundamental Rights to be Included in a Community Catalogue' (1991) 16 ELR 367; M.H. Mendelson, 'The Impact of European Community Law on the Implementation of the European Convention on Human Rights' (1983) 3 YEL 99; M.H. Mendelson, 'The European Court of Justice and Human Rights' (1981) 1 YEL 125; H.G. Schermers, 'The Eleventh Protocol to the European Convention on Human Rights' (1994) 19 ELR 367; H.G. Schermers, 'The European Community bound by Fundamental Human Rights' (1990) 27 CML Rev 249; R.M. Dallen, Jr, 'An Overview of European Community Protection of Human Rights, with some special references to the UK' (1990) 27 CML Rev 761; C. Duparc, *The European Community and Human Rights*, (EC Commission 1992); de Bùrca, 'Fundamental Human Rights and the Reach of European Law' (1992) 13 OJLS 283.
[2] J. Coppel and A. O'Neill, 'The European Court of Justice: Taking Rights Seriously' 29 (1992) CML Rev 669.
[3] J. H. H. Weiler and N. J. S. Lockhart, ' "Taking Rights Seriously" Seriously: The European Court and its Fundamental Rights Jurisprudence' (1995) 32 CML Rev 51 and 579.

European Union has increased considerably. A number of factors have contributed to this development. Fundamental rights have acquired greater prominence throughout the world. In an era where there is heightened zeal for the accountability of the State and the empowerment of the individual, respect for human rights is viewed not only as a *sine qua non* of legality but as the most important yardstick in assessing a polity's democratic credentials. In the EU, the observance of human rights by the Union institutions and by the Member States is part of the renewed calls for accountability, transparency and legitimacy. There is a shared belief that democracy is not exhausted in the majoritarian rule but encompasses respect for the individual, tolerance and pluralism.[4] Respect for human rights defines the limits of tolerance to political diversity.

According to the settled case law, fundamental rights form an integral part of the general principles of law whose observance the Court ensures.[5] Although this is a long enduring statement and the Court's rhetoric has remained the same, in substance the human rights jurisdiction of the Court has been enhanced in many ways. Firstly, the ECJ has broadened the scope of application of human rights. It is becoming increasingly difficult to find areas of national law which fall outside the scope of EU law and therefore beyond the human rights jurisdiction of the ECJ. Secondly, in its judgment in *Schmidberger*[6] the ECJ revisited the balance between fundamental freedoms and human rights, viewing the latter as being of at least equal ranking to the former. Thirdly, the level of scrutiny employed by the Court has increased: in more cases it is now prepared to reach an outcome rather than leave matters to the national courts. Finally, through respective developments in their jurisprudence and skilful judicial diplomacy, the ECJ and the ECtHR are reaching a new state of symbiosis characterised by mutual respect and deference. The two courts do not compete but cooperate. By increasing its own level of scrutiny, the ECJ has received endorsement from the ECtHR to provide a one-stop jurisdiction on human rights issues within the scope of Community law.[7]

This chapter does not intend to provide an exhaustive account of human rights law in the EU but rather to outline developments, highlight trends, and assess the current state of the case law in selected areas. After giving an overview of the development of the case law, it looks briefly at the application of fundamental rights on Community measures and the level of scrutiny exercised by the Court. It then concentrates on the application of fundamental rights on national measures and the relationship between the ECJ and the ECtHR. It concludes by a brief overview of the Charter.

---

[4] Article 2 of the EU Constitution, headed 'The Union's values', refers to 'a society of pluralism, non-discrimination, tolerance, justice, solidarity and equality between women and men'.

[5] Case 5/88 *Wachauf* [1989] ECR 2609, para 17; Case C-274/99 P *Connolly v Commission* [2001] ECR I-1611, para 17; Case C-94/00 *Roquette Frères* [2002] ECR I-9011, para 23.

[6] Case C-112/00 *Schmidberger, Internationale Transporte und Planzüge v Austria*, [2003] ECR I-5659.

[7] See the Judgment of 30 June 2005 in *Bosphorus Hava Yollari Turizm ve Ticaret AS v Ireland*, application no. 45036/98. discussed in 7.2.7 below.

Among the issues that merit particular attention are the following: should Community law adopt a minimalist approach, seeking the lowest common denominator of the national constitutions, or should it follow a maximalist approach? Another issue is the scope of protection. What types of measure should be subject to review on grounds of compatibility with human rights? Does review apply only to Community measures or does it also extend to national measures, and if so, what types of measure are covered and why? This issue also raises questions pertaining to the standard of review. Where national measures are subject to review on grounds of compatibility with human rights, what standard of review is applicable? Is it the Community standard or that applicable in the Member State concerned? The question acquires practical importance where Community and national standards differ. The final issue refers to the relationship between Community law and the European Convention on Human Rights which remains the subject of a lively debate.

7.2. Review of Community measures

7.2.1. The early years

Apart from an oblique reference in the preamble,[8] the Treaty of Rome made no reference to the protection of fundamental rights. The reason for this silence is to be found in the historical origins of the Community. In the aftermath of the Second World War, the protection of human rights at a pan-European level was the subject of a separate political structure. The Council of Europe was established in 1949 with the main task of drafting and implementing the European Convention for the Protection of Human Rights and Fundamental Freedoms (ECHR). The Convention was concluded on 4 November 1950 and came into force on 3 September 1953. The Draft Treaty for a European Political Community of 1953 provided for the application of Section I of the European Convention and its First Protocol as part of its provisions, but the Draft Treaty encountered insuperable political difficulties and its all-embracing, federalist, structure gave way to less ambitious, sectoral, economic integration. Although the EEC was perceived as a dynamic entity, bound to evolve in subsequent years, its goals were first and foremost economic. It was thought that the protection of human rights did not merit specific reference in a Treaty setting up a Community with enumerated competences mainly in the economic sphere. This applied *a fortiori* to the European Coal and Steel Community and Euratom.

In a series of early cases, the Court did not accept that the Community was bound by the fundamental rights guaranteed by the constitutions of the Member States.[9]

---

[8] The eighth recital states that the Member States are resolved 'to preserve and strengthen peace and liberty'.

[9] See e.g. Case 1/58 *Stork v High Authority* [1959] ECR 17 at 25–26; Joined Cases 36, 37, 38 and 40/59 *Geitling v High Authority* [1960] ECR 423 at 438–439; Case 40/64 *Sgarlata v*

This case law is not to be attributed to a lack of commitment to human rights protection but a more pragmatic reason. The Court was fearful of subordinating the Treaty to the laws of Member States and thus prejudicing the effect of Community law. It is ironic that an early, almost primitive, form of constitutional assertion was the denial of fundamental constitutional values. The first reluctant step was taken in *Stauder v City of Ulm*.[10] A Commission decision provided for the sale of butter at reduced prices to citizens in receipt of social assistance. The German and the Dutch versions of the decision required as a condition of entitlement the presentation of a coupon indicating the name of the beneficiary. A German national argued that the requirement to reveal his identity was an infringement of fundamental rights. On the basis of the French and the Italian versions of the decision which employed more general language, the Court held that the decision did not require the identification of beneficiaries by name but enabled Member States to employ other methods by which the coupons could refer to the person concerned. Interpreted in that way, the Court held, the provision 'contains nothing capable of prejudicing the fundamental human rights enshrined in the general principles of Community law and protected by the Court'.[11]

7.2.2. From *Internationale Handelsgesellschaft* to *Hauer*

The reference to fundamental rights in *Stauder* was incidental but paved the way for the seminal *Internationale Handelsgesellschaft*.[12] German traders challenged the system of deposits established by Community agricultural regulations on the ground that it ran counter to the fundamental rights protected by the German Constitution, in particular the principle of proportionality and the freedom to pursue trade and professional activities. Reasserting the primacy of Community law, the Court stated that it could not be overridden by rules of national law. It was not therefore possible to test the validity of Community acts *vis-à-vis* fundamental rights as protected by the constitutions of the Member States. The Court however continued:[13]

> ...respect for fundamental rights forms an integral part of the general principles of law protected by the Court of Justice. The protection of such rights, whilst inspired by the constitutional traditions common to the Member States, must be ensured within the framework of the structure and objectives of the Community.

In the constitutional development of the Community, *Internationale Handelsgesellschaft* marks a distinct development. The passage quoted above is testament to

---

Commission [1965] ECR 215 at 227. As Mendelson points out, *op. cit.*, p. 130, it is not an accident that the first cases came from Germany and Italy, the two Member States which, fearful of their troubled past, were particularly sensitive on matters of fundamental rights and had provided themselves with very strong constitutional protection.

[10] Case 29/69 [1969] ECR 419.   [11] *Ibid.*, para 7.
[12] Case 11/70 *Internationale Handelsgesellschaft v Einfuhr- und Vorratsstelle Getreide* [1970] ECR 1125. See further above p. 141.   [13] *Ibid.*, para 4.

the Court's creative jurisprudence. On the one hand, the Court reiterates the supremacy of Community law and takes the principle of primacy to its utmost limits: Community law takes precedence even over the most precious provisions of the national constitutions. On the other hand, the Court reassures the Member States that the Treaty shares their constitutional values and ensures ideological continuity. At the same time, it takes care to safeguard the autonomy of Community law. The national constitutional traditions provide 'inspiration' for respect of human rights in the Community legal order. There their function ends. The balance to be struck where fundamental rights conflict with each other and the application to specific cases of general principles borrowed from the national constitutions is a matter for the Court, since the protection of human rights must be secured 'within the framework of the structure and the objectives of the Community'. To be sure, the Court arrogates to itself important functions as it is the concrete effects of human rights that matter. One however could hardly advocate a different view. *Internationale Handelsgesellschaft* is not a paradigm of unwarranted judicial activism. The assertion that the Community is bound by fundamental rights finds justification in the constitutional traditions of the Member States. As Mancini and Keeling note, it is hardly conceivable that 'the national parliaments would have ratified a Treaty which was capable of violating the fundamental tenets of their own constitutions'.[14] Once it is accepted that human rights form part of the Community legal order and bind the Community institutions, their protection must be ensured within the four corners of the Community polity. It would simply not be possible to mechanically apply human rights as recognized in one or another national legal system without taking into account the specific qualities of Community law.

If *Internationale Handelsgesellschaft* reconciled the primacy of Community law with respect for national constitutional traditions, *Nold*[15] made the first step towards the establishment of Community standards for human rights protection. The Commission authorised new terms of business in the coal sector, as a result of which the applicant undertaking lost its status as a direct wholesaler and with it entitlement to direct supplies from the producer. It argued that the new trading rules jeopardized its profitability to the extent of endangering its very existence and therefore infringed the right to property and the freedom to trade as protected by the German Constitution. The Court held that, in safeguarding human rights, it draws inspiration from the constitutional traditions common to the Member States and cannot therefore uphold measures which are incompatible with fundamental rights recognized and protected by the Constitutions of those States.[16] It then identified as an additional source international treaties for the protection of human rights on which the Member States have collaborated or of which they are signatories. Such Treaties, the Court stated, 'can supply guidelines which would be

---

[14] G.F. Mancini and D.T. Keeling, 'Democracy and the European Court of Justice' (1994) 57 MLR 175 at 187.   [15] Case 4/73 *Nold* [1974] ECR 491.
[16] *Ibid.*, para 13.

followed within the framework of Community law'.[17] The Court also laid down the basic formula on the basis of which human rights would be protected by the Court. It held that the right to property and the right to practise freely a trade or profession do not constitute unfettered prerogatives but must be viewed in the light of their social function. They should, where necessary, be subject to certain limits justified by the overall objectives pursued by the Community, on condition that the substance of those rights is left untouched.[18] In reaching that conclusion, the Court drew inspiration from the constitutions of Member States where the right to property and the freedom to trade and practise a profession are made subject to limitations in the public interest.

The judgment in *Nold* was reiterated in *Hauer*.[19] At issue there was a Council regulation which, with a view to controlling wine surpluses, prohibited the new planting of vines for a period of three years. It was argued that the prohibition infringed the right to property and the right to trade. With regard to the former, the Court stated that it is guaranteed in the Community legal order in accordance with the ideas common to the constitutions of the Member States. The Court accepted for the first time the special significance of the European Convention for the protection of Fundamental Rights in the Community legal order. Referring to the first Protocol of the ECHR, it distinguished between a measure which deprives the owner of his right and a measure which restricts its exercise and held that the contested regulation belonged to the second category. It then referred to the constitutions of several Member States and came to the conclusion that the restriction on the planting of new vines was a type of restriction familiar to, and accepted as lawful by, the Member States. It proceeded to examine whether the contested regulation was justified in the circumstances and gave an affirmative answer. The contested measure was of a temporary nature. It was intended to deal immediately with the problem of surpluses whilst at the same time preparing the introduction of permanent structural measures. Also, in view of the underlying situation of the market, the cultivation of new vineyards would make no economic sense. It would worsen the underlying economic situation making more difficult the implementation of a structural policy and perhaps posing the risk that more restrictive measures would need to be introduced in the future.[20]

Nold and *Hauer* evince a firm but cautious approach. The determination to ensure that the Community institutions are bound by fundamental rights co-exists with the eagerness to secure the autonomy of the Community polity. The Court appeared more accommodating to the national constitutions than in *Internationale Handelsgesellschaft* declaring that measures which are incompatible with fundamental rights recognized and protected by the Constitutions of the Member States

---

[17] *Ibid.*, para 13.
[18] *Ibid.*, para 14. Cf *Geitling v High Authority, op. cit.*, where the Court had refused to recognize the protection of the right of property in the Community legal order.
[19] Case 44/79 *Hauer v Land Rheinland-Pfalz* [1979] ECR 3727. See also Joined Cases 154 etc/ 78 and 39 etc/79 *Valsabbia v Commission* [1979] ECR I-907.   [20] *Op. cit.*, paras 28–29.

cannot be upheld.[21] This more conciliatory approach was largely the result of the defiant reaction of the German Constitutional Court following *Internationale Handelsgesellschaft*.[22] It was a concession on the road to legitimacy but the Court was careful to retain residual control. Respect for the same rights does not mean reaching the same outcome on the facts. It is clear from *Nold* and *Hauer* that the content of a right as recognized in the Community legal order may be different from its content as recognized in the Constitutions of the Member States. This reflects the general position of the Court in deriving general principles of law from the national legal systems, according to which it does not seek to derive common denominators but makes a synthesis guided by the spirit of the Treaty and the requirements of Community polity. As Weiler points out, the Community is a new polity the constitutional ethos of which must give expression to a multiplicity of national traditions.[23] The frequent references to the constitutions of the Member States in *Nold* and *Hauer* however suggest that, in the field of human rights, concepts of national law are more influential than in relation to other general principles. The reason for this is that respect for rights recognized as fundamental by the laws of the Member States provides political legitimacy and ideological grounding for the Community legal order.

7.2.3. Legislative developments

In parallel with case law developments, the political institutions of the Community began to make references to the protection of fundamental rights.[24] By the end of the 1980s, the road towards the formalization of fundamental rights protection had began in earnest, as their protection at Community level was seen both as a force of integration and a source of legitimacy.[25] At Treaty level, an express reference was made in the Preamble to the Single European Act. This was followed by Article F1 (now Article 6(2)) of the Treaty on European Union, the entrenchment of the Union values by the Treaty of Amsterdam, the Charter, and the EU Constitution.[26]

Articles 6(1) and (2) of the TEU, as amended by the Treaty of Amsterdam, state as follows:

1. The Union is founded on the principles of liberty, democracy, respect for human rights and fundamental freedoms, and the rule of law, principles which are common to the Member States.

---

[21] *Nold, op. cit.*, para 13; *Hauer, op. cit.*, para 15.   [22] See 7.2.4 below.

[23] J. Weiler, 'Fundamental Rights and Fundamental Boundaries: On Standards and Values in the Protection of Human Rights', in Neuwahl and Rosas, *op. cit.*, n. 1 above, p. 66.

[24] See, among others, the 1977 Joint Declaration on human rights, OJ 1977 C 103/1, and the European Council Declaration on Democracy, EC Bull 3 -1978, p. 5.

[25] G. de Bùrca, 'The Language of Rights in European Integration', in J. Shaw and G. More (eds), *New Legal Dynamics of European Union*, Oxford University Press, 1995 p. 29.

[26] See Article 9 of the Constitutional Treaty.

2. The Union shall respect fundamental rights, as guaranteed by the European Convention for the Protection of Human Rights and Fundamental Freedoms signed in Rome on 4 November 1950 and as they result from the constitutional traditions common to the Member States, as general principles of Community law.

Notably, the Treaty of Amsterdam provided for a political enforcement mechanism in the event that a Member State fails to observe human rights and fundamental freedoms or any of the other values enshrined in Article 6(1). This mechanism was further extended by the Treaty of Nice and is found in Article 7 TEU as amended by those Treaties. Articles 7(2) and (3) provide that, if the Council determines the existence of a 'serious and persistent' breach by a Member State of one of the principles mentioned in Article 6(1),[27] it may, acting by a qualified majority, 'decide to suspend certain of the rights deriving from the application of this Treaty to the State in question, including the voting rights of the representative of the Government of that Member State in the Council'. Article 7 was included in the Treaty of Amsterdam in response to calls by certain Member States who argued that the Union or the Community should accede to the European Convention on Human Rights. It is, however, no substitute for such accession. It was envisaged by the Inter-Governmental Conference that such a draconian penalty would be used only in the most exceptional of cases. The process of enforcement is intended to be a political one involving solely the political institutions of the Union. The Court has jurisdiction 'purely' in relation to the procedural stipulations of Article 7.[28] This suggests that the concept of 'serious and persistent' breach is not amenable to judicial control.

Article 7(1) is a new provision added by the Treaty of Nice.[29] It provides that if there is 'a clear risk of a serious breach' by a Member State of the principles mentioned in Article 6(1), the Council may address 'appropriate recommendations' to that State following the procedure specified therein. The existence of such a risk is determined by the Council acting by a majority of four-fifths after obtaining the assent of the European Parliament and following a reasoned proposal by one-third of the Member States, the European Parliament or the Commission.

7.2.4. The national reaction

Although in *Internationale Handelsgesellschaft* the Court went to lengths to address the concerns of the German judiciary relating to the protection of fundamental rights at Community level, the Federal Constitutional Court (Bundesverfassungsgericht) remained unconvinced. In a subsequent judgment arising from the

---

[27] The determination is made by the Council meeting in the composition of the Heads of State or Government and acting by unanimity (but without taking into account the vote of the representative of the Member State concerned) and after obtaining the assent of the European Parliament. See Article 7(3).   [28] See Article 46(e) TEU.

[29] The amendment was prompted by the rise to power of the extreme right-wing party in Austria and press comments made by its leader.

same dispute,[30] it held that fundamental rights were insufficiently protected by Community law because the Community lacked a codified catalogue of fundamental rights and also (at that time) a directly elected Parliament. It considered that the case law of the Court of Justice did not provide adequate protection because it was subject to change and did not satisfy the requirements of legal certainty. It held that, as long as Community law did not itself provide sufficient protection, the German courts should not apply rules of Community law which infringed fundamental rights as guaranteed by the German Constitution and reserved itself jurisdiction to decide whether such infringement existed. Some years later, in the so-called *Second Solange* case,[31] the Bundesverfassungsgericht was prepared to relax its approach. It accepted that supervening developments had rendered the protection of fundamental rights at Community level commensurate with that offered by the Basic Law. It referred to *Nold* and subsequent case law, the 1977 Joint Declaration of the political institutions on human rights,[32] and the European Council Declaration on Democracy of 1978.[33] The Constitutional Court now accepted that it would not rule on whether secondary Community law was sufficiently in conformity with the German Constitution as long as the Community continued to protect human rights at the existing level.

The Constitutional Court seemed to confirm that position in the *European Union Treaty* case[34] where Germany's ratification of the Treaty on European Union was challenged on grounds of constitutionality. The Bundesverfassungsgericht affirmed that it guarantees the essential content of fundamental rights not only against German authorities but also against the sovereign powers of the Community. It does so, however, in a relationship of cooperation with the Court of Justice, under which the Court of Justice provides protection of fundamental rights in the Community legal order and the Bundesverfassungsgericht restricts itself to a general guarantee of the constitutional standards that cannot be dispensed with. In the specific case, it rejected the submission that the potential replacement of the German mark by a common currency would infringe the right to property and the freedom to trade and carry out professional activities.

The Bundesverfassungsgericht views its relationship with the ECJ as one of cooperation under which the latter has a wide but reversible mandate to guarantee respect for inalienable human rights.[35] This approach was reiterated in the *Bananas*

---

[30] See Bundesverfassungsgericht, judgment of 29 May 1974, [1974] 2 CMLR 551. A similar backlash came from Italian courts: see *Granital*.

[31] See Bundesverfassungsgericht, judgment of 22 October 1986, 2 BvR 197/83, 73 BVerfGE 339, [1987] 3 CMLR 225.   [32] OJ 1977 No C 103, p. 1.

[33] EC Bull 3–1978, p. 5.

[34] See Bundesverfassungsgericht, judgment of 12 October 1993, 2 BvR 2134/92 and 2159/92, 89 BverfGE 155, [1993] 1 CMLR 57. For a powerful critique, see J.H.H. Weiler, 'Does Europe Need a Constitution? Demos, Telos and the German Maastrich Decision' (1995) 1 ELJ 219.

[35] A similar approach was taken by the Danish Supreme Court in *Hanne Norup Carlsen and others v Prime Minister Poul Nyrup Rasmussen* [1999] 3 CMLR 854. Judgment delivered on 6 April 1998, UfR 1998.800. For a discussion, see among others, H. Rasmussen, 'Confrontation or Peaceful Coexistence? On the Danish Supreme Court's Maastricht Ratification Judgment' in

cases,[36] where the Constitutional court rejected a challenge against the Bananas Regulation on the ground that it violated the right to property, the freedom to exercise a trade, and the principle of equality as guaranteed by the Basic Law. The essence of the applicants' argument was that the ECJ, which in the *Bananas* case had rejected a challenge to the validity of the Regulation, did not provide adequate protection of fundamental rights. The tenet of the judgment is that the Bundesverfassungsgericht retains residual jurisdiction to control the compatibility of Community law with fundamental rights but that the level of deference granted to the ECJ is so high that it would be extremely difficult for the Federal Court to be persuaded to intervene.

The above case law evinces the dialectical development of Community constitutional law. In *Internationale Handelsgesellschaft* the Constitutional Court 'asked', in *Nold* and *Hauer* the Court of Justice 'gave' and in the *Second Solange* case the Constitutional Court 'conceded'. But the provisional character of the Constitutional Court's deference to the jurisdiction of the Court of Justice is of particular importance. Firmly based on the idea that sovereignty derives from the nation State, the Constitutional Court sees itself as the guarantor of universal democratic values and is keen to retain residual authority.[37]

7.2.5. What is a fundamental right?

In *Nold* and in *Hauer* the Court made it clear that the Community legal order is committed to protecting, subject to appropriate limitations set by the objectives and the scheme of the Treaty, the rights recognized in the European Convention on Human Rights and the national constitutions. Since the Treaty does not provide for a catalogue of fundamental rights, which rights are expressly recognized by the Court depends on the accidents of litigation. The rights which have been expressly recognized so far may be classified into three broad categories: economic and property rights, civil and political liberties, and rights of defence.[38]

Economic and property rights include the right to property,[39] the freedom to trade, and the right to choose and practise freely a trade or profession.[40] Civil and political liberties include human dignity,[41] religious equality,[42] freedom of

D. O'Keeffe and A. Bavasso (eds), *Judicial Review in European Union Law* (Kluwer, 2000), 377–390; K. Høegh, 'The Danish Maastricht Judgment' (1999) 24 ELR 80.

[36] See Bundesverfassungsgericht, Judgment of 7 June 2000, 2BvL 1/97, NJW 3124 (2000). For commentary, see M. Aziz, 'Sovereignty Lost, Sovereignty Regained? Some Reflections on the Bundesverfassungsgericht's Bananas Judgment', 9 (2002) Columbia Journal of European Law 109. The Federal Court took the same approach in the *Alcan* case concerning State aid: see judgment of 7 June 2000, commented by F. Hoffmeister, (2001) 38 CML Rev 791.

[37] But see Weiler, *op. cit.*, esp. pp. 222 *et seq.*   [38] For the rights of defence, see below Chapter 8.
[39] See e.g. *Hauer, op. cit.*, and below p. 313.
[40] *Nold, op. cit.; Hauer, op. cit.*; Case 240/83 *Procureur de la République v ADBHU* [1985] ECR 531.
[41] See e.g. Case C-36/02 *Omega Spielhallen- und Automatenaufstellungs v Oberbürgermeisterin der Bundesstadt Bonn*, judgment of 14 October 2004; *Stauder, op. cit.*
[42] Case 130/75 *Prais v Council* [1976] ECR 1589.

expression,[43] prohibition of discrimination based on sex,[44] including gender reassignment,[45] the right to respect privacy,[46] including family life[47] and medical confidentiality,[48] freedom of association and trade union activity,[49] and the right to an effective legal remedy.[50] More recently, the case law has pronounced on the right to public access to documents held by the Community institutions.[51] The Court has also expressly confirmed that the Community abides by the general principle of *nulla poena sine lege*,[52] and has declared as a general principle that any intervention by the Community authorities in the sphere of private activities of any person, whether natural or legal, must have a legal basis and be justified on grounds laid down by law.[53]

By contrast, it has been held that the principle of *nulla poena sine culpa* does not necessarily prohibit the imposition of strict criminal liability provided that such liability is proportionate and aims at the protection of important interests. This was first pronounced by the Court in *Hansen*[54] in relation to a measure concerning the liability of the employer for failure to respect worker protection standards and was subsequently expressly confirmed in *Ebony Maritime and Loten Navigation v Prefetto della Provincia di Brindisi and Others*.[55] That case arose from the imposition of sanctions against Yugoslavia. The Court held that Regulation No 990/93 implementing UN sanctions against Yugoslavia[56] did not preclude an Italian law which provided for confiscation of the cargo where a vessel infringed the

---

[43] Case C-100/88 *Oyowe and Traore v Commission* [1989] ECR 4285; Case C-260/89 *ERT* [1991] ECR I-2925; Case C-159/90 *SPUC v Grogan* [1991] ECR I-4685; Case C-219/91 *Ter Voort* [1992] ECR I-5485. See also for the freedom of the press, e.g. Case 246/83 *Binon v AMP* [1985] ECR 2015, para 46.   [44] Case 149/77 *Defrenne v Sabena* [1978] ECR 1365.
[45] Case C-13/91 *P v S and Cornwall County Council* [1996] ECR I-2143; but not sexual orientation, see Case C-249/96 *Grant v South-West Trains Ltd* [1998] ECR I-621.
[46] Case 136/79 *National Panasonic v Commission* [1980] ECR 2033; Case C-62/90 *Commission v Germany* [1992] ECR I-2575; Case C-76/93 P *Scaramuzza v Commission* [1994] ECR I-5173. Reference has also been made to the duty of Community institutions to protect the personal integrity and honour of the Community employees: Case T-203/95 R *Connolly v Commission* [1995] ECR II-2919.
[47] Case 249/86 *Commission v Germany* [1989] ECR 1263.
[48] Case C-62/90 *Commission v Germany, op. cit.*; Joined Cases T-121/89 and T-13/90 *X v Commission* [1992] ECR II-2195 and on appeal Case C-404/92P [1994] ECR I-4737; Case T-10/93 *A v Commission* [1994] ECR II-179.
[49] C-415/93 *Union Royale Belge des Sociétés de Football Association and Others v Bosman and Others* [1995] ECR I-4921, para 79; Case 175/73 *Union Syndicale Massa and Kortner v Council* [1974] ECR 917.
[50] Case 36/75 *Rutili v Minister for the Interior* [1975] ECR 1219, para 21; Case 222/84 *Johnston v Chief Constable of the Royal Ulster Constabulary* [1986] ECR 1651.
[51] Consideration of this right is beyond the scope of this book.
[52] Case 63/83 *R v Kirk* [1984] ECR 2689, paras 21–22; Case C-331/88 *Fedesa* [1990] ECR I-4023, paras 41–42. See also Case 85/76 *Hoffmann-La Roche v Commission* [1979] ECR 461, at 510 and 553 *et seq.*
[53] Joined Cases 46/87 and 227/88 *Hoechst v Commission* [1989] ECR 2859, para 19.
[54] Case C-326/88 *Hansen* [1990] ECR I-2911; see esp. pp. 2925 *et seq. per* van Gerven AG.
[55] Case C-177/95 [1997] ECR I-1111. See also Case C-124/95 *The Queen, ex p Centro-Com v HM Treasury and Bank of England* [1997] ECR I-81.
[56] Regulation No 990/93 concerning trade between the Community and the Federal Republic of Yugoslavia, OJ 1993 L 102, p. 14.

provisions of the Regulation even though the penalty of confiscation was imposed without any proof of fault on the part of the owner of the cargo. The Court dismissed the argument that the Italian law violated the principle *nulla poena sine culpa* and that it was contrary to the principle of proportionality. It stated that a system of strict criminal liability is not in itself incompatible with Community law. Where it is for the Member States to provide sanctions for breach of Community measures, such sanctions must be analogous to those applicable to infringements of national law of a similar nature and also, in any event, they must be effective, proportionate and dissuasive. It is for the national court to determine whether the penalty of confiscation complies with those requirements. The Court however stated that, in making that determination, the national court had to take into account that the objective pursued by Regulation No 990/93, which was to bring to an end the state of war in the region concerned and the massive violation of human rights, was one of fundamental general interest for the international Community.

An interesting example of the application of the right to medical confidentiality is provided by *X v Commission*.[57] There, it was held that the right to medical confidentiality prohibits the Commission from subjecting a candidate for employment to a pre-recruitment medical test without his consent. The Court held that, if the person concerned, after being properly informed, withholds his consent to a test which the medical officer considers necessary in order to evaluate his suitability for recruitment, the institutions cannot be obliged to take the risk of recruiting him. The Court however understood the right to medical confidentiality more broadly than the CFI. The latter held that the Commission was under an obligation to respect the candidate's refusal to undergo an AIDS test but could carry out without his consent other tests which might point to the presence of the AIDS virus. Reversing the judgment of the CFI, the Court of Justice held that, 'the right to respect for private life requires that a person's refusal be respected in its entirety'. Since the appellant had expressly refused to undergo an AIDS screening test, the administration was precluded from carrying out any test liable to point to, or establish, the existence of that illness, in respect of which he had refused disclosure.[58]

It is interesting that linguistic protection has not received recognition as a fundamental right in Community law. In *Piageme II*, for example, the Court appeared reluctant to give priority to the protection of regional languages over the free movement of goods.[59] The issue acquires particular importance in the domain of procedure. The first Council Regulation issued under the EEC Treaty provided for the citizen's right to send correspondence to the institutions in any of the official languages of the Community and to receive answers in that language.[60] The case law however has not gone further than upholding the guarantees provided by

---

[57] *Op. cit.*, n. 48 above.   [58] *Ibid.*, para 23.

[59] Case C-85/94 *Piageme and Others v Peeters* [1995] ECR I-2955.

[60] Council Regulation No 1 of 15 April 1958 determining the languages used by the European Economic Community, OJ English Sp. Ed., 1952–58, p. 59.

Community written law,[61] and there does not seem to be a general principle guaranteeing the conduct of administrative proceedings before Community bodies in the citizen's native language.[62]

The recognition of a right as fundamental by the Court marks only the beginning of the enquiry. It does not tell us much about the level of protection afforded to that right nor of its legal value *vis-à-vis* other competing interests or rights which can be determined only by studying outcomes. Two general points may be made in this context. First, the classification of a right as fundamental indicates that the Community legal order grants to that right at least a minimum of weight and consequently increases the burden on public authorities to justify restrictions upon it.[63] The individual has, to use Dworkinian terminology, 'a trump card' against public authorities given to him by Community law. Second, the case law evinces a marked difference between social rights, on the one hand, and economic rights, on the other. With regard to the former, the Court is prepared to take a pro-active approach and pioneer solutions often stretching beyond written law. Thus, since the 1970s the Court has led the way in establishing the principle of sex equality and working out the specific consequences which flow from it, forcing effectively the national judiciaries to follow.[64] More recently, the Court took a step further holding that Community law prohibits discrimination on grounds of gender reassignment.[65] By contrast, the recognition of economic rights as rights protected by Community law, for example the right to property or the freedom to trade, seems to serve a prophylactic function. The Court recognizes in the abstract a core element of such rights upon which the Community authorities are not permitted to encroach but beyond that the freedom of the individual may be required to give way to the public interest. To put it in a different way, in the field of social law and sex equality, the case law establishes positive rights. In the field of economic rights, the case law prescribes limitations on public action. The balancing exercise performed by the Court in the field of economic rights will be illustrated below by reference to the right of property and the freedom to trade.

---

[61] See K. Lenaerts, 'General Report', in 'Procedures and Sanctions in Economic Administrative Law', 17 *FIDE Congress Report*, Berlin, 1996 at 530.

[62] See Article 115 of Regulation No 40/94 on the Community Trademark, OJ 1994 L11, p. 1. The Regulation permits persons to send applications for a Community trademark to the Office in any of the official Community languages but subsequent communications will normally be conducted in one of the five languages of the Office. See also Case T-77/92 *Parker Pen v Commission* [1994] ECR II-549, where in the context of competition proceedings, the Court dismissed the argument that statements made by German-speaking parties should have been translated into English. Lenaerts, *op. cit.*, suggests that the case might have had a different outcome if protection of native language was recognized as a general principle. See also, in a different context, Case C-274/96 *Criminal Proceedings against Bickel and Franz*, [1998] ECR I-7637.

[63] The additional burden to justify restrictions applies also to the Community judicature itself. In *Scaramuzza, op. cit.*, n. 46 above, para 30, the Court held that the CFI should have provided full reasoning in rejecting an unmeritorious plea based on the alleged breach of human rights.

[64] See e.g. *Defrenne v Sabena, op. cit.*; C-262/88 *Barber v Guardian Royal Exchange Assurance Group* [1990] ECR I-1889; case c-32/93 *Webb v EMO Air Cargo (UK) Ltd* [1994] ECR I-3567

[65] *P v S and Cornwall County Council, op. cit.*

The Community's priorities have been questioned. In particular, the issue has been raised why Community law elevates certain rights to a fundamental status but refuses such status to others.[66] In the latter category belong, for example, immigration and asylum rights, rights for people with disabilities, environmental, language and cultural rights. This question refers mainly to the political institutions whose use of the language of rights in certain areas, in particular the social sphere, contrasts with the absence of such terminology in other areas. As far as the Community judicature is concerned, suffice it to say that there are no *a priori* excluded areas. The fact that certain rights but not others have been recognized as fundamental is explained by the historical origins and nature of the judicial protection of human rights in the Community legal order.

7.2.6. Searching for the appropriate standard of protection

A vexed issue is whether the Court should be bound to accept as fundamental any right which is safeguarded by the constitution of any one of the Member States. An affirmative answer was given by Warner AG in *IRCA*[67] and the same view has been supported also by Professor Schermers.[68] The reasoning goes as follows. Community law owes its existence to a partial transfer of sovereignty by the Member States. No Member State can be said to have included in that transfer power for the Community to legislate in infringement of rights protected by its own constitution. If that were so, ratification of the Treaty by a Member State would entail capacity to flout its own constitution which is not possible.[69] The problem with this reasoning is that what matters is not so much recognition of a right as fundamental but the consequences which flow from it, in particular, the weight attributed to it where it conflicts with another fundamental right. It is correct to say that, where a Member State considers a particular right so important as to incorporate it in its constitution, that right forms part of a European legal heritage.[70] The case remains that a right does not exist in a vacuum but incorporates the outcome of a balancing exercise between conflicting rights and interests within a certain polity. That balancing exercise is influenced by a number of factors which may be legal, economic, social, political or cultural in nature. The outcome reflects ultimately the values espoused by a society and may vary from State to State or even within the same State at different times. As far as the Community polity is concerned, it is for the Community judicature to draw that balance. No doubt, as Warner AG remarked, in ratifying the Treaties the Member States did not give

[66] See the thoughtful critique of G. de Bùrca, 'The Language of Rights in European Integration' in J. Shaw and G. More (eds), *New Legal Dynamics of European Union*, (Oxford University Press, 1995) 29, at 39.

[67] Case 7/76 *IRCA v Amministrazione delle Finanze dello Stato* [1976] ECR 1213, at 1237.

[68] H.G. Schermers, 'The European Community Bound by Fundamental Human Rights' 27 (1990) CML Rev 249, at 252 *et seq.*   [69] *IRCA, op. cit.*, p. 1237.

[70] Schermers, *op. cit.*, p. 254.

carte blanche to the Community nor did they agree to forego protection of their constitutionally entrenched rights. But membership is not a bilateral relationship. It is a multilateral one and no Member State has a right to expect that in a given conflict the Community, and through it the other Member States, will endorse *simpliciter* its own balance and the fundamental societal values which go with it. This in turn poses the issue what standards of protection must the Court of Justice adopt in reviewing the compatibility of measures with Community law. Should it adopt a maximalist approach searching for the highest standard provided in the national laws or a minimalist approach searching instead for the lowest common denominator? The answer is neither. The Court should aim for the solution most suitable to the Community polity and, as *Hauer* made clear, that is precisely its approach:[71]

the question of a possible infringement of fundamental rights by a measure of the Community institutions can only be judged in the light of Community law itself. The introduction of special criteria for assessment stemming from the legislation or constitutional law of a particular Member State would, by damaging the substantive unity and efficacy of Community law, lead inevitably to the destruction of the unity of the Common Market and the jeopardizing of the cohesion of the Community.

The fallacy of the minimalist–maximalist dichotomy has aptly been exposed by Weiler.[72] To think in terms of low and high standards is to think in two dimensions. What is a maximum protection of one right can be seen as a minimum protection of another. As Weiler points out, to say that Member State A provides for the highest protection of the right to property means that this Member State imposes the largest restriction on the public authorities to act in the general interest and consequently provides for the lowest level of protection for the public at large.[73] Human rights are not empty, abstract ideas but express core societal choices as to the balance between the interests of the individual and interests of the society at large.[74] The maximalist approach would have two consequences. It would favour the Member State which happens to accord the highest protection to a certain right and transpose its values to Community law even if they are unrepresentative of the values of other Member States. Also, the aggregate of maximum protection of individual rights would result in maximum restrictions being imposed on the Community. As Weiler puts it, a maximalist approach to human rights would result in a minimalist approach to Community government[75] even though that might render unworkable a Community policy.

The issue remains whether it is possible for the Court to afford a lesser level of protection to a fundamental right than that afforded by any Member State. In other words, could it be said that the national constitutions provide at least a minimum of protection below which the Court may not go? As we have seen the Court does not accept that view and the above discussion would suggest that the Court's

---

[71] *Hauer, op. cit.*, para 14.   [72] Weiler, *op. cit.*, n. 23 above pp. 51–76.
[73] *Ibid.*, p. 60.   [74] *Ibid.*, pp. 54–56.   [75] *Ibid.*, p. 61.

approach is the correct one. In practice it is difficult to envisage circumstances in which the Court would uphold a Community measure which would have been struck down by the national courts of all Member States as being contrary to fundamental rights. The reverse question may also be asked: is it possible for the Court to recognize a right which is not recognized by any of the Member States? An affirmative answer cannot be precluded. In *P v S* the Court made no reference to the laws of the Member States, although it referred to the European Convention. Tesauro AG made extensive references to the position of trans-sexuals in the laws of Member States although the findings seemed inconclusive.[76] It seems that in order for a right to be recognized by the Court without the assistance of express Community legislation, it must be based either on 'a solid consensus of generally shared values'[77] in the Member States or belong in a broader area where the Community legislature has been active.[78]

The following section examines the case law relating to the right to property and the freedom to trade. These are among the most oft-invoked fundamental rights in actions for judicial review of Community measures.

7.2.7. The right to property and the freedom to trade

The Court has held that the right to property[79] and the right to trade or choose freely a professional activity are not absolute but must be viewed in the light of their social function.[80] They may be restricted, particularly in the context of a common organization of the market, provided that two conditions are met: the restrictions imposed must correspond to objectives of general interest pursued by the Community; and they must not 'constitute a disproportionate and intolerable interference, impairing the very substance of the right'.[81] Although the language used by the Court seems to suggest that these are distinct requirements each of which must be satisfied separately, they are in fact different aspects of the same enquiry.

We saw above how in *Nold* and in particular in *Hauer* the Court scrutinized the contested regulations with a view to determining whether they infringed

---

[76] [1996] ECR I-2149 *et seq.*

[77] The expression is used by M. Jachtenfuchs, 'Theoretical Perspectives on European Governance' (1995) 1 ELJ 115 at 126.

[78] In this category belong for example, the rights of trans-sexuals: see *P v S, op. cit.*

[79] The Treaty is neutral as regards the system of ownership and property rights recognized by Member States: see Article 295. On the right to property, see further F. Campbell-White, 'Property rights: A Forgotten Issue under the Union' in Neuwahl and Rosas, *op. cit.*, pp. 249–263.

[80] *Nold, op. cit; Hauer, op. cit.; Procureur de la République v ADBHU, op. cit.*, para 12. This is the general formula used by the Court in relation to all fundamental rights. See e.g. in relation to the freedom of expression: *Ter Voort, op. cit.*, para 38; and the right to private life: *X v Commission, op. cit.*

[81] Case C-280/93 *Germany v Council* [1994] ECR I-4973, para 78; Case 265/87 *Schräder v Hauptzollamt Gronau* [1989] ECR 2237, para 15; *Wachauf op. cit.*, para 18; Case C-177/90 *Kühn v Landwirtschaftskammer Weser-Ems* [1992] ECR I-35. For recent confirmation, see e.g. Joined Cases C-37 and C-38/02 *Di Lenardo Adriano and Dilexport v Ministero del Commercio con l'Estero*, judgment of 15 July 2004, para 82.

Community law. A more recent example is provided by *Germany v Council* (*Bananas case*).[82] It will be remembered that Council Regulation No 404/93 setting up a common organization of the market in bananas limited the volume of imports from third countries by introducing a tariff quota and subdividing it among various categories of traders. The Regulation affected severely the competitive position of German importers who, before its coming into force, were able to import third-country bananas free of tariff restrictions within a quota which was adjusted annually to take into account the needs of the market. The German Government objected to the introduction of the tariff quota, its subdivision among various categories of traders, and the principle of free transferability of import licences. It alleged that the loss of market share suffered by traders in third-country bananas was an infringement of their freedom to pursue their trade. The Court stated that the restriction of the right to import third-country bananas imposed on German traders was inherent in the establishment of the common organization of the market, which was designed to promote the realization of the objectives of the common agricultural policy and to ensure that the international obligations of the Community were complied with. Restrictions on the volume of imports from third countries were necessary in order to ensure that, after the introduction of the common organization of the market, Community and ACP bananas were not displaced from the common market following the disappearance of the protective barriers enabling them to be disposed of with protection from competition from third-country bananas. In response to the argument that the principle of free transferability of import licences had adverse consequences for German importers of third-country bananas,[83] the Court held that the transfer of import licences was an option which the Regulation allowed the various categories of economic operators to exercise according to their commercial interests. The financial advantage which such a transfer might in some cases give traders in Community and ACP bananas was a necessary consequence of the principle of transferability of licences and should be assessed in the more general framework of all the measures adopted by the Council to ensure the disposal of Community and traditional ACP products. In that context, it ought to be regarded as a means intended to contribute to the competitiveness of operators marketing Community and ACP bananas and to facilitate the integration of the Member States' markets.[84] The Court concluded that the restriction imposed by the Regulation on the freedom of traditional traders in third-country bananas to pursue their trade corresponded to objectives of general Community interest and did not impair the very substance of that freedom.

---

[82] Case C-280/93 *op. cit.*; for other aspects of the case see above, pp. 85 and 154. The judgment was confirmed in Case C-104/97 P *Atlanta AG v European Community*, [1999] ECR I-6983.

[83] The argument of the German Government reflected economic reality in that the principle of free transferability of import licences resulted in transferring profit potential from traditional dealers in third-country bananas to traditional dealers in Community and ACP bananas. See further the Opinion of Gulmann AG, *op. cit.*, at 5004.   [84] *Op. cit.*, paras 81–86.

The case illustrates that the economic interests of a certain category of trader may be affected severely as a result of introducing a common organization of the market, without that constituting a breach of the right to exercise a trade or profession.[85] In the circumstances of the case the Court took the view that, although German importers suffered significant loss, that was within the normal economic risks which commercial operators could be expected to undertake. In that respect, the case is to be distinguished from the milk quota cases[86] where the producers concerned suffered specifically as a result of relying on Community legislation and were exposed to adverse financial consequences exceeding normal commercial risks. A factor which may have operated against the annulment of the Regulation in the *Bananas* case was that, before the introduction of the common organization of the market, German traders enjoyed an exceptional benefit in that imports from third countries were exempt from customs duties pursuant to the Banana Protocol.[87] The loss of market share suffered by them was perceived as the termination of an exceptional benefit rather than as the denial of a vested right. Crucially, although the judgment dealt extensively with the requirement that the restriction imposed on the right to trade must correspond to objectives of general Community interest, it did not address specifically the requirement that the very substance of the right must not be impaired. This indicates that, as already stated, the two requirements are in fact two sides of the same test.

Notably, in no case so far has the Court found a violation of the right to property or the freedom to trade. Where Community legislation seriously threatens such rights the Court prefers to address the claim on different grounds such as breach of the principle of equality, as for example in *Codorniu*,[88] or of the protection of legitimate expectations, as in the milk quota cases.[89] Save in cases of expropriation of property rights or a very extensive prohibition, without good reason, of the carrying on of a professional activity, it is not easy to imagine a violation of the

---

[85] Note however that in a subsequent case which arose from the application of the Bananas Regulation, the Court held that the Community institutions have a duty to adopt transitional measures in order to alleviate difficulties encountered by traders in the transition from national arrangements to the common organization of the market 'in particular when the transition to the common organization of the market infringes certain traders' fundamental rights protected by Community law, such as the right to property and the right to pursue a professional or trade activity': Case C-68/95 *T. Port v Bundesanstalt für Landwirtschaft und Ernährung* [1996] ECR I-6065, para 40. For a successful action in damages arising from the Commission's failure to take transitional measures in the bananas regime, see Joined Cases T-79/96, T-260/97 and T-117/98 *Camar and Tico v Commission and Council* [2000] ECR II-2193; confirmed on appeal Case C-312/00, [2002] ECR I-113555. The legal basis of the claim, however, was breach of Article 30 of the basic Bananas Regulation and not of the right to pursue a trade or profession. For an unsuccessful claim based on the new Bananas Regulation, see *Dilexport, op. cit.*, n. 81 above.

[86] See above p. 275.

[87] See Protocol annexed to the Implementing Convention on the Association of the Overseas Countries and Territories with the Community, provided for in Article 136 EC.

[88] Case C-309/89 *Codorniu v Council* [1994] ECR I-1853.

[89] See Case 120/86 *Mulder I* [1988] ECR 2321, Case C-189/89 *Spagl* [1990] ECR I-4539. In the latter case, Jacobs AG took the view that the 60 per cent rule applicable to the calculation of the reference quantities of returning producers did not violate the right to property.

former set of rights which does not also constitute a violation of one or another of the latter principles.[90] Notably, in *Sidabras & Anor v Lithuania*,[91] the ECtHR held that a far-reaching ban on taking up private sector employment affected an individual's private life within the meaning of Article 8 of the Convention. The case concerned a ban on previous KGB officers taking up state and private sector employment in various sectors and the Court found the ban was disproportionate in the circumstances of the case. In the context of EU law, a similar ban could be addressed in terms of violation of the freedom to pursue a trade or profession, provided that it somehow fell within the scope of Community law.

The affinity between the right to property and the principle of protection of legitimate expectations is illustrated in many other cases. In *SMW Winzersekt*,[92] a Council regulation restricted, subject to a transitional period, the use of the designation 'méthode champenoise' to sparkling wines which were entitled to the registered designation 'Champagne'. Before the adoption of the regulation, the designation 'méthode champenoise' could be used by all producers of sparkling wines. German wine growers challenged the regulation on the ground that it infringed the right to property and the freedom to pursue a trade or profession. The Court held that since, prior to the adoption of the regulation, all producers of sparkling wines were entitled to use the term 'méthode champenoise', the prohibition of the use of that designation could not be regarded as an infringement of a property right 'vested in the applicants'. With regard to the freedom to pursue a trade or profession, the Court held that the regulation pursued an objective of general interest, namely, the protection of registered indications of the geographical origin of wines. In accordance with that objective, in the exercise of its discretionary powers, the Council considered that a wine producer should not be able to use, in descriptions relating to the method of production of his products, geographical indications which do not correspond to the actual provenance of the wine. The regulation took sufficient account of the interests of producers who, prior to the adoption of the regulation used the term 'méthode champenoise', by adopting transitional provisions and by allowing them to use alternative expressions.

The freedom to pursue an economic activity confers the assurance that a trader may not be arbitrarily deprived of the right to pursue his professional activities but clearly does not guarantee him a particular volume of business or a specific share of the market.[93] A distinction may be drawn between access to a trade or profession

---

[90] For the combined examination of pleas based on breach of the principle of proportionality and the right to property see Joined Cases C-153 and C-205/94 *Faroe Seafood and Others* [1996] ECR I-2465 at 2549. In that case, the Court held that the post-clearance recovery of import duties in circumstances where the conditions of Article 5(2) of Regulation No 1697/79 were not met did not breach the right to property and the principle of proportionality because it fell within the sphere of normal commercial risks of the traders concerned.

[91] Judgment of 27 July 2004, para 50.

[92] Case C-306/93 *SMW Winzersekt* [1994] ECR I-5555.

[93] See e.g. Case T-521/93 *Atlanta and Others v European Community* [1996] ECR II-1707, para 62.

and restrictions on its exercise. Restrictions on access may be more difficult to justify than restrictions on its exercise. Thus in *Hauer* the Court held that the contested regulation did not affect access to the occupation of wine growing or the freedom to pursue that occupation on land at present devoted to wine growing.[94] With regard to the prohibition on planting of new vines, the Court held that this was no more than a consequence of the restriction upon the exercise of the right of property which the Court had found to be compatible with Community law. The distinction between existence and exercise, however, is not easy to make and the Court will take into account whether the measure is justified by an overriding general interest. Such an interest includes, *inter alia*, the establishment of the internal market,[95] the objective of eliminating speculative or artificial practices in relation to import licences,[96] health protection,[97] and the effectiveness of economic sanctions.[98]

With regard to the right to property, there are dicta to the effect that the substance of the right may be impaired where the measure deprives a person of his property or of the freedom to use it,[99] but the Court has not given more specific guidelines. It is evident from the case law that a right may be deprived of much of its economic value without that amounting to a breach of the right to property. It seems that the purpose of that right is to prohibit expropriation. It has been suggested that the hallmarks of an expropriation measure are two, namely, the measure must result in the deprivation of all appreciable economic value in the (tangible or intangible) asset in issue and the deprivation must be permanent.[100] By contrast, a trader cannot claim a right to property in a market share which he held at a time before the establishment of a common organization of the market, since such a market share constitutes 'only a momentary economic position exposed to the risks of changing circumstances'.[101] In *Irish Farmers Association*[102] it was held that the conversion of the temporary suspension of a percentage of the quota allocated to milk producers into permanent withdrawal without compensation did not affect the substance of the right to property inasmuch as the applicants were able to continue to pursue their trade as milk producers. Moreover, the Court noted, the reduction in milk production led to an increase in the price of milk, thus partly compensating the loss suffered.

[94] *Hauer, op. cit.*, para 32.
[95] See e.g. Case T-113/96 *Dubois et Fils v Council and Commission* [1998] ECR II-125. The CFI held that the completion of the internal market did not deprive customs agents of their right to pursue a professional activity. It only affected them indirectly, and also the completion of the internal market was an objective of evident general interest.
[96] *Dilexport, op. cit.*, paras 84, 87.
[97] Joined Cases C-20 and C-64/00 *Booker Aquaculture Ltd v The Scottish Minister*, [2003] ECR I-7411, paras 90–92 (compulsory slaughter of fish to avoid the spreading of disease).
[98] Case C-84/95 *Bosphorus Hava Yollari Turizm ve Ticaret AS v Minister for Transport and the Attorney General* [1996] ECR I-3953.
[99] See Case 59/83 *Biovilac v EEC* [1984] ECR 4057, para 22.
[100] *Hauer, op. cit., per* Capotorti AG at p.3759–62; *Wachauf, op. cit.*, at 2629–30, *per* Jacobs AG.
[101] *Germany v Council, op. cit.*, para 79.
[102] Case C-22/94 *Irish Farmers Association and Others v Minister for Agriculture, Food and Forestry (Ireland) and the Attorney General* [1997] ECR I-1809, para 29.

Among the measures which have been found by the Court not to violate the right to property or the freedom to trade are the imposition of a co-responsibility levy on cereals with a view to stabilizing the market,[103] and the imposition on vessel owners of the obligation to finance a scrapping scheme with a view to reducing the structural overcapacity in the Community's inland waterway networks.[104] More generally, it has been held that restrictions on production owing to the economic situation cannot be regarded as being an infringement of the right to property on the ground that they may harm the profitability of an undertaking.[105] The Court has also held that the right to property does not include the right to dispose for profit of an advantage, such as a milk quota allocated in the context of the common organization of the market, which does not derive from the assets or occupational activity of the person concerned.[106] In *Wachauf*, by contrast, the Court declared that Community rules which had the effect of depriving a tenant farmer of the fruits of his labour would be incompatible with fundamental rights but did not specify which rights would be infringed as a result. The context of the case suggests that the Court was referring to the right to property.[107]

An interesting case arose from the sanctions imposed by the Community on Yugoslavia. In *Bosphorus Hava Yollari Turizm ve Ticaret AS v Minister for Transport and the Attorney General*[108] at issue was Article 8 of Regulation No 990/93[109] which required Member States to impound all vessels, freight vehicles and aircraft 'in which a majority or controlling interest is held by a person or undertaking in or operating from the Federal Republic of Yugoslavia'. Pursuant to that provision, the Irish authorities impounded an aircraft which Bosphorus Airways, a Turkish company, had leased from the Yugoslav national airline. The Court interpreted Article 8 as applying to an aircraft based in or operating from the Federal Republic of Yugoslavia even though the owner had leased it to another undertaking, which was neither based in nor operating from there, and which was not controlled by Yugoslavian interests. The Court dismissed the argument of the Turkish company that such a broad interpretation of Article 8 infringed its fundamental right to

---

[103] *Schräder, op. cit.,* n. 81 above.

[104] Joined Cases C-248 and C-249/95 *SAM Schiffahrt GmbH and Heinz Stapf v Germany* [1997] ECR I-4475.

[105] See e.g. Case 258/81 *Metallurgiki Halyps v Commission* [1982] ECR 4261, para 13; Joined Cases 172/83 and 226/83 *Hoogovens Groep* [1985] ECR 283, para 29.

[106] This dictum first made in Case C-44/89 *von Deetzen II* [1991] ECR I-5119, para 27, was confirmed in Case C-2/92 *Bostock* [1994] ECR I-955, para 19. It will be noted however that the context of the two cases was different. In *von Deetzen* the applicant sought to derive an advantage by transferring for profit the special quota allocated to him as a returning producer. The Court rightly held that the purpose of allocating special quotas to returning producers was in order to enable them to resume their occupational activity following their temporary exit from the market and not to realise their economic value. In *Bostock*, on the other hand, the applicant was not a returning producer but sought compensation upon surrendering his lease for increasing the production capacity of the holding during his tenancy. The claim in *Bostock* was more meritorious although it is not suggested here that the right to property was violated in that case.

[107] See the Opinion of Jacobs AG, at p. 2630.   [108] *Op. cit.,* n. 98 above.

[109] *Op. cit.,* n. 56 above.

property and its freedom to pursue a commercial activity. It held that any measure imposing sanctions has, by definition, consequences which affect the right to property and commercial freedom, thereby causing loss to innocent third parties. The importance of the aims pursued by the Regulation was such as to justify negative consequences, even of a substantial nature. This is clearly an exceptional case where private rights had to give way to overriding objectives pertaining to public security. In subsequent proceedings, the judgment of the ECJ was confirmed by the ECtHR.[110]

Although in practice it is difficult to establish a violation of the right to property, it may be noted that the case law has adopted a functional rather than formalistic approach to the notion of 'assets' upon which property rights may be recognized. The milk quota cases imply that the right to property encompasses in principle instruments of market control, such as milk quotas, which have a market value and can be disposed for profit.[111]

The freedom to pursue a trade or profession seems to entail a higher level of judicial scrutiny in German law, from where it originates.[112] In one case, the Bundesverfassungsgericht held, applying the principle, that the administrative courts have jurisdiction to review whether the answers given by a candidate in the State examinations to obtain a legal qualification were incorrect and therefore whether the candidate could be refused admission to the legal profession on their basis.[113] This difference in the standard of scrutiny however should not be attributed to the intrinsic qualities of the freedom to pursue a trade or profession but rather to a more deeply rooted division between German and Community administrative law. The former, unlike the latter, traditionally recognizes administrative discretion, in principle, only where it is expressly granted. Unless the law employs language which signifies that the administration has a margin of discretion, it is accepted, as a general rule, that there is only one correct way of resolving the issue. This, in turn, enables the courts to exercise a higher degree of scrutiny.[114]

7.3. Review of national measures

The issue of which types of national measures are subject to review on grounds of compatibility with the general principles of law was discussed in Chapter 1.[115] This section focuses in particular on the application of fundamental rights. It will be

---

[110] Op. cit., n. 7 above.

[111] This is borne out, for example, by the judgments in *Wachauf* and *von Deetzen II*. For an express recognition, see Jacobs AG in *Wachauf, op. cit.*, at 2630.

[112] See Article 12 of the Grundgesetz.

[113] (1991) 84 BverfGE 34. The case is referred to by G. Nolte, 'General Principles of German and European Administrative Law—a Comparison in Historical Perspective' (1994) 57 MLR 191, at 196.   [114] Nolte, *op. cit.* 196.

[115] See 1.8 above.

remembered that, according to the case law, the following types of national measure are subject to review on grounds of compatibility with fundamental rights: measures implementing Community acts; measures which interfere with the fundamental freedoms but come within the ambit of an express derogation provided for in the Treaty; other measures which fall within the scope of Community law. Each of these types of measure will now be examined in turn.

7.3.1. Implementing measures

The first case which expressly established that fundamental rights bind the Member States when implementing Community measures was *Wachauf*.[116] The case arose from the Community milk quota regime, the salient features of which have been explained elsewhere in this book.[117] Suffice it to recall here that, with a view to discouraging milk production, Community regulations provided for a system of milk quotas. A key feature of the scheme was that the quota followed the land on transfer so that in the case of farm tenancies, upon the expiry of the lease, the quota reverted to the landlord. The rules also enabled Member States to grant compensation to producers who undertook to discontinue milk production definitively. German law took advantage of that option and, in the case of tenant farmers, it provided as a condition of entitlement to compensation that the authorization of the landlord must be obtained. The rationale behind this was to protect the interests of the landlord since, if the tenant obtained compensation for definitively leaving the market, the quota allocated to him could not be returned to the landlord. In *Wachauf* the applicant argued that the milk quota regime infringed fundamental rights. If the Community rules were interpreted as meaning that, upon the expiry of the lease, the tenant's milk quota must be returned to the landlord, they could have the effect of precluding the tenant from benefiting from compensation. Such a consequence would be unacceptable if the landlord had never engaged in milk production and the tenant had acquired the milk quota by his own efforts. After recalling its judgment in *Hauer*, the Court stated:[118]

> ...Community rules which, upon the expiry of the lease, had the effect of depriving the lessee, without compensation, of the fruits of his labour and of his investments in the tenanted holding would be incompatible with the requirements of the protection of fundamental rights in the Community legal order. Since those requirements are also binding on the Member States when they implement Community rules, the Member States must, as far as possible, apply those rules in accordance with those requirements.

The rationale for the Court's finding is not difficult to understand. Since Community legislation must respect fundamental rights, the national authorities in implementing such legislation, must also be so bound. As Weiler and Lockhart

---

[116] *Op. cit.*, n. 5 above See also Joined Cases 201 and 202/85 *Klensch v Secrétaire d'Etat à l'Agriculture et à la Viticulture* [1986] ECR 3477.   [117] Above, p. 275.
[118] *Wachauf, op. cit.*, para 19.

argue, far from being an arbitrary extension of the Court's jurisdiction, *Wachauf* is the natural progression of the Court's jurisprudence, its foundations resting on cases such as *Nold* and *Hauer*.[119] In areas where the national authorities act as the agents of the Community institutions, it would be inconsistent and contradictory not to subject them to the requirement to observe fundamental rights. Why should the Commission be so subject when implementing a Council regulation but not the Member States?[120] The extension of the application of human rights in that context seems 'self-evident'.[121]

Although the justification for review in an agency situation is not difficult to grasp, its implications are not inconsiderable. In effect, *Wachauf* increased the onus on the national authorities and the national courts. National authorities came under an obligation to ensure that the way they implemented Community rules did not infringe fundamental rights. The role of national courts became critical. It fell upon them to review national measures on grounds of compatibility with fundamental rights, if necessary by making a reference to the Court of Justice. This way, they acquired a power which they did not necessarily possess under national law. This was for example the case with English courts which traditionally did not have power to review the compatibility of statutes and acts of the administration with human rights as enshrined in the European Convention.[122]

In assessing whether national implementing measures comply with human rights, the question arises which standard of protection should apply. Is it the standard provided by national law, which may vary from State to State, or the standard provided by Community law? Weiler correctly argues that it is the Community standard that should apply since, in implementing Community law, Member States act as agents of the Community.[123] In such a case therefore the implementing legislation should be struck down where it violates the Community standard for the protection of fundamental rights even if it does not violate the said standard set by national law. Weiler's proposed solution in the converse situation also seems persuasive. He argues that if the implementing measure clears the human rights protection standard set by Community law but fails to clear the higher standard set by national law, the national court is entitled to strike down the measure. Where the Community provision gives the Member States discretion for its implementation, provided that the provision is fully implemented one way or another, the requirements of Community law are satisfied. Community law does not require the national standards to be violated.[124] The higher standard of protection provided by national law, however, must in any event apply equally to

---

[119] Weiler and. Lockhart, ' " Taking Rights Seriously" Seriously', *op. cit.*, n. 3 above, Part I 32 (1995) CML Rev 51 at 73.   [120] *Ibid.*, p. 74.
[121] *Wachauf, op. cit*, at 2629 *per* Jacobs AG.
[122] But see now, Human Rights Act 1998, s. 4.
[123] See Weiler, in Neuwahl and Rosas, *op. cit.*, n. 23 above, at 72–73.
[124] *Ibid.* Weiler's view seems to be supported by the Opinion of Cosmas AG in Case C-63/93 *Duff and Others v Minister for Agriculture and Food, Ireland, and the Attorney General* [1996] ECR I-569, at 583. But note now *Booker Aquaculture, op. cit.*, n. 97 above, discussed below p. 322.

domestic areas unconnected with Community law and must not prejudice the effective enforcement of the Community rules.[125]

The principle that national implementing measures must respect fundamental rights was reiterated in *Bostock*.[126] Whilst in *Wachauf* the applicant was seeking compensation for the definitive discontinuance of milk production, in *Bostock* the applicant sought compensation from the landlord upon surrendering his lease. His argument was that if the quota was transferred to the landlord, he would be deprived of the fruits of his labour, since he had made substantial improvements to the farm which had increased its milk production capacity. The Court first pointed out that the Community regulations did not require Member States to introduce a scheme for the payment of compensation by landlords nor did they confer directly on tenants a right to such compensation. It then went on to examine whether failure on the part of Member States to provide for such a scheme infringed the general principles of Community law and gave a negative reply. It seems that the Court was not willing to intervene because Community legislation left it to the Member States to provide for the protection of the economic interests of tenants and their rights *vis-à-vis* landlords. Any judicial intervention in the landlord–tenant relationship would entail direct regulation of disputes between private parties on the basis of unwritten Community law, a step which seemed too far.[127]

The cases discussed above concerned measures adopted by the national authorities to implement regulations. Subsequently, in *Booker Aquaculture Ltd and Hydro Seafood GSP Ltd v The Scottish Minister*,[128] it was held that Member States must respect fundamental rights also when they implement directives. This is undoubtedly correct. As Mischo AG stated, the discretion of Member States to choose the form and method of implementation of directives does not include 'the choice whether or not to violate fundamental rights'.[129] A directive does not stand alone but is inseparable from the norms to which it must itself conform including the general principles of Community law.[130]

Booker Aquaculture concerned Directive 93/53 which aimed at preventing and eliminating fish diseases.[131] The Directive laid down two lists of diseases. Those in List I were subject to more onerous control measures than those in List II and included the destruction and slaughter of fish stocks. The Directive permitted

---

[125] See Cosmas AG, *Duff and Others, op. cit.*, n. 124 above.

[126] *Op. cit.*, n. 106 above. See also *Duff, op. cit.*; Joined Cases 196–198/88 *Corneé and Others v Copall and Others* [1989] ECR 2309; Case C-16/89 *Spronk v Minister van Landbouw en Visserij* [1990] ECR I-3185; Case C-463/93 *St Martinus Elten v Landwirtschaftskammer Rheinland* [1997] ECR I-255; Case C-186/96 *Demand* [1998] ECR I-8529.

[127] See also above p. 48. In *Bostock, op. cit.*, at 966, Gulmann AG identified three differences between the two cases. In *Wachauf* the applicant sought compensation for the definitive discontinuance of production whereas in *Bostock* the applicant sought compensation from the landlord; in the former, the lease was ended by the landlord whereas in the latter it was the tenant who terminated the agreement; and in *Wachauf* milk production on the holding was established in its entirety by the tenant whereas in *Bostock* the tenant increased milk production already in place.

[128] *Op. cit.*, n. 97 above.   [129] *Ibid.*, at para 53 of the Opinion.

[130] *Ibid.*, at para 58 of the Opinion.   [131] Directive 93/53 OJ 1993 L 175/23.

Member States to apply stricter requirements in their own territory and in, accordance with this provision, the UK decided to apply the stricter control measures provided in List I also to the diseases in List II. The applicants argued that the provisions of the Directive which required the slaughtering of fish stocks without granting compensation to affected farmers violated the right to property. They also argued that the imposition of more onerous conditions imposed by the UK were in breach of that right. The Court rejected both arguments. After establishing that the provisions of the Directive did not constitute a disproportionate and intolerable interference with the right to property it went on to examine the national implementing measures and came to the same conclusion. A key feature of the judgment is that the examination of the compatibility of the national measures with the right to property was Community- rather than national-law-oriented. The Court centred its analysis on whether the national implementing measures furthered the objectives of the Directive and applied the Community standard for protection of the right to property. Since however the measures in issue were national ones which were not required by Community law, the control of the ECJ cannot be considered as conclusive. National implementing measures which go beyond the required minimum of directives should remain susceptible to control of compatibility with national standards for the protection of human rights by national courts. In *Booker Aquaculture* this was not an issue since the level of protection guaranteed by domestic law was lower than the level of protection that they sought to claim under Community law. If, however, the standard of protection applicable under national law is higher, the implementing legislation may be open to review in national courts insofar as the minimum rules required by the directive are observed. It is notable that in *Booker Aquaculture* the ECJ did not leave any margin of discretion to the referring court. It held that, in circumstances such as those in the main proceedings, the measures for the immediate destruction of fish implemented by the UK were not incompatible with the right to property. It thus appeared to foreclose the possibility of further review by a national court. For the reasons stated above, however, this cannot be considered as correct and it is doubtful if this was the intention of the judgment.

7.3.2. Measures derogating from the fundamental freedoms

The second type of national provision which is reviewable on grounds of compatibility with fundamental rights are measures which a Member State seeks to justify on the basis of an express derogation from a fundamental freedom, for example Article 30. The issue was settled in *ERT*[132] but before discussing that case, it may be helpful to trace the development of the law.

Earlier case law suggested that exceptions to fundamental freedoms must be construed in the light of human rights. However, the scope of application of

---

[132] Case C-260/89 [1991] ECR I-2925.

human rights was unclear and the judicial authorities equivocal. In *Rutili*[133] the Court referred to the ECHR in order to support the finding that restrictions on the right to free movement on grounds of public policy cannot be justified unless they are limited to what is necessary in order to protect the objective in view. But Directive 64/221[134] with which the Court was concerned in that case actually required Member States to protect certain fundamental rights enshrined in the European Convention. In subsequent cases, there were dicta in Opinions of advocates general to the effect that, in assessing the compatibility with Community law of national measures derogating from the fundamental freedoms, account must be taken of respect for fundamental rights.[135] An invitation to review national measures on grounds of breach of fundamental rights was rejected by the Court in *Cinéthèque*.[136] French law prohibited the release of films on video cassettes for a period of one year following their release in the cinema. It was argued that the prohibition was in breach of the principle of freedom of expression recognized by Article 10 of the ECHR and was therefore incompatible with Community law. Having established that the French law was justified under Article 30 (now 28) in the interests of encouraging the creation of cinematographic works, the Court dismissed the argument based on the Convention stating that it had no power to examine the compatibility with the Convention of national legislation which concerns an area falling within 'the jurisdiction of the national legislator'.[137] Slynn AG took a different view, stating that the exceptions of Article 36 (now 30) and the scope of mandatory requirements should be construed in the light of the European Convention.[138]

Two years later in *Demirel*[139] the Court used a slightly different formula stating that it has no power to examine the compatibility with the European Convention of national legislation 'lying outside the scope of Community law'.[140] The case concerned the interpretation of the Association Agreement with Turkey. The wife of a Turkish national, who was lawfully employed in Germany, was refused leave to stay on the ground that she did not meet the conditions for family reunification applicable to nationals of third States under German law. The Court held that the provisions of the Association Agreement concerning free movement of workers were insufficiently precise and therefore incapable of producing direct effect. In response to the argument that the provisions of German law run counter to

---

[133] Case 36/75 *Rutili v Minister for the Interior* [1975] ECR 1219.
[134] Directive no 64/221 on the coordination of special measures concerning the movement and residence of foreign nationals which are justified on grounds of public policy, public security or public health (OJ English Sp. Ed., 1963–64, p. 117). Now replaced by Directive 2004/38 OJ 2004, L 158/77, which is due to be implemented by 30 April 2006.
[135] Case 118/75 *Watson and Belmann* [1976] ECR 1185 at 1207 *per* Trabucchi AG; Case 34/79 *Regina v Henn & Darby* [1979] ECR 3795 at 3821 *per* Warner AG.
[136] Joined Cases 60 and 61/84 *Cinéthèque v Fédération Nationale des Cinémas Français* [1985] ECR 2605.   [137] *Ibid.*, para 26.
[138] *Ibid.*, at 2616.   [139] Case 12/86 *Demirel v Stadt Schwäbisch Gmund* [1987] ECR 3719.
[140] *Ibid.*, para 28.

Article 8 of the European Convention, the Court held that, at that time, there was no provision of Community law defining the conditions in which Member States must permit the family reunification of Turkish workers lawfully settled in the Community. Since the issue fell outside the scope of Community law, the Court did not have jurisdiction to determine the compatibility of the German rules in issue with the Convention.

Six years after *Cinéthèque* the Court expanded the range of national measures which may be subject to review on grounds of human rights in *ERT*.[141] In that case, it held that a national measure may not take advantage of an express derogation from the fundamental freedoms unless it respects fundamental rights. A number of issues arise from the judgment. What is the justification for extending the application of human rights to such measures? Is the jurisdiction of the Court limited to measures based on an express derogation provided for in the Treaty or does it also extend to measures justified by judge-made exceptions, e.g. mandatory requirements? What is the applicable standard of review?

At first sight, *ERT* appears striking. Where a Member State relies on a provision of the Treaty which provides expressly for a derogation, it acts within its sphere of competence. Why then should its actions be subject to review on grounds of compatibility with human rights? The underlying rationale of *ERT* is that, where a Member State takes advantage of an express derogation, its actions do not fall outside the scope of Community law. An escape clause needs to be relied on only where the national provisions in issue interfere with the fundamental freedoms. An express derogation is thus seen as a concession granted by the Community to the Member States rather than as defining the outer limits of Community competence.[142]

In *ERT* it was stated that review on human rights grounds must be exercised where national rules 'fall within the scope of Community law . . . *in particular* where a Member State relies on the combined provisions of Articles 56 and 66'.[143] It could be argued that the effect of mandatory requirements is to take a national measure outside the scope of Article 28 altogether rather than to permit a derogation from it. If that view were correct, it would follow that a restriction on the free movement of goods or services which is justified by a judge-made exception (i.e. a mandatory requirement or an imperative reason of public interest) falls outside the scope of Community law and therefore the Court has no jurisdiction to examine its compatibility with human rights.[144]

---

[141] *Op.Cit.* See P. J. Slot, comment in (1991) 28 CML Rev 978. For subsequent confirmation, see e.g. *Commission v Germany, op. cit.,* n. 46 above.

[142] See the discussion by Weiler in Neuwahl and Rosas, *op. cit.,* n. 1 above at pp. 69–71.

[143] See paras 42–43 (emphasis added). Articles 56 and 66 are now Articles 46 and 55 respectively.

[144] Support for that view could be derived from *ERT* itself. There, the Court cited *Cinéthèque* as authority for the proposition that it has no power to examine the compatibility with the ECHR of national rules which do not fall within the scope of Community law. *ERT* therefore gives the impression that *Cinéthèque*, which concerned a restriction justified by mandatory requirements, remains good law. In *Cinéthèque*, however, the effects of the French measure on the free

Such an approach however would be fallacious. It would be incongruous if a national measure could take advantage of an express derogation only if it was compatible with human rights but could be justified under mandatory requirements even though it violated such rights. Whether the State invokes an express derogation or a mandatory requirement, it relies on a provision of the Treaty and no distinction should be drawn between the two cases. This was confirmed in *Familiapress*.[145] In that case, the Austrian Government sought to justify a law which prohibited publishers from including prize crosswords and competitions in newspapers and periodicals on grounds of assisting small publishers to survive. The Court accepted that press diversity is an overriding requirement which may justify a restriction on the free movement of goods. It held however that, where a Member State relies on overriding requirements to justify rules which are likely to obstruct the exercise of free movement, such justification must be interpreted in the light of the general principles of law and, in particular, fundamental rights. It held that a prohibition on selling publications which offer the chance to take part in prize competitions may detract from the freedom of expression as guaranteed by Article 10 ECHR and carried on to apply a rigorous test of proportionality.

The effect of *ERT* and *Familiapress* is that compatibility with human rights is part of the enquiry which the Court performs in order to assess whether a national measure which interferes with the fundamental freedoms is permitted under Community law.

The issue whether a national provision which falls within the scope of Community law infringes human rights is, in the first place, for the national courts to decide. On a reference for a preliminary ruling, the Court of Justice must provide the necessary interpretation criteria in order to enable the national court to make that determination.[146] In *ERT* the Court left it, in the first place, up to the national court to decide whether the Greek television monopoly could be justified by Articles 46 and 55 of the Treaty having regard to the freedom of expression.[147] The issue which arises in this context is what standard of human rights protection must be applied. Weiler[148] argues that in contrast to national legislation implementing Community measures, in this case it is the national standard of protection that should be applicable. That is so because in this case the Member State does not act

movement of goods were only tenuous and indirect. The reason why the Court took such a restrictive view regarding the scope of application of human rights is probably because the facts of the case did not lend themselves to far-reaching pronouncements on such matters. The Court might have been reluctant to advance the case law along the lines suggested by the Advocate General in circumstances where the French legislation in issue was clearly compatible with Article 28.

[145] C-368/95 *Vereinigte Familiapress Zeitungsverlags- und Vertriebs GmbH v Bauer Verlag* [1997] ECR I-3689. The same view was earlier supported by the Opinion of van Gerven AG in *SPUC Ireland Ltd v Grogan, op. cit.*, n. 43 above, at 4723 and also by J. H. H. Weiler, 'The European Court at a Crossroads: Community Human Rights and Member State Action' in *Du Droit international au droit de l'intégration*, (Liber Amicorum Pierre Pescatore, Nomos 1987), p. 821 at 840–841.   [146] *ERT, op. cit.*, para 42, 44.

[147] *Ibid.*, para 44.   [148] See Weiler in Neuwahl and Rosas, *op. cit.*, p. 73.

as agent of the Community but implements a national policy. The Court should not seek to impose on Member States the Community's own standard but rather to prevent only the violation of core human rights as provided in the European Convention. If that view is correct, a national measure which fails to meet the standard of protection afforded by Community law but passes the lower hurdle imposed by national law need not be struck down by the national court. This is not however the view that the ECJ has embraced. In recent cases, it has been overtly interventionist, prescribing to the national court a set standard of fundamental rights protection.[149]

ERT and *Familiapress* extend the powers of national courts to review national measures on grounds of human rights protection. This is significant as, in many cases, the standard of protection provided by Community law is higher than that applicable in domestic law.[150]

7.3.3. Other measures falling within the scope of Community law

What other types of measures may be said to fall 'within the scope of Community law' for the purposes of the application of fundamental rights? Although the meaning of that expression is not entirely clear,[151] the following cases provide examples of cases where the Court, for one reason or another, rejected invitations to review national measures on grounds of fundamental rights.

The Court rejected the Advocate General's invitation to take the law one step further in *Konstantinidis*.[152] A Greek national established in Germany complained that the transliteration of his name into Latin characters by the German authorities was wrong. The Court saw the dispute solely as one of economic rights. It relied on the criterion of discrimination and held that the German rules on the transliteration of foreign names would be caught by Article 43 only if they placed the applicant in a disadvantageous position in law or in fact *vis-à-vis* German nationals. That would be the case if a Greek national was obliged to use in his professional activities a spelling of his name which distorted its pronunciation so much as to create a risk of confusion among prospective clients. Jacobs AG examined the applicant's claim not only from the point of view of Article 43 but also from the point of view of the protection of human rights. The Advocate General criticized the absence in the European Convention of an express recognition of the individual's right to his name and personal identity. He found a common principle underpinning the Constitutions of the Member States according to which the State

---

[149] See e.g. Case C-60/00 *Carpenter v Secretary of State for the Home Department*, [2002] ECR I-6279.
[150] As already stated, this has had important consequences in the UK where, prior to the Human Rights Act 1998, the Convention was not part of domestic law. See, for example, *Hodgson v Commissioners of Customs and Excise* [1997] EuLR 116, discussed below.
[151] See above pp. 36 and 39.   [152] Case C-168/91 [1993] ECR I-1191.

is required to respect not only the physical well-being of the individual but also 'his dignity, moral integrity and sense of personal identity'.[153] He argued that Article 8 of the European Convention should be interpreted broadly so as to include protection of the right to one's name and that the applicant should be able to rely on the Convention in order to avoid the wrong transcription of his name. In his view, a Community national who goes to another Member State to work is entitled not only to pursue his trade or profession and to enjoy the same living and working conditions as nationals of the host State; he is in addition entitled to assume that, wherever he goes to earn his living in the European Community, he will be treated in accordance with a common code of fundamental values and moral rights protected by law, part of which is the *jus nominis*.[154]

Konstantinidis was an ambitious attempt by the Advocate General to provide a link between European citizenship and fundamental rights. The cardinal ideas emanating from the Opinion are two: that Community law protects the *jus nominis* as a fundamental right; and that a Community citizen who exercises his freedom of movement is entitled to a certain standard of protection of his fundamental rights set by Community law, even if the host State does not guarantee that standard to its own nationals. In contrast with other cases pertaining to fundamental rights decided by the Court, Jacobs AG sought a maximalist approach to their protection. The Opinion contrasts sharply with that of van Gerven AG in *Grogan*[155] where the Advocate General followed a minimalist approach. The issues raised in the two cases however were entirely different and the former did not involve a clash of values such as that raised in the latter.

It is questionable whether *Konstantinidis* would have been decided in the same way now. First, the ECJ has been activist, almost aggressive, in deriving enforceable rights from the concept of European citizenship and, second, it is prepared to take fundamental rights much more seriously than before. It is not inconceivable that a claim could be based on the protection of fundamental rights and possibly also Article 12.[156]

An unsuccessful attempt to invoke Community law was also made in *Kremzow v Republic Österreich*.[157] The applicant had been sentenced by an Austrian court to life imprisonment for murder. In subsequent proceedings, the European Court of Human Rights held that Article 6 of the European Convention had been violated on the ground that the applicant had not been given the opportunity to defend himself in person.[158] Following the judgment of the Strasbourg Court, the

---

[153] *Ibid.*, at 1209.   [154] *Ibid.*, pp. 1211–1212.   [155] See 7.3.4 below.

[156] As a Community national exercising his fundamental freedoms, a person in the position of Mr Konstantinidis falls within the scope of the EC Treaty and may enjoy the rights deriving from Union citizenship. This triggers the fundamental rights jurisdiction of the ECJ. It is arguable that in the circumstances of the case, there was no legitimate reason justifying the intrusion on his rights emanating from the spelling imposed by the German authorities. See also Case C-148/02 *Garcia Avello v Etat Belge*, judgment of 2 October 2003, discussed above, p. 133.

[157] Case C-299/95 [1997] ECR I-2629.

[158] *Kremzow v Austria*, Judgment of 21 September 1993, Series A, No. 268-B.

applicant brought proceedings in Austrian courts seeking a reduction in his sentence and damages for illegal detention pursuant to Article 5(5) of the Convention. In the course of those proceedings, the Oberster Gerichtshof referred a number of questions seeking essentially to ascertain whether it was bound, as a matter of Community law, by the judgment of the Strasbourg Court and if so what were the legal consequences. The argument of the applicant was essentially that, as a citizen of the Union, he was entitled to protection by Community law. The Court of Justice declined jurisdiction on the ground that the dispute fell outside the scope of Community law. The applicant's situation was not connected in any way with the free movement of persons. Whilst detention may impede a person from exercising his right to free movement, a purely hypothetical prospect of exercising that right does not establish a sufficient connection with Community law to justify the application of Community rules.[159] The Court also pointed out that the applicant had been sentenced pursuant to provisions of national law which were not designed to secure compliance with rules of Community law.

Although in the light of previous cases, the judgment in *Kremzow* was wholly predictable, it does highlight the limits of the fundamental rights rhetoric as a force of integration. Citizenship of the Union does not carry with it the paramount feature of citizenship as understood in the context of the nation State, namely constitutional protection of core rights. This case would not be decided differently under Articles 17 and 18 EC.

7.3.4. The *Grogan* case: Deference or intervention?

The Court was confronted with the highly sensitive issue of abortion in *Society for the Protection of Unborn Children Ireland Ltd v Grogan*.[160] *Grogan* stands out from all the cases concerning the application of fundamental rights on national measures because it involved a conflict of fundamental values: on the one hand, the right to life of the unborn, as enshrined in the Constitution of a Member State, and on the other hand, the freedom of expression as a Community right. Irish law prohibited abortion as a criminal offence and entrenched the right to life of the unborn child as a constitutional right.[161] In *Attorney General v Open Door Counselling Limited*,[162] decided in 1988, the Irish Supreme Court held that to assist pregnant women to travel abroad to obtain abortions by providing information about specific clinics offering abortion services was contrary to the Constitution. In *Grogan* student's unions in Ireland circulated guidebooks giving details of clinics in the United Kingdom where medical termination of pregnancy was available. A pro-life organization brought proceedings in the Irish High Court seeking a declaration that the distribution of such information was unlawful and an injunction restraining distribution. The High Court considered that issues of Community law were

---

[159] *Op. cit.*, para 16. [160] Case C-159/90 [1991] ECR I-4685.
[161] See Article 40.3.3 of the Irish Constitution. [162] [1988] IR 593.

involved and made a reference for a preliminary ruling to the Court of Justice. The Court pointed out that termination of pregnancy is lawfully practised in several Member States and is a medical activity which is normally provided for remuneration. On that basis, it found that the medical termination of pregnancy, performed in accordance with the law of the State where it is carried out, is a service within the meaning of Article 50 EC. But the Court did not address the substantive issue of the compatibility of the Irish prohibition with Community law on the ground that the link between the clinics and the student's unions which circulated the information was too tenuous. Since the students were not acting in cooperation with the clinics, the circulation of the information was not the marketing of a service but a manifestation of their freedom of expression. In the circumstances, the prohibition on the distribution of information could not be regarded as a restriction within the meaning of Article 49. The student's unions argued that the prohibition of Irish law infringed their freedom of expression as enshrined in Article 10 of the ECHR. But in view of the conclusion that the prohibition was not a restriction on services, that argument was bound to fail. Referring to *ERT*, the Court pointed out that it had no jurisdiction to examine the compatibility with Community law of national legislation lying outside the scope of Community law.

The Court's reluctance to address the issue of fundamental rights in *Grogan* has been attributed to many factors.[163] There was a risk that the national judiciary might not look favourably on intervention by the Court of Justice.[164] The political climate and public opinion did not seem receptive to the imposition of external standards on moral issues. Member States may have felt that national policies reflecting basic philosophical and moral choices were unjustifiably being questioned in the name of economic freedoms. Also, the Court might have been reluctant to adjudicate on such a highly sensitive matter at a time when proceedings were pending at the European Court of Human Rights.[165] Whatever the reasons which led the Court to avoid the issue of substance, it did so only at the expense of adopting a narrow interpretation of the freedom to provide services. The Advocate General's reasoning seems more convincing. Van Gerven AG pointed out that Article 49 covers not only the right to provide but also the right to receive services and assessed the existence of a restriction from the point of view of the recipient. He stated that the right to receive services encompasses the right to obtain information about providers of services in other Member States regardless of

---

[163] See S. O'Leary, 'Aspects of the Relationship between Community Law and National Law' in Neuwahl and Rosas, *op. cit.*, p. 23 at 28–29.

[164] The Irish Supreme Court was critical of the High Court judge's decision to make a reference in *Grogan* although it did not interfere with her decision to do so: see [1990] 1 CMLR 689 and O'Leary, *op. cit.* at 27.

[165] Following the judgment of the Supreme Court in *Attorney General v Open Door Counselling Limited* the defendant clinics launched a complaint to the European Commission of Human Rights alleging that the injunctions prohibiting the dissemination of information infringed Articles 8, 10 and 14 ECHR. See further below, n. 168.

whether the information came from a person who was not himself the provider and did not act on the latter's behalf. This approach seems correct. What matters is whether prohibiting distribution of information about providers restricts the recipient's right to receive services. That may be so, even where the prohibition relates to dissemination made by a third party for non-economic reasons. To put it differently, the fact that information about services is disseminated by a third party, acting independently of the provider on a non-commercial basis, does not preclude the prohibition of disseminating such information from being a restriction on the freedom to provide services. In fact in the case of services such as medical ones, which are not normally marketed by the usual means of promotion, dissemination by independent sources is particularly important since it is one of the relatively few means that information about providers may be obtained by prospective recipients.

Having established that the prohibition of Irish law constituted a restriction on the freedom to provide services, the Advocate General proceeded to examine whether it was justified. As a non-discriminatory restriction, it could be justified not only on the basis of Article 55 but also on grounds of imperative requirements of public interest. The Advocate General had no difficulty in accepting that the Irish prohibition promoted such an imperative requirement as it related to a policy choice of moral and philosophical nature which the Member State was entitled to make. He also accepted that prohibiting dissemination of information which was designed to assist abortion was proportionate.[166] In relation to fundamental rights, he pointed out that it was a question of balancing two competing interests: on the one hand, the right to life of the unborn enshrined constitutionally in the law of a Member State and, on the other hand, the freedom of expression as guaranteed in Article 10 ECHR. The Advocate General considered that, in an area where a uniform moral standard is lacking among Member States, individual States should be allowed a fairly considerable margin of discretion.[167] He concluded that the restriction imposed by Irish law on the freedom of expression satisfied the test of proportionality.[168]

One may venture to suggest that, had the Court found a restriction on the freedom to provide services to exist, it would have probably reasoned along the lines of the Advocate General.[169] At the time when the litigation arose, his Opinion

---

[166] By contrast, a ban on pregnant women going abroad to receive abortion services or a rule under which they would be subjected to unsolicited examinations upon their return from abroad would fail the test of proportionality: *op. cit.*, at p. 4721, *per* van Gerven AG.

[167] *Ibid.*, p. 4728.

[168] Following the *Grogan* decision, the following Protocol was attached to the Treaty on European Union: 'Nothing in the Treaty on European Union, or in the Treaties establishing the European Communities...shall affect the application in Ireland of Article 40.3.3. of the Constitution of Ireland.' An addendum included in the Protocol stated that 'This protocol shall not limit the freedom to travel between Member States or to obtain or make available in Ireland legislative information relating to services lawfully available in a Member State'. This has now been attached as Protocol 31 to the EU Constitution. For the background to the Protocol, see O'Leary, *op. cit.*, at 32; D. Curtin, 'The Constitutional Structure of the Union: A Europe of Bits and Pieces' (1993) 30 CML Rev 17, at 47. Note also that the Constitution of Ireland was itself amended. The thirteenth amendment, adopted on 23 December 1992, provided that the right to life of the unborn does not limit freedom to travel between Ireland and another State.   [169] O'Leary, *op. cit.*, 33.

seemed entirely correct. Given that the legal and social orders of the Member States lack 'a uniform European conception of morals', it would have been wrong for the Court to overrule fundamental societal values espoused by a Member State in the name of economic freedoms. The problem was that, in the circumstances, Article 10 of the ECHR could only come into play indirectly, i.e. in order to establish whether prohibiting dissemination of information was an acceptable restriction on the freedom to provide services. In the absence of explicit political consensus, the Advocate General was wise to defer to the moral choices of Ireland. It is notable that subsequently in its judgment in the *Open Door* case,[170] the European Court of Human Rights found that the injunctions restraining welfare clinics in Ireland from providing information about abortion services abroad were not 'necessary in a democratic society' and run counter to Article 10(1) ECHR. The Strasbourg Court considered that the ban on counselling was too broad as it applied to all women regardless of their age, health, or reasons for seeking advice. It considered that there was no definite link between counselling and abortion as counselling advised women about options and did not direct them to have an abortion. Also, the ban gave rise to a health risk because it resulted in women seeking abortions without first having the benefit of counselling services.

7.3.5. Stretching the scope of Community law: An ever-expanding jurisdiction?

A remarkable development of the case law in the early 2000s is that the ECJ has considerably widened its human rights jurisdiction. It has done so in a number of ways. First, it has expanded the scope of application of fundamental freedoms and has also derived concrete rights from the concept of European citizenship. Such expansive interpretation has, in turn, increased the range of national measures falling within the scope of Community law whose compatibility with human rights the ECJ has jurisdiction to control. Second, in *Karner*[171] the ECJ took the view that its human rights jurisdiction is triggered where a measure is likely to constitute a potential impediment to intra-Community trade even if it is not as such a restriction on a fundamental freedom. Third, the ECJ has elevated fundamental rights to core Community values expressly accepting that their protection may justify a restriction on free movement. These developments will now be examined in turn.

7.3.5.1. From free movement to human rights protection

Since a restriction on a fundamental freedom cannot be justified unless it respects human rights, the broader the scope of fundamental freedoms, the further the reach of the human rights jurisdiction of the ECJ. This is aptly illustrated by the judgment

---

[170] *Open Door Counselling and Dublin Well Woman Centre Ltd v Ireland*, judgment of 29 October 1992, Series A, No. 246.
[171] Case C-71/02 *Herbert Karner Industrie-Auktionen GmbH v Troostwijk GmbH*, judgment of 25 March 2004.

in *Carpenter*.[172] Mrs Carpenter was a national of the Philippines who had been given leave to enter the UK as a visitor for six months. She overstayed her leave and, whilst present in the UK in breach of immigration laws, she married Mr Carpenter, a UK national. He was established in the UK but a significant proportion of his business as an advertising agent was conducted with advertisers established in other Member States, where he travelled for professional purposes. Mrs Carpenter applied to the Home Office for leave to remain in England as the spouse of a UK national but her application was refused and a deportation order was made against her on the ground that she had remained in the country in breach of the immigration laws.

Mrs Carpenter argued that she was entitled to remain in the UK under Community law on the ground that her deportation would restrict her husband's right to provide and receive cross-border services. Her argument was that since her husband's business required him to travel around in other Member States, he could do so more easily as she was looking after his children from his first marriage. She therefore had a derivative right to remain in the UK arising from Article 49 EC.

The recognition of such a right would require a leap forward from previous case law. Mrs Carpenter's situation was different from that in *Singh*.[173] There, the Court had held that where a Community national returns to his state of origin after being established in another Member State, his spouse must enjoy at least the same rights of entry and residence as would be granted to her under Community law, if he had entered and remained in another Member State.[174] In *Carpenter*, the husband had not left the national territory. He was based in the UK and simply provided services in other Member States as part of his business.

The Court however found for Mrs Carpenter. It held that, since a significant proportion of Mr Carpenter's business consisted in providing services to advertisers established in other Member States, he was covered by Article 49 EC. The separation of Mr and Mrs Carpenter would be detrimental to their family life and, therefore, to the conditions under which Mr Carpenter exercised a fundamental freedom. That freedom could not be fully effective if Mr Carpenter were to be deterred from exercising it by obstacles raised in his country of origin to the entry and residence of his spouse.[175] The Court then held that the decision to deport Mrs Carpenter constituted an interference with the exercise by Mr Carpenter of his right to respect for his family life within the meaning of Article 8 of the ECHR.

The remarkable aspect of *Carpenter* is that it favoured a very broad interpretation of the freedom to provide services. Its effect is to shrink the concept of a 'wholly

---

[172] *Op. cit.*, n. 149 above.

[173] Case C-370/90 *R v Immigration Appeal Tribunal and Surinder Singh, ex p Secretary of State for the Home Department* [1992] ECR I-4265.

[174] These rights flow from Article 10 of Regulation 1612/68 and include the right of the spouses of Community migrant workers to instal themselves with the Community workers, irrespective of their nationality.   [175] *Carpenter, op. cit.*, n. 24, para 39.

internal situation', which falls beyond the scope of the free movement provisions of the Treaty, to its irreducible minimum. It is also notable that there was no element of discrimination on grounds of nationality or against the provision of cross-border services. Mr Carpenter was in no way discriminated against because he was exercising a fundamental freedom. By contrast, the judgment enhances the reverse discrimination effect of Community law, i.e. the situation where a person who exercises the right to free movement acquires more rights *vis-à-vis* his Member State of origin than a person who has not exercised a fundamental freedom. Seen in this light, the provisions on free movement become a source of positive rights and not merely a form of negative integration.

The expansive interpretation of human rights continued in *Baumbast*[176] and *Akrich*.[177] In *Baumbast* the Court held that the American wife of a French citizen working in the UK had the right to remain in the UK as the primary carer of their children after their divorce. In reaching that conclusion, the Court stressed that Regulation No 1612/68 must be interpreted in the light of the requirement to respect family life laid down in Article 8 of the ECHR.[178] Further, the Court held that a citizen of the EU who no longer enjoys a right of residence as a migrant worker in the host Member State can, as a citizen of the Union, enjoy there a right of residence by direct application of Article 18(1) EC. *Baumbast* is important not only for the rights of third-country nationals and the application of the right to family life but also from the point of view of European citizenship. It goes further than previous judgments in that it derives enforceable rights from the provisions of the Treaty establishing the European citizenship and thus cultivates, through the recognition of social rights, the emergence of a European demos. The Court releases the potential of Article 18(1) EC by adopting a very broad interpretation of direct effect and applying a strict test of proportionality, the effect of which is to emasculate the discretion of national authorities.[179]

The right to family life also played a central role in *Akrich*. Mr Akrich, a Moroccan national, had been convicted of various offences and deported twice from the UK. He returned clandestinely and, whilst residing unlawfully, he married a UK citizen. He was deported to Ireland where his spouse had in the meantime obtained work and applied for entry to the UK as the spouse of a Community citizen. It was not disputed that Mr and Mrs Akrich had moved to Ireland for the express purpose of subsequently exercising Community rights to enable them to return to the UK relying on the *Singh* judgment.[180] The UK authorities argued that the couple's move to Ireland was no more than a temporary

---

[176] Case C-413/99 *Baumbast and R v Secretary of State for the Home Department*, [2002] ECR I-7091.

[177] Case C-109/01 *Secretary of State for the Home Department v Akrich*, judgment of 23 September 2003; see also Case C-235/99 *Kondova* [2001] ECR I-6427.

[178] See *Baumbast, op. cit.*, n. 28, para 72.

[179] See, in particular, paras 91–92 of the judgment. See further Case C-200/02 *Kunqian Catherine Zhu and Man Lavette Chen v Secretary of State for the Home Department*, judgment of 19 October 2004.   [180] See above, n. 173 and related text.

absence deliberately designed to manufacture a right of residence for Mr Akrich on his return to the UK and thus evade immigration control.

The Court held that Regulation No 1612/68 covers only freedom of movement within the Community and does not determine the right of entry into the Community of third-country nationals. Thus, in order to benefit from the rights provided in Article 10 of Regulation No 1612/68,[181] the national of a non-Member State, who is the spouse of a citizen of the Union, must be lawfully resident in a Member State when he or she moves to another Member State to which the citizen of the Union has migrated. The Court however took a restrictive view of abuse: it held that the motives which may have prompted an EU national to seek employment in another Member State are not relevant in assessing the legal situation of the couple at the time of their return to the Member State of origin. The Court held that the decision to return cannot constitute abuse even if the spouse did not, at the time when the couple installed itself in another Member State, have a right to remain in the Member State of which the worker is a national. Abuse would exist only if the parties entered into a marriage of convenience in order to circumvent the provisions on entry and residence of third-country nationals.

The Court also held that the powers of the Member State of origin are qualified by the right to protect family life. Although the judgment is somewhat cryptic and leaves a number of issues unanswered, it appears to suggest that even where the third-country spouse of an EU citizen is not lawfully resident in a Member State, where the couple returns to the State of origin of the EU citizen, the discretion of the authorities to refuse entry to the spouse is constrained by the need to respect family life. The net effect of the judgment is that the third-country spouses of Community nationals may derive from Article 8 of the ECHR an independent right to instal themselves with the Community national over and above the rights granted by Article 10 of Regulation 1612/68.

7.3.5.2. Measures which potentially interfere with free movement

In *Karner*[182] the ECJ stretched further the scope of application of fundamental rights and somewhat muddied the waters. The Austrian Supreme Court sought a preliminary ruling on the compatibility of Article 30 of the Austrian Law on Unfair Competition with Articles 28 and 49 EC. Article 30 of the Austrian Law seeks to prohibit misleading advertisement and provides that where goods are offered for sale, public announcements may not make reference to the fact that the goods originate from an insolvent estate where, even though this is their origin, the goods are no longer part of the insolvent estate. The rationale for this prohibition is to protect consumers who tend to assume that goods belonging to an insolvent estate are ordinarily offered at advantageous prices. The ECJ held that the Austrian

---

[181] See above, n. 174.   [182] *Op. cit.*, n. 171 above.

provision pertained to selling arrangements rather than the physical characteristics of goods and examined its compatibility under the *Keck* formula.[183] It came to the conclusion that it did not affect the marketing of products from other Member States more than it affected the marketing of domestic products and concluded that it was not caught by Article 28. As to the freedom to provide services, the Court held that, since the dissemination of advertising was not an end in itself but a secondary element in relation to the sale of goods, it was not necessary to consider the compatibility of Austrian law with Article 49.[184] This should have been the end of the enquiry. The ECJ, however, proceeded to examine whether the advertising restriction was compatible with the freedom of expression, stating that, where national legislation falls within the field of application of Community law, the Court must give the national court all the guidance as to the interpretation necessary to enable it to assess the compatibility of that legislation with fundamental rights. The ECJ found that there was no breach of the freedom of expression applying a soft proportionality test in view of the fact that the case involved freedom of expression in commercial matters. It is however unclear why the national measure 'fell within the field of application of Community law'[185] given that the ECJ had come to the conclusion that it was a selling arrangement outside the scope of Article 28 nor was it reviewable under Article 49. The judgment seems to imply that human rights jurisdiction is triggered where a measure is likely to constitute a potential impediment to intra-Community movement and its compatibility falls to be examined under the provisions of the Treaty. This is however an uncertain criterion which expands significantly the scope of human rights protection. In effect, the Procrustean bed of *Karner* grants to the ECJ universal jurisdiction on fundamental rights.

Two further cases deserve attention in this context. In *Rechnungshof v Österreichischer Rundfunk*[186] it was held that the protection of the right to privacy provided for by Directive 95/46 on the protection of individuals with regard to the processing of personal data and on the free movement of such data,[187] is not restricted only to activities which have a sufficient link with a fundamental freedom but applies also to purely internal situations. The Directive had been adopted under Article 95 EC but the Court stated that the determining criterion to justify recourse to that provision as a legal basis is that the measure in question must actually be intended to improve the conditions for the establishment and functioning of the

---

[183] Joined Cases C-267 and C-268/91 *Keck and Mithouard* [1993] ECR I-6097.

[184] The Court seemed here to raise a jurisdiction hurdle. The underlying reasoning seems to be that, since the applicant in the main proceedings was an auctioneer rather than a provider of advertising services he could only question the compatibility of the Austrian law with Article 28 and not with Article 49. Strictly speaking, however, this is an interference with the discretion of the national court to determine the questions to be asked for a preliminary ruling.

[185] *Karner, op. cit*, para 49.

[186] Joined Cases C-465/00, C-138/01 and C-139/01, [2003] ECR I-4989.

[187] Directive 95/46 on the protection of individuals with regard to the processing of personal data and on the free movement of such data, OJ 1995 L 281/31.

internal market. It is not necessary that there must be an actual link with inter-State movement in every situation referred to in the measure.[188]

This trend towards the broad interpretation of the personal data Directive was continued in *Lindqvist*,[189] where it was held that the Directive covered a situation where personal data of church workers had been published in a church website by one of the church wardens even though the publication in question and the activities involved pursued not economic but essentially charitable and religious aims.

7.4. Human rights versus fundamental freedoms

In the cases discussed above, respect for human rights and the fundamental freedoms operated as complementary and converging forces. But in other cases, human rights and fundamental freedoms may find themselves on a collision course. Although there are some examples in previous case law,[190] this conflict has never been so eminently illustrated as in the recent case of *Schmidberger v Austria*.[191] The Austrian authorities allowed an environmental group to organize a demonstration on the Brenner motorway, the main transit route linking Germany to Italy, the effect of which was to close the motorway for almost 30 hours. The applicant was an international transport undertaking based in Germany whose main activity was to transport goods to Italy. It brought an action seeking damages against the Austrian authorities claiming that their failure to prevent the motorway from being closed amounted to a restriction on the free movement of goods.

The Court reiterated that Article 28 EC does not prohibit only measures emanating from the State which, in themselves, create restrictions on inter-State trade but applies also where a Member State abstains from adopting the measures required in order to deal with obstacles to the free movement of goods which are caused by private parties.[192] Thus, the fact that the Austrian authorities had failed to ban the demonstration thereby resulting in the complete closure of a major transit route was a measure having equivalent effect to a quantitative restriction.[193] The Court then turned to examine whether the restriction was justified. After pointing out that, under Article 6(2) TEU, fundamental rights form an integral part of the general principles of Community law, it stated that the protection of fundamental rights 'is a legitimate interest which, in principle, justifies a restriction of the

---

[188] *Op. cit.*, para 41 of the judgment.

[189] Case C-101/01 *Lindqvist*, judgment of 6 November 2003.

[190] See e.g. *Commission v Germany, op. cit.*, n. 46 above. See also *R v Chief Constable of Sussex ex p International Trader's Ferry Ltd* [1999] 2 AC 418.

[191] Case C-112/00 *Schmidberger, Internationale Transporte und Planzüge v Austria*, [2003] ECR I-5659.

[192] See, on this issue, the earlier judgment in Case C-265/95 *Commission v France* [1997] ECR I-6959.   [193] *Schmidberger, op. cit.*, n. 36, para 64.

obligations imposed by Community law, even under a fundamental freedom guaranteed by the Treaty such as the free movement of goods'.[194] It then proceeded to examine how the conflicting principles should be reconciled.

The Court viewed the free movement of goods and the freedom of assembly and association as being of equal constitutional ranking. It pointed out that neither of the competing values was absolute. Under the EC Treaty, the free movement of goods may be subject to restrictions for the reasons laid down in Article 30 or for overriding requirements relating to the public interest. Similarly, whilst freedom of association and freedom of assembly form fundamental pillars of a democratic society, it follows from Articles 10 and 11 of the ECHR that, unlike other fundamental rights enshrined in the Convention, they are subject to certain limitations justified by objectives in the public interest.

The Court then proceeded to weigh the interests involved in order to determine whether a fair balance was struck between them. It came to the conclusion that, having regard to their wide discretion, the Austrian authorities were reasonable in considering that the legitimate aim of the demonstration could not be achieved by less restrictive measures. The ECJ took into account the following considerations.[195]

First, it distinguished the case from *Commission v France*.[196] In *Schmidberger*, the demonstration took place following a request for authorization presented on the basis of national law and after the competent authorities had taken a decision not to ban it. Also, traffic by road was obstructed on a single route, on a single occasion, and during a period of almost 30 hours. The obstacle to the free movement was limited by comparison with both the geographic scale and the intrinsic seriousness of the disruption caused in *Commission v France*. The Court attributed particular importance to the fact that, in contrast to the latter case, the objective of the Austrian demonstrators was not to restrict trade in goods but to manifest their opinion in public.

The Court also pointed out that the competent authorities had taken various administrative and supporting measures in order to limit disruption as far as possible. An extensive publicity campaign had been launched by the media and the motoring organizations in Austria and neighbouring countries and various alternative routes had been designed.

The Court then considered in some detail the argument of the less restrictive alternatives. It held that, taking account of the Member States' wide margin of discretion, the authorities were entitled to consider that an outright ban on the demonstration would have constituted unacceptable interference with the demonstrators' fundamental right to gather and peacefully express their opinion in public.[197] It also dismissed the argument that the authorities could have taken stricter measures to control the demonstration. In a statement revealing the way the Court prioritized the competing values, it held that the imposition of stricter conditions concerning both the site, for example requiring the demonstrators to

---

[194] *Schmidberger*, para 74.   [195] Paras 84–93.   [196] *Op. cit.*   [197] Para 89.

stay by the side of the motorway, and the duration of the protest 'could have been perceived as an excessive restriction, depriving the action of a substantial part of its scope'.[198] It then continued: 'an action of that type usually entails inconvenience for non-participants, in particular as regards free movement, but the inconvenience may in principle be tolerated provided that the objective pursued is essentially the public and lawful demonstration of an opinion'.[199] The Court accepted the argument of the Austrian Government that, in any event, all the alternative solutions that could be countenanced would have risked reactions which would have been difficult to control and would have been liable to cause much more serious disruption to intra-Community trade and public order, such as unauthorised demonstrations, confrontation or acts of violence on the part of the demonstrators.

Schmidberger gives the clearest sign yet that the Court takes human rights seriously and conducts itself not as the Court of an economic union but as the Supreme Court of a constitutional order. The reasoning of the Court contrasts with that in previous cases where it readily gave the benefit of the doubt to free movement.[200] Also, in previous cases,[201] it had dismissed the view that public disturbances and the risk of violence by protestors could justify protective measures. Although these cases can be distinguished on the facts, the methodology followed by the Court in *Schmidberger* is different. The ECJ attributed particular importance to the European Convention. It also paid homage to national laws. The judgment contains subtle but repeated references to the constitutional values of the Member States.[202] By acknowledging that fundamental freedoms are conditioned by human rights and giving priority to the latter, the ECJ honoured the constitutional expectations of the Member States. Seen in the background of rebellious judgments by national Supreme Courts, *Schmidberger* is a gesture of reconciliation, and an attempt to embrace the national constitutional courts.

The ECJ declared in general terms that the protection of human rights may justify restrictions on free movement but did not place them in either of the established categories of limitations, i.e. it did not state whether they should be viewed as part of the express derogations of the Treaty (Article 30 EC) or as legitimate objectives in the public interest. The classification is important because, if human rights are viewed as part of the express derogations, they can justify even discriminatory restrictions on trade whilst if they are considered as mandatory requirements they can only justify indistinctly applicable restrictions. In principle, since human rights are viewed as being of equal ranking to the Treaty there is

---

[198] Para 90.   [199] Para 91.

[200] See e.g. *Commission v Germany, op. cit.*, n. 46 above where the Court had rejected the argument that respect for private life and the protection of medical confidentiality justified restrictions on the importation of medicinal products.

[201] See C-52/95 *Commission v France* [1995] ECR I-4443, para 38; *Commission v France, op. cit.*, n. 192 above, para 55; see also Case 231/83 *Cullet v Leclerc* [1985] ECR 305, para 35.

[202] See e.g. paras 70, 71, 72, 74, 76 of the judgment.

nothing to restrict them from justifying also discriminatory measures. This also follows from the fact that the protection of human rights may justify restrictions not only on the import but also on the export of goods which, if they fall within the scope of Article 29, are *ex hypothesi* discriminatory.[203]

A distinct feature of *Schmidberger* is that the Court erred on the side of fundamental rights rather than the side of free movement. It stressed that national authorities had wide discretion and made reference to the criterion of reasonableness, thus applying to national authorities a standard of scrutiny which is usually reserved to the Community institutions themselves. This is not to say that Member States now have a free hand to restrict free movement on grounds of human rights protection. The Court did examine closely the alternative options available to the Austrian authorities. It is notable however that the pendulum swung in favour of human rights and that the ECJ went all the way, offering a ready-made solution to the national court rather than giving only general guidelines and leaving it to the latter to resolve the conflict.[204]

All the cases discussed above show that the ECJ attributes particular importance to the European Convention on Human Rights and is in a mood of convergence with the case law of the Strasbourg Court. This approach has been followed in other cases.[205] A consequence of this case law is that, by applying the Convention, the ECJ in effect pre-empts any possible intervention by the Strasbourg Court and reasserts its position as the Supreme Court of the Union, offering a one-stop forum for the protection of fundamental rights.

The tendency towards deference to national constitutional standards through a soft proportionality test continued and was, in fact, enhanced in *Omega Spielhallen*.[206] The Bonn police authority banned a game of simulated homicide played in a 'laserdrome' operated by the applicant company. The object of this game was to fire on human targets using laser guns and sensory tags fixed on jackets worn by players. The company challenged the ban, *inter alia*, on the ground that it was contrary to the freedom to provide services since its laserdrome used equipment and technology supplied by a British company under a franchise agreement. The ban was upheld by the German courts on the ground that the commercial exploitation of a killing game was an affront to human dignity as protected by Article 1(1) of the Basic Law. The ECJ was therefore faced with a constitutional

---

[203] See *Schmidberger, passim*, and also *International Trader's Ferry Ltd, op. cit.*; in Case C-12/02 *Grilli*, judgment of 2 October 2003 (paras 41, 42), the ECJ reiterated that Article 29 EC covers only discriminatory restrictions.

[204] Previous rulings of the ECJ concerning free movement and human rights have been of varied specificity. See and contrast *ERT, op. cit.*, n. 132 above; *Familiapress, op. cit.*, n. 139 above; *Carpenter, op. cit.*, n. 149 above.

[205] See e.g. Case C-276/01 *Steffensen*, [2003] ECR I-3735. There the Court held that, in addition to complying with the principles of equivalence and effectiveness, national rules of procedure and remedies must comply with fundamental rights as guaranteed by the European Convention. See also, more recently, Case C-117/01 *KB v National Health Service Pensions Agency*, judgment of 7 January 2004, dealing with discrimination against trans-sexuals.

[206] *Op. cit.*, n. 41 above.

clash, namely, on the one hand, the interest in free movement and, on the other, the protection of human dignity as understood by German courts. In a spirit reminiscent of *Schmidberger*, it resolved the conflict in favour of national choice. It reiterated that the protection of fundamental rights is a legitimate interest which may justify a restriction on the freedom to provide services. To be compatible with the Treaty, such restrictions must satisfy the principle of proportionality. The Court held however that it is not indispensable for the restrictive measure issued by the authorities of a Member State to correspond to a conception shared by all Member States as regards the precise way in which the fundamental right or legitimate interest in question is to be protected.

The importance of the judgment lies in that the ECJ rejected the notion that national restrictions on free movement imposed on grounds of public policy must conform to a legal conception common to all Member States. It thus promotes an integration model based on value diversity which views national constitutional standards not as being in a competitive relationship with the economic objectives of the Union but as forming part of its polity.

7.5. Community law and the European Convention on Human Rights[207]

7.5.1. The status of the Convention in Community law

Express reference to the Convention by the ECJ was made for the first time in *Rutili*.[208] Subsequently, in *Nold* the Court identified the Convention as one of the primary sources of fundamental rights whose observance is guaranteed in the Community legal order.[209] As the case law evolved, the function of the Convention in judicial reasoning became more instrumental: general references gave way to detailed analysis of its provisions.[210] The case law acknowledged the 'special significance' of the Convention, the underlying principles of which 'must be taken into consideration in Community law'.[211] References to its provisions have been

---

[207] Bibliography on this issue abounds. See the works quoted in subsequent footnotes and also, among others, F.G. Jacobs: 'European Community Law and the European Convention on Human Rights' in D. Curtin and T. Heukels (eds), *Institutional Dynamics of European Integration, Essays in Honour of H.G. Schermers* Vol. II, (1998) Kluwer, 561–572; H. G. Schermers, 'The European Community Bound by Fundamental Human Rights' (1990) 27 CML Rev 249; N. Grief, comment in [1991] PL 555, J; J. McBride and L.N. Brown, 'The United Kingdom, The European Community and the European Convention on Human Rights' (1981) 1 YEL 167; A. Drzemczewski, 'The Domestic Application of the European Human Rights Convention as European Community Law' (1981) 30 ICLQ 118; H. G. Schermers, 'The Communities Under the European Convention on Human Rights' (1978) 1 LIEI 1.   [208] *Op. cit.*, n. 133 above.
[209] See above p. 302.
[210] See e.g. most recently, *Grant v South-West Trains Ltd, op. cit.*, n. 45 above.
[211] *Johnston v Chief Constable of the RUC, op. cit.*, n. 50 above, para 18; *ERT op. cit.*, n. 132 above, para 41; *Connolly v Commission, op. cit.*, n. 5 above, para 17; *Roquette Frères, op. cit.*, n. 5 above, para 23.

made in numerous cases, among the most oft-quoted articles being Articles 6 and 13,[212] 8,[213] and 10.[214] References have been made in numerous Community documents[215] and measures of secondary law.[216] Article 6(2) of the TEU now commits the Union to respect fundamental rights 'as guaranteed by the European Convention . . . and as they result from the constitutional traditions common to the Member States, as general principles of Community law'.[217] It follows that, even though the Community is not formally bound by it, it is required to respect, as a minimum, the standards of the Convention which forms an integral part of Community law.[218]

7.5.2. The relationship between the ECJ and the ECtHR: Deference and convergence

Since the Court of Justice has jurisdiction to apply the Convention in areas which fall within the scope of Community law, the possibility exists that conflicting rulings may be delivered by the Court of Justice and the Court of Human Rights on the interpretation of the Convention. This is illustrated by the case law of the two courts pertaining to the right of privacy. Article 8(1) of the Convention states that 'Everyone has the right to respect for his private and family life, his home and his correspondence'. In *Hoechst v Commission* [219] the ECJ held in the context of Commission investigations in the field of competition law, that the right to the inviolability of the home applies only to the private dwellings of natural persons and does not extend to undertakings. The Court reasoned that the protective scope

---

[212] See e.g. Case 98/79 *Pecastaing v Belgium* [1980] ECR 691; Case 374/87 *Orkem v Commission* [1989] ECR 3283; *Johnston v Chief Constable of the RUC, op. cit.,* Joined Cases T-377/00, T-379/00, T-380/00, T-260/01 and T-272/01 *Philip Morris International, Inc and Others v Commission,* [2003] ECR II-1.

[213] See e.g. *Rutili, op. cit.,* n. 133 above; *National Panasonic, op. cit.,* n. 46 above; Case 249/86 *Commission v Germany* [1989] ECR 1263; *Hoechst v Commission, op. cit.,* n. 53 above; *Konstantinidis, op. cit. (per* Jacobs AG).

[214] See e.g. *ERT, op. cit.; Grogan, op. cit. (per* van Gerven AG); *Connolly v Commission, op. cit.; Lindqvist, op. cit.,* n. 189 above.

[215] See e.g. Joint Declaration on Fundamental Rights by the European Parliament, the Council and the Commission, 5 April 1977; Declaration of Fundamental Rights and Freedoms, European Parliament, 12 April 1989; Declaration on Racism and Xenophobia, Maastricht European Council, 9–10 December 1991. For other measures, see Duparc, *op. cit.,* n. 1 above.

[216] See e.g. the reference to Article 10(1) in the eighth recital of the Preamble to Council Directive 89/552/EEC on the coordination of national laws concerning the pursuit of television broadcasting activities, OJ 1989 L 298, p. 23.

[217] For references to those provisions, see e.g. *Connolly v Commission, op. cit.,* para 38; *Roquette Frères, op. cit.,* para 24; *Bosman, op. cit.,* n. 49 above, para 79.

[218] See Jacobs, *op. cit.,* p. 563; P. Pescatore, 'La Cour de justice des Communautés européennes et la Convention européenne des droits de l'Homme', in F. Matscher and H. Petzold (eds), *Protecting Human Rights: The European Dimension: Studies in Honour of Gerard J. Wiarda* (Köln: Carl Heymanns Verlag, 1988); *op. cit.,* n. 1 above, p. 108.

[219] *Op. cit.,* n. 93 above. The ruling was confirmed in Case 85/87 *Dow Benelux v Commission* [1989] ECR 3137 and Joined Cases 97–99/87 *Dow Chemical Ibérica v Commission* [1989] ECR 3165.

of Article 8(1) is concerned with 'the development of man's personal freedom and may not therefore be extended to business premises'.[220] Subsequently, in *Niemietz v Germany*[221] the European Court of Human Rights held that the protection of Article 8(1) extends to the professional offices of a lawyer. Rejecting the literal interpretation of the Court of Justice, it held that a restrictive construction of Article 8(1) posed the risk of unequal treatment because self-employed persons may carry on professional activities at home and, conversely, private activities in their place of work. The ECtHR found this broad interpretation of the right of privacy as being more compatible with the underlying objective of Article 8 which is to protect the individual from arbitrary interference from the public authorities. Subsequently, in *Roquette Frères v Commission*,[222] the ECJ heeded the interpretation of Article 8 followed by the ECtHR. It reiterated, as a general principle of Community law, that any intervention by public authorities in the sphere of private activities must not be arbitrary or disproportionate. It then continued by stating that, in determining the scope of that principle, regard must be had to the case law of the ECtHR subsequent to the judgment in *Hoechst*. According to that case law, first, the protection of the home may in certain circumstances be extended to cover business premises and, second, the power of interference established by Article 8(2) of the ECHR may be more far-reaching where professional or business activities or premises are involved.[223]

Despite the potential problems arising from conflicting rulings, it should be emphasised that the two jurisdictions are in a relationship of cooperation and not one of confrontation. In the 1990s, the ECJ began referring directly to the case law of the ECtHR.[224] Such references have been much more frequent in the 2000s[225] and, as *Roquette Frères* illustrates, the development of the ECJ case law shows a tendency towards convergence. Also, as explained above, the ECJ has considerably broadened and deepened its fundamental rights jurisdiction,[226] and has been prepared to be led by the ECtHR in recognizing or refusing to recognize rights.[227] As we shall see, this spirit of cooperation and convergence is mutual and the ECtHR, on its part, is prepared to defer in principle to the human rights standards adopted by the ECJ.

---

[220] *Hoechst, op. cit.*, para 18.

[221] Judgment of 16 December 1992, Series A, No 251–B, 16 EHRR 97.

[222] *Op. cit.*, n. 5 above.

[223] *Ibid.*, para 29, referring to *Colas Est and Others v France*, judgment of 16 April 2002, para 41; *Niemietz, op. cit.*, para 31.

[224] See e.g. Joined Cases C-74/95 and C-129/95 *Criminal proceedings against X* [1996] ECR I-6609 (Article 7); *Familiapress, op. cit.* (Article 10); Case C-185/95 *Baustahlgewebe GmbH v Commission* [1998] ECR I-8417 (Article 6).

[225] See e.g. Case C-7/98 *Krombach* [2000] ECR I-1935 (Article 6); *Connolly v Commission, op. cit.* (Article 10); *Carpenter, op. cit.* (Article 8); *Akrich, op. cit.*, (Article 8); *Steffensen, op. cit.*, n. 205 above (Article 6); *Karner, op. cit.* (Article 10).

[226] See above, *Schmidberger, op. cit.*; *Carpenter, op. cit.*

[227] See e.g. the case law on trans-sexuals and same-sex relationships: *P v S, op. cit.*, n. 45 above, para 16; *K.B. v NHS, op. cit.*, n. 205 above; *Grant v South-West Trains, op. cit.*

Pockets of divergence, however, continue to exist. The right against self-incrimination has proved a troublesome area. In *Orkem*[228] the ECJ held that Article 6 of the Convention does not include the right not to give evidence against oneself. Subsequently, in *Funke v France*[229] the ECtHR held that, under Article 6, any person charged with a criminal offence has the right to remain silent and not to contribute towards self-incrimination. These rulings evince that the two courts have, at least in some issues, different priorities. As we saw in a previous chapter, in subsequent case law the CFI and the ECJ stopped short of endorsing the ruling in *Funke*.[230]

7.5.3. The status of the advocate general

Another area where the case law has come into conflict is the status of the advocate general. In *Vermeulen v Belgium*,[231] the ECtHR found, by fifteen votes to four, that the participation of the procureur général of the Belgian Cour de Cassation in the adjudication of civil cases infringed Article 6(1) of the Convention.[232] The main duties of the procureur général are to assist the Cour de Cassation to resolve the case in issue and ensure the consistency of its case law. The Court noted that the procureur général acts with the strictest objectivity but pointed out that his opinion, intended as it is to advise and to influence the Cour de Cassation, may rebound on the legal position of the person concerned. The Court found a violation of Article 6(1) on two counts. First, the fact that the person concerned does not have the right to reply to the submissions of the procureur général before the end of the hearing infringes his right to adversarial proceedings. Second, the participation of the procureur général in the deliberations of the Cour de Cassation, even though he takes part only in an advisory capacity, violates the right to a fair hearing. Such participation, the Court noted, offers him, if only in appearance, an additional opportunity to bolster his submissions in private without the fear of contradiction.

Vermeulen raised a question mark over the office of the advocate general of the ECJ. Clearly, the second infringement of Article 6(1) established in *Vermeulen* cannot be substantiated as the advocate general does not take part in the deliberation of the ECJ. The reasoning of the Court of Human Rights regarding the first infringement however raises questions. The delivery of the opinion concludes

---

[228] *Op. cit.*, n. 212 above, para 30.   [229] Series A, No 256-A, 16 EHRR 297.

[230] See Case T-112/98 *Mannesmannröhren-Werke AG v Commission* [2001] ECR II-729 and the more nuanced approach of the ECJ in the *PVC II* cases: Joined Cases C-238, 244–245, 247, 250, 251–252 and 254/99 P *Limburgse Vinyl Maatschappij NV and others v Commission* [2002] ECR I-8375, paras 270 *et seq.*; discussed above Chapter 8.

[231] Case 58/1994/505/587 judgment of 22 January 1996, Reports of Judgments and Decisions, 1996 I, 224.

[232] Earlier, a similar finding had been made in relation to the participation of the procureur général in criminal proceedings: *Borgers v Belgium*, judgment of 30 October 1991, Series A, No. 214, (1993) 15 EHRR 92.

the oral hearing and the litigants have no right of reply. Does the fact that the advocate general has the last word infringe the right to judicial protection?[233] In *Emesa Sugar*,[234] the ECJ held that the reasoning of the Strasbourg Court was not applicable to the advocate general. It pointed out that advocates general do not perform the function of public prosecutors. It distinguished *Vermeulen* on the ground that, in contrast to the position of equivalent offices in some Member States, the advocate general does not derive his authority from any source outside the Court and is organically and functionally an integral part of it.[235]

Following the judgment in *Emesa Sugar*, the Strasbourg Court had the opportunity to revisit the issue of judicial independence, this time in relation to no lesser an authority than the commissaire du Gouvernement of the French Conseil d' Etat. In *Kress v France*,[236] the applicant claimed that her right of fair trial had been violated on the following grounds. The submissions of the commissaire had not been communicated to her before the hearing, nor had she been able to reply to him after the hearing as he always spoke last. Also, the commissaire attended the deliberations and, even if he did not vote, this was a breach of the principle of equality of arms and the right to adversarial procedure.

The Court commenced by making a eulogy of the French system of administrative justice. It hailed the very establishment and existence of administrative courts 'as one of the most conspicuous achievements of a State based on the rule of law', particularly because their jurisdiction was not accepted without a struggle.[237] It also accepted that the role of the commissaire du Gouvernement is not similar to that of a State counsel's office. It is a *sui generis* institution peculiar to the organization of administrative court proceedings in France. It noted however that the mere fact that the administrative courts and the commissaire du Gouvernement have existed for more than a century and function well cannot justify a failure to comply with the present requirements of European law.

The Court stressed that the independence and impartiality of the commissaire were not in doubt. This however was not sufficient to ensure that there was no breach of Article 6(1). Great importance must be attached to the part actually played in the proceedings, and especially, to the content and effect of his submissions. The Court pointed out that the commissaire makes his submissions

---

[233] Notably, Judges Gölcüklü, Matscher and Pettiti in their joint dissenting opinion, took the view that judgment of the majority illustrated 'excessive formalism'. They stated: 'in our view, to see the *procureur général*, when he acts in civil proceedings, as an adversary of either of the parties is to misunderstand the nature of the institution, since his rôle—of what one might call an *amicus curiae*—is solely that of a neutral and objective guardian of the lawfulness of the proceedings and of the uniformity and consistency of the case-law. To that extent, his participation in the hearing and—in an advisory capacity—in the deliberations in no way offends against the principle of equality of arms as he is placed above the parties.'

[234] Case C-17/98 *Emesa Sugar (Free Zone) NV v Aruba* [2000] ECR I-665.

[235] *Emesa Sugar, op. cit.,* paras 14–16. The Court effectively endorsed the view expressed in T. Tridimas, 'The Role of the Advocate General in the Development of Community Law: Some Reflections' (1997) CML Rev, 1381–82.

[236] Application No. 39594/98, judgment of 7 June 2001.   [237] *Ibid.*, para 69.

for the first time orally at the public hearing. The parties to the proceedings, the judges, and the public all learn of his opinion on that occasion. The fact therefore that the applicant did not have a right to have his submissions disclosed to her before the hearing was not a breach of the principle of equality of arms.

The Court then turned to examine whether there was a breach of Article 6(1) because the applicant was not able to respond to the submissions of the commissaire. It reiterated that the concept of fair trial entails the opportunity for the parties to have knowledge of, and comment on, all observations filed even by an independent member of the national legal service with a view to influencing the court's decision. It found that the procedure of the Conseil d'Etat afforded litigants sufficient safeguards and there was no breach of the right to a fair trial for three reasons. First, because lawyers may ask the commissaire before the hearing to indicate the general tenor of his submissions. Second, because the parties to the proceedings may reply to his submissions by means of a memorandum for the deliberations. Third, because if the commissaire raised an issue not raised by the parties, the presiding judge would stay the proceedings to enable the parties to present argument.[238] Notably, these safeguards are not available at the ECJ. *Kress* leaves the advocate general of the ECJ in a very precarious, indeed unsustainable, position. The ECtHR considered the second element, i.e. the fact that the parties have the opportunity to communicate to the Court their views on the opinion as particularly important because it 'helps to ensure compliance with the adversarial principle'. In fact, it was this element that distinguished the commissaire du gouvernement from similar offices in other courts. The ECJ has the power to reopen the oral hearing. It is arguable that this power is sufficient to prevent injustice but it is discretionary and does not go as far as to enable the litigants to reply to the Opinion. It may therefore fall short of the expectations of the ECtHR.[239]

It may be said that *Kress* endorses a notion of independence which is not shared by the higher courts of the contracting states since they are based on the belief that the advocate general, in its various incarnations, serves as a fundamental pillar of the justice system. In the light of the function of the advocate general and the

---

[238] The Court however took issue with one aspect of the procedure. It held that the participation of the commissaire in the deliberations of the Court, even though he did not vote, was a breach of Article 6(1) as it was liable to give the impression that he could influence the judges and ran counter to the principle of neutrality: see paras 79 *et seq.*

[239] See Article 61 of the Rules of Procedure. Following *Kress*, the compatibility of the office of the Advocate General of the ECJ with Article 6 ECHR was raised again in Case CB466/00 *Kaba* [2003] ECR I-2219. The ECJ avoided the issue but Colomer AG followed the approach in *Emesa Sugar* and found no violation of Article 6. He took the view that the procedure before the ECJ offers litigants sufficient guarantees, by interpreting Article 61 of the Rules of Procedure as meaning that, if the Advocate General has raised arguments which the parties have not been able to debate, they have a right to have the oral procedure re-opened. The Advocate General, however, questioned the reasoning of the ECtHR in *Kress* and argued against the recognition of a general right on the part of the parties to submit observations on the Opinion.

contribution of the office in the development of Community law, the suggestion that it may violate the right to legal protection does not appear wholly convincing.[240] There can be no doubt that the advocate general is an integral part of the Community judicial system. He performs *par excellence* a judicial function, being 'the embodied conscience' of the Court.[241] Arguably, the fact that the litigants may not submit observations on the opinion is no more of a threat to the right to judicial protection than the fact that the litigants have no right of appeal against the judgment of the Court itself. By the nature of things, there must be a court which is the final arbiter of a dispute and against the decision of which there is no legal remedy. It is precisely as a member of such a court that the advocate general can fulfil a most useful function.

Such divergences in the case law expose the relativity of judicial reasoning. It may be said that the existence of competing judiciaries with overlapping jurisdictions enhances the accountability of the judiciary, leads to cross-fertilization and, through the dialectical development of the case law, promotes convergence of standards which reflect a wider political and societal consensus. There is no doubt that the co-existence of the two courts enhances their legitimacy and the values of democracy. Conflicting rulings, however, raise problems of legal certainty and potentially may put national courts in a dilemma: either they have to abide by the case law of the ECJ, thus violating the Convention, or follow the Strasbourg jurisprudence thus risking a violation of Community law. The accession of the European Union to the Convention would eliminate such problems without risking judicial pluralism.[242]

---

[240] See further Tridimas, *op. cit.*, 1349 and 1380.

[241] C. Hamson, *Executive Discretion and Judicial Control* (Stevens, 1954) p. 80.

[242] Note that in contrast to *Kress* the ECtHR has not endorsed the view that the restrictive interpretation of Article 230(4) EC by the ECJ runs counter to the fundamental right to judicial protection as guaranteed by the Convention. The issue has not been examined directly by the ECtHR but in *Posti and Rahko v Finland*, judgment of 24 September 2002, the Strasbourg Court reiterated that Article 6 does not guarantee a right of access to a court with competence to invalidate or override a law enacted by the legislature. It held however that, where a decree, decision or other measure, albeit not formally addressed to any individual natural or legal person, in substance affects the civil rights or obligations of such a person or of a group of persons in a similar situation, whether by certain attributes peculiar to them or by reason of a factual situation which differentiates them from all other persons, Article 6(1) may require that the substance of the decision or measure in question is capable of being challenged by that person or group before a tribunal meeting the requirements of Article 6. The Court expressly stated that its position resembles that of EC law where a general measure such as a regulation may in certain circumstances be of individual concern to a private applicant. The judgment appears to draw a distinction between legislative and regulatory acts. Whilst Article 6 does not guarantee to individuals a right to challenge the former, it may require access to an independent tribunal to challenge the latter. The Court of Human Rights drew inspiration from the case law of the ECJ but the case should not necessarily be seen as an endorsement of the restrictive interpretation of individual concern given by the ECJ. Rather, it confirms that individuals may not *a priori* be denied *locus standi* to challenge regulatory acts, and that a person who is able to show that a regulatory measure affects in substance his interests in a distinct way should be able to challenge it. The judgement however does not settle whether an over-restrictive interpretation of individual concern by the ECJ may, in certain circumstances, amount to breach of Article 6(1). Nor is this settle by the judgment in *Bosphorus Airways*, discussed below, although the ECtHR seemed to condone it.

If it is accepted that the Convention forms part of the corpus of Community law, it must also be accepted that, on issues of law, the Court of Justice is bound to follow the interpretation given to the Convention by the Court of Human Rights. The Convention occupies a special position in the Community legal order. It is not only a source of inspiration on human rights but much more: it is the expression of a fundamental core of moral, political and social values underlying the legal systems of the Contracting States and underpinning the Community legal order. The interpretation of the Convention should be left to the Court of Human Rights, that being the competent judicial body. The Court of Justice, for its part, has jurisdiction to apply the Convention within the confines of that interpretation in the light of the distinct requirements of the Community polity. Inevitably, it will reach outcomes and concretize the weighing of interests in specific facts but will have to abide by the case law of the ECtHR with regard to the interpretation of the Convention.

7.5.4. From the Straits of Gibraltar to the straits of *Bosphorus*

Since neither the European Communities nor the European Union are Contracting Parties to the European Convention on Human Rights, it is not possible to bring an action against them before the European Court of Human Rights. For this reason, the European Commission of Human Rights traditionally declared actions against the Community inadmissible.[243] In fact the relationship between Strasbourg and Luxembourg has traditionally been one of mutual respect and deference. The Commission of Human Rights took the view that the Member States could not be held responsible for acts of an international organization to which they had transferred powers, if the organization itself provided an adequate system of judicial control for the protection of fundamental rights.[244] The issue was first examined by the Court of Human Rights itself in *Matthews v United Kingdom*.[245] Annex II of the

---

[243] See e.g. *CFDT v European Communities*, decision of 10 July 1978, application no. 8030/77.

[244] *M & Co v Federal Republic of Germany*, decision of 9 February 1990, application no. 13258/87. The European Commission rejected as inadmissible an application by a German national alleging that the execution by the German authorities of a decision of the European Court of Justice in competition law violated Article 6 of the Convention. The Commission considered that it was not competent to examine the claim in view of the transfer of powers in the field at issue from Germany to the Community. It held that such transfer of powers was compatible with the Convention provided that an equivalent standard of protection was guaranteed to fundamental rights and referred to that effect to the case law of the Court of Justice. Note also that in *Pafitis v Greece*, judgment of 26 February 1998, the ECtHR gave the ECJ a clean bill of health. In assessing whether the length of civil proceedings before the Greek courts was contrary to Article 6(1) of the Convention, the Strasbourg Court did not take into account the time during which the proceedings were stayed pending a reference for a preliminary ruling. As a result of the reference, the proceedings were prolonged by 2 years and 7 months (Case C-441/93 *Pafitis v Trapeza Kentrikis Ellados AE* [1996] ECR I-1347). The ECtHR held however that it could not take this period into consideration. Even though it might at first sight appear relatively long, to take it into account 'would adversely affect the system instituted by Article 177 of the EEC Treaty and work against the aim pursued in substance in that Article' (para 90).

[245] Judgment of 18 February 1999, application 24833/94.

Act on Direct Elections of 1976[246] excluded residents of Gibraltar from voting in elections for the European Parliament. Mrs Matthews, a British citizen resident in Gibraltar, argued that her exclusion was contrary to Article 3 of Protocol 1 of the Convention which provides that the Contracting Parties undertake to hold elections at reasonable intervals for the choice of the legislature. The alleged violation flowed from the Act on Direct Elections and the Maastricht Treaty which had extended the powers of the European Parliament.

In its judgment, the ECtHR made some important pronouncements of principle. It held that the Convention does not exclude the transfer of competences to international organizations provided that the Convention rights continue to be secured. The responsibility of the Contracting Parties therefore continues even after such a transfer.[247] The Court attributed particular importance to the fact that the Act on Direct Elections was not an act of the Community institutions but an international treaty concluded by the Member States. The alleged violation therefore derived from an act of primary law which could not be challenged before the European Court of Justice. The same was true in relation to the Maastricht Treaty. In those circumstances, the Court held that the United Kingdom, together with all the other Member States, was responsible for any violation of the Convention emanating from those Treaties. From a human rights perspective, this rationale is convincing. If the Convention is to guarantee rights which are not theoretical or illusory, the Contracting Parties should undertake responsibility for any obligations which they voluntarily enter into just as they are for the exercise of their sovereign powers within the domestic legal order.

The ECtHR further held that the European Parliament was sufficiently involved in the law-making process and in the political supervision of Community affairs as to constitute part of the legislature of Gibraltar for the purposes of Article 3 of Protocol 1 and found that there was a violation of that provision.

Although the ECtHR found a breach of the Convention emanating from the transfer of sovereign rights to the EU, in fact it pursued an agenda fully in conformity with that of the ECJ. It endorsed the project of European integration and, by viewing the European Parliament as a form of legislature, it added to the democratic legitimisation and the constitutionalisation of the EC Treaty. The underlying message is that European integration is good but only if it conforms with fundamental constitutional values. The ECtHR judged that the process of supranational constitutionalism was best served by emphasising the credentials of the Parliament as a body which guarantees electorate representation rather than the democratic deficit of the EU decision-making process. By condemning the disenfranchisement of Mrs Matthews, the ECtHR in fact promoted the idea of Union citizenship:[248]

As to the context in which the European Parliament operates, the Court is of the view that the European Parliament represents the principal form of democratic, political accountability

---

[246] Act concerning the Election of the Representatives of the European Parliament by Direct Universal Suffrage of 20 September 1976.   [247] *Matthews, op. cit.*, para 32.
[248] *Ibid.*, para 52.

in the Community system. The Court considers that whatever its limitations, the European Parliament, which derives democratic legitimation from the direct elections by universal suffrage, must be seen as that part of the European Community structure which best reflects concerns as to 'effective political democracy.

It follows from *Matthews* that Member States may be held accountable for breach of the Convention by acts of primary law which cannot be challenged before the European Court of Justice. Thus, Treaty clauses which limit the Court's jurisdiction might potentially be vulnerable on grounds of violation of Article 6 ECHR if the Member States do not offer at national level sufficient alternative protection.[249] What about acts of the Community institutions themselves? Can the Member States be held responsible for violations flowing from them? The issue was examined in *Bosphorus Hava Yollari Turizm ve Ticaret AS v Ireland*.[250]

It will be remembered that in its judgment in *Bosphorus*[251] the ECJ upheld the impounding by the Irish authorities of an aircraft leased by a Turkish company from the Yugoslav national airline pursuant to Regulation 990/93 imposing sanctions against the Federal Republic of Yugoslavia. Following the judgment of the ECJ and its enforcement by Irish courts, the applicant airline argued before the ECtHR that the impounding breached its right to property contrary to Article 1, Protocol No 1 of the Convention. The ECtHR considered that the sanctions regime imposed by the Regulation amounted to a control of the use of property which should be assessed under the second paragraph of Article 1 of the Protocol. It accepted that the seizure of the aircraft, which remained inoperative for about three years out of a four-year lease, was not the result of the exercise of any discretion by the Irish authorities but amounted to compliance by the Irish State with its legal obligations flowing from EC law. It reiterated that compliance with EC law by a contracting party to the Convention is a legitimate general interest objective within the meaning of Article 1[252] and proceeded to examine whether the interference with the applicant's property rights was justified. It concluded that it was.

The judgment represents the most important statement made so far regarding the position of the Community legal order *vis-à-vis* the Convention and the relationship between the European Court of Human Rights and the European Court of Justice. The principles emanating from the judgment are the following:

(1) The Convention does not prohibit Contracting Parties from transferring sovereign powers to an international or supra-national organization. Where such transfer occurs, the organization does not become responsible under the convention unless it is itself a Contracting Party.[253]

---

[249] See e.g. Article 68(2) EC, Article 35(5) TEU.   [250] *Op. cit.*, n.7 above.
[251] *Op. cit.*, n. 98 above.
[252] *Ibid.*, para 150; *S.A. Dangeville v France*, application no. 36677/97, judgment of 16 April 2002, paras 47 and 55.   [253] *Op. cit.*, para 152.

(2) Under Article 1 ECHR, however, a Contracting Party remains responsible for all acts and omissions of its organs regardless of whether such act or omission was a consequence of domestic law or of the necessity to comply with international obligations. The reason for this is a functional one. If Contracting Parties were absolved of their responsibilities, the guarantees offered by the Convention would become illusory and its safeguards would be undermined.[254]

(3) State action taken in compliance with such international obligations is justified as long as the relevant organization protects fundamental rights, 'as regards both the substantive guarantees offered and the mechanisms controlling their observance', in a manner which can be considered to be at least equivalent to that provided by the Convention. 'Equivalent' here means 'comparable' and not 'identical': the imposition of the latter requirement would run counter to the interest of international cooperation, the growing importance of which the ECtHR recognizes.[255]

(4) The existence of such equivalent standards raises a presumption that the State has not departed from the requirements of the Convention.[256] This presumption is limited and it is rebuttable.

(5) It is limited in that it applies only where the State does no more than implement legal obligations flowing from its membership of the organization. The State remains fully responsible under the Convention for all acts falling outside its strict international obligations.[257]

(6) The presumption can be rebutted if, in the circumstances of a particular case, it is considered that the protection of Convention rights was 'manifestly deficient'. In such a case, the interest of international cooperation would be outweighed by the Convention's role as a constitutional instrument of European public order in the field of human rights.[258]

The Court stressed that the presumption applies only insofar as a Member State acts within its strict legal obligations flowing from Community law. It follows that, where a Member State enjoys discretion under Community rules, it remains fully responsible for any breach of the Convention in the exercise of its discretion. Sometimes, it may be difficult to determine whether such discretion exists. This is a matter of interpretation of Community law to be decided ultimately by the ECJ. In *Bosphorus* the ECJ had already had the chance to pronounce on the issue and it was clear that the Irish courts did not have any margin of manoeuvring on how to apply its ruling. If there is no judgment of the ECJ, there may be opportunity for blame shifting. A Member State may argue as a defence to an alleged violation of fundamental rights that it had no discretion in implementing Community obligations. In some cases, therefore, the ECtHR may be called upon to evaluate whether a

---

[254] *Ibid.*, paras 153–154.   [255] *Ibid.*, para 155.   [256] *Ibid.*, para 156.
[257] *Ibid.*, para 157.   [258] *Ibid.*, para 156.

Member State enjoys discretion under Community law. We see here a reversal of roles: just as the ECJ may in some cases rule on the interpretation of the Convention, the ECtHR may have to rule on the interpretation of Community law. Such role shifting raises the prospect of conflicting rulings and may be seen as a source of legal uncertainty. On the other hand, it may also be seen as leading to beneficial judicial cross-fertilization.

Acts of primary Community law do not fall within the presumption and continue to be governed by *Matthews*. Since such acts are 'freely entered into' by the Member States, respect for human rights remains their responsibility.

In *Bosphorus*, the ECtHR found that the protection of fundamental rights offered by Community law was equivalent both in terms of the substantive standards of protection and in terms of the mechanisms. As regards substantive standards, the Court referred to the case law of the ECJ which grants special significance to the Convention, the reference to fundamental rights in the SEA and the TEU and the Treaty of Amsterdam, and even the Charter of Fundamental Rights. As to the mechanisms of enforcement, the ECtHR was satisfied that they also offered sufficient guarantees. Whilst acknowledging the limitations on *locus standi* of individuals to bring actions under Article 230(4), it accepted that it is essentially through national courts that the Community provides a remedy for individuals. It concluded therefore that the protection of fundamental rights by EC law is equivalent to that of the Convention system. The ECtHR devoted little effort to examining whether the presumption was rebutted in the circumstances. In the light of the nature of the interference, the general interest pursued by the sanctions regime and the ruling of the ECJ, there was no dysfunction of the mechanisms of control of the observance of Convention rights.

Bosphorus comes in the aftermath of the ECJ's activist case law on fundamental rights and can be seen as a reward for judgments such as *Carpenter* and *Schmidberger*. In some respects, the approach of the Strasbourg Court resembles that of the German Constitutional court: it views the ECJ as an agent of its own standards. The ECJ operates under a double conditional and reversible endorsement granted to it by the national courts and the ECtHR.

The Strasbourg Court however has reserved itself sufficient discretion to be able to intervene in circumstances where it considers it appropriate to do so. Much will depend on what degree of scrutiny it is prepared to exercise in reviewing whether in a particular case the presumption of equivalence that Community law enjoys has been rebutted. The test of 'manifest deficiency' in the protection of Convention rights suggests a deferential level of review and this is confirmed by what the ECtHR did in *Bosphorus* itself. However, the ECtHR may examine both the substantive and the procedural aspects of fundamental rights in a specific case with a view to establishing whether the presumption holds. As a general rule, in the context of a federal or quasi-federal organization, both the central authority and the constituent parts should observe the same standards of human rights protection. There is no reason why Member States should be subject to more stringent standards than those applicable to the Community institutions. The judgment in *Bosphorus* should not be interpreted as departing from this principle.

Still, there is no doubt that the ECtHR showed a high degree of deference to the Community legal order. *Bosphorus* can be contrasted with *Pellegrini*.[259] The applicant complained of a violation of Article 6 on the ground that the Italian courts declared the decision of the Roman Rota (an ecclesiastical court) annulling her marriage enforceable. Her argument was that her rights of defence had not been respected before the ecclesiastical courts. The ECtHR held that, since the Vatican had not ratified the Convention, its task was not to examine whether the proceedings before the ecclesiastical courts complied with Article 6 but whether the Italian courts, before authorising enforcement of the decision annulling the marriage, duly satisfied themselves that the relevant proceedings fulfilled the guarantees of Article 6. Such review is required where a decision in respect of which enforcement is requested emanates from the courts of a country which does not apply the Convention. The Court proceeded to examine the reasons given by the Italian courts in dismissing her complaints and concluded that they had not so done finding a violation of Article. 6. The Court in fact applied a high standard of scrutiny. The issue was not whether the Italian courts were reasonable in concluding that the requirements of Article 6 had been complied with but whether those requirements had actually been respected in the circumstances. In other words, it did not apply a lesser standard of scrutiny than it would if it was examining whether the Italian courts themselves had breached Article 6. In *Bosphorus* the Court distinguished *Pellegrini* on the ground that the responsibility of a Contracting State when it enforces a judgment of a non-Contracting State is not comparable to compliance with a legal obligation emanating from an international organization to which Contracting Parties have transferred part of their sovereignty.

7.5.5. EU accession to the ECHR

Although in the mid 1970s the Commission had considered that formal accession of the Communities to the European Convention was not necessary,[260] in 1979 it floated the idea that accession was a desirable objective in order to strengthen the protection of human rights.[261] This proposal re-emerged in 1990 and in 1993 the Commission published a working document entitled 'Accession of the Community to the European Convention on Human Rights and the Community

---

[259] Judgment of 20 July 2001, application no. 30882/96.

[260] See EC Commission Report, *The Protection of Fundamental Rights as Community law is created and developed*, EC Bull Suppl 5/76 and, for a general discussion, see Mc Bride and Brown, *Op. cit.*, pp. 171 *et seq.*

[261] See *Accession of the European Communities to the European Convention on Human Rights*, EC Bull Suppl 2/79.

Legal Order'. There, it considered, among others, issues pertaining to the legal basis of accession and the jurisdiction of the Court of Justice. In 1994, the Council sought the opinion of the Court pursuant to Article 300(6) EC on whether accession would be compatible with the Treaty. In its Opinion,[262] the Court distinguished between two issues: whether accession would be compatible with the Treaty, and whether the Community has competence to accede. It considered that the issue of compatibility was not admissible because, at the time when the Opinion was sought, no specific arrangements had been made concerning the way in which the Community would become subject to the machinery of judicial control established by the Convention. On the issue of competence, the Court gave a negative reply. It referred to Article 5(1) EC which provides that the Community may act only within the limits of the powers conferred upon it by the Treaty and of the objectives assigned to it therein. It stated that no Treaty provision confers on the Community institutions any general power to enact rules on human rights or to conclude international conventions in that field.[263] In the absence of express or implied powers for that purpose, the Court turned to examine whether the residual provision of Article 308 EC may provide a legal basis for accession. It stated that Article 308 cannot serve as the basis for widening the scope of Community powers beyond the general framework created by the provisions of the Treaty as a whole and, in particular, those which define the tasks and the activities of the Community.[264] It pointed out that, under the case law, respect for human rights is a condition of the lawfulness of Community acts. Accession to the Convention, however, would bring about a substantial change in the Community system for the protection of human rights, as it would 'entail the entry of the Community into a distinct international institutional system as well as integration of all the provisions of the Convention into the Community legal order'.[265]

The reasoning of the Opinion is not wholly convincing. The core argument in favour of competence submitted by the Commission and by several Member States[266] was that respect for fundamental rights is a component of all Community policies or, as the Commission put it, a transverse objective forming an integral part of the Community's objectives. The Opinion contains virtually no discussion of that argument. Clearly, Article 308 may not be used to grant the Community institutions powers in areas which fall beyond the competence of the Community. Thus, it would not be possible for the Council to legislate on

---

[262] Opinion 2/94 [1996] ECR I-1759.   [263] *Ibid.*, para 27.

[264] This point was subsequently confirmed in *Grant v South-West Trains Ltd, op. cit.*, n. 45 above; and see Case C-376/98 *Germany v Council (Tobacco Advertisement case)*, [2000] ECR I-8419, para 83.   [265] *Op. cit.*, para 34.

[266] The Commission, the Parliament, Austria, Belgium, Denmark, Finland, Germany, Greece, Italy and Sweden argued that the Community had competence to accede to the Convention. France, Portugal, Spain, Ireland and the United Kingdom argued against accession.

fundamental rights in fields which do not otherwise fall within the scope of the Treaty.[267] That does not mean however that the Community does not have competence to accede to the Convention and be bound by it within the scope of application of Community law. Whether accession is compatible with Community law will depend on the specific arrangements concerning the relationship between the European Court of Human Rights and the European Court of Justice.[268] In previous opinions the Court had accepted that, in principle, it is possible for the Community to become part of a supra-national structure with its own, separate, system of judicial control.[269] The issue of accession to the Convention therefore should not be viewed as an issue of competence but as an issue of compatibility.[270]

Finally, it should be noted that the Opinion does not stand as authority that the Community may not conclude measures in the field of human rights on the basis of Article 308.[271] It rather stated that recourse to Article 308 may not be made with a view to establishing a system for the protection of human rights which has fundamental institutional and constitutional implications. Such a system may be brought about only by way of Treaty amendment.[272]

The EU Constitution took up the Court's invitation and provided an express legal basis for accession. Article I-9(2) commits the Union to accede to the European Convention and provides that 'such accession shall not affect the Union's competences as defined in the Constitution'. Protocol 32 annexed to the Constitutional Treaty provides some general guidelines for the contents of the agreement relating to accession. Following the demise of the Constitution, the prospects of accession in the short to medium term look bleak. In the absence of accession, the relationship between the two legal orders is governed by the principles laid down in *Bosphorus*.

Accession would be desirable. It would promote legal certainty, avoid the possibility of national courts being under contradictory obligations,[273] enhance the protection of the individual, and promote the rule of law: it is an oxymoron that the Community institutions make observance of fundamental rights a *sine qua non* for the accession of aspiring Member States to the EU, whilst they themselves are not directly bound to observe the Convention. The mechanics

---

[267] See A. Arnull, 'Opinion 2/94 and its Implications for the future Constitution of the Union', (Centre for European Legal Studies, Cambridge, 1996), 7.

[268] For further comments on Opinion 2/94, see G. Gaja, Comment in (1996) 33 CMLRev 973; 'The Human Rights Opinion of the ECJ and its Constitutional Implications', CELS Occasional Paper No.1, University of Cambridge, 1996.   [269] Opinion 1/76; Opinion 1/91.

[270] Notably, Advocate General Jacobs writing extra-judicially before the Court delivered its ruling took the view that it would be compatible with the EC Treaty for the Community to accept the jurisdiction of the European Court of Human Rights, basing his views on Opinion 1/91 *on the draft agreement relating to the creation of the EEA* [1991] ECR I-6079. See Jacobs, *op. cit.*, in Schermers, p. 565.   [271] That view is espoused by Arnull, *Op. cit.*, p. 7.

[272] *Op. cit.*, para 35.   [273] See above p. 347.

of accession and the relationship between the ECJ and the ECtHR present challenges but not insuperable problems. A system of preliminary references whereby the ECJ stays proceedings pending before it and refers to the ECtHR issues pertaining to the interpretation of the Convention would not be desirable since it would unduly lengthen the proceedings before the ECJ. There is however no reason why interested parties may not be able to apply to Strasbourg following the exhaustion of remedies provided by the Community legal order, applying *mutatis mutandis* the system currently in force as regards the existing Contracting Parties.

7.6. The Charter of Fundamental Rights

7.6.1. Origins, objectives, and content of the Charter

The origins of the Charter of Fundamental Rights lie in the Cologne European Council of June 1999.[274] The Council identified the protection of fundamental rights as a founding principle of the Union and 'an indispensable prerequisite for her legitimacy' and decided to set up a body with the task of drafting a Charter of Fundamental Rights. The drafting process was indicative of constitutional aspirations:[275] the Charter was prepared by a Convention whose proceedings were public and which provided the model for the subsequent establishment and workings of the Constitutional Convention responsible for drafting the EU Constitution.[276] The Charter was approved unanimously by the Biarritz European

[274] Bibliography on the Charter is vast. See, among others, S. Peers and A. Ward, *The Charter of Fundamental Rights and the Future of Human Rights Protection in Europe*, (Hart Publishing, 2004); K. Lenaerts and E. de Smijter, 'A "Bill of Rights" for the European Union', (2001) 38 CML Rev 273; P. Eeckhout, 'The EU Charter of Fundamental Rights and the Federal Question', 39 (2002) CML Rev 945; I. Pernice, 'Integrating the Charter of Fundamental Rights into the Constitution of the European Union: Practical and Theoretcial Propositions', (2003) 10 Columbia Journal of European Law 5.

[275] See G. de Bùrca, 'The Drafting of the European Union Charter of Fundamental Rights', (2001) 26 ELR 126.

[276] The Charter Convention was composed of fifteen personal representatives of the Heads of State or Government of the Member States, one representative of the Commission, sixteen members of the European Parliament and thirty members of national Parliaments (two per Parliament). It elected as its Chairman Mr Roman Herzog, former President of the Federal Republic of Germany, who was assisted by a drafting committee (Praesidium) composed of Mr Nikula (Finland), Mr Bacelar de Vasconcelos (Portugal), and Mr Braibant (France), Vice-Chairman, representing the Group of Personal Representatives, Commissioner Vitorino, representing the Commission, Mr Mendez de Vigo, Vice-Chairman, representing the Group of Members of the European Parliament, and Mr Gunnar Jansson, Vice-Chairman, representing the Group of Members of national Parliaments. The General Secretariat of the Council provided the Convention with secretariat services. The Convention held its first meeting on 17 December 1999. The Charter was forwarded to the European Council on 2 October 2000 and adopted at Biarritz on 13 and 14 October 2000.

Council in October 2000 and was signed and proclaimed by the Presidents of the European Parliament, the Council and the Commission on 7 December 2000 in Nice. The Nice Inter-Governmental Conference however left the issue whether the Charter should be binding to be considered as part of the general debate on the future of the European Union.[277] Subsequently, the Charter was included with minor amendments as Part II of the Constitution.[278] Following the failure of France and the Netherlands to ratify the Constitution, the Charter remains non-binding. It has been 'proclaimed' by the EU institutions but has the status of a declaration and does not as such create binding legal effects.

The decision to embark on the drafting of the Charter was motivated by three factors. It sought to increase the visibility of fundamental rights for the benefit of the citizen, promote legal certainty, and enhance Union legitimacy. The Charter in effect represents an effort to bring fundamental rights home: it internalizes fundamental rights into the European Union legal order and may be seen as a statement of nationhood. It represents a further stage in the process of constitutionalization of the Treaties and, at least by some of the political actors involved, was seen as a precursor to the European Constitution.[279]

One of the most important features of the Charter is that it does not protect only the classic civil liberties and political rights but incorporates fundamental economic and social rights,[280] thus 'throw[ing] into the sharpest relief [sic] the principle of indivisibility of rights'.[281] The Charter thus follows the continental constitutional tradition and not the Anglo-Saxon model of a Bill of Rights. This policy choice to provide not only for negative rights against the State but also positive obligations in favour of the citizen attests to the character of the Charter as an instrument which is based not on a purely libertarian philosophy but on ideals of social democracy. The Commission considers that, by bringing together in a single document the rights hitherto scattered in various national and international instruments, the Charter 'enshrines the very essence of the European acquit regarding fundamental rights.'[282]

---

[277] See Annex I to the Presidency conclusions and Declaration 23 on the Future of the Union adopted by the IGC.

[278] The amendments made by the Constitution are in the Preamble to the Charter (recital 5), and Article 52 of the Charter (Article II-112 of the Constitution). See 7.6.3. below.

[279] For an account of the divergent visions of the Charter that were held by those involved in its drafting, see de Bùrca, *op. cit.*, n.5 and accompanying text.

[280] The mandate given by the Cologne European Council was that the Charter should take account of economic and social rights as contained in the European Social Charter and the Community Charter of the Fundamental Social Rights of Workers (Article 136 EC) 'in so far as they do not merely establish objectives for action by the Union'. See Presidency Conclusions, European Council of Cologne, 3 and 4 June 1999, EU Bull. 6–1999, at 35.

[281] Commission Communication on the Legal Nature of the Charter of Fundamental Rights of the European Union, COM(2000) 644, Brussels, 11 October 2000, para 2.

[282] *Ibid.*, para 1.

The rights enshrined in the Charter are grouped under five headings: dignity,[283] freedoms,[284] equality,[285] solidarity,[286] citizens' rights,[287] and justice.[288] The Charter endorses the principle of universalism: as a general rule, rights apply to all persons irrespective of their nationality or residence. Exception is made in respect to rights inextricably linked to citizenship, i.e. political rights, and rights of free movement.[289] The Charter is intended to be a contemporary statement of values. It recognizes rights which are not strictly new but which are designed to meet the challenges of current and future developments in respect to information technology and genetic engineering. It provides, for example, for data protection and rights linked to bioethics.[290]

According to the Commission, the Charter meets the 'strong and legitimate contemporary demand for transparency and impartiality in the operation of the Community administration'.[291] The Commission considers that the Charter is drafted clearly and concisely and it will be easy for all those to whom it is addressed to understand.[292] In truth, some of its provisions are so vaguely drafted or subject to open-ended limitation clauses that they give little guidance as to the constraints to which State authorities are subject in specific situations. The Charter is thus

---

[283] Human dignity (Article 1), right to life (Article 2), right to the integrity of the person (Article 3), prohibition of torture and inhuman or degrading treatment (Article 4), and prohibition of slavery and forced labour (Article 5).

[284] Right to liberty and security (Article 6), respect for private and family life (Article 7), protection of personal data (Article 8), right to marry and found a family (Article 9), freedom of thought, conscience and religion (Article 10), freedom of expression and information (Article 11), freedom of assembly and association (Article 12), freedom of the arts and sciences (Article 13), right to education (Article 14), freedom to choose an occupation and right to engage in work (Article 15), freedom to conduct a business (Article 16), right to property (Article 17), right to asylum (Article 18), and protection in the event of removal, expulsion or extradition (Article 19).

[285] Equality before the law (Article 20), non-discrimination (Article 21), cultural, religious and linguistic diversity (Article 22), equality between men and women (Article 23), rights of the child (Article 24), rights of the elderly (Article 25), and integration of persons with disabilities (Article 26).

[286] Workers' right to information and consultation within the undertaking (Article 27), right of collective bargaining and action (Article 28), right of access to placement services (Article 29), protection in the event of unjustified dismissal (Article 30), fair and just working conditions (Article 31), prohibition of child labour and protection of young people at work (Article 32), family and professional life (Article 33), social security and social assistance (Article 34), health care (Article 35), access to services of general economic interest (Article 36), environmental protection (Article 37), and consumer protection (Article 38).

[287] Right to vote and to stand as a candidate at elections to the European Parliament (Article 39); right to vote and stand as a candidate at municipal elections (Article 40); right to good administration (Article 41); right of access to documents (Article 42); right to complain to the Ombudsman (Article 43); right to petition the European Parliament (Article 44); freedom of movement and residence (Article 45); and diplomatic and consular protection (Article 46).

[288] Right to an effective remedy and fair trial (Article 47), presumption of innocence and right of defence (Article 48), principles of legality and proportionality of criminal offences and penalties (Article 49), and right not be tried or punished twice for the same criminal offence (Article 50).

[289] A heavily qualified right of movement and residence is provided for third-country nationals legally resident in the EU: see Article 45(2).

[290] See Article 3 (right to the integrity of the person which includes, among others, the prohibition of the reproductive cloning of human beings) and Article 8 (data protection).

[291] Commission Communication on the Legal Nature of the Charter, para 2.   [292] Ibid.

best viewed as a document which contains rights, principles and aspirations, not all of which can be translated into concrete political choices and much less into enforceable rights.

The Commission considers as one of the Charter's main advantages that it promotes legal certainty. It will offer a clear guide for the interpretation of fundamental rights by the Court of Justice which currently has to use disparate and sometimes uncertain sources of inspiration. However, the case for legal certainty, unlike the case for visibility, is not necessarily made. First, as stated above, some of its provisions are so vaguely drafted that they give little clue as to possible outcomes. Second, given that the Charter is not legally binding, its co-existence with the case law of the ECJ or the ECtHR may add to rather than reduce legal uncertainty, especially if it is seen to depart from the other sources of human rights.

7.6.2. Status and effect

As stated above, the Charter is not currently legally binding. It was prepared by the Convention as if it were to be binding and to be incorporated in the treaties. The objective was to produce a text that could be part of the Treaty framework leaving to the European Council the final choice as to its legal nature, i.e. whether it will be a legally binding text or a political declaration. Even a non-binding Charter is not without some, albeit limited, value. It increases visibility of rights, provides an ideological posture, and serves as a guide to the exercise of legislative power. The Commission itself noted, perhaps somewhat optimistically, that it would be difficult for the Council and the Commission to ignore in the exercise of their functions a document prepared at the request of the European Council and taking account of the full range of sources of national and European legitimacy acting in concert.[293]

The Commission's initial presentation of the Charter was an exercise in skilfull equivocation: on the one hand, it extolled its virtues as a modern constitutional document of some novelty thereby establishing its constitutional credentials but, on the other hand, it was careful to emphasise that the Charter is fully compatible with the division of competence between the Union and its Member states. This political model of 'progress without offending' is by no means novel to the EU and, at the time of its adoption, revealed the underlying tensions between political actors who viewed it as a constitutional statement with binding force and those who thought it should best remain a political declaration. In 2000, the Commission expressed the view that the Charter 'by reasons of its content, its tight drafting, and its high political and symbolic value, ought properly to be incorporated in the Treaties sooner or later'.[294] It considered that, whatever its eventual status, the Charter would be integrated into the binding norms of Community law by a process of absorption: it could reasonably be expected that the Charter would

---

[293] *Op. cit.*, para 10.   [294] Commission Communication, *op. cit.*, para 11.

'become mandatory through the Court's interpretation of it as belonging to the general principles of Community law'.[295]

So far, the ECJ has conspicuously refrained from referring to the Charter even where express reliance on it is made by the parties to the proceedings or the national court making the reference.[296] In the absence of a clear commitment on the part of the Member States to be bound by it, this is a safe choice. The Court's silence is indiscriminate. Thus, it has not commented on an argument presented by one of the governments that the Charter is of no relevance.[297]

Numerous references have been made by advocates general and some references have been made by the CFI.[298] Such references have had mostly, if not invariably, a subsidiary character. The Charter has been used to support and reinforce a result that would have been reached even in its absence. In some cases, the Charter has been an integral part of the CFI's reasoning but never the sole decisive factor and, where particular prominence has been granted to it, it has been in relation to provisions which reflect existing general principles of law deriving from the case law, or the constitutional traditions common to the Member States, or international treaties. In *max.mobil*,[299] the CFI relied on Article 41(1) of the Charter, which provides for the duty of good administration, to support the proposition that the Commission is under a general duty to undertake a diligent and impartial examination of a complaint even in the absence of specific provisions granting rights to complainants. It also referred to Article 47(1) of the Charter, which reaffirms the right to a judicial remedy, to conclude that a complainant could challenge the Commission's decision dismissing a complaint.[300] In *Jégo-Quéré*,[301] the CFI referred to Article 47(1), alongside Articles 6 and 13 ECHR, to stress the paramountcy of the right to an effective remedy and procure a more liberal interpretation of *locus standi* under Article 230(4) EC than that dictated by the case law of the ECJ.[302]

In general one could identify, among others, the following possible types of reference to the Charter. First, a court may refer to it by way of subsidiary argument to buttress or reinforce a proposition of law. Second, it may be used as an integral part of the court's reasoning as one of the principal arguments to

---

[295] *Ibid.*, para 10.

[296] See e.g. Case C-347/03 *Regione autonoma Friuli-Venezia Giulia and Agenzia regionale per lo sviluppo rurale (ERSA) v Ministero delle Politiche Agricole e Forestali* Case C-347/03 [2006] ETMR 3; Case C-136/02 P *Mag Instruments Inc v OHIM*, judgment of 7 October 2004; Joined Cases C-204/00 P, C-205/00 P, C-211/00 P, C-213/00 P, C-217/00 P and C-219/00 P *Aalborg Portland v Commission*, judgment of 7 January 2004, para 56.

[297] *Österreichischer Rundfunk, op. cit.*, n. 186 above, para 56.

[298] See e.g. Case T-77/01 *Territorio Histórico de Álava–Diputación Foral de Álava v Commission*, judgment of 11 January 2002, para 35 (Article 47).

[299] Case T-54/99 *max. mobil Telekommunikation Service GmbH v Commission* [2002] ECR II-313; reversed on appeal: C-141/02 P *Commission v T-Mobile Austria GmbH*, judgment of 22 February 2005.   [300] *Ibid.*, paras 48 and 57.

[301] Case T-177/01 *Jégo-Quéré v Commission* [2002] ECR II-02365, reversed on appeal C-263/02 P *Commission v Jégo-Quéré*, judgment of 1 April 2004.   [302] *Ibid.*, paras 42 and 47.

support the result reached. Third, it may be used as the primary or the only argument of the court. No CFI judgment or advocate general opinion belongs to the last category. Cases such as *max. mobil* and *Jégo-Quéré* could be said to belong to the second category, but it should be borne in mind that in both cases the same result could have been reached in the absence of any reference to the Charter. Still, there is here a notable difference between the ECJ, on the one hand, and the CFI, on the other hand, in that, whilst the former views the Charter as a no entry zone, the latter considers it as a legitimate source of inspiration thus setting in motion the process of absorption of the Charter into the *aquis* envisaged by the Commission. It is perhaps not accidental that in both cases the CFI referred to the Charter to procure a departure from the case law of the ECJ and that in both cases it was reversed.

Many advocates general view the Charter as a source which informs the interpretation of binding rules.[303] Although it cannot have any autonomous binding effects, some accept that it serves as a substantive point of reference, or that it constitutes an invaluable source for the purposes of ascertaining the common denominator of the essential legal values prevailing in the Member States from which general principles of law emanate.[304] References have been made to numerous provisions.[305] The most evocative endorsement of the Charter has been made by Léger AG who, in *Hautala*, encapsulated its importance as follows:[306]

Naturally, the clearly-expressed wish of the authors of the Charter not to endow it with binding legal force should not be overlooked. However, aside from any consideration regarding its legislative scope, the nature of the rights set down in the Charter of Fundamental Rights precludes it from being regarded as a mere list of purely moral principles

---

[303] See e.g. Case C-181/03 P *Nardone*, Opinion of Poiares Maduro AG of 29 June 2004 at para 126; *Booker Aquaculture, op. cit.*, n. 97 above at 7415 *per* Mischo AG.

[304] See the observations of Colomer AG in Case C-466/00 *Kaba v Secretary of State for the Home Department*, [2003] ECR I-2219 at n.74 of the Opinion and further Case C-173/99 *BECTU* [2001] ECR I-4881 at 4883 *per* Tizanno AG; Case C-208/00 *Überseering* [2002] ECR I-9919, *per* Colomer AG at para 59.

[305] See e.g. *BECTU, op. cit.*, at 4891 where Tizzano AG relied on Article 31(2) of the Charter as providing the 'most reliable and definitive confirmation' of the fact that the right to a paid annual leave is a fundamental right. See further *Baumbast and R, op. cit.*, n. 176 above (Geelhoed AG): Articles 7 (family life) and 45 (freedom of movement and residence of EU citizens); Case C-160/03 *Spain v Eurojust*, Opinion of Poiares Maduro AG delivered on 16 December 2004, Article 22 (linguistic diversity); Joined Cases C-387/02, C-391/02 and C-403/02 *Berlusconi*, Opinion of Kokott AG delivered on 14 October 2004, Article 49(1) (retroactive application of the more lenient penalty); *Omega Spielhallen, op. cit.*, n. 41 above, Opinion of Stix-Hackl AG delivered on 18 March 2004, Article 1 (human dignity); Case C-105/03 *Criminal Proceedings against Pupino*, Opinion of Kokott AG delivered on 11 November 2004, Articles 24 (rights of the child), 47 (right to an effective remedy and a fair trial) and 49(1) (legality and proportionality of criminal penalties); *ERSA, op. cit.*, n. 296 above, Opinion of Jacobs AG delivered on 16 December 2004, Article 17 (right to property); Case C-34/01 *Enirisore*, Opinion of Stix-Hackl AG delivered on 7 November 2002, Article 36 (access to services of general economic interest).

[306] Case C-353/99 P *Council v Hautala*, [2001] ECR I-9565, paras 80–83 of the Opinion (footnotes omitted).

without any consequences. It should be noted that those values have in common the fact of being unanimously shared by the Member States, which have chosen to make them more visible by placing them in a charter in order to increase their protection. The Charter has undeniably placed the rights which form its subject-matter at the highest level of values common to the Member States.

It is known that the political and moral values of a society are not all to be found in positive law. However, where rights, freedoms and principles are described, as in the Charter, as needing to occupy the highest level of reference values within all the Member States, it would be inexplicable not to take from it the elements which make it possible to distinguish fundamental rights from other rights.

The sources of those rights, listed in the preamble to the Charter, are for the most part endowed with binding force within the Member States and the European Union. It is natural for the rules of positive Community law to benefit, for the purposes of their interpretation, from the position of the values with which they correspond in the hierarchy of common values.

As the solemnity of its form and the procedure which led to its adoption would give one to assume, the Charter was intended to constitute a privileged instrument for identifying fundamental rights. It is a source of guidance as to the true nature of the Community rules of positive law.

It is possible that the Charter will be used to reinforce and supplement principles of law already recognized in binding legal norms and contribute to their broader interpretation. A move from the Charter as an instrument recording existing rights to informing their interpretation and, subsequently, redefining their content remains a possibility but, at least from the point of view of the ECJ, is not forthcoming.

7.6.3. Horizontal provisions

The final chapter of the Charter[307] contains a number of general, or so-called horizontal, provisions which determine the scope of its application and its relationship to other sources of law. Essentially, most of these provisions fulfil two purposes: they seek to ensure that the Charter can be accommodated within the Community legal order without threatening its coherence, and also control the supremacy of fundamental rights, i.e. balance their enhanced protection with government discretion.

One of the most important provisions is Article 51 which determines its scope of application. Article 51(2) states that the Charter does not establish any new power or task for the Community or the Union, or modify powers and tasks defined by the Treaties. Thus, the Union is not transformed into a human rights organization. The Charter does not apply unless a situation is governed by Union law by virtue of a connecting factor other than the Charter. Also, the Charter may not in itself

---

[307] Articles 51–54.

serve as the basis for the introduction of secondary legislation. It applies however throughout the field of Community and Union activities including the second and third pillars.

Article 51(1) states as follows:

The provisions of this Charter are addressed to the institutions and bodies of the Union with due regard for the principle of subsidiarity and to the Member States only when they are implementing Union law. They shall therefore respect the rights, observe the principles and promote the application thereof in accordance with their respective powers.

This provision draws a distinction between rights and principles laid down in the Charter. Such a distinction is also made in the Preamble which in fact recognizes three categories, namely 'rights, freedoms and principles'.[308] The distinction is material since some provisions of the Charter apply only to rights and freedoms but not to principles.[309] It is unsatisfactory that the Charter attributes legal significance to a distinction which it assumes but does not explain. Notably, some further clarification is provided in the version of the Charter included in the EU Constitution and will be revisited below.[310]

Article 51(1) gives rise to problems of interpretation as regards the scope for application of the Charter to national measures. So long as the Charter is not as such binding on Member States, these problems are more theoretical than practical but nonetheless deserve attention. On the face of it, Article 51(1) suggests that the Charter applies to Member States only when they implement Union law. This makes its scope of application narrower than the application of fundamental rights as developed by the ECJ since, under the case law, Member States are bound to respect fundamental rights not only when they implement Community law but also when they act within its scope of application, a condition which the Court has progressively interpreted more broadly.[311] The Praesidium commentary on Article 51(1) does not shed light on this problem. Confusingly, it refers to the judgment in *ERT* as support for the proposition that Member States are bound to respect fundamental rights in a Union context 'only when they act in the context of Community law',[312] thus sidelining the difference between national action for the implementation of Community law and national action falling within the scope of Community law. Insofar as the Charter and the case law protect the same rights, the limitation of Article 51(1) is ineffective since, by virtue of the case law, these rights apply to a wider category of national measures. This is countenanced by Article 53 which states that the protection afforded by the Charter may not fall below the protection guaranteed by other provisions of Community law. Insofar as the Charter incorporates rights not expressly acknowledged in the case law, by

---

[308] See Preamble, recital 7.

[309] See Article 52(1) which circumscribes the limitations on the rights defined by the Charter.

[310] See below p. 367.   [311] See above p. 332.

[312] See Explanations relating to the text of the Charter issued by the Praesidium of the Charter Convention, Doc. CHARTE 4473/00, 11 October 2000, *op. cit.*, at 46.

virtue of Article 51(1), such rights will have a narrower scope of application. This will give rise to inconsistency and confusion. In any event, given that the Charter and the case law draw inspiration from the same sources, it is possible that the ECJ might endorse a new right provided for in the Charter as a general principle of law, assuming that there is a sufficient degree of support in the constitutions or other laws of the Member States, in which case it will apply to all national measures falling within the scope of Community law.

Article 52 determines the scope of limitations of the rights guaranteed by the Charter, the relationship between the Charter and the provisions of the Treaty, and the relationship between the Charter and the ECHR.

Under Article 52(1), any limitation on the exercise of the rights and freedoms recognized by the Charter must satisfy the following conditions:

(1) it must be provided for by law;
(2) it must respect the essence of those rights and freedoms;
(3) it must comply with the principle of proportionality. This means that limitations may be made only if they are necessary and genuinely meet objectives of general interest recognized by the Union or the need to protect the rights and freedoms of others.

This provision imposes strict conditions on limitations or exceptions from the rights and freedoms laid down in the Charter. According to the Praesidium notes, its purpose is to encapsulate the *Hauer* formula[313] and serves, in effect, to relativize the rights recognized in the Charter. Article 52(1) does not serve itself as a legal basis for introducing limitations on fundamental rights. It applies only where such limitations are recognized, expressly or implicitly by the Charter. However, it applies only in relation to rights and freedoms and not to principles: those are *ex hypothesi* more general and do not acquire legal effect unless they are concretized by legislation.

The inter-relationship between the rights provided for in the Charter and those guaranteed by the Treaties and the ECHR is one of the most difficult issues. Article 52(2) provides that rights recognized by the Charter which are based on the founding Treaties must be exercised subject to the conditions and limits laid down therein. The Charter therefore does not intend to alter the content and system of rights conferred by the Treaties.[314] This means that, even where the Charter uses a broader formulation of a right that than provided for in the Treaty, the limitations contained in the latter apply.[315] This is the case for example with the right of EU citizens to move and reside freely within the Community which in Article 45(1) of the Charter appears to

---

[313] In *Hauer*, the ECJ acknowledged that, as a general rule, rights are not absolute but subject to restrictions provided that they correspond to objectives of general interest pursued by the Community and do not constitute a disproportionate and unreasonable interference undermining the very substance of the right in issue. See 7.2.2 above. For recent confirmation see *Connolly v Commission, op. cit.*, n. 9 above, para 148; Case C-292/97 *Karlsson and Others* [2000] ECR I-2737, para 45.

[314] See Praesidium Explanatory notes, p. 48.

[315] See K. Lenaerts and E. De Smijter, 'A "Bill of Rights" for the European Union', (2001) 38 CML Rev 273 at 282.

be unqualified but in Article 18(1) EC is subject to limitations.[316] The limitations of the latter must also be read in Article 45(1). In some cases, the Charter expressly subjects rights to the limitations imposed in the Treaties. This is, for example, the case with the prohibition of discrimination on grounds of nationality.[317] In other cases, the Charter provides for rights which go further than the founding Treaties. In such a case, Charter rights cannot be said to be 'based on' the founding treaties and any limitations imposed therein on similar rights are not applicable.[318]

Article 52(3) states as follows:

In so far as this Charter contains rights which correspond to rights guaranteed by the Convention for the Protection of Human Rights and Fundamental Freedoms, the meaning and scope of those rights shall be the same as those laid down by the said Convention. This provision shall not prevent Union law providing more extensive protection.

The consequences of this provision are the following. The meaning and scope of the Charter rights are to be understood in the light of the ECtHR case law pertaining to the corresponding Convention rights. Also, any limitations introduced by the legislature on Charter rights must comply with the same standards as those which apply to the ECHR.[319]

Article 52(3) seeks to ensure that the Charter incorporates, as a minimum, the standards of the ECHR but, at the same time, it safeguards the autonomy of EU law by allowing the EU to provide for a higher level of protection. The reference to 'more extensive protection' raises problems since, where rights conflict, more extensive protection of one right may lead to less extensive protection of another. The meaning of the provision appears to be that the Charter may not offer higher protection of a right (e.g. freedom of expression) if that would lead to intrusions into another (e.g. right to privacy) beyond those authorised by the case law of the ECtHR. This interpretation is countenanced by Article 53 of the Charter.

The Praesidium notes contain a list of Charter rights whose meaning and scope are the same as the corresponding articles of the ECHR[320] and a list of articles

---

[316] *Ibid.*, at 282–3.   [317] See Article 21(2) of the Charter.

[318] This applies in relation to Article 21(1) of the Charter which prohibits any discrimination based on any ground such as sex, race, colour, ethnic or social origin, genetic features, language, religion or belief, political or any other opinion, membership of a national minority, property, birth disability, age or sexual orientation. As Lenaerts and De Smijter point out, *op. cit.*, at 285, this provision is broader than Article 13(1) EC, because the latter covers only discrimination based on sex, racial or ethnic origin, religion or belief, disability, age or sexual orientation and also because it is only an empowering provision authorizing the Council to adopt legislation and does not itself contain a prohibition of discrimination. It follows that the prohibition of non-discrimination provided for in Article 21(1) of the Charter is unlimited insofar as the Community or the national legislature has not introduced limitations in accordance with Article 52(1) or (2) of the Charter. See above Chapter 2.   [319] Praesidium notes, *op. cit.*, p. 48.

[320] Article 2 (right to life); Article 4 (prohibition of torture and inhuman or degrading treatment); Articles 5(1)(2) (prohibition of slavery and forced labour; cf Article 5(3) of the Charter which in prohibiting trafficking in human beings goes further than the ECHR); Article 6 (right to liberty and security); Article 7 (respect for private and family life); Article 10(1) (freedom of religion); Article 11 (freedom of expression); Article 17 (right to property); Article 19(1)

whose meaning is the same as the corresponding Articles of the ECHR but whose scope is wider.[321]

Notably, the Charter received a cautious welcome from the Council of Europe. In its observations on the Charter, whilst it was still in draft form, the Council emphasised the need for harmony between the ECHR and the protection of fundamental rights at Community level, and considered the Charter as an extension of the ECHR and other instruments adopted under the auspices of the Council of Europe in the Community legal order. The Council of Europe is keen to ensure that this relationship of complementarity is safeguarded through respect for the Strasbourg jurisprudence. It saw however the Charter as a second best option to EU accession to the Convention and expressed concern about the possibility of conflicting rulings.[322]

Notably, Article II-112 of the EU Constitution, which corresponds to Article 52 of the Charter, added further provisions in this context. Their purpose is to limit the conceptual autonomy of the Charter and constrain its effects on national sovereignty. They were inserted as the *quid pro quo* for allowing the inclusion of the Charter in the Constitution and therefore its elevation to a fully binding legal text. Article II-112(4) states that, insofar as this Charter recognizes fundamental

---

(prohibition of collective expulsions); Article 19(2) (prohibition of extradition or expulsion to a State where there is a risk that the person expelled will be subjected to the death penalty or torture or inhuman and degrading treatment); Article 48 (presumption of innocence and rights of defence); and Article 49(1) (principle of legality and proportionality of criminal penalties).

[321] Article 9 (right to marry and found a family): it covers the same field as Article 12 ECHR but its scope may be extended to other forms of marriage if they are established by national legislation; Article 12(1) (freedom of assembly and association): it corresponds to Article 11 ECHR but its scope is extended to EU level; Article 14(1) (right to education): it corresponds to Article 2 of the Protocol to the ECHR but it also covers access to vocational and continuing training; Article 14(3) (freedom to found educational establishments and right of parents to ensure the education and teaching of their children in conformity with their religious, philosophical and pedagogical convictions): it corresponds to Article 2 of the Protocol of the ECHR as regards the rights of parents; Articles 47(2) and (3) (right to an effective remedy and a fair trial): they correspond to Article 6(1) ECHR but the limitation to the determination of civil rights and obligations or criminal charges does not apply as regards Union law and its implementation; Article 50 (right not to be tried or punished twice in criminal proceedings): it corresponds to Article 4 of Protocol 7 ECHR but its scope is extended to EU level between the courts of the Member States; finally EU citizens are not aliens within the scope of application of Community law in view of the prohibition of discrimination on grounds of nationality. The limitations provided for in Article 16 ECHR as regards the rights of aliens, therefore, do not apply to them.

[322] The Council was concerned that, if the Charter acquired binding force, it would take on a dynamic which would affect the harmonious and consistent interpretation of fundamental rights. It would generate a large number of preliminary references which would in turn increase the risk that decisions of the ECJ would be at variance with decisions of the Strasbourg Court. The Council of Europe pointed out that accession, by entrusting to a single court jurisdiction to interpret the rights guaranteed by the Convention, would avoid the risk of conflicting case law and guarantee 'perfect harmony' between the two systems. It would also enable the Community institutions to play a full role in proceedings before the ECHR which concern Community law, so avoiding the risk that Member States might find themselves obliged to bear sole responsibility under the ECHR while in some cases being unable to take the action which a Strasbourg judgment might require at Community level.

rights as they result from the constitutional traditions common to the Member States, those rights must be interpreted in harmony with those traditions. According to the updated explanations on the Charter compiled by the Praesidium of the Constitutional Convention, this rule of interpretation is based on the wording of Article 6(2) TEU and the standard formula of the ECJ in earlier case law that, in safeguarding human rights, it takes account of the constitutional traditions common to the Member States.[323] The intention therefore is not to follow a rigid approach of seeking the lowest common denominator, but to interpret the Charter as offering a high standard of protection which is adequate for the law of the Union and in harmony with the common constitutional traditions.[324] In effect, this provision adds little to existing case law and imposes only a soft and imperfect interpretative obligation. Recent judgments such as *Schmidberger* and *Omega Spielhallen*[325] suggest that the ECJ indeed respects the national constitutional traditions but Article II-112(4) neither commits the ECJ to a specific level of protection nor does it determine the requisite degree of commonality that must exist in national laws in order for the ECJ to take into account a specific right.

Article II-112(5) states as follows:

The provisions of this Charter which contain principles may be implemented by legislative and executive acts taken by institutions, bodies, offices and agencies of the Union, and by acts of Member States when they are implementing Union law, in the exercise of their respective powers. They shall be judicially cognisable only in the interpretation of such acts and in the ruling on their legality.

This provision attempts to clarify the distinction between principles and rights and, it is submitted, remains valid under the current version of the Charter. Its inclusion in the EU Constitution was not intended to make a substantive amendment to the original version of the Charter but rather clarify it. According to the updated explanations, the difference is that, whilst rights give rise to 'direct claims for positive action' by the Union and national authorities, principles must be implemented by legislative or executive action at Union or State level and become material only for the purposes of the interpretation or judicial review of such acts.[326] Although these observations go some way towards explaining the differences between principles and rights, the distinction remains elusive. For one thing, there is no reason why articles of the Charter which incorporate principles rather than rights should be denied any interpretative value in the absence of implementing action. This is the case for example with the principle of environmental protection which is proclaimed in Article 37 of the Charter.[327] For

---

[323] See e.g. *Hauer, op. cit.*; Case 155/79 *AM&S* [1982] ECR 1575.

[324] See updated Explanations relating to the text of the Charter issued by the Praesidium of the Constitutional Convention, CONV 828/1/03, 18 July 2003, *op. cit.*, p. 51.   [325] *Op. cit.*

[326] Updated Explanations, *op. cit.*, p. 51.

[327] Examples of provisions which lay down principles rather than rights are Articles 25 (rights of the elderly), Article 26 (integration of persons with disabilities), Article 37 (environmental protection).

another, as the commentary itself acknowledges, articles of the Charter may incorporate elements of both principles and rights.[328]

Further, Article II-112(6) requires that, in accordance with the principle of subsidiarity, full account must be taken of national laws and practices where the Charter refers to them as parameters conditioning the rights enshrined therein. Finally, Article II-112(7) states that the explanations drawn up as a way of providing guidance in the interpretation of the Charter must be given due regard by the courts of the Union and of the Member States. This is not the case under the pre-Constitution version of the Charter which is currently in force, under which the Praesidium notes do not have any legal force.

The Charter is not intended to lower the level of protection afforded to fundamental rights by existing provisions of the national constitutions, EU and international law. This is made clear by Article 53[329] which states that:

Nothing in this Charter shall be interpreted as restricting or adversely affecting human rights and fundamental freedoms as recognised, in their respective fields of application, by Union law and international law and by international agreements to which the Union, the Community or all the Member States are party, including the European Convention for the Protection of Human Rights and Fundamental Freedoms, and by the Member States' constitutions.

Article 53 is intended to ensure compatibility between the Charter and existing sources of human rights and incorporates an interpretative obligation. Rights enshrined in the Charter may not be interpreted as providing a lower level of protection than similar rights provided for in any of the sources listed above. In practice, however, such compatibility may not be easy to ensure. The legal systems or instruments from which the rights of the Charter originate may prioritize rights differently. Thus, one system may provide for a higher level of protection of the right to privacy than the right of expression.[330] In such a case, it is not possible for the Charter to ensure a maximalist protection of both rights where the two come into conflict. This applies *a fortiori* to economic and social rights which are closely linked, and can only be understood by reference, to national economic and social models.

Article 54, the last provision of the Charter, prohibits the abuse of rights contained therein. It states that nothing in the Charter may be interpreted as implying any right to engage in any activity or perform any act aimed at the destruction of any of the rights recognized in the Charter or at their limitation to a greater extent than is provided for therein. This provision is based on Article 17 ECHR. It seeks to prevent the subversion of democratic institutions and, more generally, to prevent reliance on Charter rights and freedoms so as to undermine their objectives or for ulterior purposes.

---

[328] This is the case, for example, in relation to Articles 23 (equality between men and women), 33 (family and professional life) and 34 (social security and social assistance).

[329] Article II-113 of the EU Constitution.

[330] For reference to such a potential conflict, see *Lindqvist, op. cit.*, para 85–87.

According to the European Commission of Human Rights, the purpose of Article 17 ECHR is to prevent totalitarian groups from exploiting the rights enshrined in the Convention for the purpose of undermining them and thus to protect the free operation of democratic institutions. Article 17 has been interpreted by the ECtHR narrowly. It prevents a person from engaging in certain activities for subversive purposes, for example, the freedom of assembly or association or the freedom of expression but does not prevent a person from enjoying the guarantees of fair trial.[331]

The Charter does not contain a provision equivalent to Article 18 ECHR which may be seen as the mirror provision of Article 17. It prohibits public authorities from applying the restrictions permitted under the Convention to the rights and freedoms enshrined in its provisions 'for any purpose other than those for which they have been prescribed'. The absence of such a provision in the Charter, however, does not reduce protection for the individual. The purpose of Article 18, which has had little impact on Strasbourg case law, is to prevent the abuse of public power. This is implicit in the provisions of the Charter which prevent public authorities from using the recognized limitations on rights for improper purposes.

---

[331] See C. Ovey, F.G. Jacobs and C.A. White, *European Convention on Human Rights* (3rd edition) (Oxford University Press, 2002).

8

The Rights of Defence

8.1. Introduction

In the Community legal order, the rights of defence, and more specifically, the right to a hearing, are judge-made rights. The EC Treaty itself does not provide for a general right to a hearing in administrative proceedings.[1] It was developed by the case law to fill the gaps in Community legislation. As the Community administration began to acquire more powers, specific measures recognized the right in relation to certain areas. Its recognition has been coincidental and piecemeal. It has been provided for expressly, e.g. in competition, anti-dumping, and trademark proceedings,[2] and more recently in proceedings for State aids.[3] Now, the EU Charter on Fundamental Rights views the right to a hearing as an integral part of the right to good administration. Under Article 41,[4] it includes 'the right of every person to be heard before any individual measure which would affect him or her adversely is taken' and, moreover, the right 'to have access to his or her file, while respecting the legitimate interests of confidentiality and of professional and business secrecy'. This is the most comprehensive and far-reaching recognition of the right to be heard so far included in Community law.[5]

At an early stage, the Court of Justice elevated the rights of defence to a general principle of law. In *Alvis v Council*,[6] a staff case, it declared:

According to a generally accepted principle of administrative law in force in the Member States... the administration of these States must allow their servants the opportunity of replying to allegations before any disciplinary decision is taken concerning them.

---

[1] See K. Lenaerts and J. Vanhamme, 'Procedural Rights of Private Parties in the Community Administrative Process', 34 (1997) CML Rev 531, at 533. General contributions include K. Lenaerts, 'Procedures and Sanctions in Economic Administrative Law', General Report, 17th FIDE Congress, Vol III, Berlin, 1996, pp. 506–577; O. Due, 'Le respect des droits de la défense dans le droit administratif communautaire' [1987] CDE 383; L. Goffin, 'La jurisprudence de la Cour de justice sur les droits de défense', 16 (1980) CDE 127; A. Braun, 'Les droits de la défense devant la Commission et la Cour de justice des Communautés européennes', 141 (1980) IRCL 2; J. Schwarze, *European Administrative Law* (Sweet & Maxwell, 1992) 1243–1371, esp. 1320 *et seq.*; see also the specialized bibliography given under the specific sections of this chapter.

[2] For competition and anti-dumping, see below 8.8 and 8.9. For trademarks, see Council Reg. No 40/94 on the Community trademark, OJ 1994 L 11, p. 1 and its implementing Commission Reg. No 2868/95, OJ L1995 L 303, p. 1.

[3] Article 88(2) EC requires the Commission to give notice to the parties concerned to submit their comments. See also Article 20 of Council Regulation No 659/1999 laying down detailed rules for the application of Article 93 (now 88) of the EC Treaty, OJ 1999 L 83/1.

[4] This corresponds to Article II-41(2) of the EU Constitution.

[5] For a discussion, see 8.12 below. [6] Case 32/62 [1963] ECR 49, at p. 55.

This rule, which meets the requirements of sound justice and good administration, must be followed by Community institutions.

The importance of the last statement lies in the fact that it encapsulates the dual rationale of the right to a hearing. It is perceived by the Court as a functional requirement promoting the quality of administration: the information supplied and the views expressed by the persons affected are seen as contributing to better decision making. It is also perceived as a requirement of formal justice akin to a human right and deriving from the rule of law: the persons concerned must be given the opportunity to defend their rights and participate in the decision-making process. Those two justifications for the right to a hearing are referred to respectively as the instrumental and the non-instrumental rationale and underlie procedural rights in general.[7]

The right to a hearing is an area where Community law more resembles common law than the systems of continental Member States in that, traditionally, it has not provided by legislation for a comprehensive right to a hearing in all administrative proceedings.[8] In English administrative law, the requirements of natural justice occupy a distinct position.[9] This is not only because of their intrinsic importance as guarantors of objective and impartial decision-making but also for reasons peculiar to the development of the law in England. Natural justice as a legal concept thrived in the nineteenth century, when extensive case law applied the principles derived from it to a wide variety of decision-making bodies.[10] Also, the traditional limitations on substantive grounds of review inherent in the Diceyan concept of unitary democracy and the *ultra vires* doctrine forced preoccupation with requirements of procedural fairness. Procedure, unlike substance, was an area which could undisputedly be said to fall within the judicial province. In contrast to English and Irish law,[11] many of the laws of the continental Member States recognize by statute a general right to a fair hearing. For example, the German Act on Administrative Procedure requires that the persons concerned must be heard before decisions are taken that affect their legal positions. Provisions of general application are found *inter alia* in the laws of Austria, the Netherlands, Luxembourg, Finland, Spain and Portugal.[12] Despite the fact that most Member States incorporate in their legislation a general right to a hearing in dealings with the administration, until the introduction of the EU Charter no enthusiasm had

---

[7] See e.g. the dicta by Lord Mustill in *R v Secretary of State for the Home Department, ex p Doody* [1993] 3 All ER 92 at 98 and see further, P. Craig, *Administrative Law* (Sweet & Maxwell, 2003), 408.

[8] Lenaerts and Vanhamme, *op. cit.*, n. 1 above, p. 534.

[9] For a discussion of English law, see S. de Smith, H. Woolf and J. Jowell, *Judicial Review of Administrative Action*, (Sweet & Maxwell, 1995) Chs. 7–12; Craig, *op. cit.* Chs. 13–14.

[10] The scope of its application was limited in the first half of the 20th century but the House of Lords breathed new air into the doctrine in the seminal *Ridge v Baldwin* [1964] AC 40. For the development of English law, see further Craig, *op. cit.*

[11] Irish law, like English law, does not provide by statute a general right to a hearing but parties affected by administrative decisions enjoy variable procedural rights under specific statutes or regulations. See 'The Irish Report' by P. Lee in the *17th FIDE Congress*, Vol. III, *op. cit.*, pp. 204–248.

[12] For a detailed review see the national reports in the *17th FIDE Congress*, Vol III, op. cit., n.1, and also Schwarze, *op. cit.*

emerged for the introduction of a similar right by Community legislation.[13] By contrast, preference seemed to lie with reliance on the general concepts of fairness and due process borrowed from the common law.[14]

Natural justice was one of the first areas where, following the accession of the United Kingdom, the influence of common law on the jurisprudence of the Court of Justice was felt. Such influence was particularly evident in the *Transocean Marine Paint case*.[15] The Commission had exempted from the prohibition provided for in Article 85(1) (now 81(1)) of the Treaty an agreement concluded between the members of the Transocean Marine Paint Association. Subsequently, it renewed the exemption but made renewal subject to an onerous condition, in relation to which the association considered that the Commission had not given to it the opportunity to make its views known in advance. The problem for the Association was that Community written law did not provide for a hearing in the circumstances. Regulation No 99/63[16] required the Commission to inform undertakings of the objections raised against them but did not provide for a hearing in relation to the conditions which the Commission intended to attach to a decision granting exemption. The Court however held:[17]

It is clear . . . both from the nature and objective of the procedure for hearings, and from Articles 5, 6 and 7 of Regulation No 99/63, that this Regulation . . . applies the general rule that a person whose interests are perceptibly affected by a decision taken by a public authority must be given the opportunity to make his point of view known. This rule requires that an undertaking be clearly informed, in good time, of the essence of conditions to which the Commission intends to subject an exemption and it must have the opportunity to submit its observations to the Commission. This is especially so in the case of conditions which, as in this case, impose considerable obligations having far reaching effects.

In *Transocean* the Court followed the lead of Warner AG who, after reviewing the scope of the *audi alteram partem* principle in the laws of the Member States, concluded that 'the right to be heard forms part of those rights which "the law" referred to in Article 164 of the Treaty upholds, and of which, accordingly, it is the duty of this Court to ensure the observance'.[18] The influence of common law concepts of procedural fairness was also evinced in *AM & S v Commission*[19] where, prompted by Warner AG and Slynn AG, the Court recognized the confidentiality of communications between lawyer and client (legal professional privilege) as a general principle of Community law, viewing it as an essential corollary to the rights of defence.[20]

In English law, the concept of natural justice connotes two ideas:[21] (a) the parties should be given adequate opportunity to be heard and, as a corollary, they should

---

[13] Lenaerts and Vanhamme, *op. cit.*, p. 534.   [14] *Ibid.*
[15] Case 17/74 *Transocean Marine Paint v Commission* [1974] ECR 1063.
[16] See further for this Regulation, below n. 153.   [17] *Transocean Marine, op. cit.*, para 15.
[18] *Ibid.*, at 1089. Article 164 corresponds to current Article 220 EC.
[19] Case 155/79 [1982] ECR 1575.   [20] *Ibid.*, para 23.
[21] de Smith, Woolf and Jowell, *op. cit.*, p. 379.

be given due notice of the hearing (*audi alteram partem*), and (b) the adjudicator should be disinterested and unbiased (*nemo judex in causa sua*). In Community law, reference is usually made to the rights of the defence (*droits de la défense*) the principal component of which is the right to be heard. By contrast, the second aspect of natural justice has received minimal reference in the case law. The reason seems to be that at Community level, decisions are not taken by tribunals or quasi-judicial bodies but by the administration itself, typically the Commission, whose decisions are reviewable by the Community judicature.[22] The principle of *nemo judex in causa sua* is, of course, guaranteed by the Statutes of the Court of Justice.[23]

Apart from the right to be heard, the rights of the defence include the following rights:

- the right to be assisted by a lawyer;[24]
- legal professional privilege; and
- in a qualified form, the right against self-incrimination.

In *AM & S* the Court recognized legal professional privilege subject to two conditions: the communications between lawyer and client in relation to which privilege is claimed must be made for the purposes and in the interests of the client's rights of defence, and they must emanate from an independent lawyer, namely a lawyer who is not bound to the client by a relationship of employment.[25] By contrast, advice given by an in-house lawyer is not covered by privilege and the Commission may rely on such advice to prove an infringement of competition law.[26]

This chapter is structured as follows. After a brief account of the right against self-incrimination, it focuses on the right to a fair hearing and examines its scope of application, its content, and consequences of failure to observe. It then discusses its application in competition, anti-dumping and staff cases. It concludes by looking at

[22] Lenaerts and Vanhamme, *op. cit.*, 555–556.

[23] See Protocol of the Statute of the Court of Justice of the EEC, Articles 2, 4, 16 and 44. For a manifestly unmeritorious claim against the impartiality of a member of the CFI, see Case T-47/92 *Lenz v Commission* [1992] ECR II-2523 and Case C-277/95 P *Lenz v Commission* [1996] ECR I-6109.

[24] See Case 115/80 *Demont v Commission* [1981] ECR 3147; Joined Cases 46/87 and 227/88 *Hoechst v Commission* [1989] ECR 2859, para 16. By contrast, the rights of defence do not entitle a person to bring a direct action at the CFI without legal representation: C-174/96 P *Lopes v Court of Justice* [1996] ECR I-6401; Case C-175/96 P *Lopes v Court of Justice* [1996] ECR I-6409.

[25] *AM & S, op. cit.*, para 21; for the application of the privilege, see Case T-30/89 *Hilti* [1990] ECR II-163. See further K.P.E. Lasok, 'The Privilege Against Self-incrimination in Competition Cases' (1990) II ECLR 90; M. Guerrin and G. Kyriazis, 'Cartels: Proof and Procedural Issues' (1993) 16 Fordham International Law Journal 266; I.S. Forrester, 'Legal Professional Privilege: Limitations on the Commission's Powers of Inspection Following the *AM & S* Judgment' (1983) 20 CMLR 75; J. Faull, 'Legal Professional Privilege (*AM & S*): The Commission Proposes International Negotiations' 10 (1985) ELR 119.

[26] See *John Deere* OJ 1985, L 35/58; [1985] 2 CMLR 554. But note that in Joined Cases T-125 and T-253/03 R *Akzo Nobel Chemicals Ltd v Commission*, [2003] ECR II-4771, in proceedings for interium relief, the President of the CFI questioned the limitation of the privilege. On appeal, the ECJ did not examine the point: Case C-7/04 P(R), Order of 27 September 2004.

its relationship with other procedural requirements, the principle of good administration and the application of the right to a hearing before national authorities.

8.2. The right against self-incrimination

The right against self-incrimination was first examined in *Orkem*.[27] The case concerned a request for information made by the Commission pursuant to Article 11 of Regulation 17 which enabled the Commission to ask undertakings to supply information in the course of its investigations to establish a possible breach of competition law.[28] The Regulation did not expressly provide for the right to remain silent. The issue raised was whether the general principles of Community law included the right of an undertaking not to supply information capable of being used in order to establish against it the existence of an infringement of Community competition law. The Court held that the Commission is entitled to compel an undertaking to provide all necessary factual information and disclose to the Commission all relevant documents which are in its possession, even if the latter may be used to establish the existence of anti-competitive conduct. The Commission however may not, by means of a decision calling for information, undermine the rights of defence of the undertaking concerned. Thus, it may not compel an undertaking to provide it with answers which might involve an admission on its part of the existence of an infringement, which it is incumbent upon the Commission to prove.[29] On that basis, the Court found that the Commission was entitled to ask the undertaking concerned to supply factual information but not information pertaining to the objectives of its actions. Nor was it entitled to procure an acknowledgement by the undertaking concerned of its participation in anti-competitive conduct.

The judgment can be understood as endorsing a qualified privilege against self-incrimination. Kerse and Khan submit that the recognition of the privilege is narrow and does not restrict seriously the Commission's investigatory powers in practice.[30] Notably, in *Orkem* the ECJ interpreted Article 6 of the European Convention on Human Rights as not including the right not to give evidence against oneself,[31] an interpretation which was rejected in subsequent case law by the European Court of Human Rights. In *Funke v France*[32] the ECtHR held that,

---

[27] Case 374/87 *Orkem v Commission* [1989] ECR 3283. See also Case 27/88 *Solvay v Commission* [1989] ECR 3355.

[28] OJ, English Spec. Ed., 1962, p. 87. See now Article 18 of Council Regulation 1/2003 on the implementation of the rules on competition laid down in Articles 81 and 82 of the Treaty, OJ 2003, L1/1.   [29] *Op. cit.*, paras 34–35.

[30] C.S. Kerse and N. Khan, *EC Anti-Trust Procedure*, (Fifth Ed) (Sweet & Maxwell, 2004) p. 135.   [31] See *Orkem, op. cit.*, para 30.

[32] Series A, No 256-A, 16 EHRR 297; [1993] 1 CMLR 897 and see above, Chapter p. 344.

under Article 6, any person charged with a criminal offence has the right to remain silent and not to contribute towards self-incrimination.

The law in this area is in a state of uncertainty to which both the Strasbourg and the Luxembourg courts have contributed. Thus, although the Strasbourg Court has consistently declared the right against self-incrimination to be part of the right to a fair hearing under Article 6(2) ECHR, it has not always applied it consistently. The Luxembourg courts, on the other hand, have remained equivocal as regards its scope of application in competition proceedings. These inconsistencies are explained to some extent by the fact that the courts are preoccupied with determining whether the proceedings are fair as a whole rather than with stipulating rigid rules.[33] The concept of fairness however is relative. Each court's internalized notion of justice is based on a hierarchy of values and, in this area, Strasbourg and Luxembourg do not share the same priorities.

In *Saunders v United Kingdom*[34] the ECtHR stated that the right against self-incrimination seeks to protect the accused against improper compulsion by the authorities and thus contributes to the avoidance of miscarriages of justice. The right presupposes that the prosecution must prove their case without resort to evidence obtained through methods of coercion or oppression in defiance of the will of the accused and, in that sense, has close affinity to the presumption of innocence.

In *Saunders* the Court confirmed that the accused in a criminal trial has the right to remain silent. It held however that the right against self-incrimination does not prohibit the use of material which may be obtained through the use of compulsory powers but which has an existence independent of the will of the suspect, such as documents acquired pursuant to a warrant, breath, blood and urine samples and bodily tissue for the purpose of DNA testing. The applicant was the chief executive of a large corporation who was suspected of financial misconduct. He had been obliged to give evidence to government-appointed inspectors who had statutory powers to require witnesses to answer questions. Failure to answer the questions would amount to contempt and might lead to the imposition of a fine or even imprisonment. The Court held that the compulsory powers of the inspectors were not *per se* a breach of Article 6 ECHR but found that the subsequent use by the prosecution of the transcripts of his interviews with the inspectors violated his right against self-incrimination.

In *JB v Switzerland*[35] the applicant was asked to produce all documents in his possession relating to a number of investments in the course of an investigation for possible tax evasion. He refused and disciplinary fines were imposed totalling 3,000 Swiss francs. The Strasbourg Court held that, in view of its amount and punitive character, the fine was of criminal nature for the purposes of Article 6(1) and concluded that the imposition of the fine violated the right against self-incrimination.

---

[33] See C. Ovey, F.G. Jacobs and C.A. White, *The European Convention on Human Rights*, 3rd Ed, Oxford University Press (2002), at 177.   [34] (1997) 23 EHRR 313.

[35] Judgment of 3 May 2001.

The Swiss authorities sought to compel the applicant to submit documents which would have provided information regarding his liability to tax and could have been used against him in a prosecution for tax evasion. *JB v Switzerland* appears to provide a more extensive protection of the right against self-incrimination than *Saunders*.

Despite the findings of the ECtHR in *Funke* and subsequent cases, the Luxembourg courts have declared their adherence to *Orkem* and made only limited efforts to align their position with Strasbourg. The right to silence was revisited by the CFI in *Mannesmannröhren-Werke AG v Commission*.[36] In the course of its investigation into a suspected cartel in the seamless tube market, the Commission posed a number of questions pertaining to meetings between members of the alleged cartel. Following the applicant's refusal to answer, the Commission adopted a decision under Article 11(5) of Regulation 17 requiring answers on pain of a periodic penalty payment. The applicant's argument was that the proceedings involved a criminal charge and that the protection afforded by Article 6 ECHR goes appreciably beyond the principles recognized in *Orkem*. Article 6 not only enables persons to refuse to answer questions or provide documents containing information on the objective of anti-competitive practices, but also establishes a right not to incriminate oneself by positive action. The CFI however rejected that view. After reiterating *Orkem* it held:

> To acknowledge the existence of an absolute right to silence, as claimed by the applicant, would go beyond what is necessary in order to preserve the rights of defence of undertakings, and would constitute an unjustified hindrance to the Commission's performance of its duty under Article 89 of the EC Treaty [now 85] to ensure that the rules on competition within the common market are observed.[37]

On that basis, the Court upheld the Commission's request for factual information and for the production of documents but annulled it insofar as it required the applicant to describe the purpose of meetings and the decisions adopted therein. It also annulled it insofar as it required the applicant to answer the questions on the relationship between the various agreements. Such questions might compel the applicant to admit its participation in an unlawful agreement and therefore run contrary to the rights of defence.

The applicants invoked the progress of the Strasbourg case law to procure a change of heart by the Luxembourg courts once more in *Limburgse Vinyl Maatschappij Nv and Others v Commission (PVC II cases)*.[38] The ECJ left the issue of principle open, rejecting the arguments of the appellants on the facts. It noted that, in order to establish a breach of the privilege against self-incrimination, both the judgment in *Orkem* and the case law of the ECtHR require, first, the exercise of coercion against the suspect in order to obtain information against him and, second, actual interference with the right. It concluded however that on the facts

---

[36] Case T-112/98, [2001] ECR II-729.   [37] *Op. cit.*, para 66.
[38] Joined Cases C-238, 244–245, 247, 250, 251, 252 and 254/99 P *Limburgse Vinyl Maatschappij NV and others v Commission* [2002] ECR I-8375, paras 270 *et seq.*

the arguments of the appellants did not justify reversing the judgment of the CFI on the basis of the developments in the case law of the ECtHR.

Thus, the case law may be summarised as follows:

The issue whether competition proceedings involve the determination of a criminal charge for the purposes of Article 6 ECHR remains open.[39] There is however no doubt that the penalties which the Commission may impose on undertakings for failure to cooperate and for substantive violations are very significant and have both a preventive and punitive character.

Although the CFI and the ECJ do not have jurisdiction to apply the Convention directly when they are reviewing an investigation under competition law, Community law does recognize as fundamental principles both the rights of defence and the right to a fair legal process and offers protection 'equivalent' to that guaranteed by Article 6 ECHR.[40]

An undertaking under investigation by the Commission in competition law proceedings is under an obligation to answer questions of a purely factual nature and produce pre-existing documents. It is however not obliged to answer questions regarding the purpose and motives of its actions or other questions which might involve the admission of an infringement.[41] As a general rule, the Luxembourg case law appears to offer less protection than the Strasbourg case law. The reason for this is that the ECJ and the CFI prioritize the values involved differently. Their obvious concern is that a full endorsement of the right against self-incrimination might render the Commission's investigatory powers ineffective.[42] It is submitted that their case law does not suggest an unduly restrictive approach and the balance drawn does not seem unfair. It should be accepted however that, from a Strasbourg perspective, the argument that competition proceedings are of a distinct nature and therefore the protection of the rights of the undertakings should give way to a higher public interest is unlikely to carry much weight. In *Saunders* the ECtHR did not accept the argument that corporate fraud is so distinct as to justify lesser protection of the rights of the accused[43] and this applies *a fortiori* to competition proceedings.

The Commission's powers of investigation are now contained in Regulation 1/2003, the successor to Regulation 17. The new Regulation provides expressly for the protection of the rights of defence[44] but makes no specific reference to the right against self-incrimination. The existing case law of the ECJ and the CFI continue to apply in this respect.

Does the principle established in *Orkem* apply also in national proceedings? In *Otto v Postbank NV*,[45] on a reference by a Dutch court, it was held that a national court which examines a claim that Articles 81 and 82 have been breached in

---

[39] See the discussion, above, pp. 253–4.
[40] *Mannesmannröhren-Werke v Commission, op. cit.*, para 77.   [41] *Orkem, op. cit.*
[42] The same concern was voiced by Warner AG in the earlier *AM & S, op. cit.*, p. 1621.
[43] *Saunders v UK, op. cit.*, para 74.   [44] Regulation 1/2003, Article 27. See 8.8.1 below.
[45] Case C-60/92 [1993] ECR I-5683.

proceedings between private parties is not bound to recognize the privilege against self-incrimination where such privilege is not recognized by national law. The Court however made such deference to the national rules of procedure subject to an important proviso: if information thus disclosed comes to the possession of the Commission, the latter may not use it to initiate proceedings for the infringement of Articles 81 and 82. The criticism may be raised that the rights of defence should not differ depending on whether proceedings for the violation of Community competition law are undertaken at Community or national level. The rationale of the judgment however is that the proceedings in issue were civil proceedings between private parties and not administrative ones initiated by the national authorities. The Court saw that as the material difference pointing out that Community law does not require respect for the qualified right against self-incrimination as laid down in *Orkem* in national proceedings between private parties which may not lead directly or indirectly to the imposition of sanctions by public authorities.[46] Given that reasoning, it would appear that the qualified privilege against self-incrimination binds not only the Commission but also national competition authorities: they should also be prevented from using information obtained in civil actions for the initiation of proceedings against the undertaking concerned.

8.3. When does the right to a fair hearing apply?

The right to a hearing was first recognized in relation to disciplinary proceedings.[47] Subsequent case law extended it to administrative proceedings which led to the imposition of sanctions on economic operators, in particular fines or penalty payments.[48] It is now well established that it is 'an absolutely fundamental principle in the administrative law of the Community',[49] which has close affinity to the right to a fair hearing,[50] and applies to all proceedings 'initiated against a person which are liable to culminate in a measure adversely affecting that person'.[51] In certain cases it may also apply in proceedings which are not initiated against a person but may lead

---

[46] *Op. cit.*, para 16.   [47] See above *Alvis, op. cit.*, n. 6 above.

[48] Joined Cases 56 and 58/64 *Consten and Grundig v Commission* [1966] ECR 299 at 338; Case 85/76 *Hoffmann-La Roche v Commission* [1979] ECR 461, para 9.

[49] Case T-1/89 *Rhône-Poulenc v Commission* [1991] ECR II-867 at 883, *per* Vesterdorf AG.

[50] Case 3/00 *Denmark v Commission* [2003] ECR 2643, para 46.

[51] Case C-135/92 *Fiskano v Commission* [1994] ECR I-2885, para 39; Case 234/84 *Belgium v Commission* [1986] ECR 2263, para 27; Case C-301/87 *France v Commission* [1990] ECR I-307, para 29; Joined Cases C-48/90 and C-66/90 *Netherlands and Others v Commission* [1992] ECR I-565, paras 37 and 44. Note also the broad formulation in *Transocean Marine Paint Association, op cit.*, according to which the right to a hearing applies in every case where a person's interests 'are perceptibly affected by a decision' (above, n. 15). For recent confirmation, see Case C-315/99 P *Ismeri Europa v Court of Auditors* [2001] ECR I-5281, para 28.

to a decision affecting his interests.[52] The specific requirements of the right however may differ depending on the type of proceedings in issue. As a general principle of Community law, the right to be heard takes priority over Community legislation and therefore 'cannot be excluded or restricted by any legislative provision'.[53] Respect for it must be ensured both where there is no specific legislation and also where legislation exists but does not in itself take account of the right.[54] In principle, it is for the party concerned to raise the plea that the rights of the defence have been violated. At least in relation to the limited rights of defence enjoyed by complainants in State aid and competition law proceedings, the CFI has held that those rights do not enjoy entrenched procedural protection and a plea that they have been infringed must be raised by the applicant in his original application unless it is based on matters of law or fact which came to light in the course of the procedure.[55]

The archetypal case where the principle of *audi alteram partem* must be guaranteed is where proceedings are initiated against a person. In *Fiskano v Commission*,[56] the Commission temporarily prohibited a Swedish vessel from fishing in Community waters on the ground that it had allegedly infringed the Agreement on Fisheries between the Community and Sweden. The company which owned the vessel was not granted the opportunity to be heard before the prohibition was imposed as neither the Agreement on Fisheries nor the Council Regulation ratifying it provided for a right to a hearing. The Court annulled the Commission's decision on the ground that right to a hearing must be respected as a general principle of Community law.

A procedure is 'initiated against' a person for the purposes of the right to a hearing where it is liable to lead to a decision which directly affects his legal position even if he is not the addressee of the decision. In *Netherlands v Commission*[57] the Commission adopted a decision finding that the Netherlands law regulating postal services infringed Article 86(1) EC because it gave an unfair advantage to PTT, a State undertaking, *vis-à-vis* private messenger services. The Court held that PTT and associated undertakings had the right to be heard because they were the direct beneficiaries of the State measure in issue, they were expressly named in the postal law, the contested decision related directly to them, and its economic consequences directly affected them.[58] Similarly, in *Air Inter SA v Commission*,[59] the Commission adopted a decision pursuant to Article 8 of Regulation No 2408/92 on access for Community carriers to intra-Community air routes[60] by which it prohibited France

---

[52] See *Ismeri*, *op. cit.*, and p. 383 below.

[53] Case T-260/94 *Air Inter v Commission* [1997] ECR II-997, para 60.

[54] Case T-32/95 P *Commission v Lisrestal and Others* [1996] ECR I-5373, para 30.

[55] Case T-106/95 *Fédération Française des Sociétés d'Assurances (FFSA) and Others v Commission* [1997] ECR II-229, paras 48–49; Case T-16/91 *Rendo and Others v Commission* [1992] ECR II-2417, para 131. The existing authorities do not preclude the possibility that in appropriate circumstances the Community judicature may raise the plea of its own motion as a matter of public policy.   [56] *Op. cit.*, n. 53 above.

[57] *Op. cit.*, n. 53 above.   [58] *Ibid.*, para 50.   [59] *Op. cit.*, n. 55 above.

[60] OJ 1992 240, p. 8.

from refusing Community air carriers traffic rights over certain internal air routes. The effect of the decision was that Air Inter SA, a company to which the French Government had granted exclusive rights over those routes, could no longer enjoy exclusivity. The CFI held that although Article 8(3) did not provide for the direct participation of air carriers in the administrative procedure, the rights of defence of the persons affected should be guaranteed. Air Inter had the right to be heard because it was the direct beneficiary of the State measure which guaranteed to it privileged position. It was expressly named in that measure and would bear the economic consequences of the contested decision.

The case law takes a similar approach in relation to decisions regarding financial assistance programmes. In *Lisrestal v Commission*[61] the Commission addressed a decision to the Portuguese authorities requiring partial repayment of the financial assistance which had been granted to the applicant undertakings from the European Social Fund. The request for repayment was made following inspections which revealed financial irregularities in the management of the assistance. The CFI held that the decision to reduce the assistance was taken by the Commission and not by the national authorities which, under the applicable Community rules, had no power to make their own assessment. Although the contested decision was addressed only to the Portuguese authorities, it expressly referred to the undertakings in issue which were directly and individually concerned by the contested decision. Under Regulation No 2950/83, the primary responsibility for repayment rested with the undertakings.[62] The CFI concluded that the Commission, which alone assumes legal liability to the undertakings concerned for the contested decision, was not entitled to adopt it without first giving them the opportunity of expressing their views on the proposed reduction in assistance. On appeal, the Court of Justice confirmed the decision of the CFI stating that, even though the Member State is the sole interlocutor of the Fund, there was a direct link between the Commission and the recipient of the assistance.[63]

A common feature of the above cases is that the person claiming the right to be heard was affected by Community decisions directly and in a manner which distinguished it from other persons. It is less certain whether a right to a hearing would be recognized in relation to administrative measures of general application. In *Air-Inter SA* the CFI left open the question whether the rights of defence must be respected in a case where a procedure initiated under Article 8(3) of Regulation No 2408/92 would affect an indeterminate number of undertakings. Absent specific justification, such as a specific and distinct impact on the rights of the applicants, it would be difficult to establish a right to a hearing in relation to measures of general application. The right to a hearing does not apply in relation to

---

[61] Case T-450/93 [1994] ECR II-1177.

[62] Council Regulation No 2950/83 on the implementation of Decision 83/516 on the tasks of the European Social Fund, OJ 1983 L 289, p. 1.

[63] Case C-32/95 P *Commission v Lisrestal and Others* [1996] ECR I-5373. For more recent confirmation, see Case T-231/97 *New Europe and Brown v Commission* [1999] ECR II-2403, para 42.

the adoption of Community legislation, the only obligation incumbent on the Community institutions in that context being the obligation of consultation as provided for in the various articles of the Treaty.[64]

In certain circumstances, the case law has extended the right to a hearing further so as to apply even in cases where proceedings cannot be said to have been initiated against a person. An important decision in this context is *Technische Universität München*.[65] Community legislation exempted from customs duty scientific instruments imported from third countries for non-commercial purposes subject to the condition that no instruments of equivalent scientific value were manufactured in the Community. Under the applicable rules, in order to reach a decision, the Commission consulted a group of experts. In *Universität München* the Commission refused the import free of customs duty of a scientific instrument brought in by the applicant on the ground that equivalent apparatus was manufactured in the Community. The decision was annulled, *inter alia*, for breach of the right to a hearing. The Court held that the importer of the scientific apparatus had the right to a hearing although the applicable regulation did not expressly provide so. It stated that the person concerned should be able to put his own case before the Commission, properly make his views known on the relevant circumstances and, where necessary, express his views on the documents taken into account by the Commission.[66] The judgment departs from previous case law which accepted that undertakings did not have the right to be heard in relation to decisions finding that scientific instruments are not eligible for duty-free importation.[67] The Advocate General considered that the Commission's decision was invalid for lack of reasoning but was content to accept that the principle of *audi alteram partem* did not apply on the ground that the applicant did not suffer a penalty but merely the refusal of a benefit applied for.[68]

Subsequently in *France-Aviation v Commission*[69] the CFI extended the application of *Universität München*. It held that the right to a hearing applies not only where the Commission makes 'complex technical evaluations', as was the case in *Universität München*, but in any procedure where it has power of appraisal, for example in procedures for the repayment on equitable grounds of customs duty. By contrast, in *Windpark Groothusen v Commission*[70] the CFI held that an undertaking, whose application for financial assistance under Community legislation for the promotion

---

[64] Case T-199/96 *Bergaderm and Goupil v Commission* [1998] ECR II-2805, para 58; Case T-521/93 *Atlanta and Others v European Community* [1996] ECR II-1707, para 70; Confirmed on appeal: Case C-104/97 P *Atlanta AG v European Community*, [1999] ECR I-6983. In some cases, the issue may arise whether the procedure in issue is a legislative or administrative one. In *Denmark v Commission, op. cit.*, n. 52 above, the ECJ held that the procedure provided for in Articles 95(4) and (6) EC is administrative and not legislative in nature.
[65] Case C-269/90 [1991] ECR I-5469.   [66] *Ibid.*, para 25.
[67] See Case 185/83 *University of Gronigen v Inspecteur der Invoerrechten en Accijnzen* [1984] ECR 3623; Case 203/85 *Nicolet Instruments v Hauptzollamt Frankfurt-am-Main-Flughafen* [1986] ECR 2049; Case 303/87 *Universität Stuttgart v Hauptzollamt Stuttgart-Ost* [1989] ECR 715.
[68] *Universität München, op. cit.*, p. 5492 per Jacobs AG.
[69] Case T-346/94 [1995] ECR II-2841, paras 33–34.
[70] Case T-109/94 [1995] ECR II-3007; confirmed on appeal C-48/96P, [1998] ECR I-2873.

of energy technology had been refused, did not have the right to be heard. The CFI held that it was in accordance with the procedure in financial support programmes for candidates not to be given a hearing during the selection procedure which is conducted on the basis of the documentation submitted by them. The CFI noted that such procedure is appropriate in situations where hundreds of applications must be evaluated and does not therefore constitute an infringement of the right to a hearing.[71]

The view has been expressed that, where no specific legislation exists granting the right to a hearing, the recognition of such a right in cases where a person applies for a benefit is the exception rather than the rule.[72] Such a right is recognized where 'the administration has gathered evidence against him or targets him with his own behaviour while handling his application'.[73] *Windpark Groothusen* is correctly decided since it cannot be accepted that the right to a hearing must be guaranteed to every applicant whose application for a benefit is unsuccessful. In such cases, the duties of the decision-making body are to assess individually the merits of each application and to give all applicants the opportunity to support their candidature. By contrast, a right to a hearing may be established if the applicant has peculiar attributes which distinguish him from other candidates.[74] One of the differences between *Windpark Groothusen* and *Universität München* is that whereas in the first the Commission enjoyed discretion as to the eligibility of projects, in the second Community legislation granted a right of free import provided that certain conditions were met. Also, in the latter case, the contested decision suffered from other procedural irregularities which rendered the decision-making procedure unfair as a whole. Finally, it is highly doubtful whether the recognition of a right to a hearing in circumstances such as those of *Windpark Groothusen* would be economically justifiable. In cases where a high number of applications is submitted it becomes more difficult to argue that the recognition of process rights would be an efficient method for ensuring the substantive correctness of the decision in issue.[75]

The right to a hearing may also be invoked against public bodies in cases where their actions do not have direct legal consequences on the person concerned if they may result in reputational or other indirect damage. In *Ismeri Europa v Court of Auditors*,[76] the ECJ held that, although the adoption and publication of reports by

---

[71] But note that, in a different context, it has been held that reliance on practical grounds may not justify infringement of the rights of defence: *Lisrestal, op. cit.*, para 37. Cf. Case T-30/91 *Solvay v Commission* [1995] ECR II-1775, para 102.   [72] Lenaerts and Vanhamme, *op. cit.*, p. 537.
[73] *Ibid.*

[74] In *Windpark Groothusen* the CFI identified a second reason why the right of defence had not been infringed. That was the fact that the applicant undertaking did not request further information from the Commission following its decision not to include the undertaking in the list of successful applicants and to place its project in a reserve list.
[75] See further for the economic analysis of procedural safeguards, Craig, *Administrative Law, op cit.*, pp. 425 *et seq.* In general, as Craig points out, three factors need to be taken into account in assessing the desirability of a safeguard and also its recognition in a specific context: the individual interest at issue; the benefits flowing from procedural safeguards; and the cost of compliance with them.   [76] *Op. cit.*, n. 53 above.

the Court of Auditors are not decisions directly affecting the rights of individuals or entities mentioned therein, its reports are capable of having such consequences for those persons that they should be able to make observations before the reports are finalised. The case represents an extension of the right to a hearing initiated by the ECJ which, on appeal, was more forthcoming than the CFI.

8.4. Member States' rights

The Community administration must respect the rights of defence not only in its dealings with natural and legal persons but also in administrative proceedings involving Member States.[77] In practice, the Member States' right to a fair hearing acquires particular importance in the following cases:

- in the administrative stage of enforcement proceedings under Article 226;[78]
- in State aid proceedings;[79]
- in proceedings for the clearance of accounts presented by Member States for agricultural expenditure to be charged to the European Guidance and Guarantee Fund (EAGGF);[80]
- in proceedings relating to financial assistance programmes under the European Social Fund.[81]

Where the legal position of an undertaking is affected adversely by a decision addressed by the Commission to a Member State, the undertaking may have an interest in claiming an infringement of the principle of *audi alteram partem* as regards the Member State. That is the case where it is an essential procedural requirement for the adoption of the contested decision that the Commission must invite the Member State to submit its observations.[82]

A Member State however does not have the right to a hearing where the Commission refuses to authorize it to depart from a harmonization measure under Article 95(4) of the Treaty. Article 95(4) was included in the Treaty to safeguard the

---

[77] *Denmark v Commission, op. cit.*, n. 52 above, para 46.

[78] See e.g. for an interesting difference of view between the Court and the Advocate General as to whether the rights of defence were breached, Case C-274/93 *Commission v Luxembourg* [1996] ECR 2019.

[79] See e.g. Case 234/84 *Belgium v Commission* [1986] ECR 2263; Case C-301/87 *France v Commission (Boussac case)* [1990] ECR I-307, para 39; Case C-288/96 *Germany v Commission* [2000] ECR I-8237.

[80] For an example of a successful challenge, see Case C-61/95 *Greece v Commission* [1998] ECR I-207.

[81] See Council Regulation No 2950/83 on the implementation of Decision 83/516 on the tasks of the European Social Fund, OJ 1983 L 289, p. 1, Article 6(1). For an example of a successful challenge, see Case C-291/89 *Interhotel v Commission* [1991] ECR I-2257.

[82] *Air Inter, op. cit.*, n. 55 above, para 80; *Interhotel, op. cit.*; Case C-304/89 *Oliveira v Commission* [1991] ECR I-2283, paras 17, 21; Joined Cases T-432–434/93 *Socurte and Others v Commission* [1995] ECR II-503, para 63.

interests of Member States as a *quid pro quo* for allowing the adoption of harmonization legislation by qualified majority in the Council. It states that, if after the adoption of a harmonization measure, a Member State deems it necessary to maintain national provisions on grounds of major needs referred to in Article 30 EC or relating to the protection of environment or working environment, it may seek approval from the Commission.[83] In *Denmark v Commission*,[84] Denmark sought approval to maintain in force national provisions prohibiting the use of certain food additives derogating from the provisions of Directive 95/2 which laid down a list of additives whose use was permitted. The Commission refused to approve the Danish measure on the ground that it was excessive in relation to the aim of ensuring public health. Denmark challenged the refusal arguing, *inter alia*, that the Commission did not grant it the right to a hearing before adopting the decision nor did it give it the opportunity to hear the opinions expressed by the other Member States. The ECJ held that the procedure for approval is administrative and not legislative in nature. It held, however, that the right to a hearing does not apply because the procedure is initiated not by a Community institution but by a Member State. When the Member State seeks approval to derogate, it should state the grounds for maintaining the national provisions in question and has, therefore, the opportunity to present its views. The Commission, in turn, must be able, within the prescribed period, to obtain the information which is necessary without being required once more to hear the applicant Member State. The Court also held that a requirement for prolonged exchanges of information would be difficult to reconcile with the objective of Article 95(6) which is to ensure the speedy conclusion of the approval procedure.[85] The ECJ's view was more restrictive than that of Tizzano AG who found that, on the facts, the right to a hearing applied but had been honoured.

The finding of the Court that the right to a hearing does not apply in the procedure provided for in Article 95(4) should also apply where a Member State seeks a derogation under Article 95(5). The difference between the two provisions is that, whilst the first enables a Member State to seek approval to maintain in force an existing national provision derogating from a harmonization measure, the second enables a Member State to ask for approval to introduce a new derogating provision after the adoption of a harmonization measure if it is necessary to do so on grounds of new scientific evidence and for problems specific to that Member State. Although the substantive conditions in each case are different the procedure is the same and the denial of the right to a hearing should apply *mutatis mutandis* also in the case of Article 95(5).[86]

---

[83] Under Article 95(6), the Commission must, within six months of their notification, approve or reject the national provisions after having verified whether they are a means of arbitrary discrimination or a disguised restriction on inter-State trade. In the absence of a decision, the national provisions are deemed to have been approved. Where justified by the complexity of the matter and in the absence of danger to human health, the Commission may delay its decision for a further period of up to six months.   [84] *Op. cit.*, n. 52 above.

[85] *Ibid.*, paras 47–49.

[86] For the difference between Article 95(4) and (5), see *Denmark v Commission, op. cit.*, paras 57 *et seq.*, and also Case C-512/99 *Germany v Commission*, [2003] ECR I-845, paras 40 *et seq.*

Articles 95(4) and (5) were introduced by the Treaty of Amsterdam. Previously, Article 100a(4) provided for the possibility of a single derogation without distinguishing between national provisions adopted before and after harmonization measures. In *Germany v Commission*,[87] this led to a claim that the rights of defence had been breached in another way. Germany argued that the Commission had infringed its right to a hearing by failing to inform it that it would examine an application for the introduction of derogating legislation, which had been submitted before the entry into force of the Treaty of Amsterdam, under Article 95(5) and not under the pre-Amsterdam provision of Article 100(a)(4) EC. The ECJ however rejected this argument stating that Germany could not have been unaware of the entry into force of the Treaty of Amsterdam and could also, on its own initiative, have provided supplementary arguments to prove that the measure was justified under Article 95(5).

In a different context, the Court has invoked the Member States' right to be heard as an argument to reject preliminary references. According to established case law, the ECJ may reject a reference as inadmissible where the national court has failed to define adequately the legal and factual background to the dispute.[88] The reason for this is twofold. Adequate information is necessary to enable the ECJ to provide a meaningful and helpful ruling to the national court. Furthermore, the information provided in the order for reference gives the Governments of the Member States and other interested parties the opportunity to submit observations pursuant to Article 20 of the EC Statute of the Court of Justice.[89] The Court places particular emphasis on this provision which is designed to protect the rights of defence of the Member States and the Community institutions which have an interest in the proceedings. In effect, compliance with Article 20 is a necessary condition for the legitimacy of the Court's rulings. Thus, the ECJ insists that minimum information must be provided in the order for reference itself since it is only the order which is circulated to the Member States and the institutions.[90]

8.5. Content of the right to a fair hearing

The right to a hearing requires that the persons adversely affected by a decision must be placed in a position where they may 'effectively'[91] or

---

[87] Case C-512/99 *Germany v Commission*.

[88] See e.g. Joined Cases 320–322/90 *Telemarsicabruzzo SpA v Circostel* [1993] ECR I-393; Case C-378/93 *La Pyramide* [1994] ECR I-3999. For a discussion, see T. Tridimas, 'Knocking on Heaven's Door: Fragmentation, Efficiency and Defiance in the Preliminary Reference Procedure', 40 (2003) CML Rev 1, at pp. 21 *et seq*.

[89] Case C-458/93 *Saddik* [1995] ECR I-511, para 13.

[90] Case C-116/00 *Laguillaumie* [2000] ECR I-4979, paras 23–25; Case C-422/98 *Colonia Versicherung and Others v Belgian State* [1999] ECR I-1279, para 8.

[91] *France v Commission, op. cit.*, n. 81 above; *Fiskano, op. cit.*, n. 53 above, para 40; *Lisrestal, op. cit.*, n. 56 above, para 21.

'properly'[92] put their own case and make known their views. The precise requirements of the right depend on the type of procedure in issue and the particular
circumstances of the case. It may be said that, in general, it requires the following:

- the party concerned must receive an exact and complete statement of the
  objections raised against it;[93]
- it must have the opportunity to make known its views on the information taken
  into account by the decision-making body to reach the contested decision,
  including observations submitted by interested third parties;[94]
- the decision-making body must not take into account information and documents which it may not disclose to the party concerned because they are covered
  by the obligation of professional secrecy.[95]

According to standard case law, the right to a hearing requires that the undertaking concerned be afforded the opportunity to make known its views on the
truth and relevance of the facts, charges and circumstances relied on by the
decision-maker.[96] Where the Commission decides to initiate a procedure against
an undertaking on its own initiative, such as a procedure for finding an infringement of competition law, it must give a full and precise statement explaining the
reasons why it decided to do so.[97] Where it initiates a procedure following a
complaint by a third party, it must communicate to the undertaking the complaint
or an exact and complete summary thereof.[98] In *Netherlands v Commission*[99] the
Court annulled the Commission decision finding that the Netherlands law regulating postal services infringed Article 86(1) on the ground that the rights of
defence of the Netherlands and of PTT had not been respected. Before adopting
the decision, the Commission had sent a telex to the Government informing it
that, in its view, the postal law was incompatible with Article 86. The Government
responded to that telex but the Court found that the rights of defence had not been
observed because in its telex the Commission had raised only in general terms the
issue of incompatibility of the postal law without setting out the various features
which constituted an infringement of Article 86(1) as they were subsequently set
out in the contested decision. Also, the Commission should have given to the
Government a further hearing after it had held consultations with organizations
representing private messenger services, since those consultations had influenced
the Commission in forming the view that the law infringed Article 86.

---

[92] *Technische Universität München, op. cit.*, n. 67 above; *France-Aviation v Commission, op. cit.*,
n. 71 above, para 32.
[93] *Netherlands v Commission, op. cit.*, n. 53 above, para 45. To state the obvious, the right to a
hearing does not impose on the authorities the obligation to accept the arguments submitted by the
person concerned: Case T-155/94 *Climax Paper Converters v Council* [1996] ECR II-873, para 118.
[94] *France v Commission, op cit.*, n. 81 above; *Netherlands v Commission, op. cit.*, para 46.
[95] See further below 8.6.
[96] See e.g. *Hoffman-LaRoche, op. cit.*, n. 50 above, paras 9 and 11; *Solvay, op. cit.*, n. 73 above,
para 59.   [97] *Air Inter, op. cit.*, n. 55 above, para 83.
[98] *Ibid.*, para 84.   [99] *Op. cit.*, n. 53 above.

The burden of proving that the necessary information has been communicated to the undertaking concerned rests on the Commission. Thus even where the information in issue can be communicated orally, the Community authorities are still under an obligation to provide evidence that the information was actually communicated.[100] Also, the Commission has the onus of proving that notification of a decision has taken place and the addressee of an unregistered letter is not required to show the reasons for any delay in the delivery.[101]

Where the Commission addresses to a Member State a decision which directly affects the interests of a person and the national authorities act as interlocutor between the Commission and the party affected, it is sufficient if the rights of defence are respected directly in the person's dealings with the Commission, or indirectly through the national authorities, or through a combination of these two administrative channels.[102] It is not sufficient however for the national authorities simply to inform the undertaking concerned that the Commission has undertaken an investigation into its conduct. They must inform it of the reservations and suspicions of the Commission.[103] Problems may arise where the procedure leading to the contested decision is 'mixed', namely comprises two stages, one before the national authorities and another before the Commission. Such problems arose in *France-Aviation v Commission*[104] which concerned the procedure for repayment of customs duties. Article 13 of Regulation No 1430/79[105] provides that import duties may be repaid or remitted in special situations 'which result from circumstances in which no deception or obvious negligence may be attributed to the person concerned'. The French authorities transmitted the applicant's case to the Commission taking the view that no negligence or deception could be imputed and proposing the repayment of customs duty. The Commission decided that repayment was not justified on the ground that the applicant had displayed obvious negligence. The applicant sought the annulment of that decision on grounds of breach of the principle *audi alteram partem*. The Commission argued that the right to be heard was observed because the applicant was able to put its arguments to the French authorities which, in turn, made them available to the Commission. The Court held that in a procedure such as that in issue the right to be heard must be secured in the first place in the relations between the person concerned and the national administration. It continued that, although Regulation No 2454/93[106]

[100] Case C-49/88 *Al Jubail Fertiliser v Council* [1991] ECR I-3187, para 20.
[101] Case 108/79 *Belfiore v Commission* [1980] ECR 1769, para 7; Case 195/80 *Michel v Parliament* [1981] ECR 2861, para 11. See also *Greece v Commission, op. cit.*, n. 82 above.
[102] *Air-Inter, op. cit.*, para 65.   [103] *Lisrestal, op. cit.*, paras 41–42.
[104] *Op. cit.*, n. 71 above. Cf Joined Cases C-121 and C-122/91 *CT Control (Rotterdam) and JCT Benelux v Commission* [1993] ECR I-3873. See also Case 294/81 *Control Data v Commission* [1983] ECR 911; Joined Cases 98 and 230/83 *van Gend en Loos v Commission* [1984] ECR 3763.
[105] See Council Regulation (EEC) No 1430/79 on the repayment or remission of import or export duties (OJ 1979 L 175, p. 1) as amended by Council Regulation (EEC) No 3069/86 (OJ 1986 L 286, p. 1).
[106] Commission Regulation No 2454/93 laying down rules for the implementation of the Community Customs Code, OJ 1993 L 253, p. 1.

does not provide for direct contacts between the Commission and the person concerned, that does not necessarily mean that the Commission may deem itself satisfied in every case with the information transmitted to it by the national administration. The Court found that the file transmitted to the Commission by the French authorities omitted material information and therefore the Commission had taken the contested decision on the basis of an incomplete file. It held that, insofar as the Commission contemplated diverging from the recommendation of the French authorities and rejecting the application for repayment, it had a duty to arrange for the applicant to be heard by the French authorities.[107]

In *France-Aviation* the purpose of the hearing was to remedy the insufficiency of the information submitted by the national authority to the Commission. The CFI took a unitary conception of public authorities, in effect making the Commission responsible for rectifying the defects in the national administrative proceedings.

8.6. Fair hearing and confidentiality

As stated above, the right to a hearing requires the Commission to inform the undertaking concerned of the facts upon which the Commission's adverse decision is based. The requirement to disclose the necessary information, however, may come into conflict with the obligation of professional secrecy incumbent upon the institutions. Article 287 EC states that Community officials and other employees must not 'disclose information of the kind covered by the obligation of professional secrecy, in particular information about undertakings, their business relations or their costs components'.[108] How are the two principles to be compromised? The general answer given in the case law is that the Commission may not use to the detriment of an undertaking facts or documents which it is under an obligation not to disclose, where the failure to make such disclosure adversely affects the undertaking's opportunity to be heard.[109] Where a document has not been disclosed by the Commission, it is for the undertaking concerned to show that it has been deprived of evidence needed for its defence.[110]

---

[107] *Op. cit.*, para 36.

[108] The obligation to respect business confidentiality receives mention also in specific Community measures, see e.g. Article 20(2) of Regulation No 17 and now, Regulation 1/2003, Art. 27(2) and (4).

[109] *Hoffman-La Roche, op. cit.*, para 14; C-62/86 *AKZO v Commission* [1986] ECR I-3359, para 21; Case 234/84 *Belgium v Commission* [1986] ECR 2263, para 29.

[110] Joined Cases 209–15 and 218/78 *van Landewyck v Commission (FEDETAB)* [1980] ECR 3125, para 39 and see Case C-310/93 P *BPB Industries and British Gypsum v Commission* [1995] ECR I-865, *op. cit.*, at 887 *per* Léger AG.

In general, the case law accords confidential status to the following categories of documents:[111] (a) confidential documents belonging to third parties; (b) internal Commission documents; (c) correspondence between the Commission and Member States or other international bodies. The first category encompasses business secrets, correspondence between undertakings and their lawyers,[112] and correspondence between the Commission and third parties, e.g. complainants or customers who collaborated with the Commission during the investigation and may fear that the undertaking will adopt retaliatory measures against them.[113] Business secrets are afforded 'very special protection' and third parties may under no circumstances be given access to documents containing business secrets.[114] Whether a document contains a business secret is for the Commission and, ultimately, the Court to decide. The Commission may not disclose a document which the undertaking subject to investigation claims contains a business secret without first giving to that undertaking the opportunity to express its views and bring an action before the Court to prevent disclosure.[115] However the obligation to protect business secrets must be balanced with two important countervailing principles: the rights of the defence and the public interest in the administration of justice.[116] The Commission's notice concerning access to the file in competition proceedings expressly provides for this balancing exercise.[117] It states as follows:

Where business secrets provide evidence of an infringement or tend to exonerate a firm, the Commission must reconcile the interest in the protection of sensitive information, the public interest in having the infringement of the competition rules terminated, and the rights of the defence. This calls for an assessment of:

(i) the relevance of the information to determining whether or not an infringement has been committed;
(ii) its probative value;
(iii) whether it is indispensable;
(iv) the degree of sensitivity involved (to what extent would disclosure of the information harm the interests of the firm?);

---

[111] Lenaerts and Vanhamme, *op. cit.*, p. 541; M. Levitt, 'Access to the File: The Commission's Administrative Procedures in Cases under Articles 85 and 86' (1997) 34 CML Rev 1413., p. 1424 and see *BPB Industries, op. cit.*, paras 25 *et seq.*   [112] See *Hilti, op cit.*, n. 25 above.

[113] *BPB, op. cit.*, para 26.

[114] Case 53/85 *AKZO Chemie v Commission* [1986] ECR 1965, para 28; Joined Cases 142 and 156/84 *BAT and Reynolds v Commission* [1987] ECR I-4487, para 21. But unauthorised disclosure does not necessarily lead to annulment of the Commission's decision finding an infringement: see below 8.7.

[115] *AKZO, op. cit.*, n. 116 above, and see for anti-dumping proceedings Case 236/81 *Celanese v Council and Commission* [1982] ECR 1183.

[116] For the protection of the administration of justice, see Case 110/84 *Municipality of Hillegom v Hillenius* [1985] ECR 3947.

[117] Commission Notice 97/C23/03 on the internal rules of procedure for processing requests for access to the file in cases pursuant to Arts. 85 and 86 EC, Arts. 65 and 66 ECSC and Council Reg (EEC) No 406/89, OJ 1997 C23/3. Note that this notice has most recently been updated by comission Notice 2005/C325/07, OJ 2005 C325/7.

(v) the seriousness of the infringement. Each document must be assessed individually to determine whether the need to disclose is greater than the harm which might result from disclosure.

The Court has held that Article 287 EC must be interpreted is such a way that rights of defence are not deprived of their substance. A notable example is provided by *Timex v Council and Commission*.[118] In that case, the Court annulled a Council regulation imposing anti-dumping duties on the ground that the Commission had wrongly failed to disclose certain information to the complainant because it considered that it was covered by the obligation of confidentiality. The Court held that the Commission ought to have made every effort, so far as was compatible with the obligation not to disclose business secrets, to supply the complainant with information relevant to the defence of its interest, choosing on its own initiative the appropriate means of providing such information. Thus a request by a party that information should not be disclosed for reasons of business secrets is not a trump card which compromises *simpliciter* the rights of defence. In the *Soda-Ash* cases[119] the CFI made it clear that the Commission must protect the business secrets of an undertaking in such as a way as to cause the least possible interference with the right to a hearing. In particular, the CFI found that in the circumstances of the case the Commission had two options. It could either prepare non-confidential versions of the documents annexed to the statement of objections by deleting confidential passages, or if that was difficult, it could send a list of the documents annexed to the statement of objections giving the opportunity to the applicant to request specific documents. If the applicant requested documents which might contain business secrets, then the Commission should contact the undertaking concerned with a view to ascertaining which passages contained sensitive information and should therefore be kept secret from the applicant.

The Commission's refusal to disclose a document is a preparatory act which cannot be challenged under Article 230 during the course of the administrative procedure. The undertaking concerned may only challenge the final decision of the Commission. This is because, until a final decision has been adopted, the Commission may abandon or amend its objections or rectify procedural irregularities which may have occurred by granting access to the file.[120] By contrast, the decision of the Commission to disclose certain documents to a third party, for example, the complainant, may be challenged by the undertaking which considers that the documents contain business secrets and objects to disclosure. This is because the decision to disclose has irreversible consequences. The damage done by disclosure cannot be repaired whether the Commission's final decision is upheld or annulled.[121]

---

[118] Case 264/82 [1985] ECR 849.
[119] *Solvay, op. cit.*, n. 73 above, paras 89 *et seq.*; Case T-36/91 *ICI v Commission* [1995] ECR I-1847, paras 99 *et seq.*
[120] Joined Cases T-10-12, 15/92 *Cimenteries CBR and Others v Commission* [1992] ECR I-2667, para 47.   [121] *AKZO Chemie, op. cit.*, n. 116 above.

8.7. Consequences of failure to observe

The Community judicature views the right to a hearing as a functional rather than as an objective requirement. Infringement of the right leads to the annulment of the act in question only if it can be shown that the outcome of the procedure might have been different had the right to a hearing been respected.[122] In *Belgium v Commission*[123] the Belgian Government sought the annulment of a decision finding that State aid which had been granted to a company was unlawful on the ground that the Commission took into account representations made by other States and by competing undertakings without giving the opportunity to the Government to comment on those representations. The Court's response was to require the Commission to produce the observations made by third parties. After examining them, it found that they contained no information in addition to that which the Commission already possessed and of which the Belgian Government was already aware. Under those circumstances, the fact that the Belgian Government had no opportunity to comment on the observations was not of such a nature as to influence the result of the administrative procedure.[124]

It may be objected that the right to a hearing is a requirement of form, not one of substance, and that whether the hearing might have made a difference to the outcome should be irrelevant. The courts should not attempt to step *ex post facto* into the shoes of the administration. *Belgium v Commission* however does not suggest that the Court attempt to second guess what would have been the outcome of the procedure had the right to a hearing been respected. It merely exercises a residual control based on the criterion of reasonableness. Is it conceivable that the outcome *might* have been different if a hearing had been given? Only if that question is answered in the affirmative, may breach of the rights of defence be sanctioned by annulment. The limits of this residual control were pinpointed by the CFI in *Solvay*.[125] The applicant's argument was that the Commission had taken into account documents which it had not disclosed to the applicant. The CFI held:[126]

> ... it is not for the Court of First Instance to rule definitively on the evidential value of all the evidence used by the Commission to support the contested decision. In order to find that

---

[122] *Germany v Commission, op. cit.*, n. 81 above, para 101; Case T-7/89 *Hercules Chemicals v Commission* [1991] ECR I-1711, para 56; Case C-142/87 *Belgium v Commission (Tubemeuse)* [1990] ECR I-959, para 48; Case 234/84 *Belgium v Commission* [1986] ECR 2263, para 30; Case 30/78 *Distillers Company v Commission* [1980] ECR 2229, para 26.   [123] *Tubemeuse, op. cit.*

[124] *Ibid.*, para 48. Confirmed in *Germany v Commission, op. cit.* A similar approach had been followed much earlier in *Alvis v Council, op. cit.*, n. 6 above. There a Community official was dismissed for gross misconduct without first being given the opportunity to express his views on the allegations made against him. The Court held that the rights of the defence had been breached but took the view that the breach was not sufficient to annul the decision of dismissal as it was correct in substance. The judgment appears to fly in the face of process rights but can be defended on the ground that the Court was exercising 'unlimited' and not merely supervisory jurisdiction.

[125] *Op. cit.*, n. 73 above.   [126] *Ibid.*, para 68.

the rights of the defence have been infringed, it is sufficient for it to be established that the non-disclosure of the documents in question might have influenced the course of the procedure and the content of the decision to the applicant's detriment. The possibility of such an influence can therefore be established if a provisional examination of some of the evidence shows that the documents not disclosed might—in the light of that evidence—have had a significance which ought not to have been disregarded. If it were proved that the rights of the defence were infringed, the administrative procedure and the appraisal of the facts in the decision would be defective.

The approach of the Community courts can best be described as pragmatic. It seeks to balance two conflicting principles: on the one hand, to uphold the rights of the defence as procedural safeguards for the protection of the individual and, on the other hand, to avoid undue formalism which might encourage abusive reliance on procedural principles. The undertaking concerned must prove that the results might be different if the documents in issue had been disclosed. It seems that, overall, the burden imposed on the undertaking is not a difficult one to discharge.[127]

The consequences of failing to observe the right to a hearing will depend on the circumstances of the case. The Court seeks to establish whether the procedure, as a whole, has been fair. In a number of cases decisions of the Commission have been annulled wholly or in part.[128] But where the breach of the right to a hearing relates to matters of secondary importance, it may not affect the validity of the decision as a whole.[129] Thus where the Commission fails to communicate to the undertaking concerned documents which it has taken into account, that may result in those documents being excluded as evidence. It would not lead to the annulment of the entire decision unless the objection raised by the Commission could be proved only by reference to those documents.[130] In one case[131] the decision to disclose confidential information to a complainant was annulled even though disclosure had already taken place. But in another case[132] disclosure to the complainant of confidential information relating to the target undertaking was held not to vitiate the Commission's final decision because it did not affect its substance.

A related issue is whether irregularities during the administrative procedure may be remedied in the course of the proceedings before the Court. As a matter of principle, to admit such *ex post facto* remedy would negate the value of process rights. The case law gives contradictory signs focusing in effect on whether the

---

[127] Depending on the circumstances, the Court may not even examine the assertion of the defendant institution that even if a hearing had been given, the outcome would not have been different. See e.g. *Al-Jubail, op. cit.* n. 102 above; cf. Opinion of Darmon AG at 3226.

[128] See e.g. *Solvay, op. cit.,* and *ICI v Commission (Soda-Ash cases), op. cit.* n. 121 above; Joined Cases C-89/85 etc. *Ahlström Osakeyhtiö and Others v Commission* [1993] ECR 1307; *Al-Jubail, op. cit.; Fiskano, op. cit.; Netherlands v Commission, op. cit., France-Aviation v Commission, op. cit.*

[129] Joined Cases 100–3/80 *Musique Diffusion Française v Commission* [1983] ECR 1825, para 30.

[130] Case 107/82 *AEG v Commission* [1983] ECR 3151, para 30; cf *Solvay, op. cit.,* paras 58 and 97.

[131] *AKZO Chemie, op. cit.,* n. 116 above, para 28.

[132] *van Landewyck v Commission, op. cit.,* n. 112 above, paras 46–47.

irregularity has been serious. In *Hoffmann-La Roche v Commission* it was held that breach of the rights of defence during the administrative procedure before the Commission may be remedied in the proceedings before the Court itself if such belated remedy does not prejudice the interests of the person concerned.[133] That finding was criticized in a subsequent Opinion.[134] In *Solvay* the CFI followed a more orthodox approach holding that the Commission's failure to disclose certain documents was not justified by the obligation to respect professional secrecy and that the ensuing breach of the rights of defence could not be regularized during the proceedings before the CFI.[135]

An interesting example is provided by *Ismeri Europa v Court of Auditors*[136] although it should be borne in mind that the case concerned an action for damages and not an action for annulment. The Court of Auditors in a special report had criticized the management of certain aid programmes to Mediterranean countries. It identified the applicant company by name as being in a conflict of interest. It had been awarded a contract in the preparation of which it had itself been involved as a member of the body responsible for conducting the management of the programmes. The company brought an action for damages to its reputation and loss arising from termination of contracts resulting from the publication of the report.

The Court reiterated that the right to a hearing is a general principle of law which applies to any procedure which may result in a decision perceptibly affecting a person's interests. Since the Court of Auditors omitted to invite the applicant to express its views on the passages concerning it, the procedure leading to the adoption of the report was vitiated by a breach of the right to a hearing. The Court rejected the argument that the infringement had been remedied by the opportunity given to the applicant to submit its observations after the publication of the report. It held that,[137]

an institution is naturally more willing to welcome observations before definitely determining its view of a matter than after publication thereof since acknowledgment after publication that criticisms were well founded would compel it to go back on its views by issuing a rectification.

Thus, the fact that the Court of Auditors refuted the applicant's criticisms made after the publication of the report did not necessarily mean that it would have reached the same conclusion if the criticisms had been made prior to the adoption of the report. Nonetheless, the ECJ considered that, in the circumstances, the failure to observe the right to a hearing did not influence the content of the report and therefore there was no causal link between the breach and the alleged damage. There was a flagrant and serious failure to observe the rules of sound management arising from the existence of conflict of interests. Thus even if the applicant had

---

[133] *Op. cit.*, n. 50 above, para. 15.
[134] *Distillers Company, op. cit.*, at 2297–98 *per* Warner AG.
[135] *Solvay, op. cit.*, para 98; 1 *ICI, op. cit.*, n. 121 above, para 113.
[136] *Op. cit.*, n. 53 above.   [137] Para 31.

been given the right to a hearing that would not have altered the view taken by the Court of Auditors.

In practice, the right to a hearing acquires particular importance in the following areas: competition, anti-dumping, State aids,[138] staff cases, and proceedings relating to financial assistance programmes.[139] By way of illustration, it will be examined by reference to the areas where it is most oft-invoked, namely competition, anti-dumping, and staff cases. There is no intention to be exhaustive but rather to show the approach of the Community judicature in selected areas.

8.8. Competition proceedings

8.8.1. The right to a hearing

The right to a hearing has given rise to extensive litigation in the context of competition proceedings.[140] Article 85 EC charges the Commission with the responsibility to enforce Community competition law and investigate suspected infringements of Articles 81 and 82. The powers of the Commission were provided for in Regulation 17,[141] which has now been replaced by Regulation 1/2003.[142] The procedure before the Commission is administrative and not judicial in character[143] but this does not affect the rights of the defence which, as already stated, must be respected in all proceedings liable to culminate in a decision having adverse consequences for the person concerned.[144]

Article 27(1) of Regulation 2003/1 states that, before taking the decisions provided for in Articles 7, 8, 23 and Article 24(2), the Commission must give the undertakings or associations of undertakings which are the subject of the proceedings the opportunity of being heard on the matters to which the Commission

---

[138] For examples on State aids, see Case 234/84 *Belgium v Commission* [1986] ECR 2263; *Belgium v Commission (Tubemeuse), op. cit.; France v Commission (Boussac case) op. cit.*

[139] See e.g. *Lisrestal, op. cit; Windpark Groothusen, op. cit.*, n. 72 above.

[140] See, among others, C.S. Kerse and N. Khan, *EC Antitrust Procedures*, (5th ed.) (Sweet & Maxwell 2004); P. Roth, C. Bellamy and G. Child, *Common Market Law of Competition*, 5th Ed., (Sweet & Maxwell, 2001) Ch. 12; A. Jones and B. Sufrin, *EC Competition Law, Text, Cases and Materials*, 2nd Ed. (Oxford University Press, 2004) Ch. 14; 'Droits de la défense et droits de la Commission dans le droit communautaire de la concurrence', Proceedings of the Colloquium held on 24 and 25 January 1994 by the Association européenne des avocats (Bruylant, 1994); V. Korah, 'The Rights of the Defence in Administrative Proceedings Under Community Law' (1980) 33 CLP 73.

[141] First Regulation implementing Articles 85 and 86 of the Treaty, OJ, English Special Edition, 1959–62, p. 87.

[142] Council Regulation 1/2003 on the implementation of the rules on competition laid down in Articles 81 and 82 of the Treaty, OJ 2003, L1/1. The Regulation came into force on 1 May 2004.

[143] According to the case law, the Commission is not a 'tribunal' within the meaning of Article 6(1) ECHR since it is an administrative authority. See *Musique Diffusion Française, op. cit.*, para 7; Case T-11/89 *Shell v Commission* [1992] ECR II-757, para 39. See also Joined Cases T-213/95 and T-18/96 *SCK and FNK v Commission* [1997] ECR II-1739, para 56.

[144] See above n. 35 and *Hoffmann-La Roche, op. cit.*, para 9.

has taken objection. These provisions concern respectively the finding of an infringement, the imposition of interim measures, the imposition of a fine, and the definitive fixing of a period penalty payment in the circumstances referred to in Article 24(2).[145] They do not cover the multitude of cases where the Commission may take decisions having adverse consequences on undertakings. Article 27 however does not prejudice the all-embracing character of the right to a hearing.[146]

The persons affected enjoy rights of defence not only where proceedings are initiated by the Commission but also where proceedings are initiated by national competition authorities in accordance with the provisions of Regulation 1/2003. This follows from the fact that, in such cases, the national authorities act within the scope of Community law and therefore are bound to respect the general principles of law as protected by the ECJ and the Community legal order. It also derives from Article 35(1) of Regulation 1/2003 which states that the Member States must designate the competent authorities responsible for the application of Articles 81 and 82 'in such a way that the provisions of this regulation are effectively complied with'. It would be incongruous and contrary to the notion of equal treatment if undertakings were subject to a lower level of procedural protection where proceedings are initiated against them by national competition authorities rather than the Commission.

Regulation 1/2003 declares that, where the Commission takes proceedings, 'the rights of defence of the parties concerned shall be fully respected'.[147] The Commission must base its decisions only on objections on which the parties concerned have been able to comment. Complainants must be associated closely with the proceedings.[148] Any other persons who are able to show a sufficient interest must be afforded the opportunity to make their views known.[149] Failure to hear third parties who are able to show sufficient interest may result in the annulment of the decision.[150]

Matters regarding the hearing are now regulated by Commission Regulation No 773/2004.[151] The Regulation provides for the right to submit written comments and the right to be heard orally. Where the Commission considers that there has been a violation, it must provide the undertakings concerned with a statement of objections raised against them.[152] The parties may provide written

---

[145] Previously, Article 19 of Regulation 17 provided that the Commission was under an obligation to give undertakings or associations of undertakings concerned the opportunity of being heard in the following cases: decisions concerning negative clearances, the finding of an infringement, individual exemptions, and the imposition of fines or periodic penalty payments.

[146] See *Transocean Marine Paint Association case, op. cit.*, n. 15 above.

[147] Reg 1/2003, Article 27(2).

[148] *Ibid.*, Article 27(1). For the rights of complainants, see below.

[149] *Ibid.*, Article 27(3).

[150] Joined Cases 228 and 229/82 *Ford v Commission* [1984] ECR 1129 at 1174–75 *per* Slynn AG. See also *van Landewyck, op. cit.*, para 17.

[151] OJ 2004 L123/18. This Regulation replaced Regulation No 2843/98 (OJ 1998 L354/18) which had, in turn, replaced Regulation 99/63 (OJ, English Special Edition, 1963–64, p. 47).

[152] Reg. No 773/2004, Article 10. The Commission must set a time limit of no less than four weeks within which the undertakings concerned may make their views known. The Commission

submissions setting out all the facts known to them which are relevant to their defence. The Commission must also give to the parties concerned the opportunity to develop their arguments at an oral hearing, if they so request in their written submissions.[153]

Complainants and any other natural and legal persons who are able to show sufficient interest have the right to make written submissions and may be invited to the oral hearing, where appropriate.[154] The Commission may likewise afford to any other person the opportunity to present written or oral observations.[155]

Hearings are held by officers appointed by the Commission for this purpose. They are conducted 'in full independence'.[156] The hearing is not public but persons attending may be assisted by their legal advisers or other qualified persons admitted by the Hearing Officer.[157] In its decision, the Commission may deal only with those objections raised against undertakings which are contained in the statement of objections and in respect of which they have been afforded the opportunity of making known their views.[158] It should be stressed that the hearing officer does not act in a judicial capacity. He is an independent administrative officer whose function is to ensure that the effective exercise of the right to be heard is respected in competition proceedings.[159] He submits a final report which is attached to the draft decision of the Commission so that, in reaching its final decision, the College of Commissioners is fully apprised of all the relevant information concerning the course of the procedure and respect of the right to be heard.[160]

---

is not required to take into account submissions received after the expiry of that time limit: Article 10(2). The undertakings concerned may waive their right to a hearing: *SCK and FNK, op. cit.*, para 219. The Commission however may omit to communicate documents only where the undertaking concerned has declared its intention unambiguously: *Solvay, op. cit.*, para 57.

[153] Reg. No 773/2004, Article 12.

[154] *Ibid.*, Articles 6 and 13. Persons with sufficient interest will include consumer associations where the proceedings concern products or services used by the end consumer or products or services that constitute a direct input into such products or services: see Preamble to Reg. No 773/2004, recital 11.

[155] *Ibid.*, Article 13(3). The Commission enjoys reasonable discretion in deciding which persons to hear: Joined Cases 43 and 63/82 *VBVB and VBBB v Commission* [1984] ECR 19, para 18; Case 43/85 *Ancides v Commission* [1987] ECR 3131.

[156] *Ibid.*, Article 14(1). The powers and duties of the Hearing Officer are governed by Commission Decision 2001/462, OJ 2001, L162/21. Since 1994, the Officer has jurisdiction also in relation to hearings regarding mergers as provided by the Merger Regulation: Regulation No 139/2004, OJ L 24/1 which replaced Regulation No 4064/89, OJ 1989 L 395/1.

[157] *Ibid.*, Article 14.

[158] *Ibid.*, Article 11(2) and Reg. No 1/2003, Article 27(1). See *SCK and FNK, op. cit.*, para 65. Note however that the Commission decision need not be a replica of the statement of objections: *van Landewyck, op. cit.*, paras 68–70; *Musique Diffusion Française, op. cit.*, paras 19–20. But the Commission must set out clearly and distinctly in the statement of objections each of the infringements which it claims to have taken place: *Ahlström Osakeyhtiö, op. cit.*, n. 130 above.

[159] See Commission Decision 2001/462 on the terms of reference of hearing officers in certain competition proceedings, OJ 2001 L 162/21, Article 1. [160] *Ibid.*, Article 15.

8.8.2. Access to the file

Where a plea is raised that the rights of the defence have been breached, the claim is often that the Commission failed to disclose to the party concerned information on which its decision was based.[161] A vexed question has been whether undertakings investigated by the Commission in relation to a violation of Articles 81 or 82 have the right of access to the administrative file established by the Commission.[162] Regulations No 17 and No 99/63 were silent on the issue. By contrast, the Merger Regulation, adopted in 1989, provided for access to the complete file in relation to mergers.[163] Regulation 1/2003 now provides more clarity by giving a general right of access to the file.[164] The case law in this area has also evolved considerably.

The traditional stance of the Court of Justice was that the rights of defence do not include the right to have access to the complete file. In *VBVB and VBBB v Commission* the Court held, confirming previous case law, that the Commission is under no obligation to divulge the contents of the complete file and, in order to respect the rights of defence, only those documents on which the Commission has based its decision must be made available.[165] An undertaking may complain that the Commission has failed to disclose a document only if it can adduce evidence that the Commission has based its decision on documents which were not made public.[166]

In fact, of its own accord, the Commission promised to adhere to higher standards. In its Twelfth Report on Competition Policy, it undertook to disclose to undertakings the documents in the file concerning them, whether incriminating or exculpatory, and to permit the undertakings involved in the procedure to inspect the file of the case.[167] The CFI held that the Commission could not depart from the rules which it had imposed on itself. In *Hercules Chemicals v Commission*[168] it derived from the Twelfth Report an obligation incumbent on the Commission to make available to the undertakings involved in proceedings under Article 81(1) all documents, whether in their favour or otherwise, which it has obtained during

---

[161] See e.g. *Musique Diffusion Française, op. cit.*, paras 24 *et seq.*

[162] See for detailed discussions, M. Levitt, *op. cit.*, 1413; C.D. Ehlermann and B.J. Drijber, 'Legal Protection of Enterprises: Administrative Procedure, in particular Access to File and Confidentiality' (1996) ECLR 375. See further Lenaerts in FIDE, *op. cit.*, pp. 519 *et seq.*

[163] See Council Regulation (EEC) No 4064/89 on the control of concentrations between undertakings, OJ 1989, l395, p. 1. Article 18(3). This is now replaced by Article 18(3) of Council Regulation No 139/2004 (OJ 2004, L 24/1), which states as follows: 'The Commission shall base its decision only on objections on which the parties have been able to submit their observations. The rights of the defence shall be fully respected in the proceedings. Access to the file shall be open at least to the parties directly involved, subject to the legitimate interest of undertakings in the protection of their business secrets.'   [164] See below p. 401.

[165] *Op. cit.*, n. 157 above, para 25. See also *Consten and Grundig, op. cit.*, n. 90 above, at 338; Case 42/69 *ACF Chemiefarma v Commission* [1970] ECR 661, para 42; *AKZO v Commission, op. cit.*, n. 111 above, para 16.

[166] Case 322/81 *Michelin v Commission* [1983] ECR 3461, paras 7 and 9; *BPB Industries, op. cit.*, at 887 *per* Léger AG; *SCK and FNK, op. cit.*, para 220.

[167] Twelfth Report on Competition Policy, pp. 40–41

[168] *Op. cit.*, n. 124 above, para 53.

the course of the investigation, save where the business secrets of other under-takings, the internal documents of the Commission or other confidential information are involved.[169]

Subsequently, in *Solvay*[170] and *ICI*[171] *(Soda ash cases)* the CFI saw the right of access to the file as an integral part of the rights of defence. It held that the purpose of providing access to the file is to allow the addressees of a statement of objections to examine the evidence in the Commission's file so that they are in a position effectively to express their views on the conclusions reached by the Commission on the basis of the evidence. Access to the file is thus one of the procedural guarantees intended to protect the rights of the defence and ensure the exercise of the right to be heard.[172]

In *BPB Industries and British Gypsum v Commission*[173] Léger AG also took the view that the right of access to the file should be recognized as an integral part of the rights of defence. He put forward three arguments.[174] First, a right of access to the file is recognized in relation to mergers. Second, such a right is enshrined in the laws of a number of Member States. It would be incongruous if undertakings enjoyed a lower degree of protection in Community law given especially that a finding of infrin-gement of Community competition law leads to more severe financial implications. Third, in its Twelfth and subsequently in its Twenty-Third Report on Competition Policy,[175] the Commission itself expressed its willingness to raise the standard of protection. He concluded that an undertaking under investigation is entitled to have access to the whole file, save where the business secrets of other undertakings, the internal documents of the Commission or other confidential information are involved.[176] In its judgment, the Court was more reticent. It did not expressly endorse the Opinion of the Advocate General and chose instead to repeat the standard formula that observance of the rights of the defence requires that the undertaking must have been enabled to express its views effectively on the docu-ments used by the Commission to support its allegation for an infringement.[177]

It may be noted that providing access to the compete file, subject to confidentiality, is not without problems. It is particularly onerous where a large number of parties are involved and some of the documents may have only remote connection with the case in issue.[178] On the other hand, it must be accepted that giving access provides added

---

[169] *Ibid.*, para 54.   [170] *Op. cit.*, n. 73 above.
[171] *Op. cit.*, n. 121 above.
[172] *Solvay, op. cit.*, para 59; *ICI, op. cit.*, para 69. See also *Cimenteries CBR, op. cit.*, n. 122 above, para 38; T-65/89 *BPB Industries and British Gypsum v Commission* [1993] ECR II-389, paras 30–31.
[173] *Op. cit.*, n. 112 above.   [174] *Ibid.*, pp. 890 *et seq.*
[175] COM(94) 161, 5 May 1994, point 202.   [176] *Ibid.*, p. 892.
[177] Para 21. The judgment could be interpreted as accepting by implication that the Com-mission may refuse disclosure of documents to the party concerned only if the document is confidential and not because the Commission did not rely on it in making its decision: see paras 23–24. It is doubtful however whether that is the true meaning of the judgment.
[178] See further V. Korah, *EC Competition Law and Practice*, Seventh Ed., Hart Publishing, 2000, p. 125, and J.M. Joshua, 'Balancing the Public Interests: Confidentiality, Trade Secrets and Disclosure of Evidence in EC Competition Procedures' (1994) 2 ECLR 68.

guarantees for the undertakings under investigation. It acquires particular importance in cases where the Commission adopts composite statements of objections, i.e. statements which assert multiple violations by a number of undertakings. The main argument in favour of giving access to the complete file is to ensure that the Commission has assessed the documents correctly. Also, it should not be left to the Commission to decide which documents are useful for the defence. In the *Soda Ash* cases the CFI expressly pointed out that, where difficult and complex economic appraisals are to be made, the Commission must give the advisers of the undertakings concerned the opportunity to examine documents which may be relevant so that their probative value for the defence can be assessed.[179]

Subsequent judgments of the CFI suggest that there is no absolute right of access to the file in the sense that the Community courts will not annul on account of failure to disclose a document in the file unless it has affected adversely the exercise of the right to a hearing.[180] The party concerned must be notified of, and have the opportunity to express its views on, the documents on which the Commission based its decision.

The issue was revisited recently by the ECJ in *Aalborg Portland A/S and Others v Commission (Cement case)*,[181] where the Court laid down the following principles:

(1) The right of access to the file means that the Commission must give the undertakings concerned the opportunity to examine all the documents in the investigation file which may be relevant for its defence. These documents include both incriminating evidence and exculpatory evidence, save where the business secrets of other undertakings, the internal documents of the Commission or other confidential information are involved.[182]

(2) The Court drew a distinction between incriminating and exculpatory evidence. The failure to disclose an incriminating document is a breach of the rights of defence only if the undertaking concerned shows, first, that the Commission relied on it to support the finding of an infringement and, second, that the infringement could be proved only by reference to that document. If the infringement can be supported by other evidence which was communicated to the undertaking, failure to disclose an incriminating document does not affect the validity of the Commission's finding. The burden of proof lies with the undertaking: it is for the applicant to show that the decision which the

[179] *Solvay, op. cit.*, para 81; *ICI, op. cit.*, para 91.

[180] See Case C-458/98 P *Industrie des Poudres Sphériques v Council and Commission*, judgment of 3 October 2000, paras 101–102; Case C-51/92 P *Hercules Chemicals NV v Commission (Polypropylene cases)* [1999] ECR I-4235, paras 75–76s; Case C-185/95 P *Baustahlgewebe GmbH v Commission* [1999] ECR I-8417, para 89 Case T-145/89 *Baustahlgewebe v Commission* [1995] ECR II-987; *SCK and FNK, op. cit.*

[181] Joined Cases C-204, 205, 211, 213, 217 & 219/00 P *Aalborg Portland A/S and Others v Commission (Cement case)*, judgment of 7 January 2004.

[182] *Ibid.*, para 68; and see Case C-199/99 P *Corus UK v Commission* [2003] ECR I-11177, paras 125–128; *Solvay, op. cit.*, para. 81.

Commission reached would have been different if the incriminating document had been disallowed as evidence.

(3) Where an exculpatory document has not been communicated, the undertaking concerned must only establish that its non-disclosure was able to influence to its disadvantage the course of the proceedings and the content of the Commission's decision. Here, it is sufficient for the undertaking to show that, had it been able to rely on these documents during the administrative procedure, it would have been able to put forward evidence which departed from the Commission's findings and would therefore have been able to have some influence on the Commission's assessment. It suffices if the documents could have an impact on the findings pertaining to the gravity and duration of the conduct and, accordingly, the level of the fine.

(4) The possibility that a document which was not disclosed might have influenced the course of the proceedings and the content of the Commission's decision can be established only if a provisional examination of certain evidence by the CFI shows that the documents not disclosed might—in the light of that evidence—have had a significance which ought not to have been disregarded. It suffices if disclosure of a document would have had even a small chance of altering the outcome of the administrative procedure had the undertaking concerned been able to rely on it during that procedure.[183]

(5) In the context of this provisional analysis, it is for the Court of First Instance alone to assess the value which should be attached to the evidence produced to it. The criteria, however, to be applied in order to determine whether the Commission's exclusion of a specific document adversely affected an undertaking's rights of the defence is a question of law amenable to review by the Court of Justice. The same applies to the question whether a document must be qualified as an exculpatory document capable of being of use in an undertaking's defence. The correct criterion to be adopted in this context is the existence of an objective link. Such a link must exist between the documents which were not made accessible during the administrative procedure and an objection adopted against the undertaking concerned in the Commission's decision.

The *Cement* judgment falls short of accepting an unqualified right of access to the file. The undertakings concerned have a right to see the file but the right is not a self-standing one in the sense that it is intended to enable the undertakings concerned to exercise their rights of defence and does not extend to all documents. In the case in issue the Commission had not communicated the great majority of the documents contained in the investigation file to the undertakings concerned but the ECJ upheld the CFI's finding that the contested decision could not be annulled unless it was established that the lack of access had prevented the undertakings from perusing documents which were likely to be of use in their defence.

---

[183] *Op. cit.*, para 131.

The arrangements for providing access to the file are contained in the Commission's Notice on Access to the file adopted in 1997.[184] That revision was made to ensure compatibility with the requirements laid down by the CFI in *Solvay*.

Article 27(2) of Regulation No 1/2003 now expressly states that the parties concerned are entitled to have access to the Commission's file, subject to the legitimate interests of undertakings in the protection of their business secrets. The right of access is granted to the parties to whom a statement of objections has been addressed.[185] Article 27(2) adds to legal certainly and provides for a general right of access to the file in proceedings for breach of Articles 81 and 82 coterminous to that provided for in the Merger Regulation. The case still remains however that failure to disclose a document will not lead to the annulment of the Commission's decision unless the applicant is in a position to show that this prevented it from effectively exercising its rights of defence.

The right of access to the file provided for in Article 27 is subject to restrictions. It operates without prejudice to the protection of business interests of other undertakings. Also, it does not extend to to confidential information and internal documents of the Commission or the competition authorities of the Member States. In particular, it does not extend to correspondence between the Commission and the competition authorities of the Member States, or between the latter, including documents drawn up pursuant to Article 11, which provides for the cooperation between the Commission and the national authorities, and Article 14, which refers to consultation of the Advisory Committee on Restrictive Practices and Dominant Positions.[186] These limitations however do not prevent the Commission from disclosing and using information necessary to prove an infringement.

8.8.3. Complainants

Complainants play an important role in the enforcement of competition law. Eligible to launch complaints are the Member States and natural and legal persons who can show a legitimate interest.[187] Complainants do not enjoy, strictly speaking, rights of defence but 'merely a right to defend their legitimate interests'.[188] Even in relation to complainants however the case law traditionally recognized more extensive process rights than those provided by written law.[189]

---

[184] OJ 1997, C 23/3. Note now the new version: *op. cit.*, n. 119.

[185] Reg. No 773/2004, Article 15(1).

[186] Regulation 1/2003, Article 27(2) and Regulation No 773/2004, Article 15.

[187] Regulation 1/2003, Article 7(2).

[188] *BPB Industries, op. cit.*, at 888 *per* Léger AG, and *BAT and Reynolds, op. cit.*, n. 116 above, para 20. In that case, the Court stated: 'the procedural rights of the complainants are not as far-reaching as the right to a fair hearing of the companies which are the object of the Commission's investigation. In any event, the limits of such rights are reached where they begin to interfere with those companies' right to a fair hearing.' For a detailed account, see C.S. Kerse, 'The Complainant in Competition Cases: A Progress Report' (1997) 34 CML Rev 213; B. Vesterdof, 'Complaints concerning infringements of competition law within the context of European Community Law' (1994) 31 CML Rev 77.

[189] The rights of complainants were governed by Regulation No. 99/33 which is now replaced by Regulation No 773/2004, *op. cit.*

Regulation No 773/2004 provides for the right of the complainants to take part in the proceedings and certain process rights where complaints are rejected. Where the Commission issues a statement of objections relating to a matter in respect of which it has received a complaint, it must provide the complainant with a copy of the non-confidential version of the statement of objections and set a time limit within which the complainant may submit its views in writing. The Commission may, where appropriate, afford complainants the opportunity of expressing their views at the oral hearing of the parties.[190]

Article 7 states that, where the Commission considers that on the information in its possession there are insufficient grounds for acting on a complaint, it must inform the complainant of its reasons and set a time limit within which the complainant may submit its views in writing.[191] The Commission is required to take into account the written submissions made. If it considers that they do not lead to a different assessment, it must reject the complaint by decision. The Commission however is not required to take account of submissions made after the expiry of the time limit.[192] The complainant may have access to the documents on which the Commission based its decision to reject the complaint, subject to the protection of business secrets and other confidential information belonging to other parties.[193]

In *Automec II*,[194] decided in 1992, the CFI held that although the Commission is not required to investigate alleged anti-competitive conduct following the submission of a complaint, it is under an obligation to examine with due care the factual and legal points raised by the complainant and, in case it decides to reject the complaint, provide a fully reasoned final decision. This judgment remains unaffected by Regulation No. 773/2004. *Automec II* is important because the CFI upheld the Commission's power to engage in priority setting on the basis of its perception of the Community interest but imposed extensive procedural requirements to counterbalance the recognition of broad discretion.[195]

All in all, the process rights established in favour of complainants are extensive but may be said to derive less from the right to a hearing and more from the general principles of legality and good administration.[196]

---

[190] Article 6.

[191] Article 7(1). This provision corresponds to Article 6 of Reg. No 99/33. In relation to that provision, the Court had held in Case C-282/95 P *Guérin Automobiles v Commission* [1997] ECR I-1503 that the notification to the complainant amounted to a definition of position for the purposes of Article 232 EC but was not a final act subject to challenge under Article 230 EC. This is also correct under Article 7(1) of the new Regulation.

[192] Regulation No 773/2004, Articles 7(1) and (2).   [193] *Ibid.*, Article 8.

[194] Case T-24/90 *Automec v Commission* [1992] ECR II-2223.

[195] For cases where the Court annulled the Commission decision rejecting a complaint on the ground that it was inadequately reasoned, see Case T-37/92 *BEUC v Commission* [1994] ECR II-285 and Case T-7/92 *Asia Motor France and Others v Commission* [1993] ECR II-669. Cf Case T-114/92 *BEMIM v Commission* [1995] ECR II-147; Case T-5/93 *Tremblay and Others* [1995] ECR II-185. See also for the same principle in State aids: Case T-95/94 *Sytraval and Brink's France v Commission* [1995] ECR II-2651, para 78.

[196] See the cases referred to in the previous footnote and *Guérin Automobiles v Commission, op. cit.*, para 37.

8.9. Anti-dumping proceedings

Regulation No 384/96[197] expressly provides for the rights of defence of interested parties. Anti-dumping proceedings are initiated at the behest of a complainant or, in special circumstances, by the Commission itself, through the publication of a notice in the Official Journal. Article 6(5) states that interested parties who have made themselves known must be heard provided that the following conditions are met: (a) they must make a written request to that effect within the period specified in the notice; (b) they must show that they are an interested party likely to be affected by the result of the proceedings, and that there are particular reasons why they should be heard. It has been noted that there are two major differences between the right to a hearing in anti-dumping proceedings and in competition proceedings.[198] Unlike Regulation 773/2004 and its predecessors, Regulation No 384/96 does not require the Commission to invite complainants to submit further comments where it intends to dismiss the complaint. Also, the oral hearing acquires more importance in anti-dumping proceedings.[199] A third difference which may be added is that the need for confidentiality is increased in anti-dumping proceedings because of their often politically sensitive nature and the involvement of governments of third states.[200]

Article 6(7) of Regulation No 384/96[201] provides that interested parties[202] may, upon written request, inspect all information made available to any party in the investigation, as distinct from internal documents prepared by the authorities of the Community or the Member States, which is relevant to the presentation of their cases provided that it is not confidential and that it is used in the investigation. In *Al-Jubail Fertilizer* v *Council*[203] it was held that the provisions of the basic regulation[204] must be interpreted in the light of the right to a hearing as a fundamental right of general application. According to the judgment, the right must be respected in anti-dumping proceedings despite the fact that anti-dumping

---

[197] Council Regulation No 384/96 on protection against dumped imports from countries not members of the European Community, OJ 1996 L 56, p.1 as amended.

[198] Lenaerts, in FIDE, *op. cit.*, at 517. See further O. Due, 'Le respect des droits de la défense dans le droit administratif communautaire' (1987) CDE 383 at 387.

[199] To this effect, Article 6(6) provides for an adversarial procedure, where importers, exporters, representatives of the government of the exporting country and complainants are given the opportunity to meet each other so that the opposing views may be presented.

[200] See further H.C. von Heydebrand, und der Lasa, 'Confidential Information in Anti-dumping Proceedings before United States Courts and the European Court' (1983) ELR 331.

[201] Council Regulation No 384/96 on protection against dumped imports from countries not members of the European Community (OJ 1996, L 65/1); see consolidated version of 8.11.2002 and last amended by Regulation No 461/2004, OJ 2004 L77/12.

[202] This includes the complainants, importers and exporters and their representative associations, users and consumer organizations which have made themselves known, as well as the representatives of the exporting country. See Article 6(7).

[203] *Op. cit.*, n. 102 above. For recent confirmation: *Industrie des Poudres Sphériques*, *op. cit.*, n. 182 above; Case T-35/01 *Shanghai Teraoka Electronic Co Ltd v Council*, judgment of 28 October 2004. (In both these cases the plea based on breach of the rights of defence was dismissed.)

[204] The basic regulation applicable at the time was Regulation No 2176/84, OJ L 1984 L 201, p. 1.

measures are imposed by means of general regulations rather than individual decisions. The main consideration which led the Court to take that view was that anti-dumping regulations, although of general scope, affect directly and individually the undertakings concerned and entail adverse consequences for them. In *Al Jubail* the Commission had relied, *inter alia*, on internal documents drawn up by its officials, the contents of which had not been placed at the disposal of the undertakings against which the duty was imposed. It was held that those documents could not be accorded any probative force. In reaching that conclusion, the Court was concerned to ensure that Community law did not provide a lesser standard of procedural protection than that which was recognized by national laws.[205] The Court held that the institutions should seek with all due diligence,[206]

to provide the undertakings concerned, as far as is compatible with the obligation not to disclose business secrets, with information relevant to the defence of their interests, choosing, if necessary on their own initiative, the appropriate means of providing such information. In any event, the undertakings concerned should have been placed in a position during the administrative procedure in which they could effectively make known their views on the correctness and relevance of the facts and circumstances alleged and on the evidence presented by the Commission in support of its allegation concerning the existence of dumping and the resultant injury.

The importance of *Al Jubail* lies in that the Court continued the trend towards a broad application of the right to a hearing, developed first in relation to competition proceedings, despite the differences between the latter and anti-dumping investigations. Following the judgment in *Al Jubail* it became increasingly common for undertakings on which anti-dumping duties were imposed to challenge the legality of the duty on grounds of breach of the rights of defence. In the overwhelming majority of those cases the challenge has proved unsuccessful.[207]

Under the case law, the undertakings concerned must be informed during the anti-dumping proceedings of the principal facts and considerations on which the Community authorities based their decision. Not all aspects of the decision-making process are subject to the right to a hearing. Thus, it is within the discretion of the Council to choose any one of the methods provided for by the Community rules for the purposes of calculating the export price and therefore the Council is under no obligation to give to the undertaking concerned the opportunity to present its observations in advance.[208] Also the CFI has held that failure to communicate information and considerations which did not form part of the statement

---

[205] See para 16 and *per* Darmon AG at p. 3224.   [206] *Op. cit.*, para 17.

[207] See e.g. Case C-69/89 *Nakajima v Council* [1991] ECR I-2069; Case T-155/94 *Climax Paper Converters v Council* [1996] ECR II-873; Cf Case C-216/91 *Rima* [1993] ECR I-6303 where a Council regulation imposing a definitive anti-dumping duty was annulled on procedural grounds.

[208] Case C-178/87 *Minolta v Council* [1992] ECR I-1577; *Al Jubail, op. cit.*, para 24.

of reasons of the contested decision, and which is simply confirmatory in character, does not amount to a breach of the right to a hearing.[209]

Article 6(5) is supplemented by Article 20. This states that the complainants, importers and exporters and their representative associations, and representatives of the exporting country may request disclosure of the details underlying the essential facts and considerations on the basis of which provisional measures have been imposed. Under Article 20(2) those parties also have the right to request final disclosure of the essential facts and considerations on the basis of which it is intended to recommend the imposition of definitive duties. In *Ajinomoto Co Inc and the NutraSweet Company v Council*[210] the CFI held that the extent to which the Commission must disclose information to the undertakings subject to investigation may depend on the relative economic strength of those undertakings in the market and the informational advantage that such strength might give them. Where the undertakings under investigation are the principal actors in the field and as a result possess a thorough knowledge of the market, their right to receive information from the Commission is conditioned by the obligation on the latter not to reveal information which might enable the undertakings to work out confidential data information regarding the complainant. The CFI also held that failure to inform exporters of the essential facts and considerations on the basis of which it is intended to impose provisional duties does not in itself vitiate the regulation imposing definitive duties. This is because the latter is distinct from the regulation imposing provisional duties and its validity must be assessed on the basis of the rules applying at the time of its adoption. If in the course of the procedure leading to the adoption of a regulation imposing a definitive duty, the institutions take steps to remedy a defect vitiating the adoption of the corresponding regulation imposing a provisional duty, the illegality of the latter does not render the former illegal.

8.10. Staff cases

As already stated, staff cases was the first area where the Court applied the rights of defence. In *Alvis v Council*[211] the Court held that, although the defendant institution had disregarded its obligation to allow the applicant to submit his defence before being dismissed, given the gravity of the irregularities committed by the applicant, breach of that obligation was not sufficient to annul the decision of dismissal. In *Moli* the Court annulled the refusal of the Commission to engage a candidate as an official on account of physical unfitness, on the ground that the Commission had not given him the opportunity to express his views despite the fact that it had promised

---

[209] Case T-121/95 *European Fertiliser Manufacturers Association (EFMA) v Council* [1997] ECR II-2391.
[210] Joined Cases T-159 and T-160/94 [1997] ECR II-2461. See further Joined Cases T-33 and T-34/98 *Petrotub SA v Council*, [1999] ECR II-3837.
[211] *Op. cit.* n. 6 above. See also Case 35/67 *van Eick v Commission* [1968] ECR 329.

to do so.[212] The right to be heard acquires particular importance in disciplinary proceedings. It requires the appointing authority to inform the official concerned of the complaints against him and grant him a reasonable time to prepare his defence.[213] In *Almini*,[214] the applicant applied for the annulment of the Commission's decision to retire him under Article 50 of the Staff Regulations, which provides for the retirement of certain categories of officials in the interests of the service. The Court held that Article 50 gives to the appointing authority wide discretionary powers, the exercise of which requires that the official concerned must have the opportunity of effectively defending his interests. The Court annulled the contested decision on the ground that the Commission had only given four days to the applicant to make his views known. Also, the reasons which were stated in the contested decision as justifying his retirement were different from those stated in the minutes of the meeting of the Commission where that decision was taken. The applicant therefore had not been given the opportunity to comment on the factors which influenced the Commission in taking the contested decision.

The rights of defence include the right of an official to have access to his personal file. Article 26 of the Staff Regulations provides that the personal file of an official must contain all documents relating to his administrative status and his performance and safeguards the official's right to have access to the file. The purpose of this provision is to ensure that decisions taken by the appointing authority concerning the administrative status and career of the official are not based on matters concerning his conduct which are not included in his personal file and have not been communicated to him.[215] In *Ojha v Commission*[216] the Court of Justice held, reversing the decision of the CFI, that where an official is redeployed in the interests of the service, redeployment may not take place on the basis of documents which concern the official's conduct in the service and which are not communicated to him. That would be contrary to Article 26 because, although redeployment is not a disciplinary offence, it affects the official's administrative status and may affect his future career.

8.11. The relationship between the right to a hearing and other procedural rights

In *Technische Universität München*[217] the Court saw the right to a hearing as part of a wider network of process rights which ensue from the principle of good administration and are essential to ensuring the protection of the individual. Those

---

[212] Case 121/76 *Moli v Commission* [1977] ECR 1971. See also *Case 2/87 Biedermann v Court of Auditors* [1988] ECR 143; Case T-154/89 *Vidrányi v Commission* [1990] ECR II-445.; *van Eick, op. cit.*   [213] Case 319/85 *Misset v Council* [1988] ECR 1861.
[214] Case 19/70 *Almini v Commission* [1971] ECR 623.
[215] For previous case law, see Case 233/85 *Bonino v Commission* [1987] ECR 739; Case 140/86 *Strack v Commission* [1987] ECR 3939.   [216] Case C-294/95 P [1996] ECR II-5863.
[217] *Op. cit.*, n. 67 above.

process rights encompass the duty of the competent institution to examine carefully and impartially all the relevant aspects of the individual case, the right of the person concerned to make his views known, and the right to a reasoned decision.[218] In the circumstances of the case, it found that all the three guarantees had been infringed. The judgment is of particular interest because the Court recognized more extensive procedural requirements than had been accepted in previous cases concerning Commission decisions on the duty-free importation of scientific apparatus.[219]

The case arose as a result of a reference by the Federal Finance Court of Germany and brought to the fore a clash of conflicting philosophies of administrative law.[220] The traditional stance of the Court of Justice had been that, in matters involving technical evaluations, the Community decision-making body enjoyed wide discretionary powers. Judicial review was limited to ascertaining whether there is manifest error of fact or law or whether there is misuse of power.[221] The starting point of German law is the opposite. It adheres to the principle of limited, as opposed to discretionary, administrative power which, in general, accepts that the administration has no discretion unless the measure under which it acts expressly provides so. Unless the enabling statute vests the administration with discretion, there is deemed to be only one correct solution to the issue involved, which the decision maker is bound to follow. The principle seeks to control the discretion of the executive and is said to derive from the right of effective judicial review guaranteed by the Basic law.[222] In *Universität München*, the strengthening of process rights was the Court's response to calls by the referring German court for a thorough substantive review of the Commission's decision-making powers. It will be remembered that the Commission adopted a decision refusing the duty-free importation of an instrument on the ground that equivalent scientific apparatus was available in the Community. The Federal Finance Court found itself in a position of divided loyalties. On the one hand, German doctrine required the reviewing court to undertake full review of the substantive merits of the Commission's decision. On the other hand, the previous case law of the Court of Justice required that the review of the Commission's discretion should be limited to determining whether there is manifest error, an approach foreign to German culture. In the words of the referring court, 'The more difficult the technical questions to be decided the more immune from challenge the Commission's decision would be. It is questionable whether such a restriction of the legal protection of Community citizens is compatible with the constitutional principle guaranteeing effective legal protection which is recognized by Community law'.[223] The response of the Court of Justice was to accommodate the

---

[218] *Ibid.*, para 14.   [219] See 8.3 above.

[220] The point is aptly illustrated by G. Nolte, 'General Principles of German and European Administrative Law—A comparison in Historical Perspective' (1994) 57 MLR 191.

[221] See e.g. *Universität Stuttgart, op. cit.*, n. 69 above, para 20.

[222] See Article 19(4) Grundgesetz and (1983) 64 BVerfGE 261, 179. See further Nolte, *op. cit.*, 196, 200.   [223] *Universität München, op. cit.*, at 5483.

concerns of the Finance Court by entrenching process rights rather than increasing the degree of substantive scrutiny. This is in a way ironic since under the influence of German law the Court increased procedural safeguards, to which German law traditionally attaches less weight. *Universität München* illustrates not only the role of the Court as the melting pot of national legal cultures but also the relative distinction in functional terms between process and substantive rights.[224] The case law now seems to accept that procedural and substantive scrutiny are in an inverse relationship. Where the Court exercises only marginal review on substantive grounds because the decision-making process involves complex technical evaluations and the Community institutions enjoy broad discretion, the need to ensure respect of process rights becomes all the more important.[225]

The question which arises in this context is what is the relationship between the right to a hearing and other procedural requirements? Is it for example possible to say that consultation in advance with representative professional organizations or pressure groups to which the person affected by the decision belongs alleviates the need to provide a right to a hearing? The answer must be in the negative since the two requirements essentially pursue different objectives. Consultation ensures indirect participation in the policy-making process whereas the right to a hearing goes beyond that: it is an individual right which is seen as an integral part of the adjudication process. The fact that Community legislation requires the Commission to consult certain bodies before taking a decision does not mean that the right to a hearing need not be observed. Article 6(1) of Regulation No 2950/83 concerning the administration of the European Social Fund requires the Commission to consult the Member State concerned before it adopts a decision to suspend, reduce, or withdraw financial assistance which has been granted from the Fund. In *Lisrestal* the Court held that the requirement of consultation 'does not justify the conclusion that a principle of Community law as fundamental as that which guarantees every person the right to be heard before the adoption of a decision capable of adversely affecting him does not apply'.[226]

An issue of particular interest is how the right to a hearing interrelates with the requirement to give reasons. In general, a breach of the requirement of reasoning exists where a decision does not contain an adequate statement of the reasons on which it is based. A breach of the right to be heard occurs where the party is denied the opportunity to express its views on the facts and considerations taken into account by the authority. The requirement of reasoning is broader in its scope of application since, under Article 253 of the Treaty, it applies not only to administrative acts but also to legislative measures. It is also perceived as serving not only the interests of the persons affected but also the public interest in the administration of justice. According to standard case law, one of the objectives of the requirement to give reasons is to enable

---

[224] See further Nolte, *op. cit.*, 207–8.
[225] *Universität München, op. cit.*, para 14; Case T-44/90 *La Cinq v Commission* [1992] ECR II-1, para 86; *Asia Motor France, op. cit.*, n. 197 above.   [226] *Lisrestal, op. cit.*, n. 56 above, para 30.

the Court to exercise its power of review.[227] This explains why the Court is more willing to examine of its own motion the adequacy of reasoning of Community acts.[228]

The two requirements are closely interconnected but distinct and an administrative procedure may be in breach of one but not the other.[229] In *Bonino* the Court found that the contested decision of the Commission was adequately reasoned but annulled it for breach of the right to a hearing.[230] In *Technische Universität München*, Jacobs AG reached the converse conclusion. In his view, the applicant university did not have the right to a hearing in relation to a decision refusing the duty-free importation of scientific apparatus but found that the decision was vitiated by defective reasoning. Notably the Advocate General took the view that the inadequacy of reasoning might have been compensated if the information on the basis of which the Commission reached its decision had been communicated to the applicant. If that happened, one of the essential functions of the requirement of reasoning would have been met, since the university would have been able to ascertain whether the decision was well founded or whether it was vitiated by an error that would allow its legality to be challenged.[231] In some cases the Court has excused paucity of reasons on the ground that the person affected by the decision had the opportunity to present his arguments and a form of dialogue took place between the Commission and the party, or at least the party concerned was given that opportunity.[232]

Insofar as a general conclusion can be drawn from the cases, the statement of reasons need not rebut all objections raised by the parties concerned in the hearing.[233] In other words, there is no obligation on the part of the Community decision maker

---

[227] Its other objectives being to give an opportunity to the parties involved of defending their rights, and to third persons of ascertaining the circumstances in which the institution concerned applied the Treaty: see e.g. Case 24/62 *Germany v Commission* [1963] ECR 63 at p. 69; Case 294/81 *Control Data v Commission* [1983] ECR 911, para 14; Joined Cases T-79/89 etc. *BASF AG and Others v Commission* [1992] ECR II-315, para 66.

[228] Case 18/57 *Nold v High Authority* [1959] ECR 41; Case 185/85 *Usinor v Commission* [1986] ECR 2079, para 19; Case C-166/95 P *Commission v Daffix* [1997] ECR I-983, para 24; *Sytraval and Brink's France v Commission*, op. cit., n. 197 above, para 75 . The Community judicature however is not under a duty to raise the issue on its own motion in all cases and, depending on the circumstances, it may reject as inadmissible a plea that the contested act is insufficiently reasoned if it is not submitted in time: Case T-106/95 *Fédération Française des Sociétés d'Assurances (FFSA) and Others v Commission* [1997] ECR II-229, para 62.

[229] In a number of cases, Community acts have been found to breach both requirements. See e.g. *Lisrestal*, op. cit. *Technische Universität München*, op. cit.

[230] *Bonino v Commission*, op. cit. The Court held that the Commission is not required to give reasons for refusing to appoint an official to a new post but annulled the procedure because the rights of defence of the unsuccessful candidate had been violated. See also *Moli v Commission*, op. cit.

[231] *Technische Universität München*, op. cit., p. 5493. See also Case C-216/91 *Rima Eletrometalurgia v Council* [1993] ECR I-6303, esp at 6345 *per* Lenz AG.

[232] Case 238/86 *Netherlands v Commission* [1988] ECR 1191; Case 240/84 *NTN Toyo Bearing Co Ltd v Council* [1987] ECR 1809.

[233] See in this context the excellent analysis of M. Shapiro, 'The Giving Reasons Requirement', in *The University of Chicago Legal Forum: Europe and America in 1992 and Beyond: Common Problems ... Common Solutions?* (University of Chicago Press, 1992), 179.

to engage in a 'dialogue' with interested parties.[234] According to consistent case law, under Article 253 the Commission is required to mention the factual and legal elements which provide the legal basis of the decision concerned and the considerations which have led it to adopt its decision, but 'it is not required to discuss all the issues of fact and law raised by every party during the administrative process'.[235] Although this still remains in general the position in law, recent case law of the CFI suggests a shift in emphasis. In *Sytraval and Brink's France v Commission*[236] the CFI accepted that in certain circumstances the Commission's duty to state reasons may require an exchange of views and arguments with the complainant, since in order to justify to the requisite legal standard its assessment of the nature of a measure characterized by the complainant as State aid, the Commission must ascertain what view the complainant takes of the information gathered by it in the course of the enquiry.

8.12. The principle of good administration

As stated above, the EU Charter of Fundamental Rights views the right to a hearing as an integral part of the principle of good administration. It may thus be appropriate at this juncture to examine the components of this principle.

Although references to the requirements of good administration can be found in earlier cases,[237] the principle of 'good'[238] or 'sound'[239] or 'proper'[240] administration was developed in the case law mainly in the 1990s.[241] Its elevation to a general principle coincides with the growth and increasing diversity of Community administrative action which led the Community courts to elaborate standards of good governance and accountability. Reliance on the principle is dictated, at least partly, by the fact that, in contrast to common law statutes, Community legislation does not usually provide for a detailed account of statutory duties incumbent on the administration. Its status as a general principle

---

[234] This is clearly the case in relation to the requirement of consultation. The statement of reasons of a legislative measure must refer to any opinions which must be obtained but the Treaty does not require that it must refer, and *a fortiori* that it must try to refute, the divergent opinions expressed by the consultative bodies: Case 4/54 *ISA v High Authority* [1954–56] ECR 91, at 100; C-62/88 *Greece v Council* [1990] ECR I-1527, para 29.

[235] Case T-114/92 *BEMIM v Commission* [1995] ECR II-147, para 41; Joined Cases 240, 242, 261, 262. 268, 269/82 *Stichting Sigarettenindustrie v Commission* [1985] ECR 3831 at 3882; Case 42/84 *Remia and Nutricia v Commission* [1985] ECR 2545.   [236] *Op. cit.*, n. 197 above.

[237] See e.g. Case 61/76 *Geist v Commission* [1977] ECR 1419, para 44; Case 270/82 *Estel v Commission* [1984] ECR I-1195, para 15.

[238] *Guérin Automobiles, op. cit.*, n. 193 above, para 37; Case T-144/02 *Eagle v Commission*, judgment of 5 October 2004; Case T-193/04 R *Tillack v Commission*, Order of 15 October 2004, para 60.

[239] *New Europe Consulting, op. cit.*, n. 65 above, para 41; Case T-73/95 *Oliveira v Commission* [1997] ECR II-381, para 32.

[240] Case T-119/02 *Royal Philips Electronics NV v Commission*, judgment of 3 April 2003.

[241] See e.g. T-167/94 *Nölle* [1994] ECR II-2589; *Lisrestal, op. cit.*; Case C-255/99 P *Burban* [1992] ECR I-2253.

of law, however, is not clear cut. It transcends specific requirements and applies to all aspects of Community action. But it binds the Community administration and not the legislature and, in that sense, it does not have constitutional status. Also, in contrast to other general principles, the principle of good administration was not built by reference to the legal systems of the Member States. More importantly, its function in judicial methodology seems to be mainly, although not exclusively, subsidiary. It incorporates diverse requirements but only rarely provides the pillar of the court's reasoning or serves as an independent ground for review. Its value lies much more in setting agency standards, breach of which may lead to liability in damages, than in serving as a ground for review of administrative action.

Express reference to the right to good administration is made in Article 41 of the EU Charter on Fundamental Rights.[242] Its inclusion in the Charter 'meets the strong and legitimate contemporary demand for transparency and impartiality in the operation of the Community administration',[243] and is designed to enshrine a right which already exists but has not yet been explicitly protected.[244]

Article 41(1) states that 'Every person has the right to have his or her affairs handled impartially, fairly and within a reasonable time by the institutions and bodies of the Union'. Under Article 41(2), this includes:

- the right of every person to be heard, before any individual measure which would affect him or her adversely is taken;
- the right of every person to have access to his or her file, while respecting the legitimate interests of confidentiality and of professional and business secrecy;
- the obligation of the administration to give reasons for its decisions.

Article 41(3) states that every person has the right to have the Union make good any damage caused by its institutions or by its servants in the performance of their duties, in accordance with the general principles common to the laws of the Member States. This highlights the close affinity between good administration and liability in damages. Finally, under Article 41(4), good administration includes the citizen's right to communicate with the institutions in the language of his/her preference.

It becomes obvious from Articles 41(1) and (2) that the duty of good administration is understood to encompass some self-standing rights (i.e. right to a hearing and obligation to give reasons) and, in addition, a matrix of ancillary, primarily procedural, requirements laid down in the case law. Article 41 intends to reflect the case law and by no means lessen the protection offered by it to the citizen.[245] In some respects, it goes further. The express reference to the right of

---

[242] This corresponds to Article II-101 of the EU Constitution.

[243] See Commission Communication on the Legal Nature of the Charter of Fundamental Rights of the European Union, COM(2000) 644, Brussels, 11 October 2000, p. 2.

[244] See Commission Communication on the Charter of Fundamental Rights of the European Union, COM(2000) 559, Brussels, 13 September 2000, para 9.

[245] This is clear from the Commission Communications referred to above and also from the Praesidium commentary on the articles of the Charter. See now: Updated Explanations Relating

access to one's personal file is a welcome development.It could be interpreted to include a citizen's right to have access to his or her file even in cases where this is not required by a strict application of the right to be heard, thus providing a wider political right akin to and supplementing the right of access to personal data which is guaranteed by Article 8 of the Charter.

The right to have one's affairs handled impartially and fairly, as stated in Article 41(1), incorporates first of all the rule that, in taking decisions, the Community administration must be unbiased and avoid conflict of interests (*nemo judex in causa sua*). It incorporates, in addition, the requirement that, in taking decisions, the Community administration must act with due diligence. This derives from the case law and it is, perhaps, somewhat surprising that it is not expressly mentioned in Article 41. It includes the duty to make decisions on the basis of all information which might have a bearing on the interests of those affected;[246] the duty to take decisions based on accurate data and following a thorough investigation of the file;[247] the duty to rectify a previous error without undue delay;[248] the duty to act fairly *vis-à-vis* the citizen; and the duty not to mislead.[249] It also includes the duty to act within a reasonable time. The Commission must act within a reasonable time in adopting decisions following administrative proceedings relating, in particular, to competition policy or State aids. The duty however derives from the principle of legal certainty[250] and applies more widely to any procedure which culminates in a decision capable of affecting the interests of the individual.[251] Whether or not the duration of an administrative procedure is reasonable must be determined in relation to the particular circumstances of each case, and especially its context, the various procedural stages to be followed by the Commission, the complexity of the case and its importance for the various parties involved.[252]

Good administration is used by the Community judiciary mainly in a subsidiary and supportive role.[253] Depending on the circumstances, breach of the principle

to the text of the Charter of Fundamental Rights issued by the Praesidium of the Constitutional Convention, CONV 828/1/03, Brussels, 18 July 2003.

[246] *Oliveira v Commission, op. cit.*, para 32; *New Europe Consulting, op. cit.*, para 41; Case T-11/03 *Afari*, judgment of 16 March 2004; Case T-180/01 *Euroagri*, judgment of 28 January 2004.

[247] Case T-139/01 *Comafrica v Commission*, judgment of 2 March 2005.

[248] Case T-514/93 *Cobrecaf and Others v Commission* [1995] ECR II-621, para 70.

[249] *Tillack; op. cit.*, n. 240 above.

[250] See *Eagle, op. cit.*; Case 52/69 *Geigy v Commission* [1972] ECR 787, paras 20–21.

[251] See e.g. Case 120/73 *Lorenz* [1973] ECR 1471, para 4, Case 223/85 *RSV v Commission* [1987] ECR 4617, paras 12–17 (State aids); *Guérin Automobiles, op. cit.*, paras 37–38 (rejection of competition complaint).

[252] Case T-190/00 *Regione Siciliana*, judgment of 27 November 2003; *SCK and FNK, op. cit.*, para 57.

[253] Note that compliance with the principle of good administration is ensured not only by the CFI but also by the Ombudsman: see Article 195 EC and Article 43 of the Charter. For the interaction between the Ombudsman and judicial remedies, see Case C-234/02 P *European Ombudsman v Lamberts*, judgment of 23 March 2004. In *Tillack v Commission*, para 60, it was held that the mere fact that the Ombudsman has found an instance of maladministration does not necessarily mean that the principle of good administration as interpreted by the Community judicature has been infringed.

may lead to a variety of remedies. It may, for example, lead to a reduction of a penalty,[254] or a decision that the Commission must bear the costs of the proceedings where, although the Commission's actions do not justify the payment of damages or annulment, they betray lack of 'good administrative practice'.[255] Successful reliance on the principle is rare and, in general, its value lies more as an obligation breach of which may lead to liability in damages than as a ground of review. Where the Community authorities breach a component of the principle which imposes a self-standing obligation, such as the right to a hearing or the duty to state reasons, such a breach may lead to annulment of the contested decision. But in the absence of such a breach, the principle is an unreliable ground for review.

This is illustrated by *max.mobil*[256] where the CFI used the principle to its full potential but was reversed by the ECJ. It is submitted that the reasoning of the CFI is in fact more persuasive. An Austrian telecom company sought annulment of a letter sent by the Commission rejecting its complaint that Austria had infringed Articles 82 and 86(1) EC by granting special privileges to a State company. In its defence, the Commission argued that, in contrast to infringements of competition and State aid rules where specific provisions grant procedural rights to individuals, Article 86(3) EC does not grant complainants access to the administrative procedure that may be undertaken by the Commission against a Member State for a suspected infringement of Article 86. In the context of Article 86(3), the Commission enjoys wide discretion and may freely decide what action to take without having regard to complainants. The Commission also argued that the applicant lacked individual concern.

The CFI started from the proposition that the diligent and impartial treatment of a complaint is associated with the right to sound administration which is one of the general principles deriving from the rule of law and common to the constitutional traditions of the Member States. It referred expressly to Article 41(1) of the Charter and established a general duty on the part of the Commission to undertake a diligent and impartial treatment of a complaint even in the absence of specific provisions to this effect giving right to complainants. It based this duty on the following arguments. First, such a duty is imposed on the Commission by the case law in the context of Articles 81 and 82 and in the context of State aids. Article 86(3) always applies in conjunction with other provisions of the Treaty, including those concerning competition which expressly grant procedural rights to complainants. The applicant was therefore in a comparable situation to that referred to in Article 3 of Regulation 17.[257] Second, the duty to undertake a diligent and impartial examination of the complaint derived from the general duty of supervision incumbent upon the Commission *vis-à-vis* Member States. This duty was

---

[254] *Estel*, n. 239 above, (although the ECJ did not expressly refer to the general principle of good administration, the case and resulting outcome may be seen as illustrations of it).

[255] Case 125/80 *Arning v Commission* [1981] ECR 2539, para 20.

[256] Case T-54/99 *max.mobil Telekommunikation Service GmbH v Commission*, [2002] ECR II-313.   [257] See now Article 7(2) of Regulation No 1/2003, above, n. 189.

imposed by Article 85(1) EC which is a specific illustration of Article 211 EC. The fulfilment of the Commission's obligation to undertake a diligent and impartial examination is amenable to judicial review. Given however the wide discretion that the Commission enjoys under Article 86(3), the CFI's review is limited to checking that the Commission's action is sufficiently reasoned, that the facts relied upon are accurate and that the *prima facie* assessment of the facts is not vitiated by any illegality. The CFI proceeded to find that, although neither the Treaty nor secondary law provides expressly for the Commission to take a decision in those circumstances, this does not mean that such a decision rejecting a complaint does not exist. Even if it were supposed that the Commission's refusal to take action should not be classified as a decision rejecting a complaint but as a measure finding that a national measure is not incompatible with the Treaty whose real addressee is a Member State, the applicant would have direct and individual concern to challenge it.

On appeal, the ECJ reversed the judgment of the CFI.[258] It held that, under the wording and scheme of Article 86(3), the Commission is not obliged to bring proceedings within the terms of those provisions, as individuals may not require the Commission to take a specific position. The fact that max.mobil had a direct and individual interest in annulling the Commission's refusal to act on its complaint did not confer on it a right to challenge that decision. According to the ECJ, the Commission's letter could not be regarded as producing binding legal effects and it was therefore not a measure amenable to judicial review. Nor could max.mobil claim a right to bring an action pursuant to Regulation No 17 since the latter was not applicable to Article 86(3) EC. The Court did not consider this interpretation to be at variance with the principle of sound administration or with any other general principle of Community law since no such principle required that an undertaking must be recognized as having standing before the Community judicature to challenge a refusal by the Commission to bring proceedings against a Member State on the basis of Article 90(3) EC.

One of the rare cases in which the CFI upheld a claim in damages on grounds of breach of good administration is *New Europe Consulting and Brown v Commission*.[259] The applicant company had carried out a number of training contracts in central and eastern Europe in the context of the PHARE financing programme. Following complaints by government officials in Hungary, the Commission circulated a fax to officials in several States blacklisting the applicant from future projects. When the fax came to its attention some months after it was issued, the applicant company made representations, following which the Commission issued a rectifying fax lifting objections to its participation in future projects. The company brought an action in damages arguing that the Commission had acted with lack

---

[258] Case C-141/02 P *Commission v T-Mobile Austria GmbH*, judgment of 22 February 2005, paras 69–71.

[259] *Op. cit.*, n. 65 above. For an example of an unsuccessful claim in the field of the common agricultural policy, see *Comafrica*, *op. cit.*, n. 249 above.

of care and contrary to the principle of proportionality. The CFI addressed the claim in terms of breach of good administration. It held that the Commission had breached the principle by failing to carry out an inquiry into the alleged irregularities committed by the company. The Commission should have sent a communication of provisional information and then opened an inquiry asking the applicant to submit its observations. As a result, the CFI found a manifest lack of care and granted damages for harm to the reputation of the company and its director.

In other cases however the CFI has been reluctant to use good administration as an independent ground for judicial review. In *Internationaler Hilfsfonds eV v Commission*,[260] it held that, where the Commission receives an application for co-financing of activities by an NGO, it is under an obligation to examine whether the applicant is eligible for co-financing under the conditions governing eligibility which have been laid down by the Commission itself. This obligation arises even where a new application is submitted by an organization which on a previous occasion was found to be ineligible, if that organization submits new evidence to prove its eligibility. On the facts of the case, the CFI annulled the Commission's decisions for breach of its obligation to re-examine the eligibility of the applicant. It did not however base the Commission's obligation on the principle of good administration although it was expressly invited to do so by the applicant. In fact, the judgment is unclear as to the legal basis of the Commission's obligations.

By way of conclusion, it may be stated that, although the principle of good administration has not made an impact as an independent ground for judicial review, it does fulfil a useful function. Its remedial value lies mainly in that in some cases it may lead to the obligation to pay damages or equitable compensation. More widely, it emphasizes the inter-relationship of procedural and substantive duties and, by articulating standards of good governance, it fills the gaps of statutory law.

8.13. The right to a hearing before national authorities

It should be accepted that a person may invoke the rights of defence not only against the Community institutions but also against national authorities where they act within the scope of Community law even in the absence of specific provisions to that effect.[261] This view derives from the general pronouncement of the Court that fundamental rights bind the national authorities where they act within the scope of Community law. In some cases, Community legislation guarantees

---

[260] Case T-321/01 *Internationaler Hilfsfonds eV v Commission*, judgment of 18 September 2003.
[261] The issue was raised in Case C-144/95 *Maurin* [1996] ECR I-2909 but was not examined by the Court because the national legislation in issue fell outside the scope of Community law. See above p. 40.

specific procedural rights to the persons concerned.[262] More generally, the case law has derived from the fundamental right to judicial protection, that decisions of national authorities which deny rights guaranteed by Community law must be reasoned and be subject to judicial remedies.[263] So far however the Court has not recognized a general right to a hearing in national administrative proceedings where Community rights are at stake. It is submitted that such a right should be recognized although its precise requirements will depend on the circumstances of the case. In principle, the rights of the individual should not differ depending on whether he or she is dealing with the Community or national authorities. Thus the general approach must be that the principles applicable to the Community administration must apply *mutatis mutandis* to the national administration unless there is a reason which justifies the application of different standards.

The application of the right to a fair hearing as guaranteed by Article 6(1) ECHR in national proceedings was examined in *Steffensen*.[264] The Court was concerned with Directive 89/397 which harmonizes the rules governing official inspection of foodstuffs in the interests of consumer protection. Article 7(1) of the Directive authorizes inspectors to take samples of foodstuffs for the purposes of analysis but states that 'Member States shall take the necessary steps to ensure that those subject to inspection may apply for a second opinion'. Article 12 (1) gives to the persons concerned the right of appeal against measures taken by the competent authorities for the purposes of inspection.

The Court held that Article 7(1) has direct effect and that a foodstuffs manufacturer has a right to a second opinion when the competent authorities claim that his sample products fail to meet the standard required by the national rules. The importance of the judgment lies in the following respects. The ECJ declared that, in addition to complying with the principles of equivalence and effectiveness, national rules of procedure and remedies must comply with fundamental rights as guaranteed by the European Convention. It also illustrates that the ECJ applies a more rigorous standard of scrutiny to rules of evidence than that applied in earlier case law. It held that, although Article 6(1) ECHR does not as a matter of principle exclude evidence obtained irregularly from being admissible, it applies to the proceedings as a whole including the way in which evidence was taken. Thus, Article 6(1) requires that, where the parties are entitled to submit to the court observations on a piece of evidence, they must be afforded a real opportunity to comment effectively on it. The Court left it for the national court to assess whether, in the light of all factual and legal evidence available to it, the admission of evidence in the circumstances of the case, which had not included a second opinion, breached the right to a fair hearing.

---

[262] See e.g. Council Directive 64/221 on the co-ordination of special measures concerning the movement and residence of foreign nationals which are justified on grounds of public policy, public security or public health, OJ English Sp. Ed., 1964, p. 117, Articles 8 and 9. Now replaced by Directive 2004/38, OJ 20004, L 158/77, Articles 30 and 31.

[263] Below, Ch. 9.　　　　　　　　　　[264] Case C-276/01 *Steffensen*, [2003] ECR I-3735.

The case refers to the right to a fair hearing as guaranteed by Article 6(1) ECHR and not the more general rights of defence provided for by Community law. Also, it is based on a specific provision of a Community directive which guaranteed the right to a second opinion in the circumstances. It illustrates however more generally the application of general principles of Community law *vis-à-vis* national authorities.

9

The Principle of Effectiveness

9.1. A decentralized model of justice

The principle of effectiveness[1] underlies a series of developments in the sphere of judicial protection and has been recognized as a general principle of Community law by the Court of Justice.[2] It requires the effective protection of Community rights and, more generally, the effective enforcement of Community law in national courts. Effectiveness differs from the general principles of law examined so far in that it is not based directly on the laws of the Member States but derives from the distinct characteristics of Community law, primacy and direct effect. The

---

[1] Academic contributions include: M. Dougan, *National Remedies Before the European Court of Justice*, (Hart, 2004); T. Tridimas, 'Enforcing Community Rights in National Courts: Some recent Developments', in D. A. O'Keeffe and A. Bavasso, (eds), *Judicial Review in European Union Law: Liber Amicorum in honour of Lord Slynn* (Kluwer, 2000), pp. 465–479; T. Tridimas, 'Judicial Review and the Community Judicature: Towards a New European Constitutionalism?' (2001) 3 Turku Law Journal 119–129; W. van Gerven, 'Of Rights, Remedies, and Procedures', (2000) 37 CML Rev 501; A. Ward, *Judicial Review and the Rights of Private Parties in EC Law* (Oxford University Press, 2000); A. Biondi, 'The European Court of Justice and Certain National Procedural Limitations: Not Such a Tough Relationship', 36 (1999) CML Rev 1271; C. Lewis, *Remedies and the Enforcement of European Community Law*, (Sweet & Maxwell, 1996); C. Kakouris, 'Do the Member States possess judicial procedural autonomy?' (1997) 34 CML Rev 1389; R. Caranta, 'Judicial Protection Against Member States: A New *Jus Commune* Takes Shape', (1997) CML Rev 703; M. Hoskins, 'Tilting the Balance: Supremacy and National Procedural Rules', (1996) 21 ELR 365; E. Szyszczak, 'Making Europe More Relevant To Its Citizens: Effective Judicial Process', (1996) 21 ELR 351; A. Ward, 'Effective Sanctions in EC Law: A Moving Boundary in the Division of Competence', (1995) 1 ELJ 205; C. Himsworth, 'Things Fall Apart: The Harmonization of Community Judicial Procedural Protection Revisited' (1997) 22 ELR 291; M. Ruffert, 'Rights and Remedies in European Community Law: A Comparative View' (1997) 34 CML Rev 307; W. van Gerven, 'Bridging the Gap Between Community and National Laws: Towards a Principle of Homogeneity in the Field of Legal Remedies?' (1995) 32 CML Rev 679; D. Curtin, 'The Decentralised Enforcement of Community Law Rights. Judicial Snakes and Ladders', in D. Curtin and D. O'Keeffe, *Constitutional Adjudication in European Community and National Law* (Butterworths, 1992), pp. 33–49. See further C. Harlow, 'Codification of EC Administrative Procedures? Fitting the Foot to the Shoe or the Shoe to the Foot' (1996) 2 ELJ 3; M. Shapiro, 'Codification of Administrative Law: The US and the Union', (1996) 2 ELJ 26.

[2] See e.g. Joined Cases C-46 and C-48/93 *Brasserie du Pêcheur v Germany and the Queen v Secretary of State for Transport, ex p Factortame Ltd* [1996] ECR I-1029, para 95 and the Opinion of Léger AG in Case C-5/94 *The Queen v Ministry of Agriculture, Fisheries and Food ex p Hedley Lomas (Ireland) Ltd* [1996] ECR I-2553 at paras 174–176. In other cases, the Court has referred to the 'effectiveness of Community law' rather than the principle of effectiveness; see e.g. Case 106/77 *Amministrazione delle Finanze dello Stato v Simmenthal* [1978] ECR 629, paras 18, 20, 22–23; Case C-213/89 *Factortame and Others* [1990] ECR I-2433, para 21; Case C-224/01 *Köbler v Austria*, judgment of 30 September 2003, para 33.

origins of the principle lie in the interpretative techniques of the Court which, even at an early stage, favoured a liberal construction of Treaty provisions so as to ensure their *effet utile*. Such an approach was particularly evident in recognising the direct effect of directives.[3] As the Community legal order matured, the Court placed more emphasis on the affinity of the principle to the fundamental right of judicial protection as guaranteed by Articles 6 and 13 ECHR.[4]

Community law is supported by a decentralized system of justice in which national courts are the primary venue for the assertion of Community rights. This decentralization is the result of the preliminary reference procedure which, in conjunction with the principle of direct effect, enables the adjudication of Community rights in national courts and unleashes the potential of 'dual vigilance'. The importance of national courts for the enforcement of Community law can hardly be overstated even in areas such as competition law and State aids, where traditionally the implementation of Community policy was entrusted directly to the Commission.[5] In fact, from the point of view of the citizen, national courts are the primary venue not only for asserting Community rights against Member States but also for challenging the validity of Community acts. The restrictive *locus standi* of individuals under Article 230(4) EC often makes indirect challenge before national courts the only viable option. Notably, in its judgment in *Commission v Jégo-Quéré* the ECJ insisted on a strict interpretation of individual concern, declining the invitation of the CFI to liberalize access to justice thus reinforcing collateral challenge as the prevailing model of judicial review for individuals.[6]

This decentralized model of justice is expressly endorsed by the (now ailing) EU Constitution, Article I-29(1), the second sub-paragraph of which states as follows:

Member States shall provide remedies sufficient to ensure effective legal protection in the fields covered by Union law.

This provision, which has no equivalent in the Treaties in force, fulfil a twofold purpose. First and foremost, it serves to underline that national courts play an

---

[3] See e.g. Case 9/70 *Frans Grad v Finanzamt Traunstein* [1971] ECR 825, Case 41/74 *van Duyn v the Home Office* [1974] ECR 1337.

[4] See also Article 47 of the EU Charter (corresponding to Article II-107 of the EU Constitution) which guarantees the rights to an effective remedy and a fair trial.

[5] For the functions of national courts in relation to competition law and State aids see respectively, Case C-234/89 *Delimitis* [1991] ECR I-935 and Case C-39/94 *SFEI and Others* [1996] ECR I-3547. See now the enhanced role of national courts under Council Regulation 1/2003 on the implementation of the rules on competition laid down in Articles 81 and 82 of the Treaty, OJ 2003, L1/1.

[6] See Case C-263/02 P *Commission v Jégo-Quéré*, judgment of 1 April 2004, reversing on appeal Case T-177/01 *Jégo-Quéré v Commission* [2002] ECR II-2365. See also the Opinion of Jacobs AG in Case C-50/00 P *Unión de Pequeños Agricultores v Council* [2002] ECR I-6677. The effect of the ECJ's judgment in *Jégo-Quéré* was to make *locus standi* of individuals under Article 230(4) narrower than that envisaged by Article III-365(4) of the EU Constitution. For a discussion of *locus standi* under the Constitution, see T. Tridimas, 'The European Court of Justice and the Draft Constitution: A Supreme Court for the Union?', in T. Tridimas and P. Nebbia (eds): *EU Law for the 21st Century: Rethinking the New Legal Order*, (Oxford, Hart Publishing, 2004), pp. 113–141 at 120 *et seq*.

important part in the application and enforcement of Union rights. It provides legal basis for making further inroads into the national law of remedies and, arguably, gives precedence to the principle of effectiveness over the principle of equivalence.[7] It also seeks to counterbalance the restrictive *locus standi* under Article 230(4) EC by mandating Member States to fill the remedial gap left by the strict interpretation of direct and individual concern. Whether this is a good alternative is a different matter.[8] Suffice it to say here that Article I-29(1) formalises the pattern of decentralised judicial review favoured by the ECJ. It thus requires the national legal systems to provide *locus standi* to individuals before national courts so as to enable them to challenge the validity of Community acts indirectly via the preliminary reference procedure. The precise scope of this obligation remains, however, unclear.[9]

9.2. Three phases in the Court's case law

Since there are no harmonized Community rules, where claims based on Community law fall to be applied by national courts they are in principle subject to the national rules of procedure and remedies. But the case law in this area has evolved beyond recognition. One can identify three phases.[10]

The first phase was one of non-intervention. Initially, the Court took the view that remedies were a matter for national laws and relied on national rules of procedure and remedies subject to the dual requirement of equivalence (or non-discrimination) and effectiveness (or minimum protection).[11] The *locus classicus* of this early stage is the *Rewe*[12] and *Comet* case law.[13] The Court's approach was encapsulated in *Rewe v Hauptzollamt Kiel* decided in 1981, where it was stated that the EC Treaty 'was not intended to create new remedies'.[14] As the case law progressed, the emphasis shifted from the requirements of non-discrimination and minimum protection to the need to provide effective remedies for the breach of

---

[7] For those principles, see 9.3 below.   [8] For a discussion, see Tridimas, *op. cit.*, n. 6.

[9] In some cases, a Community regulation may affect an individual adversely without the need for any implementing measures to be taken at national level. This may lead to a denial of justice because the individual may lack individual concern to challenge the measure directly and, at the same time, be unable to mount an indirect challenge before national courts owing to the lack of implementing measures. In *Jégo-Quéré* the ECJ stated that, even in such a case, the individual may be entitled to seek from the national authorities the adoption of a measure under the regulation which the individual can then contest before the national court and thus challenge the regulation indirectly: see para 35 of the judgment. This is however a formula which may assume from national systems more than they can deliver. It is cumbersome, inefficient and may fall short of the right to effective judicial review. Also, ironically, it finds less basis in the EC Treaty than a more liberal interpretation of individual concern.

[10] See Tridimas, 'Enforcing Community Rights in National Courts', n. 1, at 465–6.

[11] See below p. 423.

[12] Case 33/76 *Rewe v Landwirtschaftskammer für das Saarland* [1976] ECR 1989.

[13] Case 45/76 *Comet v Productschap voor Siergewassen* [1976] ECR 2043.

[14] Case 158/80 [1981] ECR 1805, para 44.

Community rights. Indeed, one of the key features of judicial constitution building at Community level has been the derivation from the general principles of primacy and direct effect of a specific duty on national courts to provide full and effective protection of Community rights. The Court was prepared to take a more assertive approach and require the removal of all obstacles posed by national law which prevent the full and effective enforcement of Community rights. The seminal judgment in *Simmenthal* marked the first step in that direction.[15] The more interventionist approach of the Court was further evinced by cases such as *Johnston*,[16] *Factortame*[17] and *Peterbroeck*,[18] and reached its apex in the establishment of State liability in damages and the cognate right to reparation for private parties. Notably, Article 10 EC proved instrumental in this development. The Court has interpreted that provision creatively. Under the case law, Article 10 requires Member States to nullify the unlawful consequences of a breach of Community law and such an obligation is owed, within the sphere of its competence, by every organ of the State.[19] Thus, the Court has read in it a principle of cooperation between the national and the Community judicature, from which it has derived specific obligations on national courts regarding the enforcement of Community rights.[20]

In the 1990s, the case law entered a third period, the chief feature of which has been the selective deference to the national rules of procedure. This trend is exemplified in particular by the following developments:

- the post-*Emmott* case-law;[21]
- developments on State liability in damages, especially, the judgment in *Brinkmann*;[22]
- the tendency of the case law, in some cases, to leave discretion to national courts in determining whether the national rules of procedure provide a sufficient level of protection for the Community rights in issue.

The above developments should not be taken as evidence of retreat on the part of the Court. Rather, they illustrate the directed use of judicial power as the legal system matures. The underlying rationale seems to be that, since the general principles of the law governing remedies have now been established, the Court can

[15] Case 35/76 *Simmenthal v Italian Minister for Finance* [1976] ECR 1871, paras 22–3.

[16] Case 222/84 *Johnston v Chief Constable of the Royal Ulster Constabulary* [1986] ECR 1651.

[17] Case C-213/89 *op. cit.*, n. 2 above.

[18] Case C-312/93 *Peterbroeck v Belgian State* [1995] ECR I-4599.

[19] See Case 6/60 *Humblet* [1960] ECR 559, at 569; Case C-8/88 *Germany v Commission* [1990] ECR I-2321, para 13; Joined Cases C-6 and 9/90 *Francovich I* [1991] ECR I-5357, para 36; Case C-201/02 *Delena Wells v Secretary of State for Transport, Local Government and the Regions*, judgment of 7 January 2004, para 64.

[20] For references to Article 10, see e.g. *Rewe, op. cit.; Comet, op. cit.; Simmenthal, op. cit.,* Case C-213/89 *Factortame, op. cit.*; Francovich, *op. cit.*; Case C-147/01 *Weber's Wine World Handels-GmbH*, judgment of 2 October 2003; Case C-453/00 *Kühne & Heitz NV v Productschap voor Pluimvee en Eieren*, judgment of 13 January 2004.

[21] Case C-208/90 *Emmott* [1991] ECR 4269, see 9.4 below.

[22] Case C-319/96 *Brinkmann Tabakfabriken GmbH v Skatteministeriet* [1998] ECR I-5255, discussed below, p. 529.

entrust national courts to apply those principles and be more selective with regard to the national rules with which it takes issue. The purpose of a remedy is to stop the breach of a legal norm and undo its detrimental effects or, to put it in a different way, 'to make constitutional ideas into living truths'.[23] The starting point of the Court's approach remains the universality of remedies. Where there is a right, there must be a remedy (*ubi jus ibi remedium*), so that national courts must in principle provide a remedy for the protection of Community rights, and offer individuals the opportunity to assert rights derived from Community law.[24] This association between rights and remedies, which is much clearer in German law,[25] is not as foreign to common law as is sometimes assumed.[26]

As we shall see, the incremental and fragmentary development of the case law has made for an unsystematic body of rules. In particular, it is not always clear which aspects of procedure and remedies are subject to Community law and which are left for the national laws to decide. This is an area where casuistry prevails. Depending on one's point of view, such obscure delineation of boundaries may be seen as inevitable, harmful, desirable or simply the lesser of two evils. It is important to emphasise however that the Court sees the development of the law in this area as a dialectical one where the co-operation of national courts is of paramount importance. The Court's reliance on Article 10 has not been accidental. The development of no other area of Community law depends as much on the cooperation of national courts as the law of remedies.

More recent case law may suggest a resurgence of interventionism. One aspect of it is the readiness on the part of the ECJ to go beyond the formal application of national law and examine the way it is applied in practice by the national administration and even the national courts with a view to establishing whether they render ineffective the protection of Community rights. This 'second level' enforcement is evidenced, for example, by the judgments in *Commission v Italy*[27] and *Köbler v Austria*.[28] The trend of neo- interventionism is further illustrated by the derivation of subjective rights from obligations imposed on private parties,[29] and the tendency to go beyond the principle of equivalence by, in some areas, turning the discretion left by national law to national authorities into an obligation so as to enhance the protection of Community rights.[30]

---

[23] *Cooper v Aaron* 358 US 1, 20 (1958).
[24] For examples in the field of sex equality, see Case C-185/97 *Coote v Granada Hospitality Ltd*, judgment of 22 September 1998; Case C-167/97 *R v Secretary of State for Employment, ex p Seymour Smith and Perez*, [1999] ECR I-623.   [25] See Ruffert, *op. cit.*, n. 1 above at 332–333.
[26] See the dissenting judgment of Oliver LJ in *Bourgoin SA v Ministry of Agriculture* [1986] 3 All ER 585.   [27] Case C-129/00 *Commission v Italy*, judgment of 9 December 2003.
[28] *Op. cit.*, n. 2 above, discussed at 11.8.1 below. For other cases illustrating this trend, see *Weber's Wine World*, *op. cit.*, paras 113–4; *Kühne & Heitz NY, op. cit.*
[29] Case C-253/00 *Munoz Cia SA and Superior Fruiticola v Frumar Ltd and Redbridge Produce Marketing Ltd*, [2002] ECR I-7289.
[30] See the judgments in Joined Cases C-430 and C-431/93 *van Schijndel and van Veen v SPF* [1995] ECR I-4705 and *Kühne & Heitz NV, op. cit.*, discussed at 9.10 below.

9.3. The dual requirement of equivalence and effectiveness

According to the *Rewe* and *Comet* case law,[31] in the absence of Community rules, it is for the domestic legal system of each Member State to designate the courts having jurisdiction and to lay down the rules governing actions intended to ensure the protection of rights conferred by Community law. Such national rules, however, must comply with two conditions:

(a) they must not be less favourable than those governing similar domestic actions (the requirement of equivalence or non-discrimination);
(b) and they must not render the exercise of Community rights virtually impossible or excessively difficult (the requirement of effectiveness or minimum protection).

More recent case law seems to have added a third requirement. National rules of procedure and remedies must comply with fundamental rights as guaranteed by the European Convention.[32] Methodologically, it would be better to view this as part of the principle of effectiveness rather than as a separate requirement.

Equivalence and effectiveness are complementary. The principle of equivalence ensures that Community rights receive the same protection as domestic ones. The notion of discrimination provides legitimacy for the Court's intervention in the field of remedies: if national law guarantees a certain level of protection to domestic rights why should that level not be extended to Community ones? Also, equivalence integrates Community law into the national legal systems of remedies. It perceives Community rights not as emanating from a separate legal order but as being an integral part of the national legal system, thus promoting the federalization of Community law.

The principle of effectiveness bypasses national standards and grants Community law a quasi-constitutional status. The combination of effectiveness and equivalence has in fact far-reaching effects. It prompts national courts to view the domestic rules of remedies from a different perspective. It forces them to consider their objectives, assess their inter-relationship, expose their limitations, and examine their merits. In short, it provokes a reassessment of national remedies which may extend to remedial rules in areas not directly affected by Community law. This reassessment has had, overall, a beneficial effect in the national legal systems and led to an increase in the protection of the individual.

---

[31] *Rewe, op. cit.*, n. 12 above, para 5; *Comet, op. cit.*, n. 13 above, paras 12 to 16. For subsequent confirmation, see *inter alia* Case 68/79 *Hans Just v Danish Ministry of Fiscal Affairs* [1980] ECR 501, para 25; Case 811/79 *Amministrazione delle Finanze dello Stato v Ariete* [1980] ECR 2545; Case 826/79 *Amministrazione delle Finanze dello Stato v MIRECO* [1980] ECR 2559; Case 199/82 *Amministrazione delle Fiannze dello Stato v San Giorgio* [1983] ECR 3595, para 14; Joined Cases 331, 376 & 378/85 *Bianco and Girard v Directeur Général des Douanes des Droits Indirects* [1988] ECR 1099, para 12; Case C-96/91 *Commission v Spain* [1992] ECR I-3789, para 12; *Francovich, op. cit.*, n. 19 above, para 43; Case C-255/00 *Grundig Italiana* [2002] ECR I-8003, para 33; *Weber's Wine World, op. cit.*, n. 20 above para 103. [32] Case C-276/01 *Steffensen*, judgment of 10 April 2003.

The ECJ has referred to the principle of national procedural autonomy[33] but the scope of that principle is difficult to pin down. Its essential minimum content can more easily be defined negatively, as the discretion left to the national court after the obligation to apply the dual safeguards of equivalence and effectiveness, rather than positively. There is no doubt that the Court takes as its starting point the principle of effectiveness rather than the principle of national procedural autonomy.

The analysis in this chapter is structured as follows. First, some general observations are made in relation to the requirements of effectiveness and equivalence. Then their application to specific rules of remedies and procedure is examined in detail.

9.3.1. The principle of effectiveness

The requirement of effectiveness is separate from, and applies in addition to, the requirement of equivalence. A rule of evidence[34] or a time limit[35] which renders the protection of Community rights ineffective must be set aside by the national court even if it applies equally to similar claims arising from an infringement of national law. In *Peterbroeck*[36] the Court held that, in order to determine whether a national procedural rule renders the application of Community law ineffective, the following enquiry should be pursued:

... a national procedural provision ... must be analysed by reference to the role of that provision in the procedure, its progress and its special features, viewed as a whole before the various national instances. In the light of that analysis the basic principles of the domestic judicial system, such as protection of the rights of the defence, the principle of legal certainty and the proper conduct of procedure, must, where appropriate, be taken into consideration.[37]

In general, over the years, the standard of scrutiny employed by the Court in assessing whether a national rule is compatible with Community law has become higher and this is reflected in judicial terminology. Earlier case law stated that national rules must not make the protection of Community rights virtually impossible or excessively difficult.[38] More recent cases have ceased to view this requirement as one of minimum protection and refer to the principle of effectiveness.[39]

9.3.2. The principle of equivalence

The principle of equivalence requires that claims based on Community law must be subject to rules which are no less favourable than those governing similar claims

---

[33] See e.g. *Delena Wells, op. cit.*, n. 19 above, paras 65, 67.
[34] See e.g. *San Giorgio, op. cit.*, n. 31 above, discussed at 9.6 below.
[35] See e.g. *Peterbroeck, op. cit.*, n. 18 above, discussed at 9.9 below.   [36] *Ibid.*
[37] *Ibid.*, p. 14.
[38] The term 'excessively difficult' first appeared in *San Giorgio, op. cit.*, para 14; it has since been used in a number of cases. See e.g. *Francovich, op. cit.*, para 43; *van Schijndel and van Veen op. cit.*, n. 30 above, para 17.
[39] See e.g. Joined Cases C-397/98 and C-410/98 *Metallgesellschaft Ltd and Hoechst AG v Commissioners of Inland Revenue* [2001] ECR I-1727, para 85; *Grundig Italiana, op. cit.*, n. 31 above, para 33; *Weber's Wine, op. cit.*, para 103.

based on national law. The requirement of equivalence applies 'where the purpose and cause of actions are similar'.[40] But what is a similar claim under national law? In principle, it is for the national court to ascertain whether the national rules of procedure comply with the principle of equivalence, since it is the national court alone which has direct knowledge of those rules.[41] Thus, it is primarily for the national court to determine what national claims may be considered to be comparable to the claim based on Community law in issue in the proceedings. The Court of Justice however may provide guidelines.

In order to ascertain whether a provision complies with the principle of equivalence, account should be taken of its function in the procedure as a whole, as well as its operation and any special features before the various national courts.[42] In some cases, it suffices that the actions are broadly similar and a detailed search for a comparable claim under national law need not be undertaken. In *BP Supergas v Greek State*,[43] a case concerning overpaid VAT contrary to the Sixth Directive, the Advocate General opined that, where a taxable person is entitled to a refund of tax in respect of a particular tax year on grounds recognized by national law, that possibility must extend to grounds based on Community law without need to find a comparable claim under national law. In particular, where national law provides for revision of a tax assessment on the ground that the taxpayer made an excusable error, it must be open to the taxpayer to claim revision on the ground that the national law in accordance with which he calculated the tax is incompatible with Community law. This is because in dealing with the tax authorities, an individual is entitled to assume that the State has correctly implemented all Community directives and complied with Community obligations.[44]

Clearly, the claims must not be unrelated. Thus the fact that, under domestic law, exceptionally a national court may take into account certain pleas of its own motion even if they have not been raised by the parties, such as the issue that the dispute is *res judicata* or that the action is time-barred, does not mean that the national court may also raise of its own motion any plea based on Community law.[45]

In order to determine whether the principle of equivalence has been complied with, the national court must consider 'the purpose and essential characteristics' of allegedly similar domestic actions.[46] In *Palmisani*[47] it was held that an action to recover the loss suffered as a result of the belated implementation of a directive is comparable to a claim for the non-contractual liability of the State brought under ordinary national law and therefore the two claims may be subject to the same limitation period. By contrast, an action to recover the loss suffered as a result of the

[40] Case C-326/96 *Levez v Jennings (Harlow Pools) Ltd*, [1998] ECR I-7835, para 41; Case C-231/96 *Edis v Ministero delle Finanze* [1998] ECR I-4951, para 15.
[41] *Levez, op. cit.*, paras 39–43. Case C-261/95 *Palmisani v Instituto Nazionale della Previdenza Sociale (INPS)* [1997] ECR I- 4025, para 33. [42] *Levez, op. cit.*, para 44.
[43] Case C-62/93 [1995] ECR I-1883. [44] *Ibid., per* Jacobs AG.
[45] See *Peterbroeck*, discussed below, paras 23–7 of the Advocate General's Opinion.
[46] *Levez, op. cit.*, para 43; *Palmisani, op. cit.*, paras 34–38. [47] *Op. cit.*, n. 41 above.

failure to implement Directive 80/987[48] is not comparable with an action to claim benefits provided by that Directive and the two actions may be subject to different time limits. In *Shingara and Radiom*[49] it was held that the right of nationals from other Member States to enter the host Member State cannot be equated with the right of the host State's own nationals to enter the national territory and therefore the remedies for breach of the two need not be the same.[50]

It seems appropriate that the requirement of equivalence should prohibit not only direct but also indirect discrimination against claims based on Community law. Where a procedural rule applies to certain categories of claim, most of which are based on Community law, and a more favourable rule applies to other categories of claim, most of which are based on national law, the first rule may run counter to the requirement of equivalence unless it is objectively justified. There is however no express judicial endorsement of that view and what case law there is may cast doubt on it.[51]

The principle of equivalence does not require Member States to extend their most favourable rules to all actions based on Community law. The Court has had the opportunity to elaborate on this issue in a series of cases arising as a result of the imposition by the Italian authorities of corporate registration charges incompatible with Directive 69/335 concerning indirect charges on the raising of capital.[52] In *Edis v Ministero delle Finanze*,[53] an Italian company sought recovery of unduly paid corporate registration charges but, under the case law of Italian courts, the charges fell within the scope of Article 13(2) of Decree No 641/72 according to which the taxpayer may request repayment of charges wrongly paid within a period of three years from the date of payment. The referring court questioned the compatibility of that time limit with Community law pointing out that, under the ordinary rules provided for in the Italian Civil Code, an action for the recovery of sums paid but not due is subject to a ten-year limitation period. The Court held that Community law does not preclude the legislation of a Member State from laying down, alongside a limitation period applicable under the ordinary law to recovery actions between individuals, special detailed rules, which are less favourable, governing claims and legal proceedings to challenge the imposition of charges and other levies. The position would be different only if those detailed rules applied solely to actions for the recovery of charges paid in breach of Community law. In the case at

---

[48] Council Directive 80/987/EEC of 20 October 1980 on the approximation of the laws of the Member States relating to the protection of employees in the event of the insolvency of the employer, OJ 1980 L 283/23.

[49] Joined Cases C-65 and C-111/95 *The Queen v Secretary of State for the Home Department, ex p Mann Singh Shingara and Abbas Radiom* [1997] ECR I-3343.   [50] See further 9.7.1 below.

[51] See *Weber's Wine World, op. cit.*, paras 91–2, discussed below.

[52] OJ, English Special Ed.1969 (II), p. 412.

[53] *Op. cit.*, n. 40 above; see also Case C-260/96 *Ministero delle Finanze v SPAC* [1998] ECR I-4997; Case C-228/96 *Aprile v Amministrazione delle Finanze dello Stato*, [1998] ECR I-7141; Joined Cases C-10 to C-22/97 *Ministero delle Finanze v IN.CO.GE'90 Srl*, [1998] ECR I-6307.

issue, the three-year time limit applied not only in relation to repayment of the contested registration charge but also to that of all government charges of the same kind. A similar time limit applied to actions for repayment of certain indirect taxes, and also to actions for repayment of charges or dues levied under domestic laws declared incompatible with the Italian Constitution.[54]

On the basis of similar reasoning, the Court held in *Ansaldo Energia SpA v Amministrazione delle Finanze dello Stato*[55] that Member States may calculate the interest payable in respect of the recovery of charges paid to national authorities contrary to Community law using methods of calculation which are less favourable than those applicable to actions between individuals, provided that the method in question applies without distinction to actions against national authorities based on Community law and those based on national law.[56]

The reasoning in the above cases seems persuasive. In general, a claim against the national authorities to recover a sum levied contrary to Community law can better be equated to a claim to recover a sum levied contrary to a superior rule of national law, such as the national constitution, rather than to claims of recovery against other individuals. The public–private law distinction reasserts itself and assists the search for comparability. Further distinctions may need to be drawn if national law provides for a variety of procedures for the recovery of levies charged in breach of national law, depending for example on whether the levy was simply miscalculated, or *ultra vires*, or contrary to a fundamental constitutional norm. In general, however, the Court is unwilling to interfere with the way legal relations between the individual and the national authorities are classified under national law.[57]

Depending on the choice of the appropriate comparator, the principle of equivalence may require Community law to be treated on an equal footing with the national constitution. In *Weber's Wine*,[58] the ECJ held that, where the claim for repayment is based on a declaration of unconstitutionality by a national court, the principle of equivalence precludes national law from laying down more advantageous conditions for the repayment of unduly paid taxes than those applicable to traders who, following a judgment of the ECJ, seek repayment of a charge levied in breach of Community law.

9.4. Limitation periods

A classic example of national procedural rules which may qualify the enforcement of Community rights is rules on limitation periods. The issue first arose in *Rewe v*

---

[54] *Edis, op. cit.*, paras 37–38; *SPAC, op. cit.*, paras 21–22.

[55] Joined Cases C-279 to C-281/96 [1998] ECR I-5025.

[56] *Ibid.*, para 30. The Court left open the question whether it makes any difference that the method of calculating the interest is fixed by the authority responsible for the breach of Community law which gave rise to the claim for repayment. See paras 31–35.

[57] See e.g. *IN.CO.GE'90, op. cit.*, para 26.   [58] *Op. cit.*, n. 20 above, para 107.

Landwirtschaftskammer für das Saarland[59] and in *Comet v Productschap voor Sierge-wassen*.[60] In *Rewe* imports of French apples had been subjected to inspection charges which, subsequently, the Court found to have equivalent effect to customs duties.[61] The appellants sought to have the charges annulled and the amounts paid refunded but their claim was rejected on the ground that the time limit of 30 days laid down by German law had expired. The Court held that, in the absence of harmonization measures, the rights conferred by Community law must be exercised before national courts in accordance with the conditions laid down by national rules. The position would be different only if those conditions made it impossible in practice to exercise Community rights. The Court held that this is not the case when reasonable periods of limitation are fixed. The fixing of such time limits is an application of the fundamental principle of legal certainty which protects both the public authorities and the person affected.[62]

The Court did not express a view as to whether the 30 day time limit was reasonable, leaving the issue to the national court. In subsequent cases it has been more forthcoming in ruling on the compatibility with Community law of specific time limits imposed by national law. Thus it has been held that a five-year limitation period provided for the recovery of port duties levied in infringement of Article 90 is reasonable[63] as is a five-year period provided for the repayment of charges imposed in infringement of Directive 69/335 concerning indirect taxes on the raising of capital.[64] A one-year limitation period for bringing an action to recover loss arising from the failure to implement a directive has also been upheld.[65] It has been held, however, that the fact that a Member State has levied a charge in breach of Community law over a long period without either the public authorities or the persons liable to pay it having been aware of its unlawful nature does not constitute excusable error justifying the dismissal of claims for recovery. If the defence of excusable error were accepted, it would be excessively difficult to obtain recovery of unduly paid charges and 'would encourage infringements of Community law which would have been committed over a long period'.[66]

In *Emmott*,[67] the Court held that so long as a directive has not properly been transposed into national law, individuals are unable to ascertain the full extent of their rights. Consequently, until a directive has been transposed properly, a

---

[59] *Op. cit.*, n. 12 above.   [60] *Op. cit.*, n. 13 above.
[61] Case 39/73 *Rewe-Zentralfinanz* [1973] ECR 1039.
[62] *Rewe*, *op. cit.* para 5; *Comet*, *op. cit.*, 18.
[63] Case C-90/94 *Haahr Petroleum v Åbenrå Havn and Others* [1997] ECR I-4085; Joined Cases C-114 and C-115/95 *Texaco and Olieselskabet Danmark* [1997] ECR I-4263.
[64] Case C-188/95 *Fantask A/S and Others v Industriministeriet (Erhvervsministeriet)* [1997] ECR I-6783. In *Edis*, *op. cit.*, the Court upheld a period of three years for bringing an action for repayment of the same charges. As the claims proliferated, the allowable time limits became shorter: in Case C-30/02 *Recheio Cash and Carry SA*, judgment of 17 June 2004, the ECJ again upheld in relation to the same charges a time limit of 90 days from the end of the period allowed for their voluntary payment. The Court held that this period was reasonable taking into account the periods fixed in the legal systems of several other Member States (para 22).
[65] *Palmisani*, *op. cit.*, n. 41 above.   [66] *Fantask*, *op. cit.*   [67] *Op. cit.*, n. 21 above.

defaulting Member State may not rely on an individual's delay in initiating proceedings against it in order to protect rights conferred upon him by the directive, and a period laid down by national law within which proceedings must be initiated cannot begin to run before that time. *Emmott* concerned Directive 7/79 on the progressive implementation of the principle of equal treatment between men and women in matters of social security,[68] which Ireland had failed to implement. Article 4(1) prohibits discrimination on grounds of sex, in particular as regards the calculation of benefits including increases due in respect of a spouse and for dependants. Mrs Emmott was married and had two dependent children. On the basis of an earlier judgment of the Court[69] which held that Article 4(1) was directly effective, she sought to obtain, as from the date when the directive should have been transposed into national law, the same amount of benefit as that paid to a married man in a situation identical to hers. The defendants argued that her delay in initiating proceedings rendered her claim time-barred under national law. The Court held that the time limit for bringing an action imposed by national law cannot be relied on before the directive is fully transposed into national law.[70]

Emmott was hailed as introducing a new, more assertive, approach on the part of the Court. In subsequent cases, however, the scope of the ruling was restricted. In *Steenhorst-Neerings*[71] it was held that the failure of a Member State to transpose Article 4(1) of Directive 7/79 properly did not preclude it from relying on a rule of national law according to which benefits for incapacity for work were payable not earlier than one year before the date when benefit was claimed. The Court held that the national rule in issue applied equally to national and Community claims and did not make virtually impossible the exercise of rights conferred by Community law. *Emmott* was distinguished on the ground that the rule of Irish law in issue in that case fixed a time limit for bringing actions and made it impossible for the applicant to rely on Article 4(1). By contrast, the rule in issue in *Steenhorst-Neerings* did not affect the right of individuals to rely on Directive 7/79 but restricted the retroactive effect of claims for benefits. That restriction was justified by the need to ensure that the claimant met the conditions for eligibility and the need to preserve the financial balance of the social security system.[72]

Steenhorst-Neerings was confirmed in *Johnson*.[73] In both cases, the Court focused on whether the national rules applicable made it impossible to exercise rights based

---

[68] OJ 1979 L 6, p. 24.

[69] Case 286/85 *McDermott and Ann Cotter v Minister for Social Welfare and Attorney General* [1987] ECR 1453.

[70] Micho AG took the view that a time limit provided for by national law should begin to run from the time when the persons concerned should reasonably have been aware of their rights: *Emmott, op. cit.,* pp. 4289–91.

[71] Case C-338/91 *Steenhorst-Neerings v Bestuur van de Bedrijfsvereniging voor Detailhandel, Ambachten en Huisvrouwen* [1993] ECR I-5475.

[72] Cf the 'dissenting' opinion of Darmon AG, *op. cit.,* pp. 5492–5493.

[73] Case C-410/92 [1994] ECR I-5483.

on Community law rather than on whether an individual suffered as a result of late transposition. The judgments do not require that an individual should be put in the same position that he would have been if a Member State had transposed Directive 7/79 properly into national law within the requisite period of implementation. The individual however may recover any loss suffered by bringing an action in damages against the State.[74]

The trend towards a restrictive interpretation of *Emmott* reached its climax in *Fantask A/S and Others v Industriministeriet (Erhvervsministeriet).*[75] The case concerned charges on the registration of companies levied by the Danish authorities which were found to be contrary to Directive 69/335 concerning indirect taxes on the raising of capital. Danish law made the recovery of such charges subject to a limitation period of five years but the applicants argued pursuant to *Emmott* that a Member State could not rely on that limitation period as long as Directive 69/335 had not been properly transposed into national law. Confirming *Johnson* and *Steenhorst-Neerings*, the Court stated that the solution adopted in *Emmott* was justified by the particular circumstances of that case where the time bar had 'the result of depriving the applicant of any opportunity whatever' to rely on her right arising from the directive in issue. The five-year limitation period imposed by Danish law was reasonable and applied without distinction to domestic claims and those based on Community law and was therefore compatible with Community law.

Fantask gave a fatal blow to *Emmott* and it is now settled that the latter must be read on its facts. It applies only in relation to directives and only given the specific circumstances of that case.[76] It does not detract from the general rule that the limitation period imposed by national law starts from the date when the claim arises rather than the date when national legislation has complied with the Community obligation in issue.[77]

Steenhorst-Neerings and *Johnson* were distinguished in *Magorrian v Eastern Health and Social Services Board.*[78] The applicants were women employed as mental health nurses. They were refused additional pension benefits payable under a voluntary contracted-out pension scheme on the ground that they did not have the status of full-time workers at the time of their retirement. The national court held that their

---

[74] See Case C-66/95 *R v Secretary of State for Social Security ex p Sutton*, [1997] ECR I- 2163 and Joined Cases C-192 to C-218/95 *Comateb and Others v Directeur Général des Douanes et Droits Indirects* [1997] ECR I-165, discussed at 9.8.2 below. [75] *op. cit.*, n. 64 above.

[76] See *Haahr Petroleum, op. cit.*, n. 63 above, paras 52–53; *Texaco and Olieselskabet, op. cit.*, n. 63 above, paras 48–49. Cf in the context of public procurement, Case C-327/00 *Santex SpA v Unità Socio Sanitaria Locale*, [2003] ECR I-1877.

[77] In Case C-2/94 *Denkavit International and Others v Kamer van Koophandel en Fabrieken voor Midden-Gelderrland and Others* [1996] ECR I-2827, at 2851 Jacobs AG held that *Emmott* applies only where 'a Member State is in default both in failing to implement a directive and in obstructing the exercise of a judicial remedy in reliance upon it, or perhaps the delay in exercising the remedy—and hence the failure to meet the time-limit—is in some other way due to the conduct of the national authorities'. The Advocate General pointed out that a further factor in *Emmott* was that the applicant was in the particularly unprotected position of an individual dependent on social welfare.   [78] Case C-246/96 [1997] ECR I-7153.

exclusion from the additional benefits amounted to indirect sex discrimination. The question then arose from which date their periods of service as part-time workers should be taken into account for the purpose of calculating the additional benefits to which they were entitled. In response to a preliminary reference, the Court held that the appropriate date was 8 April 1976, the date of the judgment in *Defrenne*.[79] The applicants however encountered an obstacle posed by national law. Regulation 12 of the Northern Ireland Occupational Regulations[80] provided that, in proceedings concerning access to membership of occupational schemes, the right to be admitted to the scheme was to have effect from a date no earlier than two years before the institution of proceedings. The Court held that Regulation 12 deprived the applicants of their rights, since benefits could be calculated only by reference to periods of service completed by them as from 1990, that is to say, two years prior to their commencing proceedings. The Court distinguished *Steenhorst-Neerings* and *Johnson* on the following ground. The rules in issue there limited the period, prior to commencement of proceedings, in respect of which backdated benefits could be obtained. By contrast, Regulation 12 prevented the entire record of service completed between 8 April 1976 and 1990 from being taken into account for the purposes of calculating the additional benefits which would be payable even after the date of the claim. Consequently, Regulation 12 was such as to strike 'at the very essence of the rights conferred by the Community legal order'.[81] Also, the effect of the Regulation was to limit in time the direct effect of Article 141 of the Treaty in cases where no such limitation has been laid down either in the Court's case law or in Protocol No 2 annexed to the Treaty on European Union.

The distinct feature of Regulation 12 was that it restricted claims for future benefits based on past service. *Magorrian* was followed in *Preston*.[82] This case also concerned claims for retroactive membership of contracted-out pension schemes. The novel issue raised was the application of a limitation period on successive short-term contracts. Under s. 2(4) of the Equal Pay Act 1970, a claim based on the principle of equal pay irrespective of sex must be brought within a period of six months following the cessation of employment. Some of the claimants in the main proceedings had been employed regularly for the same employer, but periodically or intermittently, under successive legally separate contracts. Such contracts were sometimes covered by an umbrella contract, under which the parties were required to renew their various contracts of employment, thus establishing a continuous employment relationship. Where there was no umbrella contract, the six-month time limit provided for in s. 2(4) commenced from the end of each contract and not from the end of the employment relationship. In such a case, a worker could

---

[79] Case 43/75 *Defrenne v Sabena* [1976] ECR 455.
[80] Occupational Pension Schemes (Equal Access to Membership) Regulations (Northern Ireland) 1976 No 238. [81] *Magorrian, op. cit.*, para 44.
[82] Case C-78/98 *Preston and Others v Wolverhampton Healthcare NHS Trust and Others and Fletcher and Others v Midland Bank plc* [2000] ECR I-3240.

not secure recognition of periods of part-time employment for the purposes of entitlement to pension, unless she commenced proceedings within six months following the end of each contract covering the relevant period. The House of Lords raised the question whether such restrictive effect of s. 2(4) was compatible with the principle of effectiveness. On this point, there was a notable disagreement between the Advocate General and the Court. Léger AG accepted that, where there is no umbrella contract, the parties are free to renew or not renew their employment contract. In those circumstances, it is not possible to determine precisely the time at which their employment relationship ends and, thus, reasons of legal certainty justify setting the starting point of the time limit as the expiry date of each successive contract.[83] The Court reasoned differently. It held that, in the case of successive contracts, setting the starting point of the limitation period at the end of each contract renders the exercise of the right conferred by Article 141 excessively difficult. The Court did not consider the argument of legal certainty as insurmountable.

In *Preston* the Court opted for a high level of protection giving priority to the existence of a stable employment relationship over contractual freedom. It is significant that the Court itself expressly referred to alternative points which may be fixed as the starting point of the limitation period, thus intervening in a prescriptive way unusual in the field of remedies. It held that where there is a stable relationship resulting from a succession of short-term contracts concluded at regular intervals in respect of the same employment to which the same pension scheme applies, a precise starting point for the limitation period can be determined. It may be fixed at the date on which the sequence of such contracts has been interrupted through the absence of one or more of the features that characterise a stable relationship, either because the periodicity of such contracts has been broken or because the new contract does not relate to the same employment as that to which the same pension scheme applies.[84]

Whether a limitation period meets the standards of effectiveness is judged in the circumstances of the case and not in the abstract. In *Levez*,[85] Mrs Levez took up employment as manager of a betting shop replacing a male employee. Her employer falsely told her that she received the same salary as her predecessor although in fact she was paid less. When she found out, she sought to recover arrears of equal pay but her claim was obstructed by s. 2(5) of the Equal Pay Act 1970. That provision limits a woman's entitlement to arrears of remuneration or damages for breach of the principle of equal pay to a period of two years prior to the date when proceedings are instituted. The Court held that s. 2(5) was not in itself open to criticism. Mrs Levez, however, was late in bringing proceedings precisely because of the misleading information provided by her employer. The application of s.2(5) in the circumstances would be manifestly incompatible with

---

[83] *Per* Léger AG at para 138 of the Opinion.   [84] *Preston, op. cit.*, paras 69–70.
[85] *Op. cit.*, n. 40 above.

the principle of effectiveness since it would facilitate the breach of Community law by an employer whose deceit caused the employee's delay in bringing proceedings.[86]

Levez raised also the issue of inter-relationship of domestic remedies. The UK Government argued that Mrs Levez could have recovered full compensation by bringing proceedings against her employer based on the tort of deceit before the County Court. In such proceedings, she could have relied both on the Equal Pay Act and the deceit of her employer and s. 2(5) would not have applied. The Court accepted that, where an employee can rely on the rights derived from Article 141 of the Treaty and the Equal Pay Directive before another court, s. 2(5) does not compromise the principle of effectiveness.[87] It then turned to examine whether, in the circumstances, proceedings such as those brought before the County Court would comply with the principle of equivalence. The order for reference suggested that claims similar to those based on the Equal Pay Act may include those linked to a contract of employment, to pay discrimination on grounds of race, to unlawful deductions from wages, or to sex discrimination in matters other than pay. The Court left the determination of whether any of those forms of action could be considered similar to the national court. If any of them were found to be similar, the national court would then need to determine whether the claim brought before the County Court was governed by procedural rules or other requirements which were less favourable. It would be appropriate to consider whether, in order to assert fully her Community rights before the County Court, an employee in the position of Mrs Levez would incur additional costs and delay by comparison to a claimant of a similar right based on national law who could bring an action before the Industrial Tribunal, which is simpler and, in principle, less costly.[88] Also, it was of relevance that s.2(5) applied solely to claims based on equal pay without discrimination on grounds of sex, whereas claims based on similar rights under domestic law were not limited by such a rule and therefore could be adequately protected by actions brought before the Industrial Tribunal.[89]

Levez establishes that a rule of national law which makes excessively difficult the protection of Community rights is precluded even where an alternative remedy is available, if the latter is likely to entail procedural rules or other conditions which are less favourable than those applicable to similar domestic actions. In fact, the Court could have phrased its judgment in stronger terms. Proceedings before a

---

[86] *Ibid.*, paras 31–32. The Court placed emphasis on the deceit of the employer. The Advocate General, by contrast, formulated his response to the question referred in slightly wider terms. He viewed s. 2(5) as an over-restrictive rule in that it did not grant any discretion to the national court to extend the backdating of payment beyond the two-year period in special circumstances. In the view of Léger AG, what ran counter to the principle of effectiveness was not s.2(5) itself but the lack of flexibility in its enforcement. The fact that the national court had no power to extend the time limit set, and thus mitigate its application in order to take into account special circumstances, made it excessively difficult to enforce a Community law correctly. The Advocate General therefore appeared to leave the door open to setting aside s.2(5) in other cases where its application would be inequitable. See paras 96–97 of the Opinion.   [87] *Ibid.*, para 38.

[88] *Ibid.*, para 51.   [89] *Ibid.*, para 52.

County Court based on deceit seem to be a lesser substitute for Tribunal proceedings based on sex discrimination. More generally, where national law introduces a specific remedy for the protection of Community rights, such primary remedy can be presumed to be the appropriate one and an alternative remedy is acceptable only if it is effective and equivalent to the primary one.

9.5. Rules specifically introduced to limit Community claims

The case law takes a stricter view with regard to rules which are introduced by a Member State specifically to restrict claims for the recovery of a charge which has been found by the Court to be incompatible with Community law. This issue was first confronted in *Barra*.[90] Previously, in *Gravier v City of Liége*,[91] the Court had found that the imposition by Belgian law of a registration fee on nationals of other Member States studying in Belgian universities was contrary to Article 12 EC. Following the judgment in *Gravier*, Belgium passed a law which restricted the right of reimbursement of registration fees already paid only to those who had instituted proceedings before the date when the judgment in *Gravier* was delivered. In *Barra*, the Court held that this restriction rendered the exercise of the rights conferred by Article 12 impossible and was therefore incompatible with Community law.

Barra was followed in *Deville v Administration des Impôts*.[92] This case concerned a French tax on cars which in *Humblot v Directeur des services fiscaux*[93] had been held to be incompatible with Article 90 EC. Following the judgment in *Humblot*, a French law was passed which abolished the tax and enabled taxpayers to obtain a refund. The law provided that claims for refund had to be made within a certain period from the year in which the contested tax was paid. Mr Deville argued that the time limit was more restrictive than that which would have applied if the French law had not been adopted. In the latter case, a taxpayer could have made a claim within a certain period from the time when 'the event giving rise to the claim occurred', i.e. the date when the judgment in *Humblot* was delivered. The Court held that a national legislature may not, subsequent to a judgment from which it follows that certain legislation is incompatible with the Treaty, adopt a procedural rule which specifically reduces the possibilities of bringing proceedings for recovery of taxes which were wrongly levied under that legislation.[94]

In subsequent cases, the Court has taken a narrow view of *Barra* and *Deville*. *Edis v Ministero delle Finanze*[95] arose as a result of the imposition by Italian law of an

---

[90] Case 309/85 *Barra v Belgium and another* [1988] ECR 355.
[91] Case 293/83 [1985] ECR 593. The judgment is discussed above p. 124.
[92] Case 240/87 [1988] ECR 3513.   [93] Case 112/84 [1985] ECR 1367.
[94] *Deville, op. cit.*, para 13. For subsequent confirmations, see e.g. Case C-343/96 *Dilexport* [1999] ECR I-579, paras 38–39; Case C-62/00 *Marks & Spencer v Commissioners of Customs and Excise* [2002] ECR I-6325, para 36.   [95] *Op. cit.*, n. 40 above.

annual fee in respect of the registration of companies in the corporate register. In its judgment in *Ponente Carni*,[96] the Court had held that the payment of such a fee ran counter to Directive 69/335 concerning indirect charges on the raising of capital.[97] Following the judgment in *Ponente Carni*, Edis sought repayment of unduly paid registration charges but a dispute arose as to the applicable limitation period. Under Article 13(2) of Italian Decree No 641/72, the taxpayer may request repayment of charges wrongly paid within a period of three years from the date of payment. Traditionally, the case law of Italian courts interpreted that provision as applying only in cases where a sum had been unduly paid owing to an error in the calculation of the tax. Claims for the recovery of unduly paid corporate charges were subject to the ten-year limitation period provided for in the Italian Civil Code. In 1996, however, after the judgment in *Ponente Carni* was delivered, the Corte Suprema di Cassazione departed from its previous case law, holding that repayment of the registration charge was subject to the three-year time limit provided for in Decree No 641/72. The Commission argued that, by departing from its previous case law, the Corte Suprema specifically curtailed the opportunity for the persons concerned to bring proceedings for repayment. The Court rejected that argument, distinguishing the case in issue from *Barra* and *Deville* on two grounds. First, the interpretation given by the Corte Suprema related to a national provision which had been in force for several years when judgment was delivered in *Ponente Carni*. Second, that provision was concerned not only with repayment of corporate registration charges but also with all registration charges levied by the Italian Government.[98] The Court expressly left open the issue of under what conditions the *Deville* principle might apply to *ex post facto* restrictions imposed by national case law.[99]

In *Aprile Srl v Amministrazione delle Finanze dello Stato (Aprile II)*,[100] the applicant sought to recover inspections fees charged on the importation of goods, which in *Aprile I*[101] had been found to be incompatible with Community law. The right to reimbursement, however, had become statute-barred by virtue of Article 29 of Italian Decree Law No 428/1990. That Decree Law introduced a special time limit of three years for all actions for reimbursement of customs charges instead of the ordinary ten-year limitation period laid down in the Civil Code. The Commission argued that Article 29 specifically curtailed the opportunity for the persons concerned to bring proceedings thereby disregarding the judgments in *Barra* and *Deville*. The Court did not agree. It stated that, although Article 29 reduced significantly the period within which reimbursement of unduly paid sums could be claimed, it set a time limit which was sufficient to guarantee the effectiveness of the right to reimbursement. That provision did not have retroactive effect. Also,

---

[96] Joined Cases C-71/ and C-178/91 *Ponente Carni and Cispadana Construzioni* [1993] ECR I-1915.   [97] Ibid.
[98] *Ponente Carni, op. cit.*, para 25.   [99] *Ibid.*
[100] *Op. cit.*, n. 53 above; see also *Dilexport, op. cit.*, n. 94 above.
[101] Case C-125/94 [1995] ECR I-2919.

the time limit at issue was applicable not solely to a specific kind of charge which had previously been declared incompatible with Community law but to a whole range of internal charges and taxes for which the legislation had standardized the rules on time limits. The Court also pointed out that the adoption of the contested law preceded its judgment in *Aprile I.*

Thus national legislation curtailing the period within which recovery may be sought of sums charged in breach of Community law is compatible with Community law only if it meets the following conditions:[102]

(a) it must not be intended specifically to limit the consequences of a judgment of the Court to the effect that national legislation concerning a specific tax is incompatible with Community law; and

(b) the time set for its application must be sufficient to ensure that the right to repayment is effective.

In fact, the case law attributes more importance to the second rather than the first condition. In *Marks & Spencer*,[103] however, it was held that the principle of effectiveness prohibits the retroactive curtailment of a limitation period applicable to the recovery of unduly paid monies. The UK Government decided to reduce the time limit within which traders could seek refund of unduly paid VAT from six years to three years. The reason for this was to minimise the exposure of the Treasury to increasing claims for refund owing to the fact that, for a number of years, the UK had failed to implement correctly the 6th VAT Directive. The Government announced its intention in Parliament on 18 July 1996. The new limitation period was to be introduced in the Finance Bill 1997 but would apply immediately to claims already made on the date of the announcement so as to prevent the change in the law from being deprived of its effect. The Court found the retroactive application of the new limitation period incompatible with the principles of effectiveness and protection of legitimate expectations. It held that whilst national legislation reducing the period within which repayment of sums collected in breach of Community law may be sought is not incompatible with the principle of effectiveness, it is subject to the condition not only that the new limitation period is reasonable but also that the new legislation includes transitional arrangements allowing an adequate period after the enactment of the legislation for lodging the claims for repayment which persons were entitled to submit under the original legislation. Such transitional arrangements are necessary where the immediate application to those claims of a limitation period shorter than that which was previously in force would have the effect of retroactively depriving some individuals of their right to repayment, or of allowing them too short a period for asserting that right.[104]

---

[102] See *Aprile II, op. cit.*, para 28; *Dilexport, op. cit.*, paras 41 and 42; *Marks & Spencer, op. cit.*

[103] *Op. cit.*, n. 94 above; see also Case C-396/98 *Schlossstrasse* [2000] ECR I-4279.

[104] *Op. cit.*, para 38. In *Grundig Italiana SpA, op. cit.*, n. 31 above, the Court held that, where a limitation period of five years is replaced with a time limit of three years, a transitional period of

A less generous views was taken in *Weber's Wine World Handels- GmbH.*[105] Following the Opinion of the Advocate General in *EKW*,[106] who opined that an Austrian duty on alcoholic beverages was contrary to Community law, the Vienna Tax Code was amended to restrict possible future claims for repayment of duties charged on traders. The amending law made recovery subject to the duty not having been passed on other persons, a condition which hitherto had not been applicable. The law was passed one week before the Court delivered its judgment in *EKW* and applied retroactively. In that judgment, the ECJ confirmed the opinion of the Advocate General but restricted the retroactive effect of its ruling recognizing the existence of overriding grounds of legal certainty.

In *Weber's Wine World* the applicants sought repayment of duties claiming that the amending law infringed the duty of loyal cooperation laid down in Article 10 EC and was in breach of the protection of legitimate expectations. The ECJ accepted that the purpose of the amending law was to preclude the effects of the *EKW* judgment but held that this was not in itself sufficient to establish whether the law sought specifically to reduce the possibilities of bringing proceedings for recovery of the duty on alcoholic drinks. In view of the circumstances surrounding the adoption of the amending law and the fact that the Parliamentary debates of the Land of Vienna referred expressly to the Opinion of Saggio AG in *EKW*, the Court's finding seems strange. The Court relied on the fact that the amending law did not refer solely to repayment of duties which were levied in breach of Community law. It seems however clear that this was, at least, a case of indirect discrimination. The amending law restricted mainly recovery of indirect taxes levied against Community law and, undoubtedly, the judgment of the ECJ in *EKW* was the *fons et origo* of the amendment. The ECJ preferred to be reticent. It held that the adoption by a Member State of rules which retroactively restrict the right to repayment in order to forestall the possible effects of a judgment of the ECJ is contrary to Article 10 EC only insofar as it is aimed specifically at the duty which the ECJ has found to be incompatible with EC law. Whether that is the case is a matter for the national court to decide.[107] The ECJ however proceeded to scrutinize the amending law with a view to establishing whether its provisions met the requirements of equivalence and effectiveness.

The judgment suggests that the Court is less concerned with the retroactive character of national restrictions and the objectives they seek to pursue, even if they target Community rights, than with their actual effect on such rights which are assessed through the dual requirement of equivalence and effectiveness.

---

90 days is insufficient and, by a marvelous and unusual piece of judicial legislation, set at six months the minimum period required to ensure that the exercise of rights of recovery is not rendered excessively difficult. See further: Joined Cases C-216/99 and C-222/99 *Riccardo prisco Srl v Amministrazione delle Finanze dello Stato*, [2002] ECR I-6761.

[105] *Op. cit.*, n. 20 above.   [106] Case C-437/97 *EKW and Wein & Co* [2000] ECR I-1157.

[107] *Weber's Wine World, op. cit.*, para 92.

9.6. Unjust enrichment and the defence of passing on

The right to recover charges levied by a Member State in breach of Community law is a consequence of, and an adjunct to, the rights conferred on individuals by the Community provisions as interpreted by the Court.[108] In principle therefore a Member State is required to repay charges levied in breach of Community law. In the absence of Community rules governing the issue, however, the recovery of unduly paid charges is governed by national law subject to the dual requirement of equivalence and effectiveness.[109] Thus, the recovery of unduly paid sums is subject not only to time limits but also to other rules of substance and procedure provided by national law. In *Pigs and Bacon Commission v McCarren*, it was held that it is for the national court to assess whether an unduly paid levy may be set off against sums paid to the trader by way of an export bonus.[110] Also, whether a trader is entitled to the payment of interest, and if so the rate of interest and the date from which it must be calculated, is in principle a matter for the national law to decide.[111]

Issues of particular interest have arisen in relation to the defence of unjust enrichment. In *Just*[112] an importer of spirits sought repayment of excise duties levied in breach of Article 90 [95] by the Danish authorities. Under Danish law, a claim for recovery will not succeed if the charge may be presumed to have been passed on to the consumer. The Danish Government argued that the plaintiff had recovered the unlawful taxes by passing them on to consumers as part of the normal profit margin. After referring to the dual requirement of non-discrimination and effectiveness , the Court held that Community law does not require an order for the recovery of unduly paid charges to be granted in conditions which would involve the unjust enrichment of those entitled. National courts therefore can take into account, in accordance with national law, the fact that the unduly levied taxes have been incorporated in the price of goods and thus passed on.[113] Although the principle enunciated by the Court is correct, it is highly doubtful whether the argument of the Danish Government was economically justifiable. Where the amount of an unduly paid levy has been recovered by the undertaking selling its

---

[108] *San Giorgio, op. cit.*, n. 31 above para 12; *Barra*, op. cit., n. 90 above, para 17; *Comateb*, op cit., n. 74 above, para 20.

[109] The principles of equivalence and effectiveness apply not only where a person relies on Community law to obtain a benefit against the national authorities but also in the reverse situation, namely where an individual seeks to rely on national law to retain monies paid to him in breach of Community law: see Joined cases 205 to 215/82 *Deutsche Milchkontor v Germany* [1983] ECR 2633; Case C-132/95 *Jensen* [1998] ECR I-2975.

[110] Case 177/78 [1979] ECR 2161. For set-off, see also *Jensen, op. cit.*

[111] See Case 130/79 *Express Dairy Foods v Intervention Board for Agricultural Produce* [1980] ECR 1887; Case 54/81 *Fromme v Balm* [1982] ECR 1449. On the issue of interest, however, the Court has not followed a consistent approach: see 9.8.2 below.

[112] Case 68/79 *Just v Ministry for Fiscal Affairs* [1980] ECR 501.   [113] *Op. cit.*, para 26.

products at the normal, as opposed to a higher, profit margin it cannot be said that the tax has been passed on to the consumer.[114] In *Just*, as earlier in *Rewe*, the Court followed a non-interventionist approach. It referred to the general requirements of Community law, leaving ample discretion to the national court.

The Court gave more specific directions in *San Giorgio*.[115] The plaintiff had been required to pay health inspection charges contrary to Community law upon importation to Italy of dairy products from other Member States. Italian law provided that a person was not entitled to the repayment of sums unduly paid where the charge had been passed on in any way to other persons. It also provided that the charge was presumed to have been passed on whenever the goods in respect of which the charge was paid had been transferred, in the absence of documentary proof to the contrary.[116] The Court repeated its finding in *Just* that national courts may take into account the fact that the unduly paid charges have been passed on to the purchasers. It stated however that any requirement of proof which made it virtually impossible or excessively difficult to obtain repayment was incompatible with Community law. It continued:[117]

That is so particularly in the case of presumptions or rules of evidence intended to place upon the taxpayer the burden of establishing that the charges unduly paid have not been passed on to other persons or of special limitations concerning the form of the evidence to be adduced, such as the exclusion of any kind of evidence other than documentary evidence. Once it is established that the levying of the charge is incompatible with Community law, the court must be free to decide whether or not the burden of the charge has been passed on, wholly or in part, to other persons.

Of particular interest is the presence in the judgment of elements of an economic analysis which was absent in *Just*:[118]

In a market economy based on freedom of competition, the question whether, and if so to what extent, a fiscal charge imposed on an importer has actually been passed on in subsequent transactions involves a degree of uncertainty for which the person obliged to pay a charge contrary to Community law cannot be systematically held responsible.

It is noteworthy that the Court has been less willing to accept the defence of unjust enrichment in the field of social law than in has been in the field of economic law. In *Cotter and McDermott v Minister for Social Welfare and AG*[119] it held that Article 4(1) of Directive 79/7 had to be interpreted as meaning that married women were entitled to the same increases in benefits and compensatory payments as those awarded to married men in family situations identical to theirs even if that would

---

[114] The judgment has been criticised by P. Oliver, 'Enforcing Community Rights in the English Courts', (1987) 50 MLR 881 at 889.   [115] *Op. cit.*, n. 31 above.
[116] See Decree Law No 688/1982, Article 19.   [117] *Op. cit.*, para 14.
[118] *Op. cit.*, para 15.
[119] Case C-377/89 [1991] ECR I-1155. See also the previous case law from which the issue of unjust enrichment arose: *McDermott and Cotter, op. cit.*, n. 69 above; Case 71/85 *Netherlands v federatie Nederlandse Vakbeweging* [1986] ECR 3855.

result in double payments or infringe the prohibition of unjust enrichment laid down by Irish law.

In the commercial field also the Court tightened its approach to the passing on defence, its initial scepticism gradually developing into a positive dislike. In *Société Comateb and Others v Directeur Général des Douanes et Droits Indirects*[120] a dispute arose from the imposition of dock dues (*octroi de mer*) on the importation of goods from other Member States to the French overseas departments. In *Administration des Douanes et Droits Indirects v Legros and Others*[121] the Court had found that dock dues were charges having equivalent effect to customs duties. It had, however, limited the temporal effect of its judgment so that claims for refund could not be brought in relation to dock dues paid before the date of the judgment except by claimants who had initiated proceedings before that date. In *Comateb*, the applicants sought the recovery of dock dues paid on the importation of goods into Guadeloupe in the period between 17 July 1992, the day after the judgment in *Legros* was delivered, and 31 December 1992. They were unable to obtain recovery because, under the French Customs Code, a person may obtain reimbursement of unlawfully paid duties only where they have not been passed on to the purchaser. The obstacle encountered by the applicants was that French law in fact required a person liable to pay dock dues to incorporate them into the cost price of the goods sold. The Court first pointed out that, in principle, a Member State is required to reimburse charges levied in breach of Community law. Referring to *San Giorgio*, it stated that repayment need not be made where it is established that the trader has actually passed the charges on to other persons. The fact, however, that there is an obligation under national law to incorporate the charge in the cost price does not mean there is a presumption that the entire charge has been passed on, even when failure to comply with that obligation carries a penalty. Accordingly, a Member State may resist repayment to the trader concerned only where it is established that the charge has been borne in its entirety by someone else and that reimbursement would constitute unjust enrichment. If the burden of the charge has been passed on only in part, the national authorities must repay the amount not passed on. The Court also held that, even where the charge has been passed on, its repayment to the trader does not necessarily entail his unjust enrichment. He may claim that, although the charge has been passed on, its inclusion in the cost price has, by increasing the price of goods and reducing sales, caused him damage which excludes, in whole or in part, any unjust enrichment.[122] Where domestic law permits the trader to plead such damage in the main proceedings, it is for the national court to give such effect to the claim as may be appropriate. Furthermore, traders may not be prevented from applying to the courts having jurisdiction, in accordance with the conditions laid down in *Brasserie du Pêcheur and Factortame*[123]

---

[120] *Op. cit.*,n. 74 above. For an example of previous case law, see Cases 331, 376 and 378/85 *Bianco and Girard* [1988] ECR 1099.   [121] Case C-163/90 [1992] ECR I-4625.
[122] See further Joined Cases C-441/98 and C-442/98 *Michailidis* [2000] ECR I-7145, paras 34–35.   [123] *Op. cit.*, n. 2 above.

for reparation of loss caused by the levying of charges not due, irrespective of whether those charges have been passed on.[124]

Comateb went further than *San Giorgio* in signifying that the standards of protection expected of national law are much higher than previous case law suggested. Emphasis lies not so much on the requirement of equivalence as on the requirement that the protection of Community rights must be effective. Subsequent cases have reinforced this trend. In *Weber's Wine World* the ECJ stated that as 'a restriction on a subjective right' derived from Community law, the defence of passing on must be interpreted restrictively taking account in particular of the fact that shifting a charge to the consumer does not necessarily neutralise the economic effects of the tax on the trader concerned.[125] The national court is required to carry out an economic analysis in which all relevant circumstances are taken into account with a view to establishing whether the charge has actually been passed on and, if so, whether this has given rise to unjust enrichment.[126] Community law precludes not only a statutory presumption to the effect that a duty has been passed on but also the *de facto* reversal of the burden of proof by the practice of the tax authorities.[127]

The process towards the constitutionalization of remedies however would not be complete if the Court ignored 'second level non-compliance', namely, obstacles to the effective protection of Community rights posed not by national legislative measures but by administrative and judicial practice. Once the principle of effectiveness was firmly established, it was this second level that became the battleground.

Following the judgment in *San Giorgio*,[128] Italy introduced Law No 428/1990 which abolished the requirement of documentary evidence as a condition for the recovery of unduly paid sums. Article 29(2) of Law No 428 provided that duties levied under national provisions incompatible with Community law must be repaid unless the amount thereof has been passed on to others. Disputes arose however regarding the way the provision was applied in practice. In *Dilexport*,[129] the referring court observed that Article 29(2) was applied by Italian courts as incorporating a presumption. They were content to allow the administrative authorities to rely on the assumption that unduly levied sums are normally passed on to third parties. The ECJ held that such a presumption would be contrary to Community law. If, by contrast, Article 29(2) was interpreted as meaning that it was for the administrative authorities to prove that the charge was passed on, it would not be contrary to Community law. Given that *Dilexport* was a reference for a preliminary ruling, the ECJ was jurisdictionally limited to providing an interpretation of EC law and leaving it to the referring court to rule on national law.

---

[124] On the relationship between claims for the recovery of unduly paid charges and State liability in damages, see below Chapter 10.   [125] *Weber's Wine World, op. cit.*, para 95.

[126] *Ibid.*, para 101; *Michailidis, op. cit.*, paras 34–35.

[127] *Weber's Wine World, op. cit.*, paras 113–14.

[128] *San Giorgio* had been confirmed in Case 104/86 *Commission v Italy* [1988] ECR 1799.

[129] *Op. cit.*, n. 94 above.

Dilexport was not the end of the story. In *Commission v Italy*,[130] the Commission brought an enforcement action seeking a declaration that Italy had failed to meet its obligations by maintaining in force Article 29(2). The novel element in this case was that the Commission was effectively attacking the judicial interpretation of Article 29(2). Its argument was that Article 29(2) was applied by Italian courts, including the Supreme Court of Cassation, so as to give rise to a *de facto* presumption of passing on, and thus made excessively difficult the right to repayment of unduly paid charges. The Court upheld the Commission's action. It held that Article 29(2) is in itself neutral in relation both to the burden of proof and the evidence which is admissible to prove it. Its effect must be established in the light of the construction given to it by national courts. It then continued:[131]

In that regard, isolated or numerically insignificant judicial decisions in the context of case-law taking a different direction, or still more a construction disowned by the national supreme court, cannot be taken into account. That is not true of a widely-held judicial construction which has not been disowned by the supreme court, but rather confirmed by it.

Where national legislation has been the subject of different relevant judicial constructions, some leading to the application of that legislation in compliance with Community law, others leading to the opposite application, it must be held that, at the very least, such legislation is not sufficiently clear to ensure its application in compliance with Community law.

After reviewing the evidence, the Court concluded that a certain number of judgments of the Corte suprema di cassazione were based on the premise that indirect taxes are in principle passed on by economic operators. It held that such a premise was merely a presumption which was not justified and could not be accepted in the context of the examination of claims for repayment of indirect taxes contrary to Community law. The ECJ took issue also with certain other aspects of administrative practice followed by the Italian authorities and upheld by the national courts.[132] Effectively, the Court found that although Article 29(2) of the Law was in itself compatible with Community law, it was applied by the authorities and 'a substantial proportion of the courts' with undue formalism so as to give rise to a *de facto* presumption and thus failed to meet the requirement of effectiveness. The solution was for Italy to amend the law and thus end the possibility of deviation.

---

[130] *Op. cit.*, n. 27 above.   [131] Paras 32–33.

[132] There were two such aspects: first, the authorities required, as a condition to repayment, the production of the accounting documents of the undertaking concerned. The Court held that, insofar as they required the production of such documents after the expiry of their statutory preservation period and in the event of failure to produce drew a presumption of passing on, they made excessively difficult the protection of Community rights. Where the authorities required the production of accounting documents during the period for which they must be preserved by law, the Court held that failure to produce them could be regarded as a factor to be taken into account in showing that the charges had been passed on but was not in itself sufficient to create a presumption. The second aspect of administrative practice which was at issue was that the authorities considered that the charge had been passed on if the payee had not credited it as an asset in its balance-sheet for the year of its payment. The Court, understandably, held that, in view of the difficulties of obtaining reimbursement, the requirement to make such entry was unfair and could even be said to be contrary to the principles of lawful accounting.

Commission v Italy is the clearest illustration of second level enforcement. The effective enforcement of Community rights is incompatible with administrative formalism on the part of national authorities and requires the active cooperation of the national judiciary. It is the first case where the Commission brings, and the ECJ upholds, an action for breach of Community law which is owing, to a large extent, to a national supreme court.

Provided that the dual requirements of minimum protection and equivalence are respected, it falls on the Member States to determine the entities from which unduly paid charges may be recovered. In one case it was held that, where the proceeds of a duty levied contrary to Community law have been allocated to independent operators subject to local authority control, national law may require that the action for repayment lies against such persons.[133]

9.7. Effective judicial review

9.7.1. The right to judicial review before national courts

Although the Court has declared that the right to judicial protection is one of the general principles of law stemming from the constitutional traditions of the Member States,[134] this declaration gives us little guidance as to the specific contents of that right, the constraints to which it may be subject, and the way it is to be balanced with other, conflicting, interests. In general, it includes the right of access to the courts and the right to obtain effective judicial review before the Court itself and before national courts. The need for effective judicial review before the Community judicature was highlighted in *les Verts*.[135] Notably, however, access of individuals to the CFI to annul Community measures remains severely restricted. The ECJ has followed a strict interpretation of Article 230(4) and has fended off calls by Jacobs AG and the CFI to liberalise *locus standi*.[136]

National courts are also under a duty to provide effective judicial review for the protection of Community rights. The leading case is *Johnston v Chief Constable of the Royal Ulster Constabulary*.[137] Because of the high number of police officers assassinated in Northern Ireland, the Chief Constable decided that only male officers would carry fire-arms and that existing contracts of women officers serving in the RUC would not be renewed except when they had to perform duties assigned only to female officers. As a result of the new policy, Mrs Johnston,

---

[133] *Texaco and Olieselskabet Danmark, op. cit.*, n. 63 above, paras 42–43.

[134] See e.g. *Johnston, op. cit.*, n. 16 above, para 18; *Unión de Pequeños Agricultores, op. cit.*, n. 6 above, para 39; *Commission v Jégo Quéré, op. cit.*, n. 6 above, para 29.

[135] Case 294/83 *les Verts v Parliament* [1986] ECR 1339, para 23. See above ch. 1

[136] See *Jégo Quéré, op. cit., Unión de Pequeños Agricultores, op. cit.* (cf the Opinion of Jacobs AG) and see above n. 6.

[137] *Op. cit.* Note See also Case C-97/91 *Borelli v Commission* [1992] ECR I-6313.

a member of the RUC full-time Reserve, was refused renewal of her contract. She brought proceedings in the Industrial Tribunal challenging the refusal on grounds of sex discrimination. The applicable measure was the Sex Discrimination (Northern Ireland) Order 1976 which banned sex discrimination in relation to employment with the police. Article 53(1) of the Order stated that none of its provisions rendered unlawful an act done for the purpose of safeguarding national security or of protecting public safety or public order. Article 53(2) provided that a certificate issued by the Secretary of State certifying that an act was done for a purpose mentioned in Article 53(1) provided conclusive evidence to that effect. In the proceedings before the Industrial Tribunal, the Secretary of State produced such a certificate in relation to the decision to refuse the renewal of Mrs Johnston's contract. On a reference for a preliminary ruling, the Court referred to Article 6 of the Sex Discrimination Directive[138] and stated that the requirement of judicial control stipulated in that provision reflects 'a general principle of law which underlies the constitutional tradition common to the Member States' and which is laid down in Articles 6 and 13 of the ECHR. By virtue of Article 6 of the Directive, interpreted in the light of that principle, all persons have the right to obtain 'an effective remedy in a competent court against measures which they consider to be contrary to the principle of equal treatment for men and women laid down in the directive'. The Court concluded that a provision which requires a certificate to be treated as conclusive evidence that the conditions for derogating from the principle of equal treatment are met allows the competent authority to deprive an individual of judicial protection and is therefore contrary to the principle of effective judicial control laid down in Article 6 of the Directive.[139]

This was a landmark case which showed that Community law was able to provide individuals not only with rights but also remedies and illustrated the affinity between the principle of effectiveness and the right of judicial protection as a fundamental right. On the basis of the Court's reasoning, it seems that, as a general rule, any provision of Community or national law which enables a certificate issued by the administration to exclude recourse to the courts in circumstances where the rights of the individual are adversely affected will be struck down as 'unconstitutional'. The judgment is particularly notable because in that case the clause excluding recourse to the courts pertained to matters of national security, an area not easily susceptible to judicial scrutiny.[140]

---

[138] Article 6, in the version applicable at the time, stated as follows: 'Member States shall introduce into their national legal systems such measures as are necessary to enable all persons who consider themselves wronged by failure to apply to them the principle of equal treatment within the meaning of Articles 3, 4 and 5 to pursue their claims by judicial process possibly after recourse to other competent authorities.' Note that it has now been amended (and become much more specific in relation to the remedies that it requires) by Directive 2002/73 amending Council Directive 76/207, OJ L 269/15.   [139] *Johnston, op. cit.*, paras 18–20.

[140] The Court's approach in *Johnston* is consistent with its application of the principle of proportionality. As we saw in Chapter 4, acts done in the interests of national security do not escape control on grounds of proportionality although the degree of scrutiny exercised by the Court may be less strict than in other areas.

The importance of providing effective judicial review has been stressed in subsequent cases. In *UNECTEF v Heylens*[141] the Court held that, since free access to employment in the host Member State is a fundamental Community right, the existence of a judicial remedy against any decision of a national authority refusing that right is essential in order to secure effective protection. Thus, a refusal by the authorities of the host State to recognize as equivalent a diploma granted to a migrant worker by another Member State must be subject to judicial proceedings in which its legality under Community law can be reviewed. The Court has followed a similar approach in relation to the free movement of goods.[142] The case law regards the availability of judicial review against restrictions on fundamental freedoms as necessary in order to ensure that such restrictions meet the requirement of proportionality.[143]

The right to effective judicial review requires national authorities to give reasons to justify decisions which affect adversely Community rights.[144] The case law views the requirement of reasoning as a general principle incumbent on all national authorities.[145] As Fennelly AG stated in *Sodemare and Others v Regione Lombardia*,[146]

The obligation to give reasons for national decisions affecting the exercise of Community-law rights does not arise from any extension of Article 190[147] of the Treaty, but from the general principle of Community law, flowing from the constitutional traditions of the Member States, that judicial remedies should be available to individuals in such cases.

The right to a judicial remedy and the duty to state reasons are limited to final decisions and do not extend to preparatory decisions or opinions.[148] Also, the duty to state reasons applies only to individual decisions against which the person concerned may have some remedy of a judicial nature and not to national rules of general application.[149]

---

[141] Case 222/86 [1987] ECR 4097. The case concerned the refusal of French authorities to recognize a Belgian football trainers' diploma. See further C-340/89 *Vlassopoulou* [1991] ECR I-2357; Case C-104/91 *Colegio Oficial des Agentes de la Propiedad Immobiliaria v Aguirre Borrell and Others* [1992] ECR I-3003; Joined Cases C-286/94, 340/95, 341/95 and 47/96 *Molenheide* [1997] ECR I-7281.

[142] See Case 178/84 *Commission v Germany* [1987] ECR 1227, para 46. See also C-18/88 *GB-INNO-BM* [1991] ECR I-5941; Joined Cases C-46/90 and C-93/91 *Lagauche* [1993] ECR I-5267.

[143] See C-19/92 *Kraus v Land Baden-Württemberg* [1993] ECR I-1663 and above Chapter 4.

[144] *UNECTEF v Heylens*, *op. cit.*, para 15; *Vlassopoulou*, *op. cit.*, para 22; *Kraus*, *op. cit.*, para 40; Case C-249/88 *Commission v Belgium* [1991] ECR I-1275, para 25.

[145] Cf *R v Secretary of State for the Environment, Transport and Regions, and Parcelforce, ex p Marson*, judgment of 8 May 1998. In that case the Court of Appeal held that the Secretary of State was under no obligation to give reasons for refusing to carry out an environmental impact assessment under the Town and Country Planning (Assessment of Environmental Effects) Regulations 1988 implementing Directive 85/337 on the assessment of the effect of certain public and private projects on the environment, OJ 1985 L 175, p. 40. This case is now an unreliable precedent.

[146] Case C-70/95 *Sodemare SA and Others v Regione Lombardia* [1997] ECR I-3395 at 3405.

[147] See now Article 253 EC.   [148] *UNECTEF v Heylens*, *op. cit.*, para 16.

[149] *Sodemare*, *op. cit.*, para 19.

In *The Queen v Secretary of State for the Home Department, ex p Mann Singh Shingara and Abbas Radiom*,[150] on a reference from the Queen's Bench Division, the Court had the opportunity to examine the legal remedies available to Community nationals who are refused entry into the territory of a Member State on grounds of public security. Mr Shingara, a French national, was refused leave to enter the United Kingdom on grounds of national security. Mr Radiom, who had both Iranian and Irish nationality, applied for a residence permit but his application was rejected on grounds of national security. Under s. 13(5) of the Immigration Act 1971, where a foreign national is refused leave to enter on such grounds, he has no right of appeal although he may seek leave to apply for judicial review. One of the issues referred for a preliminary ruling was whether Community law granted the applicants a right to appeal to an immigration adjudicator. Article 8 of Directive 64/221[151] provides that a Community national shall have the same remedies in respect of any decision concerning entry, or refusing the issue or renewal of a residence permit, or ordering expulsion from the territory, 'as are available to nationals of the State concerned in respect of acts of the administration'. The applicants and the Commission argued that where nationals of a Member State have a specific right of appeal against any refusal of recognition of their right to entry, nationals of other Member States must have the same right of appeal in respect of a similar refusal even if the reasons for the refusal differ. Dismissing that argument, the Court stated:[152]

The two situations are . . . in no way comparable: whereas in the case of nationals the right of entry is a consequence of the status of national, so that there can be no margin of discretion for the State as regards the exercise of that right, the special circumstances which may justify reliance on the concept of public policy as against nationals of other Member States may vary over time and from one country to another, and it is therefore necessary to allow the competent national authorities a margin of discretion . . .

Consequently, the reply to the . . . question is that on a proper construction of Article 8 of the directive, where under the national legislation of a Member State remedies are available in respect of acts of the administration generally and different remedies are available in respect of decisions concerning entry by nationals of that Member State, the obligation imposed on the Member State by that provision is satisfied if nationals of other Member States enjoy the same remedies as those available against acts of the administration generally in that Member State.

It follows that it is permissible for a Member State to treat nationals of other Member States less favourably than its own nationals with regard to the remedies available against decisions refusing entry or ordering expulsion from the national

---

[150] *Op. cit.*, n. 49 above.

[151] Council Directive 64/221 on the coordination of special measures concerning the movement and residence of foreign nationals which are justified on grounds of public policy, public security or public health (OJ, English Special Edition 1963–64, p. 117).

[152] Paras 30–31.

territory. The obligation incumbent on the Member State is to make available to nationals of other Member States the same remedies as those provided against acts of the administration generally. The Court did not express a view as to what the minimum content of such remedies must be. Two points must be made however in this context. First, it follows from the case law that such remedies must provide full and effective protection. Second, Article 9 of Directive 64/221 provides for minimum procedural guarantees for the persons concerned. Colomer AG stated that a Community national is entitled to challenge a decision refusing him leave to enter or ordering his expulsion on grounds of public security or public policy by means of an effective remedy which ensures that 'the entire administrative decision, including its substantive grounds, is subjected to judicial scrutiny'.[153] He took the view that, in English law, the requirements of Article 8 are in principle satisfied by allowing the person concerned to apply for judicial review. He added however the *caveat* that if judicial review of decisions concerning the entry or expulsion of foreign nationals did not allow the courts to undertake complete and effective examination of such decisions, including review of their substance, Community law would require such restrictions to be set aside.[154]

Directive 64/221 has now been replaced by Directive 2004/38,[155] which lays down specific requirements as regards the procedural safeguards available and the standards of judicial review. Article 31(1) states that the persons concerned must have access to judicial and, where appropriate, administrative redress procedures in the host Member State to appeal against or seek review of any decision taken against them on grounds of public security, public policy or public health. Under Article 31(3), the redress procedures must allow for an examination of the legality of the decision, as well as of the facts and circumstances on which the proposed measure is based. They must also examine the proportionality of the decision in the light of the requirements laid down in Article 28 of the Directive.

Directive 2004/38 lays down more specific requirements than Directive 64/221 and in some respects goes further in protecting the interests of Community citizens but, it is submitted, it does not contradict the judgment in *Shingara* which would have been decided in the same way under it.

9.7.2. Intensity of review

Whilst the case law guarantees the right to judicial review before national courts against any decision denying or restricting Community rights, it is more difficult to provide specific guidelines regarding the intensity of review. As we saw in the

---

[153] See the final paragraph of the Opinion.   [154] Para 64 of the Opinion.
[155] Directive 2004/38 of the European Parliament and of the Council on the right of the citizens of the Union and their family members to move and reside freely within the territory of the Member States amending Regulation No 1612/68 and repealing Directives 64/221, 68/360, 72/194. 73/148, 75/34, 75/35, 90/364, 90/365 and 93/96, OJ 20004, L 158/77. The Directive is due to be implemented by 30 April 2006.

previous section, in some areas such as the free movement of workers Community law provides for specific remedies.[156] In general, effective judicial review means that the national court must have jurisdiction to determine the legality, including proportionality and the substantive grounds, of the measure. They must also comply with the requirements laid down in Article 6 of the ECHR as interpreted by the Strasbourg court. The precise scope of review, however, will depend on a number of considerations, including the nature of the right and the circumstances of the case.

An example is provided here by *Upjohn v Licensing Authority*.[157] In 1993, the UK Licensing Authority revoked the marketing authorization relating to Triazolam, a prescription drug for the treatment of insomnia, which had first been authorized for marketing in the UK in 1978. Upjohn Ltd sought judicial review of the decision revoking the authorization before the English courts. It argued that Directive 65/65 on proprietary medicinal products[158] and, more generally, Community law required national courts to exercise full review of the merits of the decisions of national competent authorities, i.e. to verify on the basis of a fresh, comprehensive examination of the issues of fact and law, whether the decision taken was correct. In the view of Upjohn, the right to full review derived from the direct effect of Article 11 of Directive 65/65 which lays down the criteria for revocation of a marketing authorization. The Court however declined to accept that argument. Referring to its established case law, it pointed out that, in the absence of Community rules, it is for the domestic legal system of each Member State to designate the courts having jurisdiction and to lay down the detailed procedural rules governing actions for safeguarding rights which individuals derive from Community law, subject to the principles of effectiveness and equivalence.[159] It held that, with regard to decisions revoking marketing authorizations following complex assessment in the medico-pharmacological field, the effective protection of Community rights does not require a procedure empowering the national courts to substitute their assessment of the facts and of scientific evidence for the assessment made by the national authority revoking authorization. The Court then proceeded to draw a parallel between judicial review of Community measures and review of national measures. It recalled its case law according to which, where a Community authority is called upon to make complex assessments in the exercise of broad discretionary powers, judicial review is limited to ascertaining the accuracy of facts, manifest error, misuse of powers, and clear excess of discretion.[160]

---

[156] See above Articles 8 and 9 of Directive 64/221 and the discussion in 9.7.1 above.

[157] Case C-120/97 [1999] ECR I-223.

[158] Council Directive 65/65/EEC on the approximation of provisions laid down by law, regulation or administrative action relating to proprietary medicinal products (OJ, English Sp. Ed., 1965–66, p. 20) as amended especially by Directive 83/570/EEC (OJ 1983 L 332, p. 1).

[159] See *Rewe* and *Comet*, op. cit.

[160] *Upjohn*, op. cit., para 34 referring, *inter alia*, to Joined Cases 56 and 58/64 *Consten and Grundig v Commission* [1966] ECR 299; Case 55/73 *Balkan-Import-Export v Hauptzollamt Berlin-Packhof* [1973] ECR 1091, para 8; Case C-157/96 *National Farmers' Union and Others* [1998] ECR I-2211, para 39.

Consequently, the Court held, Community law does not require the Member States to establish a procedure for judicial review of national decisions revoking marketing authorizations which involves a more extensive review than that carried out by the Court of Justice itself in similar cases. It pointed out however that any national procedure for judicial review must enable the court seised of the dispute to apply effectively the relevant principles of Community law when reviewing the legality of national decisions.[161]

In *Upjohn*, the Court declined an invitation to raise the standards of judicial review across the Community. By disabling the principle of effectiveness and relying instead on the principle of equivalence, it left national laws to dictate the intensity of review. The judgment promotes the internalization of Community law at the expense of uniformity and, in effect, allows national courts to play the leading role: it opts for convergence 'from below' rather than convergence 'from above'.

Upjohn illustrates a tendency to view Community and national authorities as part of one and the same constitutional structure and subject them to equivalent standards of accountability. This approach seems to be countenanced by similar developments in other areas.[162] It is not suggested here that Community and national authorities are assimilated in every respect. In some areas, the analogy between Community and national authorities breaks down. Traditionally, for example, the Court applies a much stricter test of proportionality over national provisions restricting free movement than over Community measures which constrain the freedom of the individual even where the grounds of restriction are the same.[163] Also, as we saw, in *Shingara and Radiom*, the ECJ accepted that Community nationals were not in a comparable situation to nationals of the host State with regard to the national territory.

Whilst *Upjohn* and the other cases discussed above concerned the power of national courts to review national measures which allegedly violate Community law, *Roquette Frères v Commission*,[164] concerned the power of national courts to review the execution of Community decisions by national authorities. In both cases the power of review is based ultimately on Community law but there are important differences: first, in the latter case, the national court is called upon to review not a national measure but, essentially, a Community postulation. Second, in contrast to the previous cases where Community law was relied upon to provide a higher level of protection for the individual than that guaranteed by national law, here national constitutional principles were relied upon to champion individual rights *vis-à-vis* intervention by the Community authorities. These differences led

---

[161] *Upjohn, op. cit.*, paras 35–36.
[162] See e.g, in relation to liability, Case C-352/98 P *Laboratoires Pharmaceutiques Bergaderm and Goupil v Commission* [2000] ECR I-5291, and, in relation to the rights of defence, Case T-346/94 *France-Aviation v Commission* [1995] ECR II-2841.
[163] For examples, see Tridimas, *op. cit.*, n. 3, Chapter 4.
[164] Case C-94/00 *Roquette Frères v Commission*, [2002] ECR I-9011.

the Court to circumscribe the outer limits of the national court's jurisdiction thus following a maximalist approach rather than relying on the application of the principles of equivalence and effectiveness.

The case concerned the powers of national courts to refuse authorization for the conduct of investigations carried out on business premises ordered by the Commission in the field of competition law. Article 14 of Regulation 17 enables the Commission to carry out investigations in order to establish the possible violation of competition law.[165] The powers of the Commission in this context are wide-ranging and include the power to examine business records, ask for oral explanations on the spot, and enter any premises of undertakings. The Commission may order such investigations by formal decision which, *inter alia*, must specify the subject-matter and purpose of the investigation, appoint the date on which it is to begin and indicate the penalties in case of non-compliance. Under Article 14(6), where an undertaking opposes an investigation ordered by the Commission, the Member State concerned must afford the necessary assistance to the officials authorized by the Commission to enable them to carry out their investigation. Under French law, such investigations are subject to prior judicial authorization being granted by the President of the Tribunal de grande instance which, under the French Constitution, has the duty to verify whether, in the specific circumstances, the authorization is justified.

Roquette Frères challenged an authorization granted by the President of the Tribunal de grande instance of Lille authorising the French authorities to enter its premises pursuant to a Commission decision ordering an investigation. It argued that it was not open to the President of the Tribunal to order entry into private premises without first satisfying himself that there were reasonable grounds for suspecting the existence of anti-competitive practices. The Cour de cassation made a reference seeking clarification of the ruling in *Hoechst*[166] in particular, the extent to which, in exercising its investigatory powers, the Commission must respect the procedural principles laid down by national law. The Cour de cassation asked, in particular, whether a national court may refuse authorization to enter premises where (a) it considers that the information or evidence provided in the Commission decision is not sufficient; and (b) if the court is not entitled to call for the submission of such information or evidence, on the ground that the Commission decision does not state sufficient reasons to enable the court to verify whether the application before it is sufficiently justified.

The Court laid down the following principles:

- Under Article 14(6), where the Commission intends to carry out an investigation with the assistance of national authorities, it is required to respect the relevant procedural guarantees laid down by national law.

---

[165] Note that this has now been replaced by Articles 20 and 21 of Regulation 1/2003.
[166] Joined Cases 46/87 and 227/88 *Hoechst v Commission* [1989] ECR 2859.

- Member States, for their part, are subject to a twofold requirement. On the one hand, they are required to ensure that the Commission's actions are effective; on the other hand, they must respect the constraints imposed by various general principles of Community law.
- It is for the competent national body to consider whether the coercive measures envisaged are arbitrary or excessive having regard to the subject-matter of the investigation.

The Court then proceeded to provide guidelines concerning the purpose and scope of the national court's power of review.

As to the purpose, the national court does not have jurisdiction to examine the need for the investigations ordered by the Commission. The lawfulness of the Commission's decision is a matter for the Community judicature to decide. The national court's jurisdiction is exhausted in examining whether the coercive measures in question are arbitrary and proportionate. The Court referred to the context in which the national court exercises its jurisdiction. It pointed out that Community law provides a range of guarantees for the protection of the undertaking concerned. These include the obligation of the Commission to give reasons and also state in its decision, as precisely as possible, what it is looking for and the matters to which the investigation relates. Further, the undertaking concerned may challenge the Commission's decision ordering the investigation before the CFI under Article 230(4) EC.

As to the scope of review, it drew a distinction between review to ensure that the coercive measures are not arbitrary and review of their proportionality. In reviewing whether the measures are arbitrary, the national court is required to satisfy itself that there exist reasonable grounds for suspecting an infringement of the competition rules by the undertaking concerned. There is no fundamental difference between this review and the review that the Community judicature may be called upon to carry out for the purposes of ensuring that the investigation decision itself is not arbitrary, that is to say, it has not been adopted in the absence of facts capable of justifying the investigation. Although the nature of the review in the two cases is similar, their objectives are different: the Community judicature carries out a review of the investigatory powers of the Commission whilst the national court reviews the coercive measures adopted by the national authorities. In view of the fact that such coercive measures entail an invasion of privacy, the national court has an autonomous power to satisfy itself that the measures are not arbitrary. The Commission is therefore required to provide the national court with explanations showing, in a properly substantiated manner, that it is in possession of information and evidence providing reasonable grounds for suspecting infringement of the competition rules by the undertaking concerned. On the other hand, the national court may not demand that it is provided with the information and evidence on the Commission's file as this may prejudice or delay the investigation by requiring for example the disclosure of the Commission's informants.

Review of proportionality means that the national court must establish whether the coercive measures are appropriate to ensure that the investigation can be carried out. Thus, coercive measures may be requested on a precautionary basis only if there are grounds for believing that the undertaking concerned will oppose the investigation or will attempt to conceal evidence if notified in advance. Review on proportionality grounds also requires the national court to ensure that the investigation does not constitute an intolerable interference in view of its objectives. In this context, the national court may take into account the seriousness of the suspected infringement, the nature of the involvement of the undertaking concerned and the importance of the evidence sought. The test to be followed here is whether, in view of the circumstances of the case, the granting of coercive measures 'necessarily appears manifestly disproportionate and intolerable'.[167]

Although in its judgment the Court goes to great lengths to determine the relative powers of the Community and the national authorities and circumscribe the review powers of national courts, it is in fact not possible for the ECJ to provide ready-made guidance to the national court. A striking feature of the judgment is a constant equivocation between, on the one hand, the need to defer to the Commission's discretion so as to ensure the effective enforcement of Community law and, on the other hand, the need to avoid undue interference with the right to privacy.

In *Roquette Frères* the Court placed particular emphasis on the duty of cooperation provided for in Article 10 EC. This is an area where cooperation is particularly crucial since national and Community authorities are called upon to assist in the attainment of Treaty objectives by coordinating the exercise of their respective powers. The duty of loyal cooperation means that, where the national court considers that the information supplied by the Commission does not justify the coercive measures, it cannot simply dismiss the application. It must as rapidly as possible inform the Commission or the national agency of the difficulties encountered and, if necessary, ask for additional information. Only if the Commission fails to provide the necessary clarifications may the national court refuse to grant the assistance sought.[168] This imposes on national courts a far-reaching duty of cooperation which may lead them to exceed their passive role as defined by the national rules of procedure. It views national courts as agents of the executive rather than independent tribunals.

Where a national court dismisses the application for coercive measures in breach of Community law, the national competition agency may be under an obligation, imposed by Community law, to appeal against the decision so as to achieve the carrying out of the investigation.

The case illustrates vividly that, although the principles and standards of legality are based on Community law, the Community and the national legal orders are closely intertwined since reliance on national courts is a *sine qua non* condition for the enforcement of Community law.

---

[167] Para 80.   [168] Paras 91–94.

9.7.3. *Locus standi* before national courts

The Court has had the opportunity to pronounce on the minimum standards that should be guaranteed as regards *locus standi* to challenge national measures infringing Community law only in few cases.[169] In *Verholen*[170] it declared that, although in principle it is for national law to determine an individual's standing and legal interest in bringing proceedings, national law must not undermine the right to effective judicial protection. On that basis, it held that an individual who did not come *ratione personae* within the scope of Directive 7/79 could rely on it if he had a direct interest in ensuring that the principle of non-discrimination was respected *vis-à-vis* persons who were protected by its provisions, for example, his spouse. Thus, national law must provide *locus standi* not only to the addressee of an individual act but also to its 'direct victim'.[171] For example, the dependents of an employee claiming payment of a survivor's pension may rely on Article 141 to contest an occupational pension scheme involving sex discrimination.[172]

Safalero,[173] however, took a somewhat restrictive view. The Italian authorities had seized remote control units imported from other Member States because they did not bear the approval stamp required by Italian regulations. The units had been imported by Safalero Srl and sold to a retailer from whom they were seized. Safalero argued that the regulations were contrary to Community law but encountered a procedural obstacle: under Italian law, opposition proceedings against confiscation could be brought only by the person who committed the administrative offence in issue, i.e. the retailer. As a result, the importer's challenge was rejected for lack of standing. On the basis of previous case law, the Court confirmed that the Italian regulations requiring approval stamps were contrary to Community law.[174] It reiterated its judgment in *Verholen* stating that national legislation must not undermine the right to effective judicial protection. It noted however that Safalero had been fined by the Italian authorities as the seller of the remote control units and could challenge the fine. In the circumstances, its interests as an importer were sufficiently protected and, consequently, the fact that it could not challenge the confiscation against the retailer did not violate Community law.

The judgment brings echoes of *Levez*. The denial of a remedy is acceptable if an alternative effective remedy exists. The Court however reached the conclusion that the applicant's interests were well protected without entering into an assessment of the relative merits of the alternative procedural routes of challenge.

---

[169] See further P. Oliver, 'State Liability in Damages Following *Factortame III*: A Remedy Seen in Context', in Beatson and Tridimas (eds), *New Directions in European Public Law*, (Hart Publishing, 1998) 49 at 54–56. For public procurement, see Case C-410/01 *Fritsch, Chiari & Partner, Ziviltechniker GmbH and Others v Autobahnen- und Schnellstraßen-Finanzierungs-AG(Asfinag)*, [2003] ECR I-6413.

[170] Joined Cases C-87 to C-89/90 *Verholen and Others v Sociale Verzekeringsbank Amsterdam* [1991] ECR I-3757, para 24. [171] Oliver, *op. cit.*, 55.

[172] See Case C-200/91 *Coloroll Pension Trustees v Russell* [1994] ECR I-4389.

[173] Case C-13/01 *Safalero Srl v Prefetto di Genova*, judgment 11 September 2003.

[174] Joined Cases C-338/00 and C-429/00 *Radiosistemi* [2002] ECR I-5845.

Indeed, no reasons are given in the judgment. The Advocate General by contrast found that Safalero's procedural restriction fell short of the principle of effectiveness and his views are persuasive.[175] Although *Safalero* might appear restrictive, it should be read on its facts. It does not provide general guidance regarding the extent to which national laws may restrict challenge against a national measure on grounds of incompatibility with Community law by persons directly affected by the measure.

In other cases the ECJ has made pronouncements of principle which may have a bearing on standing without examining the issue directly. In *Unilever*[176] it held that an individual may invoke the inapplicability of national technical regulations which have not been notified to the Commission in breach of Directive 83/189 even in proceedings against another individual arising from a contractual dispute. The case did not specifically raise issues of standing but, nonetheless, sanctions collateral challenge against a national measure on grounds of incompatibility with Directive 83/189 and, in that respect, it appears to trump national rules which would prohibit such challenge.[177]

The pronouncement in *Verholen* that national rules on *locus standi* must not undermine the right to effective judicial protection is further underlined by two provisions. The first is Article I-29(1) of the Constitution which would require Member States to provide sufficient remedies to ensure effective legal protection of Community rights. As already stated,[178] this provision was included in the Constitution, at least partly, to compensate for the restrictive standing of individuals to challenge the validity of Community acts directly in the CFI. Article I-29(1), however, has a wider scope. It requires the national legal systems to ensure that individuals have *locus standi* to challenge not only national measures based on allegedly invalid Community measures but also national measures which are claimed to be incompatible with Community law. In both cases, the underlying rationale is the same, namely the effective protection of rights flowing from Community law. The second provision which limits Member State discretion is Article 47 of the Charter which lays down the right to an effective remedy. In any event, as argued by Oliver,[179] in determining the standards that national laws governing *locus standi* must respect, Article 230 provides a misleading comparator. In other words, it cannot be argued that, because Article 230(4) makes *locus standi* subject to establishing direct and individual concern, national laws should be permitted to impose equally restrictive requirements. On the contrary, liberal *locus standi* rules should be favoured precisely because Article 230 is so restrictive.

---

[175] Stix-Hackl AG argued that, since Safalero had placed the products on the market, their confiscation led to adverse economic repercussions, reflected badly on its reputation, and exposed it to potential lawsuits from other retailers; also, Safalero should not be considered as a third party to the dispute as it was in a contractual relationship with the retailer from whom the goods had been confiscated.   [176] Case C-443/98 *Unilever* [2000] ECR I-7535.

[177] Note that subsequently the Court backtracked, leaving more discretion to national laws but none of the cases raised specifically the issue of *locus standi*. See Case C-159/00 *Sapoc Audic v Eco-Emballages SA*, [2002] ECR I-5031; and *Delena Wells, op. cit.*, n. 19 above.

[178] See above p. 420.   [179] *Op. cit.*, p. 56.

The cases discussed above concerned standing to challenge decisions of national authorities. Problems also surround the recognition of *locus standi* to challenge conduct of private parties infringing Community law. The judgment in *Munoz*[180] is of particular importance here. The Court held that an agricultural regulation which imposed marketing standards entitled a competitor to bring proceedings against a trader who failed to comply with those standards, thus establishing a right to a civil remedy flowing directly from a regulation which did not create subjective rights. The judgment is discussed in detail below.[181] Suffice it to state here that it does not create an *actio popularis* although it does expand significantly the private enforcement of Community obligations.

It should also be accepted that national law must guarantee to a competitor *locus standi* to challenge unnotified State aid.[182] Such an approach receives implicit support from the case law,[183] is necessary to secure effective enforcement of the provisions on State aid, and conforms with the tendency of the case law to encourage greater involvement of national jurisdictions in the resolution of such disputes.[184] The same may be said in relation to conduct violating Articles 81 and 82 of the Treaty.

9.7.4. The right to an effective remedy under the Charter

The right to an effective remedy and the right to a fair trial now receive express recognition in Article 47 of the EU Charter of Fundamental Rights (Article II-107 of the Constitution). Article 47(1) states that 'Everyone whose rights and freedoms guaranteed by the law of the Union are violated has the right to an effective remedy before a tribunal in compliance with the conditions laid down in this Article'. This provision is based on Article 13 of the ECHR but offers more extensive protection because it provides for an effective remedy before a national court and not merely before a national authority.[185] It guarantees the right to an effective remedy against both national and Community authorities. It is not intended however to change the system of judicial review established by the EC Treaty nor the restrictive *locus standi* of individuals under Article 230(4).[186]

Article 47 is all-embracing in that it applies to all rights and freedoms guaranteed by Union law but presupposes the existence of a right or freedom which is a matter

---

[180] *Munoz Cia SA, op. cit.*, n. 29 above.   [181] See 11.15.2 below.

[182] Oliver, *op. cit.*, 55.

[183] See Case C-254/90 *Fédération Nationale du Commerce Extérieur v France* [1991] ECR I-5505.

[184] See *SFEI and Others, op. cit*, n. 5 above.

[185] See the Explanations relating to the text of the Charter of Fundamental Rights, provided by the Praesidium of the Charter Convention, document CHARTE 4473/00, 11 October 2000, p. 41, and the Updated Explanations issued by the Praesidium of the Constitutional Convention, document CONV/828/1/03, Rev 1, 18 July 2003, p. 41.

[186] *Ibid.* Note however that in *Jégo-Quéré v Commission op. cit.*, n. 6 above, the CFI relied on Article 47 of the Charter to support a liberalization of *locus standi* under Article 230(4): see para 42 of the judgment.

of interpretation of Union law. Whether such a right or freedom exists is not determined by Article 47 itself. In one respect, Article 47 is narrower than the right to judicial protection as guaranteed by the case law of the ECJ because it applies to Union institutions and the Member States but only insofar as the latter implement Union law.[187] The case law, by contrast, applies to Member States insofar as they act within the scope of application of Union law, which is a wider concept. This limitation is important only to the extent that Article 47 offers a higher level of protection than that guaranteed by the Court's case law.

Article 47(2) corresponds to Article 6(1) of the ECHR. It states that everyone is entitled to a fair and public hearing within a reasonable time by an independent and impartial tribunal previously established by law. It also guarantees the right to legal representation. The provision is wider than Article 6(1) because it is not confined to disputes relating to civil rights and obligations. This is an important extension but, for the rest, the guarantees provided by Article 6(1) apply also to Article 47(2).[188]

Finally, Article 47(3) states, reflecting Strasbourg jurisprudence, that legal aid must be made available to those who lack sufficient resources insofar as such aid is necessary to ensure effective access to justice.[189]

The right to an effective remedy is supplemented by Articles 48 to 50 of the Charter which provide respectively for the presumption of innocence and the right of defence in relation to criminal charges, the legality and proportionality of criminal penalties, and the right not to be tried twice for the same criminal offence (*non bis in idem*).

9.8. Compensation

9.8.1. Damages

The effective protection of Community rights may require national courts to award compensation for breach of obligations prescribed by Community measures. The first cases arose in relation to Article 6 of the Equal Treatment Directive.[190] In *von Colson and Kamann*,[191] the applicants in the main proceedings had been refused employment in breach of sex equality laws but, under the applicable German law, they were entitled only to compensation for the loss that they suffered as a result of their expectation that they would not be discriminated on grounds of sex. On that basis, they could recover only the travel expenses that they had incurred in

---

[187] See Article 51(1) of the Charter and also the Praesidium Explanations, *op. cit.*, p. 41.
[188] Praesidium Explanations, *op. cit.*, p. 41.
[189] See *Airey*, judgment of 9 October 1979, Series A, vol. 32, 11.
[190] For the text of Article 6 in the version applicable at that time, see n. 138 above.
[191] Case 14/83 *von Colson and Kamann v Land Nordrhein-Westfalen* [1984] ECR 1891. See also Case 79/83 *Harz v Deutsche Tradax* [1984] ECR 1921.

connection with their interviews for obtaining employment. The Court held that the objective of the Equal Treatment Directive is to provide equality of opportunity between men and women as regards access to employment and that real equality of opportunity cannot be achieved without an appropriate system of sanctions. Although Article 6 does not require any specific form of sanction, it requires that sanctions must be such as to guarantee real and effective judicial protection and have a real deterrent effect on the employer. On that basis, the ECJ found the limitation of compensation to a purely nominal amount incompatible with the Directive.

The judgment in *von Colson* indicated for the first time that the sanctions available under national law may not be sufficient for the enforcement of Community measures even in areas where such measures do not provide for specific sanctions, and that it is primarily by reference to the objectives of Community measures that the appropriate sanctions should be determined. In *Marshall II*[192] the Court went further. Miss Marshall was dismissed from her employment on the ground that she had passed the retirement age applied by her employer to women. In *Marshall II*,[193] the Court held that her dismissal constituted discrimination on grounds of sex contrary to the Equal Treatment Directive. Following that ruling, the Industrial Tribunal awarded Miss Marshall compensation, including a sum by way of interest, in excess of the statutory maximum provided for by section 65(2) of the Sex Discrimination Act 1975. In *Marshall II*, the House of Lords referred to the Court questions seeking primarily to determine (a) whether it is contrary to Article 6 of the Directive for national provisions to lay down an upper limit on the amount of compensation recoverable by a victim of discrimination; and (b) whether Article 6 requires that the compensation for the damage sustained as a result of the illegal discrimination should be full and that it should include an award of interest. Referring to *von Colson*, the Court held that the objective of the Directive cannot be attained unless there are measures appropriate to restore equality of opportunity when it has not been observed. The Court continued:[194]

Where financial compensation is the measure adopted in order to achieve the objective indicated above, it must be adequate, in that it must enable the loss and damage actually sustained as a result of the discriminatory dismissal to be made good in full in accordance with the applicable national rules.

... the fixing of an upper limit of the kind at issue in the main proceedings cannot, by definition, constitute proper implementation of Article 6 of the Directive, since it limits the amount of compensation *a priori* to a level which is not necessarily consistent with the requirement of ensuring real equality of opportunity through adequate reparation for the loss and damage sustained as a result of discriminatory dismissal.

With regard to ... the award of interest, suffice it to say that full compensation for the loss and damage sustained as a result of discriminatory dismissal cannot leave out of account

---

[192] Case C-271/91 *Marshall v Southampton and South-West Hampshire Area Health Authority* [1993] ECR I-4367.
[193] Case 152/84 *Marshall v Southampton and South-West Hampshire Area Health Authority* [1986] ECR 723. [194] Paras 26, 30 and 31.

factors, such as the effluxion of time, which may in fact reduce its value. The award of interest, in accordance with the applicable national rules, must therefore be regarded as an essential component of compensation for the purposes of restoring real equality of treatment.

Article 6 of the Equal Treatment Directive has now been amended in the light of these findings.[195] In *Marshall II* the Court also took a broad view of direct effect. In *von Colson* it had held that Article 6 required Member States to provide sufficiently effective remedies to achieve the objectives of the Equal Treatment Directive but left Member States free to choose between various solutions suitable for achieving those objectives. The Directive therefore did not contain unconditional and sufficiently precise obligations as regards sanctions. In *Marshall II* the Court went a step further. It held that the combined provisions of Articles 5 and 6 gave rights against the State to a person who had been injured as a result of discriminatory dismissal. In other words, the Directive allows Member States discretion to determine the remedies available for breach of its provisions but once the United Kingdom chose to provide the remedy of compensation, the requirement that compensation must be adequate meant that the national authorities had no degree of discretion in applying the chosen solution.[196]

9.8.2. The payment of interest

As a general principle and subject to the qualifications stated below, the requirement to pay compensation due under Community law entails the payment of interest. This has not been stated unequivocally by the ECJ but seems to derive from the case law.

In the context of the non–contractual liability of the Community, the ECJ accepted in *Ireks-Arkady* that entitlement to interest derives from the general principles common to the laws of the Member States.[197] This was reiterated in *Grifoni*[198] which concerned injury arising from an accident. The Court stated that compensation for loss is intended so far as possible to provide restitution for the victim of an accident and it is, accordingly, necessary to take account of inflation

---

[195] Article 6(2) as amended by Directive 2002/73 amending Council Directive 76/207, OJ L 269/15, now provides as follows: 'Member States shall introduce into their national legal systems such measures as are necessary to ensure real and effective compensation or reparation as the Member States so determine for the loss and damage sustained by a person injured as a result of discrimination contrary to Article 3, in a way which is dissuasive and proportionate to the damage suffered; such compensation or reparation may not be restricted by the fixing of a prior upper limit, except in cases where the employer can prove that the only damage suffered by an applicant as a result of discrimination within the meaning of this Directive is the refusal to take his/her job application into consideration.'

[196] See further Case C-180/95 *Draehmpaehl v Urania Immobilienservice OHG* [1997] ECR I-2195.

[197] Case 238/78 *Ireks-Arkady v Council and Commission* [1979] ECR 2955, para 20. For a discussion, see A. van Casteren, 'Article 215(2) and the Question of Interest' in T. Heukels and A. McDonnell (eds), '*The Action for Damages in a Community Law Perspective*' (Kluwer, 1997).

[198] Case C-308/87 *Grifoni v EAEC* [1994] ECR I-341, para 40.

since the event occasioning the loss. In addition, interest must be paid on the final sum awarded as compensation from the date of the judgment.[199]

The Court appears to take a similar approach where entitlement to compensation is required by a provision of Community law. The determining criterion here is whether payment of interest is required by the objectives of the measure which provides the right to compensation. As we saw, *Marshall II* held that compensation for breach of the Equal Treatment Directive must include the award of interest. The issue was examined again in *Evans v Secretary of State for the Environment, Transport and the Regions and the Motor Insurers' Bureau*.[200] The case concerned the Second Motor Insurance Directive,[201] which requires Member States to take all appropriate measures to ensure that civil liability for damage caused by motor vehicles is covered by compulsory insurance. One of the issues raised before the Court was whether the correct implementation of the Directive obliged Member States to provide for the payment of interest on sums awarded as compensation to victims of accidents caused by an unidentified vehicle and, if so, whether the failure to provide for the payment of interest was a serious breach of Community law. The ECJ started from the observation that the Directive did not contain any provision on the payment of interest. It pointed out that, under Article 4(1) of the Directive, the body responsible for paying compensation must do so at least up to the limits of the insurance obligation specified in the Directive so as to guarantee victims adequate compensation. The Court interpreted Article 4(1) as meaning that the compensation awarded must take account of the effluxion of time until actual payment of the sums awarded in order to guarantee adequate compensation for victims. In the absence of Community rules, it was incumbent on the Member States to lay down the rules to be applied for that purpose. In particular, Member States were free to choose between awarding interest or paying compensation in the form of aggregate sums which took into account the effluxion of time.[202]

The above cases suggest that interest forms part of a claim for compensation.[203] The claim however must be compensatory in nature. Different considerations appear to apply in restitutionary claims. *R v Secretary of State for Social Security, ex p Sutton*[204] concerned Directive 79/7 which provides for sex equality in social

---

[199] *Op. cit.*, para 43; the Court fixes the amount of interest not by reference to the legal rate in force in the applicant's Member State but at a rate varying between 6 and 8 percent: see e.g. *Grifoni, op. cit.*; case 152/88 *Sofrimport v Commission* [1990] ECR I-2477; Joined Cases C-104/89 and C-37/90 *Mulder v Commission* [1992] ECR I-3061.

[200] C-63/01 *Evans v Secretary of State for the Environment, Transport and the Regions and the Motor Insurers' Bureau*, judgment of 4 December 2003.

[201] Council Directive 84/5 on the approximation of the laws of the Member States relating to insurance against civil liability in respect of the use of motor vehicles, OJ 1984 L 8, p. 17.

[202] *Evans, op. cit.*, paras 70–71. The ECJ left to the national court to establish whether there was a serious breach for the purposes of state liability in damages: see para 88. It also left to the national court to decide the prior issue whether in the circumstances of the case the calculation of compensation breached the Directive.

[203] See also for this view: *Evans, op. cit.* Alber AG at para 45 of the Opinion.

[204] *Op. cit.*, n. 74 above.

security.[205] Article 7(1)(a) of the Directive states that its provisions are without prejudice to the right of Member States to exclude from its scope the determination of pensionable age for the purposes of granting retirement pensions and 'the possible consequences thereof for other benefits'. Mrs Sutton had been refused invalid care allowance on the ground that she had reached retirement age. Following the judgment in *Thomas*,[206] the Social Security Commissioner held that Article 7(1)(a) could not be relied on to refuse to award an invalid care allowance to women over 60. He awarded to Mrs Sutton the allowance with effect from 19 February 1986, i.e. one year before her application. Mrs Sutton claimed interest on the arrears of benefit on the basis of Article 6 of Directive 79/7 or, alternatively, on the basis of the principle that a Member State is liable in damages for breach of Community law. Article 6 of the Directive requires Member States to introduce the necessary measures to enable persons who consider themselves wronged by failure to apply the principle of equal treatment to pursue their claims by judicial process. Despite the similarity between that provision and Article 6 of Directive 76/207 on Equal Treatment, the Court refused to transpose the principle laid down in *Marshall II*[207] to the effect that full financial compensation must include the award of interest. It held that *Marshall II* concerned the award of interest on amounts payable by way of reparation for damage sustained as a result of discriminatory dismissal. By contrast, the case at issue concerned the right to receive interest on social security benefits. According to the judgment, payment in arrears of such benefits is not compensatory in nature and therefore interest on them cannot be regarded as an essential component of the right to equal treatment. Oliver correctly criticizes the judgment[208] on the ground that it runs counter to the principle of effectiveness. It focused on the wrong criterion since what matters is not the compensatory or otherwise nature of the claim but the need to ensure that the effluxion of time does not deprive a pecuniary right from its substance. The Court however left open the possibility that Mrs Sutton could obtain the amount of interest by means of an action based on State liability in damages.

Sutton was distinguished in *Metallgesellschaft*[209] which concerned the repayment of unduly paid tax. The Income and Corporation Taxes Act 1988 enabled companies to defer payment of tax when they paid dividends to their shareholders but this option was not available to subsidiaries of companies having their seat outside the UK. The applicants were UK subsidiaries of German companies who argued that, because they were unable defer payment, they suffered a cash flow disadvantage. The Court held that the differential tax regime was contrary to the

---

[205] Directive 79/7 on the progressive implementation of the principle of equal treatment for men and women in matters of social security, OJ 1979 L 6, p. 24.

[206] Case C-328/91 *Secretary of State for Social Security v Thomas and Others* [1993] ECR I-1247. In that case, the Court gave a restrictive interpretation to the derogation of Article 7(1)(a) holding that it was limited to the forms of discrimination existing under the other benefit schemes which are necessarily and objectively linked to the difference in retirement ages.   [207] *Op. cit.*, n. 67.

[208] See Oliver, 'State Liability in Damages following Factortame III' *op. cit.*, 49 at 60.

[209] *Op. cit.*, n. 39 above.

right of establishment and that UK subsidiaries of companies based in other Member States should have an effective legal remedy in order to obtain reimbursement of the advance payment of tax. On the basis of previous case law,[210] the Court held that, subject to the requirements of equivalence and effectiveness, it is for national law to settle all ancillary questions relating to the reimbursement of charges improperly levied, such as the payment of interest, its rate and the date from which it must be calculated. It noted however that, in this case, the claim for payment of interest was not ancillary but the very objective sought by the plaintiff's action. Where the breach of Community law arises not from the payment of the tax itself but from the fact it was levied prematurely, the award of interest represents the reimbursement of that which was improperly paid and is essential in restoring the equal treatment guaranteed by Article 43 EC.[211] The plaintiffs could recover a sum equal to the interest accrued either by way of restitution or by way of an action for damages for breach of Community law. *Sutton* was distinguished on the ground that in *Metallgesellschaft* it was precisely the interest itself which represented what would have been available to the plaintiffs but for the inequality of treatment, and which constituted the essential component of the right conferred upon them.

9.9. Is a national court required to raise a point of Community law on its own motion?

Does the duty of national courts to provide effective protection of Community rights extend so far as to require them to raise a point of Community law on their own motion where the parties to the proceedings have failed to do so? That issue arose in *Peterbroeck*[212] and in *van Schijndel*.[213] Both cases are of constitutional importance and were treated as such by the Court.[214]

Peterbroeck concerned the compatibility with Community law of certain provisions of the Belgian Income Tax Code. Under the Code, a taxable person may contest the imposition of a tax before the Regional Director of direct contributions. If his complaint fails, he may appeal to the Court of Appeal where he may submit new arguments within a period of 60 days. Arguments presented after that period are rejected as inadmissible. In *Peterbroeck* the applicant raised new arguments based on

---

[210] See e.g. *Express Dairy Foods, op. cit.,* n. 111 above; *Fromme v Balm, op. cit.,* n. 111 above.
[211] Para 87. [212] *Op. cit.,* n. 18 above.
[213] *Op. cit.,* n. 30 above. For a comment on both cases, see T. Heukels, (1996) 33 CML Rev 337.
[214] In *Peterbroeck* the Court decided to reopen the oral hearing and invited all Member States to submit argument on the power of a national court to raise on its own motion points based on Community law. A joined hearing was held for *Peterbroeck* and *van Schijndel*. In the litigation as a whole, eight Member States submitted argument. Only two of them, Spain and Greece, suggested that a national court is required to consider on its own motion points of Community law notwithstanding any national procedural rules to the contrary.

Community law after the expiry of the 60-day time limit. The Court of Appeal stated that the provisions of the Income Tax Code prevented it from examining on its own motion a point which had not been raised by the parties and referred to the Court of Justice the question whether those provisions were compatible with Community law. The Court gave a negative reply. After recalling its case law that a national procedural provision must not render the application of Community law excessively difficult, the Court held that although a 60-day time limit is not objectionable *per se*, the time limit provided by the Belgian Code was incompatible with Community law in the light of the special features of the procedure at issue. The Court relied on four arguments.[215] First, it pointed out that the Court of Appeal was the first authority capable of making a reference for a preliminary ruling since the Director of Taxes was an administrative body and as such not a court or tribunal within the meaning of Article 234. Second, it stated that the 60-day time limit started to run from the time when the Director lodged a certified copy of the contested decision. That meant that the period during which new pleas could be raised by the appellant had expired by the time the Court of Appeal held its hearing so that it was denied the possibility of considering the question of compatibility with Community law. Third, no other national court in subsequent proceedings could consider on its own motion the question of compatibility. Fourth, the Court held that the impossibility of national courts raising points of Community law on their own motion did not appear to be reasonably justifiable by principles such as the requirement of legal certainty or the proper conduct of procedure.

The reasoning of the Court is not beyond criticism and the above arguments are not necessarily conclusive.[216] In relation to the first argument, it may be noted that the fact that the Court of Appeal is the first court capable of making a reference under Article 234 does not prohibit, nor indeed does it make it any more difficult, for the taxable person to raise a point of Community law either before the Director or before the Court of Appeal. Similarly, the fact that no other Belgian court can consider issues of Community law *ex propriu motu* should not have any bearing on the 60-day time limit. The second argument used by the Court is difficult to compromise with Article 42(2) of its own Rules of Procedure. That article provides that no new plea in law may be introduced in the course of proceedings unless it is based on matters of law or of fact which come to light in the course of the procedure.[217] It will also be noted that Article 230(5) EC provides for a restrictive two-month time limit for actions for judicial review before the Community courts. Finally, the generality of the fourth argument appears to contradict statements made in the judgment in *van Schijndel*.[218] The latter judgment lays down the general principle and *Peterbroeck* should be read on its facts.

---

[215] *Op. cit.*, paras 17 to 20.

[216] In contrast to the Court, the Advocate General considered that the 60-day time limit was not unreasonably short and did not prevent a taxable person from claiming rights based on Community law.   [217] See also Article 48(2) of the Rules of Procedure of the CFI.

[218] See paras 21–22 of the judgment in *van Schijndel*.

In *van Schijndel* the Court was asked to rule, on a preliminary reference by the Hoge Raad, on whether a national court is required to raise on its own motion a point of Community law in civil proceedings pending before it. Applying the principle of equivalence, the Court held that where, by virtue of domestic law, national courts must raise on their own motion points of law based on binding domestic rules which have not been raised by the parties, such an obligation also exists in relation to binding rules of Community law. The Court went a step further holding that national courts must raise on their own motion points based on binding rules of Community law, where domestic law does not require but confers discretion on them to apply on their own motion binding rules of national law. That obligation is based on Article 10 EC and the duty to ensure the legal protection which persons derive from the direct effect of Community law.[219]

The Court held, however, that a national court is not required to raise on its own motion an issue of Community law where its examination would oblige the court to abandon the passive role assigned to it by going beyond the ambit of the dispute defined by the parties themselves and relying on facts other than those on which the parties base their claim.[220] That limitation is correct. As the Court pointed out, in a civil action it is for the parties to take the initiative, the court being able to act on its own motion only in exceptional cases where the public interest requires its intervention. That principle reflects conceptions prevailing in most of the Member States as to the relation between the State and the individual. It also safeguards the rights of defence and ensures proper conduct of the proceedings.[221]

The approach of the Court in *van Schijndel* accords broadly with that of the Advocate General. In his Opinions in *Peterbroeck* and *van Schijndel*, Jacobs AG concluded that Community law does not require that a national court must be free to raise an issue of Community law on its own motion irrespective of any time limit imposed by national law.[222] In the view of the Advocate General, the

---

[219] *van Schijndel, op. cit.*, para 14. Those findings were confirmed in Case C-72/95 *Kraaijeveld and Others v Gedeputeerde Staten van Zuid-Holland* [1996] ECR I-5403. It is not clear whether the duty of national courts to raise points of Community law on their own motion applies only in relation to directly effective provisions. Paragraph 14 of the judgment in *van Schijndel* suggests so but it is probably sufficient that the provision is binding and that it is intended to confer rights even if it is not directly effective. Contra: Heukels, *op. cit.*, n. 213 above.

[220] *van Schijndel, op. cit.*, para 22.   [221] *Ibid.*, para 21.

[222] The Advocate General rejected the argument that such a requirement derives from *Simmenthal* and *Factortame*. Those judgments establish that it must always be possible for an individual to bring a claim before a national court and to require it to protect Community rights. They do not establish that it must in all circumstances be open to the national court, as a matter of Community law, to raise *ex propriu motu* issues which the parties have failed to raise. Nor does such a requirement derive from Article 234. The Advocate General interpreted the Court's case law as meaning that where a question of Community law is raised before the national court, no rule of national law may preclude the national court from making a reference. However, Article 234 does not address the prior question in what circumstances a national court may itself raise on its own motion a point of Community law. See *Peterbroeck, op. cit.*, p. 4612.

principle of effectiveness requires that individuals are given, by the national procedural rules, an effective opportunity of enforcing their rights.[223] He stated:[224]

...if the view were taken that national procedural rules must always yield to Community
law, that would...unduly subvert established principles underlying the legal systems of the
Member States. It would go further than is necessary for effective judicial protection. It
could be regarded as infringing the principle of proportionality and, in a broad sense, the
principle of subsidiarity, which reflects precisely the balance which the Court has sought to
attain in this area for many years. It would also give rise to widespread anomalies, since the
effect would be to afford greater protection to rights which are not, by virtue of being
Community rights, inherently of greater importance than rights recognized by national law.

The picture which emerges from *Peterbroeck* and *van Schijndel* is that, whilst the
Court is ready to scrutinize vigorously national rules with a view to determining
whether they offer an adequate level of protection, it is keen not to upset the
adversarial character of civil proceedings.

Subsequently, *Eco Swiss China Time Ltd v Benetton International NV*[225] accepted
that certain provisions of Community law must be granted the status of rules of
public policy (*ordre public*), where such status is recognized by the national rules of
procedure. Eco Swiss commenced arbitration proceedings against Benetton in
relation to the premature termination of a licencing agreement, under the terms of
which all disputes between the parties were to be settled by arbitration in accordance with Netherlands law. The arbitrator found against Benetton who applied to
the Dutch courts for annulment of the arbitral award. It claimed that it was contrary to public policy (*ordre public*) because the licencing agreement infringed
Article 81 EC and was therefore void. During the arbitration proceedings, neither
the parties nor the arbitrator had raised any point of Community law. Netherlands
law provides for a limited number of grounds on which an arbitration award may
be annulled, one of them being that the award is contrary to public policy or
accepted principles of morality.[226] Under Dutch law, however, failure to respect
competition law is not regarded as a ground of public policy.

On a reference from the Hoge Raad, the Court elevated Article 81 to a rule of
ordre public on the basis of two arguments that can be termed the public policy
argument and the judicial protection argument. The Court accepted that, in the
interests of efficiency, review of arbitration awards should be possible only in
exceptional cases. It stated however that Article 81 is a fundamental provision
which is essential for the functioning of the internal market. It concluded that
where, under the domestic rules of procedure, a national court must annul an
arbitration award for failure to observe national rules of public policy, it must also

---

[223] *van Schijndel, op. cit.,* p. 4715.   [224] *Ibid.,* pp. 4715–4716.
[225] Case C-126/97 *Eco Swiss China Time Ltd v Benetton International NV* [1999] ECR I-3055. For
a comment, see A. P. Komninos, (2000) 37 CML Rev 459. See further C-53/96 *Hermes* [1998]
ECR I-3603, Joined Cases C-300/98 and 392/98 *Parfums Christian Dior SA v Tuk Consultancy BV*
[2000] ECR I-11307; Case C-89/99 *Schieving-Nijstad and Others* [2001] ECR I-5851.
[226] See Article 1065(1)(e) of the Code of Civil Procedure.

annul such an award for failure to comply with the prohibition laid down in Article 81(1).[227] The second argument, based on judicial protection, runs as follows. An arbitration award should be open to challenge in a court of law on grounds of incompatibility with EC competition law so as to ensure respect for the principle of judicial protection and also access to the preliminary reference procedure. Arbitration tribunals set up by private agreement are not courts or tribunals within the meaning of Article 234 and cannot therefore make preliminary references to the Court of Justice.[228] To meet the overriding requirement of uniform interpretation of Community law, a national court which is asked to determine the validity of an arbitral award should be able to examine the compatibility of the award with Article 81 EC and, if necessary, refer questions for a preliminary ruling.[229]

The net effect of the judgment is that failure of an arbitration award to observe the competition rules of the Treaty is a ground for its annulment.[230] The Court declared Article 81 as a rule of *ordre public*, even though Dutch law did not grant similar status to rules of competition law. This evinces a more prescriptive approach and surpasses the principle of equivalence. The obvious question which arises in this context is what other provisions of the Treaty should be treated as rules of *ordre public*. It is difficult to give a general answer. Much may depend on the type of proceedings in issue, i.e. whether they are civil or criminal or administrative in nature. In view of the Court's reasoning, there is a strong argument to be made that, in some contexts, the provisions of the Treaty on which the internal market is founded and which are directly effective deserve to be treated as public policy rules. This would encompass, for example, the provisions on the fundamental freedoms, and equality of sexes. But if so, what about other norms which are fundamental to the Community legal order such as the protection of fundamental rights or the principle of primacy? It may also be noted that the fact that a Community norm is included not in the Treaty itself but in a Community measure does not preclude it from being a rule of *ordre public*.

The issue whether a national court must raise a point of Community law on its own motion was examined once more in *Océano Grupo Editorial SA v Rocío Murciano Quintero*.[231] It was there held that a national court may determine on its own motion whether a contractual clause conferring exclusive jurisdiction on the courts of the supplier's domicile is unfair within the meaning of Directive 93/13 on

---

[227] *Eco Swiss, op. cit.*, paras 36–37.

[228] See Case 102/81 *Nordsee v Reederei Mond* [1982] ECR I-1095.

[229] *Eco Swiss, op. cit.*, para 40. See also Case C-393/92 *Municipality of Almelo v NV Energiebedrijf Ijsselmij* [1994] ECR I-1477, para 23.

[230] By contrast, the Court left the principle of *res judicata* of arbitral awards undisturbed. It held that the rules of Dutch civil procedure under which an arbitration award is open to appeal only within a period of three months and thereafter acquires the force of *res judicata* was compatible with Community law: see para 45.

[231] Joined Cases C-240 to C-244/98 *Océano Grupo Editorial SA v Rocío Murciano Quintero* and *Salvat Editores SA v Sánchez Alcón Prades and Copano Badillo*, [2000] ECR I-4941.

unfair terms in consumer contracts.[232] The Court held that the aim of Article 6 of the Directive, which requires Member States to lay down that unfair terms are not binding on the consumer, would not be achieved if the consumer were himself obliged to raise the unfair nature of such terms.[233] Although *Océano Grupo* referred only to a jurisdiction clause, subsequently, *Codifis*[234] extended the protection offered to consumers by holding that the unfairness of any contractual term may be raised even after the expiry of a limitation period provided for by national law. The Court held, in particular, that a provision which in proceedings brought by the seller against the consumer prohibits a national court, on the expiry of a limitation period, from finding on its own motion or following a plea raised by the consumer that a contractual term is unfair infringes the Directive. The Court justified this intervention on the ground that, otherwise, sellers would be able to avoid the application of the Directive simply by waiting until the expiry of the time limit fixed by national law before bringing proceedings.

9.10. Obligation to review final administrative decisions

A ruling on interpretation delivered by the ECJ in preliminary reference proceedings has retroactive effect. It defines the meaning of the Community provision in issue as it ought to have been understood and applied from the time of its coming into force unless the Court itself restricts the retroactive effect of its ruling.[235] Thus the national administrative authorities must apply the interpretation provided by the ECJ even to legal relationships which arose before its judgment. This duty is subject to limits imposed by the principle of legal certainty. It does not go as far as to require a national authority to reopen an administrative decision which became final under national law before the ECJ delivered its ruling. In *Kühne & Heitz NV v Productschap voor Pluimvee en Eieren,*[236] however, the Court held that, under certain conditions, the duty of cooperation provided for by Article 10 EC requires the national authorities to review a final administrative decision in order to take into account the interpretation of Community law provided by the ECJ. The obligation to reopen arises where the following conditions are met:

- national law confers on the administrative body the power to reopen a final decision;
- the administrative decision became final as a result of a judgment of a national court against whose decisions there is no judicial remedy;

---

[232] Council Directive 93/13/EEC of 5 April 1993 on unfair terms in consumer contracts, OJ 1993 L 95, p. 29.   [233] Para 26.

[234] Case C-473/00 *Codifis* [2002] ECR I-10875.

[235] See, *inter alia*, Case 61/79 *Denkavit Italiana* [1980] ECR 1205, para 16, and Case C-50/96 *Deutsche Telekom* [2000] ECR I-743, para 43.   [236] *Op. cit.*, n. 20 above.

- that judgment was based on an interpretation of Community law which, in the light of a subsequent judgment of the Court, was incorrect and which was adopted without a preliminary reference to the Court;
- the person concerned complained to the administrative body immediately after becoming aware of that judgment of the Court.

As in *van Schijndel*, in *Kühne & Heitz NV* the ECJ used Article 10 to transform a discretionary power provided under national law to an obligation. In this case, it is the power of a national authority to revisit a final administrative decision. The judgment strengthens the remedies for failure of a national court of last instance to make a reference. Interestingly, the Court made no reference to the principle of equivalence and treated the issue as one of effective protection of Community rights. *Kühne* suggests that a national administrative authority must revisit its decisions even if it would not be required to do so in a similar claim based purely on national law.

9.11. Interim measures

In direct actions, the Court of Justice and the Court of First Instance have wide powers to grant interim relief.[237] In proceedings before national courts interim relief is a matter for the national court to decide even where a reference for a preliminary ruling is made. The matter however is not governed exclusively by national law. The Court has laid down certain principles regarding the availability of interim measures.

9.11.1. Interim relief in national courts to protect Community rights

In *Factortame I*[238] it was held that national courts may be required to provide interim relief for the protection of Community rights even in cases where they would be unable to do so under national law. The litigation arose as a result of changes made by Part II of the Merchant Shipping Act 1988 and the Merchant Shipping (Registration of Fishing Vessels) Regulations 1988 to the system for the registration of British vessels. The Act tightened the conditions for the registration of vessels on the British register in order to stop the practice known as quota hopping whereby, according to the United Kingdom, its fishing quotas were plundered by vessels flying the British flag but having no genuine link with the United Kingdom. The applicants in the main proceedings were the owners or

---

[237] See Articles 242 [185] and 243 [186] EC. The CFI has similar powers: see Article 4 of Council Decision 88/591 of 24 October 1988 establishing a Court of First Instance of the European Communities, OJ 1988 L 319/1, as amended.   [238] *Op. cit.*, n. 2 above.

operators of 95 fishing vessels which were registered in Britain under the previous legislation but failed to satisfy the new conditions imposed by the Merchant Shipping Act 1988. The applicants challenged the compatibility of the Act with Community law by means of an application for judicial review and also applied for the grant of interim relief. The House of Lords[239] held that the grant of interim relief was precluded by the common law rule that an interim injunction may not be granted against the Crown and also by the presumption that an Act of Parliament is in conformity with Community law until such time as a decision on its compatibility with that law has been given. It referred however to the Court of Justice the question whether, notwithstanding the rules of national law, an English court has the power to grant an interim injunction against the Crown where it has sought a preliminary ruling. The Court replied in the affirmative relying on Article 10, Article 234, and the requirement to provide effective protection of Community rights. After referring to its judgment in *Simmenthal*, it held:[240]

... the full effectiveness of Community law would be just as much impaired if a rule of national law could prevent a court seised of a dispute governed by Community law from granting interim relief in order to ensure the full effectiveness of the judgment to be given on the existence of the rights claimed under Community law. It follows that a court which in those circumstances would grant interim relief, if it were not for a rule of national law, is obliged to set aside that rule.

That interpretation is reinforced by the system established by Article 177 of the EEC Treaty whose effectiveness would be impaired if a national court, having stayed proceedings pending the reply by the Court of Justice to the question referred to it for a preliminary ruling, were not able to grant interim relief until it delivered its judgment following the reply given by the Court of Justice.

In *Factortame* therefore the Court established that, where a national court considers that it is necessary to grant interim relief for the protection of Community putative rights, it is under a duty to make such relief available, setting aside a rule of national law which prevents it from doing so.[241] The effect of the judgment was to lead to reverse discrimination in the procedural plain. With regard to claims based on Community law, English courts acquired a power which hitherto they did not possess, namely, the power to suspend the application of an Act of Parliament pending a preliminary reference to the Court regarding its compatibility with Community law. With regard to claims based on national law, the old common law rule which prevented the suspension of Acts of Parliament continued to apply. Such differential treatment was clearly unsatisfactory and was criticized by the Law

---

[239] [1989] 2 WLR 997.   [240] Paras 21–22.
[241] In subsequent proceedings, the House of Lords granted interim relief to the applicants: see [1991] 1 All ER 70. For a critique of the *Factortame* litigation from the point of view of English law, see H.W.R. Wade, (1991) 107 LQR 1 and 4. In Case C-393/96 P(R) *Antonissen v Council and Commission* [1997] ECR I-441 it was held that the CFI may award provisional damages by way of interim measure in proceedings under Article 288(2) EC. It is arguable that national courts also have jurisdiction to grant interim damages. See Oliver, *op. cit.*, p. 59.

Commission.[242] It has since partly been remedied as a result of the House of Lords decision in *M. v Home Office*[243] where it was established that an injunction can be obtained against a Minister of the Crown as a matter of English law. One of the reasons which led the House of Lords to recognize injunctive relief against Ministers was precisely the need to avoid reverse discrimination.[244]

9.11.2. Interim relief in national courts to suspend national measures implementing Community regulations

The *Factortame* litigation involved a conflict between national legislation and Article 43 of the Treaty and therefore raised the issue of interim relief in the context of primacy of Community law. The judgment however opened the way to developments in the sphere of interim measures extending beyond primacy. If interim relief is 'a fundamental and indispensable instrument of any judicial system' as Tesauro AG declared,[245] the requirement to provide such relief derives from the rule of law rather than the principle of primacy. The question therefore arises whether a national court may suspend by way of interim relief the application of national measures implementing Community rules. That question was examined in *Zuckerfabrik*.[246] A Council regulation required sugar manufacturers to pay a special levy. The applicant undertakings challenged the demand for payment in the Finance Court of Hamburg claiming that the regulation was void. They also sought suspension of enforcement of the demand pending the outcome of the proceedings concerning its validity. Earlier, in *Foto-Frost*[247] the Court had held that national courts do not have the power to declare Community acts invalid but had expressly left open the possibility that a national court may be able to order the temporary suspension of a Community measure by way of interim relief. In *Zuckerfabrik* the Court saw the availability of interim protection as emanating from the right to judicial protection itself. It stated that the right of individuals to challenge the legality of regulations before national courts under Article 234 would be compromised if, pending delivery of the judgment of the Court in the preliminary reference proceedings, individuals did not have the right to obtain suspension of enforcement. Referring to Article 242 EC, the Court held that the coherence of the system of interim legal protection requires that national courts should also be able to order suspension of enforcement of a national administrative

---

[242] Law Commission Consultation Paper No 126, para 6.6.

[243] [1994]1 AC 377, [1993] 3 All ER 537.

[244] Note the dicta of Lord Woolf, *op. cit.*, at 551. See also the dicta by Lord Donaldson MR in the Court of Appeal: *M v Home Office* [1992] QB 270, 306H–307A. Note that the extension of the common law rule to cover injunctions against Ministers has been strongly criticized: see H.W.R. Wade, New Law Journal, 18 and 25 Sept. 1992.

[245] *Factortame, op. cit.*, at p. 2457.

[246] Joined Cases 143/88 and C-92/89 [1991] ECR I-415.

[247] Case 314/85 *Foto-Frost v Hauptzollamt Lübeck-Ost* [1987] ECR 4199.

measure based on a Community regulation, the legality of which is contested. The Court concluded as follows:[248]

The interim legal protection which Community law ensures for individuals before national courts must remain the same, irrespective of whether they contest the compatibility of national legal provisions with Community law or the validity of secondary Community law, in view of the fact that the dispute in both cases is based on Community law itself.

The Court's reasoning is instructive of its general approach in the area of remedies. It views national measures and measures adopted by the Community institutions as belonging to different tiers of the same legal order rather than as emanating from different legal orders. The principle of effective protection of Community rights is a constituent of the rule of law and binds not only the Member States but also the Community institutions. The task of national courts to uphold Community rights extends not only to protecting such rights against State action but also against Community action. However, the power of national courts to question Community action is made subject to limitations deriving from the principle of primacy and the need to ensure, as much as possible, the uniform application of Community law.

In *Zuckerfabrik* the Court held that the following conditions must be satisfied in order for a national court to be able to suspend the application of national measures based on a Community regulation:[249]

(1) The national court must have serious doubts as to the validity of the Community regulation on which the contested administrative measure is based.
(2) The national court must refer the question of validity of the Community regulation in issue to the Court of Justice if the question is not already before it.
(3) The granting of relief must be subject to uniform conditions in all the Member States.

Drawing an analogy with Articles 242 and 243 EC, the Court held that suspension may only be granted if there is urgency, namely if it is necessary to do so in order to avoid serious and irreparable damage to the applicant, and if the national court takes due account of the Community's interests.

On the requirement of urgency, it was held that the damage invoked by the applicant must be liable to materialize before the Court has been able to rule on the validity of the contested Community measure. In accordance with the case law under Article 242 EC, the Court stated that purely financial damage cannot in principle be regarded as irreparable.[250] The Court pointed out, however, that it is for the national court to examine the circumstances before it. In particular, the national court must consider whether immediate enforcement of the measure

---

[248] *Zuckerfabrik, op. cit.*, para 20.   [249] *Op. cit.*, paras 23 *et seq.*
[250] The case law however has held that, exceptionally, pecuniary damage may be regarded as irreparable where compensation cannot restore the injured person to the position prior to the occurrence of the damage: Case C-195/90 R *Commission v Germany* [1990] ECR I-3351, para 38.

would be likely to result in irreversible damage to the applicant which could not be made good if the Community act were to be declared invalid. On the requirement to take into account the interests of the Community, the Court emphasised that national courts are under an obligation to give full effect to Community law and consequently the application of regulations must not be suspended without proper guarantees. The national court must examine whether the regulation in issue would be deprived of all effectiveness if not immediately implemented.[251] The Court added that if suspension of enforcement is liable to involve a financial risk for the Community, the national court must be in a position to require the applicant to provide adequate guarantees, such as the deposit of money or other security.

The conditions for the granting of interim relief laid down in *Zuckerfabrik* are strict and may be seen as limiting the scope of interim protection available under some national laws.[252] It is submitted however that the judgment is a successful attempt to strike a balance between competing principles namely, on the one hand, the principle of effective judicial protection which requires that interim protection must be made available and, on the other hand, the requirement to ensure the full effect and uniform interpretation of Community law. It need hardly be emphasised that the power of national courts to suspend the application of Community law must be exercised with caution. Otherwise, the uniform application of Community law would be jeopardized and distortions of competition may ensue.[253] It has been suggested that the power to order interim relief against Community measures should be transferred from national courts to the CFI. A new procedure should be introduced, under which a national court could make a fast-track reference on interim relief to the CFI enabling the latter to issue a Union-wide interim order pending a ruling on its validity. This proposal would ensure the uniform application of Community law and deal with the argument of distortions

---

[251] The balancing exercise which the national court is called upon to perform is analogous to that which the Community judicature carries out in the context of Article 242. The Community court hearing the application for interim measures examines whether the possible annulment of the contested Community act in the main action would make it possible to reverse the situation that would have resulted from its immediate implementation, and conversely whether suspension of the operation of the act would be such as to prevent it being fully effective in the event of the main application being dismissed. See e.g. Joined Cases 76, 77 & 91/89 R *RTE and Others v Commission* [1989] ECR I-1141; Case C-149/95 P (R) *Commission v Atlantic Container Line and Others* [1995] ECR I-2165.

[252] For an interesting discussion, see S. de la Sierra, 'Provisional Court Protection in Administrative Disputes in Europe: The Constitutional Status of Interim Measures Deriving from the Right to Effective Court Protection. A Comparative Approach', (2004) 10 ELJ 42.

[253] The danger of distortions in the conditions of competition being created was identified by the United Kingdom in its submissions in *Zuckerfabrik*. If national courts are able to release undertakings from the obligation to pay levies imposed by Community law, temporary exemption from the payment of a levy may give a competitive advantage to the undertakings so exempted. Whilst the possibility of such distortions cannot deny the power of national courts to provide interim measures, it does underline that national courts are entrusted with a high degree of responsibility and that they should exercise their power cautiously in accordance with the case law of the Court of Justice.

in competition but gives rise to considerable difficulties both from the point of view of principle and the point of view of its practical application.[254]

An important consideration is whether, in the absence of interim relief, the applicant is likely to suffer irreversible damage. An interesting issue is how much reliance can be placed on the possibility that the applicant may be able to obtain damages against the Community institution which authored the measure in the event that it is declared invalid. Suffice it to say here that this factor may not necessarily be decisive as the case law under Article 288(2) does not enable a national court to predict with a sufficient degree of certainty that liability for damages may ensue. In *Foto-Frost*, Mancini AG had suggested as one of the requirements for the granting of interim relief that it must be impossible for the applicant to have recourse to other remedies, such as an action under Article 288(2), under which interim measures are available.[255] In *Zuckerfabrik* the Court did not refer to that condition. Failure of the applicant to have recourse to alternative remedies however may well be relevant to the national court in deciding whether to grant interim measures.

The requirement to make a reference for a preliminary ruling, if such a reference has not already been made, is a *sine qua non* condition for the granting of interim relief. The following points may be noted in this context. First, one presumes that the national court may still need to make a reference even where the validity of the regulation is already pending before the Court of Justice or the CFI as a result of another preliminary reference or a direct action, if the national court questions the validity of the regulation on grounds different from those already pending before one of the Community courts. Second, it seems that a reference should be made by the court hearing the application for interim measures. This derives from paragraph 24 of the judgment in *Zuckerfabrik*. However, if that court is different from the court hearing the main action, it may be possible for the reference to be made by the latter. What matters is that interim relief should not be granted without a reference being made. The remaining procedural issues are for national law to decide. The final point concerns the issue of appeal. In *Krüger v Hauptzollamt Hamburg-Jonas*,[256] it was held that the national court which has suspended the application of national measures based on a Community act and has made a reference for a preliminary ruling is not precluded from granting leave to appeal against its decision to grant interim relief. This is because the granting of leave does not compromise the application of Community law. If the interim order were to be reversed on appeal, Community law would again be fully applicable. Nor does a successful appeal compromise the preliminary ruling procedure. If the interim decision was set aside, that would not prevent the court of last instance from making a reference, as it is required to do under Article 234(3), if it has doubts regarding the validity of the Community act in

---

[254] See A.Ward, 'The Draft EU Constitution and Private Party Access to Judicial Review of EU Measures', in Tridimas and Nebbia (eds): '*EU Law for the 21st Century: Rethinking the New Legal Order*', Vol. 1, (Oxford, Hart Publishing, 2004), pp. 209–221, at 219.
[255] See *Foto-Frost, op. cit.*, at p. 4221. [256] Case C-334/95 [1997] ECR I-4517.

question. It is submitted however that the decision to refer cannot be set aside on appeal by a superior national court without the interim suspension also being set aside. If the superior court quashes the decision to refer, the interim measures must also be withdrawn. The opposite solution would be tantamount to accepting that national courts may suspend the application of Community law without the safeguard of the preliminary reference and question the monopoly of the Court of Justice to determine the validity of Community acts.

The power of national courts to provide interim relief was extended in *Atlanta*.[257] The difference between *Zuckerfabrik* and *Atlanta* is that whereas in the first interim protection was sought to preserve the status quo, in the second it was sought to establish a new situation. The applicants were importers of bananas from third countries who challenged the validity of the Bananas Regulation[258] in proceedings before a German court, and by way of interim relief requested import licences in addition to those which they had been granted pursuant to that Regulation. The Court held that the interim protection which national courts must afford to individuals must be the same whether they seek suspension of enforcement of a national measure adopted on the basis of a Community regulation or the grant of interim measures 'settling or regulating the disputed legal positions or relationships for their benefit'.[259] The Court dismissed the argument that the grant of such interim relief had more radical consequences for the Community legal order. It held that the consequences of the interim measure for the Community legal order, whatever they may be, must be assessed as part of the balancing exercise between the Community interest and the interests of the individual which the national court is required to perform. This approach is correct. The argument that national courts may only grant interim relief in order to preserve the status quo and not otherwise to settle provisionally the dispute runs counter to the fundamental objective of interim protection which requires that such measures as are necessary in the circumstances must be granted. On the other hand, it should be accepted that the balancing exercise performed by the national court may be affected by the type of relief sought and account may be taken of the fact that positive rather than negative action is requested by the individual.

In *Atlanta* the Court also clarified the conditions for granting interim relief laid down in *Zuckerfabrik*, providing the following guidelines:

- When making the interim order, the national court must set out the reasons why it considers that the Court of Justice should find the regulation invalid in the preliminary reference proceedings.[260]

---

[257] Case C-465/93 *Atlanta Fruchthandelsgesellschaft I v Bundesamt für Ernährung und Forstwirtschaft* [1995] ECR I-3761. For an example of an English case concerning interim relief pending the outcome of a preliminary reference, see *R v The Licensing Authority established by the Medicines Act 1968, ex p Generics (UK) Limited and E.R. Squibb & Sons* [1997] 2 CMLR 201.

[258] Council Regulation No 404/93, OJ 1993 L 47/1 examined by the Court in Case C-280/93 *Germany v Council* [1994] ECR I-4973 discussed above pp. 85 and 154.

[259] *Atlanta, op. cit.*, para 28.   [260] *Atlanta, op. cit.*, para 36; *Zuckerfabrik, op. cit.*, para 24.

- In assessing whether the regulation may be declared invalid by the Court of Justice, the national court must take into account the discretion enjoyed by the Community institutions in the sector concerned.[261] Thus, in the field of the common agricultural policy, regard must be had to the established case law according to which the Community institutions enjoy a wide margin of discretion which reflects their political responsibilities.
- In considering the damage which may be caused to the regime established by the regulation if interim measures are ordered, the national court must take into account, on the one hand, the cumulative effect which would arise if a large number of national courts were also to adopt interim measures for similar reasons and, on the other hand, the special features of the applicant's situation which distinguish him from all other operators concerned.[262]
- In accordance with Article 10 EC, the national court must respect the case law of the Community courts. Thus if the Court of Justice has dismissed on its merits an action for annulment of the regulation in issue, the national court can no longer order interim measures, or must revoke existing ones, unless the grounds of illegality submitted to it differ from those rejected by the Court in its judgment. The same applies if the CFI has dismissed on its merits an action for annulment of the regulation by a final judgment.[263]

In *Atlanta* the Court left open the possibility that a national court might grant interim measures even in a case where the Court of Justice itself has refused to grant interim measures against the same regulation in previous proceedings brought by a Member State under Article 230. This is understandable given that the type of damage which an interim order seeks to avoid differs in the two cases. Where a Member State brings annulment proceedings and seeks interim measures, it acts in the national public interest and is entitled to invoke damage suffered by a whole sector of the economy. By contrast, where individual traders bring proceedings and seek interim protection, they invoke damage suffered by them in their private capacity.

In *Atlanta* the Court stressed that, in assessing whether interim relief should be granted, the national court hearing the application must take due account of the Community interest. But how is the Community represented in national proceedings? In *Krüger v Hauptzollamt Hamburg-Jonas*,[264] the Commission argued that, where a national court is minded to grant interim relief, the Community institution which adopted the act whose validity is in issue should be given the opportunity to express its views. But the Court did not heed that request, holding that it is for the national court to decide, in accordance with its own rules of procedure, which is the most appropriate way of obtaining all relevant information pertaining to the Community act in question. This, it is submitted, is the correct approach. If the Commission's view were followed, that would lead to the

---

[261] *Atlanta, op. cit.*, para 37.   [262] *Ibid.*, para 44.   [263] *Ibid.*, para 46.
[264] *Op. cit.*, n. 256 above. See also the Opinion of Cosmas AG in Case C–183/95 *Affish BV v Rijksdienst Keuring Vee en Vlees* [1997] ECR I-4315, at 4335–6.

proceedings before the national court becoming unduly complicated. The intervention of a Community institution would impose a heavy burden on national courts, especially on those at the lower tiers of the national judicial system. It would lead to undue formalism in the proceedings and be liable to lengthen what is by definition a summary procedure.[265]

National courts do not have the power to order interim protection where, by virtue of a Community regulation, the existence and scope of individual rights must be established by another Community measure implementing the regulation and that measure has not yet been adopted. In *T. Port GmbH v Bundesanstalt für Landwirtschaft und Ernährung*,[266] an undertaking importing bananas claimed that additional import licences should be allocated to it. On a reference for a preliminary ruling by the Higher Administrative Court of Hesse, the Court held that Article 30 of the Bananas Regulation enables and, depending on the circumstances, even requires the Commission to lay down transitional rules providing for the allocation of additional import licences in cases of hardship. The Court held however that the national court did not have power to grant additional import licences by way of interim measure. It distinguished the case in issue from *Zuckerfabrik* and *Atlanta* on the following basis. The case in issue concerned granting traders interim protection in a situation where, by virtue of a Community regulation, the existence and scope of traders' rights was to be established by a Commission measure which the Commission has not yet adopted.[267] The Treaty however makes no provision for a preliminary reference procedure by which a national court can ask the Court of Justice to rule that an institution has failed to act. Consequently, national courts have no jurisdiction to order interim measures pending action on the part of an institution. Judicial review of alleged failure to act can be exercised only by the Community courts.[268]

In *Port* the applicants were seeking to obtain by way of interim order a remedy which went beyond the scope of the main action. That is what distinguishes the case from Atlanta. The issue arises: what are the alternative remedies available to a trader in the position of the applicants? The Court stated that Article 232 EC entitles an individual to bring an action for failure to act against an institution which he claims has failed to adopt a measure which would concern him directly and individually.[269] It also stated that interim measures may be adopted in proceedings for failure to act. What is of particular interest is the implied suggestion that a banana trader in the applicant's position would be able to establish direct and

---

[265] Note that under Article 15(3) of Regulation 1/2003 on the implementation of Articles 81 and 82 EC (OJ 2003, L1/1), the Commission may, acting on its own initiative, submit written observations in national court proceedings, where the coherent application of Article 81 or Article 82 so requires and, with the permission of the court in question, it may also make oral observations. This is however a different situation. It applies to a specialist area and refers, as a general rule, to main actions rather than proceedings for interim relief.

[266] Case C-68/95 [1996] ECR I-6065.   [267] *Ibid.*, para 52.   [268] *Ibid.*, para 53.

[269] In Case C-107/91 *ENU v Commission* [1993] ECR I-599 the Court had made a similar finding in relation to Article 148 Euratom which is equivalent to Article 175 (now Article 232).

individual concern so as to require the Commission to adopt rules of general application catering for cases of hardship pursuant to Article 30 of the Banana Regulation. If that is correct, it means that in *Port* the Court was prepared to interpret the requirements of direct and individual concern liberally. Another remedy would be for the applicant to bring an action in damages against the Community for failure to act. Despite the significant practical difficulties surrounding such an action, it may still prove successful.[270]

By way of conclusion, it may be helpful to summarise the conditions which must be satisfied in order for a national court to be able to grant interim relief as stated by the Court in *Atlanta* and confirmed in subsequent cases.[271] Interim relief can be granted only if:

- the court entertains serious doubts as to the validity of the Community act, and if the validity of the contested act is not already in issue before the Court of Justice, itself refers the question to the Court of Justice;
- there is urgency, in that the interim relief is necessary to avoid serious and irreparable damage being caused to the party seeking such relief;
- the court takes due account of the Community interest; and
- in its assessment of all those conditions, it respects any decisions of the Court of Justice or the Court of First Instance ruling on the lawfulness of the regulation or on the application for interim measures seeking similar interim relief at Community level.

The Court of Justice entrusted national courts with wide powers to grant interim protection suspending the application of Community regulations. That development was inevitable given that the enforcement of Community law is a matter not only for the Community judicature but also for the national courts. As the Court observed, the interim protection available to individuals should be the same irrespective of whether they contest the legality of national measures or Community measures since in both cases the challenge is based on Community law itself. There is no denying however that the power of national courts to suspend the application of Community law creates risks as it is liable to be applied diversely. If the coherence of legal remedies and the uniformity of Community law are to be observed, this power must be exercised with caution.

---

[270] See Joined Cases T-79/96, T-260/97 and T-117/98 *Camar and Tico v Commission and Council* [2000] ECR II-2193 and, on appeal, Case C-312/00, [2002] ECR I-11355.

[271] *Atlanta, op. cit.*, para 51; *Port, op. cit.*, para 48; *Krüger, op. cit.*, para 44.

10

The Liability of Community Institutions

This chapter gives an overview of the principles which govern the liability of the Community institutions under Article 288(2) EC.[1] The development of the case law in this area is important for a number of reasons. Article 288(2) is one of the few provisions of the founding Treaties which make express reference to the laws of Member States. Thus, the case law under Article 288(2) illustrates how the Court has understood its mandate to build up a common law on the liability of Community authorities. Also, it highlights the role of general principles, such as equality and proportionality, as rules of law breach of which may give rise to liability. Finally, an understanding of the rules governing the liability of the Community institutions is necessary to evaluate the liability of Member States. The ECJ itself views the liability of the Community institutions and the Member States as two sides of the same coin and, in its judgment in *Bergaderm*,[2] sought to establish a set of uniform conditions applicable to both.

The chapter does not intend to provide an exhaustive account. It gives an overview, focusing on the notion of breach of Community law as a condition of liability, the possibility of liability for lawful acts, and the requirement of causation.[3]

10.1. Article 288(2)

Article 288(2) provides that the Community must make good any damage caused by its institutions or by its servants in the performance of their duties, 'in accordance with the general principles common to the laws of the Member States'. The express reference to the laws of the Member States is less helpful than it appears. Save for very

---

[1] Formerly, Article 215(2) EC. It corresponds to Article III-431(2) of the EU Constitution.
[2] Case C-352/98 P *Laboratoires Pharmaceutiques Bergaderm and Goupil v Commission* [2000] ECR I-5291.
[3] For bibliography, see among others, T.C. Hartley, *The Foundations of European Community Law* (Oxford, 2003) Ch. 17; H. G. Schermers and D. Waelbroeck, *Judicial Protection in the European Union* (6th Ed., Kluwer, 2001), pp. 519 *et seq.*; T. Tridimas, 'Liability for Breach of Community Law: Growing Up and Mellowing Down?' (2001) 38 CML Rev. 301; K. Lenaerts and D. Arts, *Procedural Law of the European Union*, (Sweet & Maxwell, 1999) Ch 11; T. Heukels and A. McDonnell (eds), *The Action for Damages in Community Law* (Kluwer, 1997). For comparative material, see D. Fairgrieve, M. Andenas and J. Bell (eds), *Tort Liability of Public Authorities in Comparative Perspective*, (London, BIICL, 2002.)

general principles which themselves offer little guidance to the judicial inquiry, there is in fact no common corpus of rules governing the non-contractual liability of public authorities in the national laws. The search for appropriate standards is perforce selective. Far from looking for the lowest common denominator, the ECJ has approached the interpretation of Article 288(2) creatively.[4]

According to the case law, in order for the Community to incur liability, the following conditions must be met: (a) there must be illegal conduct; (b) there must be damage, (c) and there must be a causal link between the illegal conduct and the damage claimed.[5] In its seminal judgment in *Zuckerfabrik Schöppenstedt* the Court held that liability may arise not only as a result of an individual act but also as a result of legislation.[6] The following sections seek to give a short survey of the way the Court has approached the interpretation of Article 288(2) especially in relation to the concept of illegal conduct.[7]

In *Laboratoires Pharmaceutiques Bergaderm and Goupil v Commission* the Court recast the conditions of liability.[8] Before *Bergaderm*, the case law attributed particular importance to whether the breach was the result of administrative or legislative action. In *Bergaderm*, the Court held that the determining criterion is not the administrative or legislative character of the measure but the degree of discretion available to the institution in question. The following sections examine the pre-*Bergaderm* case law, the judgment in *Bergaderm* and its aftermath.

10.2. The case law before *Bergaderm*

10.2.1. Administrative action

The case law traditionally accepted that, in the field of administrative action, any infringement of law might give rise to liability.[9] Thus, it was held that the Commission may be liable for the improper application of protective measures

---

[4] Note that in relation to the liability of the ECB the EC Treaty requires rather than simply permits a higher standard of liability than that provided by national law. Member States generally make their central banks immune from liability actions in relation to monetary decisions. Article 288(3) by contrast, as amended by the TEU, states that the ECB may also be held liable in accordance with the conditions of Article 288(2). The language is clearer in Article III-431(3) of the EU Constitution.

[5] See e.g. Case 4/69 *Lütticke v Commission* [1971] ECR 325, para 10; Case T-575/93 *Koelman v Commission* [1996] ECR II-1, para 89.

[6] Case 5/71 *Zuckerfabrik Schöppenstedt v Council* [1971] ECR 975.

[7] This chapter examines only liability as a result of action attributable to the Community institutions *(faute de service)*. Liability as a result of action attributable to the servants of the Community *(faute personelle)* falls beyond the scope of this book.   [8] *Op. cit.*, n. 2 above.

[9] Case 145/83 *Adams v Commission* [1985] ECR 3539; Case T-390/94 *Aloys Schröder v Commission* [1997] ECR II-501, para 51. For an extensive discussion, see M. H. van der Woude, 'Liability for Administrative Acts under Article 215(2) EC' in T. Heukels and A. McDonnell, *op. cit.*, 109–128. An administrative act in this context is defined as one 'by which the administration applies general rules in individual cases or otherwise exercises its executive powers in an individual manner'. See van der Woude, at 112 where further references are given.

suspending the issue of import licences,[10] for failing to keep secret the identity of an informant who provided information regarding the breach of competition law,[11] and for cooperating unlawfully with national authorities investigating the conduct of a Community official in the context of a criminal enquiry.[12] The Court, however, had not articulated any standards of liability based expressly on the concept of duty of care or the degree of discretion enjoyed by the Commission. In one case, it was held that the adoption by the Commission of an incorrect interpretation of Community law did not constitute illegality and could not give rise to liability. The Commission's delay in correcting that information, however, could be actionable.[13]

Liability may arise as a result of omission only where an institution has infringed a legal obligation to act. It follows that where the institutions enjoy discretion it would be difficult for such an action to succeed.[14] In *KYDEP v Council and Commission*,[15] a cooperative of Greek producers sought compensation arguing that the Council's failure to adopt special measures in favour of the cereals sector in Greece discriminated against Greek products which were affected much more than other Community products from the Chernobyl nuclear accident. The Court dismissed the claim holding that Greece was not the only region to have been affected seriously by the accident. More recently, however, in *Camar* the CFI found the Commission liable for failing to adopt transitional measures in favour of the applicant.[16]

10.2.2. Legislative measures

Liability arising as a result of legislative acts (normative injustice) was subject to more stringent conditions.[17] Clearly, a finding of invalidity is not in itself sufficient for the Community to incur liability.[18] In *Zuckerfabrik Schöppenstedt* the Court stated that, with regard to measures of economic policy, the Community does not

---

[10] Joined Cases 5, 7 and 13–24/66 *Kampffmeyer v Commission* [1967] ECR 245.

[11] Case 145/83 *Adams v Commission* [1985] ECR 3539.

[12] Case 108/87 *Hamill v Commission* [1988] ECR 6141.

[13] Joined cases 19, 20, 25 & 30/69 *Richez-Parise v Commission* [1970] ECR 325, para 36. See also Case T-514/93 *Cobrecaf and Others v Commission* [1995] ECR II-621, para 70.

[14] This applies *a fortiori* where the Council enjoys wide discretion in the exercise of legislative policy, for example, in the conclusion of international agreements on fishing: Case T-572/93 *Odigitria v Council and Commission* [1995] ECR II-2025, confirmed on appeal: C-293/95 P [1996] ECR I-6129.   [15] Case C-146/91 [1994] ECR I-4199, para 58.

[16] Joined Cases T-79/96, T-260/97 and T-117/98 *Camar and Tico v Commission and Council* [2000] ECR II-2193 discussed at 10.4 below.

[17] For the purposes of determining the conditions of liability, the case law treated as a legislative act any measure of general application irrespective of whether it might be of individual concern to the applicant for the purposes of Article 230(4): see Case C-152/88 *Sofrimport v Commission* [1990] ECR I-2477; Joined Cases T-480 and T-483/93 *Antillean Rice Mills and Others v Commission* [1995] ECR II-2305, confirmed on this point on appeal in C-390/95 P [1999] ECR I-769. See also *Aloys Schröder, op. cit.*, paras 54 *et seq.* and the Opinion of the Advocate General in *Bergaderm, op. cit.*

[18] See e.g. Case C-282/90 *Vreugdenhil v Commission* [1992] ECR I-1937, para 19.

incur liability for damage suffered by individuals 'unless a sufficiently flagrant violation of a superior rule of law for the protection of the individual has occurred'.[19] It follows that the conditions for liability in relation to measures of economic policy[20] are the following: (a) there must be violation of a superior rule of law, (b) the rule must be intended for the protection of the individual, and (c) such violation must be sufficiently serious. The reason why liability is subject to such strict conditions is not difficult to understand. Policy makers should be able to enjoy wide discretion and their decision making must not be inhibited by the threat of liability in cases where a measure is subsequently found to be illegal. It is not the objective for liability in damages to be a sword of Damocles over the legislature. Also, where an action in damages is successful, it is ultimately the taxpayer who is called upon to cover the costs. Viewed from that perspective, a public authority should incur liability as a result of legislative action only where the interest of compensating the persons who suffer loss as a result is judged as more worthy of protection than the interest of the taxpayer. The *Schöppenstedt* formula is designed to meet the legitimate concern that liability in damages should not be a readily available remedy in relation to all invalid legislative acts.

10.2.2.1. Superior rule of law for the protection of the individual

In order for liability to arise, the superior rule of law whose violation is alleged must be for the protection of the individual.[21] This requirement borrows from the German *Schutznormtheorie*, according to which the State is liable only where it breaches a legal norm which protects a subjective public right of the injured party. The legal norm in issue must be intended to protect a specific group to which the injured party belongs rather than merely the public in general.[22] Under Community law, this condition is not difficult to meet. It suffices that the rule is intended to protect interests of a general nature, for example the interests of producers in a certain sector. The test is therefore less stringent than the requirement of direct and individual concern applicable to establish *locus standi* under Article 230(4) EC.[23]

Certain principles are fundamental to the Community legal order but do not have as their purpose the protection of individual rights. This is for example the case with the principle of institutional balance. The objective of the rules governing the division of powers between the institutions is not to protect the individual but to maintain a balance between the institutions. Therefore, illegality of a

---

[19] *Op. cit.*, para 11.   [20] For other types of measures, see 10.2.3 below.

[21] So far, the case law has not addressed the issue whether a Member State or a regional authority may claim damages against the Community. This remains an open issue but there is no reason why such liability should be excluded *a priori*.

[22] See A. Arnull, 'Liability for Legislative Acts under Article 215(2) EC' in Heukels and McDonell, *op. cit.*, 129–151 at 136 and see Darmon AG in *Vreugdenhil, op. cit.*, at 1956.

[23] See *Kampffmeyer, op. cit.*, at 263; see also *Schöppenstedt, op. cit.*; Joined Cases 9 and12/60 *Vloeberghs v High Authority* [1961] ECR 197; Case 9/56 *Meroni v High Authority* [1958] ECR 133; Joined Cases 9 and 11/71 *Compagnie d'Approvisionnement v Commission* [1972] ECR 391.

measure which arises from failure to observe the institutional balance, as for example where the Commission exceeds its implementing powers, is not sufficient on its own to give rise to liability in damages.[24]

The principles of equality, proportionality, protection of legitimate expectations and fundamental rights are superior rules of law for the protection of the individual. It is less clear whether a breach of a procedural requirement can give rise to a right to compensation. The Court has held, for example, that breach of the requirement of reasoning may not give rise to liability in damages,[25] even though in a different context it has stressed the importance of Article 253 EC for enabling individuals to protect their rights and the Court to exercise its judicial function.[26] Liability for breach of procedural requirements may not be excluded as a matter of principle subject to the requirements of damage and causal effect. The case law has accepted that moral damage may also be compensated.[27] Damages may be awarded under this heading, for example, in appropriate cases where fundamental rights have been infringed but the individual has not suffered any material loss.

The overwhelming majority of actions for damages against legislative acts have been unsuccessful.[28] The principles most usually pleaded are equal treatment and respect for legitimate expectations. In some cases, they have been pleaded successfully.[29] By contrast, it is extremely difficult for compensation claims based on breach of fundamental rights[30] or the principle of proportionality[31] to succeed.

The Court has not placed much importance on the requirement that the rule of law must be 'superior' as an independent condition of liability. Save in very

---

[24] *Vreugdenhil, op. cit.*

[25] Case 106/81 *Kind v EEC* [1982] ECR 2885, para 14, and see more recently the CFI's case law: Case T-167/94 *Nölle v Council and Commission* [1994] ECR II-2589, para 57; *Aloys Schröder, op. cit.*, para 66.

[26] See e.g. Case 294/81 *Control Data v Commission* [1983] ECR 911, para 14, Case 250/84 *Eridania v Cassa Conguaglio Zucchero* [1986] ECR 117, para 37.

[27] See e.g. Case 110/63 *Williame* [1965] ECR 667 and see further Schermers and Waelbroeck, *op. cit.*, p. 359.

[28] For examples of unsuccessful actions see *Zuckerfabrik Schoppenstedt op. cit.*; Case 49/79 *Pool v Council* [1980] ECR 569 (alleging breach of the principle of non-discrimination as expressed in Article 34(2) EC as a result of the conversion rate fixed for the pound sterling); Case 20/88 *Roquette Frères v Commission* [1989] ECR 1553 (breach of the principle of equal treatment resulting from the miscalculation of monetary compensatory amounts was an insufficiently serious technical error); *KYDEP v Council and Commission, op. cit.*, (alleged breach of Article 34(2) by the fixing of maximum permitted levels of radioactive contamination); *Aloys Schröder, op. cit.* (alleged breach arising from measures seeking to contain the spreading of swine fever).

[29] For examples of successful actions, see Joined Cases C-104/89 and C-37/90 *Mulder v Council and Commission (Mulder II)* [1992] ECR I-3061; *Sofrimport, op. cit.*, n. 17 above. In Case 74/74 *CNTA* [1975] ECR 533 which concerned monetary compensatory amounts, the Court found violation of the principle of protection of legitimate expectations but, in subsequent proceedings, the applicant company failed to establish loss: [1976] ECR 797.

[30] In a number of cases, applicants have unsuccessfully sought to recover damages allegedly flowing from breach of the right to property or the freedom to trade. See e.g. Case 59/83 *Biovilac v EEC* [1984] ECR 4057; *Aloys Schröder, op. cit.*; but see *Camar, op. cit.*, discussed at 10.4 below.

[31] See e.g. Joined Cases 83 and 94/76, 4, 15 and 40/77 *HNL v Council and Commission* [1978] ECR 1209, cf Opinion of Capotorti AG; Joined Cases 63 to 69/72 *Werhahn v Council* [1973] ECR 1229, cf Opinion of Roemer AG.

exceptional circumstances,[32] a legislative act cannot give rise to a right to reparation unless it is illegal, namely, it breaches a higher-ranking rule of law. Such a rule may fall into one of three categories:[33] (a) it may be a provision of the Treaty or other primary Community law; (b) it may be a general principle of law, such as equal treatment or protection of legitimate expectations; (c) it may be a Community act which in formal ranking stands higher than the Community act which caused damage, as for example where a Commission regulation breaches the terms of its parent Council regulation. The crucial issue is to establish that the rule breached is for the protection of the individual rather than that it is superior in some technical sense.

The Community cannot be liable in damages for loss suffered by individuals as a result of primary law. In *Dubois et Fils v Council and Commission*[34] a French company providing custom agency services sought compensation, arguing that the completion of the internal market and the abolition of internal frontiers on 1 January 2003 led to the complete cessation of its activities. The CFI pointed that the Single European Act, which was the direct and determining cause of the applicant's loss of business, forms part of primary Community law and is not an act of the Community institutions. Under the hierarchy of rules, Articles 235 and 288(2) could not be brought to bear on norms belonging to an equivalent level where this is not expressly provided for.[35]

10.2.2.2. Seriousness of the violation

The violation of a superior rule of law does not *per se* give rise to liability in damages. In order for such liability to arise the violation must be sufficiently serious. But what is a sufficiently serious breach? The case law in this area has evolved. Although few actions have been successful, more recent cases evince a relaxation of the strict approach of earlier case law. In *HNL v Council and Commission* the Court held that in legislative areas where the exercise of wide discretion is essential for the implementation of a Community policy, the Community may not incur liability 'unless the institution concerned has manifestly and gravely disregarded the limits on the exercise of powers'.[36] The case concerned the Community regime for the compulsory purchase of skimmed milk power. Owing to imbalance between supply and demand, the Community accumulated a skimmed-milk 'mountain'. With a view to disposing of the surpluses, Council Regulation No 563/76[37] provided for the compulsory purchase of skimmed milk powder by producers for use in feedstuffs. In a series of cases, the Court declared the Regulation void for being contrary to the principles of equality and proportionality.[38] In *HNL* the

---

[32] See 10.5 below.

[33] See P. Craig and G. de Bùrca, *EU Law, Text, Cases, and Materials* (Oxford University Press, Third Ed., 1998), pp. 449–50.

[34] Case T-113/96 *Dubois et Fils v Council and Commission* [1998] ECR II-125.

[35] Para 41.   [36] *Op. cit.*, n. 31 above, para 6.   [37] OJ 1976 L 67, p. 18.

[38] Case 114/76 *Bela-Mühle v Grows-Farm* [1977] ECR 1211, Case 116/76 *Granaria* [1977] ECR 1247, Joined Cases 119 and 120/76 *Ölmühle and Becher* [1977] ECR 1269.

applicants were animal producers who, following the annulment of the Regulation, applied for compensation for the damage which they allegedly suffered. After
explaining that liability in damages should be subject to strict conditions so as not to
hinder the institutions in taking policy decisions, the Court stated that individuals
may be required to accept within reasonable limits harmful effects on their economic interests as a result of a legislative measure even if the measure has been
invalidated. On the facts of the case, the Court found that there was no manifest
and grave disregard by the institutions of the limits of their powers. It based its
judgment on two considerations. First, the Regulation in issue affected very wide
categories of traders so that its effects on individual undertakings were considerably
lessened. Second, the effects of the Regulation on the production costs of those
traders were only limited. The Court concluded that the effects of the Regulation
on the profit-earning capacity of the traders 'did not ultimately exceed the bounds
of the economic risks inherent in the activities of the agricultural sectors concerned'.[39] It is interesting that in his Opinion Capotorti AG took a different view
concluding that the Community was liable.[40]

Subsequently in the quellmehl and gritz cases,[41] which involved breach of the
principle of equal treatment, the Court found that there was 'manifest and grave
disregard'. The Court held that in the circumstances, the violation of the principle
of equality affected a limited and clearly defined group of commercial operators;
the damage suffered by the applicants went beyond the bounds of the economic
risks inherent in the sector concerned; and equality of treatment between the
products in issue had been terminated without sufficient justification. The last
ground indicates that discrimination in those cases was linked to a loose notion of
vested rights: it was the result of terminating without good reason equality in
treatment which existed under previous regulations. In the isoglucose cases,[42]
however, the Court found that a breach of the principle of equality did not lead to
liability in damages on the ground that the conduct of the defendant institutions
was not 'verging on the arbitrary',[43] despite the fact that the group of traders
involved was equally limited and clearly defined. One of the considerations which
the Court took into account was that the regulation imposing a levy on isoglucose,
which had been found to infringe the principle of equal treatment in
previous proceedings, had been adopted to deal with an emergency situation. The

[39] Op. cit., para 7.   [40] See HNL, op. cit., pp. 1231–7.
[41] Case 238/78 Ireks-Arkady v Council and Commission [1979] ECR 2955; Joined Cases 261 and
262/78 Interquell Stärke-Chemie v Council and Commission [1979] ECR 3045; Joined Cases 241,
242 and 245–250/78 DGV v Council and Commission [1979] ECR 3017; Joined Cases 64 and
113/76, 167 and 239/78, 27, 28 and 45/79 Dumortier Frères v Council [1979] ECR 3091. Cf Case
90/78 Granaria v Council and Commission [1979] ECR 1081 where the action was unsuccessful
since no breach of the principle of equality was established.
[42] Joined Cases 116 and 124/77 Amylum v Council and Commission [1979] ECR 3497; Case
143/77 Koninklijke Scholten-Honig v Council and Commission [1979] ECR 3583.
[43] See Amylum v Council and Commission, op. cit., para 19. Note, however, that it is not
a separate requirement of liability that the conduct verges on the arbitrary: Case C-220/91
Commission v Stahlwerke Peine-Salzgitter [1993] ECR I- 2393, para 51.

isoglucose cases are not easy to reconcile with the quellmehl and gritz cases[44] and illustrate how difficult it is to quantify legally the existence of a sufficiently serious breach. That difficulty has led in some cases to divergence of views between the Advocates General and the Court.[45]

It follows from the above cases that, in determining whether there is a manifest and grave disregard of the limits on discretionary powers, the Court refers to two elements:[46] (a) the effect of the measure on individuals, in other words, the degree of harm suffered by them as a result of the measure; and (b) the extent to which the law has been violated. The first element refers to the nature of the damage suffered rather than to the infringement *per se*. Under the case law, however, it is a necessary condition for the establishment of unlawfulness.[47] In particular, a requirement which consistently appears in the case law is that, in order for liability to ensue, the damage alleged by the applicants must go beyond the bounds of the economic risks inherent in the activities in the sector concerned.[48]

The Court was more generous to the applicants in *Mulder II*,[49] a case which determines with greater accuracy than any other the requisite threshold of seriousness. The case concerned breach of legitimate expectations and arose from the Community milk quota regime. It is discussed elsewhere in this book.[50] Suffice to mention here certain conclusions which may be drawn with regard to the liability of Community institutions. In contrast to previous cases, in *Mulder II* liability was established although the measure in issue affected a wide category of traders. It is notable that whereas in the quellmehl and gritz cases the Court referred to 'a *limited* and clearly defined group of commercial operators'[51] in *Mulder II* reference was made merely to 'a clearly defined group of economic agents'.[52] It follows that it is no longer a strict requirement of liability that the group of persons affected must be limited in number. It does not follow, however, that the limited number of the persons affected may never be a relevant issue. It is a consideration to be taken into account together with other considerations, in particular, the extent to which the law has been violated. *Mulder II* makes clear that liability is more likely to arise where, in exercising its discretion, the Community legislature totally fails to take into account relevant interests rather than where it does take such interests into account but fails to grant them due consideration. The Community institutions were found liable to the extent that they totally excluded returning producers from the allocation of a quota but were not found liable for allocating to them a quota reduced to 60 per cent of their production.

---

[44] See further, Hartley, *op. cit.*, p. 472.

[45] See e.g. *HNL, op. cit.*; Case C-63/89 *Assurances du Credit v Council and Commission* [1991] ECR I-1799. Cf *Sofrimport, op. cit.*, n. 17 above.   [46] Hartley, *op. cit.*, pp. 472–3.

[47] See further, F. Grondman, 'La Notion de violation suffisamment caractérisée en matière de responsabilité non contractuelle', 1979 CDE, No 1, p. 86; E-W Fuss, 'La responsabilité des Communautés européennes pour le comportement illégal de leurs organs', 1981 RTDE 1.

[48] See e.g. *Mulder, op. cit.*, n. 29 above, para 13.   [49] *Ibid.*   [50] See above p. 275.

[51] *Ireks-Arcady v Council and Commission, op. cit.*, para 11 (emphasis added).

[52] *Mulder II, op. cit.*, para 16.

The action succeeded also in *Sofrimport v Commission*.[53] The applicant was refused an import licence for goods in transit as a result of Commission protective measures suspending import licences. The Court found that the suspensory measures ran counter to the principle of protection of legitimate expectations insofar as they applied to goods in transit and that the Community was liable to make good the damage caused thereby. In that case, the legitimate expectation of the applicant was based on a Council Regulation which specifically intended to protect goods in transit from the unfavourable consequences of protective measures.

Overall, the cases decided since the 1990s evince a more liberal attitude towards establishing liability of Community institutions than the cases decided in the 1970s.[54] The number of cases, however, is relatively small and it is difficult to draw reliable conclusions.[55] Indeed, it may be said that this area of law does not lend itself to certainty as the existing authorities make it difficult to predict whether in a given case the requirements of liability are likely to be met.

10.2.3. Measures other than measures of economic policy

The requirement of 'manifest and grave disregard' applies not only in relation to measures of economic policy but also in relation to all measures where the institution concerned enjoys wide discretion. In *Assurances du Crédit v Council and Commission*,[56] the Court applied the same test to determine whether the Community was liable for the alleged breach of the principle of non-discrimination by a harmonization directive. Also, the definition of a measure of economic policy for the purposes of Article 288(2) is a broad one. It covers all decisions adopted in the exercise of a discretion and intended to organize a sector, in particular a common organization of the market.[57]

By contrast, where the Commission does not enjoy wide discretionary powers, the requirement that the violation must be sufficiently serious is not exemplified by the condition that it must manifestly and gravely have disregarded the limits of its powers.[58] The case law, however, was not consistent. In the *Live Pigs* case, for example, the CFI seemed to suggest that the requirement of serious breach applied only where the measure was legislative in character *and* the author of the act enjoyed wide discretion.[59] Also, in some cases the Court did not even refer to the *Schöppenstedt* formula even though the alleged loss arose as a result of legislative

---

[53] *Op. cit.*, n. 17 above.   [54] Hartley, *op. cit.*, p. 473.

[55] Note also *Stahlwerke Peine-Salzgitter, op. cit.*, n. 43 above where the Court upheld on appeal a judgment of the CFI finding the Commission liable in damages in an action under Articles 34 and 40 of the ECSC Treaty.   [56] *Op. cit.*, n. 45 above.

[57] See e.g. *Aloys Schröder op. cit.*; T-472/93 *Campo Ebro Industrial and Others v Council* [1995] ECR II-421.

[58] See e.g. *Sofrimport, op. cit.*; cf the Opinion of Tesauro AG at 2502; Joined Cases 44–51 *Union Malt v Commission* [1978] ECR 57.

[59] Joined cases T-481 and T-484/93 *Vereniging van Exporteurs in Levende Varkens and Another v Commission* [1995] ECR II-2941, para 81.

action.[60] In any event, the test of manifest and grave disregard applied only in relation to legislative measures. The case law had not extended it to administrative measures, even where such measures entailed the exercise of wide discretionary powers.[61]

10.3. The judgment in *Bergaderm*

The importance of the judgment in *Bergaderm*[62] is twofold. First, the Court unified the conditions of State and Community liability. Second, it recast the conditions of liability holding that the determining factor is not the general or individual nature of the act in question but the discretion available to the institution concerned.

In *Brasserie du Pêcheur*,[63] decided some years earlier, the Court had declared that the conditions under which a Member State may incur liability for breach of Community law cannot, in the absence of particular justification, differ from those governing the liability of the Community institutions in like circumstances.[64] On that basis, the Court proceeded to define serious breach, in cases where the national authorities enjoy wide discretion, by reference to the test of 'manifest and grave disregard'.[65] Although the Court did not pursue the analogy consistently,[66] the basic premise that the liability of Community and national authorities must be governed by similar principles is well-founded. As the Court expressly stated, the protection of the rights of the individual cannot vary depending on whether a national or a Community authority is responsible for the damage.[67] In *Brasserie*, the correlation between State and Community liability served a dual purpose:[68] it underlined the affinity between State liability and the rule of law, and served as a source of legitimacy for the Court's bold move to recognize a right to reparation against Member States. It should be borne in mind that, as there are strong similarities between Community and State liability, so there are important disparities

---

[60] See Case 81/86 *de Boer Buizen v Council and Commission* [1987] ECR 3677 and the *Christmas Butter* cases (Joined Cases 279, 280, 285 and 286/84 *Rau v Commission* [1987] ECR 1069, Case 27/85 *Vandemoortele v Commission* [1987] ECR 1129, Case 265/85 *van den Bergh en Jurgens v Commission* [1987] ECR 1155). See further van der Woude, *op. cit.*, at 113–114.

[61] See van der Woude, *ibid.* This view is said to receive support from Joined Cases T-458 and T-523/93 *ENU v Commission* [1995] ECR II-2459, para 67 (loss allegedly arising from the Commission's failure to guarantee disposal of the applicant's uranium production pursuant to Article 53 Euratom). That case however does not provide conclusive authority that the CFI rejected the test of manifest and grave disregard in relation to administrative acts.

[62] *Op. cit.*, n. 2 above. For a detailed discussion, see T. Tridimas, *op. cit.*, n. 3 above.

[63] Joined Cases C-46 and C-48/93 *Brasserie du Pêcheur v Germany and the Queen v Secretary of State for Transport, ex p Factortame Ltd* [1996] ECR I-1029.   [64] *Ibid.*, para 42.

[65] *Ibid.*, para 45.   [66] See the criticism below p. 512.   [67] *Brasserie, op. cit.*, para 42.

[68] Already, in his Opinion in *Francovich*, Mischo AG had sought inspiration from the case law under Article 215(2) (now 288(2)) EC to establish the right to reparation against the State. In its judgment, the Court did not draw any analogy between Community and Member State liability probably because the type of breach in issue, namely failure to implement a directive, did not lend itself to such a comparison.

between the two. Suffice it to refer here to the different constraints under which the Community and the national legislature operate within the bounds of the Community legal order: whilst the first act as primary legislature, the second are bound by the principle of primacy.[69]

Be that as it may, the Court's dicta in *Brasserie* inevitably opened the way for the dialectical development of the law: if Community liability is capable of influencing State liability, the reverse must also be true. Indeed, in *Bergaderm* the Court reversed the correlation by relying, for the first time, on its case law on State liability to determine the conditions applicable to the liability of the Community institutions.

The factual background to *Bergaderm* was defined by the Cosmetics Directive,[70] which requires Member States to prohibit the marketing of cosmetic products containing the substances specified in Annex II to the Directive. It also provides for the updating of Annex II through adoption of adaptation directives. Bergaderm SA brought an action against the Commission seeking to recover compensation for the loss that it had allegedly suffered by the adoption of an adaptation directive restricting the use of a carcinogenic molecule used by Bergaderm in the manufacture of a sun oil called Bergasol. Bergaderm claimed that the directive in issue concerned exclusively Bergasol and therefore was to be regarded as an administrative act. It claimed that the Commission had adopted it in breach of the procedural requirements laid down in the Cosmetics Directive and also Bergaderm's rights of defence. The CFI held that the adaptation directive was a measure of general application and therefore, under the established case law, liability would ensue only if, in adopting it, the Commission had disregarded a superior rule of law for the protection of the individual. It found that it was not necessary to examine whether the provisions governing the procedure for the adoption of the adaptation directive were such rules since, in any event, the Commission had not infringed them.

On appeal, Bergaderm argued, *inter alia*, that the CFI had erred in law by considering the adaptation directive as a legislative measure and also that the CFI was incorrect in deciding that there was no breach of a superior rule of law. The Court rejected the appeal. The importance of the judgment lies not so much in the outcome reached on the facts but in certain pronouncements of principle.

The Court held that the conditions under which a Community institutions or a Member State may become liable in damages for breach of Community law are the following:[71]

(a) the rule of law infringed must be intended to confer rights on individuals;
(b) the breach must be sufficiently serious;
(c) there must be a direct causal link between the breach of the obligation resting on the author of the act and the damage sustained by the injured parties.

---

[69] This was expressly recognized in *Brasserie*: see para 46 of the judgment.
[70] Council Directive 76/768 of 27 July 1976 on the approximation of the laws of the Member States relating to cosmetic products (OJ 1976 L 262, p. 169). The Directive has been amended, *inter alia*, by Council Directive 93/35/EEC of 14 June 1993, OJ 1993 L 151, p. 32.
[71] *Op. cit.*, paras 41 and 42.

The decisive test for finding that a breach is sufficiently serious is whether the Community institution concerned manifestly and gravely disregarded the limits of its discretion. Where the institution has only considerably reduced, or even no, discretion, the mere infringement of Community law may be sufficient to establish the existence of a sufficiently serious breach.[72] The determining factor, therefore, in deciding whether there has been such an infringement is not the general or individual nature of the act in question but the discretion available to the institution concerned.[73]

The most important aspect of *Bergaderm* is that it links liability with discretion irrespective of the administrative or legislative character of the measure. In doing so, it does away with the need to draw artificial distinctions between legislative and administrative measures. It also recognizes that, in certain cases, the Community administration may enjoy ample discretion and may be called upon to make choices which are equally difficult, complex and sensitive to those of the legislature, and its liability should therefore be governed by the same conditions. It thus opens the way for the test of manifest and grave breach to be applied as a condition governing liability for administrative acts, where the administration enjoys wide discretion.

Bergaderm lays down the requirement of serious breach as a general condition of liability. As stated above, in its previous case law, the Court had not articulated that requirement as a condition of liability arising as a result of administrative action. The reason for this may be that there was not much need to develop such a conceptual tool. The cases where a natural or legal person suffers loss directly as a result of Community action are relatively few since Community law is administered mainly at national level. By contrast, in the context of normative injustice, the notion of seriousness has served both a constitutional and an economic rationale by underscoring the exceptional character of liability. It is submitted that the introduction of seriousness as a general condition of liability is helpful both from the methodological and the substantive point of view. In terms of methodology, it serves to structure the judicial inquiry better. In terms of substance, it highlights the growth in Community administrative powers and recognizes that in certain cases the Community administration may be called upon to make difficult policy choices entailing the exercise of broad discretion.

The introduction of serious breach as a condition of liability, however, was not intended to make liability for Community administrative action more difficult. It is submitted that in the few pre-*Bergaderm* cases where an action in damages was successful, the result would have been the same under the *Bergaderm* formula.

With regard to legislative acts, *Bergaderm* has replaced the previous formula that there must be *a violation of a superior rule of law for the protection of the individual* with the condition that the defendant institution must have infringed '*a rule of law intended to*

---

[72] *Ibid.*, paras 43 and 44.

[73] *Ibid.*, para 46. For subsequent confirmation of these dicta, see *Camar and Tico*, *op. cit.*, n. 16 above, paras 53–55; Case C-472/00 P *Commission v Fresh Marine*, [2003] ECR I-7541, paras 25–27.

confer rights on individuals.[74] Despite the difference in phraseology, in fact these requirements do not differ in substance and nothing turns on the new formula. As shown above, the Court has placed little importance on the requirement that the rule of law must be 'superior'. The omission of this term in *Bergaderm* makes no difference.

10.4. The post-*Bergaderm* case law: Discretion and duty of care

Although in *Bergaderm*, the ECJ elevated discretion to the main criterion for determining the seriousness of the breach, subsequent case law illustrates that this is by no means the only consideration to be taken into account. A Community institution may be found to have committed a serious breach even though it enjoys broad discretion and, conversely, a breach may not be serious even though the institution has committed an error in a field where its discretion is limited.

In *Camar*[75] the Court found the Commission liable for failure to adopt transitional measures even though it possessed wide discretionary powers. The case concerned the common organization of the market in bananas set up by Regulation No 404/93, which provided for a common quota regime for the importation of bananas from third countries.[76] Article 30 of the Regulation requires the Commission to take measures to assist the transition from the previous national regimes to the common organization of the market.

The applicant company was the main importer of Somalian bananas into Italy. Owing to the outbreak of civil war in 1990, its normal supply of imports was interrupted. It requested the Commission to increase its quota for bananas from third countries in order to offset the impossibility of making use of its quota for Somalian bananas but the Commission refused. The CFI held that the Commission's refusal was a breach of Article 30 and proceeded to examine the claim for compensation. At that time, the ECJ had not yet delivered its judgment in *Bergaderm*, so the CFI followed the *Schöppenstedt* formula, starting from the proposition that, in the field of administrative action, any infringement of law constitutes illegality which may give rise to liability. It held that the Commission's refusal to take provisional measures, even though it was based on Article 30 which gives the Commission broad discretionary power, was an individual decision and therefore administrative in nature. It followed that the first condition of liability, i.e. breach of law, was satisfied without any further enquiry.

On appeal,[77] the ECJ referred to the conditions of liability as recast in *Bergaderm* and found that the CFI had committed an error of law by holding that the

---

[74] *Op. cit.*, para 62. Emphasis added.
[75] *Op. cit.*, n. 16 above. Cf Case 26/81 *Oleifici Mediterranei* [1982] ECR 3057.
[76] OJ 1993 L 47/1 as amended by Regulation No 3029/94, OJ 1994 L 349/105.
[77] Case C-312/00 *Commission v Camar and Tico*, [2002] ECR I-11355.

Commission's liability could arise from the mere illegality of its decision without taking account of the discretion which it enjoyed. Nevertheless, the ECJ upheld the CFI's finding that there was an actionable breach because the Commission's failure to take transitional measures amounted to a manifest and grave disregard of the limits of its discretionary powers. This was the first case where the ECJ applied the test of manifest and grave disregard to an administrative measure.

By contrast, in *Dieckmann & Hansen GmbH v Commission*,[78] the CFI upheld the wide discretion of the Commission in matters of health protection and dismissed an action for compensation for loss arising from a decision banning the import of fish products from Kazakhstan. Shortly before the decision, the applicant had contracted for the import of caviar, but the CFI held that public health, as an overriding public interest, may preclude the adoption of transitional measures in respect of contracts which had been concluded before the new rules came into force. Also, the Commission was entitled to impose a ban on the basis of the general risk which imports from a country represent rather than proof of actual risk which certain products or consignments pose.

Where the Commission commits an error of law in circumstances where it does not enjoy much discretion, liability will not ensue automatically. The post-*Bergaderm* case law of the CFI suggests that, in the field of administrative action, an error on the part of an institution will not give rise to liability unless it is the result of lack of due diligence.[79] In *Comafrica*,[80] importers of bananas from third countries brought an action seeking the annulment of a number of regulations by which the Commission had fixed the annual reduction coefficients for the determination of the quantity of bananas to be allocated to each trader. They also sought damages for the loss that they had allegedly suffered as a result. The CFI stated that, where the Commission acts in an administrative capacity, the test of liability is whether the Commission has committed a mistake which would not have been committed in similar circumstances by an administrative authority exercising ordinary care and diligence.[81] An error or irregularity is not sufficient in itself to give rise to liability.[82] In *Comafrica* the CFI attributed importance to the fact that the Commission acted in an administrative rather than legislative capacity[83] and linked the

---

[78] Case T-155/99 *Dieckmann & Hansen GmbH v Commission*, judgment of 23 October 2003.
[79] Joined Cases T-198/95, T-171/96, T-230/97, T-174/98 and T-225/99 *Comafrica and Dole Fresh Fruit Europe v Commission* [2001] ECR II-1975, para 144.   [80] *Op. cit.*
[81] Para 138.
[82] Para 144. In the circumstances, the CFI found that there was no such lack of care by the Commission because although there were discrepancies in the data used by the Commission to calculate the coefficients, the Commission had done everything it could to establish the figures correctly. The CFI took into account the complexity of the import regime, the time constraints involved, the vast magnitude of the transactions, 'the difficulties linked with operations spread over the administrations of 15 Member States' and the extensive efforts made by the Commission to reduce inconsistencies in the figures.
[83] An interesting aspect of the case is that, in the action for damages, the CFI considered that the regulations in issue were of an administrative character even though earlier in the judgment it had rejected the applicant's contention that they were bundles of individual decisions and found that they were measures of general application, for the purposes of the action for annulment.

seriousness of the breach to the degree of care shown by the Commission rather than the degree of discretion enjoyed by it.

In *Fresh Marine Company AS v Commission*,[84] the applicant was a Norwegian company which, in order to avoid the imposition of anti-dumping and anti-subsidy duties, had given the Commission an undertaking that it would not sell salmon in the Community below a minimum price. On the basis of a report submitted by the applicant, the Commission took the view that, during the third quarter of 1997, the applicant had failed to observe its undertaking, and adopted a regulation imposing a provisional anti-dumping duty. Subsequently, following clarifications provided by the applicant, the Commission concluded that it had not broken its undertaking and repealed the provisional duties. The applicant brought an action seeking to recover the damage which it had allegedly suffered by not being able to export salmon to the Community during the period when the provisional duties were in force.

Referring to its earlier case law, the CFI reiterated that, in principle, anti-dumping measures are legislative acts involving choices of economic policy and therefore the Community may incur liability only if there is a sufficiently serious rule of law for the protection of the individual.[85] It pointed out however the special features of that case. Although the anti-dumping duties had been imposed by a regulation, the Commission was not in fact exercising economic policy.[86] In view of this, the CFI held that there was no need to satisfy the *Schöppenstedt* test and that the mere infringement of Community law would be sufficient to lead to liability. Although it referred to *Bergaderm*,[87] it proceeded to examine whether the Commission had failed to exercise ordinary care and diligence in monitoring compliance by the applicant with its undertaking. It came to the conclusion that the Commission had breached its duty of diligence although it also found contributory negligence on the part of the applicant.

On appeal,[88] the ECJ followed a discretion-based approach but upheld the outcome of the CFI. It stated that the Commission may impose provisional anti-dumping duties only where it has reason to believe that an undertaking offered by a company has been breached, and that the decision imposing such duties must be taken on the best information available. The Commission, however, had imposed provisional duties on Fresh Marine's imports, relying solely on the analysis of a report which it had amended on its own initiative, without taking the precaution of asking Fresh Marine what impact its unilateral action might have on the reliability of the information provided by the latter. Such conduct was to be regarded as a sufficiently serious breach of Community law.

The judgments discussed above suggest that discretion, although important, is not as decisive as suggested in *Bergaderm*. The concept of 'broad discretion' is in itself relative. In *Camar* both the CFI and the ECJ declared that the Commission

---

[84] Case T-178/98 *Fresh Marine Company AS v Commission*, [2000] ECR II-3331.
[85] *Ibid.*, para 57, and see *Nölle v Council and Commission op. cit.*, n. 25 above.
[86] *Fresh Marine Company, op. cit.*, paras 58–60.   [87] *Ibid.*, para 61.
[88] Case C-472/00 P *Commission v Fresh Marine*, 10 July 2003.

has wide discretion to adopt transitional measures but, in fact, they interpreted the Commission's powers restrictively and made it subject to severe constraints.[89] Also, the CFI and the ECJ seem to follow different methodology. The ECJ focuses on discretion whilst the CFI prefers an analysis which attributes importance to the legislative or administrative nature of the breach and is dominated by the concept of the duty of care. This difference in approach does not necessarily lead to different outcomes but inserts a degree of uncertainty in the case law. The ECJ's approach is based on an ad hoc evaluation of the limits of discretion and appears to lack in structure and principle. It contrasts with its methodology on State liability where it has provided criteria for determining the seriousness of the breach. In the case of purely administrative, as opposed to policy measures, it is preferable to apply the CFI test, namely that an error or irregularity on the part of an institution does not give rise to liability unless it is the result of lack of diligence or care. This opens the way for articulating standards of good administration and brings Community liability closer to the liability of Member States which was the Court's intention in *Bergaderm*.

Despite the deficiencies of the case law, the action for damages remains a universal remedy. In *European Ombudsman v Lamberts*,[90] it was held that an action may also lie against the European Ombudsman. The Court stressed that the Ombudsman has very wide discretion in dealing with complaints and that he is merely under an obligation to use his best endeavours and under no obligation as to the results to be achieved. Consequently, review by the Community judicature must be limited. It is however possible in very exceptional circumstances that a citizen may be able to demonstrate that the Ombudsman has committed a sufficiently serious breach in the performance of his duties.[91] The test applicable is the manifest and clear disregard of discretionary powers although, given the distinct function of the Ombudsman, it would be difficult for an action for damages to succeed.

10.5. Liability for lawful acts

Although, in practice, illegality of a measure is a necessary condition of liability,[92] the case law has not excluded the possibility that, in exceptional cases, liability may arise as a result of a lawful legislative act. The case law has been persistently non-committal in this respect.

---

[89] This was also the case in Case C-68/95 *T. Port* [1996] ECR I-6065. Cf *Dieckmann & Hansen, op. cit.*, n. 78 above, where the CFI held that the Commission enjoys wide discretion in the field of health policy the requirements of which enabled it to act without adopting transitional measures.

[90] Case C-234/02 P *European Ombudsman v Lamberts*, judgment of 23 March 2004, confirming on appeal Case T-209/00 *Lamberts v Ombudsman* [2002] ECR II-2203.   [91] *Op. cit.*, para 52.

[92] This is not to say that the measure must have already been declared invalid in order for an action for damages to succeed. The action for damages is an autonomous form of action: see *Zuckerfabrik Schöppenstedt, op. cit.*

Liability for lawful acts is based on the notion of 'special sacrifice' or 'equality before the public burdens', developed in French and German law.[93] According to this notion, the State may be held liable to make good loss suffered by a trader as a result of lawful measures taken in the public interest if he was harmed in a distinct way and much more severely than other traders.[94]

In *Compagnie d'Approvisionnement v Commission*,[95] the applicants argued that they had suffered damage because, following the devaluation of the French franc, the Commission had fixed the level of subsidies on imports of wheat from third countries at too low a level. They claimed that the Community should incur liability even in the absence of illegality because they had suffered unusual and special damage in that they had been treated less favourably than importers from other Member States. In his Opinion, Advocate General Mayras took the view that the application of the principle of special sacrifice should not be excluded but found that, on the facts, the applicants were not entitled to compensation.[96] The ECJ laconically rejected the claim stating that, in a situation such as that at issue, any liability for a valid legislative act was inconceivable since the measures adopted by the Commission were in fact intended to alleviate the adverse consequences which resulted from the devaluation of the franc.[97]

In *Biovilac*,[98] the Court expressly left open the possibility of liability arising without illegality on the basis of the theory of special sacrifice.[99] It held however that, even if that theory were accepted in Community law, it could not cover loss from a measure which was or should have been foreseeable. Also, the damage allegedly suffered must exceed the limits of the economic risks inherent in the sector concerned.[100]

Liability for lawful acts has been claimed unsuccessfully in other cases but the Community judicature has always left the door ajar.[101] The conditions of such liability were articulated by the CFI in *Dorsch Consult v Council and Commission*.[102] The applicants, a German firm of consultant engineers, had rendered services to the Ministry of Works Housing of Iraq. Following the invasion of Kuwait in 1990, the Council adopted a regulation preventing trade with Iraq pursuant to the trade embargo imposed by the UN Security Council Resolution 661 (1990). In

---

[93] In German law the notion is known as 'Sonderopfer' and in French law it is referred to as '*rupture de l'egalité devant les charges publiques*'.

[94] Note that, procedurally, liability for a lawful act is a new plea in law which must be raised in the application. It cannot be raised for the first time at a subsequent stage in the proceedings if the action in damages was initially based only on liability arising from illegality: Case C-104/97 P *Atlanta v European Community* [1999] ECR I-6983, paras 27–29.

[95] *Op. cit.*, n. 23 above. See also Case 169/73 *Compagnie Continentale v Commission* [1975] ECR 117; *Vloeberghs, op. cit.*, n. 23 above. [96] *Op. cit.*, pp 422–423.

[97] *Op. cit.*, para 46. [98] *Op. cit.*, n. 30 above.

[99] In *Biovilac, op. cit.*, at p. 4091, Slynn AG drew parallels between the requirement to pay compensation for the expropriation of property and the notion of special sacrifice.

[100] *Ibid.*, para 28.

[101] See Case 267/82 *Développement and Clemessy v Commission* [1986] ECR 1907, para 33; *de Boer Buizen, op. cit.*, n. 60 above, paras 16–17; *Dubois et Fils, op. cit.*, n. 34 above.

[102] Case T-184/95 *Dorsch Consult v Council and Commission* [1998] ECR II-667; confirmed on appeal: C- 237/98 P [2000] ECR I-4549.

response, the Iraqi Government adopted a law freezing all assets and income of enemy country firms. The applicant argued that the outstanding debts owed to it by Iraq had become irrecoverable and sought compensation from the Community alleging that its loss was the result of the trade embargo. The CFI rejected the action on the ground that there was no direct causal link and also that the applicant had failed to prove actual and certain damage. It examined however in some detail the conditions of liability for lawful acts. It stated that, in the event that such liability was recognized, it would be subject to the existence of 'special' and 'unusual' damage.[103] These conditions merit more detailed consideration.

The alleged damage must be special. This means that liability can be incurred only if the damage alleged affects a particular circle of economic operators in a disproportionate manner by comparison with others.[104] This is in effect a participatory requirement which is based on considerations of equality. The applicants must establish that they are part of a group which suffered particularly compared to other groups which are perceived to be in similar circumstances. The size of the group appears to be important. It must be small and arguably closed. In *Dorsch Consult* the CFI rejected the applicant's claim that it suffered special damage because, unlike other undertakings, it could not obtain insurance cover by State guarantees in Germany. The applicant had failed to establish that it was the only undertaking or that it belonged to a small group of economic operators for which the benefit of insurance cover of that kind was unavailable.[105] Also, it was not only their claims but also those of all other Community undertakings that were affected by the refusal of the Iraqi authorities to honour their debts.

The second requirement is that the damage must be unusual. This has two components. The damage must exceed the limits of the economic risks inherent in operating in the sector concerned. Also, the legislative measure that gave rise to the alleged damage must not be justified by a general economic interest.[106]

In *Dorsch Consults* the CFI found that the alleged damage was not unusual. By reason of its involvement in the Iran war, Iraq was regarded as a high risk country so that its possible involvement in renewed warfare and the suspension of payment of its debts for foreign policy reasons constituted foreseeable risks inherent in any provision of services to Iraq. Finally, the CFI held that the objectives of the embargo, which were to end the occupation of Kuwait and maintain international peace and security, were of such fundamental importance for the international community that, even if the alleged damage could be said to be substantial, it could not render the Community liable in the circumstances of the case.[107]

The last requirement, namely that the damage must be unjustified, enables the Court to balance the conflicting interests involved and underscores the exceptional

---

[103] *Dorsch Consult, op. cit.*, para 80. These conditions were confirmed on appeal by the ECJ: *Dorsch, op. cit.*, para 18. For subsequent confirmation, see: Case T-195/00 *Travelex Global and Financial Services Ltd v Commission*, judgment of 10 April 2003, para 161; Case T-196/99 *Area Cova v Council and Commission* [2001] ECR II-3597, para 171. [104] *Ibid.*
[105] *Op. cit.*, para 82. [106] *Op. cit.*, para 80. [107] *Op. cit.*, paras 82–89.

character of liability. Often, however, the claim fails on the condition of special damage without the need to enter into an enquiry as to whether the damage is justified. In *Area Cova v Council and Commission*,[108] the applicants claimed compensation for the loss arising from the reduction of their fishing opportunities following the fixing of a Community quota for halibut. The CFI held that they had not suffered special damage. The reduction of fishing opportunities in the area in question was not unforeseeable nor did it totally prevent the pursuit of fishing. Also, the applicants could not claim a right to fish halibut in specific waters. The Court pointed out that 'economic operators cannot rely on an acquired right to the maintenance of an advantage arising from Community legislation especially legislation worked out in the context of an international organization in which the Community participates'.[109]

The requirements of special and unusual damage establish a normative framework which makes it virtually impossible for liability to arise. Indeed, in no case so far has the ECJ or the CFI found the conditions to be satisfied. There is a justifiable fear that liberalization of the conditions will open the floodgates to a host of unmeritorious claims. Also, the high threshold accords with the theoretical underpinnings of EU public law. A wider acceptance of liability for lawful acts would imply a transition from our understanding of the State as a regulator to the State as an insurer. In practice, such liability can be established only if the measure has an expropriatory character but, even in such a case, the Court might prefer to address the issue in terms of a violation of the right to property rather than the theory of special sacrifice. The case law remains open to criticism on doctrinal grounds. Although it has repeatedly discussed the conditions which would apply if it were accepted that the Community could be liable to compensate damage arising from a lawful act, it has not unequivocally stated whether such liability may arise as a matter of principle. This approach is not satisfactory. It puts the cart before the horse and is liable to maintain uncertainty.

10.6. Causal link

The requirement of causation is satisfied where the damage is the 'direct' consequence of the breach. This was established in *Dumortier* and repeated in subsequent cases[110] but the case law has not articulated specific criteria on the basis of which to determine the remoteness of damage. The burden of proving a direct link rests with the applicant.[111]

---

[108] *Op. cit.*, n. 103 above.   [109] *Ibid.*, para 177.

[110] *Dumortier Frères v Council, op. cit.*, n. 41 above, para 21; Joined Cases C-363 and C-364/88 *Finsider and Others v Commission* [1992] ECR I-359, para 25; Case T-175/94 *International Procurement Services v Commission* [1996] ECR II-729, para 55; Case T-7/96 *Perillo v Commission* [1997] ECR II-1061, para 41.

[111] Case T-168/94 *Blackspur and Others v Council and Commission* [1995] ECR II-2627, para 40. For an example where the applicant failed to prove causation, see: Case T-1/99 *T. Port v*

In *Dorsch Consults* the CFI denied the existence of a direct causal link on two grounds. It held that the adoption of the Iraqi Law pursuant to which Dorsch was refused payment was not an objectively foreseeable consequence, in the normal course of events, of the adoption of the Community regulation imposing the trade embargo. It also held that, even if the Iraqi Law could be considered as a foreseeable consequence of the Community regulation, the alleged damage could not in fact be attributed to the regulation but to the United Nations Security Council resolution pursuant to which the regulation was adopted.[112] This suggests that the chain of causation is broken if the Community is required to adopt an act under the United Nations Charter and possibly also under other international law. It will be remembered however that in *Dorsch* the claim was based on liability for a lawful act. It is uncertain if the Court would take the same view if the measure was found to be unlawful as a matter of Community law.

The chain of causation may be broken where the applicant has contributed to the damage.[113] In some cases, the ECJ has used the concept of a prudent trader to deny causation. In *Compagnie Continentale France v Council* the Court held that, as a prudent exporter, the applicant should have been aware at the time that it concluded contracts for the export of agricultural products to a new Member State that the world prices were rising and that, as a result, the Community would lower the subsidies granted for the exportation of products to new Member States.[114] In *Odigitria*[115] the applicant's vessel held a licence to fish in Senegalese waters pursuant to an agreement concluded between the Community and Senegal. The Community had concluded a similar agreement with Guinea-Bissau. The dispute arose because both Senegal and Guinea-Bissau claimed sovereignty over a certain marine area. The applicant's vessel, which was fishing in the disputed area, was seized by the Guinea-Bissau coast guard on the ground that it did not hold a licence to fish in its territorial waters. The Court accepted that the Commission might be liable for failing to warn the licence holder of the risks of fishing in waters whose sovereignty was disputed. It found however that the damage suffered was not the result of the Commission's failure to provide information. The master of the vessel knew of the dispute between the two countries so that the seizure of the vessel could only be attributed to his deliberate decision to fish there or to navigational error.

In *Kampffmeyer*[116] the Court found that the damage suffered by the applicants was the direct result of the Commission's decision authorizing Germany to maintain in force protective measures. More recently, however, in *DLD Trading*

Commission [2001] ECR II-465, confirmed on appeal: C-122/01 P *T. Port v Commission*, [2003] ECR I-4261.

[112] *Dorsch Consults, op. cit.*, paras 73–74.
[113] *Adams, op. cit.*, n. 9 above; Case C-308/87 *Grifoni* [1990] ECR I-1203.
[114] Case 169/73 [1975] ECR 117, para 28; see also *Oleifici Mediterranei, op. cit.*, n. 75 above, para 22.
[115] *Odigitria v Council and Commission, op. cit.*, n. 14 above.
[116] *Kampffmeyer v Commission, op. cit.*, n. 10 above.

Community legislation authorised a new Member State to derogate from the Community rules ordinarily applicable but it was held that any damage suffered by traders was not attributable directly to the Community since authorization merely granted a power and did not require the Member State to follow a specific course of action.[117] By contrast, in staff cases a less strict standard is applied.[118]

[117] Case T-146/01 *DLD Trading Co v Council*, judgment of 17 December 2003. This case however is distinguishable from *Kampffmeyer* on the facts. It is submitted that Article 288(2) should be interpreted in a way similar to that of Article 230(4) where the ECJ has accepted the existence of *de facto* direct concern. Under the case law, an individual is directly concerned by a Community measure which leaves discretion to a Member State where it can be predicted with certainty how the State will exercise its discretion: See Case 11/82 *Piraiki-Patraiki v Commission* [1985] ECR 207; Case C-403/96 P *Glencore Grain Ltd v Commission* [1998] ECR I-2405. Thus, in cases where the Community authorizes a Member State to take certain action and such authorization runs counter to Community law, the Community may not avoid liability simply on the ground that it authorized rather than required the State to take the action if no real exercise of discretion is involved.

[118] In cases where, by failing to recruit a person, the Community administration has committed a serious breach of law, a right to reparation is borne if, in the circumstances of the case, it seems 'eminently probable' that the administration would have recruited that person. Thus, it is sufficient to prove a genuine chance of being recruited. See Case T-144/02 *Eagle v Commission*, judgment of 5 October 2004, para 149.

11

State Liability for Breach
of EU Law

There is no doubt that the most important aspect of the principle of effectiveness is the establishment by the Court of State liability in damages for breach of Community law and the cognate right to reparation of injured parties. The development of the case law in this area eminently illustrates the creative function of the Court. The subject has attracted vast bibliography[1] and will be examined here in some detail.

11.1. The legal basis of State liability

The EC Treaty is silent on the issue of whether Member States may be liable in damages to injured parties for breach of Community law. Traditionally, it was accepted that the matter was governed by national law. In its case law under

---

[1] See *inter alia*, M. Dougan, 'What is the Point of *Francovich*?' In T.Tridimas and P. Nebbia, *European Union Law for the 21st Century* (Hart Publishing 2004) pp. 239–258; J. E. Pfander, 'Member State Liability and Constitutional Change in the United States and Europe', (2003) 51 Am. J. Comp. Law. 237; C.Kremer, 'Liability for Breach of European Community Law: An Analysis of the new Remedy in the Light of English and German Law', (2003) 22 YEL 203; D. Fairgrieve, M. Andenas and J. Bell (eds), *Tort Liability of Public Authorities in Comparative Perspective*, (London, BIICL, 2002); T.Tridimas, 'Liability for Breach of Community Law: Growing Up and Mellowing Down?' (2001) 38 CML Rev. 301; J. Beatson and T. Tridimas (eds), *New Directions in European Public Law*, (Hart Publishing, 1998); T. Heukels and A. McDonnell (eds), *The Action for Damages in Community Law* (Kluwer, 1997); P. Craig, 'Once More unto the Breach: The Community, the State and Damages Liability', (1997) 113 LQR 67; M. Wathelet and S. van Raepenbusch, 'La responsabilité des États Membres en cas de violation du droit Communautaire. Vers un alignement de la responsabilité de l'État sur celle de la Communauté ou l' inverse?' (1997) 33 CDE 13; W. van Gerven, 'Bridging the Unbridgeable: Community and National Tort Laws after *Francovich* and *Brasserie*', (1996) 45 ICLQ 507; C. Harlow, '*Francovich* and the Problem of the Disobedient State' (1996) 2 EurLJ 199; T. Downes, 'Trawling for a Remedy: State Liability under Community Law' (1997) 17 LS 286; N. Gravells, case notes in (1996) PL 567; N. Emiliou, case notes in (1996) 21 ELR 399; L. Neville Brown, 'State Liability to Individuals in Damages: An Emerging Doctrine of EU Law', (1996) 31 IrJur. 7; T. Tridimas, case notes in (1996) 55 CLJ 412; W. van Gerven, 'Non-Contractual Liability of Member States, Community Institutions and Individuals for Breaches of Community Law with a View to Common Law for Europe', (1994) 1 MJ 6; P. Craig, *Francovich*, Remedies and the Scope of Damages Liability (1993) 109 LQR 595; C. Lewis and S. Moore, 'Duties, Directives and Damages in European Community Law', (1993) PL 151.

Article 226 EC, the Court had repeatedly pointed out that a judgment finding an infringement of Community law may serve as the basis for liability that a Member State might incur under national law against private parties.[2] In *Russo v AIMA*,[3] decided in 1976, an Italian producer claimed that he had suffered loss as a result of action by the Italian intervention agency which made available in the market products at prices lower than those guaranteed to producers by Community agricultural regulations. The Court held that, under Community law, a producer may claim that he should not be prevented from obtaining a price at least equal to the intervention price guaranteed by Community regulations. It then stated that it was for the national court to decide, on the basis of the facts of each case, whether an individual producer has suffered damage. If damage had been caused through an infringement of Community law, the State was liable to the injured party in accordance with the provisions of national law on the liability of public authorities.[4] The traditional approach of the Court towards remedies was encapsulated in a dictum, made in *Rewe v Hauptzollamt Kiel* in 1981, that the EC Treaty 'was not intended to create new remedies'.[5]

The issue of liability for breach of Community law was not addressed again by the Court until 1991.[6] In its seminal judgment in *Francovich*,[7] the Court established that a Member State may be liable in damages to an injured party for breach of Community law. The case concerned loss arising as a result of failure by a Member State to implement a directive. The Court based liability on two grounds: the principle of effectiveness and Article 10 EC. Its reasoning is instructive of the way it interprets the Treaty and of the way it understands its function in developing Community law. It first recalled that Community law gives rise to rights for individuals which become part of their legal heritage. Such rights arise not only where they are expressly provided in the Treaty but also impliedly by virtue of specific obligations which the Treaty imposes on Member States. It also stated that national courts must provide full protection to rights which Community law confers on individuals. It then continued:[8]

The full effectiveness of Community rules would be impaired and the protection of the rights which they grant would be weakened if individuals were unable to obtain redress when their rights are infringed by a breach of Community law for which a Member State can be held responsible.

---

[2] See e.g. Case 39/72 *Commission v Italy* [1973] ECR 101, para 11; Case 154/85 *Commission v Italy* [1987] ECR 2717, para 6.   [3] Case 60/75 *Russo v AIMA* [1976] ECR 45.

[4] *Ibid.*, paras 8–9. See also Case 181/82 *Roussel* [1983] ECR 3849 and the earlier dicta in Case 101/78 *Granaria v Hoofdproductschap voor Akkerbouwprodukten* [1979] ECR 623, para 14.

[5] Case 158/80 [1981] ECR 1805, para 44. See 9.1 above.

[6] The question whether liability might arise for breach of Community law by national administrative measures was referred but not examined by the Court in Case 380/87 *Enichem Base and Others v Comune di Cinisello Balsamo* [1989] ECR 2491. The issue of damages as a remedy for breach of the Equal Treatment Directive was discussed briefly by van Gerven AG in Case C-188/89 *Foster and Others v British Gas* [1990] ECR I-3301, at 3341.

[7] Joined Cases C-6 and C-9/90 *Francovich* [1991] ECR I-5357.   [8] *Ibid.*, paras 33–35.

The possibility of obtaining redress from a Member State is particularly indispensable where, as in this case, the full effectiveness of Community rules is subject to prior action on the part of the State and where, consequently, in the absence of such action, individuals cannot enforce before the national courts the rights conferred upon them by Community law.

It follows that the principle whereby a State must be liable for loss and damage caused to individuals as a result of breaches of Community law for which the State can be held responsible is inherent in the system of the Treaty.

The Court found a further basis of liability in Article 10 EC, stating that among the measures which Member States must take to ensure fulfilment of their obligations, as required by Article 10, is the obligation to nullify the unlawful consequences of a breach of Community law.

The question may well be asked what changed between 1981, when the Court declared that the Treaty is not intended to create new remedies, and 1991 when the Court proclaimed that State liability in damages 'is inherent in the system of the Treaty'? Why did the Court take such a fundamentally different approach in *Francovich*? The answer may be found only if one looks at the development of the case law on judicial remedies as a whole.

In the early 1990s the case law moved from an approach based on rights to an approach based on remedies. Establishment of State liability in damages is the high point in the evolution of the principle of primacy from a general principle of constitutional law to a specific obligation on national courts to provide full and effective remedies for the protection of Community rights.[9] It has been noted that the principles of direct and indirect effect of directives were developed in the light of persistent failures by Member States to meet their obligations with a view to securing the enforcement of Community law.[10] *Francovich* could be seen as another such 'expedient'. Viewed in that perspective, direct effect and State liability in damages can be seen merely as the means to achieve results or, to put it in a different way, as the directed use of judicial power. This analysis is correct but does not give the whole picture. It is an implicit premise in every legal system that the courts which are entrusted with upholding its laws must avoid consequences which would undermine its fundamental presuppositions. The Court's approach can be encapsulated in the principle *ubi jus, ibi remedium*. According to this approach, the value of a right is determined by the legal consequences which ensue from its violation, namely the

---

[9] Traces of the Court's approach in *Francovich* can already be found in the Opinion of the Advocate General in *Russo v AIMA*. Reischl AG stated that the issue of Member State liability was one for the national courts in accordance with the national legal system. He added however that, in order to avoid the risk of unequal treatment of individuals under the national legal systems, it was necessary to work out principles, as the Court had done in other cases, upon which a uniform and effective enforcement of Community rights could be established. *Russo v AIMA, op. cit.* n. 2, p. 62.

[10] J. Steiner, 'From Direct effects to *Francovich*: shifting means of enforcement of Community law', (1993) 18 ELR 3, at 10. That view received judicial recognition by Léger AG in Case C-5/94 *The Queen v Ministry of Agriculture, Fisheries and Food ex p Hedley Lomas (Ireland) Ltd* [1996] ECR I-2553, at p. 2575.

remedies available from its enforcement. The common thread underlying the Court's case law on remedies is the concern to ensure the availability of effective judicial protection. Such reasoning is by no means unique to the Community judicature. In his dissenting judgment in *Bourgoin*,[11] Oliver LJ (as he then was) followed a similar approach. At the risk of becoming 'too metaphysical', he distinguished between a general right to have the provisions of the law observed, shared by everyone, and an individual right requiring protection. He then continued:

It is only when the breach of the public duty inflicts loss or damage on the individual that he has, as an individual, a cause of complaint. *If the law gives him no remedy for that damage then he would not ordinarily be said to have any 'individual right'.*[12]

In *Francovich* the Court viewed State liability as the natural consequence of the breach of individual rights granted by Community law. Its primary objective was to vindicate rights by opening the road to claims for compensation. It also sought to internalise the negative externalities caused by the non-compliance with Community law. Where a public authority fails to comply with Community law, such failure gives rise to external costs in that the intended recipients of Community rights are unable to benefit from them. By rendering States liable in damages the ECJ sought to satisfy the requirements of corrective justice and also provided a powerful deterrent: Member States now acquired a strong incentive to comply with the requirements of Community directives.[13]

The question still remains why the Court felt able to establish a right to reparation in *Francovich* although it had been so reticent in previous cases. It seems that three factors precipitated a change of attitude. First, the Commission's internal market programme, heralded by the 1985 White Paper, provided a new impetus for the completion of the internal market and made all the more important the provision of adequate remedies for failure to implement directives. Thus, the recognition of a right to reparation became a constitutional imperative because it was supported by a strong instrumental rationale. Second, previous case law, in particular the judgment in *Factortame*,[14] had prepared the ground for increasing judicial intervention in the area of remedies. Third, the facts of *Francovich* lent themselves to the recognition of State liability in damages given the manifest and inexcusable breach of Community law in the circumstances of the case. In short, the legal and political climate was such as to enable the Court to make a quantum leap.

The next step came in *Brasserie du Pêcheur and Factortame*.[15] In *Brasserie du Pêcheur*, a French company was forced to discontinue exports to Germany because the German authorities considered that the beer it produced did not satisfy the requirements of

[11] *Bourgoin SA v Ministry of Agriculture* [1986] 3 All ER 585.
[12] *Ibid.*, at 616, emphasis added.
[13] See further G. Anagnostaras, 'The Principle of State Liability for Judicial Breaches: The Impact of European Community Law', (2001) 7 EPL 281 at 282–283.
[14] Case C-213/89 *Factortame and Others* [1990] ECR I-2433.
[15] Joined Cases C-46 and C-48/93 *Brasserie du Pêcheur v Germany* and *the Queen v Secretary of State for Transport, ex p Factortame Ltd* [1996] ECR I-1029.

German law. Earlier, in the *Beer* case[16] the Court had found in enforcement proceedings brought by the Commission that German law infringed Article 28 in two respects: first, by prohibiting the marketing under the designation 'beer' of beers lawfully produced in other Member States by different methods (the designation prohibition) and, second, by prohibiting the import of beers containing additives (the additives prohibition). The French company brought an action for reparation of the loss that it suffered as a result of the import restrictions. In *Factortame*, the applicants sought to recover the loss that they incurred as a result of the registration conditions imposed by the Merchant Shipping Act 1988, which in previous proceedings had been found by the Court to be incompatible with Article 43 of the Treaty.[17]

The difference between *Francovich* and *Brasserie du Pêcheur* is that, whereas the former concerned liability arising from inaction, the latter concerned liability arising from an act of the national legislature. The Court did not find that to be a material difference. It held that, since the principle of State liability is inherent in the system of the Treaty, it 'holds good for any case in which a Member State breaches Community law, whatever be the organ of the State whose act or omission was responsible for the breach'.[18] It follows that a Member State is liable irrespective of whether the breach which gave rise to the damage is attributable to the legislature, the judiciary or the executive. The Court rejected the argument submitted by some Member States that, where a provision is directly effective, it is unnecessary to provide a right to reparation, viewing the latter as a 'the necessary corollary' rather than a substitute for direct effect.[19]

In *Brasserie*, the German Government argued that a general right of reparation for individuals could be created only by legislation and that for such a right to be recognized by judicial decision would be incompatible with the allocation of powers between the Community institutions and Member States. Dismissing that argument, the Court held that the existence and extent of State liability for breach of Community law are questions of interpretation of the Treaty which fall within the jurisdiction of the Court. Referring to Article 220 EC, it stated that since the Treaty contains no provision governing the consequences of breaches of Community law by Member States, it is for the Court to rule on such questions, in accordance with general principles of interpretation, by reference in particular to the fundamental principles of the Community legal system and, where necessary, legal principles common to the legal systems of the Member States.[20] That reasoning is indicative of the way the Court approaches Article 220 and understands its function in the development of Community law.[21]

The extension of State liability to cases where a breach of Community law is the result of action by the national legislature was to be expected. Once the principle of State liability in damages was established in *Francovich*, there did not seem to be any

---

[16] Case 178/84 *Commission v Germany* [1987] ECR 1227.
[17] See Case C-221/89 *Factortame II* [1991] ECR I-3905; Case C-246/89 *Commission v United Kingdom* [1991] ECR I-4585.   [18] *Brasserie du Pêcheur, op. cit.*, para 32.
[19] *Op. cit.*, para 22.   [20] *Op. cit.*, para 27.   [21] See above, Chapter 1.

valid reason why such liability should be excluded *a priori* in the case of other breaches. However, the basis of State liability arising as a result of acts of the legislature is not identified with sufficient clarity in *Brasserie*. That basis is to be found in the distinct nature of Community law and the principle of primacy. It is not based on principles common to the laws of the Member States as the Court implied. As Léger AG stated in *Hedley Lomas*, with regard to State liability arising from acts of the legislature 'there are no general principles which are *truly common* to the Member States'.[22]

Recognition of state liability for breach by the national legislature signals the transition from the perception of the nation-state as a sovereign legislature to its perception as a constituent part of a quasi-federal legal order. Historically, Member States have acted as primary legislatures. In the case of primary legislative action, liability must be imposed, if at all,[23] only in exceptional circumstances since, as the Court pointed out in *Brasserie*, the freedom of the legislature must not be obstructed by the prospect of action for damages. As Capotorti AG put it in an earlier case, the 'power to express the sovereignty of the people'[24] may justify immunity of the legislature from the general rules of liability. By contrast, within the scope of Community law, Member States no longer act as primary legislatures. As Léger AG stated, it is no longer possible to seek refuge behind the sovereign nature of legislation.[25] Reparation for damage is the corollary of the principle of primacy which requires not only that legislation contrary to Community law should be disapplied but also that reparation must be made for damages resulting from its past application.[26]

11.2. The conditions of State liability: An overview

In early case law, the Court emphasised that the conditions of State liability differed depending on the nature of the breach giving rise to damage.[27] In *Dillenkofer*, however, an attempt was made to unify the requirements of liability, and the Court laid down the following as generally applicable conditions:[28]

- the rule of law infringed must be intended to confer rights on individuals;
- the breach must be sufficiently serious;
- there must be a direct causal link between the breach of the obligation resting on the State and the damage sustained by the injured party.

---

[22] *Hedley Lomas, op. cit.*, n. 10 above at p. 2579 (emphasis in the original).

[23] The legal systems of many Member States do not recognize State liability for legislative action: this is the case for example in Italy, Germany, Belgium, Ireland, Luxembourg and the United Kingdom. See Léger AG in *Hedley Lomas, op. cit.*, at p. 2579.

[24] See Joined Cases 83 and 94/76, 4.15 and 40/77, *HNL v Council and Commission*, [1978] ECR 1209, at p. 1229. [25] Léger AG, *Hedley Lomas, op. cit.*, p. 2580.

[26] *Ibid.*

[27] See e.g. *Francovich, op. cit.*, n. 7 above, para 35; *Brasserie, op. cit.*, n. 15 above, para 31.

[28] Joined Cases C-178, C-179, C-188–190/94 *Dillenkofer and others v Federal Republic of Germany* [1996] ECR I-4845, paras 21–24.

Subsequent case law has consistently referred to those conditions which, since *Bergaderm*, also govern the liability of the Community institutions.[29] The above conditions are necessary and sufficient to found State liability but the possibility remains open that liability may be incurred under less strict requirements on the basis of national law.[30]

For the first condition of liability to be met, it suffices that a provision is intended to confer rights on individuals. The fact that it may be designed to protect general, as opposed to individual, interests does not prevent the provision from being for the protection of individuals for the purposes of the right to reparation.[31] Whether this condition is met is a matter of interpretation of Community law and therefore falls within the exclusive remit of the ECJ.[32] Liability may arise from breach of the Treaty or any other binding provision of Community law. It may also arise from breach of a directly effective provision of an international agreement. The crucial issue here is whether the agreement is capable, in the light of its objectives, context and wording, of producing direct effect.[33] If so, a State may be held liable for breach of a provision of the agreement which is intended to confer rights on individuals.[34] Liability may further arise from breach of a general principle of law provided that an individual may derive enforceable rights from it.

So far, the Court has examined the following types of breach: failure to transpose a directive into national law; breach of Community law by the national legislature; breach by the national administration; incorrect transposition of a directive; and breach by the national judicature. These types of violation will be examined in turn in the sections that follow.

11.3. Failure to transpose a directive into national law

Where a Member State fails to transpose a directive into national law, liability arises only where the result prescribed by the directive entails the grant of rights to individuals and it is possible to identify the content of those rights on the basis of

---

[29] See e.g. Joined Cases C-283, C-291 and C-292/94 *Denkavit Internationaal BV and others v Bundesamt für Finanzen* [1996] ECR I-5063, para 48; Case C-424/97 *Haim v Kassenzahnärztliche Vereinigung Nordrhein* [2000] ECR I-5123, para 36; Case C-63/01 *Evans v Secretary of State for the Environment, Transport and the Regions and the Motor Insurers' Bureau*, judgment of 4 December 2003, para 83. For an analysis of *Bergaderm*, see above, Chapter 10.

[30] *Brasserie du Pêcheur, op. cit.*, n. 15 above, para 66; C-224/01 *Köbler v Austria*, judgment of 30 September 2003, para 57.

[31] *Brasserie, op. cit.*, at p. 1107 per Tesauro AG. This applies not only to Treaty provisions but also to provisions of directives. See *Dillenkofer, op. cit.*, n. 28 above, paras 36–39.

[32] For the distinction between the first condition of liability and the concept of direct effect, see below p. 505.

[33] See Case 104/81 *Hauptzollamt Mainz v Kupferberg* [1982] ECR 3641; case 12/86 *Demirel v Stadt Schwäbisch Gmünd* [1987] ECR 3719.

[34] The issue was raised but not examined in Case C-235/99 *Kondova* [2001] ECR I-6427.

the provisions of the directive.[35] In *Francovich* the Court drew a distinction between provisions which are sufficiently precise and unconditional as to be able to produce direct effect and provisions which, although they lack sufficient precision for that purpose, are nonetheless capable of giving rise to a right to reparation. This distinction is well founded. The right to reparation is a co-relative right, separate in law from direct effect. The provisions of Directive 80/987[36] in issue in *Francovich* were sufficiently precise with regard to the identity of the right holder and the content of the right but not with regard to the persons on whom the corresponding obligation was imposed.[37] The right granted by the Directive was therefore incomplete. The right to reparation however was complete since there could be no doubt about the identity of the entity on which the obligation to implement a directive is imposed. *Ex hypothesi*, that obligation burdens the State.

Where a Member State fails to adopt implementing measures to transpose a directive, such failure is considered to be *per se* a serious breach. This was unequivocally established in *Dillenkofer*,[38] a case which arose from Germany's failure to implement Directive 90/314 on Package Travel.[39] This Directive seeks to protect the purchaser of package travel in the event of the insolvency of the travel operator and, to that effect, Article 7 provides that the organizer or retailer of package travel must provide the consumer with 'sufficient evidence of security for the refund of money paid over and for the repatriation of the consumer in the event of insolvency'. The Directive required implementation by 31 December 1992 but it was not implemented in Germany until 1994. The applicants were purchasers of package tours who, following the insolvency of their tour operators in 1993, either never left for their destination or incurred expenses to return home. Having failed to obtain reimbursement of the sums paid to the operators or the repatriation expenses, they sought compensation from the German State on the ground that, if Germany had implemented the Directive within the prescribed time-limit, they would have been protected against the insolvency of the tour operators.

In *Dillenkofer* it was argued by several governments that a State may incur liability for late transposition of a directive only where there has been a serious breach of Community law. The Court declined to accept that argument. It stated that failure of a Member State to implement a directive within the prescribed period is *per se* a serious breach and, consequently, it gives rise to a right of reparation for individuals subject to the conditions of liability provided for in *Francovich*. No other condition

---

[35] See *Francovich, op. cit.*, para 40; *Dillenkofer, op. cit.*, para 22.

[36] Council Directive 80/987 on the approximation of the laws of the Member States relating to the protection of employees in the event of the insolvency of their employer, OJ 1980 L283/23.

[37] The Directive required Member States to set up guarantee institutions responsible for paying arrears of unpaid wages to employees of insolvent undertakings but left significant discretion to the Member States in setting up those institutions.   [38] *Op. cit.*, n. 27 above.

[39] Council Directive 90/314/EEC on package travel, package holidays and package tours, OJ 1990 L 158, p. 59.

need be taken into consideration.[40] In particular, liability does not depend on the circumstances which caused the period of transposition to be exceeded. Also, liability does not depend on the prior finding by the Court of an infringement of Community law attributable to the State nor on the existence of intentional fault or negligence on the part of the State.[41]

Despite the generality of the judgment in *Dillenkofer*, which appears to recognize no exceptions, the question may be asked whether there may be circumstances in which failure to transpose a directive within the prescribed period does not in itself constitute a serious breach. The following cases may be examined.

Transposition through existing legislation. Where a Member State does not transpose a directive on the assumption that existing national legislation already complies with its provisions,[42] and subsequently it transpires that the legislation does not satisfy the requirements of the directive, it is submitted that liability should not be automatic.[43] This case should be equated with the situation where a Member State implements a directive incorrectly and should be subject, *mutatis mutandis*, to the same conditions of liability. It will be necessary therefore to establish that the error of interpretation committed by the Member State constitutes a serious breach.[44] This view is supported by *Evans v Secretary of State for the Environment, Transport and the Regions and the Motor Insurers' Bureau,*[45] which concerned the Second Motor Insurance Directive.[46] The directive was implemented in the UK by a series of agreements with the Motor Insurers' Bureau predating the Directive. Although the Court did not examine the issue directly, it held that liability would arise only if defects in transposition amounted to a serious breach. The point was expressly examined by Alber AG who, in contrast to the Court, took the view that the UK had committed a serious breach.[47]

Failure to implement attributable to the national administration. Where a Member State fails to implement a directive but, despite the lack of implementing measures, the national administration attempts to apply the directive, any damage suffered by individuals as a result of its incorrect application may be causally connected with the actions of the administration rather than the failure to implement. This is not, strictly speaking, an exception from *Dillenkofer* but may lead to the Member State

---

[40] *Dillenkofer, op. cit.*, para 27.   [41] *Ibid.*, para 28.

[42] The case law accepts that, subject to certain safeguards, where national law already complies with the requirements of a directive, a Member State need not take implementing measures. See e.g. Case 29/84 *Commission v Germany* [1985] ECR 1661. Note however the safeguards: national law must guarantee that the national authorities will apply the directive effectively in full, that the legal position under national law should be sufficiently precise and clear, and that individuals are made fully aware of their rights and, where appropriate, may rely on them before the national courts. Case C-365/93 *Commission v Greece* [1995] ECR I-499, para 8; Case C-144/99 *Commission v Netherlands* [2001] ECR I-3541, paras 17–18. See further chapter 10 on legal certainty.

[43] For an example of unsuccessful transposition by existing legislation, see Case C-334/92 *Wagner Miret* [1993] ECR I-6911.

[44] See 11.6 below, the *BT* case and the guidelines given by the Court there.

[45] *Op. cit.*, n. 29 above.   [46] Council Directive 84/5, OJ 1984 L 8/17.

[47] See paras 154–157 of the Opinion.

avoiding liability even in the case of a complete failure to take implementing measures of general application.[48]

Illegality of directive as defence. May a State plead as a defence that the unimplemented directive is vitiated by illegality? This question gives rise to intricate issues and, so far, has not been addressed by the Court. It should be noted that a Community measure is voidable and not void in that it can be annulled by the Court of Justice or the Court of First Instance only if it is challenged via certain procedural routes by an applicant having *locus standi* within the specified time limit. The case law under Article 226 EC may be instructive here. Where the Commission initiates enforcement proceedings for failure to implement a directive, the defendant Member State may not plead the unlawfulness of the directive as a defence.[49] The rationale behind this approach is that enforcement actions under Article 226 and actions for judicial review under Article 230 are different remedies, which pursue different objectives and are subject to different rules.[50] The case law recognizes an exception only where the Community measure in issue contains such particularly serious and manifest defects that it could be deemed to be non-existent.[51] The precise scope of this exception remains uncertain.[52] Still, there is no doubt that the Court follows a strict approach. This is in conformity with its view in other cases, such as *TWD* [53] and, more generally, illustrates a formalistic

---

[48] See Case C-319/96 *Brinkmann Tabakfabriken GmbH v Skatteministeriet* [1998] ECR I-5255. For a full discussion, see 11.9 below.

[49] This approach was first introduced in relation to collateral challenges in enforcement proceedings against Commission decisions adopted under Article 93(2) (now Article 88(3)) and Article 90(3) (now 86(3)) EC. It was subsequently extended to directives: see Case 156/77 *Commission v Belgium* [1978] ECR 1881, para 24; Case 52/84 *Commission v Belgium* [1986] ECR 89, para 13; Case 226/87 *Commission v Greece* [1988] ECR 3611, para 14; Case C-74/91 *Commission v Germany* [1992] ECR I-5437, para 10; Case C-183/91 *Commission v Greece* [1993] ECR I-3131, para 10; Case C-404/97 *Commission v Portugal* [2000] ECR I-4897, para 34. Note, however, that the ECJ allowed such a collateral challenge in enforcement proceedings in relation to a regulation in Case C-116/82 *Commission v Germany* [1986] ECR 2519. Note also that a Member State which has not challenged a Commission decision addressed to it within the time limit laid down in Article 230(5) cannot subsequently invoke its unlawfulness before a national court in order to dispute the merits of an action brought against it: C-241/01 *National Farmers' Union* [2002] ECR I-9079.

[50] *Commission v Greece, op. cit.*, n. 49 above para 14; Case C-74/91 *Commission v Germany, op. cit.*, n. 49 above para 10.

[51] *Commission v Greece, op. cit.*, n. 49 above, para 16; *Commission v Germany, op. cit.*, n. 49 above, para 11.

[52] The language used by the Court suggests that the possibility of a collateral challenge in the context of enforcement proceedings is limited to cases where the act in question is non-existent, i.e. it is vitiated by such manifest and serious defects as to be immediately obvious not only to the body which adopted the act but also to its addressee: see Case C-137/92P *Commission v BASF AG* [1994] ECR I-2555, paras 49–52 and *per* van Gerven AG at 2623. In previous cases, however, the Court formulated the exception to the prohibition of collateral challenge in wider terms. It appeared to accept that a Member State may challenge the lawfulness of an act in enforcement proceedings where the act in question 'would lack all legal basis in the Community legal system' or infringe 'a principle of a constitutional nature', for example where the Community lacked competence to adopt it because the subject-matter of the act fell within the competence of Member States. See Case 226/87 *Commission v Greece, op. cit., per* Mancini AG at 3617 and Joined Cases 6 and 11/69 *Commission v France* [1969] ECR 523, para 13.

[53] See Case C-188/92 *TWD v Germany* [1994] ECR I-833, discussed above p. 249.

understanding of the law of remedies. The Court's approach is not without its critics. It has been argued that the position would be different in relation to enforcement proceedings for failure to comply with regulations.[54] In such a case, the defendant State could challenge the applicability of the regulation by virtue of the plea of illegality. This view finds support in Article 241 EC which states that the inapplicability of regulations may be invoked 'in proceedings in which a regulation . . . is at issue', and therefore should be taken to include enforcement proceedings under Article 226. If that view were correct, it should apply not only to regulations but to all acts of normative character, including directives. As we have seen, however, this view has been rejected by the Court.

In the context of actions for liability in damages, the following points may be made. In some cases, the defendant Member State may not succeed in its attempt to plead illegality. Thus, a Member State which considers that a directive has been adopted in violation of an essential procedural requirement but does not bring an action for its annulment within the time limit provided for in Article 230 and chooses instead not to implement it, may not necessarily succeed in pleading procedural impropriety as a defence in an action for damages. Since the directive was not annulled, it continues to produce legal effects. In any event, even if it had been annulled in proceedings under Article 230, the Court might have declared its effects definitive pursuant to Article 231, in which case there would still be an obligation on Member States to implement it. It could be argued that the individual's right to reparation should not depend on whether the State was diligent enough to seek clarification of the status of the directive by bringing an action for annulment.

On the other hand, where a directive is vitiated by a substantive defect such as to make the right which the directive is intended to grant to the individual incompatible with a higher rule of Community law,[55] it might appear odd to impose liability on the State. How can the individual be said to have a 'right' under Community law, if the legal measure which confers that right on him infringes a superior rule of the Community legal order? Imposing liability in those circumstances would run counter to the principle of legality. It would also give rise to odd consequences. For example, an individual could bring proceedings to recover damages for failure to implement a directive in the courts of a Member State whereas, in another State which has implemented the directive, another individual, whose interests are thereby affected adversely, could challenge its validity and obtain its annulment with the assistance of Article 234. That would be an oxymoron and breach 'the coherence of the system of judicial protection established by the Treaty'.[56] The counter-argument would be

---

[54] H. G. Schermers and D. Waelbroeck, *Judicial Protection in the European Communities* (Sixth ed, Kluwer, 1992), p. 624. This view is supported by Case 116/82 *Commission v Germany, op. cit.,* n. 49 above.

[55] E.g. where the directive in issue lies beyond the competence of the Community or exceeds the powers of the institution which adopted it. Cf *Commission v France, op. cit.*

[56] Case 314/85 *Foto-Frost v Hauptzollamt Lübeck-Ost* [1987] ECR 4199, para 16.

that the inability of the Member State to plead the unlawfulness of the directive in an action for damages is the logical consequence of its failure to challenge it in time. This argument however appears over-formalistic.

11.4. Breach of Community law as a result of action by the national legislature

11.4.1. The case law

In *Brasserie* the Court modelled the liability of Member States for breach of Community law on the liability of the Community institutions. Such an approach had been advocated by Mischo AG in *Francovich* but the Court did not follow his view. This is probably because the breach in issue, namely failure to implement a directive, was of such a nature that it was not necessary for the Court to draw an analogy with Article 288(2). In *Brasserie* the Court stated that the conditions under which a State may incur liability to individuals for breach of Community law may not, in the absence of particular justification, differ from those governing the liability of the Community in like circumstances.[57] It then referred to its case law under Article 288(2) and stated that the strict conditions which govern Community liability for legislative measures are justified by two considerations. First, the exercise of the legislative function must not be hindered by the prospect of actions for damages; second, it is in the public interest that, in taking policy decisions, the legislature must enjoy ample discretion. It follows that in a legislative context characterised by the exercise of a wide discretion, which is essential for implementing a Community policy, the Community may not incur liability unless the institution concerned has manifestly and gravely disregarded the limits on the exercise of its powers (*Schöppenstedt* test).[58] Turning to State liability, the Court held that where the breach emanates from the national legislature in circumstances where the legislature has wide discretion comparable to that of the Community institutions, Community law confers a right of reparation where three conditions are met:[59]

(1) the rule of law infringed must be intended to confer rights on individuals;
(2) the breach must be sufficiently serious;
(3) there must be a direct causal link between the breach of the obligation resting on the State and the damage sustained by the injured parties.

The Court stated that these conditions satisfy the need to ensure that Community provisions are fully effective and also that they correspond in substance to the

---

[57] *Brasserie, op. cit.*, n. 15 above, para 42. [58] See Chapter 10 above.
[59] *Brasserie, op. cit.*, para 51.

conditions which must be satisfied in order for liability to arise on the part of the Community institutions as a result of legislative action.[60]

The innovation of *Brasserie* is that it introduced the requirement for serious breach as a condition of liability. Drawing a parallel with the liability of the Community institutions under Article 288(2), the Court stated that the decisive test for finding that a breach of Community law is sufficiently serious is whether the Member State concerned manifestly and gravely disregarded the limits of its discretion.[61] The Court listed the following factors as being material in determining whether the infringement passes the threshold of seriousness:[62]

- the clarity and precision of the rule breached;
- the measure of discretion left to the national authorities;
- whether the infringement and the damage caused was intentional or involuntary;
- whether any error of law was excusable or inexcusable;
- the fact that the position taken by a Community institution may have contributed towards the omission;
- the adoption or retention of national measures or practices contrary to Community law.

In any event, a breach of Community law will be sufficiently serious if it has persisted despite a judgment which establishes the infringement in question or a preliminary ruling or settled case law of the Court on the matter from which it is clear that the conduct in question constitutes an infringement.[63] The existence of previous case law, however, is not a prerequisite of liability. In *Lindöpark*,[64] Swedish law exempted from VAT the supply of premises and other facilities and related services for the practice of sport or physical education. The Court held that there was no reasonable doubt that such a wholesale exemption was contrary to Articles 13A and 13B of the Sixth VAT Directive.[65] Given the clarity of these provisions, the breach committed by the Swedish legislature was a serious breach notwithstanding the absence of any case law on the issue and the fact that the Commission had not initiated enforcement proceedings.

The notion of serious breach incorporates the notion of 'fault'. The Court stated that the obligation to make reparation cannot be made dependent on any notion of fault going beyond that of a sufficiently serious breach. Given that the notion of 'fault' does not have the same meaning in the laws of the Member States,[66] the Court was keen to avoid reliance on concepts of national law which might lead to the right of reparation being subject to different conditions in the national legal systems.

In its judgment, the Court proceeded to give more specific guidelines with regard to the cases in issue. In relation to *Brasserie*, it drew a distinction between the

---

[60] *Op. cit.*, paras 52–53.   [61] *Brasserie, op. cit.*, para 55.
[62] *Ibid.*, para 56.   [63] *Ibid.*, para 57.
[64] Case C-150/99 *Stockholm Lindöpark* [2001] ECR I-493.
[65] Council Directive 77/388, OJ 1977 L 145/1.   [66] *Op. cit.*, para 76.

provisions of German law prohibiting the marketing as beer of beverages which did not conform to the German purity laws and those prohibiting the import of beers containing additives. With regard to the first, the Court held that it would be difficult to regard the breach of Article 28 as an excusable error, since the incompatibility of the purity requirements with Article 28 was manifest in the light of earlier case law. By contrast, in the light of the existing case law, the criteria available to the national legislature to determine whether the prohibition of the use of additives were contrary to Community law was significantly less conclusive until the judgment in the *Beer* case.

The Court also gave guidelines with regard to the situation in *Factortame*. It stated that different considerations apply to the provisions of the Merchant Shipping Act 1988 making registration of fishing vessels subject to the requirement of nationality and those imposing residence and domicile requirements for vessel owners and operators. The requirement of nationality constitutes direct discrimination manifestly contrary to Community law. The breach committed therefore by imposing that requirement is sufficiently serious. In assessing whether the requirements imposing residence and domicile are sufficiently serious the national court may take into account, *inter alia*, the particular features of the common fisheries policy, the attitude of the Commission, which made its position known to the United Kingdom in good time, and the assessments as to the state of certainty of Community law made by the national courts in the interim proceedings brought by individuals affected by the Merchant Shipping Act. A further consideration was whether the United Kingdom failed to adopt immediately the measures needed to comply with a previous interim order issued by the President of the ECJ.[67]

11.4.2. A critique of the Court's reasoning

The notion of 'serious breach' provides a flexible tool for the development of State liability in damages. The fundamental premise of the Court's rationale in *Brasserie* was that, unless specific reasons dictate otherwise, the liability of Member States and the liability of the Community institutions must be governed by the same principles. As a starting point, that is undoubtedly correct. The following points however may be made in this context.

First, there is a fundamental difference between the liability of Community institutions arising from legislation and the liability of Member States for breach of Community law. That difference was identified by Léger AG in *Hedley Lomas*.[68] Within the scope of application of Community law, the Community institutions act as a primary legislature. Member States, by contrast, are confined by the norms of Community law which, according to the principle of supremacy, are higher ranking. Thus, the discretion enjoyed by the Member States may not necessarily be

---

[67] See Case 246/89 R *Commission v United Kingdom* [1989] ECR 3125.
[68] See 11.1 above.

comparable with that of the Community institutions. The Court acknowledges this only indirectly by stating that the conditions must be the same 'in the absence of particular justification'[69] and that 'the national legislature . . . does not systematically have a wide discretion when it acts in a field governed by Community law'.[70] The judgment does not emphasise sufficiently the differences between Community liability and State liability for breach of Community law nor does it do justice to the multifarious nuances of the concept of discretion. The case where Member State liability for breach of Community law may be most akin to the liability of the Community institutions is where a Member State exercises discretion conferred upon it by Community regulations in the field of the common agricultural policy in breach of one of the fundamental principles, e.g. equality or proportionality.[71] Even in such a case however considerable differences exist as the discretion of the national authorities is confined by the relevant Community measures.

Further, it is not clear that the conditions of State liability for legislative acts correspond fully to those defined by the case law in relation to the liability of the Community institutions for legislative acts. In its case law under Article 288(2), the Court refers to two elements in determining whether there is a manifest and grave disregard of discretionary powers, namely, the effect of the measure on individuals and the extent to which the law has been violated. The damage alleged by the applicants must go beyond the bounds of the economic risks inherent in the activities in the sector concerned.[72] That requirement, however, was not mentioned in *Brasserie* as a prerequisite for the establishment of State liability in damages. The case law reveals only limited cross-fertilisation between Article 288(2) and State liability.[73] The difficulties are compounded by the fact that the analytical tools employed by the ECJ and the CFI are not always the same. *Bergaderm* went a long way towards unifying the conditions of liability but subsequent case law of the CFI under Article 288(2) is based on a criterion of duty of care rather than solely on discretion.[74] The case law of the ECJ is less nuanced.

Finally, an important difference is that, whilst the liability of Community institutions is solely for the ECJ and the CFI to decide, the liability of national authorities involves by necessity some input from national courts.

11.5. Breach of the Treaty by the national administration

A national administrative authority may commit a serious breach of Community law in diverse situations. It may, for example, commit a serious breach where it fails

---

[69] *Brasserie, op. cit.*, para 42.   [70] *Ibid.*, para 46.
[71] Cf 5/88 *Wachauf v Bundesamt für Ernährung und Forstwirtschaft* [1989] ECR 2609.
[72] See chapter 10 above.
[73] See here the criticism by W. van Gerven, 'Taking Article 215(2) EC Seriously', in J. Beatson and T. Tridimas (eds), *New Directions in European Public Law*, (Oxford: Hart Publishing, 1998), pp. 35–47.   [74] See above, chapter 10.

to comply with a clear and unambiguous provision of the Treaty, or where it misinterprets a clear and unambiguous Community measure, or where it fails to apply a judgment of the ECJ. The concept of discretion is crucial here. Liability will be easier to establish where the national authority has limited discretion or no discretion at all.

In *Hedley Lomas*[75] the United Kingdom imposed a general ban on the export of animals to Spain for slaughter on the ground that their treatment in Spanish slaughterhouses was contrary to Directive 74/577.[76] In accordance with the general ban, Hedley Lomas was refused a licence to export sheep to a Spanish slaughterhouse. The licence was refused on grounds of Article 30 EC even though the authorities had no evidence to suggest that the slaughterhouse was not complying with the Directive. The Court held that recourse to Article 30 is not possible where Community directives provide for harmonization of the measures necessary to achieve the specific objective which would be furthered by reliance upon that provision. The fact that Directive 74/755 did not lay down any Community procedure for monitoring compliance with its provisions made no difference in this respect. The Court added that a Member State may not unilaterally adopt corrective or protective measures to obviate any breach by another Member State of Community rules.

On the issue of damages, the Court found that the conditions of liability were met. With regard to the first condition, it recalled that Article 29 EC creates rights for the individual which national courts must protect. With regard to the seriousness of the breach, it held that where, at the time when it committed the infringement, the Member State was not called upon to make any legislative choices and had only considerably reduced discretion, or even no discretion, the mere infringement of Community law may be sufficient to establish the existence of a sufficiently serious breach. The Court noted that in the circumstances of the case, the United Kingdom authorities were not even in a position to produce any proof of non-compliance with the Directive by the slaughterhouse concerned.

In *Larsy II*,[77] the Court found that the Belgian authorities had committed a serious breach by misinterpreting Regulation 1408/71 and by failing to apply the judgment in *Larsy I*.[78] Mr Larsy was a self-employed gardener in Belgium and France. Inasti, the Belgian social security institution for self-employed persons, had reduced his pension with effect from 1 March 1987 on the ground that he was also receiving a pension from the French State. Mr Larsy challenged that decision before a Belgian court but his action was dismissed as unfounded. In its judgment in *Larsy I*, delivered in 1993 as a result of litigation initiated by Mr Larsy's brother who was in a similar factual situation, the ECJ held that Articles 12(2) and 46 of Regulation 1408/71[79] precluded the application of a national rule against

---

[75] *Op. cit.*, n. 10 above.
[76] Council Directive 74/577 on stunning of animals before slaughter, OJ 1974 L 316, p. 10.
[77] Case C-118/00 *Larsy II* [2001] ECR I-5063.
[78] Case C-31/92 *Larsy* [1993] ECR I-4543.
[79] Council Regulation No 1408/71 on the application of social security schemes to employed persons, to self-employed persons and to members of their families moving within the

overlapping benefits where a person had worked in two Member States during the same period and had been obliged to pay pension contributions in both. Following the judgment in *Larsy I*, Mr Larsy requested that his situation should be resolved on the same terms. Inasti, relying on Article 95a(5) of Regulation No 1408/71, asked him to submit a new application, in response to which he was awarded a full retirement pension but with effect from 1 July 1994. In subsequent proceedings, the issue arose whether Inasti's refusal to grant Mr Larsy his full pension retro-actively was a serious breach of Community law.

The Court held that it was on two counts. It recalled that a breach of Community law will be sufficiently serious if it has persisted despite a preliminary ruling from the Court from which it is clear that the conduct in question constituted an infringement. By refusing to grant Mr Larsy a full retirement pension retroactively, Inasti had failed to draw all the consequences from, and comply with, the judgment in *Larsy I*. Inasti had also misapplied Article 95a of Regulation No 1408/71. The Court held that the inapplicability of that provision should not have been in any doubt given its clarity and precision.

11.6. Incorrect transposition of a directive

In *The Queen v H.M. Treasury ex p British Telecommunications*[80] the Court held that the conditions provided for in *Brasserie* must also be met in order for liability to arise where a Member State incorrectly transposes a directive into national law. In such a case therefore liability does not ensue automatically and it must be established that the breach is sufficiently serious. A strict approach to State liability in this case is justified for the same reasons as those given in *Brasserie*, namely the concern to ensure that the exercise of legislative functions is not hindered by the prospect of actions for damages.

In order to determine whether the incorrect transposition amounts to a serious breach account must be taken of all the circumstances of the case and, especially, the factors provided by the Court in *Brasserie* and repeated in subsequent case law.[81] The determination whether the breach is serious will be made by the national court unless the ECJ considers that it has sufficient information at its disposal to be able to reach an outcome. Thus, in *Evans v Secretary of State for the Environment, Transport and the Regions and the Motor Insurers' Bureau*,[82] the Court left it to the national court to decide whether the UK had committed a serious breach by transposing incorrectly the Second Motor Insurance Directive.[83] It took the view that in the

Community, as amended and updated by Council Regulation No 2001/83 (OJ 1983 L 230/6), as amended by Council Regulation No 1248/92 (OJ 1992 L 136/7).

[80] Case C-392/93 [1996] ECR I-1631.

[81] See above, and for a more recent confirmation, *Evans v Motor Insurers' Bureau*, *op. cit.*, n. 29 above, para 86.   [82] *Op. cit.*

[83] Council Directive 84/5 on the approximation of the laws of the Member States relating to insurance against civil liability in respect of the use of motor vehicles, OJ 1984 L 8, p. 17.

circumstances the extent to which, and even the question whether, the UK had breached the Directive depended on an assessment of the procedures established by national law which could only be made by the national court.[84] In other cases, the ECJ has decided itself the issue of seriousness of the breach.

In *British Telecommunications*, the Court was concerned with Article 8(1) of Directive 90/531 on the procurement procedures of entities operating in the water, energy, transport and telecommunications sectors.[85] The Court found that the United Kingdom had interpreted the Directive erroneously and, as a result, it had implemented it incorrectly, but held that the incorrect implementation did not amount to a serious breach. The Court stated that Article 8(1) was imprecisely worded and was reasonably capable of bearing the interpretation given to it by the United Kingdom in good faith. That interpretation was shared by other Member States and was not manifestly contrary to the wording of the Directive and the objectives pursued by it. Also, no guidance was available to the United Kingdom from the case law of the Court with regard to the interpretation of Article 8. Finally, the Commission did not raise the matter when the implementing legislation was adopted. It is submitted that the last consideration is of lesser importance. The fact that the Commission considers that the interpretation which a Member State has given to a directive is incorrect is not conclusive since the Commission has no power to give authentic interpretation to Community law. The most important factors seem to be the existence of previous case law and whether the interpretation given by the Member State may be considered to be reasonable.

In *Denkavit*[86] the Court found that the incorrect transposition by Germany of a taxation directive[87] did not amount to a serious breach relying on the following considerations. First, it noted that the interpretation given to the directive by Germany, which proved to be incorrect, had been adopted by a number of other Member States. Second, those Member States had taken the view that they were entitled to adopt such an interpretation, following discussions within the Council. Third, the incorrect interpretation furthered the objective of preventing tax fraud which was compatible with the Directive. Fourth, the case law did not provide any indication as to how the contested provision was to be interpreted.

The second point mentioned above is of interest. In *Denkavit*, to support the interpretation of the directive given by Germany, a number of Member States referred to discussions in the Council while the directive was being adopted. Following previous case law, the Court held that expressions of intent made in

---

[84] CF the Opinion of Alber AG who concluded that the UK had committed a serious breach.

[85] OJ 1990 L 297, p. 1. That Directive has now been superseded by Directive 93/38 coordinating the procurement procedures of entities operating in the water, energy, transport and telecommunications sectors, OJ 1993, L 199, p. 84.

[86] *Denkavit Internationaal BV, op. cit.*, n. 29 above.

[87] Council Directive 90/435 on the common system of taxation applicable in the case of parent companies and subsidiaries of different Member States, OJ 1990 L 225, p. 6.

Council have no legal status unless they are actually expressed in the legislation. This difference in treatment appears odd.[88] If observations made in the Council cannot have any bearing on interpretation unless they are expressed in the legislation, neither should they be attributed any legal significance for the purposes of establishing the seriousness of breach.

A Member State may be held liable for failure to implement a directive only after the time limit for its implementation has expired. In the case of new Member States, the Treaties of Accession provide as a standard term that they must put into effect the measures necessary to comply with directives from the date of accession unless another time limit has been provided in the Act of Accession.[89] Thus, as a general rule, a new Member State may not be held liable for failure to implement a directive if the material facts occurred prior to accession, unless transposition of a directive was a condition of accession.[90] But a new Member State may not delay the application of the provisions of a directive until a certain date after the date of accession. Such temporal limitation would be a serious breach unless the State has a specific derogation granted by the Treaty of Accession.[91]

11.7. Seriousness of breach and Member State discretion

As we saw, in *Brasserie du Pêcheur* the Court laid down a number of guidelines to be taken into account by the national court with a view to determining whether the threshold of seriousness has been reached.[92] Suffice it to make two points in this context. First, other things being equal, the margin of discretion enjoyed by the Member State is in an inverse relationship to the likelihood of establishing a serious breach. The less the margin of discretion left to the national authorities by the Community rules, the easier it would be to establish that a breach of those rules is serious.[93] Second, in determining whether a breach is serious, the precision and clarity of the provision breached is of cardinal importance.[94] In *Rechberger*, a case concerning Austria's failure to implement the Travel Package Directive, the Court

---

[88] *Denkavit, op. cit.*. Compare paras 29 and 51 of the judgment.

[89] See Article 54 of the 2003 Act of Accession; Article 168 of the 1995 Act of Accession.

[90] Case C-321/97 *Ulla-Brith Andersson and Susanne Wåkerås-Andersson v Swedish State* [1999] ECR I-3551.

[91] Case C-140/97 *Rechberger, Greindl and Others v Austria*, [1999] ECR I-3499, para 51. The Court also held that it has no jurisdiction to rule on whether a Member State is liable under the EEA Agreement for failure to implement a Community directive prior to its accession to the European Union, where the obligation to implement arises under the EEA Agreement. See also on the same point, *Andersson, op. cit.* The liability of an EFTA State for infringement of a directive referred to in the EEA Agreement was examined in the EFTA Court's judgment E-9/97 *Sveinbjörnsdóttir*, 10 December 1998.   [92] *Op. cit.*, paras 56–57, n. 15 above.

[93] *Hedley Lomas, op. cit.*, para 28; *Dillenkofer, op. cit.*, para 25; Case C-127/95 *Norbrook Laboratories Ltd v Ministry of Agriculture* [1998] ECR I-1531, para 109.

[94] See especially *BT, op. cit.*, n. 80 above.

considered that the temporal limitation of the financial guarantees provided by Article 7 of the Directive was a serious breach since none of its provisions gave Member States any discretion to limit those guarantees in time. In that case the Court also confirmed that the seriousness of the breach is a qualitative rather than a quantitative concept: the fact that Austria had implemented all the other provisions of the Directive did not exonerate it from liability for breach of Article 7.[95]

The case law declares that it is for the national court to establish whether a breach is serious. But how much freedom does the Court of Justice leave to the national court? The Court's intervention is highly selective. In *Rechberger* it made no effort to examine whether Austria's incomplete transposition of the Package Travel Directive amounted to a serious breach. By contrast, as we saw, in *BT*,[96] *Denkavit*[97] and *Larsy II*[98] it provided the national court with a specific outcome.

A hands-off approach was favoured in *Konle v Austria*.[99] The Tyrol Law on the Transfer of Land of 1993[100] made the acquisition of building land in the Tyrol region by foreign nationals subject to prior authorization. The 1993 Law was replaced with effect from 1 October 1996 by a new Law which extended the authorization requirement to Austrian and foreign nationals alike.[101] Subsequently, by a judgment of 10 December 1996, at a time when the 1993 Law was no longer in force, the Austrian Constitutional Court declared it unconstitutional on the ground that it was in breach of the fundamental right to property.

In 1994, Mr Konle, a German national, sought to acquire a plot of land in the Tyrol region but was refused authorization by the Land Transfer Commission pursuant to the 1993 Law. The refusal was subsequently annulled by the Austrian Constitutional Court on the ground that the 1993 Law had been declared unconstitutional. The effect of the Constitutional Court's judgment was to bring Mr Konle's application back before the Land Transfer Commission but, without waiting for the Commission's new decision, he brought an action for State liability in damages.

On a reference for a preliminary ruling, the Court held that the 1993 Law discriminated against nationals of other Member States in respect of inter-State capital movements and that such discrimination was prohibited by Article 56 EC unless it was justified on grounds permitted by the Treaty. The Austrian Government sought to rely on Article 70 of the Act of Accession which states that 'Notwithstanding the obligations under the Treaties on which the European Union is founded, the Republic of Austria may maintain its existing legislation regarding secondary residences for five years from the date of accession'. The question arose whether the 1993 Law could be considered as 'existing legislation' on the date of accession, i.e. 1 January 1995, given that it was subsequently declared

---

[95] *Rechberger, op. cit.*, para 52.   [96] *Op. cit.*   [97] *Op. cit.*   [98] *Op. cit.*
[99] Case C-302/97, [1999] ECR I-3099. Another case where the ECJ did not examine the issue of seriousness of breach is *Rechberger*, discussed at 11.9 below.
[100] Tiroler Grundverkehrsgesetz 1993, Tiroler LGB1. 82/1993.
[101] Tiroler Grundverkehrsgesetz 1996, Tiroler LGB1. 61/1996.

unconstitutional by the Constitutional Court. The Court of Justice held that the concept of 'existing legislation' is based on a factual criterion and does not require an assessment of the validity in domestic law of the legislation in issue. Any rule of Austrian law concerning secondary residences which was in force on the date of accession is, in principle, covered by the derogation of Article 70 unless it was withdrawn subsequently with retroactive effect.[102] The Court added, uncontroversially, that it is for the national court to assess the temporal effects of declarations of unconstitutionality made by the Austrian constitutional court.[103]

The answer to the national court's question was inconclusive since it was interlinked with matters of national law. If the 1993 Law was deemed to be in force on 1 January 1995, it would be covered by the derogation of Article 70. If, by contrast, the 1993 Law was deemed not to be in force on that date because of its subsequent annulment by the Constitutional Court, then it could not benefit from Article 70. In the latter case, the Law would be in breach of Community law, but would it be a serious breach for the purposes of State liability in damages?

By its second and third questions, the referring court asked respectively whether it is for the Court of Justice to assess whether a breach of Community law is sufficiently serious, and if so whether the breach met that condition in the circumstances of the case. The Court provided a laconic response. Referring to previous case law, it held that it is, in principle, for the national courts to apply the criteria to establish the liability of Member States in damages.[104] In view of that reply, it was not necessary to respond to the third question.

The Court's reticence is understandable given that, in the circumstances, the seriousness or otherwise of the breach was to a good extent dependent on interlinking issues of national law. It should be borne in mind however that 'serious breach' is, as a legal notion, a matter of Community law and therefore ultimately for the Court of Justice to determine. It is notable that la Pergola AG was more forthcoming. His starting point was the same as that of the Court, namely that it is for the national court to verify whether the conditions governing State liability for breach of Community law are met. He argued however that the Court of Justice has the task of providing 'centralized supervision' through the dialogue facilitated by the preliminary reference procedure. It is thus for the Court to define the scope of a sufficiently serious breach by establishing the conditions in which an individual may claim protection of the right to reparation, and for the national court to determine whether those conditions are met on the facts of the case.[105] The Advocate General took the view that, in the circumstances, the breach was not sufficiently serious.

In contrast to *Konle* which concerned liability arising from legislation, *Haim*[106] raised issues pertaining to liability arising from acts of the administration. Mr Haim was an Italian national who, after obtaining a diploma in dentistry from the University of Istanbul and practising in Turkey, obtained permission to practise as a

---

[102] *Konle, op. cit.*, paras 28–29.   [103] *Ibid.*, para 30.   [104] *Ibid.*, paras 58–59.
[105] *Ibid.*, Opinion of la Pergola AG, para 24.   [106] Op. cit., n. 29 above.

self-employed dentist in Germany. His diploma was also recognized as equivalent to the domestic dentistry qualification in Belgium where, for a period, he worked as a dental practitioner under a social security scheme. When however he applied to the KVN, the German competent authority, to become eligible for appointment as a dental practitioner under a social security scheme, his application was refused. The reason for the refusal was that he did not hold a qualification from another Member State but only a diploma from a non–member country recognized by a Member State as equivalent to it own diplomas. In *Haim I*[107] the Court held that Directive 78/686 on the mutual recognition of dentistry qualifications[108] could not assist a person in the position of Mr Haim since he did not possess a diploma from another Member State. It held however that such a person had a right under Article 43 EC to have his practical experience in another Member State taken into account for the purposes of establishing whether he had completed the preparatory period required by German law.

Following the judgment in *Haim I*, the German authorities enrolled Mr Haim on the register of dental practitioners eligible for appointment as dentists under a social security scheme. On account of his age, Mr Haim did not seek appointment but brought an action against the competent authority seeking compensation for the loss of earnings he had allegedly suffered in the past by its refusal to enrol him in the register. The Landgericht Düsseldorf absolved the KVN from liability on the ground that, although it had erred in refusing enrolment, it had acted in good faith. At the time the decision to refuse him enrolment was taken, the question whether the freedom of establishment required professional experience gained in another Member State to be taken into account had not been decided. That question was only decided subsequently in *Vlassopoulou*.[109] On those grounds, the Landgericht Düsseldorf concluded that Mr Haim's action for damages had no basis in domestic law but sought a preliminary ruling in order to determine whether Mr Haim could derive a right to reparation directly from Community law.

The reference gave rise, *inter alia*, to issues pertaining to administrative discretion. The national court asked in particular whether, where a national official has applied national law in a manner not in conformity with Community law, the mere fact that the official did not have any discretion in taking his decision gives rise to a serious breach of Community law. Recalling its judgment in *Hedley Lomas*, the Court held that where, at the time when it committed an infringement, a Member State had only considerably reduced, or even no discretion, the mere infringement of Community law may be sufficient to establish the existence of a serious breach.[110] In *Haim* the Court clarified that what matters is the discretion left

---

[107] Case C-319/92 *Haim* [1994] ECR I-425.

[108] Council Directive 78/686/EEC of 25 July 1978 concerning the mutual recognition of diplomas, certificates and other evidence of the formal qualifications of practitioners of dentistry, including measures to facilitate the effective exercise of the right of establishment and freedom to provide services, OJ 1978 L 233, p. 1.   [109] Case C-340/89 [1991] ECR I-2357.

[110] *Haim, op. cit.*, para 38, and see above p. 512.

to the Member State by Community law. The existence and scope of that discretion are determined by reference to Community law and not by reference to national law. The discretion which may be conferred by national law on the official or the institution responsible for the breach of Community law is, in this respect, irrelevant.[111]

In *Haim* the Court was more forthcoming than in *Konle*. Although it reiterated that it was for the national court to examine whether there was a serious breach of Community law in the circumstances of the case, it recalled the factors laid down in *Brasserie* and gave some guidelines as to how those factors were to be applied. It stated that, when the German legislature adopted the regulation in question and the competent authority refused to enrol Mr Haim, the Court had not yet given judgment in *Vlassopoulou*.[112] The implication of the judgment appears to be that neither the German legislature nor the KVN had committed a serious breach.[113] That view was shared by Mischo AG and also the Commission and the governments who submitted observations in the proceedings.

Given the allocation of competence between the Court of Justice and the national courts in the context of the preliminary reference procedure, the Court's input in some cases will be limited perforce. Thus, whilst the general direction of the remedy depends on the Court of Justice, its application on the facts depends on the referring court. Of the three conditions of liability, the only one which will be decided conclusively by the Court is the first, namely whether the provision breached is intended to grant rights to the injured party. That condition pertains to the interpretation of Community law which falls squarely within the jurisdiction of the Court of Justice. The other two conditions may be left to the national court, depending on the circumstances of the case. This point is reiterated by *Norbrook*[114] which concerned the interpretation of Directives 81/851 and 81/852 on veterinary medicinal products.[115] Directive 81/851 provides that no such product may be marketed in a Member State unless authorization has previously been issued by its competent

---

[111] *Ibid.*, para 40. It will be noted however that the discretion conferred by national law on a public authority may be relevant for the purposes of determining which body is responsible for making reparation, and therefore for identifying the proper defendant. See 11.11 below.

[112] *Haim, op. cit.*, para 46.

[113] The law was clarified in *Haim I* and, as we saw, the KVN revised its decision following that judgment. Clearly, if the German authorities had persisted in refusing to recognize Mr Haim's practical experience after that judgment, they would have committed a serious breach. Should the German authorities have revised their view already after *Vlassopoulou* which was delivered before *Haim I*? In other words, did the breach become serious as from *Vlassopoulou*? The answer is probably not. *Vlassopoulou* did not concern qualifications from third countries and the law did not become crystal clear until *Haim I*. Notably, after *Haim I*, the Commission proposed a corresponding amendment to Directive 78/686.

[114] *Norbrook Laboratories Limited, op. cit.*, n. 93 above.

[115] Council Directive 81/851/EEC on the approximation of the laws of the Member States relating to veterinary medicinal products (OJ 1981, L317, p. 1) and Council Directive 81/852/EEC on the approximation of the laws of the Member States relating to analytical pharmaco-toxicological and clinical standards and protocols in respect of the testing of veterinary medicinal products (OJ 1981 L 317, p. 16).

authorities. In examining the issue of possible State liability in damages arising as a result of the refusal to issue authorization, the Court held that the Directives granted a right to obtain authorization if certain conditions were met. Since those conditions were laid down precisely and exhaustively in their provisions, the scope of the right conferred on applicants was sufficiently identified. As regards the other two conditions of liability, the Court simply referred to its previous case law, and left it to the national court to determine whether they were met.

In effect, in interpreting the condition of serious breach, the ECJ enjoys discretion. Whether it will leave the issue entirely to the national court, or provide guidance or reach an outcome on the facts depends on several factors which include the following:

- whether the existence of a serious breach depends on findings of fact which are for the national court to decide;
- whether in the circumstances of the case Community and national law are closely interlinked;
- whether the breach is obvious and can readily be ascertained as, for example, when a Member State completely fails to implement a directive;
- whether the ECJ considers, as a matter of judicial policy, that it should provide leadership thereby reaching an outcome or defer to the Member States.

The last point is vividly illustrated by the case law on liability for judicial breaches.

11.8. Breach of Union law by the national judiciary

11.8.1. The judgment in *Köbler*

In *Brasserie du Pêcheur* the Court established the universality of State liability, thus opening the way for recognizing a right to reparation against the State for breach of Community law by the national judiciary.[116] This was unequivocally established in *Köbler v Austria*.[117] The judgment introduces a new principle and has important repercussions for national courts.[118]

The facts of the case were as follows. Mr Köbler brought an action against the Austrian State seeking damages for the alleged loss he had suffered from breach of Community law by the Austrian Supreme Administrative Court (Verwaltungsgerichtshof). Austrian law provided for the award of a special length-of-service

---

[116] *Brasserie, op. cit.*, see n. 15 above, para 32.   [117] *Op. cit.*, n. 30 above.

[118] For a general discussion of judicial liability, see, among others, A. Olowofoyeku, *Suing Judges*, (Oxford University Press, 1993). For Community law, see H. Toner, 'Thinking the Unthinkable? State Liability for Judicial Acts after *Factortame (III)*,' (1997) 17 YEL 165; G. Anagnostaras, 'The Principle of State Liability for Judicial Breaches: The Impact of European Community Law', (2001) 7 European Public Law, 281.

increment to university professors who had completed fifteen years' service in an Austrian university. He claimed that, although he had not served fifteen years in Austrian universities, he had completed the requisite length of service if the duration of his employment in universities in other Member States was taken into account. His claim gave rise to a dispute in the course of which the Supreme Administrative Court made a preliminary reference. In response to the reference, the Registrar of the ECJ asked the Supreme Court whether, in the light of the judgment in *Schöning-Kougebetopoulou*,[119] it considered it necessary to maintain its request for a reference. Compliance with Community law required that the Supreme Court should do one of two things: either uphold Mr Köbler's claim, if it considered that the *Schöning-Kougebetopoulou* judgment was applicable, or maintain the reference, if it considered that this judgment did not cover the point. The Supreme Court, however, misunderstood the judgment. It withdrew the reference and dismissed Mr Köbler's application. Its reasoning was that the special length of service increment was a loyalty bonus which legitimately required a certain length of service as a professor in an Austrian university and thus justified a derogation from the free movement of workers. Mr Köbler brought an action for damages before the Regional Court of Vienna alleging that the judgment of the Administrative Court directly infringed effective provisions of Community law.

On a reference from the Vienna court, the ECJ laid down the principles governing liability for breach of EU law by the national judiciary. In a reasoning reminiscent of *Brasserie du Pêcheur*, the Court derived arguments from international, national, and Community law to support the conclusion that a right to reparation for breach by a last instance court must be recognized. It held that in international law, a State which incurs liability for breach of an international commitment is viewed as a single entity, irrespective of whether the breach is attributable to the legislature, the judiciary or the executive. This principle must apply *a fortiori* in the Community legal order. In terms of Community law, the Court relied on the principle of effectiveness and, by way of supporting argument, to Article 234 EC. It pointed out the essential role played by the judiciary in the protection of Community rights and stated that the full effectiveness of Community rules would be weakened if individuals were precluded from being able to obtain reparation when their rights are affected by a breach attributable to a national court of last instance.[120]

The Court further pointed out that State liability for judicial decisions is recognized in one way or another by most of the Member States and also by the ECHR. In relation to the latter, the ECJ referred to Article 41 which enables the European Court of Human Rights to order a State which has infringed a fundamental right to provide reparation of the damage suffered. It pointed out that, under the case law of the Strasbourg Court, reparation may be granted when the infringement stems from a decision of a national court of last instance.[121]

---

[119] Case C-15/96 [1998] ECR I-47.   [120] *Köbler, op. cit.*, paras 33–35.
[121] See ECtHR, *Dulaurans v France*, judgment of 21 March 2000.

The Court turned the argument that the recognition of liability would prejudice the independence and the authority of the judiciary on its head. It viewed the possibility of questioning final judgments of last instance courts not as risking the diminution of judicial authority but rather 'as enhancing the quality of a legal system and thus in the long run the authority of the judiciary'.[122] This argument is premised on a federal reasoning. If one accepts the primacy of Union law and the principle of State liability for its breach why should courts be the only branch of government that enjoys *a priori* immunity? More generally, in a polity governed by the rule of law, why should the judicial branch be the only one which is exempt from the possibility of challenge?[123]

The judgment in *Köbler* reiterates that, in elaborating remedies, the Court firmly views the Union as a federal structure. This federal perception of the Union underlies other developments in the law of remedies. The Court, however, appears to follow double standards. Where it comes to judicial control of the acts of State and Community political actors, it views the judiciary, (that is to say, itself and by extension the national judiciaries) as being external to the system of government over which it exercises monitoring and control. This perception of the judiciary as an independent power outside the government structure coexists with an understanding of the national judiciary as being part of the state imperium in a federal structure and therefore in a vertical relationship *vis-à-vis* the Court of Justice itself.[124]

With regard to the conditions of liability, the Court resisted suggestions by some governments to make liability subject to additional normative conditions, for example, the requirement that the breach of Community law must be not only objectively indefensible but also subjectively intentional.[125] It stated that the conditions which govern liability for judicial acts are the same as the general conditions for liability, namely the provision infringed must confer rights on individuals, the breach must be sufficiently serious, and there must be a direct causal link.[126] In relation to the seriousness of the breach, however, the Court held that regard must be had to the specific nature of the judicial function and the requirements of legal certainty. Thus, liability will ensue 'only in the exceptional case where the court has manifestly infringed the applicable law'.[127]

---

[122] *Köbler, op. cit.*, para 43.

[123] In accord: Toner, *op. cit.*, at 181; Anagnostaras, *op. cit.*, at 293–4.

[124] For a discussion of courts as institutions external or internal to the government structure, see R. Cotterell, 'Judicial Review and Legal Theory' in G. Richardson and H. Genn (eds), *Administrative Law and Government Action*, (Oxford University Press, 1994) 13–34.

[125] This was proposed by the German and the Dutch Governments. Some years earlier, in Case 30/77 *Boucherau* [1977] ECR 1999 at 2020, Warner AG had suggested that a Member State might be found in breach of Community law in enforcement proceedings for failure of its judiciary to comply with Community law only if a national court deliberately ignored or disregarded Community law. This view was recently rejected by the ECJ: see Case C-129/00 *Commission v Italy*, judgment of 9 December 2003. Note however that the intentional or otherwise character of the breach is still important as one of the factors to be taken into consideration for deciding the seriousness of the breach. See *Köbler, op. cit.*, para 55.

[126] *Köbler, op. cit.*, para 51–52.   [127] *Ibid.*, para 53.

It is notable that the Court made reference to 'manifest' infringement rather than the test of manifest and grave disregard used in previous case law. This terminological inconsistency does not mean that liability for judicial acts is subject to less stringent conditions. On the contrary, the judgment acknowledges the special position of courts and refers to liability for judicial acts as 'exceptional', an epithet not used in the case law for State liability in general. The reason for this terminological variation lies elsewhere. The terms 'manifest and grave' disregard refer to the cases where the national legislature or administration enjoy wide discretionary powers in the exercise of their policy making. Courts, however, do not enjoy any discretion in the way that policy makers do. Discretion therefore is not an appropriate criterion on which to base liability for judicial breaches and it is notable that in *Köbler* neither the ECJ nor the Advocate General attributed importance to it.[128]

The Court held that, in determining whether there is a serious breach, all factors must be taken into account, including the degree of clarity and precision of the rule infringed, whether the infringement was intentional, whether the error of law was excusable or inexcusable, any position which might have been taken by a Community institution, and non-compliance by the court in question with its obligation to make a reference for a preliminary ruling under Article 234(3).[129] In any event, as the Court had already stated in *Brasserie du Pêcheur*, violation will be sufficiently serious where the decision concerned was made in manifest breach of the case law of the ECJ on the area in issue.[130]

On the specific case, the Court held that the fact that Austrian law precluded periods of employment in a university in another Member State from being taken into account was an obstacle to free movement and was, in principle, contrary to Article 39 EC and Article 7(1) of Regulation No 1612/68. It came to the conclusion, however, that the breach committed by the Supreme Administrative Court was not manifest. This is because Community law does not expressly cover the point whether a loyalty bonus which impedes freedom of movement can be justified. No reply was to be found to that question in the Court's case law nor was the reply to the question obvious. Also, the Court noted that the fact that the Supreme Administrative Court ought to have maintained its request for a preliminary ruling did not change that conclusion. The reason why the national court

---

[128] See the Opinion of Léger AG, para 138.   [129] *Köbler, op. cit.*, para 55.

[130] *Ibid.*, para 56. By contrast, the Advocate General considered that the decisive factor is whether the error of law committed by the national court is excusable or inexcusable. This will depend on the clarity and the precision of the rule infringed and the existence or the state of the case law on the matter: see para 139 of the Opinion. Also, the Advocate General took the view that the issue of whether the breach was intentional or involuntary was problematic and no particular weight should be attached to it: this would be difficult to establish, especially where the judgment was collegiate, and would put national judges in a delicate position since they would have to decide whether one of their brethren had acted with the intention of breaching the law. Similarly, the Advocate General considered that no particular weight should be attached to the views of the Commission: see paras 154–155 of the Opinion.

had decided to withdraw the request for a reference was its incorrect reading of the judgment in *Schöning-Kougebetopoulou*. Notably, the Advocate General was less generous opining that the Austrian Supreme Court had made an 'inexcusable error' in considering that the length of service allowance was justified despite being indirectly discriminatory.[131]

11.8.2. Assessment and implications

The judgment in *Köbler* has important constitutional implications. It provides a remedy for the failure of a national court of last instance to make a preliminary reference. It views the relationship between the ECJ and national supreme courts as one of hierarchy rather than one of cooperation since, ultimately, it is for the ECJ to determine whether the breach is 'manifest'. A possible effect of the judgment may be to increase the number of preliminary references to the ECJ as national courts may prefer 'to play it safe', thus operating as a countervailing force to persistent efforts to reduce the number of references and the workload of the ECJ. It is interesting here to note that the ECJ does not allow its internalized notion of justice to be influenced by organizational considerations: whilst, as a bureaucracy, the Court has repeatedly rung the alarm bells in relation to its mounting workload, in its case law, it has opted for an expansive view of its jurisdiction thus encouraging more preliminary references.[132] This tendency is reiterated by *Köbler*.

There is no doubt that the judgment also encourages litigation at the national level as the pronouncement of a last instance court may no longer be viewed as the final step in the litigation. It also increases the power of lower national courts *vis-à-vis* higher ones since it opens the possibility of actions in damages before national courts at the lower tiers of national judicial hierarchy against judgments of superior national courts. It thus accentuates the dispersal of judicial power at national level. Liability for judicial acts, however, is not without problems. An action for damages may be heard in the first instance by a lower court but, on appeal, may ultimately come to be heard by the same court whose decision allegedly caused the damage. This puts the lower national court under a considerable strain. More importantly, it raises serious questions as to the compatibility of the jurisdiction of the higher court to hear an action for damages against its own previous decision with Article 6 ECHR, since it will not be an impartial tribunal.[133]

---

[131] *Köbler, op. cit.*, Opinion of Léger AG, para 170.

[132] This is evidenced by, among others, two tendencies in the preliminary reference procedure: the ECJ adopts a wide view of what is a 'court or tribunal' under Article 234 EC and also accepts references where Community law applies by virtue of national law under the *Dzodzi* line of cases. See Joined Cases C-297/88 and C-197/89 *Dzodzi v Belgian State* [1990] ECR I-3763 and T. Tridimas, 'Knocking on Heaven's Door: Fragmentation, Efficiency and Defiance in the Preliminary Reference Procedure', (2003) 40 CML Rev 9.

[133] See e.g. the ECtHR judgments in *Piersak*, 1 October 1982 (Series A, No 11); *McGonnell*, 8 February 2000 (Series A, No 2112). In Case C-185/95 P *Baustahlgewebe v Commission* [1998] ECR I-8417, at 8437–8 Léger AG stated that it would be contrary to Article 6(1) to entrust a

The practical effect of *Köbler* will depend mainly on how the ECJ understands the meaning of a 'manifest' breach and how it interprets the requirement of direct causal link. It is interesting that, in the circumstances of the case, the ECJ was content to give the Austrian Court the benefit of the doubt despite the fact the latter's approach to Article 39 EC was casual.[134] *Köbler* however leaves a number of issues unclear. Some of these are examined below.

Liability for breach by a last instance court may arise in the following cases: (a) where the court fails to apply a clear provision of Community law; (b) where it fails to abide by existing ECJ case law; (c) where it refuses to make a reference (as was the case in *Köbler*); or (d) where it makes a reference but commits a manifest breach in applying the ruling of the ECJ.

Where the national court refuses to make a reference, liability presupposes that two breaches have occurred. First, the national court must have failed to make a reference in circumstances where it is under an obligation to do so under Article 234(3) EC (procedural violation). In addition, the national court must have misinterpreted or misapplied the provisions of Community law relevant to the case in issue (substantive violation). The judgment in *Köbler* does not make it clear whether both violations must be manifest in order for liability to arise. One could distinguish here the following situations. If both the procedural and the substantive breach are manifest, liability arises. This will be the case, for example, where a national court fails to make a reference on a point which is clearly covered by ECJ case law and does not apply that case law (e.g. direct discrimination on grounds of nationality). Where neither breach is manifest, no liability arises. The more difficult situation is where, by failing to make a reference, the national court commits a manifest breach of Article 234 but the breach that it commits by misinterpreting or misapplying Community law is not manifest. Would liability arise in such a case? It seems that here there is no liability for material damage because any such damage suffered by the applicant is not directly causally connected to the failure to refer but the misapplication of Community law by the national court. Under this approach, liability for material damage arises only if the substantive violation is manifest.

---

judicial body with the task of determining whether its own conduct is wrongful or unlawful, even if it did so under a different composition. In his Opinion in *Köbler*, the Advocate General considered that a guarantee of impartiality may be provided by the preliminary reference procedure but stopped short of imposing a requirement on the national court to make a reference to the ECJ in order for the latter to establish whether the national supreme court committed a manifest breach: see paras 111–112 of the Opinion.

[134] The Austrian court inferred from the *Schöning-Kougebetopoulou* judgment that, since the benefit at issue was to be classified under national law as a loyalty bonus, it could be justified even if it was in itself contrary to the principle of non-discrimination. This, however, does not seem persuasive: the national court only reclassified the benefit as a loyalty bonus after it was alerted to the *Schöning* judgment by the ECJ. Beforehand, it had sought a preliminary reference on the express finding that the benefit was not a loyalty bonus but a component of the salary. Also, the *Schöning* judgment does not support the finding that, if the benefit in question was a loyalty bonus, it would be automatically justified. The issue was not *acte clair* and the Austrian court had clearly committed a breach of Article 234 by not referring.

Where the substantive violation is not manifest but the refusal to make a reference is arbitrary, there could only be liability for non-material damage arising from the loss of opportunity.[135] This approach seems preferable given the exceptional character of liability and is supported by the judgment in *Brinkmann* where the ECJ took a narrow view of direct causal link.[136]

The task of establishing that the substantive breach is manifest is not an easy one. The applicant would have to satisfy the national court hearing the application for damages that the Community right in issue was so obvious that the national court of last instance should have applied it without making a reference or that, if a reference had been made, the ECJ would have upheld the claim. For a right to reparation to arise here, it is not sufficient to prove simply that the ECJ would have upheld in general terms the legal right claimed by the applicant but also that the preliminary ruling would have determined the outcome of the proceedings without leaving any discretion to the national court. This is an important limitation of liability because, where it ascertains the meaning and the scope of Community rights, the ECJ often leaves proportionality to be applied by the national courts and thus allows discretion on how to apply its ruling on the facts of the case. Thus, liability for loss of opportunity is much easier to establish than liability for material damage.

A condition of liability is that the rule of law infringed must be intended to confer rights on individuals. How is this rule to be applied in the context of liability for judicial acts? As already stated, an integral part of the infringement of Community law is the failure of the national court to make a reference contrary to Article 234(3). Is the breach of the obligation to refer sufficient to satisfy this condition of liability or is it a requirement that the rule of Community law which the national court was called upon to apply must be intended to confer rights on individuals? The judgment in *Köbler* appears to support the second solution, i.e. that the Community rule relied upon intends to give rights to individuals.[137] It appears however that it is not necessary for the rules of Community law in question to give positive or express rights to the person concerned. An implied right appears to suffice.[138] Also, failure of a national court to apply the *Marleasing* doctrine,[139] i.e. to interpret national law in accordance with non-directly effective provisions of Community law, might give rise to liability.[140]

---

[135] See the Opinion of Léger AG, paras 148 *et seq.* As the Advocate General noted, the case law of the Strasbourg Court may be instructive here. It has held that, where there is a breach of Article 6 of the Convention, it is not possible to speculate what would have been the outcome of the proceedings if they had been conducted in accordance with Article 6 and thus allow a claim for reparation of material damage. It allows however the award of a certain sum by way of reparation in view of the seriousness of the non-material damage sustained. See *Coëme v Belgium* (application numbers 32492/96, 32547/96, 33209/96 and 33210/96, judgment of 22 June 2000), *McMichael v UK*, (1995) 20 EHRR 205. [136] *Op. cit.*, n. 48 above, discussed at 11.9 below.

[137] See paragraphs 33 to 36 of the judgment where the Court finds the essential basis of liability for judicial acts in the need to guarantee the full effectiveness of 'rights derived by individuals from Community law' (para 33).

[138] For example, a right similar to that in issue in *Munoz*, see 11.15.2 below.

[139] C-106/89 *Marleasing* [1990] ECR I-4135. [140] See Toner, *op. cit.*, 183.

In its judgment, the Court stressed that the recognition of liability does not call into question the principle of *res judicata*. Liability proceedings do not have the same purpose, and do not necessarily involve the same parties, as the proceedings resulting in the decision which has acquired the status of *res judicata*. The need to ensure effective protection translates to a right to reparation but not a right to revision of the judicial decision which was responsible for the damage.[141] It is however questionable whether the principle of *res judicata* remains unaffected. Clearly, the right to reparation undermines the finality of the judgment since it opens the possibility of litigation involving the same issue of substance. Further, the precise limits of *res judicata* are unclear here. In *Köbler*, the Court held that its finding that the Supreme Administrative Court had not committed a serious breach was 'without prejudice to the obligations arising for the Member State concerned' from the Court's finding that the Austrian regime was contrary to Article 39 EC and Article 7(1) of Regulation 1612/68.[142] It follows that other persons in the position of Mr Köbler would be able to benefit from the judgment. Since the ECJ did not restrict the retroactive effect of its ruling, a free mover in the position of Mr Köbler would be able to claim the length of service allowance on the basis of past service in another Member State.[143] What about Mr Köbler himself? The judgment of the ECJ does not undo the judgment of the Supreme Administrative Court denying him the allowance but might not prevent him from reapplying for that allowance in the future.[144] It is, in any event, difficult to avoid the conclusion that the recognition of a right to reparation for failure of a last instance court to comply with Community law has a corrosive effect on the finality of judgment and *res judicata*. The real issue is not whether those principles are undermined but whether such undermining effect is outweighed by the need to ensure respect for the rule of law and the effectiveness of EC law which liability for judicial acts in intended to serve.

A final issue arising from *Köbler* is the following. In its judgment, the Court was concerned with a breach committed by a national court of last instance. Is it possible for a right to reparation to arise where a breach is committed by a lower national court? It is submitted that, in principle, the answer must be in the negative. Insofar as the person who has suffered loss has the right to appeal and thereby obtain an effective remedy, he must exercise that right. The reason for this is twofold. First, State liability arises where the national judiciary as a branch of government fails to uphold Community rights. The person concerned therefore is required to pursue the judicial means of redress available to him before seeking damages.[145] Second, as has been pointed out, the initiation of parallel litigation through an action in damages

---

[141] *Köbler, op. cit.*, para 39.   [142] *Ibid.*, para 125.

[143] Such a claim would be subject to the national rules of procedure and remedies which, however, must satisfy the requirements of equivalence and effectiveness.

[144] See also in this context Case C-453/00 *Kühne & Heitz v Productschap voor Pluimvee en Eieren*, judgment of 13 January 2004.

[145] See also here *Brasserie du Pêcheur, op. cit.*, n. 15 above, para 84; cf Cases C-397/98 and C-410/98 *Metallgesellschaft Ltd and Hoechst AG v Commissioners of Inland Revenue* [2001] ECR I-1727, para 106.

when the judicial recognition of the substantive rights in issue is not finally settled, 'would hardly serve the interests of justice and legal certainty'.[146] It is therefore submitted that the right of action for loss arising from judicial acts is, in principle, subject to the prior exhaustion of judicial remedies provided that such remedies provide adequate redress for the person concerned.

Köbler opened a new chapter in State liability. The Court rejected the absolute immunity of the State and recognized, in limited circumstances, State liability for judicial acts. It is submitted that this is correct. In a mature democracy, such liability can co-exist with the independence of the judiciary and the separation of powers.[147] Seen in the light of previous case law, the judgment appears principled and balanced. The Court reaffirms the primacy of Community law and the universality of remedies. The price of this is to undermine the finality of last instance judgments and project a more hierarchical relationship between the ECJ and the national supreme courts. The right to reparation for judicial acts seems subject to such stringent conditions that, in practice, liability would be established in few and exceptional cases where a national court manifestly violates Community law and disregards existing case law of the ECJ. However new remedies, once established, tend to acquire a dynamic of their own and the way this new right of action will be used may be difficult to predict. Even though an action in damages may have few chances of success, it may be used as an instrument to obtain a ruling by the Court that a national court of last instance has violated Community law. An important aspect of the case is that State liability for judicial acts, as all remedies provided by Community law, is a 'co-operative remedy' in the sense that it requires the active collaboration of national courts. They are the gatekeepers entrusted with the delicate task of judging their brethren, filtering out unmeritorious claims, and finding an acceptable balance between finality and legality.

11.9. Causation

State liability arises only if there is a direct causal link between the breach of an obligation resting on the State and the damage sustained by the injured parties.[148] The requirement that causation must be direct has been borrowed from the case law under Article 288(2) EC.[149]

In *Brinkmann*[150] the applicant was a German company which produced 'Westpoint', a patented tobacco product. This product consists of tobacco rolls enveloped in porous cellulose which need to be wrapped in cigarette paper in order to be

---

[146] See Anagnostaras, *op. cit.*, at 290.   [147] See Toner, *op. cit.*, 169.

[148] See e.g. *Brasserie, op. cit.*, para 51; *Norbrook, op. cit.*, para 107; *Brinkmann, op. cit.*, para 25; *Rechberger, op. cit.*, n. 91 above, para 72.

[149] See above, p. 495. The term 'direct' did not appear in *Francovich* where the Court referred to the 'existence of a causal link': see para 40 of the judgment. It was added in *Brasserie* and has appeared since in subsequent cases.   [150] *Op. cit.*, n. 48 above.

smoked. In Germany, Westpoint was taxed as smoking tobacco but on importation into Denmark, it was taxed at the higher rate applicable to cigarettes. The Court upheld the applicant's contention that Westpoint must be classified as smoking tobacco within the meaning of Directive 79/32.[151] It then turned to examine whether the erroneous classification of the product gave rise to liability in damages. It found that Articles 3(1) and 4(1) of the Directive, which contain the definitions of cigarettes and smoking tobacco, were not properly transposed into Danish law since the competent Minister authorized to introduce the relevant provisions had not adopted any implementing measures. The Court recalled that failure to implement a directive is *per se* a serious violation. It found however that, in the circumstances, there was no direct causal link between the breach of Community law and the damage allegedly suffered by the applicant. This was because, despite the failure to implement the Directive by ministerial decree, the Danish authorities gave immediate effect to the relevant provisions of the Directive.[152] The Court proceeded to examine whether the Danish authorities had committed a sufficiently serious breach of the Directive and found that they had not. It came to that conclusion on the following grounds. Westpoint did not correspond exactly to either of the definitions of the Directive, being a new product which did not exist at the time when the Directive was adopted. In view of the nature of Westpoint, the classification made by the Danish authorities was not manifestly contrary to the wording or the aim of the Directive. Notably, the Commission and the Finnish Government had supported the same classification.[153]

Brinkmann is the first case where the Court relied on causation to restrict state liability. In doing so, it was able to limit liability without technically qualifying its strict approach that failure to implement is *per se* a serious breach.[154] This has important repercussions. It means that, where a Member State fails to adopt implementing measures in order to transpose a directive into national law, the national administrative authorities may present as a valid defence that, despite the lack of implementing measures, they themselves endeavoured to comply with the requirements of the directive. In such a case, the State would incur liability only if their failure to comply with the directive was serious. This inserts an important *caveat* on State liability and provides an exit route in cases of non-transposition. It also offers an incentive to public authorities to observe the requirements of directives even where the legislature has failed to take implementing measures. It is possible that, in the absence of implementing measures, separate administrative authorities in one and the same Member State may understand the meaning of a directive differently. It is conceivable then that some of them might be found to have committed a serious breach but others might not.[155]

---

[151] Second Council Directive on taxes other than turnover taxes which affect the consumption of manufactured tobacco, OJ 1979 L 10/8.   [152] *Op. cit.*, para 29.
[153] *Ibid.*, para 31.   [154] See *Dillenkofer, op. cit.*, above n. 28.
[155] This begs the question which authority would be the appropriate defendant in an action for damages, i.e. whether it would be the Member State itself or the agency that made the decision on the specific circumstances. On this issue, see 11.11 below.

A criticism which might be levelled against *Brinkmann* is that it is not based on a structured view of causation. Why was the alleged loss of the applicants more attributable to the erroneous interpretation of the directive by the Danish administration than the failure to adopt implementing measures? After all, proper transposition requires binding measures of general application and, if the Minister authorized by national law to adopt implementing provisions had done so, the authorities would not have had to improvise. The approach of the Court was pragmatic. In the circumstances, it was satisfied that the Member State, through the administrative authorities, had paid due respect to its obligations under Community law and intended to comply with the requirements of the Directive in its dealings with the affected traders. Also, the Directive in issue lent itself to application by administrative action in that the absence of transposing legislation did not make it impossible for the authorities to give effect to its requirements. The outcome in *Brinkmann* seems correct. It is submitted however that *Brinkmann* applies only to cases where it is possible for the national administration to apply the provisions of a directive in the absence of implementing legislation. In some cases, the requirements of a directive may be such that the administration may not be able to cover the failure to adopt implementing measures of general application, in which case liability will ensue automatically irrespective of any efforts made by the authorities.

The cautious generosity shown in *Brinkmann* was not forthcoming in *Rechberger, Greindl and Others v Austria*,[156] a case which raised issues pertaining both to the requirement of serious breach and causation. *Rechberger* concerned Directive 90/314 on package travel,[157] which was in issue also in *Dillenkofer*. It will be remembered that the purpose of the Directive is to protect the purchaser of package travel. To that effect, Article 7 requires the package tour organizer to provide sufficient security for the refund of money paid over and for the repatriation of the consumer in the event of the organizer's insolvency. In *Dillenkofer* the Court had decided that Article 7 confers on individuals rights whose content is determinable with sufficient precision, and therefore the first condition for the right to reparation to arise was met.[158] In *Rechberger*, an Austrian newspaper offered to its subscribers a holiday trip at substantially reduced prices as a gift to thank them for their loyalty. The offer proved more popular than had been anticipated. This caused the travel organizer which had undertaken the organization of the trips logistical and financial difficulties which, in turn, led to bankruptcy proceedings being initiated against it. The plaintiffs in the main proceedings were subscribers who had taken part in the newspaper's offer. They had all paid the travel costs in advance but their trips were cancelled and, as a result, they suffered financial loss. Since they were unable to recover against the travel organizer, they brought an action against Austria claiming that their loss was attributable to the State's failure to implement the Package Travel Directive in full.

---

[156] *Op. cit.*, n. 91 above.
[157] Council Directive 90/314/EEC of 13 June 1990 on package travel, package holidays and package tours, OJ 1990 L 158, p. 59. [158] *Dillenkofer, op. cit.*, para 44.

One of the issues raised in *Rechberger* concerned the method by which Austria gave effect to Article 7. The implementing measures required a travel organizer to have a contract of insurance or a bank guarantee covering at least five per cent of the organizer's business turnover in the corresponding quarter of the previous calendar year. In the first year of business, the amount of cover was to be based on the estimated turnover from the intended business of the organizer. Some of the plaintiffs in the main proceedings had suffered loss because the bank guarantee issued by the travel organizer was insufficient to reimburse their travel costs. The referring court asked whether the Austrian legislation correctly transposed Article 7. It also asked whether there was a direct causal link between the late or incomplete transposition of Article 7 and loss or damage caused to the consumer.

The Court interpreted Article 7 strictly as imposing an obligation of result. It held that national legislation transposes that provision properly only if it achieves the result of providing the consumer with an effective guarantee.[159] The guarantee required by the Austrian legislation was limited both in terms of its amount and in terms of the basis on which the cover was calculated. It was therefore 'structurally incapable' of catering for events in the economic sector in question, such as a significant increase in the number of bookings in relation to either the turnover for the preceding year or the estimated turnover.[160] The Court concluded that the Austrian legislation did not transpose Article 7 properly but, curiously, did not express a view on whether the incorrect transposition of the Directive was a serious breach. This is presumably because the referring court did not ask that question *expressis verbis*. The issue of seriousness, however, appeared to be crucial for determining whether the plaintiffs in the main proceedings had a right to reparation. As we shall see, in answering the final question posed by the national court, the Court of Justice held that there was direct causal link between Austria's failure to transpose and the loss suffered by the plaintiffs. This finding in itself does not settle the outcome since liability would ensue only if the loss was causally connected to a serious breach. It may seem surprising then that no attempt was made to address the issue of the seriousness of the breach in the judgment. Arguably, the Court left the glass half-full in circumstances where the spirit of cooperation of the preliminary reference procedure invited it to fill it.[161]

Turning now to the issue of causation, the Austrian Government argued that there was no direct causal link between late or incomplete transposition of Article 7 and the loss or damage suffered by consumers because the unsuccessful transposition had contributed to the damage only as a result of a chain of wholly exceptional and unforeseeable events. By this, the Government meant that the loss of the plaintiffs was due to the imprudent conduct of the travel agent and the atypical character of the case. The Court declined to accept that argument.

---

[159] *Rechberger, op. cit.*, para 64.   [160] *Ibid.*, para 62.

[161] By contrast, Saggio AG expressly stated that Austria's defective transposition amounted to a sufficiently serious and clear breach: see paras 46–48 of the Opinion. Cf the Austrian Government's submissions in paras 56–58 of the judgment.

It pointed out that Article 7 requires a guarantee specifically aimed at arming consumers against the consequences of bankruptcy, whatever the causes of bankruptcy may be. State liability for breach of Article 7 cannot be precluded by imprudent conduct on the part of the travel organizer or by the occurrence of exceptional and unforeseeable events.[162] This is correct: the chain of causation cannot easily be broken by the conduct of the travel organizer since it is against the financial risks associated with that very trader that the Directive is intended to safeguard the consumer.

It may be helpful at this juncture to attempt to draw some conclusions regarding causation as they emerge from the case law. The starting point is that there must be a direct causal link between the alleged damage and the breach of Community law. It is for the national court to determine whether such link exists.[163] This means that the national court must determine whether causation exists on the facts. It does not mean that the rules governing causation depend on national law. That would amount to a 're-nationalization' of the conditions of liability. Although the case law is equivocal on this point, this view is supported by *Brinkmann* and *Rechberger* and derives also from the nature of State liability as a Community remedy. Causation, as with the other conditions of liability, must be determined in the first place by Community law. At the very least, the Court will discard the national rules of causation which do not provide an effective standard of protection. So far, however, the Court has not elaborated any systematic principles of causation but has approached the issues which arise on a case-by-case basis.

11.10. The right to reparation: The importance of national law

Although the conditions of liability are provided for by Community law, the remedy of reparation is subject to national law. In *Brasserie* the Court held that the State must make reparation for the consequences of the loss caused in accordance with the domestic rules on liability, provided that the dual requirements of equivalence and effectiveness laid down in the *Rewe* and *Comet* case law[164] are respected.[165] The Court identified two conditions which breach the principle of effectiveness. Under German law, where a legislative act is in breach of a higher-ranking national law, for example the Constitution, a right of reparation ensues only where the applicant can be regarded as the beneficiary of the obligation

---

[162] *Op. cit.*, paras 74–75.

[163] *Brasserie, op. cit.*, para 65; *Norbrook, op. cit.*, para 110; *Rechberger, op. cit.*, para 72.

[164] Case 33/76 *Rewe v Landwirtschaftskammer für das Saarland* [1976] ECR 1989; Case 45/76 *Comet v Productschap voor Siergewassen* [1976] ECR 2043.

[165] *Brasserie, op. cit.*, n. 15 above, para 83; *Francovich, op. cit.*, n. 7 above, paras 41–43; *Haim, op. cit.*, n. 29 above, paras 30, 33; *Konle, op. cit.*, n. 99 above, para 63; *Norbrook Laboratories, op. cit.*, n. 93 above, para 111.

breached. The Court held that such a restriction would make it extremely difficult to obtain reparation, since the tasks falling to the national legislature relate in principle to the public at large and not to identifiable persons or classes of person. Referring to English law, the Court held that proof of misfeasance in public office as a condition of liability would make it impossible in practice to obtain reparation for loss arising from breach by the national legislature.[166]

Reparation for damage resulting from breaches of Community law must be commensurate with the damage sustained.[167] In the absence of Community provisions, it is for the domestic legal system of each Member State to set the criteria for determining the extent of reparation. The Court laid down the following guidelines:

- The national court may inquire whether the injured person showed reasonable diligence in order to avoid the loss or damage or limit its extent and whether, in particular, he availed himself in time of all the legal remedies available to him.[168]
- Total exclusion of loss of profit as a head of damage for which reparation may be awarded in the case of a breach of Community law is not acceptable. The Court pointed out that in the context of economic or commercial litigation, such a total exclusion of loss of profit would make reparation of damage practically impossible.[169]
- An award of exemplary damages pursuant to a claim or an action founded on Community law cannot be ruled out if such damages could be awarded pursuant to a similar claim or action founded on domestic law.[170]

Subject to these guidelines and the general conditions laid down in the *Rewe* and *Comet* case law, the remedy of reparation is governed by national law. Reliance on the laws of Member States is a source of divergence but lack of uniformity is inevitable given that the right to reparation is an entirely judge-made right. One would expect that, as the case law develops, Community law will gradually occupy some of the area currently left to national laws.

11.11. Which authority is responsible for providing reparation?

In *Konle* and, especially, in *Haim*[171] the Court had the opportunity to provide some guidance on the question of which national authority bears the obligation to

---

[166] *Brasserie* therefore put it beyond doubt that the judgment of the Court of Appeal in *Bourgoin* is no longer good law. After *Francovich*, doubt had already been expressed about the correctness of that decision by the House of Lords in *Kirklees M.B.C. v Wickes Building Supplies Ltd* [1992] 3 WLR 170.   [167] *Brasserie, op. cit.*, para 82.
[168] *Op. cit.*, para 84. The obligation to act with due diligence and within reasonable time to minimise the loss also arises in the context of the liability of Community institutions; see e.g. Case T-144/02 *Eagle v Commission*, judgment of 5 October 2004, paras 57 *et seq.*
[169] *Op. cit.*, para 87.   [170] *Ibid.*, para 89.
[171] Op. cit., n. 99 above (*Konle*), n. 29 above (*Haim*).

provide reparation and is the proper defendant in an action for damages. The principles which emerge from the cases can be summarised as follows.

As a general rule, the question of which authority is liable to provide compensation is for national law to decide. Community law imposes limitations which derive, in the first place, from the right to reparation itself and, in the second place, the principles of effectiveness and equivalence. The basic obligation incumbent on Member States is to ensure that individuals obtain reparation for loss or damage caused to them by non-compliance with Community law. This principle must be honoured whichever public authority is responsible for the breach and whichever public authority is, under national law, responsible for making reparation.[172] A Member State may not escape liability by pleading the distribution of powers between various State bodies as defined by national law or by claiming that the public authority responsible for the breach does not have 'the necessary power, knowledge, means or resources'.[173]

The dictum that a Member State may not avoid liability by claiming that the body responsible for the breach of Community law did not have the necessary power, knowledge, means or resources is of considerable importance. It is phrased in general terms and appears to be a minimum requirement deriving from the principle of effectiveness. If that is correct, it must be honoured in all cases, i.e. even if national law does not guarantee an equivalent degree of protection for comparable claims based on national law. The issue may be crucial in relation to independent public bodies which enjoy budgetary autonomy.

Subject to those requirements, it is up to each Member State to ensure the way individuals obtain reparation. Thus, in Member States with federal structure, reparation for damage need not necessarily be provided by the federal State.[174] Where a Member State devolves legislative or administrative tasks to a public law body legally distinct from the State, reparation for loss caused by measures taken by that body may be made by it and not by the State.[175] Nor does Community law preclude a public law body from being liable to make reparation in addition to the State itself.[176]

The requirement of equivalence may fetter, or even remove altogether, national discretion. If domestic law provides for the liability of a public body for a comparable breach of national law, the principle of equivalence requires that the body must also be held responsible for the breach of EC law. The converse is also true: an action for damages against the State for breach of Community law by an independent public authority must be available if it is available for comparable breaches of national law.

The crucial consideration here is that the claims must be comparable.[177] What if there is more than one comparable claim in national law? Does the individual have

---

[172] *Konle, op. cit.*, para 62, *Haim, op. cit.*, 27.   [173] *Haim, op. cit.*, para 28.
[174] *Konle, op. cit.*, para 64.   [175] *Haim, op. cit.*, para 31.   [176] *Ibid.*, para 32.
[177] For the meaning of this term, see pp. 424 *et seq.*

a choice? In some cases, it may not even be possible to specify in general terms which alternative cause of action is more favourable to the individual because an action may be more favourable in some respects but less so in other respects. It is submitted that the individual is not necessarily entitled to choose the most favourable treatment in the circumstances. The objective of the case law is not to treat claims based on Community law preferentially over claims of domestic law. It suffices if the national legal system affords the injured party an effective opportunity to seek reparation. If a claimant under Community law had unlimited choice or were allowed to 'cherry pick'and combine elements from different causes of action, that would lead to uncertainty and disrupt the national systems of procedure and remedies.[178]

The issue of whether an independent administrative authority as opposed to the State itself is liable may depend on whether it had any discretion in taking the decision which amounted to a serious breach of Community law. If the administrative authority was bound by national legislation in taking the decision, it might be more difficult to hold it liable for the ensuing breach of Community law. If, by contrast, it enjoyed discretion under national law and could have exercised it in such a way as not to commit a serious breach, it would be easier to allocate liability to the authority itself. These are, however, considerations to be taken into account by national law. Community law does not appear to impose any hard and fast rules in this respect.[179]

What if a Member State has delegated functions to a private body? Although *Haim* refers to the liability of 'public-law bodies', it is submitted that national law is not in principle precluded from devolving liability to a body governed by private law to which public functions have been delegated and which, in the exercise of those functions, is responsible for an actionable breach of Community law. A host of consequential issues arise here. If an individual successfully brings an action for reparation against an independent public agency, may that agency in turn seek to recover its loss against the State on the ground that the breach of Community law was in fact attributable to the latter? This question acquires importance where the authority is independent from central government and enjoys budgetary auto-nomy, for example a professional association enjoying public law status. A further question relates to causation. What happens in cases where the applicant has successfully established a breach of Community law but there is uncertainty as to whether the breach is attributable to the State or an independent public authority? In other words, is it a condition for the success of the action that the applicant must

---

[178] See also M. Hoskins, 'Rebirth of the Innominate Tort?' in Beatson and Tridimas, *op. cit.*, 91–100, at 100.

[179] See the Opinion of Mischo AG in *Haim*, *op. cit.*, para 32. In a different context, the Court has declared that all national authorities are under an obligation to uphold the principle of primacy and ensure the effective protection of Community rights, if necessary, by setting aside any obstacles posed by national law, including national legislation. See e.g. Case 106/77 *Simmenthal* [1978] ECR 629 and Case 103/88 *Fratelli Costanzo v Commune di Milano* [1989] ECR 1839. The Court recently reiterated the application of this principle in relation to administrative authorities: see Case C-224/97 *Ciola v Land Vorarlberg*, judgment of 29 April 2000.

be able to establish firmly a direct causal link with the action of a specific body? In principle, the question should be answered in the affirmative. In some cases, however, it may not be easy to determine which body should be sued and failure to identify the proper defendant may cost the success of the action. A claim for reparation against an independent public agency may need to be brought in a different court from a claim against the State. The danger is that an applicant who decides to bring an action against the agency and finds his claim rejected on the ground that the action should have been brought against the State, may find his action against the latter time-barred. It should be emphasised here that, in addition to the requirements laid down above, Community law imposes an additional requirement founded on the principle of legal certainty. The rules of national law pertaining to the right of reparation for breach of Community law must give to individuals an effective opportunity to claim reparation and must be clear and precise so that citizens are able to understand them.[180]

Finally, if national law makes the right to reparation for loss suffered as a result of breach of domestic law subject to less stringent conditions than those laid down in the Court's case law, the principle of equivalence requires that those conditions must also apply to a claim for reparation based on breach of Community law. The issue of comparability of claims arises here once again and, with it, some interesting questions. For example, the law of a Member State may provide for a right to damages for the breach of the general principle of non-discrimination as guaranteed in the national constitution or, more specifically, for discrimination on grounds of race, including nationality.[181] Would then an applicant who had suffered loss as a result of the breach of a fundamental freedom, such as the right of establishment, be able to rely on that cause of action and thus avoid the requirement of a 'serious' breach? This of course assumes that the 'comparable' cause of action under national law is more favourable to the individual but this may not be excluded in some cases.

11.12. The aftermath of *Francovich*

To illustrate the importance of national law in defining the right to reparation, it may be interesting to look at the response of the Italian State to the judgment in *Francovich*. Following the judgment, by a Legislative Decree adopted on 27 January 1992, Italy took steps to implement Directive 80/987[182] and provide compensation to those who suffered loss as a result of its belated implementation. The Legislative

---

[180] Cf the case law on national measures transposing directives: Case 29/84 *Commission v Germany* [1985] ECR 1661; Case C-119/92 *Commission v Italy* [1994] ECR I-393; Case C-236/95 *Commission v Greece* [1996] ECR I-4459.

[181] This is the case with the Race Relations Act in the United Kingdom.

[182] Council Directive 80/987 on the approximation of the laws of the Member States relating to the protection of employees in the event of the insolvency of their employer, OJ 1908 L 283, p. 23. The Directive has been amended by Directive 87/164, OJ 1987 L 66, p. 11.

Decree provided that actions for reparation must be brought within a period of one year from the date of its entry into force. Also, it applied retroactively to claims for reparation in respect of the implementing measures and the limitations imposed therein on the liability of the guarantee institutions to meet outstanding wage claims of employees of insolvent employers. Both these aspects of the Legislative Decree were challenged on grounds of compatibility with Community law.

11.12.1. Time limit

The time limit of one year was challenged in *Palmisani v INPS*.[183] In *Palmisani* the Court had no difficulty in finding that the one-year time limit satisfied the principle of effectiveness. It was a reasonable period within which persons harmed by the belated transposition could protect their rights. The requirement of equivalence was more contentious. The national court referred for the purposes of comparison to time limits applicable to other claims. Thus, in implementation of Directive 80/987, the Legislative Decree provided a limitation period of one year for benefits payable under the Directive, running from the date of submission of the application for the benefit to the Guarantee Fund. The Court held that applications for payments provided by the Directive and those made under the compensation scheme for its belated transposition differ as to their objective. The former aim to provide employees with specific guarantees of payment of unpaid remuneration in the event of the insolvency of their employer. The latter, by contrast, seek to make good the loss sustained by the beneficiaries of the Directive as a result of its belated transposition. The Court also noted that reparation cannot always be ensured by retroactive and proper application in full of the measures implementing the Directive. Given the different nature of the claims, it was not necessary to undertake a comparison of the time limits applicable to them. For the same reason, the Court rejected a comparison with the time limit applicable under Italian law for obtaining social security benefits.[184]

The national court also referred to the limitation period applicable under ordinary law to claims for non-contractual liability. This is set by the Italian Civil Code at five years. The Court held that compensation for the belated implementation of a directive and the ordinary system of non-contractual liability pursued essentially the same objective, namely to effect reparation of the loss sustained as a result of unlawful conduct. They were therefore comparable. The Court did not possess all the information necessary to determine whether an action for damages brought by an individual pursuant to the Italian Civil Code could be directed against public authorities and left it to the national court to undertake that examination. The Court stated that if the ordinary system of non-contractual liability were to prove incapable of serving as a basis for an action against public

---

[183] Case C-261/95 *Palmisani v Instituto Nazionale della Previdenza Sociale (INPS)* [1997] ECR I-4025.   [184] *Palmisani, op. cit.,* n. 2, paras 33–37.

authorities and the national court were unable to undertake any other relevant comparison between the time limit in issue and the conditions relating to similar claims of a domestic nature, the conclusion would have to be drawn that the one-year time limit was not precluded by Community law.[185]

11.12.2. Retroactive application of implementing measures

Article 4(2) of Directive 80/987 allows Member States to limit the liability of the guarantee institutions to payment of outstanding claims for certain periods of the employment relationship and grants to Member States a number of options for determining those periods. In implementation of the Directive, the Legislative Decree took advantage of Article 4(2) and applied the same limitation of liability retrospectively to the compensation payable to employees who suffered loss from the belated transposition of the Directive. The Legislative Decree also provided for an upper limit on payments by guarantee institutions pursuant to Article 4(3) of the Directive[186] and applied the same limitation to reparation.

In *Maso v INPS*[187] and *Bonifaci v INPS*,[188] the question was referred whether a Member State is entitled to apply implementing measures retroactively to claims of reparation belatedly adopted, including the limitations provided for in Article 4(2). The Court held that retroactive application in full of the measures implementing the Directive to employees who have suffered loss as a result of belated transposition enables in principle the harmful consequences of the breach to be remedied, provided that the Directive has been transposed properly.[189] Such application, should have the effect of guaranteeing to those employees the rights from which they would have benefited if the Directive had been transposed within the prescribed period. With regard to Directive 80/987, retroactive application of implementing measures necessarily implies that a limitation of the guarantee institution's liability may also be applied, in accordance with Article 4(2), where the Member State has in fact exercised that option when transposing the Directive into national law. The Court however added a *caveat*. It stated that it is for the national court to ensure that reparation for the loss sustained is adequate. Retroactive and proper application in full of the measures implementing the Directive will suffice unless the beneficiaries establish the existence of complementary loss sustained on account of the fact that they were unable to

---

[185] Ibid., paras 38–39.

[186] Article 4(3) allows Member States to set a ceiling on payments by guarantee institutions in order to avoid the payment of sums going beyond the social objective of the Directive.

[187] Case C-373/95 *Maso, Graziana and Others v Instituto Nazionale della Previdenza Sociale (INPS) and Italian Republic* [1997] ECR I-4051.

[188] Joined Cases C-94 and C-95/95 *Bonifaci, Berto and Others v Instituto Nazionale della Previdenza Sociale (INPS)* [1997] ECR I-3936.

[189] This has been reiterated in subsequent cases. See Case C-131/97 *Carbonari and Others v Università degli Studi di Bologna and Others* [1999] ECR I-1103, para 53; Case C-371/97 *Gozza v Università degli Studi di Padova and Others*, judgment of 3 October 2000, para 39.

benefit at the appropriate time from the financial advantages guaranteed by the Directive. In such a case, the complementary loss must also be made good.[190]

11.13. The national reaction

Following the judgment in *Brasserie and Factortame*, it fell upon the national courts which made the references to the Court of Justice to determine whether the applicants' claim for damages could succeed on the facts. In its judgment of 24 October 1996, the Bundesgerichtshof rejected the claim of Brasserie du Pêcheur for damages against the State as unfounded.[191] By contrast, in its judgment of 31 July 1997 in *R v Secretary of State* for Transport *ex p Factortame*, the Divisional Court held that the breach committed by the United Kingdom was serious.

The Bundesgerichtshof referred to the judgment of the ECJ in *Brasserie* and held that the damage suffered by the applicant was the result of the additives prohibition imposed by German law, which was not a serious breach, and not the result of the designation prohibition which constituted a serious breach.[192] It referred to the Opinion of Tesauro AG in *Brasserie* who stated that, if the damage suffered by the applicant was causally connected with the prohibition on additives rather than the designation prohibition, the failure of the claim 'could not be ruled out'.[193]

It should be accepted that, where there are separate breaches of Community law, only the damage which is actually causally connected with the serious breach must be compensated. In the case of overlapping breaches one of which is serious and the other of which is not, identifying the damage which is connected with the serious breach may give rise to difficulties. In the case in issue, the German court took the view that the additives prohibition would have in itself made the importation of the plaintiff's beers to Germany impossible even in the absence of the designation prohibition.

The Bundesgerichtshof also rejected the claim of the applicant for the damage which it allegedly incurred after 12 March 1987, the date when the judgment in the *Beer* case was delivered. Brasserie argued that it had suffered loss of profits during the transitional period that it needed after the judgment in the *Beer* case in order to build a distribution network. The court accepted however that the German authorities took immediate steps to comply with the judgment and held that the loss suffered during the transitional period was the result of the previous additives prohibition which was not a serious breach.

By contrast, in *R v Secretary of State for Transport ex p Factortame Ltd*,[194] the House of Lords held that the deliberate adoption of legislation which was clearly contrary

---

[190] *Maso, op. cit.*, paras 39–42; *Bonifaci, op. cit.*, paras 51–54.
[191] See [1997] 1 CMLR 971.   [192] See above, pp. 510–11.
[193] *Brasserie, op. cit.*, n. 15 above, p. 1126.
[194] [1997] 1 All ER 736; affirmed by the Court of Appeal: [1999] 2 All ER 640; and the House of Lords: [2001] AC 524.

to the fundamental principle of equal treatment on grounds of nationality was a serious breach. It accepted that the Government had acted in good faith in the public interest but that was not sufficient to exonerate it from liability. The House of Lords took into account the following considerations: the breach was clear and referred to a fundamental rule of the Treaty; the breach was grave both intrinsically and as regards the consequences it was likely to have for the applicants; the registration requirements had been introduced by primary legislation which made it impossible for the applicants to obtain interim relief or even challenge it and no adequate transitional measures had been provided; the Government had taken a calculated risk by choosing to disregard the Commission's opinion that the legislation contravened Community law; finally, it continued to apply the registration requirements even though it became progressively clear that they would be found incompatible with the Treaty.[195]

11.14. Relationship with other remedies

The relationship between State liability and other remedies for breach of Community law remains largely uninvestigated. Is State liability a residual remedy to be used only where all other remedies are unavailable or exhausted? The case law does not provide a clear answer to this question but the following points may be made. In *Brasserie*, the Court stated that, in determining the extent of reparation, a national court may take into account whether the injured party availed himself in time of alternative remedies available.[196] This is an illustration of a more general principle of tort law according to which the injured party must take the steps necessary to minimise the effects of the damage. This does not mean that State liability is necessarily a residual remedy. An injured party cannot be faulted for failing to apply first for an alternative right or remedy where it is clear that national law will refuse it or where the remedy is not adequate.[197]

The case law suggests that the right to reparation is an independent remedy which may be sought in addition to other remedies available in national courts, where those remedies do not provide full satisfaction to the applicant. This is best illustrated by *Sutton* and *Comateb*.[198] In *Sutton*, Mrs Sutton was entitled to receive arrears of a social

---

[195] See the judgments in Case C-3/87 *R v Ministry of Agriculture, Fisheries and Food ex p Agegate* [1989] ECR 4459 and Case C-216/87 *R v Ministry of Agriculture, Fisheries and Food ex p Jaderow* [1989] ECR 4509 and the interim order in Case C-246/89 R *Commission v United Kingdom* [1989] ECR 3125. The failure of the Government to comply with the Order of the President of the Court in that case by suspending immediately the nationality requirement amounted to a serious breach giving rise to a right to reparation. [196] See above.

[197] *Metallgesellschaft Ltd and Hoechst AG v Commissioners of Inland Revenue, op. cit.*, n. 145 above, paras 103–106.

[198] Case C-66/95 *Sutton* [1997] ECR I-2163. Joined Cases C-192 to C-218/95 *Comateb and Others v Directeur Général des Douanes et Droits Indirects* [1997] ECR I-165. Both cases are discussed in detail above p. 440 and p. 459, respectively.

security benefit which had been denied to her in breach of Directive 79/7. The Court held that since her claim was restitutive and not compensatory in nature she could not claim interest on the amount of social security benefits owed to her by virtue of the Directive. It left open however the possibility that she could obtain the amount of interest by means of an action based on State liability in damages, if a serious breach has occurred. In *Comateb*, it was held that, even where a levy paid contrary to Community law has been passed on to the consumer, the trader concerned may still seek to recover it by bringing an action in damages. *Comateb* muddled rather than clarified the relationship between State liability and claims arising directly from provisions of Community law which give rise to substantive rights. If the defence of passing on is available to the public authorities in a claim based directly on breach of Article 25 EC why should it not be available to them in a *Francovich* claim? It could be argued that, in contrast to a claim for the recovery of unduly paid charges, the conditions of a claim based on State liability are governed totally by Community law. This however runs counter to express dicta made by the Court in *Francovich* and *Factortame* where it was held that reparation is governed by national law subject to the requirements of equivalence and effectiveness.

As a general rule, where the claim is purely restitutive in nature, an action for damages is not necessary. In *Stockholm Lindöpark*[199] the question referred was whether the exemption from VAT of certain sport-related services by Swedish legislation was a serious breach of Community law. The Court found that, in the circumstances, a serious breach had occurred but at the start of its reasoning, it observed that, since the provisions of the Sixth VAT Directive were directly effective, the applicant in the main proceedings could pursue any debts owed to it by the Swedish State retroactively before national courts so that 'at first sight, . . . an action for damages founded on the Court's case-law relating to the liability of Member States for breaches of Community law does not seem necessary'.[200] This is because the recovery of monies paid contrary to Community law is the necessary corollary of direct effect. An individual may recover unduly paid sums without the need to prove a serious breach of Community law, subject to the requirements of equivalence and effectiveness. What however if those requirements prevent recovery? Can the individual bring an action in damages instead? This could occur, for example, where the individual misses the time limit for the recovery claim but seeks to take advantage of a longer time limit available in actions in damages. As the case law stands at the moment, it appears that there is nothing to prevent him from doing so, provided that the conditions of State liability are met.[201]

---

[199] *Stockholm Lindöpark, op. cit.*, n. 64 above.　　　[200] Para 35.

[201] This view is supported by *Comateb, op. cit.*; *Metallgesellschaft, op. cit.*; paras. 102 and 107; see also the Opinion of Jacobs AG in Case C-188/95 *Fantask a/S and Others v Ministry of Trade and Industry* [1997] ECR I-6783. See further M. Dougan, *op. cit.*, n. 1; P. Eeckhout, 'Liability of Member States in Damages and the Community System of Remedies', in Beatson and Tridimas, *op. cit.*, 63; G. Anagnostaras, 'State Liability and Alternative Courses of Action: How Independent Can an Autonomous Remedy Be?' (2002) 21 YEL 355.

11.15. Liability of private parties

11.15.1. Horizontal provisions

Following *Francovich* and *Brasserie*, the question arose whether liability for breach of Community law might extend to individuals. The archetypal situation where such liability may arise is breach of competition law, since in this area the Treaty imposes express obligations on non-state entities. The issue was first examined by van Gerven AG in *Banks*,[202] a case which concerned the competition rules of the ECSC Treaty. The Advocate General opined that *Francovich* should also apply where an individual infringes a provision of Community law thereby causing damage to another individual. He derived the right to damages from the general principle of effectiveness and found that, in the field of competition law, there were powerful militating arguments in favour of recognizing it. He saw the right to reparation as the logical consequence of the horizontal effect of competition provisions, and considered that it would make the Community competition rules more 'operational', by facilitating their full enforcement by national courts.[203]

In *Banks* the Court did not examine the right to damages, but the issue re-emerged some years later in *Courage Ltd v Crehan*.[204] The defendant in the main proceedings had concluded two twenty-year leases for the use of public houses. The lease agreements contained an exclusive purchase obligation under which he had to purchase a fixed minimum quantity of beer from Courage Ltd, a brewery which in 1990 held a 19 per cent share of the UK market. When Courage Ltd brought an action to recover unpaid deliveries of beer, the defendant argued that the beer tie was contrary to Article 81 EC and counter-claimed damages. The difficulty was that, under the principle *pari delicto*, espoused by English law, a party to an illegal contract may not claim damages from the other party. Mr Crehan's defence that the lease was contrary to Article 81 EC would thus bar his claim in damages. The ECJ did not have much sympathy for this argument. In a judgment reminiscent of the approach of the US Supreme Court, it highlighted 'the inappropriateness of invoking broad common-law barriers to relief where a private suit serves important public purposes'.[205]

Echoing the Opinion of van Gerven AG in *Banks*, the Court based liability for breach of competition law on the effectiveness of Article 81, in particular the need to safeguard the practical effect of the prohibition laid down in Article 81(2). It thus

---

[202] Case C-128/92 *Banks v British Coal Corporation* [1994] ECR I-1209. Note that earlier in *Garden Cottage Foods v Milk Marketing Board* [1983] 3 WLR 143, the House of Lords (Lord Wilberforce dissenting) was prepared to accept that in English law a violation of Article 82 EC would give rise to a claim in damages for breach of statutory duty.

[203] *Op. cit.*, pp. 1250–1251.

[204] Case C-453/99 *Courage Ltd v Bernard Crehan*, judgment of 20 September 2001.

[205] See *Perma Life Mufflers Corporation v International Parts Corp.* 392 US 134 (1968) where the Supreme Court disregarded the *pari delicto* principle and allowed a party to an anti-competitive contract to recover damages against the other party.

concluded that a party to a contract liable to restrict or distort competition can rely on Article 81 to obtain relief from the other contracting party. The Court did not delve into the conditions of liability but provided some guidelines. The matters to be taken into account by the national court include the economic and legal context in which the parties find themselves, their respective bargaining power, and their conduct within the contractual setting. Community law does not preclude national law from denying the right to damages to a party who bears significant responsibility for the distortion of competition. The Court stressed that it is for the national court to ascertain whether the claimant is in a markedly weaker position than the other party, such as seriously to compromise or even eliminate his freedom to negotiate the terms of the contract and his capacity to avoid the loss or reduce its extent, in particular by availing himself in good time of all the legal remedies available to him.[206]

Crehan brings EC law closer to US law and sits well with the decentralization of the enforcement of competition law.[207] It allows liability for breach not only of Article 81 but also Article 82 EC, as the Court referred to compensation for loss caused by a contract 'or by conduct liable to restrict or distort competition'.[208] Even though the concept of abuse under this provision is an objective one, that does not exclude liability in favour of the injured parties.

Crehan also opens up the potential for liability in a host of other cases where Community norms impose obligations on private parties. Such obligations may be imposed by provisions of primary law or Community acts such as regulations. In *Angonese*,[209] for example, the Court held that Article 39 EC, which guarantees the free movement of workers, may be invoked not only *vis-à-vis* public bodies but also private entities. It follows that national courts must in principle entertain an action for damages against a private employer for breach of Article 39. The details of such liability remain for national private law to decide subject to the requirements of equivalence and effectiveness. As to the conditions of liability, it is clear that the rule of EU law infringed must be intended to grant rights to individuals and there must be a causal connection between the breach and the damage suffered. There appears however no reason why the seriousness of the breach must be a general condition for the liability of private parties. The requirement of serious breach emanates from the sovereign nature of the State and serves public interest purposes, namely to safeguard the decision making of the *imperium* and limit the exposure of public authorities to potential claims in damages. These reasons do not apply in relation to the liability of private parties. In any event, according to the principle of

---

[206] *Courage Ltd v Crehan, op. cit.,* para 33.

[207] Following the ruling of the ECJ, the High Court (Park J) dismissed Mr Crehan's damages claim on the ground that the network of lease agreements concluded by the brewery were not such as to foreclose access to the market for competitors and therefore the agreement in issue was not anti-competitive under the *Delimitis* test: *Crehan v Inntrepreneur Pub Company and Brewman Group Ltd* [2003] EuLR 663.   [208] *Courage Ltd v Crehan, op. cit.,* para 21.

[209] Case C-281/98 *Angonese v Cassa di Risparmio di Bolzano SpA,* [2000] ECR I-4139, para 36.

equivalence, a claim against a private party for breach of Community law must not be subject to more stringent conditions than those applicable to a comparable claim for breach of national law. A lot will therefore depend here on national tort laws which are centred on issues of rights, causation, and damages and not on the seriousness of breach.

As a general rule, the liability of private parties for breach of Community law, precisely because of its private law nature, is much more dependent on the national rules of remedies than the liability of public authorities where the Court is more confident to lay down the parameters.[210]

Another case where liability against private parties may arise is where a public authority has delegated regulatory powers to a private entity. This is, however, not a genuinely horizontal case as it involves, in effect, the exercise of public power. In such a case, therefore, the general conditions of liability laid down in *Francovich* and *Bergaderm* will apply.

11.15.2. Implied rights of action

A right of action against a private party may be implied by Community provisions which impose obligations without containing specific subjective rights. In *Munoz SA v Frumar Ltd*[211] the Court held that a regulation which imposes standards for the marketing of a product entitles a competitor to bring civil proceedings against a trader who fails to comply with those standards. The measures at issue were agricultural regulations which laid down quality standards for grapes and provided that each package must bear the name of the variety to which the grapes belonged. The applicants in the main proceedings were Spanish producers who grew the 'Superior Seedless' variety. They brought an action arguing that the defendant traders marketed in the UK, under different names, table grapes which were in fact of the 'Superior Seedless' variety, and as result violated Community law. The High Court found that the defendants had infringed the Community rules in issue but dismissed the action on the ground that those rules did not give other producers the right to bring a civil action.

On a reference to the ECJ made by the Court of Appeal, the Court held that the regulations in issue were capable of enforcement by means of civil proceedings instituted by a trader against a competitor. The Court based this solution on two arguments, namely, the objectives of the regulations and the principle of effectiveness of Community law. It held that the purpose of common quality standards

---

[210] In English law there is some uncertainty as to what would be the suitable cause of action for breach of Articles 81 and 82. Under the *Garden Cottage* case, it is a private law claim for damages for the tort of breach of statutory duty but the *remedium* has been characterised as a mixture of EU competition law and English domestic law: *Provimi Ltd and Others v Aventis Animal Nutrition SA and others* [2003] EuLR 517 at 541.

[211] Case C-253/00 *Munoz Cia SA and Superior Fruiticola v Frumar Ltd and Redbridge Produce Marketing Ltd*, [2002] ECR I-7289.

was to keep products of unsatisfactory quality off the market, and promote fair competition. The full effectiveness of the rules implied that it must be possible to enforce the obligations which they imposed by means of civil proceedings instituted by a trader against a competitor. The Court placed particular emphasis on the 'dual vigilance' principle familiar from *van Gend en Loos*. It stated that the possibility of bringing civil proceedings strengthens the practical working of the Community rules on quality standards. As a supplement to the power of the national authorities to make inspections, it helps to discourage practices which distort competition and are often difficult to detect and contributes substantially to ensuring fair trading and market transparency.[212]

Munoz sets an important precedent by transposing the principle of horizontal direct effect to the procedural and remedial plain. An individual whose interests are adversely affected by the failure of another individual to comply with an obligation imposed by Community law may derive a right of action against the latter. The judgment establishes a right to a civil remedy as a matter of Community law. Such remedy must be effective and may include an injunction or a right to damages, as appropriate. The existence and scope of such a right depends on the Community rules in issue. The potential class of beneficiaries appears wide and it will depend on the range of interests that the norm of Community law in issue intends to protect. Thus, depending on the circumstances, it may include not only competitors but also consumers, employees, representative associations, trade unions or pressure groups.[213] The *Munoz* principle, however, does not extend to directives. Since directives may not by themselves impose obligations on individuals, a private party may not derive a right of action to enforce an obligation imposed by an unimplemented directive on another individual.

---

[212] *Munoz, op. cit.*, para 31.

[213] In his Opinion, Geelhoed AG took the view that the requirements concerning access to the national courts by an interested third party may be inferred from the conditions governing access to the Community judicature itself. He stated that the case law does not recognize an *actio popularis* against infringements of Community law. Drawing inspiration from the case law under Article 230(4) EC, he came to the conclusion that national law must afford a right of action to an interested third party who has suffered loss as a result of the infringement of a provision of a Community regulation where the following conditions are met: (a) the person concerned invokes an economic interest which is protected by the regulation; (b) the interest differentiates him from other economic operators; (c) the person concerned has availed himself first of other rights of recourse as required by national law. The analogy, however, between *locus standi* under Article 230(4) and a right to initiate proceedings before a national court against a private party for breach of a Community norm is questionable. The purpose of the two actions is different. In the first case, it is to obtain the annulment of a public act whereas in the second it is to enforce an obligation and obtain a remedy for breach of a Community provision; also, the Court has followed a restrictive interpretation of individual concern under Article 230(4) on policy grounds taking into account the possibility of indirect challenge against Community acts before national courts under Article 234 EC. It would be unwise to make private rights of action before national courts dependent on the existence of individual concern. In *Munoz* itself, the applicant company would not have been able to satisfy the requirement of individual concern and therefore have *locus standi* to seek the annulment of the regulations in issue before the CFI.

Munoz unleashes the private enforcement potential of myriads of regulatory measures. The establishment of a private right of action is seen by the Court as an integrative mechanism and seems to be part of a wider strategy to provide effective enforcement of internal market legislation. *Munoz*, like the earlier judgments in *CIA* and *Unilever*,[214] grants individuals a stake in the enforcement of internal market legislation, and views private remedies as fulfilling also an important public law function.

---

[214] Case C-194/94 *CIA Security International v Signalson SA* [1996] ECR I-2201; Case C-443/98 *Unilever Italia SpA v Central Food SpA* [2000] ECR I-7535.

12

Conclusions

An attempt was made in the preceding chapters to show how the Community judicature uses the general principles of law as sources of rights and obligations. A number of descriptive and prescriptive conclusions may be drawn from the above analysis.

The study of the case law makes it clear that the use of the general principles is not exhausted in their gap-filling function. They form an integral part of the Court's methodology and express constitutional values. There can be no doubt that, as sources of rights and obligations, the general principles pose significant limitations on the policy-making power of the Community institutions. It is true that the cases where they have been successfully invoked leading to the annulment of Community acts are concentrated mainly in certain areas, such as agriculture and staff cases. Measures have also been annulled in other fields, however, and no area of Community action remains immune from their application. This all-embracing, character of the general principles should not hide their relative nature. Far from establishing a uniform standard, concepts such as proportionality and equality are used to protect diverse interests and entail varying degrees of judicial scrutiny depending on the context in which they are applied. It is appropriate to emphasise here once more the dual nature of judicial review exercised by the Community judicature. Where it exercises judicial review of Community measures, it seeks to protect the individual *vis-à-vis* arbitrary conduct of the Community authorities and balances private *vis-à-vis* public interests. Where it exercises 'judicial review' of national measures, it controls State action *vis-à-vis* the Community objectives and uses the concepts of non-discrimination and proportionality as instruments of market integration. The standard of judicial scrutiny is higher in the latter case than it is in the former. This differential is less prominent in recent case law which, at least in some areas, shows evidence towards equivalence of standards.[1]

The general principles derive from the laws of the Member States but in the Court's case law they acquire, by a process of 'creative appropriation', independent normative value and are applied subject to the exigencies of the Community polity. The Community judiciary subscribes to a substantive rather than a formal version of the rule of law. The Court perceives the general principles as expressing fundamental democratic values enshrined in the common cultural and political heritage of the Member States. In that sense, general principles can be seen as the

---

[1] See below p. 558.

expression of a 'shared political morality'.[2] This line of reasoning can be accepted only if it is read subject to an important proviso, namely, that the Court not only reflects but also shapes political morality. Judicial intervention is not only negative but also positive in the sense that it not only seeks to protect the citizen *vis-à-vis* public authority but also to promote political and social values. The judgments in *Chernobyl*[3] and, in a different context, *P v S*[4] provide testament to the cultivation of positive judicial standards. In terms of their ideological foundations, the general principles make a hybrid. They incorporate standards deriving from the liberal constitutional tradition but also promote a model of European integration influenced by ideas founded on the notion of social market economy.

One may identify the following as the underlying objectives of the case law on general principles:

1) to protect the individual *vis-à-vis* arbitrary public power;
2) to promote European integration in accordance with the putative intentions of the authors of the founding treaties;
3) to achieve a balance of powers among the political institutions of the Community inspired by ideas of participatory democracy;[5]
4) to uphold the paramountcy of the principle of judicial protection;
5) to preserve the autonomy of the Community judicial system.[6]

Under the case law of the ECJ, the right to an effective remedy is the most valuable right of all.[7] Still, it is qualified by public interest exigencies. Cases like *Jégo-Quéré*[8] and possibly also *Safalero*[9] suggest that it is under serious, some would say, unacceptable limitations.

As grounds for review of Community action, the general principles seek to impose on the institutions a high burden to justify their actions, enhance the protection of the individual and, ultimately, contribute to better decision making. The contribution of the Court of First Instance in this context should not be underestimated. Although, to paraphrase Dworkin, the judgments of the Court of Justice remain the most dramatic expression of judicial power, the CFI has made its own mark in the case law especially, but by no means exclusively, by the elaboration and application of procedural principles. In fact, more recent case law suggests that the CFI has increased its endeavours to shape the law and is willing to

---

[2] See T. R. S. Allan, *The Limits of Parliamentary Sovereignty*, (Oxford: Oxford University Press, 1985) PL 614, 621.   [3] Case C-70/88 *Parliament v Council* [1990] ECR I-2041.

[4] Case C-13/91 *P v S and Cornwall County Council* [1996] ECR I-2143.

[5] *Parliament v Council, op. cit.*

[6] See Opinion 1/91 *on the Draft Agreement relating to the creation of the European Economic Area* [1991] ECR I-6079; Opinion 2/94 *on the accession of the Community to the ECHR* [1996] ECR I-1759.

[7] This is best illustrated by reference to cases such as Case 294/83 *les Verts v Parliament* [1986] ECR 1339, *Chernobyl case op. cit*; Case 222/84 *Johnston* [1986] ECR 1651; Case C-97/91 *Borelli v Commission* [1992] ECR I-6313; Case C-224/01 *Köbler v Austria*, judgment of 30 Septemeber 2003.   [8] Case C-263/02 P *Commission v Jégo-Quéré*, judgment of 1 April 2004.

[9] See Case C-13/01 *Safalero Srl v Prefetto di Genova*, judgment of 11 September 2003.

challenge precedent and established principles of the ECJ[10] or venture bravely into uncharted waters.[11]

A specific comment may be appropriate here in relation to the principle of proportionality. It is submitted that the principle structures the judicial enquiry better than the concept of *Wednesbury* unreasonableness traditionally applicable under English law. This is because proportionality enables the court to identify better the various competing interests and to ascribe normative value to them. It will be noted that the intervention of the Court remains perforce negative rather than positive in that the Court may annul a measure but has no jurisdiction to give directions to its author as to the precise course of action which needs to be followed in order to redress illegality. The institution concerned must try again attempting to second-guess the Court's standards. As the milk quota litigation and the mushrooms cases poignantly prove,[12] that may not be an easy task: successive measures dealing with the same issue may be annulled. It is true that the use of proportionality, in particular, encourages the Court to replicate the balancing process which the decision maker himself performs. It must be emphasised however that the Court does not act as an appellate body. Although the threshold of legality is higher than that applicable under English law, a range of options remains available to the Community legislature.

This book identifies three principal functions of proportionality: as a ground for review of Community measures, as a ground for review of national measures interfering with fundamental freedoms, and as a principle seeking to protect the nation state from excessive intervention by the Community legislature. A fourth function may be identified as having acquired particular prominence in recent years: the Court appears to engage in what can be termed collateral review on grounds of proportionality. It assesses the proportionality of a national measure not *vis-à-vis* its adverse impact on the primary Community interest (i.e. free movement), which is what brings the measure within the scope of Community law in the first instance, but on an incidental Community objective (i.e. human rights) with which the measure must conform.[13] Thus, in some ways, free movement has been transformed into the gateway for the Court to assert its fundamental rights jurisdiction.[14]

---

[10] See especially Case T-54/99 *max.mobil Telekommunikation Service GmbH v Commission* [2002] ECR II-313; reversed on appeal: C-141/02 P *Commission v T-Mobile Austria GmbH*, judgment of 22 February 2005; Case T-177/01 *Jégo-Quéré v Commission* [2002] ECR II-2365, reversed on appeal: Case C-263/02 P, *op. cit.*

[11] See the very recent judgments in Case T-315/01 *Kadi v Council and Commission*, judgment of 21 September 2005, and Case T-306/01 *Yusuf v Council and Commission*, judgment of 21 September 2005.   [12] See above, 5.4.2. and 3.6.

[13] See e.g. Case C-60/00 *Carpenter v Secretary of State for the Home Department*, [2002]; ECR I-6279; Case C-413/99 *Baumbast and R v Secretary of State for the Home Department*, [2002] ECR I-7091; Case C-109/01 *Secretary of State for the Home Department v Akrich*, judgment of 23 September 2003; C-112/00 *Schmidberger*, [2003] ECR I-5659; Case C-71/02 *Herbert Karner Industrie-Auktionen GmbH v Troostwijk GmbH*, judgment of 25 March 2004.

[14] The same occurred in cases such as Case C-491/01 *The Queen v Secretary of State for health ex p British American Tobacco Ltd* [2002] ECR I-11453, in relation to the policy of public health.

The general principles of law are closely inter-related. Proportionality, as a principle requiring that the means used must correspond to the objective sought, has a transverse character and forms part of all other principles. It is a component of fundamental rights since, although certain restrictions on such rights may be permitted, no restriction may be justified if it constrains the freedom of the individual more than is necessary to serve the public interest. Similarly, the principle of protection of legitimate expectations may need to give way to overriding public interests. That assessment entails a balancing exercise which involves considerations of proportionality.

The affinity between equality and proportionality requires closer examination. The starting point of the two principles is different. Equality is a principle of participation whereas proportionality is a principle of merits. But the link between them is evident in a number of respects. A test of proportionality is inherent in the concept of 'objective justification', which negates breach of the principle of equal treatment. Also, proportionality incorporates an element of participation. In order to assess whether a burden imposed on a product or an individual is proportionate, the Court will have regard to the way other related products or individuals are treated even if they are not in a strictly comparable situation.[15] The participatory character of proportionality was particularly evident in the skimmed milk powder cases. It will be remembered that in annulling the contested regulation, the Court declared that the obligation on feedstuff producers to purchase milk powder at a disproportionate price amounted to a discriminatory distribution of burdens between different agricultural sectors.[16] A central point in the reasoning of the Court was that the measure in issue made a particular group of producers bear unevenly the economic burden of an unfavourable situation which had developed in another economic sector.

A further area where the interaction between equality and proportionality is vividly illustrated is the imposition of flat-rate charges. Claims that such charges infringe equal treatment and proportionality have been countered by the Court by the use of virtually identical reasoning irrespective of the principle, breach of which is pleaded.[17]

The link between equal treatment and legitimate expectations is also evident in the case-law. Examples abound. In *Spagl*,[18] the Court and the Advocate General were at odds as to which principle was applicable. The Court found an infringement of the

---

[15] See e.g. Case C-24/90 *Werner Faust* [1991] ECR I-4905; Case C-25/90 *Wünsche* [1991] ECR I-4939; Case 122/78 *Buitoni v Forma* [1979] ECR 677; Case C-256/90 *Mignini* [1992] ECR I-2651, cf Opinion of Jacobs AG.

[16] Case 114/76 *Bela-Mühle v Grows-Farm* [1977] ECR 1211. See above 3.5.2.4.

[17] See e.g. Joined Cases C-267 to C-285/88 *Wuidart and Others* [1990] ECR I-435; Case C-27/90 *SITPA* [1994] ECR I-133; Joined Cases C-133, C-300 and C-363/93 *Crispoltoni II* [1994] ECR I-4863; Case 5/73 *Balkan-Import-Export v Hauptzollamt Berlin-Packhof* [1973] ECR 1091.

[18] Case C-189/89 [1990] ECR I-4539. See also Case C-217/89 *Pastatter* [1990] ECR I-4585 and above 6.4.2.

principle of respect for legitimate expectations which, in the circumstances, it understood as a principle of participation, namely as dictating the equitable allocation of burdens among different classes of producers. The Advocate General, on the other hand, saw the issue as one of equal treatment between returning producers and continuing ones and found that objective justification existed. In *Spagl* the issue could justly be seen as involving the application of both principles but in *Meiko*[19] the Court was less exacting by establishing a legitimate expectation where none should exist: the issue there was clearly one of equal treatment.[20] Finally, in *Ruckdeschel*[21] the claim of the applicants that the principle of equality was breached was helped by the fact that an existing advantage had been withdrawn.

This fusion of general principles is not surprising given that they share common ideological foundations and pursue common objectives. Their functional equivalence denotes their character as methodological tools facilitating the judicial enquiry. In a word, these general principles are the primary tools for the enforcement of negative rights against public authorities.

In substantive terms, the reasoning of the Court is not always convincing. The preceding chapters identified certain cases where, in the view of this author, consistency is lacking[22] or the result reached is not supported by compelling arguments.[23] It may not be coincidental that the general principles of law is an area characterised by a relatively high proportion of cases where the Court has disagreed with the advocate general. This may be explained by the fact that the application of general principles, especially the principle of proportionality, sometimes involves a subjective evaluation, and also by the fact that the Court invokes general principles of law to exercise an equitable jurisdiction. A notable example of disagreement is provided by the *Staff Salaries* case.[24] In a number of other cases, the Court applied the principle of legitimate expectations and reached a result more favourable to the individual than that of the advocate general.[25] In other cases, by contrast, the advocate general has found an infringement of a general principle but the Court has disagreed.[26] In general, it may be said that advocate generals' opinions are distinguished by a more compelling reasoning but are not necessarily more generous to the individual than the Court.

---

[19] Case 224/82 *Meiko-Konservenfabrik v Germany* [1983] ECR 2539.

[20] See above 6.3.4.

[21] Joined Cases 117/76 and 16/77 *Ruckdeschel v Hauptzollamt Hamburg-St.Annen* [1977] ECR 1753.

[22] See e.g. the rules governing the retroactive application of laws.

[23] See e.g. Case 127/80 *Grogan v Commission* [1982] ECR 869, above 6.7; Case C-312/93 *Peterbroeck v Belgian State* [1995] ECR I-4599, see above 9.9.

[24] Case 81/72 *Commission v Council* [1973] ECR 575.

[25] See e.g. Case 74/74 *CNTA v Commission* [1975] ECR 533 (Trabucchi AG); Case 5/75 *Deuka v Einfuhr- und Vorratsstelle Getreide* [1975] ECR 759 (Trabucchi AG); *Grogan, op. cit.*, (Capotorti AG); Joined Cases C-260 and C-261/91 *Diversinte and Iberlacta* [1993] ECR I-1885 (Gulmann AG).

[26] See e.g. Case 195/87 *Cehave v Hoofdproduktschap voor Akkerbouwprodukten* [1989] ECR 2219 (equality, Tesauro AG); Case C-345/88 *Butterabsatz Osnabrück- Emsland* [1990] ECR I-159 (proportionality, Jacobs AG).

To some extent, consistency of reasoning is inhibited by the collegiate character of the judgment. The inherent limitations imposed by collegiality have led at least one former member of the Court of Justice to suggest that dissenting judgments should be allowed as is the case in the European Court of Human Rights.[27] It is true that in recent years the Court employs more expansive reasoning. This is partly owing to the fact that, as the Community expanded and more legal cultures came to be reflected in the composition of the Court, the French influence on the style of the judgment waned and the output became more international. It has also been necessitated by the growing importance of the case law for the legal community and the public in general, and the national courts in particular. As more and more disputes at national level raise issues of Community law, national courts increasingly need to rely on the case law of the Court for their solution. It therefore becomes necessary for the Court to explain its reasoning in more detail.

It has become obvious from the preceding chapters that the relationship between Community law and the laws of Member States is a dialectical one. On the one hand, Community law borrows elements from national laws in order to fill the gaps in the Treaties and provide solutions to questions left unanswered by Community written law. On the other hand, Community law feeds back into the national legal systems principally through the national courts. This dialectical relationship deserves to be examined in more detail.

In the early stages of the development of Community law, the Court sought inspiration from national laws to cover the *lacunae* in written Community law. Thus in the early years, the general principles of law fulfilled a dual function: they provided a unifying theme adding cohesiveness and rationality and, at the same time, they ensured that Community law was the legal and ideological continuum of the laws of the Member States, acting as a force of legitimacy. As the case law developed and the Community legal order reached a stage of relative maturity, the general principles came to embody constitutional values attuned to the special needs of the Community polity. It should be stressed that, even nowadays, the Community judicature continues to heed, and seek inspiration from, the laws of the Member States on procedural and substantive issues. National law influences are sometimes overt but more often covert and indirect. We saw for example above,[28] how in *Technische Universität München*[29] calls by the German judiciary for greater substantive scrutiny of the decisions of the Community administration led to the elaboration by the Court of Justice of stricter procedural requirements.

In turn, the principles elaborated at Community level feed back to the national legal systems. Community law influences national laws in two ways. First, there is direct influence. Where national authorities act within the scope of Community

---

[27] See the evidence presented by Lord Slynn to the House of Lords Select Committee on the European Communities, Sub-committee on the 1996 Inter-Governmental Conference, *1996 Inter-Governmental Conference, Minutes of Evidence, House of Lords, Session 1994–95, 18th Report,* p. 246.   [28] Above p. 407.
[29] Case C-269/90 [1991] ECR I-5467.

law, they are bound to comply with Community principles and standards. National courts acquire powers to review national measures on the basis of grounds which may not be accepted under purely domestic law. Such direct influence is aptly illustrated in the Court's case law on fundamental rights. Following the judgment in *ERT*,[30] national courts acquired jurisdiction to review the compatibility with fundamental rights of national measures which fell within the scope of Community law. The case law of the ECJ effectively let the European Convention of Human Rights into the English legal system by the back door and precipitated a shift in the balance of power between the judiciary and the executive in favour of the former. It may be thought that the influence of Community law on English law is particularly pervasive because the latter shares neither the ideological underpinnings nor the methodological tools of the former. But as already stated in the first chapter, it would be wrong to divide national law between borrowers and lenders. The Court's case law has had far-reaching and penetrating influence on the laws of all Member States. Its net effect has been to raise the standards of accountability of national public authorities through the introduction of new remedies and higher standards of judicial scrutiny.

Apart from its direct influence, Community law also has indirect influence on national laws. By indirect influence, it is meant that the case law of the Court of Justice influences the development of national laws in areas unconnected with Community law. Such spill-over effect is inevitable for two reasons. First, to a great extent, the courts of all European countries face similar problems. It is natural for the judges of one Member State to turn to the Community courts and, to the extent that it is practically possible, to their brethren in other Member States, with a view to gaining inspiration. Cross-fertilization between national and supra-national legal systems is a sign of our times, perhaps more so than in other eras, and can be expected to increase.[31] That is especially so in areas where domestic law does not provide a clear answer or is perceived as suffering from deficiencies. The second reason is more powerful. Once different standards of judicial scrutiny are infused into a legal system, it is difficult to restrict their application only to certain areas of law unless such restriction can be justified not only on grounds of doctrinal reasoning but also on grounds of fairness. The expanding presence of Community law in the area of remedies and the higher standards introduced by the Court have led in many a case to reverse discrimination, namely, the situation where claims based on purely domestic law are treated less favourably than claims based on Community law. Such reverse discrimination flies in the face of justice. That is particularly so since the intrinsic value of Community rights which enjoy superior protection may be lower than the intrinsic value that rights governed by domestic

---

[30] Case C-260/89 [1991] ECR I-2925.

[31] See J. Beatson and T. Tridimas (eds), *New Directions in European Public Law*, Hart Publishing, 1998, Ch.1; for a judge's perspective, see Lord Justice Schiemann, 'The Application of General Principles of Community Law by English Courts', in A. Andenas and F. G. Jacobs, *European Community Law in the English Courts*, (Oxford University Press, 1998) 136–148.

law possess. How, for example, can it be justified that action by a public authority which restricts the free movement of goods is reviewable on grounds of proportionality but public action which restricts fundamental rights in areas unconnected with Community law is not? In English law, the indirect influence of Community law is clearly illustrated in cases like *M v Home Office*[32] and *Woolwich Equitable Building Society v Inland Revenue Commissioners*.[33] Overall, it may be said that, so far, English courts have followed a cautious approach and have been selectively receptive to such indirect influences. It is possible that the indirect influence of Community law, where visible, is not based on a genuine effort on the part of the national judiciary to follow the lead of Community law. Rather Community law is used as a catalyst to promote solutions which the national judiciary favours in terms of policy but feels unable to endorse being constrained by the principle of binding precedent or, more generally, by traditional ideas and concepts underpinning the legal system. Whichever way it is seen, the influence of the case law on the public laws of the Member States has been extensive, pervasive and, at times, subversive. It has been described by a member of the French Constitutional court as 'a peaceful revolution in the law'. Such indirect influences and cross-fertilization, it is submitted, should not be viewed with consternation but be welcomed as an enrichment of the national legal traditions.[34]

There is of course no doubt that, as the Community legal order evolves, the law on general principles also develops. The most important developments since the end of the 1990s may be said to be following:

- first, the enhanced importance and prominence of fundamental rights in the case law of the ECJ;
- second, the formalization of Community law;
- third, the expansion of the application of general principles on national measures;
- fourth, the development of the principle of equivalence;
- fifth, the development and articulation of the principle of selective deference.

These developments will be commented on in brief.

The most remarkable development in the case law has undoubtedly been that the ECJ has widened and deepened its fundamental rights jurisdiction. It has done so in a number of ways. It has expanded the scope of application of fundamental freedoms which has, in turn, broadened the range of national measures subject to the Court's human rights control.[35] It has asserted jurisdiction where a measure is likely to constitute a potential impediment to intra-Community trade even if it is not as such a restriction on a fundamental freedom. As noted above, the

---

[32] [1994] 1 AC 377.
[33] [1992] 3 WLR 366. See further Lord Justice Schiemann, *op. cit.*, at 143 *et seq.* and the discussion in de Smith, Woolf and Jowell, *Judicial Review of Administrative Action* (Sweet & Maxwell, 1995) pp. 897–899.
[34] A leading member of the English judiciary described extra-judicially the growing direct and indirect influence of Community law as 'eminently sensible'. See Schiemann LJ (as he then was), *op. cit.*, at 140.   [35] See e.g. *Carpenter*, *op. cit.*; *Akrich*, *op. cit.*

procrustean bed of *Karner* grants to the ECJ universal jurisdiction on fundamental rights.[36] Most importantly, the ECJ has elevated fundamental rights to core Community values accepting that their protection may take priority over free movement.[37] Finally, the ECJ is more prescriptive as to the standards of review. In an increasing number of preliminary references, it prefers to provide the referring court with a ready-made solution rather than defer to national standards of review. The outcome provided by the ECJ often upholds the national measure whose compatibility with Community law is contested. Thus, the Court provides leadership without necessarily stifling national choice.[38]

All in all, the ECJ continues to practise assertive constitutionalism except that nation building through economic integration has given way to nation building through fundamental rights. This has enhanced its role as the Supreme Court of the Union and, at the same time, brought it closer to the ECtHR and national constitutional courts. There is little doubt that the success of the ECJ in constructing the edifice of European law and attaining the constitutionalization of the Treaties owes much to the approval, encouragement and cooperation of national courts. As the Maastricht decisions of the German Constitutional Court[39] and the Danish Supreme Court[40] show, however, such cooperation cannot be equated with submission. Primacy means different things to different courts. The ECJ has the delicate task of embracing the national legal orders and addressing the sensitivities of the national supreme courts without endangering the fundamental principles of Union law. The case law has responded to that challenge. Judgments such as *Schmidberger* and *Omega Spielhallen*[41] show that the Court promotes an integration model based on value diversity which views national constitutional standards not as being in a competitive relationship with the economic objectives of the Union but as forming part of its polity. In that respect, general principles of law are not only an instrument for empowerment of supra-national government but also an instrument of legitimacy. The judgment of the ECtHR in *Bosphorus*[42] is an endorsement of the ECJ's enhanced presence in human rights and, as noted above, the approach of the Strasbourg Court resembles that of the German Constitutional court: it views the ECJ as an agent of its own standards which operates under a double conditional and reversible endorsement granted to it by the national courts and the ECtHR. Despite the fact that the case law of the ECJ and the ECtHR are not always in harmony, there can be no doubt that both courts share the same liberal underpinnings. They both understand democracy in the same way, namely not

---

[36] *Herbert Karner Industrie-Auktionen GmbH, op. cit.*

[37] See e.g. Case C-112/00 *Schmidberger, op. cit.*, n. 13; Case C-36/02 *Omega Spielhallen- und Automatenaufstellungs v Oberbürgermeisterin der Bundesstadt Bonn*, judgment of 14 October 2004; and in a different context: *Köbler v Austria op. cit.*, n. 7 above.

[38] See e.g. *Schmidberger, op. cit., Omega Spielhallen, op. cit.*; and in a different context: *Köbler v Austria, op. cit.*   [39] *Brunner* [1994] 1 CMLR 57.

[40] *Hanne Norup Carlsen and Others v the Prime Minister* [1999] 3 CML Rev 854.

[41] *Op. cit.*   [42] Judgment of 30 June 2005, application no. 45036/698.

merely as majoritarianism but as 'tolerance, pluralism, and broadmindedness'.[43] Democracy is not exhausted in ensuring that the wishes of the majority are respected but also that minorities are not oppressed. They adopt a pluralist vision of democracy which includes the right to be different. To be sure, the two courts share a substantive idea of the rule of law viewing the Convention and the EU Treaties not merely as procedural documents but as including also substantive standards of justice.

The second development outlined above is the formalization of Community law. This was examined in some detail in the first chapter and need not detain us for long here. As discussed, there has been an explosion of constitutional or legislative measures seeking to occupy fields hitherto left to the case law. This is a sign of maturity in the development of Community law, a further stage in the process of constitutionalization of the Treaties, which in fact enhances rather than weakens the role of the ECJ. The avowed objectives of the formalization process are to strengthen legitimacy and add legal certainty. The demise of the Constitution shows, however, that the legitimacy gap remains wide open and that citizens may suffer from treaty-fatigue.

The third development of recent years has been the increasing application of general principles to national measures. There has been a growth in the litigation concerning the application of principles, such as equality, proportionality, legitimate expectations, and fundamental rights to national measures which implement or fall within the scope of Community law. In general, the case law has failed to articulate objective criteria determining what types of national measures are reviewable on grounds of compatibility with the general principles. This is evident in particular from the judgment in *Karner* which appeared to depart from precedent.[44] Be this as it may, there is no doubt that the ECJ contributes to the establishment of a *jus communae*. More generally, the Court has understood its jurisdiction very broadly, viewing the national and the Community legal orders not as separate systems but as different tiers of the same legal order.[45] It extends its franchise by encouraging the application of Community norms even to situations which fall outside the scope of Community law, thus encouraging the indirect influence of Community law and the emergence of a *jus communae europeum*.[46]

[43] See e.g. *Smith and Grady v United Kingdom*, (2000) 29 EHRR 493, judgment of 27 September 1999, para 87.   [44] See the discussion above p. 335.

[45] A prime example of this is the duty of consistent interpretation laid down in Case C-106/89 *Marleasing* [1990] ECR I-4135. For more recent applications of the principle, see e.g. C-456/98 *Centrosteel Srl v Adipol GmbH*, [2000]; ECR I-6007 Joined Cases C-240 to C-244/98 *Océano Grupo Editorial SA v Rocío Murciano Quintero* and *Salvat Editores SA v Sánchez Alcón Prades and Copano Badillo*, [2000] ECR I-4941

[46] This is evident especially in the *Dzodzi* line of case law where the Court accepts jurisdiction under the preliminary reference procedure to interpret Community law where it applies not by virtue of the EC Treaty but by virtue of national law: See e.g. Joined Cases C-297/88 and C-197/89 *Dzodzi v Belgian State* [1990] ECR I-3763, and more recently, Case C-267/99 *Adam v Administration de l'enregistrement et des domaines*, judgment of 11 October 2001, Case C-1/99 *Kofisa Italia* [2001] ECR I-207.

A further trend which has been prevalent in the case law of the ECJ is a trend towards equivalence. This is to say that the Court increasingly subjects the Community institutions and the Member States to the same standards of scrutiny and accountability. This applies, in particular, to the liability in damages for breach of Community law[47] and also to some extent, to the fields of fundamental rights[48] and judicial review.[49] The Court, in other words, increasingly views supra-national and State agencies as being part of the same administration.

The final development identified is the trend towards selective deference. By this, it is meant that in some areas the Court of Justice is content to defer to choices made at national level, uphold the powers of the Member States, or leave matters to the national courts to decide. But in other areas, the Court is willing to provide leadership and dictate the results. This is best illustrated by reference to the case law on the protection of Community rights in national courts, where the following phases in the evolution of the case law were identified. To start with, the ECJ relied on national rules on procedure and remedies subject to the *Rewe* and *Comet* principles. This was followed by a phase of interventionism which reached its apex in the judgment in *Francovich* and the articulation of the conditions governing State liability in damages. In the 1990s, interventionism gave way to a more selective approach and the targeted use of judicial power, through corrective adjustments, such as the post-*Emmott* case law. In some respects, recent case law suggests a resurgence of interventionism. One aspect of it is the readiness on the part of the ECJ to go beyond the formal application of national law and examine the way it is applied in practice by the national administration and even the national courts with a view to establishing whether the protection of Community rights is truly effective in practice. This 'second level' enforcement is evidenced, for example, by the judgments in *Commission v Italy*,[50] and *Köbler v Austria*.[51] The trend of neo-interventionism is further illustrated by the derivation of subjective rights from obligations imposed on private parties,[52] and the tendency to go beyond the principle of equivalence by turning, in some areas, the discretion left by national law to national authorities into an obligation so as to enhance the protection of Community rights.[53] In other areas, however, the Court seems to defer to national standards.[54] Overall, it is submitted that the case law in this area is balanced, seeks to strike a compromise

---

[47] Case C-352/98P *Laboratoires Pharmaceutiques Bergaderm and Goupil v Commission* [2000] ECR I-5291.   [48] See *Schmidberger, op. cit.*, n. 13.

[49] See e.g. Case C-120/97 *Upjohn v Licensing Authority* [1999] ECR I-223.

[50] Case C-129/00 *Commission v Italy*, judgment of 9 December 2003.

[51] *Köbler v Austria, op. cit.*, discussed above, p. 521. For other cases illustrating this trend, see Case C-147/01 *Weber's Wine World Handels- GmbH*, judgment of 2 October 2003, paras 113–4; Case C-453/00 *Kühne & Heitz NV v Productschap voor Pluimvee en Eieren*, judgment of 13 January 2004.

[52] Case C-253/00 *Munoz Cia SA and Superior Fruiticola v Frumar Ltd and Redbridge Produce Marketing Ltd*, [2002] ECR I-7289.

[53] See the judgments in Joined Cases C-430 and C-431/93 *van Schijndel and van Veen v SPF* [1995] ECR I-4705 and *Kühne & Heitz NV, op. cit.*, discussed above, pp. 463 and 466, respectively.

[54] See *Safalero, op. cit.; Weber's Wine World, op. cit.*

between the need to ensure the effective protection of Community rights and respect for the autonomy of national legal systems.[55] The resulting uncertainty is an inevitable consequence of the fragmentary development of the law inherent in the process of judicial harmonization.

---

[55] *van Schijndel and van Veen, op. cit.*, at 4713 per Jacobs AG.

Bibliography

Adamovich, L., 'Marge d'appréciation du législateur et principe de proportionnalité dans l'appréciation des "restrictions prévues par la loi" au regard de la Convention européenne des droits de l'homme', (1991) R Trim Dr Homme, 291

Alexander, W., 'Perte de la caution en droit agricole communautaire', (1988) CDE 384

Allan, T.R.S., *The Limits of Parliamentary Sovereignty*, (Oxford: Oxford University Press, 1985) PL 614

——, *Law, Liberty and Justice* (Oxford: Oxford University Press, 1993)

Alston, P., (ed.), *The EU and Human Rights*, (Oxford University Press, 1999)

Anagnostaras, G., 'The Principle of State Liability for Judicial Breaches: The Impact of European Community Law', (2001) 7 European Public Law 281

——, 'State Liability and Alternative Courses of Action: How Independent Can an Autonomous Remedy Be?' (2002) 21 YEL 355

Anderas, A. and Jacobs, F.G. (eds), *European Community Law in the English Courts* (Oxford University Press, 1998)

Arnull, A., 'Does the Court of Justice have inherent jurisdiction?', (1990) 27 CML Rev 683

——, *The General Principles of EEC Law and the Individual* (Leicester: Leicester University Press, 1990)

——, 'Opinion 2/94 and its Implications for the future Constitution of the Union', (Cambridge, Centre for European Legal Studies, 1996)

——, 'Liability for Legislative Acts under Article 215(2) EC' in Heukels, T. and McDonnell, A. (eds), *The Action for Damages in Community Law* (The Hague: Kluwer, 1997)

——, *The European Union and its Court of Justice* (Oxford: Oxford University Press, 1999)

Association européenne des avocats, Colloquim of 24/25 January 1994, 'Droits de la défense et droits de la Commission dans le droit communautaire de la concurrence' (Brussels: Bruylant, 1994)

Aziz, M., 'Sovereignty Lost, Sovereignty Regained? Some Reflections on the Bundesverfassungsgericht's Bananas Judgment' 9 (2002) Columbia Journal of European Law 109

Barents, R., *The Agricultural Law of the EC* (Kluwer, 1994)

Barnard, C., '*P v S*: Kite Flying or a New Constitutional Approach?' in A. Dashwood and S. O'Leary, *The Principle of Equal Treatment in E.C. Law* (London: Sweet & Maxwell, 1997)

Barnard, C., 'The Principle of Equality in the Community Context: *P, Grant, Kalanke,* and *Marschall*: Four Uneasy Bedfellows?', (1998) CLJ 352

——, *EC Employment Law,* 2nd Ed, (Oxford University Press, 2000)

——, 'Fitting the Remaining Pieces into the Goods and Services Jigsaw?' (2001) 26 ELR 35

——, *The Substantive Law of the EU: The Four Freedoms* (Oxford University Press, 2004)

Barrett, G., 'Protecting Legitimate Expectations in European Community Law and in Domestic Irish Law', (2001) 20 YEL 191

——, 'Re-examining the Concept and Principle of Equality in EC Law', 22 (2003) YEL 117

Beatson, J. and Tridimas, T. (eds), *New Directions in European Public Law,* (Oxford: Hart Publishing, 1998)

Bell, M., 'The New Article 13 EC Treaty: A Sound Basis for European Anti-Discrimination Law?' (1999) 6 Maastricht Journal of Eur. Comp. Law, 9

——, *Anti-Discrimination Law and the EU* (Oxford: Oxford University Press, 2002)

——, 'Beyond European Labour Law? Reflections on the EU Racial Equality Directive', (2002) 8 ELJ 384

Bercusson, B., *European Labour Law* (London, Butterworths, 1996)

Bermann, G., 'Competences of the Union' in Tridimas, T. and Nebbia, P. (eds), *EU Law for the 21st Century: Rethinking the New Legal Order* (Oxford: Hart Publishing, 2004) Vol. 1

Bernard, N., 'Discrimination and Free Movement in EC Law', (1996) 45 ICLQ 82

Bernitz, U. and Nergelius, J. (eds), *General Principles of European Community Law* (Kluwer, 2000)

Biondi, A., 'The European Court of Justice and Certain National Procedural Limitations: Not Such a Tough Relationship' 36 (1999) CML Rev 1271

Boulois, B.J., *Droit Institutionnel des Communautés Européennes* 4th Ed (Paris: Montcherstein, 1993)

Boyron, S., 'Proportionality in English Administrative Law: A Faulty Translation?' (1992) 12 OJLS 237

Braun, A., 'Les droits de la défense devant la Commission et la Cour de justice des Communautés européennes', 141 (1980) IRCL 2

Brennan, F., 'The Race Directive, Institutional Racism and Third Country Nationals' in Tridimas, T. and Nebbia, P. *European Union Law for the Twenty-first Century: Rethinking the New Legal Order,* Volume 2, (Oxford: Hart Publishing, 2004) 371–386

——, 'The Race Directive: Recycling Racial Equality', (2004) Cambridge Yearbook of European Legal Studies 311

Brown, N., 'The First Five Years of the Court of First Instance and Appeals to the Court of Justice: Assessment and Statistics', (1995) 32 CML Rev 743

Brown, L. Neville & Jacobs, F.G., *The Court of Justice of the European Communities,* 5th Ed. (by Brown, L. Neville and Kennedy, T.) (London: Sweet & Maxwell, 2000).

Brownlie, I., *Principles of Public International Law*, Fourth Ed. (Oxford: Oxford University Press, 1990)

Campbell-White, F., 'Property rights: A Forgotten Issue under the Union' in Neuwahl, N. and Rosas, A. (eds), *The European Union and Human Rights* (The Hague: Kluwer, 1995), 249–263

Caranta, R., 'Judicial Protection Against Member States: A New *Jus Commune* Takes Shape', (1997) CML Rev 703

Carey, N., 'From Obloquy to Equality: In the Shadow of Abnormal Situations', (2001) 20 YEL 79

Cassese, A., Clapham, A., and Weiler, J. (eds), *Human Rights and the European Community*, Vols II–III, (Nomos: 1991)

Casteren, van A., 'Article 215(2) and the Question of Interest' in Heukels, T. and McDonnell A. (eds), *The Action for Damages in a Community Law Perspective*, (The Hague: Kluwer, 1997)

Centre for European Legal Studies, (several authors), 'The Human Rights Opinion of the ECJ and its Constitutional Implications', CELS Occasional Paper No. 1, University of Cambridge, 1996

Chalmers, D., 'Repackaging the internal market: the ramifications of the *Keck* judgment', (1994) 19 ELR 385

Clapham, A., 'A Human Rights Policy for the European Community' (1990) 10 YEL 309

——, *Human Rights in the Private Sphere* (Oxford University Press, 1993)

Constantinesco, V., Kovar, R., Simon, D., *Traité sur l'Union Européenne*, Economica, 1995

Cooke, Sir Robin, 'The Struggle for Simplicity in Administrative Law' in M. Taggart (ed), *Judicial Review of Administrative Action in the 1980s* (Oxford: Oxford University Press, 1986)

Coppel, J. and O'Neill, A., 'The European Court of Justice: Taking Rights Seriously', 29 (1992) CML Rev 669

Cotterell, R., 'Judicial Review and Legal Theory' in Richardson, G. and Genn, H. (eds), *Administrative Law and Government Action*, (Oxford: Oxford University Press, 1994) 13–34

Craig, P., 'Legitimate Expectations: A Conceptual Analysis', (1992) 108 LQR 79

——, '*Francovich*, Remedies and the Scope of Damages Liability' (1993) 109 LQR 595

——, 'Substantive Legitimate Expectations in Domestic and Community Law', (1996) 55 CLJ 289

——, 'Once More unto the Breach: The Community, the State and Damages Liability', (1997) 113 LQR 67

——, *Administrative Law* 5th Ed., (London: Sweet & Maxwell, 2003)

Craig, P. and de Burca, G. (eds), *The Evolution of EU Law*, (Oxford University Press, 1998)

——, *EU Law, Text, Cases, and Materials*, 3rd Ed, (Oxford University Press, 2002)

Craig, P., and Schonberg, S., 'Substantive Legitimate Expectations after *Coughlan*' [2000] PL 684

Curtin, D., 'The Decentralised Enforcement of Community Law Rights. Judicial Snakes and Ladders', in D. Curtin and D. O'Keeffe, *Constitutional Adjudication in European Community and National Law* (London: Butterworths, 1992)

——, 'The Constitutional Structure of the Union: A Europe of Bits and Pieces', (1993) 30 CML Rev 17

——, and Heukels, T. (eds), *Institutional Dynamics of European Integration, Essays in Honour of H.G. Schermers* (Vols I–III) (The Hague: Kluwer, 1998)

da Cruz Vilaca, J. L., 'The Precautionary Principle in EC Law', (2004) 10 EPL 369

Dallen, R.M., Jr, 'An Overview of European Community Protection of Human Rights, with some special references to the UK' (1990) 27 CML Rev 761

Daniele, L., 'Non-Discriminatory Restrictions to the Free Movement of Persons', (1997) 22 ELR 191

Dashwood, A., 'The Limits of European Community Powers', (1996) 21 ELR 113 at 114

——, and O'Leary, S. (eds), *The Principle of Equal Treatment in E.C. Law*, (London: Sweet & Maxwell, 1997)

——, 'Non-Discriminatory Restrictions After *Keck*' (2002) 61 CLJ 35

Dauses, M., 'The Protection of Human Rights in the Community Legal Order', (1985) ELR 398

de Bùrca, G., 'Fundamental Human Rights and the Reach of European Law', (1992) 13 OJLS 283

——, 'The Principle of Proportionality and its Application in EC Law', (1993) 13 YEL 105

——, 'The Language of Rights in European Integration', in Shaw, J. and More, G. (eds), *New Legal Dynamics of European Union* (Oxford: Oxford University Press, 1995)

——, 'The Drafting of the European Union Charter of Fundamental Rights', (2001) 26 ELR 126

de la Sierra, S., 'Provisional Court Protection in Administrative Disputes in Europe: The Constitutional Status of Interim Measures Deriving from the Right to Effective Court Protection. A Comparative Approach', (2004) 10 ELJ 42

de Smith, S., Woolf, H. and Jowell, J., *Judicial Review of Administrative Action*, 5th Ed., (London: Sweet & Maxwell, 1995) p. 833

——, Woolf L. J. and Jowell, J., *Judicial Review of Administrative Action* (London: Sweet & Maxwell, 1995)

Dicey, A.V., *The Law of the Constitution* 10th Ed., (London: Macmillan, 1959)

Dougan, M., *National Remedies Before the European Court of Justice*, (Oxford: Hart Publishing, 2004)

——, 'What is the Point of *Francovich*?' In Tridimas T. and Nebbia P., *European Union Law for the 21st Century: Rethinking the new legal order* (Oxford: Hart Publishing, 2004)

Downes, T., 'Trawling for a Remedy: State Liability under Community Law', (1997) 17 LS 286

Drzemczewski, A., 'The Domestic Application of the European Human Rights Convention as European Community Law', (1981) 30 ICLQ 118

Due, O., 'Le respect des droits de la défense dans le droit administratif communautaire', [1987] CDE 383

Duparc, C., *The European Community and Human Rights* (EC Commission, 1992)

Dworkin, R., *Taking Rights Seriously* (London: Duckworth, 1994)

EC Bulletin, 'The Development and future of the Common Agricultural Policy', Suppl. 5/91

Eeckhout, P., 'Liability of Member States in Damages and the Community System of Remedies', in Beatson, J. and Tridimas, T. (eds), *New Directions in European Public Law*, (Oxford: Hart Publishing, 1998)

——, 'The EU Charter of Fundamental Rights and the Federal Question', 39 (2002) CML Rev 945

Egger, A., 'The Principle of Proportionality in Community Anti-Dumping Law', (1993) 18 ELR 367

Ehlermann, C.D. and Drijber, B.J., 'Legal Protection of Enterprises: Administrative Procedure, in particular Access to File and Confidentiality' (1996) ECLR 375

Elias, P., 'Legitimate Expectation and Judicial Review' in Jowell, J. and Oliver, D. (eds), *New Directions on Judicial Review*, CLP Special Issue, 1988

Ellis, E., *European Community Sex Equality Law*, 2nd Ed., (Oxford University Press, 1998)

Emiliou, N., Case notes in (1996) 21 ELR 399

——, *The Principle of Proportionality in European Law* (Kluwer, 1996)

Enchelmaier, S., 'The Awkward Selling of a New Idea', (2003) YEL

Fairgrieve, D., Andenas, M. and Bell, J. (eds), *Tort Liability of Public Authorities in Comparative Perspective* (London: BIICL, 2002)

Faull, J., 'Legal Professional Privilege (*AM & S*): The Commission Proposes International Negotiations', 10 (1985) ELR 119

Feldman D., (ed.), *English Public Law* (Oxford: Oxford University Press, 2003)

Fitzmaurice, Sir Gerald, 'The General Principles of International Law' (1957) 92 Collected Courses of the Hague Academy of International Law

Flynn, L., 'The Implications of Article 13—After Amsterdam, Will Some Forms of Discrimination Be More Equal than Others?' (1999) 36 CML Rev 1132

Forrester, I.S., 'Legal Professional Privilege: Limitations on the Commission's Powers of Inspection Following the *AM & S* Judgment', (1983) 20 CMLR 75

Forsyth, C., 'The Provenance and Protection of Legitimate Expectations', (1988) 47 CLJ 238

——, '*Wednesbury* Protection of Substantive Legitimate Expectations', [1997] PL 375

Fredman, S., 'Combating Racism with Human Rights: the Right to Equality' in Fredman, S. (ed.), *Discrimination and Human Rights*, (Oxford University Press, 2001)

Fredman, S. (ed.), *Discrimination and Human Rights—The Case of Racism* (Oxford University Press, 2001)

Fuss, E-W., 'La responsabilité des Communautés européennes pour le comportement illégal de leurs organes', 1981 RTDE 1

Gaja, G., Comment in (1996) 33 CML Rev 973

Galmot, Y., 'L'apport des principes généraux du droit communautaire à la garantie des droits dans l'ordre juridique français' (1997) 33 CDE 67

Goffin, L., 'La jurisprudence de la Cour de justice sur les droits de défense', 16 (1980) CDE 127

Gormley, L., 'Reasoning renounced? The remarkable judgment in *Keck and Mithouard*' [1994] Eur Bus L Rev 63

Gravells, N., Case notes in (1996) PL 567

Greaves, R., 'Advertising Restrictions and the free Movement of Goods and Services', (1998) 23 ELR 305

Greenawalt, K., 'How Empty is the Idea of Equality?' (1983) 83 Columbia Law Review 1186

Grief, N., Comment in [1991] PL 555

Grondman, F., 'La Notion de violation suffisamment caractérisée en matière de responsabilité non contractuelle', 1979 CDE, No 1

Groussot, X., *Creation, Development and Impact of the General Principles of Community Law: Towards a jus commune europeum?* (Lund, Sweden: Lund University Press, 2005)

Guerrin, M. and Kyriazis, G., 'Cartels: Proof and Procedural Issues' (1993) 16 Fordham International Law Journal, 266

Hall, S., 'Loss of Union Citizenship in Breach of Fundamental Rights' (1996) 21 ELR 129

Hamson, C., *Executive Discretion and Judicial Control* (Stevens, 1954)

Harlow, C., 'Codification of EC Administrative Procedures? Fitting the Foot to the Shoe or the Shoe to the Foot', (1996) 2 ELJ 3

——, 'Francovich and the Problem of the Disobedient State', (1996) 2 EurLJ 199

——, 'Back to Basics: Reinventing Administrative Law' (1997) PL 245

Harris, D.J., O'Boyle, M., and Warbrick, C., *Law of the European Convention on Human Rights* (London: Butterworths, 1995)

Hart Ely, J., *Democracy and Distrust* (Boston: Harvard University Press, 1980)

Hartley, T.C., 'The European Court and the EEA', (1992) 41 ICLQ 841

——, *The Foundations of European Community Law*, 5th Ed., (Oxford, 1994)

——, *The Foundations of European Community Law* (5th Ed.), (Oxford: Oxford University Press, 2003).

Herdegen, M., 'The Origins and Development of the General Principles of Community Law' in Bernitz, U. and Nergelius, J. (eds), *General Principles of European Community Law* (Kluwer, 2000)

Heukels, T., Comment on *Peter broeek* and *van Schijndel*, in (1996) 33 CML Rev 337

——, and McDonnell, A. (eds), *The Action for Damages in Community Law* (The Hague: Kluwer, 1997)

Hilson, C., 'Discrimination in Community Free Movement', (1999) 24 ELR 445

Himsworth, C., 'Things Fall Apart: The Harmonization of Community Judicial Procedural Protection Revisited', (1997) 22 ELR 291

Høegh, K., 'The Danish Maastricht Judgment' (1999) 24 ELR 80

Hoskins, M., 'Tilting the Balance: Supremacy and National Procedural Rules', (1996) 21 ELR 365

——, 'Rebirth of the Innominate Tort?' in Beatson, J. and Tridimas, T., (eds), *New Directions in European Public Law*, (Oxford: Hart Publishing, 1998)

Issac, G., *Droit Communautaire Général*, 3rd Ed., (Masson, 1992)

Jachtenfuchs, M., 'Theoretical Perspectives on European Governance', (1995) 1 ELJ 115

Jackson, J.H., *The World Trading System* (Boston: MIT Press, 1989)

Jacobs, F.G., (ed.), *European Law and the Individual* (Oxford University Press, 1976)

——, 'Human Rights in Europe: New Dimensions' (1992) 3 King's College Law Journal 49

——, 'European Community Law and the European Convention of Human Rights' in Curtin, D. and Heukels, T. (eds), *Institutional Dynamics of European Integration, Essays in Honour of H.G. Schermers* Vol. II, (The Hague: Kluwer, 1998)

Jarvis, M., *The Application of EC Law by National Courts: The Free Movement of Goods* (Oxford University Press, 1998)

Joliet, R., 'La Libre Circulation des Merchandises: L'arrêt *Keck et Mithouard* et les nouvelles orientations de la jurisprudence', (1994) Journal des tribunaux, *Droit Européen*, 145

Jones, A. and Sufrin, B., *EC Competition Law, Text, Cases and Material* (2nd Ed.), (Oxford: Oxford University Press, 2004)

Joshua, J.M., 'Balancing the Public Interests: Confidentiality, Trade Secrets and Disclosure of Evidence in EC Competition Procedures', (1994) 2 ECLR 68

Jowell, J., 'Is Equality a Constitutional Principle?'(1994) 47 CLP 1

——, and Lester, A., 'Proportionality: neither novel nor dangerous' in (1988) CLP Special Issue, *New Directions in Judicial Review*, 51

Jowell, J. and Oliver, P. (eds), *New Directions on Judicial Review*, CLP Special Issue, 1988

Kakouris, C., 'Do the Member States possess judicial procedural autonomy?', (1997) 34 CML Rev 1389

Kapteyn, P.J.G. and Verloren van Themaat, P., *Introduction to the Law of the European Communities,* 3rd Ed., (The Hague: Kluwer, 1998)

Karst, K., 'Why Equality Matters', (1983) Ga L Rev 245

Kerse, C.S., 'The Complainant in Competition Cases: A Progress Report', (1997) 34 CML Rev 213

Kerse, C.S., and Khan, N., *EC Anti-Trust Procedures*, 5th Ed., (London: Sweet & Maxwell, 2004)

Komninos, A.P., Comment on *Eco Swiss China Time*, in (2000) 37 CML Rev 459

Koopmans, T., 'The Birth of European Law at the Crossroads of Legal Traditions', (1991) 39 AJCL 493

Koopmans, T., 'Comparative Law and the Courts', (1996) 45 ICLQ 545

Korah, V., 'The Rights of the Defence in Administrative Proceedings Under Community Law' (1980) 33 CLP 73

——, *EC Competition Law and Practice*, 7th Ed., (Oxford: Hart Publishing, 2000)

Koutrakos, P., 'On Groceries, Alcohol and Olive Oil; More on Free Movement of Goods after *Keck*', (2001) 26 ELR 391

Kremer, C., 'Liability for Breach of European Community Law: An Analysis of the new Remedy in the Light of English and German Law', (2003) 22 YEL 203

Krogsgaard, L.B., 'Fundamental Rights in the European Community after Maastricht' (1993) LIEI 99

Kvjatkovski, V., 'What is an "Emanation of the State"? An Educated Guess', (1997) 3 EPL 329

Lamoureux, F., 'The Retroactivity of Community Acts in the Case Law of the Court of Justice', (1983) 20 CML Rev 269

Lasok, K.P.E., 'The Privilege Against Self-incrimination in Competition Cases', (1990) II ECLR 90

Law Commission, Consultation Paper No. 126

Lee, P., 'The Irish Report', 17th FIDE Congress, Vol. III, Berlin, 1996, pp. 204–248

Lenaerts, K, *Le Juge et la Constitution aux États-Unis d'Amérique et dans l'Ordre Juridique Européen*, 1988

——, 'Fundamental Rights to be Included in a Community Catalogue', (1991) 16 ELR 367

——, 'L'Egalité de Traitement en Droit Communautaire', (1991) 27 CDE 3

——, 'General Report', in 'Procedures and Sanctions in Economic Administrative Law' 17th FIDE Congress, Vol. III, Berlin 1996

——, 'Respect for Fundamental Rights as a Constitutional Principle of the European Union', 6 (2000) Columbia Journal of European Law 1

——, and Arts, D., *Procedural Law of the European Union* (London: Sweet & Maxwell, 1999)

——, and Corthaut, T., 'Judicial Review as a Contribution to the Development of European Constitutionalism' in Tridimas, T. and Nebbia, P., *European Union Law for the Twenty-first century: Rethinking the New Legal Order*, volume 1, (Oxford: Hart Publishing, 2004) pp. 17–64

——, and de Smijter, E., 'A "Bill of Rights" for the European Union', (2001) 38 CML Rev 273

——, and van Ypersele, P., 'Le principe de subsidiarité et son contexte: Étude de l'article 3B du traité CE' (1994) 30 CDE 3

——, and Vanhamme, J., 'Procedural Rights of Private Parties in the Community Administrative Process', 34 (1997) CML Rev 531

Levitt, M., 'Access to the File: The Commission's Administrative Procedures in Cases under Articles 85 and 86' (1997) 34 CML Rev 1413

Lewis, C., Remedies and the Enforcement of European Community Law, (London: Sweet & Maxwell, 1996)

——, and Moore, S., 'Duties, Directives and Damages in European Community Law', (1993) PL 151

Livingstone, S., 'Article 14 and the Prevention of Discrimination in the ECHR' (1997) European Human Rights Law Review 25

Mancini, G.F. and Keeling, D.T., 'Democracy and the European Court of Justice' (1994) 57 MLR 175 at 187

Manolkidis, S., Granting Benefits through Constitutional Adjudication, (Thessaloniki, Sakkoulas Press, 1999)

Markezinis, B.S., The Gradual Convergence: Foreign Ideas, Foreign Influences and English Law on the Eve of the 21st Century, (Oxford: Oxford University Press, 1994)

Matscher, F. and Petzold, H., (eds), Protecting Human Rights: The European Dimension: Studies in Honour of Gerard J. Wiarda (Köln: Carl Heymanns Verlag, 1988)

McBride, J. and Brown, L.N., 'The United Kingdom, The European Community and the European Convention on Human Rights' (1981) 1 YEL 167

McCrudden, C. (ed), Women, Employment and European Equality Law, (Eclipse, 1987)

——, 'Equality and Discrimination' in Feldman, D. (ed.), English Public Law (Oxford: Oxford University Press, 2003)

——, 'The New Concept of Equality', paper presented in the Conference on 'Fight Against Discrimination: The Race and Framework Employment Directives', Trier, 31 March–1 April 2003

McKean, W., Equality and Discrimination under International Law (Oxford: Oxford University Press, 1983), p. 283

Mendelson, M.H., 'The European Court of Justice and Human Rights', (1981) 1 YEL 125

Mendelson, M.H., 'The Impact of European Community Law on the Implementation of the European Convention on Human Rights', (1983) 3 YEL 99

Millns, S., 'Bio-Rights, Common Values and Constitutional Strategies' in Tridimas, T. and Nebbia, P. (eds), EU Law for the 21st Century, Vol II, 387–402 (Oxford: Hart Publishing, 2004)

Moore, S., 'Nothing Positive from the Court of Justice', (1996) 21 ELR 156.

More, G., 'The Principle of Equal Treatment: From Market Unifier to Fundamental Right?' in Craig, P. and de Burca, G. (eds), The Evolution of EU Law (Oxford: Oxford University Press, 1999)

Mortelmans, K., 'Article 30 of the EEC Treaty and Legislation relating to Market Circumstances: Time to Consider a New Definition', (1991) 28 CML Rev 115

Neil, Sir Patrick, QC, 'The European Court of Justice: a Case Study in Judicial Activism', Evidence submitted to the House of Lords Select Committee on the European Communities, Sub-committee on the 1996 Inter Governmental Conference, *1996 Inter Governmental Conference, Minutes of Evidence, House of Lords, Session 1994–95, 18th Report*

Neri, S., 'Le principe de proportionnalité dans la jurisprudence de la Cour relative au droit communautaire agricole', (1981) 17 RTDE 652

Neuwahl, N. and Rosas, A. (eds), *The European Union and Human Rights* (The Hague: Martinus Nijhoff, 1995)

Neville Brown, L., 'State Liability to Individuals in Damages: An Emerging Doctrine of EU Law', (1996) 31 IrJur7

Nolte, G., 'General Principles of German and European Administrative Law—A comparison in Historical Perspective', (1994) 57 MLR 191

O'Keeffe, D. and Bavasso, A., 'Four Freedoms, One Market and National Competence: In search of a Dividing Line', in O'Keeffe and Bavasso (eds), *Judicial Review in European Union Law, Liber Amicorum in Honour of Lord Slynn* (The Hague: Kluwer, 2000), 554

O'Leary, S., 'Aspects of the Relationship between Community Law and National Law' in Neuwahl, N. and Rosas, A. (eds), *The European Union and Human Rights*, (The Hague: Martinus Nijhoff, 1995)

Oliver, P., 'Enforcing Community Rights in the English Courts', (1987) 50 MLR 881 at 889

——, 'State Liability in Damages Following Factortame III: A Remedy Seen in Context', in Beatson, J. and Tridimas, T. (eds), *New Directions in European Public Law*, (Oxford: Hart Publishing, 1998) 49

——, 'Some Further Reflections on the Scope of Articles 28–10 EC', (1999) 36 CML Rev 783

——, and Jarvis, M., *Free Movement of Goods in the European Community*, 4th Ed., (London: Sweet & Maxwell, 2002)

Olowofoyeku, A., *Suing Judges*, (Oxford University Press, 1993)

Ovey, C., Jacobs, F. G. and White, C. A., *The European Convention on Human Rights* (3rd edition) (Oxford University Press, 2002)

Papadopoulou, L., 'Indivisible Citizenship: Same Sex Partners in European Union Immigration Law' (2002) 21 YEL 229

Papadopoulou, R.E, *Principes Généraux du Droit et Droit Communautaire* (Bruylant, 1996)

Peers, S., 'Who's Judging the Watchmen? The Judicial System of the "Area of Freedom Security and Justice"', 18 (1998) YEL 337, at 376

——, and Ward, A., *The Charter of Fundamental Rights and the Future of Human Rights Protection in Europe* (Oxford: Hart Publishing, 2004)

Pernice, I., 'Integrating the Charter of Fundamental Rights into the Constitution of the European Union: Practical and Theoretcial Propositions', (2003) 10 Columbia Journal of European Law 5

Pescatore, P., 'Les objectifs de la CEE comme principes d'interprétation dans la jurisprudence de la Cour de justice', in *Miscellanea Ganshof van der Meersch*, (Brussels, Bruylant, 1972) II

——, 'La Cour de justice des Communautés européennes et la Convention européenne des droits de l'Homme', in Matscher and Petzold (eds), *Protecting Human Rights and Freedoms: The European Dimension* (1988)

Pfander, J. E. , 'Member State Liability and Constitutional Change in the United States and Europe', (2003) 51 Am J Comp Law 237

Picheral, C. and Olinga, A.D., 'La théorie de la marge d'appréciation dans la jurisprudence récente de la Cour européenne des droits de l'homme', (1995) R.Trim Dr. Homme 567

Plender, R., 'Equality and Non-discrimination in the Law of the European Union', (1995) 7 Pace Internl. L R. 57

Poiares Maduro, M., '*Keck*: the end? Or just the end of the beginning?' (1994) Irish Journal of European Law 33

——, 'Reforming the Market or the State? Article 30 and the European Constitution: Economic Freedom and Political Rights', (1997) 3 ELJ 55

——, *We, the Court: The European Court of Justice and the European Economic Constitution* (Oxford: Hart Publishing, 1998)

Posner, R.A., *The Problems of Jurisprudence*, (Boston: Harvard University Press, 1990)

——, *The Federal Courts: Challenge and Reform* (Boston: Harvard University Press, 1999)

Posner, R., *Law and Legal Theory in the UK and the USA* (Oxford University Press, 1996)

Presidency Conclusions, European Council of Edinburgh (11–12 December 1992), Annex to Part 1 A (Agence Europe, Special Ed., No. 5878 BIS, 13/14 December 1992)

Prechal, S. and Burrows, N., *Gender Discrimination Law of The European Community* (Dartmouth, 1990)

Raitio, J., *The Principle of Legal Certainty in EC Law* (The Hague: Kluwer, 2003)

Rasmussen, H., *On Law and Policy in the European Court of Justice*, (The Hague: Martinus Nijholf, 1986)

——, 'Confrontation or Peaceful Coexistence? On the Danish Supreme Court's Maastricht Ratification Judgment' in O'Keeffe, D. and Bavasso, A. (eds), *Judicial Review in European Union Law. Liber Amicorum in Honour of Lord Slynn* (The Hague: Kluwer, 2000), 377–390

Rawls, J., *A Theory of Justice* (Oxford: Clarendon Press, 1972)

Reich, N., 'The "November Revolution" of the European Court of Justice', (1994) 31 CML Rev 459

Richardson, G. and Genn, H. (eds), *Administrative Law and Government Action*, (Oxford: Oxford University Press, 1994)

Roth, P., Bellamy, C. and Child G., *Common Market Law of Competition*, 5th Ed., (London: Sweet & Maxwell, 2001)

Ruffert, M., 'Rights and Remedies in European Community Law: A Comparative View', (1997) 34 CML Rev 307

Sauter, W., *Competition Law and Industrial Policy in the EU* (Oxford University Press, 1997)

Schermers, H.G., 'The Communities Under the European Convention on Human Rights' (1978) 1 LIEI 1

——, 'The European Community Bound by Fundamental Human Rights' (1990) 27 CML Rev 249

——, 'The Eleventh Protocol to the European Convention on Human Rights' (1994) 19 ELR 367

——, and Waelbroeck, D., *Judicial Protection in the European Union* (6th Ed) (The Hague: Kluwer, 2001)

Schiemann, Lord Justice, 'The Application of General Principles of Community Law by English Courts', in Andenas, A. and Jacobs, F.G., *European Community Law in the English Courts*, (Oxford: Oxford University Press, 1998) 136–148

Schonberg, S., 'Legal Certainty and Revocation of Administrative Decisions: A Comparative Study of English, French, and EC Law' (1999–2000) 19 YEL 257

Schwarze, J., *European Administrative Law*, (London: Sweet & Maxwell, 1992)

——, *European Influences in Administrative Law*, (London, Sweet & Maxwell, 1998)

Shapiro, M., 'The Giving Reasons Requirement', in *The University of Chicago Legal Forum: Europe and America in 1992 and Beyond: Common Problems . . . Common Solutions?* (Chicago: University of Chicago Press, 1992), 179

——, 'Codification of Administrative Law: The US and the Union', (1996) 2 ELJ 26

Sharpston, E., 'Legitimate Expectations and Economic Reality', (1990) 15 ELR 103

Shaw, J. and More, G. (eds), *New Legal Dynamics of European Union*, (Oxford: Oxford University Press, 1995)

Shiubhne, N., 'The Free Movement of Goods and Article 28 EC: An Evolving Framework', (2002) 27 ELR 35

Simon, D., 'Y a-t-il des principes généraux du droit communautaire?', (1991) 14 *Droits*, 73

Slot, P.J., Comment in (1991) 28 CML Rev 978

Snell, J., *Goods and Services in EC Law* (Oxford University Press, 2002)

——, 'Who's got the Power? Free Movement and Allocation of Competences in EC Law', (2003) 22 YEL 323

Soulier, G., *L'Europe*, (Paris: Armand Colin, 1994)

Spielmann, D., *L'effet potentiel de la Convention européenne des droits de l'homme entre personnes privées* (Brussels: Bruylant, 1995)

Steiner, J., 'From Direct effects to *Francovich*: shifting means of enforcement of Community law', (1993) 18 ELR 3

Strozzi, G., 'Le principe de subsidiarité dans la perspective de l'intégration européenne: une énigme et beaucoup d'attentes', (1994) 30 RTDE 373

Sunstein, C.R., *Legal Reasoning and Political Conflict* (Oxford University Press, 1996)

Szyszczak, E., 'Making Europe More Relevant To Its Citizens: Effective Judicial Process', (1996) 21 ELR 351

——, *EC Labour Law* (London: Longman, 2000)

Taggart, M., (ed.), *Judicial Review of Administrative Action in the 1980s* (Oxford: Oxford University Press, 1986)

Thirlway, H., 'The Law and Procedure of the International Court of Justice 1960–1989', (1990) 61 BYIL 1

Timmermans, C., 'The Constitutionalisation of the European Union', (2002) 21 YEL 1

Tomuschat, C., 'Le principe de proportionnalité: *Quis iudicabit?*' (1977) 13 CDE 97

Toner, H., 'Thinking the Unthinkable? State Liability for Judicial Acts after *Factortame* (III)', (1997) 17 YEL 165

——, 'Non-Discriminatory Obstacles to the Exercise of Treaty-rights: Articles 39, 43, 49 and 18', (2004) 23 YEL 275

Toth, A.G., *The Oxford Encyclopaedia of European Community Law* (Oxford University Press, 1990)

Trachtman, J.P., 'L'Etat, C'est Nous: Sovereignty, Economic Integration and Subsidiarity', (1992) 33 *Harvard International Law Journal* 459

Triantafyllou, D., *La Constitution de l'Union européenne*, (Brussels: Bruylant 2005)

Tridimas, G. and Tridimas, T., 'The European Court of Justice and the Annulment of the Tobacco Advertisement Directive: Friend of National Sovereignty or Foe of Public Health?' (2002) 14 European Journal of Law and Economics 171

Tridimas, T., 'The European Court of Justice and Judicial Activism', (1996) 21 ELR 199

——, 'The Principle of Proportionality in Community Law: From the Rule of Law to Market Integration', (1996) 31 The Irish Jurist, 83

——, 'The Role of the Advocate General in the Development of Community Law: Some Reflections' (1997) 34 CML Rev 1349

——, 'Enforcing Community Rights in National Courts: Some recent Developments', in O'keeffe and Bavasso, (eds), *Judicial Review in European Union Law: Liber Amicorum inhonour of Lord Slynn* (Kluwer, 2000) 405

——, 'Judicial Review and the Community Judicature: Towards a New European Constitutionalism?' (2001) 3 Turku Law Journal 119

——, 'Liability for Breach of Community Law: Growing Up and Mellowing Down?', (2001) 38 CML Rev 301

Tridimas, T., Hart 'Knocking on Heaven's Door: Fragmentation, Efficiency and Defiance in the Preliminary Reference Procedure', 40 (2003) CML Rev 1

———, 'The European Court of Justice and the Draft Constitution: A Supreme Court for the Union?', in Tridimas, T. and Nebbia, P. (eds): *EU Law for the 21st century: Rethinking the New Legal Order*' (Oxford: Hart Publishing, 2004) 113

———, 'The European Court of Justice and Judicial Federalism' in Markezinis, B. S. and Fedtke J., (ed.), *Patterns of Federalism and Regionalism: Lessons for the UK* (Oxford: Hart Publishing, 2006) 149

———, and Eeckhout, P., 'The External Competence of the Community and the Case-Law of the Court of Justice: Principle versus Pragmatism', (1994) 14 YEL 143

Turner, C., and Munoz, R., 'Revisiting the Judicial Architecture of the European Union', (1999–2000) 19 YEL 1

Usher, J. A., *General Principles of EC Law* (Longmans, 1998)

van den Berghe, F., 'The European Union and the Protection of Minorities: How Real is the Alleged Double Standard?', (2003) 22 YEL 155

van den Bogaer, S., 'Horizontality: Rowing with Square or Feathered Blades?', paper delivered in the conference on 'Unpacking the Internal Market', organised in CELS, Cambridge, 2001

van der Woude, M.H., 'Liability for Administrative Acts under Article 215(2) EC' in Heukels, T. and McDonnell, A. (eds), *The Action For Damages in Community Law* (The Hague: Kluwer, 1997)

van Gerven, W., 'Non-Contractual Liability of Member States, Community Institutions and Individuals for Breaches of Community Law with a View to Common Law for Europe', (1994) 1 MJ 6

———, 'Bridging the Gap Between Community and National Laws: Towards a Principle of Homogeneity in the Field of Legal Remedies?' (1995) 32 CML Rev 679

———, 'Bridging the Unbridgeable: Community and National Tort Laws after *Francovich* and *Brasserie*', (1996) 45 ICLQ 507

———, 'Taking Article 215(2) EC Seriously', in Beatson, J. and Tridimas, T. (eds), *New Directions in European Public Law* (Oxford: Hart Publishing, 1998), pp. 35–47

———, 'Of Rights, Remedies, and Procedures', (2000) 37 CML Rev 501

Vesterdof, B., 'Complaints concerning infringements of competition law within the context of European Community Law' (1994) 31 CML Rev 77

von Bogdandy, A., 'The European Union as a Human Rights Organisation? Human Rights and the Core of the European Union', (2000) 37 CML Rev 1307

———, 'The Preamble' in Bruno de Witte (ed.), *Ten Reflections on the Constitutional Treaty for Europe* (EUI, 2003), 3–10

———, and Bast, J., 'The European Union's Vertical Order of Competences: The Current Law and Proposals for its Reform', (2002) 39 CMLR 227

von Heydebrand, und der Lasa, H.C., 'Confidential Information in Anti-dumping Proceedings before United States Courts and the European Court' (1983) ELR 331

Wade, H.W.R., Comment on the *Factortame* litigation, (1991) 107 LQR 1 and 4

——, Comment on *M v Home Office*, NLJ 18 and 25 September 1992

Ward, A., 'Effective Sanctions in EC Law: A Moving Boundary in the Division of Competence', (1995) 1 ELJ 205

——, *Judicial Review and the Rights of Private Parties in EC Law* (Oxford University Press, 2000)

——, 'The Draft EU Constitution and Private Party Access to Judicial Review of EU Measures', in Tridimas, T. and Nebbia, P. (eds), *EU Law for the 21st Century: Rethinking the New Legal Order*, Vol. 1, (Oxford, Hart Publishing, 2004)

Wathelet, M. and van Raepenbusch, S., 'La responsabilité des États Membres en cas de violation du droit Communautaire. Vers un alignement de la responsabilité de l'État sur celle de la Communauté ou l' inverse?' (1997) 33 CDE 13

Weatherill, S., *Law and Integration in the European Union* (Oxford: Oxford University Press, 1995)

——, 'After *Keck*: Some thoughts on How to Clarify the Clarification', (1996) 33 CML Rev 885

——, 'Recent Case law concerning the free movement of goods', (1999) 36 CML Rev 51

——, 'Competence Creep and Competence Control', (2004) YEL

Weiler, J.H.H., 'The European Court at a Crossroads: Community Human Rights and Member State Action' in *Du Droit international au droit de l'intégration, Liber Amicorum Pierre Pescatore*, (Nomos, 1987)

——, 'Does Europe Need a Constitution? Demos, Telos and the German Maastrich Decision', (1995) 1 ELJ 219

Weiler, J.H.H 'Fundamental Rights and Fundamental Boundaries: On Standards and Values in the Protection of Human Rights' in Neuwahl, N. and Rosas, A., *The European Union and Human Rights*, (Martinus Nijhoff, 1995), pp. 51–76 at pp. 69–71

——, 'Text and Context in the Free Movement of Goods', in Craig, P. and de Burca, G. (eds), *The Evolution of EU Law* (Oxford University Press, 1998)

——, and Lockhart N.J.S., ' "Taking Rights Seriously" Seriously: The European Court and its Fundamental Rights Jurisprudence—Part I' 32 (1995) CML Rev 514

Westen, P., 'The Empty Idea of Equality' (1982) 95 HLR 537

——, 'To Lure the Tarantula from its Hole: A Response', (1983) Columbia Law Review 1186

——, *Speaking of Equality: An Analysis of the Rhetorical Force of 'Equality' in Moral and Political Discourse*, (Princeton, NJ: Princeton University Press, 1990)

White, E., 'In Search of the Limits to Article 30 of the EEC Treaty' (1989) 26 CML Rev 235

Wintemute, R. and Andenas, M. (eds), *Legal Recognition of Same-Sex Partnerships* (Oxford: Hart Publishing, 2001)

Wyatt, D., 'European Community Law and Public law in the United Kingdom', in Markezinis B.S., *The Gradual Convergence*, (Oxford: Oxford University Press, 1994) 188–201

Wyatt, D.F., 'Subsidiarity and Judicial Review', in O'Keeffe, D. and Bavasso, A. (eds), *Judicial Review in European Union Law, Liber Amicorum in Honour of Lord Slynn*, (The Hague: Kluwer, 2000)

Ziller, J., *La nouvelle Constitution européenne* (Paris: Editions la Découverte, 2004)

Index